WORLD HISTORY IN BRIEF

Major Patterns of Change and Continuity

COMBINED VOLUME

SEVENTH EDITION

PETER N. STEARNS

George Mason University

Longman

Boston   Columbus   Indianapolis   New York   San Francisco   Upper Saddle River
Amsterdam   Cape Town   Dubai   London   Madrid   Milan   Munich   Paris   Montreal   Toronto
Delhi   Mexico City   Sao Paulo   Sydney   Hong Kong   Seoul   Singapore   Taipei   Tokyo

Editorial Director: Leah Jewell
Executive Editor: Charles Cavaliere
Editorial Project Manager: Rob DeGeorge
Editorial Assistant: Lauren Aylward
Senior Marketing Manager: Maureen Prado Roberts
Marketing Assistant: Marissa O'Brien
Production Manager: Kathy Sleys
Design Director: Jayne Conte
Cover Designer: Bruce Kenselaar
Manager, Visual Research: Beth Brenzel
Manager, Rights and Permissions: Zina Arabia
Image Permission Coordinator: Cynthia Vincenti

Manager, Cover Visual Research & Permissions:
  Karen Sanatar
Cover Art: Don Arove and His Two Sons,
  Colombia/Museo De America
Media Editor: Sarah Kinney
Associate Supplements Editor: Emsal Hassan
Full-Service Project Management: Karpagam
  Jagadeesan
Composition: GGS Higher Education Resources,
  A Division of PreMedia Global Inc.
Printer/Binder/Cover Printer: Courier Companies
Text Font: Bembo 11/12

Credits and acknowledgments borrowed from other sources and reproduced, with permission, in this textbook appear on pages 668–670.

Many of the designations by manufacturers and seller to distinguish their products are claimed as trademarks. Where those designations appear in this book, and the publisher was aware of a trademark claim, the designations have been printed in initial caps or all caps.

Library of Congress Cataloging-in-Publication Data
Stearns, Peter N.
  World history in brief : major patterns of change and continuity / Peter N. Stearns. — 7th ed.
    p. cm.
  Includes bibliographical references and index.
  ISBN 978-0-205-70973-1 (alk. paper) — ISBN 978-0-205-70974-8 (alk. paper) —
  ISBN 978-0-205-73555-6 (alk. paper) 1. World history. I. Title.
  D21.3.S77 2010
  909—dc22

                                                2009027304

Longman
is an imprint of

www.pearsonhighered.com

10 9 8 7 6 5 4 3 2 1

Student ISBN 10:   0-205-70973-7
Student ISBN 13: 978-0-205-70973-1
  Exam ISBN 10:   0-205-70975-3
  Exam ISBN 13: 978-0-205-70975-5

Brief Contents

Contents

CHAPTER 22   **World Economy and Western Imperialism: Africa and South Asia   399**

CHAPTER 23   **The Settler Societies: The West on Frontiers   417**

CHAPTER 27   World War I and the End of an Era   476

PART VI   The Contemporary World, 1918 to Present   487

CHAPTER 28   The West in the Contemporary Period   491

CHAPTER 29   Eastern European Civilization   517

List of Maps

List of Features

Preface

The study of world history is steadily gaining ground at the college level for several reasons. Global issues dominate our newspapers, television screens, and computer monitors daily. Americans must gain a perspective on the dynamics of these issues and understand the diverse societies around the globe that help shape them and our future. History—even history that might seem rather remote—explains how the world became what it is now, including why global influences loom larger than ever before. Global issues are at work even within the United States, because the United States is increasingly a nation of people of different heritages from around the world. Finally, world history raises some classic issues of historical interpretation, allowing its students to sharpen their understanding of how to interpret change and historical causation and providing a rich field for comparative analysis. Some educators still prefer to concentrate on Western civilization, arguing that it lies at our origins and, sometimes, that it is measurably superior. Although Western heritage must be included in any study of world history, it is clear that a purely Western interpretation cannot describe the world as we need to know it.

APPROACH

World History in Brief, now entering its seventh edition, has always had two goals. The first is to present a truly global approach to world history. This is accomplished through the focus on *forces that cut across individual societies*, through a *balanced treatment* of major societies themselves, and through *invitations to comparisons on a global scale*. The second goal is brevity and manageability. It is no secret that many world history texts are large and demand a major commitment from instructors and students. *World History in Brief* offers an alternative. Its length is compatible with a serious treatment of the major issues in world history, but it is concise enough to set aside time for careful analysis and to use with other types of materials beyond the textbook. The purpose here is to allow instructors and students to have some cake while eating it, too: to have the advantages of a coherent textbook overview, but also the opportunity to spend serious time with documents and with other kinds of historical scholarship.

World history demands a commitment to a *global* rather than a Western-centered approach. *World History in Brief* shows how different civilizations have encountered the various cross-cutting factors—for example, population growth, economic changes, and international currents in diplomacy and art—over the centuries. Western civilization is included as one of the major world societies, but east Asian, Indian, Middle Eastern, east European, African, and Latin American civilizations are all subjects of study in order to achieve a genuine worldwide perspective. World history also demands a balance between the examination of individual societies, within which the lives of most people are played out, and attention to the larger interactions across regional boundaries. These global interactions include trade, cultural contact, migrations, and disease. *World History in Brief* presents the major civilizations through a narrative overview combined with emphasis on regional and global political, cultural, social, and economic characteristics and trends. A grasp of these characteristics, in turn, facilitates comparisons and assessments of change.

World History in Brief is also designed to inspire additional readings and analytical exercises. World history teaching must follow the precedent of other survey history courses in reducing the emphasis on coverage and sheer memorization in favor of materials that provide facts that can be used to build larger understandings. Overwhelming detail, therefore, is not the chief goal of this book. Instead, *World History in Brief* presents enough data to facilitate comparison and assessment of changes and to highlight major developments in the world's history. Students can readily refer to large reference works if they wish to follow up on themes of special interest with greater factual detail. For this purpose, a list of suggested readings and Web sites follows each chapter.

PERIODIZATION

Chronological divisions—the basic periods of world history—reflect successive stages of international contact, from relative isolation to regional integration to the formation of global systems. This periodization is not conveniently tidy for the whole of world history, but it captures the leading dynamics of change at the global level. *World History in Brief* focuses on six major periods. The first involves the early features of human development, particularly the emergence of agriculture and the creation of civilization as a form of organization. The second examines the great classical societies from 1000 B.C.E. to 500 C.E. and their relationships with surrounding regions. The third, the postclassical period, from 500 C.E. to 1450 C.E., highlights the emergence of new contacts in trade and culture, the spread of world religions, and the development of civilizations in new as well as established centers. The fourth, the early modern period,

from 1450 C.E. to 1750 C.E., treats the emergence of a truly global trade system. It deals with not only the changing world role of Europe, but also the diverse and often quite independent developments in many other societies. The fifth period emphasizes the age of European industrialization and imperialism in the "long" 19th century and again the opportunity for varied reactions. The emergence of a new period in world history during the 20th–21st centuries draws the text to a close. In all these periods, major themes are carefully defined, both as a springboard for assessing the interactions of individual societies with more global forces and as a basis for comparison and discussion of change and continuity over time.

THEMES

Using the global focus plus international periodization, students can follow the themes of change and continuity across time and comparative analysis. For example, we can track and compare the juxtaposition of the traditions and novel forces that have shaped the modern world; the response of China or Latin America to the issues of the modern state; or the conditions of women in developing and industrial economies. How different societies respond to common issues and contacts, and how these issues and contacts change over time—this is the framework for examining world history. By focusing on these problems of comparison and assessment of change, the text uses the leading patterns of world history to provide experience in analysis that will apply to other historical studies beyond a survey.

FEATURES

World History in Brief is the most accessible world history text available in the market. Its brevity allows instructors and students flexibility about what additional readings will be included in their study of world history. The text focuses only on substantive topics, so students understand major themes and developments in world history rather than memorize an array of unconnected facts. The text is organized chronologically by civilizations, allowing for easy and orderly understanding by students. A number of features distinguish *World History in Brief,* and they have been carefully constructed over seven editions.

- *History Debates*, included in every chapter, offer students a brief synopsis (usually two paragraphs long) of some topic over which historical debate currently rages. Among the many topics explored are the causes of the abolition of slavery in the European colonies, women in patriarchal societies, the contributions of nomads, the political implications of Islam, how Western is Latin America, and consumerism and industrialization. Students are given an opportunity to see that the discipline of world history is focused on actively debating the past.

- *World Profiles* provide additional emphasis on the human component of world history through biographies. These profiles explore the history of an individual and how his or her story illuminates aspects of his or her society or a particular cultural interaction.

- *Key Questions*, which appear after each chapter's introduction, help students focus on the major issues they will grapple with as they read the chapter.

- *Part Openers*. A brief Part Opener highlights the major themes of each major period in world history. These are themes most major societies had to grapple with during the period—such as new trading patterns or new technologies—though various societies often reacted in different ways.

- *Global Connections*. At the end of each Part Opener, this section briefly explores the major types of contact among societies in the period. Understanding the unfolding and impact of the different patterns of contact, over time, is a crucial aspect of world history.

- *Paths to the Present* sections close each chapter and briefly suggest how the developments discussed in the chapter help explain our world today. Using the past to understand the present is not the only use of history, but it is a crucial one.

- *Part Retrospectives*. Following the final chapter in each part is a retrospective essay that recaps the dominant cross-civilizational (or cross-regional) contacts and divisions that occurred during the era under examination.

NEW TO THIS EDITION

- A new *Solving Problems* feature, in about half of the book's chapters, focuses on how human societies encountered and tried to resolve common issues, ranging from how to handle death (in early society) to how to react to the railroad. The goal here is to emphasize both shared concerns and the diversity of responses that developed among major societies, from early history on toward the present.

- Each chapter has been reviewed and revised, in some cases substantially, in light of new historical work and reactions to the previous edition. Significant changes in the treatment of Persia and the analysis of World War I are two results.

- Rewritten *Contacts and Identities* sections at the end of each chronological part highlight the interregional contacts occurring during each historical period and the defining issues that helped shape or influence the developing identity of individual civilizations. In this edition, these sections focus more directly on the relative importance of interaction and imitation in shaping societies' identities.

- New coverage is included in the areas of social history, particularly gender history, childhood, and consumerism, including new coverage of the impact of agriculture's advent on the nature of childhood in Chapter 1 and new treatment of consumerism in premodern China in Chapter 13.

- *Chapter 35*, the last chapter in the text, brings the book up to date on recent developments, including terrorism, and gives much more attention to *globalization*, including resistance to it, and globalization's meaning in the perspective of world history.

- The revisions in this edition also take into account new knowledge about particular societies and periods, which is reflected in revisions to individual chapters. Chapters on the contemporary world incorporate not only recent developments but also the wider perspectives provided by ongoing trends such as globalization.

SUPPLEMENTS

The following supplements are available to qualified college adopters for use in conjunction with *World History in Brief*.

For Instructors

Instructor's Manual and Test Item File. Written by Peter N. Stearns, this tool provides guidance in using the textbook and suggestions for structuring the syllabus for a world history course complete with assignment ideas; chapter summaries; multiple-choice, short-answer, and essay questions; and map exercises.

MyTest. This is a computerized test management program for Windows and Macintosh environments. The program allows instructors to select items from the Test Item File in order to create tests. It also allows for online testing.

The Instructor's Resource Center (www.pearsonhighered.com). Text-specific materials, such as the instructor's manual, and the test item file, are available for downloading by adopters.

Discovering World History Through Maps and Views, Updated Second Edition, by Gerald A. Danzer, University of Illinois, Chicago, winner of the American History Association's James Harvey Robinson Award for his work in developing map transparencies. This set of more than 100 four-color transparency acetates is an unparalleled supplement that contains historical reference maps, source maps, views and photos, urban plans, building diagrams, and works of art. Available to qualified college adopters on the Instructor Resource Center (IRC) at www.pearsonhighered.com.

For Instructors and Students

 MyHistoryLab (www.myhistorylab.com). MyHistoryLab provides students with an online package complete with the Pearson eText and numerous study aids. With several hundred primary sources, many of which are assignable and link to a gradebook, pre- and post-tests that link to a gradebook and result in individualized study plans, videos, and images, as well as map activities with gradable quizzes, the site offers students a unique, interactive experience that brings history to life. The comprehensive site also includes a History Bookshelf with 50 of the most commonly assigned books in history classes and a History Toolkit with tutorials and helpful links. Other features include gradable assignments and chapter review materials and a Test Item File. Available at no additional cost when packaged with *World History in Brief*, Seventh Edition.

For Students

Titles from the renowned **Penguin Classics** series can be bundled with *World History in Brief*, Seventh Edition, for a nominal charge. Please contact your Pearson Arts and Sciences sales representative for details.

CourseSmart **CourseSmart Textbooks Online.** This is an exciting new choice for students looking to save money. As an alternative to purchasing the print textbook, students can subscribe to the same content online and save up to 50 percent off the suggested list price of the print text. With a CourseSmart eTextbook, students can search the text, make notes online, print out reading assignments that incorporate lecture notes, and bookmark important passages for later review. For more information, or to subscribe to the CourseSmart eTextbook, visit www.coursesmart.com.

 The Prentice Hall Atlas of World History, **Second Edition.** Produced in collaboration with Dorling Kindersley, the leader in cartographic publishing, the updated second edition of *The Prentice Hall Atlas of World History* applies the most innovative cartographic techniques to present World History in all of its complexity and diversity. Copies of the atlas can be bundled with *World History in Brief,* Seventh Edition, for a nominal charge. Contact your Pearson Arts and Sciences sales representative for details. (ISBN 0-13-604247-3)

Longman Atlas of World History. Featuring 52 carefully selected historical maps, this atlas provides comprehensive global coverage for the major historical periods, ranging from the earliest of civilizations to the present and including maps such as the Conflict in Afghanistan 2001, Palestine and Israel from Biblical Times to Present, and World Religions. Each map has been designed to be colorful, easy to read, and informative, without sacrificing detail or accuracy. Available at no additional cost when packaged with *World History in Brief,* Seventh Edition. (ISBN 0-321-20998-2)

World History Map Workbook Volume I (to 1600) and Volume II (from 1600), both prepared by Glee Wilson of Kent State University. Each volume includes more than 40 maps accompanied by more than 120 pages of exercises and is designed to teach the location of various countries and their relationship to one another. Also included are numerous exercises aimed at enhancing students' critical-thinking capabilities. Available at no additional cost when packaged with *World History in Brief,* Seventh Edition. (Vol. 1: ISBN 0-321-06632-4 Vol. 2: ISBN 0-321-06633-2)

Documents in World History Volume I, Fifth Edition (The Great Traditions: From Ancient Times to 1500) and Volume II (The Modern Centuries: From 1500 to the Present), both edited by Peter N. Stearns, Stephen S. Gosch, and Erwin P. Grieshaber, is a collection of primary source documents that illustrate the human characteristics of key civilizations during major stages of world history. (Vol. 1: ISBN 0-205-61789-1; Vol. 2: ISBN 0-205-61947-9)

Study Card for World Civilization. Colorful, affordable, and packed with useful information, Study Cards make studying easier, more efficient, and more enjoyable. Course information is distilled to the basics, helping students quickly master the fundamentals, review a subject for understanding, or prepare for an exam. Because they are laminated for durability, they will keep for years and can be referred to for quick review. Available at no additional cost when packaged with *World History in Brief,* Seventh Edition. (ISBN 0-321-29234-0)

World History Study Site (www.ablongman.com/longmanworldhistory). Students can take advantage of this online resource that supports the world history curriculum. The site includes practice tests, Web links, and flash cards that cover the scope of topics discussed in a typical world history classroom.

A Guide to Your History Course: What Every Student Needs to Know. Written by Vincent A. Clark, this concise, spiral-bound guidebook orients students to the issues and problems they will face in the history classroom. Available at a discount when bundled with *World History in Brief,* Seventh Edition. (ISBN 0-13-185087-3)

A Short Guide to Writing About History, Seventh Edition. Written by Richard Marius, late of Harvard University, and Melvin E. Page, Eastern Tennessee State University, this engaging and practical text helps students get beyond merely compiling dates and facts. Covering both brief essays and the documented resource paper, the text explores the writing and researching processes, identifies different modes of historical writing, including argument, and concludes with guidelines for improving style. (ISBN 0-205-67370-8)

mysearchlab www.mysearchlab.com Pearson's MySearchLab™ is the easiest way for students to start a research assignment or paper. Complete with extensive help on the research process and four databases of credible and reliable source material, MySearchLab™ helps students quickly and efficiently make the most of their research time.

ACKNOWLEDGMENTS

Many people helped shape this book. I am grateful to Barry Beyer, Donald Schwartz, William McNeill, Andrew Barnes, Donald Sutton, Erick Langer, Jayashiri Rangan, Paul Adams, Merry Wiesner-Hanks, and Michael Adas, who aided my understanding of world history in various ways. Comments by Steven Gosch and Donald Sutton, and editorial assistance by Clio Stearns and Holly Moir, greatly aided in the preparation of this revised edition. Other colleagues who have furthered my education in world history include Ross Dunn, Judith Zinsser, Richard Bulliet, Jerry Bentley, and Stuart Schwartz. I also thank the various readers of earlier drafts of this manuscript, whose comments and encouragement improved the end result: Jay P. Anglin, Richard D. Lewis, Kirk Willis, Arden Bucholz, Richard Gere, Robert Roeder, Stephen Englehart, Marc Gilbert, John Voll, Erwin Grieshaber, Yong-ho Choe, V. Dixon Morris, Elton L. Daniel, Thomas Knapp, Edward Homze, Albert Mann, J. Malcom Thompson, Peter Freeman, Patrick Smith, David McComb, Charles Evans, Jerry Bentley, John Powell, B. B. Wellmon, Penelope Ann Adair, Linda Alkana, Samuel Brunk, Alexander S. Dawson, Lydia Garner, Surendra Gupta, Craig Hendricks, Susan Hult, Christina Michelmore, Lynn Moore, Joseph Norton, Elsa Nystrom, Diane Pearson, Louis Roper, Thomas O'Toole, John D. Boswell, Connie Brand, Robert Cassanello, John K. Hayden, Ben Lowe, Kenneth Wilburn, Dennis A. Frey Jr., Matthew Maher, Kenneth J. Orosz, Warren Rosenblum, Brian Williams, and Robert H. Welborn. J. Michael Farmer's assistance has been invaluable. The following reviewers provided helpful suggestions regarding the latest revision: Marybeth Carlson, University of Dayton; and Stephen S. Gosch, University of Wisconsin—Eau Claire.

My gratitude extends also to Laura Bell, whose editorial assistance has been vital. I have been taught and stimulated as well by my students in world history courses at George Mason University. And thanks, finally, to my family, who have put up with my excited babble about distant places for some time now.

PETER N. STEARNS

About the Author

Peter N. Stearns is Provost and Professor of History at George Mason University. He has taught previously at Harvard, the University of Chicago, Rutgers, and Carnegie Mellon; he was educated at Harvard University. He has published widely in modern social history, including the history of emotions, and in world history. Representative works in world history include *World History: A Survey, The Industrial Revolution in World History, Gender in World History, Consumerism in World History*, and *Growing Up: The History of Childhood in Global Context*. His publications in social history include *Old Age in Preindustrial Society, Anxious Parents: A History of Modern American Childrearing, American Cool: Developing the Twentieth-Century Emotional Style, Fat History: Bodies and Beauty in Western Society, American Fear: The Causes and Consequences of High Anxiety, Revolutions in Sorrow: A History of American Experiences and Policies Toward Death in Global Context, From*

Alienation to Addiction: Modern American Work in Global Historical Perspective, and *Educating Global Citizens in Colleges and Universities: Challenges and Opportunities*. While under Dr. Stearns's leadership, George Mason University was awarded the 2006 Andrew Heiskell Award for Innovation in International Education. He has also edited encyclopedias of world and social history, and since 1967, he has served as editor-in-chief of *The Journal of Social History*.

In most of his research and writing, Dr. Stearns pursues three main goals. First, as a social historian, he is eager to explore aspects of the human experience that are not generally thought of in historical terms, and with attention to ordinary people as well as elites. Second, he seeks to use an understanding of historical change and continuity to explore patterns of behavior and social issues. Finally, he is concerned with connecting new historical research with wider audiences, including of course classrooms. Dr. Stearns is also eager to promote comparative analysis and the assessment of modern global forces—for their own sake and as they illuminate the American experience and impact.

PART I

Early World History: From Origins to Agriculture and New Forms of Human Organization

INTRODUCTION: BEGINNING WORLD HISTORY

World historians continue to discuss when the effective history of the human experience began. A strong impulse has emerged to push treatment earlier, to take fuller account of the origins and evolution of the human species and the many migrations that brought humans from their starting point, in East Africa, to almost every habitable part of the world by about 27,000 years ago.

This very early history is fascinating and important. Scientific work has steadily expanded what we know about early humans. Discoveries multiply about previously unknown species that served as intermediaries between apes and early semi-humans, or about the startling amount of genetic material humans share with species such as chimpanzees. There's every reason to explore these diverse and complex beginnings.

At the same time, however, it's important to keep sight of main points. Without slighting far more detailed inquiry, or the possibilities of lifetimes of fruitful new research, the long early stages of the human journey highlight three points, which are covered in Chapter 1. First, evolution gradually improved human capacities—adding, for example, unprecedented facility in speech—yet with the arrival of the current species the evolutionary process halted at least for a time. There have been no fundamental changes in the species for about 120,000 years. Second, humans were tool-using animals and gradually improved their abilities, moving from picking up potential tools to shaping them deliberately. And third, humans were often on the move. Their hunting and gathering economy dictated recurrent migration in search of additional space. The wide

In 1940 in Lascaux, France, four boys playing together discovered a long-hidden cave filled with thousands of complex and beautiful Stone Age paintings like this one. Most of the paintings are of animals, some of which were extinct by the time they were painted. No one knows for sure why Stone Age artists painted these pictures, but they remain a powerful reminder of the sophistication of so-called primitive peoples.

dispersion of people was a fundamental feature of early history and a precondition of much that would follow.

After early history comes the first great transformation of the human economy, from hunting and gathering to agriculture or herding. This transformation, one of the great systems changes in the human experience, added to the framework for world history. This change is covered in Chapter 1 also.

Fundamental transformation is easy to claim, but it is also abstract. Childhood provides a concrete example. In hunting and gathering societies, children were important but they could not be handled in large numbers. Families could not support many children, who were not very useful; and trying to travel with many young children during migrations to new hunting spots was impractical. But with agriculture, children gained new utility—they could do useful work and indeed provided families with a vital labor force. So their number increased greatly, and human groups began approaching childhood in terms of labor expectations. This was one reason agricultural people normally placed such emphasis on obedience, to try to shape children into useful workers. Another huge transformation for all concerned.

Many agricultural societies ultimately created new organizational forms that we call civilizations. This subsequent change and the four specific centers of the earliest civilizations are discussed in Chapter 2. Chapter 3 turns to peoples who made a different transition, to nomadic herding, avoiding both agriculture and civilization. These peoples too played a vital role in world history for many centuries.

Chapters in this part thus deal with crucial building blocks of the human experience: evolution and migration; tool use that ultimately helped lead to agriculture and the domestication of animals; and new organizational forms for many human societies. The stretch of time involved is massive, but the chapter primarily emphasizes changes that took shape between 10,000 and 4000 years ago. The result was a set of practices and institutions that have not required reinvention in human history since that point.

GLOBAL CONNECTIONS

One of the key features of the early human experience involves the separateness that could come from dispersion. As people fanned out in search of space—each hunter-gatherer required an average of 2.5 square miles to operate, so even small population bumps could create big pressures—they normally lost contact with their points of origin.

Two obvious examples of this, late in the dispersion process, involve Australia and the Americas. People reached Australia about 60,000 years ago. At this point, because of the ice age, the Indian Ocean was smaller than it now is, so land extended south from Asia; the distance across water was not too great. But then the waters expanded, and the people who had reached Australia were cut off from further contacts. Only 300 years ago were new forms of contact developed, to the great disadvantage of the native Australians who simply lacked the experience, including disease immunities, to handle the new interactions without huge damage.

On the other end of the planet, people reached the Americas about 25,000 years ago, crossing what was then a land bridge from northeast Asia to Alaska. Several surges of migration may have occurred before the land bridge was flooded and the process halted. It would be many millennia before peoples in the Americas had any contact, or at least meaningful contact, with other humans in other regions.

These are two dramatic examples, but even migrants to Asia or Europe or other parts of Africa might easily lose connection with their relatives and ancestors. The emergence of different physical characteristics was a sign of this process. So was the welter of separate languages that emerged—more than 6000 at a high point (the number is smaller today). To be sure, basic language groups were far less numerous—many separate tongues sprang from common cores such as the Semitic or Indo-European or Bantu stems. Still, the process of diffusion and separation was both illustrated and encouraged when groups of people, even in the same linguistic family, lost the capacity to talk with each other in case of encounter.

Yet too much emphasis on separation misses the mark, even in these very early parts of the human experience, because connections of several sorts developed as well.

Migration and invasion, for example, proved to be recurrent processes. The Middle East, the cradle of civilization, was frequently overrun by new peoples, often coming in from central Asia. Egypt, though invaded less often, saw attacks from the Middle East and from farther south in Africa. These processes mixed peoples. Stone tablets have been found in the Middle East with

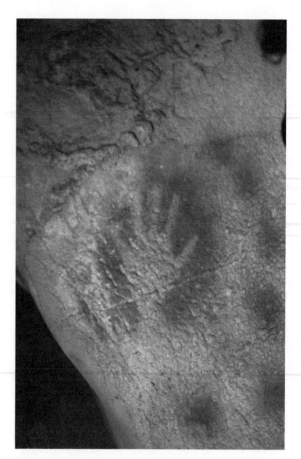

Prehistoric art in Europe depicting a handprint, red in color, believed to be female—a rare theme in cave art.

inscriptions both in the local language and in ancient Egyptian, showing the need and ability to translate. Egyptian pictures present people from Africa along with Semitic peoples from the Middle East—as well as local Egyptians.

Mixing of this sort also brought knowledge of new technologies. Several of the technological changes vital to extend agriculture, such as knowledge of the wheel, came into the Middle East from peoples migrating or attacking from central Asia.

Beyond outright invasion, contacts also developed by a vaguer process often called diffusion, in which people in one region learned from their neighbors. Occasional travelers or traders might also bring new ideas. Thus we will see that agriculture, though separately invented in several places, gradually spread through diffusion. It took centuries for knowledge of this new system to reach southern Europe from the Middle East, for contacts were doubtless limited and there was outright resistance to change. But same diffusion process occurred, bringing knowledge of how to work metals and introducing foodstuffs from one region to another, where they might be adopted as basic crops.

And, of course, there was trade. We know that earlier agricultural communities often traded with nearby hunting and gathering groups, if only to provide symbolic exchanges that helped keep the peace. By the time of the early civilizations there was a certain amount of interregional trade—linking, for example, parts of the Middle East to northwestern India.

Separateness, in sum, was not an absolute. A few peoples truly became isolated, at least from population centers in other parts of the world. Contacts were sporadic for many groups. But the advantages of exchanges, in terms of trade and

new knowledge, made contact an important part of the early human experience. And advantage or not, the force of migration and invasion made interaction inescapable for many of the world's peoples, at least recurrently.

SUGGESTED READINGS

Important explorations of world history that provide greater detail or a somewhat different vantage point from this study include: W. McNeill, *Rise of the West: A History of the Human Community* (1970) and *A History of the Human Community* (1996); J. M. Roberts, *The Pelican History of the World* (1984); Peter N. Stearns, Michael Adas, and Stuart B. Schwartz, *World Civilizations: The Global Experience* (2003); Richard Bulliet et al., *The Earth and Its Peoples* (1997); Jerry Bentley, *Traditions and Encounters: A Global Perspective on the Past* (2000). Also useful for background on the geographic distribution of the world's people is Gerald Danzer, *Atlas of World History* (2000); see also Peter N. Stearns, *Childhood in World History* (2005).

CHAPTER

1

From Human Prehistory to the Rise of Agriculture

GETTING STARTED IS ALWAYS HARD

The human species has accomplished a great deal in a relatively short period of time. There are significant disagreements over how long an essentially human species, as distinct from other primates, has existed. However, a figure of about 2.5 million years seems acceptable. This is approximately 1/4000 of the time the earth has existed. If one thinks of the whole history of the earth to date as a 24-hour day, the human species began at about five minutes until midnight. Human beings have existed for less than 5 percent of the time mammals of any sort have lived. Yet in this brief span of time—by earth-history standards—humankind has spread to every land-mass (with the exception of the polar regions) and, for better or worse, has taken control of the destinies of countless other species.

To be sure, human beings have some drawbacks as a species, compared to other existing models. They are unusually aggressive against their own kind: while some of the great apes, notably chimpanzees, engage in periodic wars, these conflicts can hardly rival human violence. Human babies are dependent for a long period, which requires some special family or child-care arrangements and often has limited the activities of many adult women. Certain ailments, such as back problems resulting from an upright stature, also burden the species. And, the distinctive human awareness of the inevitability of death imparts some unique fears and tensions.

Distinctive features of the human species account for considerable achievement as well. Like other primates, but unlike most other mammals, human beings can manipulate objects fairly readily because of the grip provided by an opposable thumb on each hand. Compared to other primates, human beings have a relatively high and regular sexual drive, which aids reproduction; being omnivores, they are not dependent exclusively on plants or on animals for food, which helps explain why they can live in so many different climates and settings; the unusual variety of their facial expressions aids communication and enhances social life. The distinctive human brain and a facility for elaborate speech are even more important: much of human history depends on the knowledge, inventions, and social contracts that resulted from these assets. Features of this sort explain why many human cultures, including the Western culture that many Americans share, promote a firm separation between human and animal, seeing in our own species a power and rationality, and possibly a spark of the divine, that "lower" creatures lack.

Although the rise of humankind has been impressively rapid, its early stages can also be viewed as painfully long and slow. Most of the 2 million plus years during which our species has existed are described by the term *Paleolithic*, or *Old Stone Age*. Throughout this long-time span, which runs until about 14,000 years ago, human beings learned only simple tool use, mainly through employing suitably shaped rocks and sticks for hunting and warfare. Fire was tamed about 750,000 years ago. The nature of the species also gradually changed during the Paleolithic, with emphasis on more erect stature and growing brain capacity. Archeological evidence also indicates some increases in average size. A less apelike species, whose larger brain and erect stance allowed better tool use, emerged between 500,000 and 750,000 years ago; it is called, appropriately enough, *Homo erectus*. Several species of *Homo erectus* developed and spread in Africa, then to Asia and Europe, reaching a population size of perhaps 1.5 million 100,000 years ago.

Considerable evidence suggests that more advanced types of humans killed off or displaced many competitors over time. Intermarriage also occurred. And even *Homo sapiens sapiens* coexisted with other human species in several regions for considerable periods, as recent archeological and genetic evidence suggests. Ultimately, however, the single species predominated throughout the world, rather than a number of rather similar human species, as among monkeys and apes. The newest human breed, *Homo sapiens sapiens*, of which all humans in the world today are descendants, originated about 120,000 years ago, also in Africa. The success of this subspecies means that there have been no major changes in the basic human physique or brain size since its advent.

Part of human evolution in this decisive later phase involved a probably modest genetic modification in the brain that allowed much more elaborate patterns of speech. A number of animals and birds have some power of speech, in terms of varied sounds that communicate. But with the advent of this "language gene," people became capable of a much wider variety of sounds. From this, it was possible to invent languages. Scientists have wondered what the first people who had this gene must have thought, surrounded by other people who were still confined to a series of grunts plus elaborate facial expressions.

■**KEY QUESTIONS**   *What were the most significant human achievements before the rise of agriculture? How did agriculture change human life?*

HUMAN DEVELOPMENT AND CHANGE

Even after the appearance of *Homo sapiens sapiens,* human life faced important constraints. People who hunted food and gathered nuts and berries could not support large numbers or elaborate societies. Most hunting groups were small, and they had to roam widely for food. Two people required at least one square mile for survival. Population growth was slow, partly because women breast-fed infants for several years to limit their own fertility. On the other hand, people did not have to work very hard—hunting took about seven hours every three days on average. Women, who gathered fruits and vegetables, worked harder, but there was significant equality between the sexes based on common economic contributions.

Paleolithic people gradually improved their tool use, beginning with the crude shaping of stone and wooden implements. The development

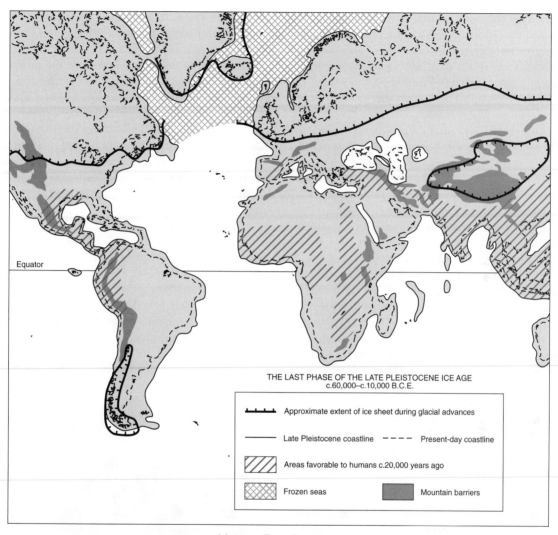

THE LAST PHASE OF THE LATE PLEISTOCENE ICE AGE
c.60,000–c.10,000 B.C.E.

⊢⊣⊢⊣	Approximate extent of ice sheet during glacial advances
——— Late Pleistocene coastline	– – – Present-day coastline
⫽⫽⫽⫽	Areas favorable to humans c.20,000 years ago
⊠⊠⊠ Frozen seas	▨ Mountain barriers

Human Development

of speech allowed more group cooperation and the transmission of technical knowledge. By the later Paleolithic period, people had developed rituals to lessen the fear of death and created cave paintings to express a sense of nature's beauty and power. Goddesses often played a prominent role in the religious pantheon. Thus, the human species came to develop systems of belief that helped explain the environment and set up rules for various kinds of social behavior. The development of speech provided rich language and symbols for the

transmission of culture and its growing sophistication. At the same time, different groups of humans, in different locations, developed quite varied belief systems and languages.

The greatest achievement of Paleolithic people was the sheer spread of the human species over much of the earth's surface. The species originated in eastern Africa; most of the earliest types of human remains come from this region, in the present-day countries of Tanzania, Kenya, and Uganda. But gradual migration, doubtless caused by the need to find scarce food, steadily pushed the human reach to other areas. Key discoveries, notably fire and the use of animal skins for clothing—both of which enabled people to live in colder climates—facilitated the spread of Paleolithic groups. The first people moved out of Africa about 750,000 years ago. Human remains (Peking man, Java man) have been found in China and southeast Asia dating from 600,000 and 350,000 years ago, respectively. Humans inhabited Britain 250,000 years ago. Later, migrations of *Homo sapiens sapiens* from Africa took people not only to Eurasia, but well beyond. They first crossed to Australia 60,000 years ago, followed by another group 20,000 years later; these combined to form the continent's aboriginal population. Dates of the migration from Asia to the Americas have been debated, but most scholars now believe that humans crossed what was then a land bridge from Siberia to Alaska about 25,000 years ago and quickly began to spread out, reaching the tip of the South American continent possibly within a mere thousand years. Settlers from China reached Taiwan, the Philippines, and Indonesia 4500 to 3500 years ago.

In addition, soon after this time—roughly 14,000 years ago—the last great ice age ended, which did wonders for living conditions over much of the Northern Hemisphere. Human development began to accelerate. A new term, *Mesolithic,* or *Middle Stone Age,* designates a span of several thousand years, from about 12,000 to 8000 B.C.E.,* in which human ability to fashion stone tools and other implements improved greatly.

*In Christian societies, historical dating divides between years "before the birth of Christ" (B.C.) and after (A.D., *anno Domini,* or "year of our Lord"). This system came into wide acceptance in Europe in the 18th century as formal historical consciousness increased (although ironically, 1 A.D. is a few years late for Jesus' actual birth). China, Islam, Judaism, and many other societies use different dating systems, referring to their own history. This text, like many recent world history materials, uses the Christian chronology (one has to choose some system) but changes the terms to B.C.E. ("before the common era") and C.E. ("of the common era") as a gesture to less Christian-centric labeling.

People learned to sharpen and shape stone, to make better weapons and cutting edges. Animal bones were used to make needles and other precise tools. From the Mesolithic also date the increased numbers of log rafts and dugouts, which improved fishing, and the manufacture of pots and baskets for food storage. Mesolithic people domesticated additional animals, such as cows (dogs had been tamed earlier), which again improved food supply. Population growth accelerated, which also resulted in more conflicts and wars. Skeletons from this period show frequent bone breaks and skull fractures caused by weapons.

In time, better tool use, somewhat more elaborate social organization, and still more population pressure led people in many parts of the world to the final Stone Age—the *Neolithic,* or *New Stone Age.* And from Neolithic people, in turn, came several more dramatic developments that changed the nature of human existence—the invention of agriculture, the creation of cities, and other foreshadowings of civilization, which ended the Stone Age altogether throughout much of the world.

Stone tools.

SOLVING PROBLEMS

DEALING WITH DEATH

■ Two related problems human societies faced concerning death involving devising appropriate rituals for those who died—so people could be assured that loved or powerful figures were taken care of properly and could have some confidence their own death would be handled well—and making sure that dead bodies did not cause disease. Members of various species have some awareness of death immediately around them, but presumably humans are the only species with knowledge of death as an inevitable experience. It is not surprising that death figures strongly in early human culture, including the world's first known literary epic, the *Gilgamesh* from the Middle East in the 3rd millennium B.C.E. We cannot know when people figured out that death was an issue, or that dead bodies could be sources of contagion. It is possible that earlier versions of the human species, such as Peking man, (500,000 B.C.E.) developed burial sites (there are stacks of bones, but this might be a result of cannibalism). Certainly by the time of *Homo sapiens sapiens*, and the possibility of speech, deliberate burial practices were becoming common.

■ Various hunting and gathering groups buried people with ornaments and tools (and, sometimes, with wives and servants). This implies a belief that an afterlife must be prepared for, and also a recognition that while death occurred to everyone, people of high status could claim special monuments.

■ While efforts to solve problems posed by death are seemingly universal, and persist today, widely separated societies also forged very different specific approaches. North American hunting tribes often urged that death was a normal part of life, to be faced fearlessly, while many Australian aborigines viewed it as a disruption caused by forces of evil and magic. Reflecting mixed feelings about the dead, some African groups established a custom of creating a special hole in the wall of the home to remove a corpse, then sealing it up so that the spirit would have a harder time figuring out a way back.

■ Early civilizations elaborated the rituals associated with death, but again with many distinctive cultural variants. Mesopotamians tended to emphasize gloomy aspects of death; the *Gilgamesh* epic stressed that the dead lived on in darkness, with dust for good. Egyptians, on the other hand, emphasized the need to organize for an afterlife, with expensive funeral rituals even for relatively ordinary people, and with large numbers of professionals associated with preparing bodies and creating art for monuments. Egypt's *Book of Death* is the earliest surviving sacred literature, emphasizing assurances for the afterlife. Egyptians believed that the gods would judge individuals, with sinners possibly eaten by a crocodile-headed monster, but in contrast to Mesopotamian gloom about the cessation of life tended to assume most people would be evaluated favorably. Egyptian beliefs and rituals developed over a 6000 year span, changing fundamentally only with the arrival of Islam after 600 C.E.

■**QUESTIONS:** *What kinds of evidence best show widely shared human concerns about death? Why did specific cultures concerning death and ritual vary so widely?*

THE NEOLITHIC REVOLUTION

Human achievements during the various ages of stone are both fascinating and fundamental, and some points are hotly debated. Our knowledge of Stone Age society is of course limited, although archeologists have been creative in their interpretations of tool remains and other evidence, such as cave paintings and burial sites, that Stone Age people produced in various parts of the world. What people accomplished during this long period of prehistory remains essential to human life today; our ability to make and manipulate tools thus depends directly on what our Stone Age ancestors learned about physical matter.

However, it was the invention of agriculture that most clearly moved the human species toward more elaborate social and cultural patterns that people today would recognize. With agriculture, human beings were able to settle in one place and focus on particular economic, political, and religious goals and activities. Agriculture also spawned a great increase in the sheer number of people in the world, a tenfold increase over several millennia.

The initial development of agriculture—that is, the deliberate planting of grains for later harvest—was probably triggered by two results of the ice age's end. First, population increases, stemming from improved climate, prompted people to search for new and more reliable sources of food. Second, the end of the ice age saw the retreat of certain big game animals, such as mastodons. Human hunters had to turn to smaller game, such as deer and wild boar, in many forested areas. Hunting's overall yield declined. Here was the basis for new interest in other sources of food. There is evidence that by 9000 B.C.E., in certain parts of the world, people were becoming increasingly dependent on regular harvests of wild grains, berries, and nuts. This undoubtedly set the stage for the deliberate planting of seeds (probably accidental to begin with) and the improvement of key grains through the selection of seeds from the best plants.

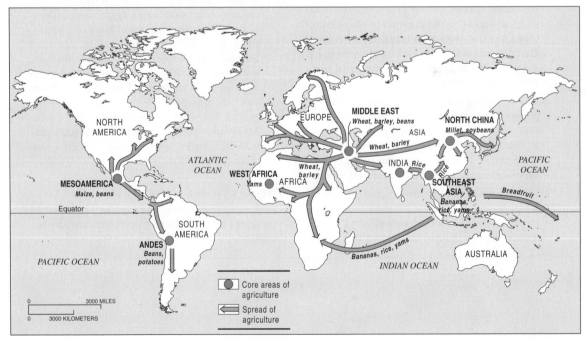

The Spread of Agriculture

As farming evolved, new animals were also domesticated. Particularly in the Middle East and parts of Asia, by 9000 B.C.E. pigs, sheep, goats, and cattle were being raised. Farmers used these animals for meat and skins and soon discovered dairying as well. These results not only contributed to the development of agriculture, but they also served as the basis for nomadic herding societies.

Farming was initially developed in the Middle East and Black Sea regions, in an arc of territory running from present-day Turkey to Iraq and Israel. This was a very fertile area, more fertile in those days than at present. Grains such as barley and wild wheat were abundant. At the same time, this area was not heavily forested, and animals were in short supply, presenting a challenge to hunters. In the Middle East, the development of agriculture may have begun as early as 10,000 B.C.E., and it gained ground rapidly after 8000 B.C.E. Gradually during the Neolithic centuries, knowledge of agriculture spread to other centers, including parts of India, North Africa, and Europe. Agriculture, including rice cultivation, soon developed independently in China (the second of at least three separate inventions of the new economic systems). We will see that agriculture spread later to much of Africa south of the Mediterranean coast, reaching west Africa by 2000 B.C.E., although here too there were additional developments with an emphasis on local grains and also root crops such as yams. Agriculture had to be invented separately in the Americas, based on corn cultivation, where it was also a slightly later development (about 5000 B.C.E.).

Many scholars have termed the development of agriculture a *Neolithic revolution*. The term is obviously misleading in one sense: agriculture was no sudden transformation, even in the Middle East, where the new system had its roots. Learning the new agricultural methods was difficult, and many peoples long combined a bit of agriculture with considerable reliance on the older systems of hunting and gathering. A "revolution" that took more than a thousand years, and then several thousand more to spread to key population centers in Asia, Europe, and Africa, is hardly dramatic by modern standards.

The concept of revolution is, however, appropriate in demonstrating the magnitude of change involved. Early agriculture could support far more people per square mile than hunting ever could; it also allowed people to settle more permanently in one area. The system was nonetheless not easy. Agriculture required more regular work, at least of men, than hunting did. Hunting-and-gathering groups today, such as the Kung or Khoisan peoples of the Kalihari Desert in southwest Africa, work an average of 2.5 hours a day, alternating long, intense hunts with periods devoted to such pursuits as music, dance, and decorative art. Settled agriculture concentrated populations and encouraged the spread of disease. As much as agriculture was demanding, it was also rewarding: agriculture supported larger populations, and with better food supplies and a more settled existence, agricultural peoples could afford to build houses and villages. Animals provided not only hides but also wool for more varied clothing.

We know next to nothing of the debates that must have raged when people were first confronted with agriculture, but it is not hard to imagine that many would have found the new life too complicated, too difficult, or too unexciting. Most evidence suggests that gathering and hunting peoples resisted agriculture as long as they could. Gradually, of course, agriculture did gain ground. Its success was hard to deny. And as farmers cleared new land from forests, they automatically drove out or converted many hunters. Disease played a role: settled agricultural societies suffered from more contagious diseases because of denser population concentrations. Hunting-and-gathering peoples lacked resistance and often died when agriculturists who had developed immunities carried the diseases into new areas.

Not all the peoples of the world came to embrace the slowly spreading wave of agriculture, at least not until very recently. Important small societies in southern Africa, Australia, the islands of southeast Asia, and even northern Japan were isolated for so long that news of this economic system simply did not reach them. The white-skinned hunting tribes of northern Japan disappeared only

PEOPLE IN THE AMERICAS

As early as the 17th century, a Catholic scholar suggested that American Indians had come from Asia. But it was only in the late 19th century that speculation about where the Indians had come from turned into scientific inquiry. For some time, using carbon dating techniques from Indian cities and artifacts, it was generally agreed that immigrants from Siberia poured across the land bridge that then connected to Alaska around 12,000–15,000 years ago. They moved relatively rapidly, reaching South America within a few hundred years. Archeological finds seemed to support this view. So did the belief that people would not have moved in this fashion, in the far north, before the end of the ice age.

More recently, new techniques—including better carbon dating but, above all, genetic analysis—have called this long-established view into question. Among other things, we realize that it would be very unlikely for migrants to develop sophisticated settlements in South America so quickly. Now it is widely agreed that migrations began about 25,000 years ago. The migrants knew how to make boats, which allowed them to move down the Pacific Coast, bypassing ice-age glaciers. (Boats, after all, had allowed humans to reach Australia even before this.) There is still debate over the best scientific techniques to use, and over whether there was one migration or several. Some authors, though now a declining number, also long defended the older migration model. Is a debate of this sort significant? How does it affect judgments about human experience and capacity before the rise of agriculture?

about a hundred years ago. Northern Europeans and southern Africans converted to agriculture earlier, about 2000 years ago, but well after the Neolithic revolution had transformed other parts of their continents. Agriculture was initiated in the Americas as early as 5000 B.C.E. and developed vigorously in Central America and the northern part of South America. However, most Indian tribes in North America continued a hunting-and-gathering existence, though it was often combined with seasonal agriculture, until recent centuries. Finally, the peoples of the vast plains of central Asia long resisted a complete conversion to agriculture, in part because of a harsh climate; herding, rather than grain growing, became the basic socioeconomic system of this part of the world. From this area came waves of tough, nomadic invaders and migrants whose role in linking major civilizations was a vital force in world history until a few centuries ago.

Development possibilities among people who became agriculturists were more obvious than those among smaller populations who resisted or simply did not know of the system: agriculture set the basis for more rapid change in human societies. Greater wealth and larger populations freed some people for other specializations, from which new ideas or techniques might spring. Agriculture itself depended on control over nature that could be facilitated by newly developed techniques and objects. For example, during the Neolithic period itself, the needs of farming people for storage facilities, for grains and seeds, promoted the development of basket-making and pottery. The first potter's wheel came into existence around 6000 B.C.E., and this, in turn, encouraged faster and higher-quality pottery production. Agricultural needs also encouraged certain kinds of science, supporting the human inclination to learn more about weather or flooding.

THE NATURE OF AGRICULTURAL SOCIETIES

Much of what we think of as human history involves the doings of agricultural societies—societies, that is, in which most people are farmers and in which the production of food is the central economic activity. Nonagricultural groups, such as the nomadic herders in central Asia, made their own mark, but their greatest influence usually occurred in interactions with agricultural peoples. Many societies remain largely agricultural today. The huge time span we have thus far considered, including the Neolithic revolution itself, is all technically "prehistorical"—involved with human patterns before the invention of writing allowed the kinds of recordkeeping historians prefer. In fact, because we now know how to use surviving tools and burial sites as records, the pre-historic–historic distinction means less than it once did. The preagricultural–agricultural distinction is more central. Fairly soon after the development of agriculture—although not, admittedly, right away—significant human change began to occur in decades and centuries, rather than in the sizable blocks of time, several thousand years or more, that describe preagricultural peoples.

From their origins until about 200 years ago, and in some cases more recently, agricultural societies had a number of features in common. They varied, of course, depending on what kinds of crops they grew and a host of other factors. But it is vital to consider the shared characteristics.

All agricultural societies, for example, invented some kind of week. This is the only division of time that is entirely human-constructed, with no relationship to phenomena in nature. Agricultural weeks varied, from four days to nine, and this is a big difference. But all agricultural societies had something that marked an interruption in normal work. Usually, this interruption had or developed religious significance, seen as a special day of prayer or observance. Even more often, weeks were ended (or begun) by market days, and this need to exchange certain goods, even in villages where families produced most of their own requirements, may help explain why weeks were invented. It is also true that agricultural work was hard, so some interruption may have been essential in order to motivate people to resume their work when the next week began.

In agricultural societies, not surprisingly, most people farmed, at least part of the time. Agricultural societies often produced some surplus, but never enough to allow more than 20–25 percent of the population to specialize in something other than agriculture, or to live away from the land (in cities). Often, the agricultural percentage of the population was even higher. Agricultural societies also always developed certain rituals around planting and harvesting, often including special festivals. Here too, religion usually picked up some of the tasks of seeking a good season or giving thanks when the harvest was in, though there was great variety among the religions that arose among agricultural peoples. Agricultural societies always emphasized certain kinds of science and mathematics, in order for example to calculate seasons and permit the development of calendars. Sometimes, science became far more elaborate than this, but agricultural needs always figured in intellectual life.

Agricultural societies always emphasized the superiority of men over women, in what is called the *patriarchal system*. The exact form and extent of male and fatherly power varied, but it was always there. Some historians have argued that, because agriculture encouraged the emergence of ideas of property, men tended to think of women as part of the property package. Trying to control women's sexual activity, so a father could be sure that his children were his, and so feel comfortable in passing on his land to them, may have been part of the arrangement as well. Certainly, patriarchal societies place a high premium on women's sexual faithfulness. Agricultural societies also encouraged higher birth rates than hunting-and-gathering societies had done, because a number of children were useful as labor on the land. This meant that more of women's time was taken up with bearing and caring for young children, which reduced their ability to match men's economic activities. Growing the staple grain crop was almost always seen as a male activity, which meant that men were more important economically.

Agriculture brought many disadvantages to many people involved, including greater liability to disease and an increase in human inequality. But it did allow societies to support a larger number of people than hunting and gathering had done, because the food supply became more reliable despite frequent bad harvests and famines. Before agriculture, and for many thousands of years, the global human population had fluctuated between 5 and 8 million. By 4000 B.C.E. the global population stood at 60 to 70 million. And this proved to be only the beginning.

AGRICULTURE AND CHANGE

Agriculture encouraged the formation of larger as well as more stable human communities than had existed before Neolithic times. A few Mesolithic groups had formed villages, particularly where opportunities for fishing were good, as around some of the lakes in Switzerland. However, most hunting peoples moved in relatively small groups, or tribes, each containing anywhere from 40 to 60 individuals, and they could not settle in a single spot without the game running out. With agriculture, these constraints changed. To be sure, some agricultural peoples did move around. A system called *slash and burn* agriculture developed in a few parts of the world, including parts of the Americas, and it still operates in some rain forest regions. Here, people burn off trees in an area, farm intensively for a few years until the soil is depleted, and then move on. Herding peoples also moved in tribal bands, with strong kinship ties. But most agricultural peoples did not have new lands close by to which they could move after a short time. And there were advantages to staying

put: houses could be built to last, wells built to bring up water, and other "expensive" improvements afforded because they served many generations. In the Middle East, China, and parts of Africa and India, a key incentive to stability was the need for irrigation devices to channel river water to the fields. This same need helps explain why agriculture usually generated communities and not a series of isolated farms. Small groups simply could not regulate a river's flow or build and maintain irrigation ditches and sluices. Irrigation and defense encouraged villages—groupings of several hundred people—as the characteristic pattern of residence in almost all agricultural societies from Neolithic days until our own century.

One Neolithic town, Çatal Hüyük in southern Turkey, has been elaborately studied by archeologists. It was founded about 7000 B.C.E. and was unusually large, covering about 32 acres. Houses were made of mud bricks set in timber frameworks, crowded together, with few windows. People seem to have spent a good bit of time on their rooftops in order to experience daylight and make social contacts—many broken bones attest to frequent falls. Some houses were lavishly decorated, mainly with hunting scenes. Religious images, both of powerful male hunters and "mother goddesses" devoted to agricultural fertility, were common, and some people seem to have had special religious responsibilities. The town produced almost all the goods it consumed. Some trade was conducted with hunting peoples who lived in the hills surrounding the village, but apparently it was initiated more to keep the peace than to produce economic gain. By 5500 B.C.E., important production activities developed in the village, including those of skilled toolmakers and jewelers. With time also came links with other communities. Towns such as Çatal Hüyük ruled over smaller communities. This meant that some families began to specialize in politics, and military forces were organized. Some towns became small cities, ruled by kings who were typically given divine status. Here were developments that led to bigger changes in the organization of some agricultural societies.

The discovery of metal tools dates back to about 4000 B.C.E. Copper was the first metal with which people learned how to work, although the more resilient metal, bronze, soon entered the picture. In fact, the next basic age of human existence was the Bronze Age. By about 3000 B.C.E., metalworking had become so commonplace in the Middle East that the use of stone tools dissipated, and the long stone ages were over at last— although, of course, an essentially Neolithic technology persisted in many parts of the world, even among some agricultural peoples.

Metalworking was extremely useful to agricultural or herding societies. Metal hoes and other tools allowed farmers to work the ground more efficiently. Metal weapons were obviously superior to those made from stone and wood. Agricultural peoples now supported the small number of individuals such as toolmakers, who specialized in this activity and exchanged their products with farmers for food. Specialization of this sort did not, however, guarantee rapid rates of invention; indeed, many specialized artisans seemed very conservative, eager to preserve methods that had been inherited. But specialization did improve the conditions or climate for discovery, and the invention of metalworking was a key result. Like agriculture, knowledge of metals gradually fanned out to other parts of Asia and to Africa and Europe.

Gradually, the knowledge of metal tools created further change, not only for farmers but also for manufacturing artisans benefited from better tools. Woodworking, for example, became steadily more elaborate as metal replaced stone, bone, and fire in the cutting and connecting of wood. We are, of course, still living in the metal ages today, although we rely primarily on iron—whose working was introduced around 1500 B.C.E. by herding peoples who moved into the Middle East from Central Asia—rather than copper and bronze.

By about 4000 B.C.E., other changes began to accumulate in several agricultural centers,

A headless reconstruction of an enthroned stone fertility goddess, from Çatal Hüyük.

particularly in the Middle East, beyond metalworking and the expansion of towns. These changes depended on the extent to which agricultural production could free up a few people to specialize in craft manufacturing, initially on products used in the agriculture process, such as the manufacture of pots. Gradually, certain other inventions cropped up that could benefit agricultural production, while also spilling over into other human activities such as warfare. Around 4000 B.C.E., for example, the wheel was introduced, probably by peoples who migrated into the Middle East. Here was a vital contribution to the movement of goods and, soon, to certain kinds of fighting.

PATHS TO THE PRESENT

By definition, the initial human experiences were in many ways remote from what we do and how we live today. They do, however, illustrate human capacities that we see around us—including adaptability to many different situations and geographies. A basic feature of today's world—that people exist in virtually every place that can support human life—occurred quite early. To be sure, the number of people was miniscule by contemporary standards, but humans had moved to all the inhabitable continents and most of the island groups where we find people today.

Agriculture's arrival is more obviously relevant to how we live now. Just recently, in the early 21st century, the majority of humans began to live in cities, rather than the countryside, for the first time. But many agricultural societies still exist, societies in which characteristics that emerged several millennia ago still apply.

Even in societies no longer dominated by agriculture, such as our own, questions derived from agriculture have not disappeared. We know, in industrial society, that the patriarchal gender relations generated by agriculture need to be rethought. But no society has yet fully resolved the question of what new gender model should replace patriarchy; traces of the older system, and groups committed to its values, still exist almost everywhere.

Early human activities and changes thus established key aspects of the framework in which global societies still function—including wide geographic distribution and the capacity to increase food supply through agriculture. They also set up issues that have survived a long time as well, because of the force and durability of agricultural forms. As world society debates gender rights or even appropriate roles for children, it must take this agricultural legacy into account.

SUGGESTED WEB SITES

For more information on the Stone Age, see www.stoneageinstitute.org/; on archeology, see www.ucl.ac.uk/archaeology/; on the Field Museum, see www.fieldmuseum.org/; on first peoples and cultures, see www.indians.edu/~arch/saa/matrix/ia/ia03_mod_10.html.

SUGGESTED READINGS

David Christian's *Maps of Time: An Introduction to Big History* (Berkeley, 2005) provides insight into perspectives on early human history and on; other rich accounts of human prehistory include John H Morgan's *"In the Beginning—": The Paleolithic Origins of Religious Consciousness* (2007); Brian Fagan *Peoples of the Earth* (1998 ed.); Pamela R. Willoughby, *The Evolution of Modern Humans in Africa: A Comprehensive Guide* (2007). See also Ronald Wright's *A Short History of Progress* (2004); John Mears, *Agricultural Origins in Global Perspective* (2000); Donald R. Kelley, "The Rise of Prehistory," *Journal of World History* (2003); www.historycooperative.org/jounals/jwh/14.1/kelley.html (2006); John Robb, *The Early Mediterranean Village: Agency, Matial Culture, and Social Change in Neolithic Italy* (2007); Michael Balter, *The Goddess and The Bull: Çatalhöyük—An Archaeological Journey to the Dawn of Civilization* (2006); Marcel Mazoyer and Laurence Roudart, *A History of World Agriculture: From the Neolithic Age to the Current Crisis* (2006); Raymond Corbey and Wil Roebrocks, eds., *Studying Human Origins: Disciplinary History and Epistemology* (2001); Joy Hakim, *The First Americas* (1999); David Tandy, ed., *Prehistory and History: Ethnicity, Class and Political Economy* (2001); Chris Gosden, *Prehistory: A Very Short Introduction* (2003); John F. Hoffecker, *A Prehistory of the North* [electronic resource]: *Human Settlement of the Higher Latitude* (2005); Steven Mithen, *After the Ice: A Global Human History, 20,000–5000 B.C.* (2004); and Barbara Sher Tinsley, *Reconstructing Western Civilization: Irreverent Essays on Antiquity* (2006).

On specific regions, see Douglas Price, *Europe's First Farmers* (2000); Ian Kuijt, *Life in Neolithic Farming Communities* (2000); P. D. Hunt, *Indian Agriculture in America* (1985); James Mellaart, *The Neolithic of the Near East* (1975); Chris Scarre, ed., *Monuments and Landscape in Atlantic Europe* (2002). Jared Diamond's *Guns, Germs and Steel: The Fate of Human Societies* (1997) deals powerfully with agriculture. On debates over human nature (culture and genetics), see Matt Ridley's *Nature Via Nurture* (2003). For a splendid guide to world history, from beginnings on, see Patrick Manning's *Navigating World History* (2003).

CHAPTER

2

Early Civilizations 3500–1000 B.C.E.

By 3000 B.C.E., Çatal Hüyük, the agricultural city discussed in Chapter 1, had become part of a civilization. Although many of the characteristics of civilization had existed by 6000 or 5000 B.C.E. in this Middle Eastern region, the origins of civilization, strictly speaking, approximately date to only 3500 B.C.E. From this point on to roughly 1000 B.C.E., the emergence of several civilization centers defined key developments in world history more generally. The first civilization arose in the Middle East along the banks of the Tigris and Euphrates rivers. Another center of civilization started soon thereafter in northeast Africa (Egypt), and a third by around 2500 B.C.E. along the banks of the Indus River in northwestern India. These three early centers of civilization had some interaction. The fourth early civilization center arose in China along the Yellow River, although a bit later and more separately. A fifth center would emerge in central America, though it was not river-based.

▉KEY QUESTIONS   *What did the river valley civilizations have in common? What were the main differences between them? How did developments in other parts of the world relate to the early civilization centers?*

CIVILIZATION

After the rise of agriculture, the introduction of civilization as a form of human organization was a crucial step for many people. Civilization first developed in Mesopotamia, after about 3500 B.C.E., on the heels of several changes in technology and communication. This form of human organization spread to several other places, and separately developed in China and Central America. Human organization along civilization lines did not emerge

17

everywhere at the same time, and many regions—even some successful agricultural economies—avoided it altogether, at least until much more recently. Hunting and gathering and nomadic societies lacked the economic surplus necessary to develop civilization, and often actively disliked the constraints they saw in civilization as well.

Civilizations normally demonstrated four distinctive features, operating powerfully in combination. First, they developed greater amounts of economic surplus, beyond subsistence needs, and they distributed this surplus unequally. This provided funds for new kinds of monuments. It also heightened social inequalities, compared to other, "non-civilized" kinds of societies. Second, civilizations developed formal governments, with at least small bureaucracies. Leadership thus became more specialized than in simpler agricultural or nomadic societies. Third,

almost all civilizations, including all the early ones, had writing. This facilitated trade over long distances by facilitating standardized communication; it enhanced recordkeeping, which aided both commerce and bureaucracy. And fourth, they developed larger and more important urban centers as cities emerged as concentrations of populations.

In agricultural civilizations, most people lived in the countryside, and most people remained illiterate. But cities and writing were nonetheless influential in shaping societies with different characteristics from those of the earliest agricultural settlements.

There are problems with the definition of civilization. Some scholars prefer to use a smaller number of criteria, which would allow other societies—those that had surpluses and some formal leadership, for example, but not cities and writing—to be included as civilizations.

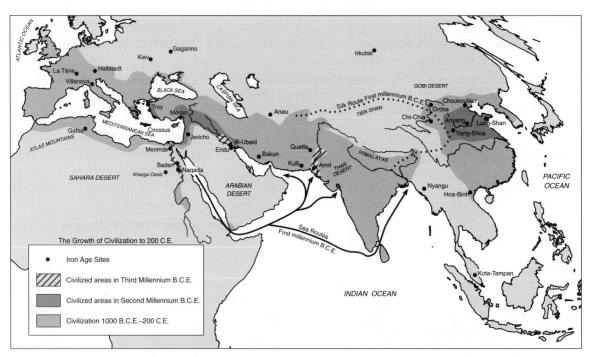

Afro-Eurasia: The Growth of Civilization to 200 C.E.

More serious is the common connotation of civilization as being unusually refined and restrained. Leaders of early civilizations often argued that their way of life was more cultivated than that of non-civilized peoples—barbarians—around them. But people in civilizations could be cruel and rude. To groups such as North American Indians, encountering Europenas in the 17th century, the behavior of the "civilized"—including drinking, violence to children, and the like—seemed far cruder than their own, whose habits and capacities for emotional control were often quite refined. Civilization as meaning greater impulse control should not be included in the definition of civilization as a form of human organization. The two meanings might, but also might very well not, overlap.

Civilizations also increased human impact on the environment. For example, the first center of copper production in Europe, along the Danube valley, led to such deforestation that the fuel supply was destroyed, and the industry collapsed after about 3000 B.C.E. The extensive agriculture needed to support Indus river cities opened the land to erosion and flooding because of overuse of the soil and removal of trees.

The areas where early civilization developed covered only a tiny portion of the inhabited parts of the world, although they were the most densely populated. Such early civilizations, all clustered in key river valleys, were in a way pilot tests of the new form of social organization. Only after about 1000 B.C.E. did a more consistent process of development and spread of civilization begin—and with it came the main threads of world history. However, the great civilizations unquestionably built on the achievements of the river valley pioneers, so some understanding of this contribution to the list of early human accomplishments is essential.

Tigris-Euphrates Civilization

The most noteworthy achievements of the earliest civilizations were early versions of organizational and cultural forms that most of us now take for granted—writing; formal codes of law; city planning and architecture; and institutions for trade, including the use of money. Once developed, most of these building blocks of human organization did not have to be reinvented, although in some cases they spread only slowly to other parts of the world.

It is not surprising then, given its lead in agriculture, metalworking, and village structure, that the Middle East generated the first example of human civilization. Indeed, the first civilization, founded in the valley of the Tigris and Euphrates rivers in a part of the Middle East long called Mesopotamia, forms one of only a few cases of a civilization developed absolutely from scratch—and with no examples from any place else to imitate. (Chinese civilization and civilization in Central America also developed independently.) By 4000 B.C.E., the farmers of Mesopotamia were familiar with bronze and copper working and had already invented the wheel for transportation. They had a well-established pottery industry and interesting artistic forms. Farming in this area, because of the need for irrigation, required considerable coordination among communities, and this in turn served as the basis for complex political structures.

By about 3500 B.C.E., a people who had recently invaded this region, the Sumerians, developed a cuneiform system, the first known case of human writing. Their system at first used different pictures to represent various objects but soon shifted to the use of geometric shapes to symbolize spoken sounds. Early Sumerian writing may have had as many as 2000 such symbols, but this number was later reduced to about 300, as later people adapted the system for their own languages. Even so, writing and reading remained complex skills, which only a few had time to master. Scribes wrote on clay tablets, using styluses shaped quite like the modern ballpoint pen.

Sumerian art developed steadily as statues and painted frescoes were used to adorn the temples of the gods. Statues of the gods also decorated individual homes. Sumerian science aided a complex agricultural society, as people sought to learn more about the movement of the sun and stars—thus founding the science of astronomy—and improved their mathematical knowledge. (Astronomy defined the calendar and provided the astrological forecasts widely used in politics and religion.) The Sumerians employed a system of numbers based on units of 10, 60, and 360 that we still use in calculating circles and hours. In other words, Sumerians and their successors in Mesopotamia created patterns of observation and abstract thought about nature that a number of civilizations, including our own, still rely on, and they also introduced specific systems, such as charts of major constellations, that have been in use, at least among educated people, for 5000 years not only in the Middle East but, by later imitation, in India and Europe as well.

Sumerians developed complex religious rituals. Each city had a patron god and erected impressive shrines to please and honor this and other deities. Massive towers, called ziggurats, formed the first monumental architecture in this civilization. Professional priests operated these temples and conducted the rituals within. Sumerians believed in many powerful gods, for the

nature on which their agriculture depended often seemed swift and unpredictable. Prayers and offerings to prevent floods as well as to protect good health were a vital part of Sumerian life. Sumerian ideas about the divine force in natural objects—in rivers, trees, and mountains—were common among early agricultural peoples; a religion of this sort, which sees gods in many aspects of nature, is known as *polytheism*. More specifically, Sumerian religious notions, notably their ideas about the gods' creation of the earth from water and about the divine punishment of humans through floods, later influenced the writers of the Old Testament and thus continue to play a role in Jewish, Christian, and Muslim cultures. Sumerian religious ideas also included a belief in an afterlife of punishment—an original version of the concept of hell.

Sumerian political structures stressed tightly organized city-states, ruled by a king who claimed divine authority. The Sumerian state had carefully defined boundaries, unlike the less formal territories of precivilized villages in the region. Here is a key early example of how civilization and a more formal political structure came together. The government helped regulate religion and enforce its duties; it also provided a court system in the interests of justice. Kings were originally military leaders during times of war, and the function of defense and war, including

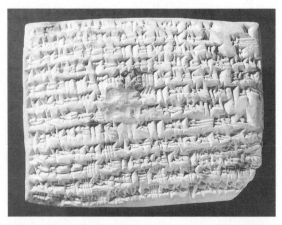

Cuneiform and Chinese lettering. *Left:* Cuneiform tablet from the Middle East. *Right:* A Shang dynasty oracle bone with ideographs.

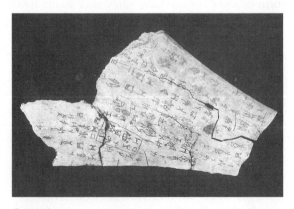

Oracle bone.

leadership of a trained army, remained vital in Sumerian politics. Kings and the noble class, along with the priesthood, controlled considerable land, which was worked by slaves. Thus began a tradition of slavery that long marked Middle Eastern societies. Warfare remained vital to ensure supplies of slaves, taken as prisoners during combat. At the same time, slavery was in a variable state of existence, and many slaves were able to earn money and even buy their freedom.

Mesopotamian civilization developed a strongly patriarchal family structure. By 3000, only men were shown as wielding a plow in Middle-Eastern art. Laws insisted that women remain sexually faithful, but they granted greater latitude to men. Women had a few legal protections, at least in principle: husbands were supposed to support their wives, and wives could legitimately leave if this support failed. Outside the law, customs developed, particularly in the cities, that further marked off women. By 2000 B.C.E., veiling of respectable women became common, in order to shield them from the eyes of men outside their family.

The Sumerians added to their region's agricultural prosperity not only by using wheeled carts but also by learning about fertilizers and by adopting silver as a means of exchange for buying and selling—an early form of money. However, the region was also hard to defend and proved a constant temptation to outside invaders from Sumerian times to the present. The Sumerians themselves fell to a people called the Akkadians, around 2400 B.C.E. The Akkadians continued much of Sumerian culture. It was an Akkadian king, Sargon, who came to be the first identifiable figure in world history, in terms of surviving records. He unified the empire and added to Sumerian art the theme of royal victory. Sargon maintained 5400 troops, a larger professional army than had existed before. Akkadians sent troops as far as Egypt and Ethiopia.

After about 200 years, another period of decline was followed by conquest by the Babylonians, who extended their own empire and

Bronze head of Sargon.

thus helped bring civilization to other parts of the Middle East. It was under Babylonian rule that the king Hammurabi introduced the most famous early code of law, boasting of his purpose:

> to promote the welfare of the people, me Hammurabi, the devout, god-fearing prince, to cause justice to prevail in the land, to destroy the wicked and the evil, that the strong might not oppress the weak.

Hammurabi's code established rules of procedure for courts of law and regulated property rights and the duties of family members, setting harsh punishments for crimes.

For many centuries during and after the heyday of Babylon, peace and civilization in the Middle East were troubled by the invasions of hunting and herding groups. Indo-European peoples pressed in from the north, starting about 2100 B.C.E. In the Middle East itself, invasions by Semitic peoples from the south were more important, and Semitic people and languages increasingly dominated the region. The new arrivals adopted the culture of the conquered peoples as their own, so the key features of the civilization persisted. But large political units declined in favor of smaller city-states or regional kingdoms, particularly during the centuries of greatest turmoil, between 1200 and 900 B.C.E. Thereafter, new invaders, first the Assyrians and then the Persians, created large new empires in the Middle East.

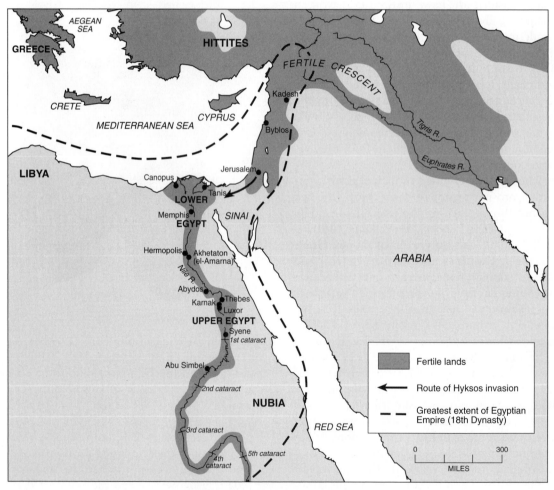

Ancient Egypt and Mesopotamia

SOLVING PROBLEMS

THE USE OF CULTURE

All human societies develop cultures—that is, patterns of beliefs, values, and assumptions that help them explain the world around them, define mutual obligations, and serve as a shared identity. Humans are not the only species that have cultures; several primates and a few bird species do. One group of chimpanzees in Africa, for example, has a quiet culture, in contrast to the noisy chattering of most chimp societies—presumably because they live amid gorillas and have learned (and taught their young) not to call attention to themselves. Here, as with humans, culture serves the basic function of facilitationg adaptation to different environments. But human culture is unusually elaborate and important. With the power of speech, *Homo sapiens sapiens* had opportunities to construct more culture than other species. Also, spreading to very diverse environments, humans were able to use culture as part of basic adjustment—cultures in this sense solved problems by organizing learning patterns. Compared to many other species, humans had fewer pure instincts but had more learned or partially learned behavior. This helped them cope. It also helps explain why it takes so long to train a human into what we regard as full adulthood.

Cultures provoke two kinds of discussion. First, and most fundamental, is the question of how much of human behavior is explained by culture, how much by innate characteristics. This distinction is often called nature versus nurture. Cultural analysts note what a wide variety of ideas and practices can develop even around seemingly basic natural phenomena—such as whether urine is disgusting or useful, or how to regard homosexuality, or whether anger is a useful emotion or should be repressed.

A second culture discussion involves the two edges of diversity itself. Human societies generated very pronounced and different cultures. These different characteristics or strategies helped members of a society cope with their particular circumstances, and they also established another function for culture: the provision of group identity. These cultural differences could also greatly complicate relationships with other groups, causing or complicating the resolution of conflict. Different cultures can disagree fiercely over how children should be raised, or how to understand disease, or whether tolerance is a good quality or a dangerous distraction from the truth. Some cultural variance is simply interesting, but some can generate misunderstandings and clashes. We live with this dilemma of culture today, with a vengeance.

■**QUESTIONS:** *Can a specific culture shape how humans express basic emotions? How did different cultures address specific problems, such as the health danger of eating undercooked pork?*

Egyptian Civilization

A second center of civilization sprang up in northern Africa, along the Nile River. Egyptian civilization, formed by 3000 B.C.E., benefited from the trade and technological influence of Mesopotamia, but it produced quite a different society and culture. Less open to invasion, Egypt retained a unified state throughout most of its history. With some fluctuations, the kingdom lasted almost 3000 years, though its period of greatest vitality had passed by 1000 B.C.E. Farming had developed along the Nile by about 5000 B.C.E., but economic activity increased before 3200, in part because of greater trade with Mesopotamia. This acceleration provided the basis for the formation of regional kingdoms and soon a unified empire along the great river.

Ushabti, a carved blue figure, of an Egyptian pharaoh wearing a royal headdress and carrying agricultural tools.

The Egyptian economy was more fully government-directed than its Mesopotamian counterpart, which had a more independent business class. Government control may have been necessary because of the complexity of coordinating irrigation along the Nile. It nonetheless resulted in godlike status for the pharaohs, who built splendid tombs for themselves—the pyramids—from 2700 B.C.E. on. During periods of weak rule and occasional invasions, Egyptian society suffered a decline, but revivals kept the framework of Egyptian civilization intact until after 1000 B.C.E. At key points, Egyptian influence spread up the Nile to the area now known as Sudan, with an impact on the later development of African culture. The kingdom of Kush interacted with Egypt and invaded it at some points.

Neither Egyptian science nor the Egyptian alphabet was as elaborate as its Mesopotamian equal, although mathematics was more advanced in this civilization. Egyptian art was exceptionally lively; cheerful and colorful pictures decorated not only the tombs—where the belief in an afterlife made people want to be surrounded by objects of beauty—but also palaces and furnishings. Egyptian architectural forms were also quite influential, not only in Egypt but in other parts of the Mediterranean as well. Egyptian mathematics produced the idea of a day divided into 24 hours, and here too Egypt influenced the development of later Mediterranean cultures.

The most famous Egyptian art form was of course the pyramid, which the pharaohs built to house themselves and their families after death. The largest pyramids required labor forces of up to 100,000 people, and they were amazing achievements given the state of Egyptian technology. Workers rolled the huge stones, weighing more than 5 tons, over logs and onto Nile barges. The pyramids attested to royal power. They also illustrated Egypt's ability to generate agricultural surpluses and to command a labor force.

Egypt interacted periodically with the Middle East, but the contacts were not very influential in either direction. Egypt's interactions with the upper reaches of the Nile, deeper into Africa, were more

Because of its early unity and its cohesion along the banks of the Nile, Egypt had fewer problems with political unity than Mesopotamia did. The king, or pharaoh, possessed immense power.

significant. After about 1570 B.C.E., in the final main phase of the great kingdoms, Egypt also expanded trade with the islands of the eastern Mediterranean, which extended the empire's influence to southern Europe, particularly in terms of monumental art but also in the area of mathematics.

EGYPT AND MESOPOTAMIA COMPARED

Comparisons in politics, culture, economics, and society suggest that the two civilizations varied substantially because of largely separate origins and environments. The distinction in overall tone was striking, with Egypt more stable and optimistic than Mesopotamia not only in its beliefs about gods and the afterlife but also in the colorful and lively pictures the Egyptians emphasized in their decorative art. The distinction in internal history was also striking: Egyptian civilization was far less marked by disruption than its Mesopotamian counterpart.

Egypt and Mesopotamia differed in many ways thanks to variations in geography, exposure to outside invasion and influence, and different beliefs. Despite trade and war, they did not imitate each other much. Egypt emphasized strong central authority, whereas Mesopotamian politics shifted more often over a substructure of regional city-states. Mesopotamian art focused on less monumental structures and embraced a literary element that Egyptian art lacked.

The economies differed as well. Mesopotamia developed more technological improvements because the environment was more difficult to manage than the Nile valley. Trade contacts were more wide-ranging, and the Mesopotamians gave considerable attention to a merchant class and commercial law.

Social differences between the two civilizations are less obvious because we have less information on daily life for this early period. It is probable, though, that the status of women was higher in Egypt than in Mesopotamia (where

Relief from the temple of Aten at Tel el-Amarna.

women's position seems to have deteriorated after Sumer). Egyptians seem to have paid great respect to women, at least in the upper classes, in part because marriage alliances were vital to the preservation and stability of the monarchy. Vivid love poetry indicated a high regard for emotional relations between men and women. Also, Egyptian religion included more pronounced deference to goddesses as sources of creativity. Egyptians did not practice female infanticide—the killing of baby girls—which most societies used for population control.

Differences were not the whole story, as river valley civilizations, Egypt and Mesopotamia

HISTORY DEBATE

WOMEN IN PATRIARCHAL SOCIETIES

In contrast to hunting-and-gathering societies, agricultural civilizations were generally *patriarchal;* that is, they were not only run by men but were based on the assumption that men directed political, economic, and cultural life. Furthermore, as agricultural civilizations developed and became more prosperous and more elaborately organized, the status of women increasingly deteriorated.

Patriarchal family structure rested on men's control of most or all property, starting with land. Marriage was based on property relationships, and it was assumed that marriage, and therefore subordination to men, was the normal condition for women. A revealing symptom of patriarchy in families was the fact that after marrying, a woman usually moved to the orbit (and often the residence) of her husband's family.

Characteristic patriarchal conditions developed in Mesopotamian civilization. Thus, in Sumerian law, the adultery of a wife was punishable by death, whereas a husband's adultery was treated far more lightly—a double standard characteristic of patriarchalism. Mesopotamian societies after Sumerian times began to emphasize the importance of a woman's virginity at marriage and to require women to wear veils in public to emphasize their modesty. A good portion of Mesopotamian law (such as the Hammurabic code) was devoted to prescriptions for women, ensuring certain basic protections but clearly emphasizing limits and inferiority.

Patriarchal conditions varied from one agricultural civilization to another. Egyptian civilization gave women, at least in the upper classes, considerable credit and witnessed several powerful queens. Nefertiti, wife of Akhenaton, seems to have been influential in the religious disputes during his reign; artistic works suggest her religious role. Some agricultural societies traced descendants from mothers rather than from fathers. This was true of Jewish law, for example. But even these matrilineal societies held women to be inferior to men; for example, Jewish law insisted that men and women worship separately, with men occupying the central temple space. These variations are important, but they usually operated within a basic framework of patriarchalism. It was around 2000 B.C.E. that an Egyptian writer, Ptah Hotep, put patriarchal beliefs as clearly as anyone in the early civilizations: "If you are a man of note, found for yourself a household, and love your wife at home, as it beseems. Fill her belly, clothe her back. . . . But hold her back from getting the mastery."

As agriculture improved with the use of better techniques, women's labor, though still vital, became less important than it had been in hunting-and-gathering or early agricultural societies. This was particularly true in the upper classes and in cities, where men often took over the most productive work (e.g., craft production or political leadership). The inferior position of women in the upper classes, relative to men, usually was more marked than in peasant villages, where women's labor remained essential.

Patriarchalism raises important questions about women themselves: Why did they put up with it? Many women internalized the culture of patriarchalism, holding that it was their job to obey and to serve men and accepting arguments that their aptitudes were inferior to those of men. But patriarchalism did not preclude some important options for women. In many societies, a minority of women could gain expression through religious tasks, such as prayer or service in ceremonies. These could allow them to act independently of family structures. Patriarchal laws defined some rights for women even within marriage, protecting them in theory from the worst abuses. Babylonian law, for example, gave women as well as men the right to divorce under certain conditions when the spouse had not lived up to obligations. Women could also wield informal power in patriarchal societies by their emotional hold over husbands or sons. Such power was indirect, behind the scenes, but a forceful woman might use these means to figure prominently in a society's history. Women also could form networks, if only within a large household.

Older women, who commanded the obedience of many daughters-in-law and unmarried daughters, could shape the activities of the family.

Patriarchalism was a commanding theme in most agricultural civilizations from the early centuries on. Its enforcement, through law and culture, was one means by which societies tried to achieve order. In many agricultural civilizations, patriarchalism dictated that boys, because of their importance in carrying on the family name and the chief economic activities, were more likely to survive: when population excess threatened a family or a community, female infants sometimes were killed as a means of population control.

shared important features. Both emphasized social stratification, with a noble, landowning class at the top and masses of peasants and slaves at the bottom. A powerful priestly group also figured in the elite. Although specific achievements in science differed, both civilizations emphasized astronomy and related mathematics and produced durable findings about units of time and measurement. Both Mesopotamia and Egypt changed slowly by more modern standards. Having developed successful political and economic systems, both societies tended strongly toward conservation. Change, when it came, usually was brought by outside forces (natural disasters or invasions).

Finally, both civilizations left important heritages in their regions and adjacent territories. Several smaller civilization centers were launched under the impetus of Mesopotamia and Egypt, and some produced important innovations of their own by about 1000 B.C.E.

INDIAN AND CHINESE RIVER VALLEY CIVILIZATIONS

River valley civilizations developed in two other centers. A prosperous urban civilization emerged along the Indus River by 2500 B.C.E., supporting several large cities, including Harappa, whose houses even had running water. Toilets, in fact, connected to citywide drainage systems, were perhaps the first that humans ever invented. Indus River peoples had trading contacts with Mesopotamia, but they developed their own distinctive alphabet

and artistic forms. The large cities, including Harappa itself, contained buildings that were probably palaces, with audience rooms for people to appeal to the rulers for assistance. Public baths were also available. Governments stored grain for times of shortage and for festival days. Trade was extensive, and precious stones from China and southeast Asia have been found. Priests had great power in this civilization, servings as intermediaries between the people and the gods and goddesses who were believed to control fertility.

For all their achievements, the Harappan people seem to have been somewhat conservative. Though they used bronze, they did not keep up with the tools available in Mesopotamia, though they had contact with this area. Notably, they did not manufacture swords, relying on bronze-tipped arrows instead. They became vulnerable to attack.

Harappa remains something of a mystery. Its ruins began to be discovered only in the mid-19th century, when it began to become clear that this had been a major center of ancient civilization but also rather unlike what later developed in India, for example in terms of the styles of writing. We also do not fully know what caused the civilization to decline after about 1500 B.C.E. The decline was gradual and probably resulted from several factors, including massive flooding. Invasions and, even more, migrations by a cattle-herding people, the Indo-Europeans, probably challenged the control of the priestly group. Some violence was probably involved, and skeletons with crushed skulls and in postures of flight, either from

Statuette of a mother goddess from Harappa, Indus River.

invaders or from floods, have been found. The Harappan decline resulted in such complete destruction of this culture that we know little about its nature or its subsequent influence on India. Harappan writing, for example, has yet to be deciphered. It remains true that civilization never had to be fully reinvented in India. The Indo-European migrants combined their religious and political ideas with those that had taken root in the early cities. In recent times, Indians' pride in their early civilized history has become an important part of their national identity.

Civilization along the Huanghe (Yellow River) in China developed in considerable isolation, although some overland trading contact

with India and the Middle East did develop. Huanghe civilization was the subject of much later Chinese legend, which praised the godlike kings of early civilization, starting with the mythic ancestor of the Chinese, Pan Gu. The Chinese had an unusually elaborate concept of their remote origins, and they began early to record a part-fact, part-fiction history of their early kings. What is clear is the following: first, a well-organized state developed that carefully regulated irrigation in the fertile but flood-prone river valley. Early kings sponsored a considerable network of dikes and canals. Second, by about 2000 B.C.E., the Chinese had produced an advanced technology and developed an elaborate intellectual life. They had learned how to ride horses and were skilled in pottery; they used bronze well and by 1000 B.C.E. had introduced iron, which they soon learned to work with coal. Their writing progressed from knotted ropes to scratches of lines on bone to the invention of ideographic symbols. By 1500 B.C.E., at least 3000 pictographic characters had been devised. This standardized writing began to provide some unity to the very diverse peoples assembled in this river valley kingdom, who originally spoke a wide array of languages. Science, particularly astronomy, also arose early. Chinese art emphasized delicate designs, and the Chinese claim an early interest in music. Because of limits on building materials in the region, the Chinese did not construct many massive monuments, choosing to live in simple houses built of mud. By about 1500 B.C.E., a line of kings called the Shang ruled over the Huanghe valley, and these rulers did construct some impressive tombs and palaces. Invasions disrupted the Shang dynasty and caused a temporary decline in civilization. However, there was less of a break between the river valley society and the later, fuller development of civilization in China than occurred in other centers.

River valley civilization in China generated a number of features of importance for later periods. Silk manufacturing developed. Some form of ancestor worship began. Emphasis on a

Early Chinese art. An elaborate clay vase, imitating bronze, from the Shang dynasty.

strong, expansionist state, particularly under the Shang, set the basis for later Chinese politics. The Shang fought on horseback and from chariots, using conquered peoples as foot soldiers. They maintained fuller control over their armies than was characteristic of many other early societies. Shang rulers also directed important rituals, devoted to fertility. In times of famine or drought, the state provided dancers to woo the gods with their performance, and the dancers were later buried alive to calm the spirits who had caused the natural disaster. The state, in other words, took on cultural responsibilities, and this too characterized the Chinese political tradition.

TRANSITIONS: THE END OF THE RIVER VALLEY PERIOD

The river valley societies were widely separated, though they had trading contacts with their neighbors and, in the case of the Middle East and north Africa, an occasional military encounter. With this separation, it is not surprising that there was no single development, or even a single century, to signal the transition away from the river valley period. Several developments did, however, roughly coincide.

In China, the control of the Shang had loosened, and then a central Asian people, the Zhou, probably of Turkic origin, began to migrate into Shang territory. They initially recognized Shang rule but then seized power themselves, by about 1100 B.C.E. Zhou rulers used kinsmen to rule particular regions, granting them land and insisting on elaborate oaths of mutual loyalty, in what amounted to a feudal system that decentralized political power. The vassals passed on some of the local tax revenues to the central government. This system worked effectively for a while, though it burdened the heavily taxed peasants.. Ultimately, the political system broke down. But it was under the Zhou that improvements in agriculture, use of iron, extensive cultural changes, and the sheer expansion of Chinese territory began to mark a new stage in Chinese history. Important ties to the river valley period remained, but changes were accumulating.

The end of the river valley period in northwestern India was of course far more decisive, given the gradual but conclusive decline of Harappan society. Migrating and invading Indo-European peoples even ignored agriculture for many centuries, relying on animal herding. The Indo-Europeans were more warlike than the Harappans, with far less emphasis on orderly government. They brought in different ideas about gods and goddesses, though some emphasis on the power of goddesses may have been borrowed from Harappan religion. The Indo-Europeans also fanned out over a wider area of India than the Harappans had controlled. Gradually, they began to settle down, adopting agriculture and expanding trade. But in the process, most traces of Harappan civilization became a dim memory. A few symbols remained, including the mother goddess and yoga positions. So did certain artistic images, including a swastika that became prominent in later Indian religious art. Public bathing facilities, another Harappan legacy, persisted in some Indian cities, particularly in the south. Agricultural techniques, including the growing of cotton, were not abandoned, and the Indo-Europeans ultimately took them over. But with the passing of Harappa, a decisive new period in Indian history clearly began.

A different set of developments took place in the Middle East and north Africa. In Egypt, we have seen that the power of the pharaohs began to weaken by around 1000 B.C.E. Invasions, including from other African peoples in the south, became more common. At times, the kingdom was divided in half. After 500 B.C.E. Persian, then Greek, then Roman invasions effectively brought an end to Egypt's independence.

In the Middle East, the pattern of outside invasion continued to 1000 B.C.E. and even beyond. As before, the new states tended to adopt Mesopotamian culture and legal forms. Around 1100 invasions by an Assyrian ruler were marked by unusual cruelty, including mass execution and the deporting of civilian populations. But the Assyrians did not maintain consistent control, though parts of their empire revived periodically. This inconsistency, and the decline of Egypt, allowed the formation of a number of smaller states for several centuries around 1000 B.C.E.

THE HERITAGE OF THE RIVER VALLEY CIVILIZATIONS

Many accomplishments of the river valley civilizations had a lasting impact. Monuments such as the Egyptian pyramids have long been regarded as one of the wonders of the world. Other achievements, although more prosaic, are fundamental to world history even today: the invention of the wheel, the taming of the horse, the creation of usable alphabets and writing implements, the production of key mathematical concepts such as square roots, the development of well-organized monarchies and bureaucracies, and the invention of functional calendars and methods for other divisions of time. These basic achievements, along with the awe that the early civilizations continue to inspire, are vital legacies to the whole of human history. Almost all the major alphabets in the world today are derived from the writing forms pioneered in the river valleys, apart from the even more durable concept of writing itself. Almost all later civilizations, then, built on the massive foundations first constructed in the river valleys.

Despite these accomplishments, we have seen that most of the river valley civilizations were in decline by 1000 B.C.E. The civilizations had flourished for as many as 2500 years, although of course with periodic disruptions and revivals. But, particularly in India, the new waves of invasion did produce something of a break in the history of civilization, a dividing line between the river valley pioneers and later cultures.

This break raises one final question: besides the vital achievements—the fascinating monuments and the indispensable advances in technology, science, and art—what legacies did the river valley civilizations leave for later ages? The question is particularly important for the Middle East and Egypt. In India, we must frankly admit much ignorance about possible links between Indus River accomplishments and what came later; in China, there is a definite connection between the first civilization and subsequent forms. Indeed, the new dynasty in China, the Zhou, took over from the Shang about 1100 B.C.E., ruling a loose coalition of regional lords; recorded Chinese history flowed smoothly at this point. But what was the legacy of Mesopotamia and Egypt for later civilizations in or near their centers?

Europeans, even North Americans, are sometimes prone to claim these cultures as the "origins" of the Western civilization in which we live. These claims should not be taken too literally. It is not altogether clear that either Egypt or Mesopotamia contributed much to later political traditions, although the Roman Empire emulated the concept of a godlike king, as evidenced in the trappings of the office, and the existence of strong city-state governments in the Middle East continued to be significant. Ideas about slavery may also have been passed on from these early civilizations. Specific scientific achievements are vital, but scholars argue over how much of a connection exists between Mesopotamian and Egyptian science and later Greek thinking, aside from certain techniques of measuring time or charting the stars. Some historians of philosophy have asserted a basic division between a Mesopotamian and Chinese understanding of nature, which they claim affected later civilizations around the Mediterranean in contrast to China. Mesopotamians were prone to stress a gap between humankind and nature, whereas Chinese thinking developed along ideas of basic harmony. It is possible, then, that some fundamental thinking helped shape later outlooks, but the continuities here are not easy to assess. Mesopotamian art and Egyptian architecture had a more measurable influence on Greek styles, and through these, in turn, later European and Islamic cultures. The Greeks thus learned much about temple building from the Egyptians, whose culture had influenced island civilizations, such as Crete, which then affected later Greek styles.

NEW STATES AND PEOPLES AROUND 1000 B.C.E.

There was a final connection between early and later civilizations in the form of regional cultures that sprang up under the influence of Mesopotamia and Egypt, along the eastern shores of the Mediterranean, and in northeastern Africa mainly after 1200 B.C.E. Although the great empires from Sumer through Babylon were disrupted and the Egyptian state finally declined, civilization in the Middle East and north Africa had spread widely enough to encourage a set of smaller cultures capable of surviving and even flourishing after the great empires became weak. These cultures produced important innovations that affected later civilizations in the Middle East and throughout the Mediterranean. They also created a diverse array of regional identities that continued to mark the Middle East even as other forces, such as the Roman Empire or the later religion of Islam, took center stage. Several of these small cultures proved immensely durable, and in their complexity and capacity to survive, they influenced other parts of the world as well.

Kingdoms began to develop south of Egypt, for example. A kingdom in Kush emerged about 2000 B.C.E., under strong Egyptian influence. Egypt conquered the area after 1500, setting up an elaborate bureaucracy and building large temples. At this point, the population of Kush was about 100,000. Trade with southern Arabia expanded. In the 8th century, Kushites conquered Egypt, though they soon were driven out by Assyrians. Kingdoms in northeastern Africa continued to flourish, with a growing population. Local artistic styles combined with the use of Egyptian forms such as pyramids and obelisks. Much of this tradition continued in the later kingdom of Ethiopia.

Along the Mediterranean cost of the Middle East, another mixture of societies emerged. A people called the Phoenicians, for example, devised a greatly simplified writing system with 22 letters around 1300 B.C.E.; this alphabet, in turn, became the predecessor of Greek and Latin alphabets. The Phoenicians also improved the Egyptian numbering system. Great traders, they set up colony cities in north Africa and on the coasts of Europe. Phoenicians traded as far away as England, where they purchased tin to make

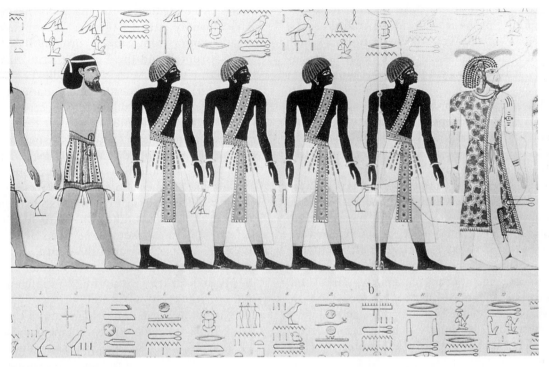

Egyptian tomb painting.

bronze. Another regional group, the Lydians, first introduced coined money.

The most important of the smaller Middle Eastern groups in terms of ultimate historical impact were the Jews, who gave the world the first clearly developed monotheistic religion. We have seen that early religions, both before and after the beginnings of civilization, were polytheistic, claiming that many gods and goddesses worked to control nature and human destiny. The Jews, a Semitic people influenced by Babylonian civilization, settled near the Mediterranean around 1200 B.C.E. The Jewish state was small and relatively weak, retaining independence only when other parts of the Middle East were in political turmoil. What was distinctive about this culture was its firm belief that a single God, Jehovah, guided the destinies of the Jewish people. Priests and prophets defined and emphasized this belief, and their history of God's guidance of their people formed the basis for the Hebrew Bible. The Jewish religion and moral code persisted even as the Jewish state suffered domination by a series of foreign rulers, from 772 B.C.E. until the Romans seized the state outright in 63 B.C.E. Jewish monotheism has sustained a distinctive Jewish culture to this day; it also served as a basis for the development of both Christianity and Islam as major world religions.

Because Judaism stressed God's special compact with the chosen Jewish people, there was no premium placed on converting non-Jews. This belief helps explain the durability of the Jewish faith itself; it also kept the Jewish people in a minority position in the Middle East as a whole.

However, the elaboration of monotheism had a wide, if not immediate, significance. In Jewish hands, the concept of God became less humanlike, more abstract. This represented a basic change in not only religion but also humankind's overall outlook. Jehovah had not only a power but also a rationality far different from what the traditional gods of the Middle East or Egypt possessed. These gods were whimsical and capricious; Jehovah was orderly and just, and individuals knew what to expect if they obeyed God's rules. God was also linked to ethical conduct, to proper moral behavior. Religion for the Jews was a way of life, not merely a set of rituals and ceremonies. The full impact of this religious transformation on Middle Eastern civilization was realized only later, when Jewish beliefs were embraced by other, proselytizing faiths. However, the basic concept of monotheistic religion was one of the legacies of the end of the first great civilization period to the new cultures that soon arose.

PATHS
TO THE PRESENT

Some of the achievements of the early civilizations invoke a sense of awe that is expressed as our wonder at what people so long ago could achieve, but also as our awareness of how separate they are from us today. We gape at pictures of the pyramids, and study how a society relying on human labor alone could build them; but we also know that the idea of building such massive monuments to individual leaders is a product of an earlier age.

Nonetheless, connections exist between the early civilizations and the present beyond our sense of wonder. Most obviously, early civilizations created a foundation that has not required reinvention. Different writing systems emerged, but the idea of writing flows directly from these early systems. The same holds for basic concepts of government, including codes of law. Some parts of early law codes might strike us as pioneering even today—such as the idea of society compensating victims of crimes, which was part of the Hammurabic code. Money is another staple that links present systems to the inventiveness of early civilization. In these and other respects, the early civilizations created implements for human activity, in trade or government, that we take for granted.

There is debate about how many of the less tangible characteristics of human activity have survived from the early period. Does a Chinese interest in political order—still strong in China today—date back to the Shang dynasty, or was this a value that was instilled at a later time? The many rival groups and traditions in the Middle East today are not what they were 4000 years ago, but some of the components of these conflicts date back to the mixture of peoples and invasions operating at that point. Certainly, there is a straight line between the Jewish identity and religion forged late in the early civilization period and the Jewish people today. Historians debate how much legacy Egypt or Mesopotamia created for later history, much less for today, because of the impact of later cultures and institutions on these regions. But there are at least some connections, for example, in architectural styles and scientific ideas, beyond the apparatus of civilization itself.

SUGGESTED WEB SITES

To visit the Oriental Institute Museum, go to http://oi.uchicago.edu/OI/MUS/GALLERY/EAST/New_East_Gallery.html; to explore ancient world cultures, see http://eawc.evansville.edu/; to learn more on the mysteries of Çatal Hüyük, go to www.smm.org/catal/top.php; visit the Weaving Art Museum and Research Institute at www.weavingartmuseum.org/. See also the

Ancient History Sourcebook from Fordham University at www.fordham.edu/halsall/ancient/asbook.html.

SUGGESTED READINGS

Robert Chadwick, *First Civilizations: Ancient Mesopotamia and Ancient Egypt* (2005); Robert G. Morkot, *The Egyptians: An Introduction* (2005); Ian Shaw, *Exploring Ancient Egypt* (2003); Francis Joannès, *The Age of Empires: Mesopotamia in the First Millennium B.C.* (2004); Christiance Cesroches Noblecourt, *Gifts from the Pharaohs: How Egyptian Civilization Shaped the Modern World* (2007); Mu-Chou Poo, *Enemies of Civilization: Attitudes Toward Foreigners in Ancient Mesopotamia, Egypt, and China* (2005); Kwang-chih Chang, *The Formation of Chinese Civilization: An Archaeological Perspective* (2005); "Formation of Chinese Civilization," found at www.china.org.cn/e-gudai/; Li Liu, *The Chinese Neolithic: Trajectories to Early States* (Cambridge, 2004); David N. Keightley, *The Ancestral Landscape: Time, Space, and Community in Late Shang China, ca. 1200–1045 B.C.* (Berkeley, 2000); Jayantanuja Bandyopadhyaya, *Class and Religion in Ancient India* (2008); Kiran Kumar Thaplyal, *Village and Village Life in Ancient India* (2004); Mark Kenoyer, *Ancient Cities of the Indus Valley Civilizations* (1998); Gregory L. Possehl, *Indus Age: The Beginnings* (1999); A.C. Pandey, *Government in Ancient India* (2000); Nicola Di Cosmo, *Ancient China and Its Enemies* (2002); and Donald B. Redford, *From Slave to Pharaoh: The Black Experience of Ancient Egypt* (Baltimore, 2004).

On the environment, see I. G. Simmons, *Environmental History* (1993). On patterns of contact, see Philip D. Curtin, *Cross-Cultural Trade in World History* (1984); Xinru Liu, *Ancient India and Ancient China: Trade and Religious Exchanges* (1988); and Shereen Ratnagar, *Encounter: The Westerly Trade of the Harappan Civilization* (1981). On the science and technology of the ancient world are discussed in Richard Bulliet, see *The Camel and the Wheel* (1975); George Ifrah, *From One to Zero: A Universal History of Numbers* (1985); and Edgardo Marcorini, ed., *The History of Science and Technology: A Narrative Chronology* (1988). The nature and influence of early science, particularly from Egypt, is also covered in Dick Teresi's *Lost Discoveries: The Ancient Roots of Modern Science* (2002). See also M. E. Auber, *The Phoenicians and the West* (1996); Donald Redford, *Egypt, Canaan, and Israel in Ancient Times* (1995); Gay Robbins, *Women in Ancient Egypt* (1993); and J. Curtis, *Ancient Persia* (1989).

3 Nomadic Societies

Not everyone nor every area was folded into the embrace of agricultural civilizations and societies. World historians are paying increasing attention to nomadic herding peoples, whose economy and society contrasted with the more standard pattern. These smaller groups of people were capable of great impact because, of necessity, they moved around considerably. They were in a position to contact and influence civilizations, and to link civilizations through trade.

Nomadic populations were smaller than those of the civilizations, with economies that developed fewer resources. This was one reason that nomads recurrently pressed into other areas, to relieve population pressure. Indeed, nomadic peoples show up in world history particularly when they migrated into more settled areas, or when they invaded. But they also, more systematically, provided trading contacts, through which ideas and techniques could spread. And they introduced some important techniques of their own.

■ **KEY QUESTIONS**   *How did nomadic societies differ from civilizations? Why might a herding economy be preferred over agriculture? What kinds of contacts did nomadic peoples have with civilizations?*

EARLY NOMADIC SOCIETIES

We do not know when nomadic societies developed, for they have left few written records and no real architectural monuments. They may have begun before the first civilizations emerged. Nomadic societies ultimately developed particularly in the region of the huge grassy plains of central Asia, on the fringes of the Sahara desert in Africa, and also in southern Arabia. Smaller nomadic societies also developed in the Americas, in the Andes Mountains, the only place where there were relevant domesticated animals. Nomadic regions generally are characterized by rainfalls sufficient for developing grasslands but less adequate for settled agriculture.

The first groups of nomads to break into the historical record were the Indo-Europeans, who periodically intervened in the civilizations of the Middle East and India for a thousand years, beginning about 1500 B.C.E. Some Indo-European groups invaded civilized areas and established their own empires—such as the Hittites, who fit into the series of empire-invaders in Mesopotamia. Others, such as the Greeks, migrated into new territory and settled down, ultimately trying to fight off later groups of Indo-European invaders with whom they finally intermingled. Indo-European incursions into India increasingly threatened the later phases of Harappan civilization. Early Indo-

Europeans used war chariots drawn by horses, but gradually they developed the equipment needed to ride horses directly.

Another early nomadic group that played an important role in larger world history, also from central Asia, was the Xionghu, known in Europe as the Huns. The Hun invasions in China caused great devastation from the 4th century B.C.E. on. Like the Indo-Europeans before them, Hun movements were probably initially due to droughts and internal warfare in central Asia, but then, achieving success, they took on a life of their own.

Other early nomadic groups included reindeer herders in northern Europe (the Lapps). More important were the camel herders in Arabia and north central Africa. The camel was domesticated by 1700 B.C.E. as a pack animal. Its capacity for traveling with huge loads, for more than 20 days without new water, was ideal

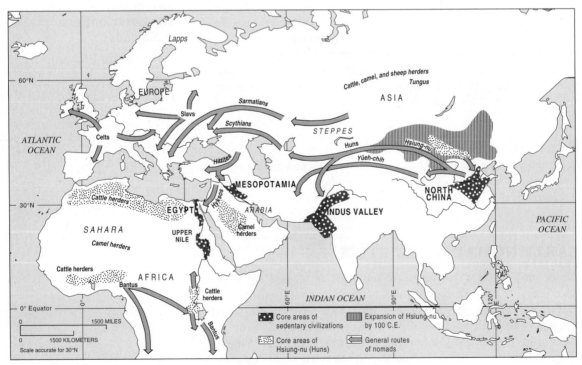

Earliest Civilizations and Migrations of Nomads

for nomadic life in the deserts. Cattle-raising nomads also played a role in parts of Africa.

NOMADIC SOCIETY AND CULTURE

Seasonal travel was fundamental to the nomadic way of life. Harsh weather forced movement in search of adequate food, and too much time in one place exhausted the available vegetation. Most nomadic groups usually traveled the same routes, year after year. But droughts or other hardships could promote change. While nomadic groups usually respected each other's routes, problems could cause conflicts as one group tried to muscle into the territory of another.

Animals formed the core of the cultural interests of nomadic societies, with religion usually emphasizing animal sacrifices. Size of herd was the measure of wealth in nomadic societies. Animals were also the core of the nomadic economy. Nomads traded in leather, wool, milk products, and bone sculptures.

The harshness of the nomadic environment, plus periodic warfare, introduced a common note of violence into nomadic life. Nomadic societies emphasized the importance of honor, or what anthropologists call courage culture. Strong, warlike men dominated, and their leadership was dependent on a willingness to meet physical challenge. Nomadic cultures valued courage and heroic action above all other achievements. In addition to recognizing brave

Desert nomads.

Mongol hunter in pursuit of game.

leaders, nomadic organization depended on kinship relations in small bands, usually of 30 to 150 people. These bands could, however, assemble into much larger groups in response to crisis.

Hospitality was another keynote of nomadic culture. Honor required that travelers be aided, a recognition of the harshness of the nomadic life. Acts of great generosity contributed to the reputation of leaders.

Nomads were outstanding fighters. Because their economic activity required much less time than that of agricultural peoples, there was more opportunity to train for battle. Easy familiarity with horses (or other animals) made for excellent military skills as well. Nomads' ability to ride for long distances often allowed them to draw the armies of civilizations out, where, exhausted, they could later be picked off. This technique was used successfully against Persian armies in the 6th century B.C.E., in western Asia, and against the British in 19th-century Africa.

Because of their fighting skills, nomads had a reputation for cruelty. This was sometimes exaggerated, but not always. Hun invaders in China had drinking cups made from the skulls of defeated rivals. Some nomadic groups routinely killed the wives and children of leaders they defeated.

Persian miniature depiction of a camp.

Nomadic societies were male-dominated, with care of animals and skill in their use reserved for men. Marriages were arranged to promote the interests of kinship groups, though nomads liked to tell stories about great romance and love of beautiful women. Polygamy was common for wealthier men. Women's tasks, besides childrearing, involved making and breaking camp, cooking, and sewing. In a few nomadic societies, however, women held positions of greater prestige, occasionally even participating in wars and holding leadership positions.

NOMADS AND CIVILIZATIONS

Nomads are particularly famous in history when they invade. Civilized peoples, from the Chinese to the Romans, feared and condemned nomads as offspring of evil spirits, the ultimate barbarians. Without question, nomadic invasions were important, particularly when they were part of larger migrations that could change the population structure as well as political leadership. The role of the Indo-Europeans in shaking up civilizations in the Middle East and India is obvious, and this basic pattern repeated in the classical and postclassical periods.

But nomads often had a peaceful, mutually beneficial relationship with agricultural societies, and this pattern had its own historical significance. Nomads often traded with farmers for useful goods, including vegetables, silks, and iron tools and weapons. In turn, the meat and milk products provided by the nomads could supplement meager diets for frontier farming

HISTORY DEBATE

THE CONTRIBUTIONS OF NOMADS

Violence and war grab the history headlines where nomads are concerned, but they may not be the main point. Nomads pioneered all the great overland trade routes that joined civilized areas in Asia, Europe, and Africa, from the river valley period through the postclassical centuries. They showed the way across the Sahara desert, though other merchants and missionaries might follow. They cut through central Asia, along the fringe of the Himalayan Mountains.

To be sure, nomads often threatened the trade routes, and Roman or Chinese emperors might send troops against these land-based pirates. But they also served as facilitators along the routes, offering protection for merchant groups, providing animals and hospitable way-stations. Sometimes they traded directly; more often, they cooperated with merchant groups. At key points in world history, before the definitive rise of ocean-based transport and then the railroad, nomadic-shaped trade routes were the lifeline of connections among the major civilizations. Religions such as Buddhism and Islam spread peacefully along these routes, while artistic styles from centers such as Greece fanned out along the routes as well. The mobility of nomads was long fundamental to world trade.

Sometimes, when nomads picked up some additional pointers from civilizations with which they were in contact, contributions were more direct. Warfare against Chinese forces in western China in the 8th century, by nomadic armies that had converted to Islam, brought the capture of several Chinese craftsmen who knew how to make paper. This, in turn, resulted in the rapid spread of papermaking in the Middle East and north Africa, and then more widely.

Nomads also contributed to the spread of knowledge of new crops, even when they did not cultivate them directly. Sometimes they carried new diseases as well, the downside of contact. More obviously still, they recurrently added to the technology of war, with their equipment for horses and skill in hit-and-run attacks copied by the armies of civilizations.

How do the nomads compare to other intermediaries among early civilizations? What's the most accurate verdict on nomads' role in world history? What agents now serve the roles that nomads once did?

communities. Nomads also provided warhorses for civilizations in China, India, the Middle East, and sub-Saharan Africa.

Atristic interactions with settled societies also occurred. Scythians, a nomadic people in what is now southern Russia, influenced, and were influenced by, Greek artisans in colonies around the Black Sea. The result was elaborate and intricate jewelry in which Greek techniques married Scythian styles and artistic themes.

Nomadic societies were also sources of invention, for limited resources did not preclude some specializations and indeed could encourage new techniques. Iron working probably first developed among nomads in Central Asia, who later brought it into the Middle East. Felt, the cloth that mixed wool and fur, was another creative product from nomadic Central Asia.

Nomads often received tribute payments from agricultural societies, to keep them at bay. Chinese silk trade began with tribute shipments to nomads in central Asia. Civilization governments often hired nomads as mercenary soldiers. At the end of the Roman Empire, nomads were hired to protect frontiers—Germans in Europe, Arabs in the Middle East. The Zhou, in China, began their careers as border guards for the Shang dynasty. Obviously, this practice could backfire when the guards gained additional organizational skills and turned against the host society. Not surprisingly, many civilizations spent a great deal of money trying to keep nomads out—as with the Great Wall in China, or the frontier garrisons of the Roman Empire.

Nomadic invaders, including former border guards, often incorporated the institutions and values of a civilization when they were able to take over, changing more than the societies around them. It was often hard to maintain a nomadic identity. Many nomads feared the lures of civilization, worrying that they would become soft, and often pulled back lest they be corrupted. An Arab nomad put it this way: "A tent flapping in the desert air is dearer than [a] towering house, Wind rustling over the sandy waste has a sweeter sound than all the king's trumpets."

The skills and values of nomadic peoples gave them a world history role greater than their relatively small populations suggest. At the same time, their conditions of life made it difficult to develop durable civilizations of their own, or even to dominate farming societies for very long. To be sure, there were great nomadic leaders; and early Mayan civilization, in central America, developed even amid a nomadic economy, though agriculture emerged later. So there are exceptions to generalizations about the limitations of the nomadic way of life. Generally, however, when it came to setting up more complex states, nomadic peoples depended on picking up techniques, and some of the personnel, of established civilizations.

So the nomadic intrusions into world history tended to be dramatic but brief. Often, they caused more change by what they prompted agricultural societies to do in defense, in organizing government resources to guard against attack, than by what they did themselves.

PATHS TO THE PRESENT

In today's world, nomads are at most a curiosity, living on the fringes of settled societies, because agricultural civilizations gobbled up most of the nomadic lands 500 years ago or more, particularly in central Asia. Bedouin groups, for example, continue to roam the Middle East, but they are small and do not have much impact on the cultures around them other than generating a certain amount of nostalgia. Despite nomads' modern invisibility, nomadic early contributions to world history were concrete. Nomadic societies challenged civilizations at various points through invasions and migrations, facilitating trade, and bringing new techniques and ideas.

Some societies retain a historical memory of a nomadic past. The nation of Mongolia understandably celebrates the achievements of nomadic Mongols, even though those achievements occurred 700 years ago. Other societies arguably retain particular traditions from earlier, nomadic ways. Arab hospitality, for example, is justly famous and possibly a nomadic legacy, even though most Arabs abandoned nomadism many centuries ago.

Contemporary world history has revived attention to one of the classic nomadic regions, central Asia. The collapse of the Soviet Union, and the crucial location of central Asia near Russia, the Middle East, India, and China, make the new nations of central Asia intriguing players in international relations. But the region gains notice now not because of nomadic economies, which have largely ended, but because of its rich resources, including oil, and its strategic position. Descendants of the nomads have new assets to affect the lives of the larger populations that surround them.

SUGGESTED WEB SITES

On the Silk Road Foundation, see http://www
.silkroadfoundation.org/toc/index.html; to
learn more about early nomads, go to www
.hermitagemuseum.org/html_En/03/_hm3_
2_7.html; on nomadic challenges and civilized
responses, see http://history-world.org/nomads
.htm. See also www.harappa.com.

SUGGESTED READINGS

An excellent general work is A. M. Khazanov's
Nomads and the Outside World (1984). Though not
the explicit subject, the role of nomads in contacts
is treated in Jerry Bentley, *Old World Encounters*
(1993). See also Alicia Sanchez-Mazas, ed., *Past
Human Migrations in East Asia* (2008); Nils Anfinset,
*Metal, Nomads and Culture Contact: The Middle East
and North Africa* (2008); Rene Grousset, *Empire of the
Steppes: A History of Central Asia* (1970), and
Richard Bulliet, *The Camel and the Wheel* (1975);
recent works include Ben Fitzhugh, ed., *Beyond For-
aging and Collecting: Evolutionary Change in Hunter-
Gatherer Settlement Systems* (2002); G. E. R. Lloyd,
*Ancient Worlds, Modern Reflections: Philosophical Per-
spectives on Greek and Chinese Science and Culture*
(2004); Steven Mithen, *After the Ice: A Global Human
History, 20,000–5000 BC* (2004); Morris Berman,
Wandering God: A Study of Nomadic Spirituality
(2000); A. M. Khazanov, *Nomads in the Sedentary
World* (2001); Peter S. Ungar, *Human Diet: Its Origins and Evolution* (2002); Steven A. LeBlanc, *Constant Battles: The Myth of the Noble Savage* (2003); and
Richard Lee, *The Cambridge Encyclopedia of Hunters
and Gatherers* (1999).

The Rise of Agriculture and Agricultural Civilizations

CONTACTS AND IDENTITIES

The most important global contacts during the early periods of human history involved the spread of techniques and foods, gradually, usually through ways we know little about. The diffusion of agriculture and iron use, from centers of initial invention, is the most important example. But foods also spread. For example, African farmers by 1000 B.C.E. were growing foods, including bananas, that originated in southeast Asia, which greatly enriched the variety available to them. This suggests some trade through the Indian Ocean, through which seeds or tubers were transported, but we don't know the mechanisms. Direct contacts among the river valley centers were less important, though trade and some warfare periodically brought Egypt and the Middle East into contact, and Harappan civilization traded widely. What resulted, beyond exchange of goods, is unclear. We have seen that Harappans ignored examples of technology available to them from societies with which they traded.

Because contacts were limited, it is also unclear how conscious people were of their identities. Egyptians surely had some sense of their culture and institutions when they encountered Kushites or peoples in the eastern Mediterranean; they often tried to impose some of their standards. The Middle East, so often invaded, must have seen efforts to retain identity. The Jewish people, certainly, worked hard to maintain their religion and language even when overtaken by Assyrians and others; identity proved crucial in Jewish history from this point on. Only a bit later, a strong Vietnamese identity emerged amid fears of being overwhemed by Chinese conquest.

Many agricultural peoples were aware of different identities from the hunting or nomadic groups around them, and vice versa. We have seen that nomads, even when attracted by the more abundant wealth of civilizations, often insisted on the importance of maintaining their own values and greater simplicity. But surviving records make many identity issues a matter of speculation; here the Jewish experience, with its explicit chronicles, is atypical.

TENSIONS

The problem: Many aspects of the world today can be described in terms of the tensions between international exchanges and outside influences, on the one hand, and the clear human need to maintain identities, on the other. These tensions affect whole societies, which are called upon to decide how much identity to sacrifice in favor of possible benefits from wider interactions, as well as groups and individuals.

Several years ago, a French farmer won international attention and wide praise for driving his tractor into a local McDonald's to protest globalization of fast food. He struck a blow for traditional French identity and its connotation of creating fine cuisine. Yet, over a third of French restaurant meals are taken in fast-food operations, either foreign or imitative domestic—another case of an unresolved tension between global links and local identities.

The argument: Tensions between local practices and loyalties and the lure or inevitability of wider contacts are endemic to world history. The balance has gradually shifted toward the global, over the local—one sign is the disappearance, mainly in the past two centuries, of several thousand languages. But the tension remains. World history helps us understand how it evolved and helps explain why some societies and groups, even today, react to the tension in terms of identity protection while others are more open to the larger world.

The early history: The most striking point about the early human experience involves the wide dispersion of people, which explains how strong local identities emerged in the first place. Additionally, differences in economic systems, between agriculturalists and nomads for instance, provided bases for separate identities. Most polytheistic religions, to take one illustration, were highly regional in specific beliefs and practices, even if they shared wider elements because of the human need to explain the forces of nature or the inevitability of death. In contrast, the forces that pushed for wider contacts were usually more sporadic and diffuse.

Admittedly, we do not know as much about the nature and passion of early identities as we would like. Egyptians surely had some sense of their culture and institutions when they encountered Kushites or peoples in the eastern Mediterranean. They could and did identify non-Egyptians as "others" or outsiders. But we do not know details about the Egyptians' response to these outsiders. Phoenicians, to take another case, clearly had distinctive practices, which they exported to settlements in North Africa and southern Europe, providing a Phoenician identity that supported wider trading ventures. Theirs was a case of a people who managed to further wider economic contacts but maintain a set of values and institutions separate from the groups they dealt with.

The most durable identity launched in this period was that of the Jewish people. Possessing a distinctive religion, and despite the lack of a durable Jewish state, Jewish people began quite early to maintain their sense of identity, even when overrun by conquerors such as the Assyrians. Maintenance of this identity, even amid wide geographic dispersion, was and is a fundamental feature not only of Jewish history, but of the role of Jews in the wider world.

Other identities took shape as well. Many Chinese scholars later claimed that some of their political and cultural features emerged with the Shang dynasty or even before, but it is hard to sort myth from reality. It is clear that a Chinese identity emerged and claimed deep historical roots, but it is not easy to sort out when this happened in fact. Another example of cultural identity is that of the Harappan people, who maintained an awareness of their values and achievements, even as their cities declined and Indo-European migrants overran their settlements. But this identity did not survive wider contacts. Similarly, Sumerians and other Mesopotamian groups, beset by invasions, left a legacy, in the form of surviving institutions and values, but not a durable identity.

Early human history illustrates and explains the process of identity formation in the various regions of the world. Migrations and diffusions challenged identities, but these larger connecting forces did not yet predominate. The tensions that resulted were sporadic, in contrast to the regular interactions with—and tensions that result from—global influences that form the framework of life today.

PART II

The Classical Period, 1000 B.C.E.–500 C.E.

INTRODUCTION: NEW ISSUES FOR EXPANDING SOCIETIES

The classical period in world history began between 1000 and 800 B.C.E. and ended with the fall of great empires between the 2nd and 6th centuries C.E. So, it lasted about 1500 years, from roughly 1000 B.C.E. to roughly 500 C.E.

Slightly before 1000 B.C.E., the Zhou dynasty took shape in China. The Zhou began expanding Chinese territory; it was under them that characteristic Chinese cultural systems, such as Confucianism, emerged. In the Middle East, the Persian empire developed in the 6th century. A bit before this, Greek city-states emerged and began to spread settlements to other parts of the eastern Mediterranean. Classical Indian culture gained greater coherence between 1000 and 600 B.C.E. as key religious epics were written down, though the first Indian empires emerged only in the 4th century B.C.E. So, although starting points varied, the notion of a distinctive classical past gained traction in many parts of Asia, southern Europe, and north Africa from 1000 B.C.E. on.

At the other end, the classical period did not close tidily, at a single date; but it did close noisily. Majestic empires in China, the Mediterranean, and India all collapsed by or before 600 C.E. Clearly, an important human experience had ended, at least in part.

45

THEMES

If the classical period has reasonably clear boundaries in time—a start and a finish—what did it contain? Amid a host of specific developments, two major themes emerge:

First, several societies gained the capacity to expand territorially, much more widely than the river valley civilizations had done. Indeed, all the classical civilizations covered the river valley territories but then went much farther. Territorial expansion was possible not only because of the experience gained from the earlier societies but also because of the use of iron tools and weapons, which were much more effective than bronze weapons had been.

Second, the leading classical societies worked hard to create values and institutions that would help internally tie these expanded territories together. They promoted internal trade, so different regions within the civilization could specialize effectively. Wheat-growing north China thus interacted with rice-growing south China. The societies promoted ideas and artistic styles that provided people across the civilization with common beliefs and expressions. Rome built its temples and coliseums from Iraq to Britain. Chinese leaders pressed elites in all regions to practice Confucian values. Finally, all the classical civilizations worked, at least periodically, toward political integration, seeking to meld the disparate expanded territories into a single political unit.

In the process of integration, all the classical societies created certain beliefs and institutions that had great survival power. Indian religions, Greek science, Chinese bureaucracy—these were achievements that continued to influence the regions in question long after the classical period was over. Some later influenced other regions. The classical period was thus a formative one, generating many practices that affected the experience of millions of people over many centuries.

Given classical societies' achievements and durability, it is small wonder that many people look on them with awe and reverence. Our awe stems from wondering how people in early cultures could attain such greatness. Our reverence comes from wondering, if they did so much, can we also be inspired to great things?

In 2005, the nation of Iran was seeking, against considerable world resistance, to develop a nuclear power program, and possibly nuclear weaponry. Some young Iranians were interviewed amid the great temple ruins of Persepolis, the capital of the Persian Empire. They argued that if their classical ancestors built monuments that were the envy of the world, surely contemporary Iranians can claim their place in the international sun. This is a sentiment that many people experience—though without the nuclear twist—as they contemplate the classical pasts of their own societies, from Spain to China's Pacific coast.

Many people and regions continued apart from the major classical civilizations. Classical populations were unusually large: China's tripled to about 60 million; Rome at its height held sway over 54 million souls; and India contained about 50 million people. But during this period people lived elsewhere, in other parts of Africa, in northern Europe, in Japan, and, of course, in the Americas, who were not yet strongly influenced by the classical achievements, and whose histories were quite different. Even many of these regions, however, were later influenced by some of the ideas and institutions one or more of the classical civilizations had generated.

THE GEOGRAPHY OF THE CLASSICAL PERIOD

Four major centers of classical civilization emerged: China, India, the Middle East, and the Mediterranean. Persia interacted with the Mediterranean and at one point was conquered by Greek armies, but on the whole it established and maintained a separate tradition.

Each of the classical civilizations influenced adjacent regions. Chinese power and example affected Korea and Vietnam. Japan, now developing agriculture, became aware of Chinese example. Mediterranean societies traded actively with Ethiopia, a pattern that explains why Ethiopia became predominantly Christian (though with a Jewish minority). Indian merchants strongly influenced many parts of southeast Asia. Even with outreach, however, the classical experience was bounded in terms of place, it was far from representing the whole world. In west Africa and much of northern Europe, and even in Japan, the big developments during the classical period involved the spread of agriculture and iron working, with the emergence of some regional kingdoms. New migrations also occurred, for example, slave peoples moving into eastern Europe. During much of the classical period, from 800 to 400 B.C.E., a new center emerged in Central America under the Olmec peoples, who produced major religious monuments and who furthered the cultivation of corn. In yet another pattern, Polynesian peoples, operating from islands like Samoa, extended explorations in the Pacific using large outrigger canoes; they reached Hawaii by 400 C.E., where they established agricultural settlements. These varied regions were not really connected to the classical world—in the case of Olmecs and the Polynesians, not connected at all. They would become a clearer part of the larger fabric of world history later on, but their formative developments, during these centuries, helped prepare this role.

GLOBAL CONNECTIONS

Aside from their regional outreach, the achievements of the classical civilizations rested largely on separate developments. This was the period in which durable but distinctive features in India, or in China, were created, though they may have utilized some earlier, river valley precedents. Of course, the civilizations showed common tendencies: they all expanded, they all worked at integration, and they all relied heavily on social and gender inequality. But they implemented these common themes in different ways. This means, in turn, that a key feature of the classical period was internal development.

Yet contacts with other cultures were also important, even if they had limited impact in shaping specific institutions or cultures within each civilization. The contacts were significant at that time and for later, they insured the maintenance of connective channels.

Trade opportunities increased as a result of these contacts between societies. During the classical period, a series of overland routes developed from western China, through central Asia, into India and the Middle East (and thence to the Mediterranean). These routes are called the Silk Road, for merchants used them to carry Chinese silk westward, and to return with gold, exotic animals, and other products. Trade along the Silk Road was regional: one group of merchants carried goods through their region—nomads were sometimes involved—then another group took the goods to the next stage. Persian institutions such as a good road system and inns for travelers helped Asian goods reach the rest of the Middle East and Mediterranean.

Interregional trade also emerged in the Indian Ocean. Indian merchants actively traded with southeast Asia, including present-day Indonesia. Various Middle Eastern merchants developed commercial ties with India. So did the Romans, when they reached the eastern Mediterranean. Regular convoys were sent from the Red Sea, into the Indian Ocean, and on to India, seeking pepper and other spices; some Roman merchants resided in India to drum up trade. China also traded with India by sea. One emperor sent a special mission to India to buy a rhinoceros for his zoo.

Classical civilizations occasionally encountered each other more directly than via trade. Alexander the Great's conquests, in the 4th century B.C.E., brought Greeks not only to Persia but also to northwestern India (present-day Pakistan), where they set up the kingdom of Bactria. For two centuries Indians and Greeks

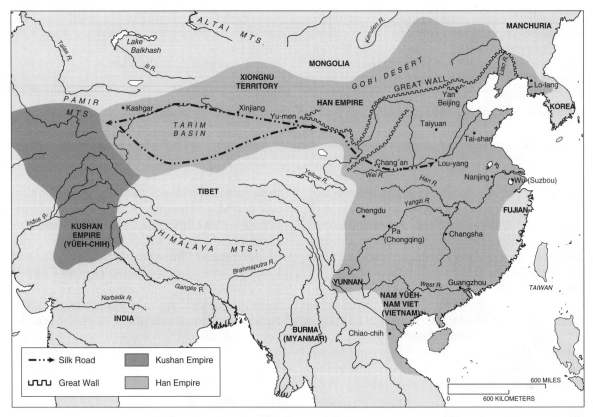

The Silk Road

interacted here, pooling mathematical knowledge, among other things. For a time, as a result, Indian artists in the region portrayed Buddha with Greek hairstyles and costumes.

Late in the classical period, Chinese overland trade with India reached such a high level that Chinese merchants gained unusually active knowledge of Indian culture. Some began to convert to Buddhism, leading to other Chinese delegations being sent to India to learn more about this religion. Chinese importation of Buddhism was one of the great interregional cultural events in Chinese history.

Exchanges of products and ideas thus form an active part of the classical period, even amid the separate self-definitions of the key civilizations.

There were limits to the exchanges, however. Greeks learned from Indian mathematicians, and vice versa, but the Greeks did not import the efficient Indian numbering system—an odd omission, at least by our standards today. Also, while Roman elites valued silks from China, they had virtually no knowledge of China itself, and there is no definite evidence that anyone went from China to Rome or vice versa. Travelers did not venture too far outside their own region; the intensity of trade was rarely sufficient to inspire other kinds of exchange. Even the Greek-Indian interaction, in Bactria, led to few permanent achievements—for instance, the fad of dressing Buddhas in Greek attire lasted for only a century or so, then disappeared without much trace.

SUGGESTED READINGS

There are several useful treatments of cross-cultural themes and topics in antiquity. See, for example, Richard A. Gabriel, *War in the Ancient World* (1992); Milo Kearney, *The Indian Ocean in World History* (2004); W. H. McNeill, *Plagues and People* (1977); Irving Rouse, *Migrations in Prehistory* (1986); and Chester G. Starr, *The Influence of Sea-power on Ancient History* (1989). The role of women in the ancient world is the subject of A. Sharma, ed., *Women in World Religions* (1987); Bonnie S. Anderson and Judith P. Zinsser, *A History of Their Own: Women in Europe from Prehistory to the Present* (1988); and Bella Vivante, ed., *Women's Roles in Ancient Civilizations: A Reference Guide* (1999). The nature and impact of some of the most influential individuals of the classical world are the focus of S. N. Eisenstadt, ed., *The Origins and Diversity of the Axial Age* (1986). More recent works include Johann P. Arnason, *Axial Civilizations and World History* (Boston, 2005); Ralph W. Mathisen, *People, Personal Expression, and Social Relations in Late Antiquity, with Translated Texts from Gaul and Western Europe* (Ann Arbor, 2003); Barbara Sher Tinsley, *Reconstructing Western Civilization: Irreverent Essays on Antiquity* (Selinsgrove, 2006); and J. W. Roberts, *The Oxford Dictionary of the Classical World* (Oxford, 2005).

4 Classical Civilization: China

China generated the first of the great classical societies. The region faced periodic nomadic invasions, which encouraged an intense, and distinctive, Chinese identity. The decline of the Shang dynasty did not result in as much internal chaos as did invasions of parts of the Middle East and particularly India. Hence, the Chinese could build more strongly on Huanghe precedents. Particularly important was a general, if somewhat vague, worldview developed by Huanghe thinkers and accepted as a standard approach in later Chinese thinking. This intellectual heritage stressed the basic harmony of nature: every feature is balanced by an opposite, every *yin* by a *yang*. Thus for hot there is cold, for male, female. According to this philosophy, an individual should seek a way, called *Dao,* to relate to this harmony, avoiding excess and appreciating the balance of opposites. Individuals and human institutions existed within this world of balanced nature, not, as in later Mediterranean philosophy, on the outside. Chinese traditions about balance, Dao, and yin/yang were intrinsic to diverse philosophies and religions established in the classical period, and they provided some unity among various schools of thought in China.

Despite important cultural continuity, classical China did not simply maintain earlier traditions. The formative centuries of classical Chinese history were witness to a great many changes. The religious and particularly the political habits of the Shang kingdom were substantially modified as part of building the world's largest classical empire. As a result of these new centuries of development, leading to much diversity but often painful conflict, the Chinese emerged with an unusually well-integrated system in which government, philosophy, economic incentives, the family, and the individual were intended to blend into a harmonious whole.

■**KEY QUESTIONS** *How did classical China fit the general definition of a classical civilization? Are there ways it did not fit? What were the main changes during the classical period: how was China different by 200 C.E. from what it had been 1200 years earlier; but, also, what had survived through the period as a whole?*

PATTERNS IN CLASSICAL CHINA

Of all the societies in the world today, it is China that has maintained the clearest links to its classical past—a past that has been a source of pride but also the cause of some problems of adaptation. Already, in the period of classical Chinese history a pattern was set in motion that lasted until the early part of the 20th century. A family of kings, known as a *dynasty,* began its rule of China with great vigor, developing strong political institutions and encouraging an active economy. Subsequently, the dynasty grew weaker and tax revenues declined, while social divisions increased in the larger society. Internal rebellions and sporadic invasions from the outside hastened the dynasty's decline. As the ruling dynasty declined, another dynasty emerged, usually from the family of a successful general, invader, or peasant rebel, and the pattern started anew. Small wonder then that many Chinese conceive of history in terms of cycles, in contrast to the Western tendency to think of steady progress from past to present.

Three dynastic cycles cover the many centuries of classical China: the Zhou, the Qin, and the Han. The Zhou dynasty lasted from 1029 to 258 B.C.E. Although lengthy, this dynasty flourished only until about 700 B.C.E.; it was then beset by a decline in the political infrastructure and frequent invasions by nomadic peoples from border regions. Even during its strong centuries, the Zhou did not establish a powerful government, ruling instead through alliances with regional princes and noble families. The early

Zhou and the introduction of a feudal system were discussed in Chapter 2. The dynasty initially came into China from the north, displacing its predecessor, the Shang rulers. The alliance systems the Zhou used as the basis for their rule were standard in agricultural kingdoms. (We will see similar forms later emerge in Japan, India, Europe, and Africa.) Rulers lacked the means to control their territories directly and so gave large regional estates to members of their families and other supporters, hoping that their loyalties would remain intact. The supporters, in exchange for land, were supposed to provide the central government with troops and tax revenues. In this Chinese feudal period, rulers depended on a network of loyalties and obligations to and from their landlord-vassals. Such a system was, of course, vulnerable to regional disloyalties, and the ultimate decline of the Zhou dynasty occurred when regional landowning aristocrats solidified their own power base and disregarded the central government.

The Zhou did, however, contribute in several ways to the development of Chinese politics and culture in their active early centuries. First, they extended the territory of China by taking over the Yangzi River valley. This new stretch of territory, from the Huanghe in the north to the Yangzi in the south, became China's core—often called the "Middle Kingdom." It provided rich agricultural lands plus the benefits of two different agricultures—wheat-growing in the north, rice-growing in the south—a diversity that encouraged population growth. The territorial expansion obviously complicated the problems of central rule, for communication and transport from the capital to the outlying regions were difficult. This is why the Zhou relied so heavily on the loyalty of regional supporters.

Despite these circumstances, the Zhou did actually heighten the cultural focus on the central government itself. Zhou rulers claimed direct links to the Shang rulers. They also asserted that heaven had transferred its mandate to rule China to the Zhou emperors. This political concept of a mandate from heaven remained a key justification for Chinese imperial rule from the Zhou on. Known as Sons of Heaven, the emperors lived in a world of awe-inspiring pomp and ceremony.

The Zhou worked to provide greater cultural unity in their empire. They discouraged some of the primitive religious practices of the Huanghe civilization, banning human sacrifice and urging more restrained ceremonies to worship the gods. They also promoted linguistic unity, beginning the process by which a standard spoken language, ultimately called Mandarin Chinese, prevailed over the entire Middle Kingdom. This resulted in the largest single group of people speaking the same language in the world at this time. Regional dialects and languages remained, but educated officials began to rely on the single Mandarin form. Oral epics and stories in Chinese, many gradually recorded in written form, aided in the development of a common cultural currency.

Increasing cultural unity helps explain why, when the Zhou Empire began to fail, scholars were able to use philosophical ideas to lessen the impact of growing political confusion. Indeed, the political crisis spurred efforts to define and articulate Chinese culture. During the late 6th and early 5th centuries B.C.E., the philosopher known in the West as Confucius (see p. xx) wrote an elaborate statement on political ethics, providing the core of China's distinctive philosophical heritage. Other writers and religious leaders participated in this great period of cultural creativity, which later reemerged as a set of central beliefs throughout the Middle Kingdom.

Cultural innovation did not, however, reverse the prolonged and painful Zhou downfall. Regional rulers formed independent armies, ultimately reducing the emperors to little more than figureheads. Between 402 and 201 B.C.E., a period known aptly enough as the Era of the Warring States, the Zhou system disintegrated. In reaction, new political ideas emerged, called Legalism, that urged rulers to establish order at all costs.

At this point, China might have gone the way of civilizations such as India, where centralized government was more the exception than the rule. But a new dynasty arose to reverse the process of political decay. One regional ruler deposed the last Zhou emperor and within 35 years made himself sole ruler of China. He took the title Qin Shihuangdi, or First Emperor. The dynastic name, Qin, conferred on the whole country its name of China. Qin Shihuangdi was a brutal ruler, but effective given the circumstances of internal disorder and supported as well by Legalist ideas. He understood that China's problem lay in the regional power of the aristocrats, and like many later centralizers in world history, he worked vigorously to undo this force. He ordered nobles to leave their regions and appear at his court, assuming control of their feudal estates. China was organized into large provinces ruled by bureaucrats appointed by the emperor; and Qin Shihuangdi was careful to select his officials from nonaristocratic groups, so that they would owe their power to him and not dare to develop their own independent bases. Under Qin Shihuangdi's rule, powerful armies crushed regional resistance.

The First Emperor followed up on centralization by extending Chinese territory to the south, reaching present-day Hong Kong on the South China Sea and even influencing northern Vietnam. In the north, to guard against barbarian invasions, Qin Shihuangdi built a Great Wall, extending more than 3000 miles, wide enough for chariots to move along its crest. This massive mud wall, probably the largest construction project in human history up to that point, was built by forced labor, conscripted by the central bureaucracy from among the peasantry.

The Qin dynasty was responsible for a number of innovations in Chinese politics and culture. To determine the empire's resources, Qin Shihuangdi ordered a national census, which provided data for the calculation of tax revenues and labor service. The government standardized coinage, weights, and measures through the entire realm. Even the length of axles on carts was regulated to promote coherent road planning. The government also made Chinese written script uniform, completing the process of creating a single basic language in which all educated Chinese could communicate. The government furthered agriculture, sponsoring new irrigation projects, and promoted manufacturing, particularly for silk cloth. The activist government also attacked formal culture, including Confucian ideas, burning many books. Thinking, according to Qin Shihuangdi, was likely to be subversive to his autocratic rule.

Although it created many durable features of Chinese government, the Qin dynasty was short-lived. Qin Shihuangdi's attacks on intellectuals, and particularly the high taxes needed to support military expansion and the construction of the Great Wall, made him fiercely unpopular. One opponent described the First Emperor as a monster who "had the heart of a tiger and a wolf. He killed men as though he thought he could never finish, he punished men as though he were afraid he would never get around to them all." On the emperor's death, in 210 B.C.E., massive revolts organized by aggrieved peasants broke out. One peasant leader defeated other opponents and in 202 B.C.E. established the third dynasty of classical China, the Han.

It was the Han dynasty, which lasted more than 400 years, to 220 C.E., that rounded out China's basic political and intellectual structure. Han rulers retained the centralized administration of the Qin but sought to reduce the brutal repression of that period. Like many dynasties during the first flush of power, early Han rulers expanded Chinese territory, pushing into Korea, Indochina, and central Asia. This expansion gave rise to direct contact with India and also allowed the Chinese to develop contact with the Parthian empire in the Middle East, through which trade with the Roman Empire around the Mediterranean was conducted. The most famous Han ruler, Wudi (140–87 B.C.E.), enforced peace throughout much of the continent of Asia, rather

Han Hsin, a famous general from the early part of the Han dynasty, is represented on horseback, in carved, decorated tile.

like the peace the Roman Empire would bring to the Mediterranean region a hundred years later, but embracing even more territory and a larger population. Peace brought great prosperity to China itself. A Han historian conveys the self-satisfied, confident tone of the dynasty:

> The nation had met with no major disturbances so that, except in times of flood or drought, every person was well supplied and every family had enough to get along on. The granaries in the cities and the countryside were full and the government treasuries were running over with wealth. In the capital the strings of cash had stacked up by the hundreds of millions until . . . they could no longer be counted. In the central granary of the government, new grain was heaped on top of the old until the building was full and the grain overflowed and piled up

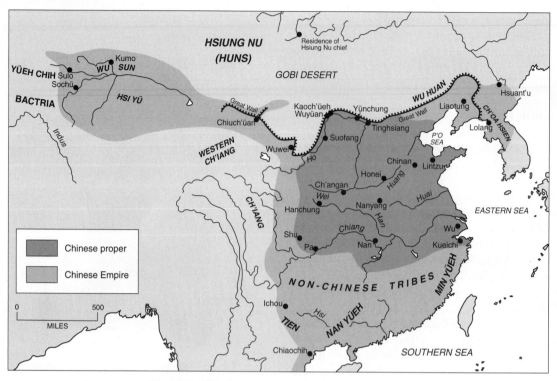

China Under Emperor Wudi, About 100 B.C.E.

outside, where it spoiled and became unfit to eat. . . . Even the keepers of the community gates ate fine grain and meat.

Under the Han dynasty, the workings of the state bureaucracy also improved and the government was linked to formal training that emphasized the values of Confucian philosophy. Reversing the Qin dynasty's policies, Wudi urged support for Confucianism, seeing it as a vital supplement to formal measures on the government's part; shrines were established to promote the worship of the ancient philosopher as a god.

The quality of Han rule declined after about two centuries. Central control weakened, and invasions from central Asia, spearheaded by a nomadic people called the Xiongnu, who had long threatened China's northern borders, overturned the dynasty entirely. Between 220 and

589 C.E., China was in a state of chaos. Order and stability were finally restored, but by then the classical or formative period of Chinese civilization had ended. Well before the Han collapse, however, China had established distinctive political structures and cultural values of unusual clarity, capable, as it turned out, of surviving even three centuries of renewed confusion.

POLITICAL INSTITUTIONS

The Qin and Han dynasties of classical China established a distinctive, and remarkably successful, kind of government. The Qin stressed central authority, whereas the Han expanded the powers of the bureaucracy. More than any other factor, it was the structure of this government that explained how such a vast territory could be effectively ruled—for the Chinese empire was indeed the largest political system in the classical world. This structure changed after the classical period, particularly in terms of streamlining and expanding bureaucratic systems and procedures, but it never required a fundamental overhaul.

The political framework that emerged as a result of the long centuries of China's classical period had several key elements. Strong local units never disappeared. Like most successful agricultural societies, China relied heavily on tightly knit patriarchal families. Individual families were linked to other relatives in extended family networks that included brothers, uncles, and any living grandparents. Among the wealthy landowning groups, family authority was enhanced by the practice of ancestor worship, which joined family members through rituals devoted to important forebears who had passed into the spirit world. For ordinary people, among whom ancestor worship was less common, village authority surmounted family rule. Village leaders helped farming families regulate property and coordinate planting and harvest work. During the Zhou dynasty, and also in later periods when dynasties weakened, the regional power of great landlords also played an important role at the village level. Landed nobles provided courts of justice and organized military troops.

Strong local rule was not the most significant or distinctive feature of Chinese government under the Qin and Han dynasties, however. Qin Shihuangdi not only attacked local rulers; he also provided a single law code for the whole empire and established a uniform tax system. He appointed governors to each district of his domain, who exercised military and legal powers in the name of the emperor. They, in turn, named officials responsible for smaller regions. Here indeed was a classic model of centralized government that other societies later replicated: the establishment of centralized codes and appointment of officials directly by a central authority, rather than by reliance on arrangements with numerous existing local governments. The effectiveness of a central government was further enhanced by the delegation of special areas and decisions to the emperor's ministers. Some dealt with matters of finance, others with justice, others with military affairs, and so on.

Able rulers of the Han dynasty resumed the attack on local warrior-landlords. In addition, they realized the importance of creating a large, highly skilled bureaucracy, one capable of carrying out the duties of a complex state. By the end of the Han period, China had about 130,000 bureaucrats, representing 0.2 percent of the population. The emperor Wudi established examinations for his bureaucrats—the first example of civil service tests of the sort that many governments have instituted in modern times. These examinations covered classics of Chinese literature as well as law, suggesting a model of the scholar-bureaucrat that later became an important element of China's political tradition. Wudi also established a school to train men of exceptional talent and ability for the national examinations. Although most bureaucrats were drawn from the landed upper classes, who alone had the time to learn the complex system of Chinese characters, individuals from lower ranks of society were occasionally recruited under this system. China's bureaucracy thus provided a slight check on complete upper-class rule. It also tended to limit the exercise of arbitrary power by the emperor himself. Trained and experienced bureaucrats, confident in their own traditions, could often control the whims of a single ruler, even one who, in the Chinese tradition, regarded himself as divinely appointed—the "Son of Heaven." It was no accident then that the Chinese bureaucracy lasted from the Han period until the 20th century, outliving the empire itself.

Small wonder that from the classical period at least until modern times, and possibly still today, the Chinese were the most tightly governed people in any large society in the world. When it worked well—and it is important to recall that the system periodically broke down—Chinese politics

HISTORY DEBATE

WAR

Historians debate how to fit war and military developments into general patterns, beyond noting major wars as significant events. Military history is something of a specialty, and some historians stay away from it. Ironically, military history is one of the most popular kinds of history with the general American public, as indicated by the History Channel and the purchases of books directed at a wide audience.

The classical period—classical China in particular—offers ways to relate military history to wider developments, while recognizing its importance and interest. Classical civilizations, with expanding territory and tax revenues, inevitably changed the ways wars were handled. Wider use of iron weaponry, a key underpinning of the classical period, had the same effect. Wars began to involve more soldiers, more casualties, and extend over longer spans of time.

In most early civilizations, war had involved a good bit of ritual, along with contests among individual fighters. Leaders avoided war during harvest season or winter; they announced intentions of attack in advance, and they used priests to consult signs in order to determine when to strike. Battles involved contests among well-armed and trained elite warriors, along with a confused mass of ordinary foot soldiers who were peasants or slaves. Codes of honor dominated; it was not proper, for example, to strike from behind. There was great emphasis on heroic deeds, and early literature in India and the Mediterranean continued to highlight competition among individual heroes.

In the Shang and early Zhou dynasties, Chinese wars showed this common pattern. But Chinese leaders, with their concern for order, began to worry about the waste this system involved. In the 4th century B.C.E., one official, Sunzi, responded with a careful treatise, *The Art of War*, probably the most important book ever written in the military field. Sunzi urged that wars be carefully organized and moved away from macho contests among heroes. Armies should strike quickly, seeking to end wars rapidly. He recommended special schools to train military leaders. Chinese governments began to set these up. Under Sunzi's influence, a wider array of strategies were used in war, with the goals of winning and winning quickly. These strategies included bluffing, spying, sneak attacks, and committing sabotage. Psychological attacks to demoralize the enemy were also emphasized. At the same time, Chinese governments paid a great deal of attention to organizing large armies, including maintaining supply lines.

Sunzi's influence showed in the military success of the Qin dynasty. Quite independently, Greek armies began introducing similar kinds of careful organization and discipline, which underpinned their conquests and those of Alexander the Great. War as a contest among champions did not end—it showed up later in Europe and Japan—but the trend was clear, as war became part of the growing organization of government.

represented a remarkable integration of all levels of authority. The edicts of an all-powerful emperor were administered by trained scholar-bureaucrats, widely respected for their learning and, often, their noble birth. Individual families also emphasized this strong principle of authority, with the father in charge, presumably carrying on the wishes of a long line of ancestors to which the family paid obeisance. The Chinese were capable of periodic rebellions, and gangs of criminals more regularly came to disrupt the social scene—indeed,

frequently harsh punishments reflected the need of the government to eradicate such deviant forces. Nevertheless, whether within the family or the central state, most Chinese in ordinary times believed in the importance of respect for those in power.

Government traditions established during the classical period included an impressive list of state functions. Like all organized states, the Chinese government operated military and judicial systems. Military activity fluctuated, as China did not depend on steady expansion. Although classical China produced some enduring examples of the art of war, the state was not highly militaristic by the Han period. Judicial matters—crime and legal disputes—commanded more attention by local government authorities.

The government also sponsored much intellectual life, organizing research in astronomy and the maintenance of historical records. Under the Han rulers, the government played a major role in promoting Confucian philosophy as an official statement of Chinese values and in encouraging the worship of Confucius himself. The government developed a durable sense of mission as the primary keeper of Chinese beliefs.

The imperial government was active in the economy. It directly organized the production of iron and salt. Its standardization of currency, weights, and measures facilitated trade throughout the vast empire. The government additionally sponsored public works, including complex irrigation and canal systems. Han rulers even tried to regulate agricultural supplies by storing grain and rice in good times to control price increases—and potential popular unrest—when harvests were bad.

China's ambitious rulers in no sense directed the daily lives of their subjects; the technology of an agricultural society did not permit this. Even under the Han, it took more than a month for a directive from the capital city to reach the outlying districts of the empire—an obvious limit on imperial authority. A revealing Chinese proverb held that "heaven is high, and the emperor is far away." However, the power of the Chinese state did extend considerably. Its system of courts was backed by a strict code of law; torture and execution were widely employed to supplement the preaching of obedience and civic virtue. The central government taxed its subjects and also required some annual labor on the part of every male peasant—this was the source of the incredible physical work involved in building canals, roads, and palaces. No other government had the organization and staff to reach ordinary people so directly until virtually modern times, except in much smaller political units such as city-states. The power of the government and the authority it commanded in the eyes of most ordinary Chinese people help explain why its structure survived decline, invasion, and even rebellion for so many centuries. Invaders such as the Xiongnu might topple a dynasty, but they could not devise a better system to run the country, and so the system and its bureaucratic administrators normally endured.

RELIGION AND CULTURE

The Chinese way of viewing the world, as this belief system developed during the classical period, was closely linked to a distinct political structure. Upper-class cultural values emphasized a good life on earth and the virtues of obedience to the state, more than speculations about God and the mysteries of heaven. At the same time, the Chinese tolerated and often combined various specific beliefs, so long as they did not contradict basic political loyalties.

Rulers in the Zhou dynasty maintained belief in a god or gods, but little attention was given to the nature of a deity. Rather, Chinese leaders stressed the importance of a harmonious earthly life that maintained proper balance between earth and heaven. Harmony included carefully constructed rituals to unify society and prevent individual excess. Among the upper classes, people were trained in elaborate exercises and military skills such as archery. Commonly, ceremonies venerating ancestors and even marking special meals were conducted. The use of chopsticks began at the end of the Zhou dynasty; it encouraged a code of politeness at meals. Soon after this, tea was introduced, although the most elaborate tea-drinking rituals developed later on, in Japan more than China.

Even before these specific ceremonies arose, however, the basic definition of a carefully ordered existence was given more formal philosophical backing. Amidst the long collapse of the

Zhou dynasty, many thinkers and religious prophets began to challenge Chinese traditions. From this ferment came a restatement of the traditions that ultimately reduced intellectual conflict and established a long-lasting tone for Chinese cultural and social life.

Confucius, or Kong Fuzi (which means Master Kong), lived from roughly 551 to 478 B.C.E.

His life was devoted to teaching, and he traveled through many parts of China preaching his ideas of political virtue and good government. Confucius was not a religious leader; he believed in a divine order but refused to speculate about it. Chinese civilization was unusual, in the classical period and well beyond, in that its dominant values were secular rather than religious.

WORLD PROFILES

CONFUCIUS, OR KONG FUZI (C. 551–479 B.C.E.)

Confucius was the single most important thinker in Chinese history. He was responsible for developing an orderly political and social philosophy as the Zhou dynasty became more unstable. He believed that an emphasis on personal virtue would preserve Chinese tradition and restore what he regarded as the great days of the Chinese state. He spent much of his life traveling to many parts of China, preaching his ideas of personal virtue, which included respect for one's social superiors and a reverence for tradition. Tempering this emphasis on hierarchy, Confucius maintained that society's leaders must also exhibit personal virtue through moderation in behavior, veneration of custom and ritual, and a love of wisdom. The 18th-century Chinese nobleman who painted the image shown here depicts the philosopher with the costume and headdress of his own scholar-gentry class. What does the portrait suggest about the characteristics later generations attributed to Confucius?

Eastern Asia, Shanghai, China: Wen Maio Temple, statue of Confucius in courtyard.

Confucius saw himself as a spokesman for Chinese tradition and for what he believed were the great days of the Chinese state before the Zhou declined. He maintained that if people could be taught to emphasize personal virtue, which included a reverence for tradition, a solid political life would naturally result. The Confucian list of virtues stressed respect for one's social superiors—including fathers and husbands as leaders of the family. However, this emphasis on a proper hierarchy was balanced by an insistence that society's leaders behave modestly and without excess, shunning abusive power and treating courteously those people who were in their charge. According to Confucius, moderation in behavior, veneration of custom and ritual, and a love of wisdom should characterize the leaders of society at all levels. And with virtuous leaders, a sound political life would inevitably follow: "In an age of good government, men in high stations give preference to men of ability and give opportunity to those who are below them, and lesser people labor vigorously at their husbandry to serve their superiors."

Confucianism was primarily a system of ethics—do unto others as your status and theirs dictate—and a plea for loyalty to the community. It confirmed the distaste that many educated Chinese had developed for religious mysteries, as well as their delight in learning and good manners. Confucian doctrine, lovingly preserved in a book called the *Analects,* was revived under the Han emperors, who saw the usefulness of Confucian emphasis on political virtue and social order. Confucian learning was also incorporated, along with traditional literary works, into the training of aspiring bureaucrats.

The problems Confucius set out to rectify, notably political disorder, were approached through an emphasis on individual virtuous behavior, both by the ruler and the ruled. "When the ruler does right, all men will imitate his self-control. What the ruler does, the people will follow." According to Confucius, only a man who demonstrated proper family virtues, including respect for parents and compassion for children and other inferiors, should be considered for political service. "When the ruler excels as a father, a son, and a brother, then the people imitate him." Confucius thus built into his own system the links among many levels of authority that came to characterize larger Chinese politics at their best. His system also emphasized personal restraint and the careful socialization of children.

Confucianism emphasized the importance of the gentleman, a member of what came to be known as the *shi* class. A superior man controlled his emotions, observed all the proper manners and rituals. He was a generalist, not a specialist, capable of serving in all sorts of government positions, capable of contributing also to art and poetry. His authority rested on his morality, not his expertise. Confucius believed that if such men ruled China, harmony would prevail forever.

For subordinates, Confucius largely recommended obedience and respect; people should know their place, even under bad rulers. However, he urged a political system that would not base rank simply on birth but would make education accessible to all talented and intelligent members of society. The primary emphasis still rested nonetheless on the obligations and desirable characteristics of the ruling class. According to Confucius, force alone cannot permanently conquer unrest, but kindness toward the people and protection of their vital interests will. Rulers should also be humble and sincere, for people will grow rebellious under hypocrisy or arrogance. Nor should rulers be greedy; Confucius warned against a profit motive in leadership, stressing that true happiness rested in doing good for all, not individual gain. Confucius projected the ideal of a gentleman, best described by his benevolence and self-control, a man always courteous and eager for service and anxious to learn.

Confucianism was accepted and amplified by many disciples. Mencius (Meng Ko) was an important figure who emphasized the goodness of human nature. People should be ruled in ways that brought out their goodness. Mencius' ideas, less hierarchical than pure Confucianism, set the basis for the belief that it was legitimate for peasants to rebel against oppressive rulers.

During the Qin and early Han periods, the alternate system of political thought called "Legalism" sprang up in China. Legalist writers prided themselves on their pragmatism. They disdained Confucian virtues in favor of an authoritarian state that ruled by force. Human nature for the Legalists was evil and required restraint and discipline. In a proper state, the army would control and the people would labor; the idea of pleasures in educated discourse or courtesy was dismissed as frivolity. Although Legalism never captured the widespread approval that Confucianism did, it too entered the political traditions of China, where a Confucian veneer was often combined with strong-arm tactics.

Confucianists did not explicitly seek popular loyalty. Like many early civilizations, China did not produce a single system of beliefs, as different groups embraced different values, with the same individual even turning to contrasting systems depending on his or her mood. Confucianism had some obvious limits in its appeal to the masses and, indeed, to many educated Chinese. Its reluctance to explore the mysteries of life or nature deprived it of a spiritual side. The creed was most easily accepted by the upper classes, which had the time and resources to pursue an education and participate in ceremony. However, elements of Confucianism, including a taste for ritual, self-control, and polite manners, did spread beyond the upper classes. But most peasants needed more than civic virtue to understand and

survive their harsh life, where in constant toil they eked out only a precarious and meager existence. During most of the classical period, polytheistic beliefs, focusing on the spirits of nature, persisted among much of the peasant class. Many peasants strove to attract the blessing of conciliatory spirits by creating statues and emblems, and household decorations honoring the spirits, and by holding parades and family ceremonies for the same purpose. A belief in the symbolic power of dragons stemmed from one such popular religion, which combined fear of these creatures with a more playful sense of their activities in its courtship of the divine forces of nature. Gradually, ongoing rites among the ordinary masses integrated the Confucian values urged by the upper classes.

Classical China also produced a more religious philosophy—Daoism—which arose at roughly the same time as Confucianism, during the waning centuries of the Zhou dynasty. Daoism first appealed to many in the upper classes, who had an interest in a more elaborate spirituality. Daoism embraced traditional Chinese beliefs in nature's harmony and added a sense of nature's mystery. As a spiritual alternative to Confucianism, Daoism produced a durable division in China's religious and philosophical culture. This new religion, vital for Chinese civilization, although never widely exported, was furthered by Laozi, who probably lived during the 5th century B.C.E. Laozi stressed that nature contains inherent principles that, if not recognized, lead to strife and unhappiness. True human understanding comes in withdrawing from the world and contemplating this life force. Dao, which means "the way of nature," refers to this same basic, indescribable force:

There is a thing confusedly formed,
Born before heaven and earth.
Silent and void
It stands alone and does not change,

Goes round and does not weary.
It is capable of being the mother of the
  world.
I know not its name,
So I style it "the way."

Along with secret rituals, Daoism promoted its own set of ethics. Daoist harmony with nature best resulted through humility and frugal living. According to this movement, political activity and learning were irrelevant to a good life, and general conditions in the world were of little importance.

Daoism, which combined with a strong Buddhist influence from India during the chaos that followed the collapse of the Han dynasty, guaranteed that China's people were not united by a single religious or philosophical system. Individuals did come to embrace some elements from both Daoism and Confucianism, and indeed many emperors favored Daoism. They accepted its spread with little anxiety, partly because some of them found solace in Daoist belief but also because the religion, with its otherworldly emphasis, posed no real political threat. Confucian scholars disagreed vigorously with Daoist thinking, particularly its emphasis on mysteries and magic, but they saw little reason to challenge its influence. As Daoism became an increasingly formal religion, from the later Han dynasty on, it provided many Chinese with a host of ceremonies designed to promote harmony with the mysterious life force. Finally, the Chinese government from the Han dynasty on was able to persuade Daoist priests to include expressions of loyalty to the emperor in their temple services. This heightened Daoism's political compatibility with Confucianism.

Confucianism and Daoism were not the only intellectual products of China's classical period, but they were the most important. Confucianism blended easily with the high value of literature and art among the upper classes. In literature, a set of Five Classics, written during the early part of the Zhou dynasty and then edited during the time of Confucius, provided an important tradition. They were used, among other things, as a basis for civil service examinations. The works provided in the Five Classics included some historical treatises, speeches, and other political materials, and a discussion of etiquette and ceremonies; in the *Classic of Songs,* more than 300 poems dealing with love, joy, politics, and family life appeared. The Chinese literary tradition developed on the basis of mastering these early works, plus Confucian writing; each generation of writers found new meanings in the classical literature, which allowed them to express new ideas within a familiar framework. Several thinkers during the Han dynasty elaborated Confucian philosophy. In literature, poetry commanded particular attention because the Chinese language featured melodic speech and variant pronunciations of the same basic sound, a characteristic that promoted an outpouring of poetry. From the classical period on, the ability to learn and recite poetry became the mark of an educated Chinese. Finally, the literary tradition established in classical China reinforced the Confucian emphasis on human life, although the subjects included romance and sorrow as well as political values.

Chinese art during the classical period was largely decorative, stressing careful detail and craftsmanship. Artistic styles often reflected the precision and geometric qualities of the many symbols of Chinese writing. Calligraphy became an important art form. In addition, Chinese artists painted, worked in bronze and pottery, carved jade and ivory, and wove silk screens. Classical China did not produce monumental buildings, aside from the Great Wall and some imperial palaces and tombs, in part because of the absence of a single religion; indeed, the entire tone of upper-class Confucianism was such that it discouraged the notion of temples soaring to the heavens.

This elaborate bronze vase dates from the late Zhou dynasty (c. 300 B.C.E.). It might be compared with the simpler, more primitive Chinese designs depicted earlier from the Shang dynasty.

In science, important practical work was encouraged, rather than imaginative theorizing. Chinese astronomers had developed an accurate calendar by 444 B.C.E., based on a year of 365.5 days. Later astronomers calculated the movement of the planets Saturn and Jupiter and observed sunspots—more than 1500 years before comparable knowledge developed in Europe. The purpose of Chinese astronomy was to make celestial phenomena predictable, as part of the wider interest in ensuring harmony between heaven and earth. Chinese scientists steadily improved their instrumentation, inventing a kind of seismograph to register earthquakes during the Han dynasty. The Chinese were also active in medical research, developing precise anatomical knowledge and studying principles of hygiene that could promote longer life.

Chinese mathematics also stressed the practical. Daoism encouraged some exploration of the orderly processes of nature, but far more research focused on how things actually worked. For example, Chinese scholars studied the mathematics of music in ways that led to advances in acoustics. This focus for science and mathematics contrasted notably with the more abstract definition of science developed in classical Greece.

Horse figure from Han dynasty, 2nd century C.E. The Chinese imported new horse breeds as they expanded into central Asia. This statue celebrates the improvement over the early, short-legged horses that were known to the Chinese.

ECONOMY AND SOCIETY

Although the most distinctive features of classical China centered on politics and culture, developments in the economy, social structure, and family life also shaped Chinese civilization and continued to have an impact on the empire's history for a significant period of time.

As in many agricultural societies, considerable gaps developed between China's upper class, which controlled large landed estates, and the masses, farmer-peasants who produced little more than what was needed for their own subsistence. The difficulty of becoming literate symbolized these gaps, for landlords enjoyed not only wealth but also a culture denied to most common people. Prior to the Zhou dynasty, slaveholding may have been common in China, but by the time of the Zhou, the main social division existed between the landowning gentry—about 2 percent of the total population—and peasants, who provided dues and service to these lords while also controlling some of their own land. The Chinese peasantry depended on intensive cooperation, particularly in the southern rice region; in this group, property was characteristically owned and regulated by the village or the extended family, rather than by individuals. Beneath the peasantry, Chinese social structure included a group of "mean" people who performed rough transport and other unskilled jobs and suffered the lowest possible status. In general, social status was passed from one generation to the next through inheritance, although unusually talented individuals from a peasant background might be given access to an education and rise within the bureaucracy.

Officially then and to a large extent in fact, classical China consisted of three main social groups. The landowning aristocracy plus the educated bureaucrats formed the top group. This top group, first known as the "shi", then the scholar-gentry, under the Han combined education and bureaucratic service, with landowning. Scholar-gentry families cooperated to run the estates and also provide bureaucrats. They were marked by their special attire, including silks, which commoners were not supposed to wear. Most gentry families employed some toughs to help protect them and to make sure commoners stayed in their place, but they also received great deference from most ordinary people. Under the gentry next came the laboring masses, peasants, and also urban artisans who manufactured goods. These people, far poorer than the top group and also condemned to a life of hard manual labor, sometimes worked directly on large estates but in other cases had some economic independence. Finally, were the mean people, the general category we have identified as applying to those without meaningful skills. Interestingly, performing artists were ranked in this group, despite the fact that the upper classes enjoyed plays and other entertainments provided by actors. Mean people were punished for crime more harshly than other groups and were required to wear identifying green scarves. Household slaves also existed within this class structure, but their number was relatively few and China did not depend on slaves for actual production.

Trade became increasingly important during the Zhou and particularly the Han dynasties. Much trade focused on luxury items for the upper class, produced by skilled artisans in the cities—silks, jewelry, leather goods, and furniture. There was also food exchange between the wheat- and rice-growing regions. Copper coins began to circulate, which facilitated trade, with merchants even sponsoring commercial visits to India. Although significant, trade and its attendant merchant class did not become the focal points of Chinese society, and the Confucian emphasis on learning and political service led to considerable scorn for lives devoted to moneymaking. The gap between the real importance and wealth of merchants and their officially low prestige was an enduring legacy in Confucian China.

If trade fit somewhat uncomfortably into the dominant view of society, there was no question about the importance of technological advance. Here, the Chinese excelled. Agricultural implements improved steadily. Ox-drawn plows were introduced around 300 B.C.E., which greatly increased productivity. Under the Han, a new collar was invented for draft animals, allowing them to pull plows or wagons without choking—this was a major improvement that became available to other parts of the world only many centuries later. Chinese iron mining was also well advanced, as pulleys and winding gear were devised to bring material to the surface. Iron tools and other implements such as lamps were widely used. Production methods in textiles and pottery were also highly developed by world standards. Under the Han, the first water-powered mills were introduced, allowing further gains in manufacturing. Finally, during the Han, paper was invented, which was a major boon to a system of government that emphasized the bureaucracy. In sum, classical China reached far higher levels of technical expertise than Europe or western Asia in the same period, a lead that it long maintained.

Technological advances, emphasis on manufacturing, and the particular mastery of silk production also positioned China strongly in the world trade of the period. The quality of Chinese goods helped sustain the network of the Silk Roads.

The relatively advanced technology of classical China did not, however, steer Chinese society away from its primary reliance on agriculture. Farming technology helped increase the size of the population in the countryside; with better

Peasants transplanting rice seedlings in south China.

tools and seeds, smaller amounts of land could support more families. But China's solid agricultural base, backed by some trade in foodstuffs among key regions, did permit the expansion of cities and manufacturing. There were many towns with more than 10,000 people; China was probably the most urbanized of the classical civilizations. Nonagricultural goods were mainly produced by artisans, working in small shops or in their homes. Even though only a minority of the workforce was involved in such tasks that used manual methods for the most part, the output of tools, porcelain, and textiles increased considerably, aided in this case as well by the interest in improving techniques.

In all major social groups, tight family organization helped solidify economic and social views as well as political life. The structure of the Chinese family resembled that of families in other agricultural civilizations in emphasizing the

WORLD PROFILES

BAN ZHAO
(c. 48–117 C.E.)

Ban Zhao, now known as China's most famous woman scholar, was long esteemed as an advisor on female humility and an example of chaste widowhood. Her life and ideas illustrate the complexities of a patriarchal society in action, and also the several sides of Confucianism.

Ban Zhao was the daughter of a leading scholar, with two able brothers, one a historian, the other a general. She received a good education. Ban Zhao married and had a son but was widowed at an early age. Living with her historian-brother, she collaborated with him on a history of the Han dynasty. When her brother died, the emperor insisted she complete the history, and she seems to have been responsible for some of its most original sections. She also tutored women at the imperial court, in literature, history, mathematics, and astronomy, and exerted considerable influence when one of her students became empress, serving as regent for a time. Ban Zhao wrote widely, although most of her works have been lost over the centuries. Her most famous effort was *Lessons for Women,* reprinted and actively circulated in China through the 19th century. In this work, Ban Zhao urged humility and domestic skills, a point of view that seemed at odds with, although not in complete contrast to, her own life. Young girls, for example, were urged to sleep at the foot of a brother's bed, so they would begin to learn their proper station. Accepting a Confucian family hierarchy, Ban Zhao also insisted that men had specific obligations to women, particularly to provide an appropriate education—and she emphasized that this aspect of their reciprocal relationship was not being met. Still, the dominant tone of *Lessons for Women* was subservient. Her work raises obvious questions. Why would an educated, self-sufficient woman condone the notion of women's inferiority to men? How can the contradiction between Ban Zhao's life and her public views be explained?

This woodcut of Ban Zhao appeared in 1690, obviously long after her death. The drawing is a sign of her ongoing importance as an advisor on gender. Because it reflects no knowledge of what the famous author actually looked like, the drawing should be interpreted in terms of what symbolic qualities artists had decided to emphasize.

importance of unity and the power of husbands and fathers. Within this context, however, the Chinese stressed authority to unusual extremes. Confucius said, "There are no wrongdoing parents"—and in practice, parents could punish disobedient children freely. Law courts did not prosecute parents who injured or even killed a disobedient son, but they severely punished a child who scolded or attacked a parent. In most families, the emphasis on obedience to parents, and a corresponding emphasis on wives' obedience to husbands, did not produce great friction. Chinese popular culture stressed strict control of one's emotions, and the family was seen as the center of such an orderly, serene hierarchy. Indeed, the family served as a great training ground for the principles of authority and restraint that applied to the larger social and political world. Women, although subordinate, had their own clearly defined roles and could sometimes gain power through their sons and as mothers-in-law of younger women brought into the household. The mother of a famous Confucian philosopher, Mencius, continually claimed how humble she was, but during the course of his life, she managed to exert considerable influence over him. But the basic subordination was clear. A Confucian poet stated, "A woman with a long tongue is a stepping stone to disorder. Disorder does not come down from Heaven—It is produced by women." There was even a clear hierarchical order for children, with boys superior to girls and the oldest son having the most enviable position of all. Chinese rules of inheritance, from the humblest peasant to the emperor himself, followed strict primogeniture, which meant that the oldest male child inherited property and position alike.

HOW CHINESE CIVILIZATION FIT TOGETHER

Classical Chinese technology, religion, philosophy, and political structure evolved with very little outside contact. Although important trade routes did lead to India and the Middle East, most Chinese saw the world in terms of a large island of civilization surrounded by barbarian peoples with nothing to offer save the periodic threat of invasion. Proud of their culture and its durability, the Chinese had neither the need nor the desire to learn from other societies. Nor, except to protect their central territory by exercising some control over the mountainous or desert regions that surrounded the Middle Kingdom, did Chinese leaders have any particular desire to teach the rest of the world. A missionary spirit was foreign to Chinese culture and politics. Of course, China displayed key patterns that were similar to those of the other agricultural civilizations. Further, the spread of Buddhism from India, during and after the Han decline, was a notable instance of a cultural diffusion that altered China's religious map and also its artistic styles. Nevertheless, the theme of separators and superiority, developed during the formative period of Chinese civilization, was to prove persistent in later world history—in fact, it has not entirely disappeared to this day.

Chinese civilization was also noteworthy for the relative harmony among its various major features. We have, in this chapter, examined the pattern of leading historical events in classical China and then the systems of government, belief, economy, and social structure. All these facets were closely meshed. Although the centralized government, with its elaborate functions and far-reaching bureaucracy, gave the clearest unity and focus to Chinese society, it did not do so alone. Confucianism provided a vital supplement, making the bureaucracy more than a collection of people with similar political objectives, but rather a trained corps with some common ideals. In appreciation of distinctive artistic styles, poetry and the literary tradition added to this common culture. Cohesive government and related beliefs about human ideals and aesthetics were linked, in turn, to the economy. Political stability over a large and fertile land aided economic growth, and the government took a direct role in encouraging both agriculture and industry. A strong economy, in turn, provided the government with vital tax revenues. Economic interests were also related to the pragmatic Chinese view of science, whose aim was to determine how nature worked. Finally, social relationships reinforced all these systems. The vision of a stable hierarchy and tight family structures meshed with the strong impulse toward orderly politics and helped instill the virtues of obedience and respect that were important to the larger political system.

Not surprisingly, given the close links between the various facets of their civilization, the Chinese tended to think of their society as a whole. They did not distinguish clearly between private and public sectors of activity. They did not see government and society as two separate entities. In other words, these Western concepts that we have used to define classical China and to facilitate comparisons with other societies do not really fit the Chinese view of their own world. Confucius himself, in seeing government as basically a vast extension of family relationships, similarly suggested that the pieces of the Chinese puzzle were intimately joined.

A grasp of Chinese civilization as a whole, however, should not distract us from recognizing some endemic tensions and disparities. The division in belief systems, between Confucianism and Daoism, modifies the perception of an ultimately tidy classical China. Confucianists and Daoists tolerated each other. Sometimes their beliefs coincided, so that an individual who behaved politically as a Confucianist might explore deeper mysteries through Daoist rituals. However, between both groups there was considerable hostility and mutual disdain, as many Confucianists found Daoists superstitious and overexcited. Daoism did not inherently disrupt the political unity of Chinese culture, but at times the religion did inspire attacks on established politics in the name of a mysterious divine will.

Tension in Chinese society showed in the way Confucian beliefs were combined with strict policing. Chinese officials believed in fundamental human goodness and the importance of ceremony and mutual respect. However, they also believed in the force of stern punishment, not only against criminals but also as warnings to the larger, potentially restless population. People arrested were presumed guilty and often subjected to torture before trial. The Chinese, in fact, discovered early on the usefulness of alternating torture with benevolence, to make accused individuals confess. In the late Han period, a thief who refused to confess even under severe torture was then freed from chains, bathed, and fed, "so as to bring him in a happy mood"—whereupon he usually confessed and named his whole gang. In sum, both Confucianism and the Chinese penal system supported tight control, and the combination of the two was typically effective; however, they involved quite different approaches and quite different moral assumptions.

All of this suggests that classical China, like any vigorous, successful society, embraced a diversity of features that could not be fully united by any single formula. Elites and masses were divided by both economic interests and culture. Some shared the same values, particularly as Confucianism spread, and upper-class concern for careful etiquette and the general welfare of the population mitigated the tension. But such calm was a precarious balance, and when overpopulation or some other factor tipped the scale, recurrent and often violent protest could be the result.

Despite any divisions, the symbiosis between the various institutions and activities of many people in classical China deserves strong emphasis. It helps account for the durability of Chinese values. Even in times of political turmoil, families transferred beliefs and political ideals by the ways in which they instructed their children. The wholeness of Chinese society also helps account for its relative immunity to outside influence and for its creativity despite considerable isolation.

Chinese wholeness, finally, provides an interesting contrast to the other great Asian civilization that developed in the classical period. India, as fully dynamic as China in many ways, produced different emphases, but also a more disparate society in which links among politics and beliefs and economic life were less well defined. Many argue that this contrast between the two Asian giants persists to this day.

PATHS
TO THE PRESENT

The astonishing durability of the classical civilizations' features—a durability that extends to the present—is a key reason to study their formation and characteristics. Nowhere is this more the case than in China.

Huge changes have occurred, of course, between the fall of the Han dynasty and emergence of a modern China, and it is important to examine later world history, to avoid stereotyping Chinese culture and people.

But the basic list of early China's enduring accomplishments is intriguing. China was once a center of world manufacturing, as evidenced by its centrality in Silk Roads trade, and modern China is reemerging in that role. Modern China, though no longer Confucian, continues to emphasize the importance of political order and a strong state. Strong family structures, including a preference for boys over girls in the countryside, suggest additional links to the past; this has led, in recent decades, to a striking gender imbalance in contemporary Chinese society, which is a potentially serious problem. Even the current widespread enthusiasm for higher education—though in modern subjects, not traditional ones—likely builds on values created during the Han dynasty.

China's classical experience, in other words, forms part of the framework that has created China as it exists today. This raises vital questions about the reasons so many traditional elements survived so well—questions that can be answered by looking at the nation's experience in later world history periods.

SUGGESTED WEB SITES

For a view of the formation of Chinese civilization, see http://www.china.org.cn/e-gudai/; on Confucius, see http://plato.stanford.edu/entries/confucius/; for more information on the Great Bronze Age of China, see http://www.humanities-interactive.org/ancient/bronze/brochure_bronze_age.htm. Information on classical China can be found at http://eawc.evansbille.edu/chpage.htm.

SUGGESTED READINGS

Important works include Nicola DiCosmo, *Ancient China and Its Enemies: The Rise of Nomadic Power in East Asian History* (2002); Michael Loewe, ed., *The Cambridge History of Ancient China* (1999); Grant Hardy, *Worlds of Bronze and Bamboo: Sima Qian's Conquest of History* (1999); and Michael Neiberg, *Warfare in World History* (2001).

Several sources offer original materials on classical Chinese thought and politics: Walter Scheidel, ed., *Rome and China: Comparative Perspectives on Ancient World Empires* (2008); Chun-shu Chang, ed., *The Rise of the Chinese Empire* (2007); Grant Hardy and Anne Behnke Kinney, *The Establishment of the Han Empire and Imperial China* (2005); John Fairbank, ed., *Chinese Thought and Institutions* (1973); Wing-stit Chan, *A Source Book in Chinese Philosophy* (1963); and P. Ebrey, *Chinese Civilization and Society: A Sourcebook* (1981). Two excellent general surveys for this period and later ones are John Fairbank and Albert Craig, *East Asia: Tradition and Transformation* (1993), and E. O. Reischauer and John Fairbank, *A History of East Asian Civilization,* Vol. 1: *East Asia, The Great Tradition* (1961); see also Arthur Cotterell, *The First Emperor of China* (1981). On more specialized topics, see E. Balazs, *Chinese Civilization and Bureaucracy* (1964); J. Needham, *Science and Civilization in China,* 4 vols. (1970); Richard J. Smith, *Traditional Chinese Culture: An Interpretive Introduction*

(1978); Benjamin Schwartz, *The World of Thought in Ancient China* (1983); Michael Loewe, *Everyday Life in Early Imperial China* (1968); and Bella Vivante, ed., *Women's Roles in Ancient Civilizations: A Reference Guide* (1999); Steven Shankman, *Early China/Ancient Greece: Thinking Through Comparisons* (2002); Constance A. Cook, *Defining China: Image and Reality in Ancient China* (2004); Kwang-chih Chang and Sarah Allan, *The Formation of Chinese Civilization: An Archaeological Perspective* (2005); Steven Shankman and Stephen Durrant, *The Siren and the Sage: Knowledge and Wisdom in Ancient Greece and China* (2000); Paul Rakita Goldin, *The Culture of Sex in Ancient China* (2002); and Mu-chou Poo, *Enemies of Civilization: Attitudes Toward Foreigners in Ancient Mesopotamia, Egypt, and China* (2005).

5 Classical Civilization: India

The classical period of Indian history includes a number of contrasts to that of China—and many of these contrasts have proved enduring. Whereas the focus in classical China was on politics and related philosophical values, the emphasis in classical India shifted to religion and social structure; a political culture existed, but it was less cohesive and central than its Chinese counterpart. Less familiar but scarcely less important were distinctions that arose in India's scientific tradition and the tenor of the economy and family life. Here, too, the classical period generated impulses that are still felt in India today—and that continue to distinguish India from other major civilizations in the world.

India's distinctiveness was considerable, but a comparison must not be one-sided. India was an agricultural society, and this dictated many similarities with China. Most people were peasant farmers, with their major focus on food production for their own family's survival. The clustering of peasants in villages, to provide mutual aid and protection, gave a strong localist flavor to many aspects of life in China and India alike. In addition, agriculture influenced family life, with male ownership of property creating a strongly patriarchal flavor, and women held as inferiors and often treated as possessions. As agricultural civilizations, both China and India produced important cities and engendered significant trade, which added to social and economic complexity and also created the basis for most formal intellectual life, including schools and academies. Both societies, finally, generated ideas that helped explain and confirm social inequality—though the cultural systems were rather different.

KEY QUESTIONS *What were the main changes in India from the early classical period until the Gupta dynasty at the end? How did Hinduism and Buddhism relate in Indian history in this period? How did extensive merchant activity coexist with India's strong religious emphasis?*

THE FRAMEWORK FOR INDIAN HISTORY: GEOGRAPHY AND A FORMATIVE PERIOD

Important reasons for India's distinctive paths lie in geography and early historical experience. India was much closer to the orbit of other civilizations than China. Trading contacts with China expanded late in the classical period. India was also frequently open to influences from the Middle East and even the Mediterranean world. Persian empires spilled over into India at several points, bringing new artistic styles and political concepts. Briefly, Alexander the Great invaded India; while he did not establish a durable empire, he did allow important Indian contacts with Hellenistic culture. Periodic influences from the Middle East continued after the classical age, prompting India to react and adapt in ways that China, more isolated save for nomadic pressures, largely avoided.

In addition to links with other cultures, India's topography shaped a number of vital features of its civilization. The vast Indian subcontinent is partially separated from the rest of Asia, and particularly from east Asia, by northern mountain ranges, notably the Himalayas, though important passes through the mountains, especially in the northwest, linked India to the Middle East and central Asia. At the same time, divisions within the subcontinent made full political unity difficult: India was thus marked by greater diversity than China's Middle Kingdom. The most important agricultural regions are those along the two great rivers, the Indus and the Ganges. However, India also has mountainous northern regions, where a herding economy took root, and a southern coastal rim, separated by mountains and the Deccan Plateau, where an active trading and seafaring economy arose. India's separate regions help explain not only economic diversity but also the racial and language differences that, from early times, have marked the subcontinent's populations.

Much of India is semitropical in climate. In the river valley plains, heat can rise to 120°F during the early summer. Summer also brings torrential monsoon rains, crucial for farming. But the monsoons vary from year to year, sometimes bringing too little rain or coming too late and causing famine-producing drought, or sometimes bringing catastrophic floods. Certain features of Indian civilization may have resulted from a need to come to terms with a climate that could produce abundance one year and grim starvation the next. In a year with favorable monsoons, Indian farmers were able to plant and harvest two crops and could thus support a sizable population.

Indian civilization was shaped not only by its physical environment but also by a formative period, lasting several centuries, between the destruction of the Indus River (Harappan) civilization and the revival of full civilization elsewhere on the subcontinent. During this formative period, called the Vedic and Epic ages, the Indo-European migrants—nomadic herding peoples originally from central Asia, and sometimes called Aryans—gradually came to terms with agriculture but had their own impact on the culture and social structure of their new home. Also during the Vedic Age, from about 1500 to 1000 B.C.E., Indian agriculture extended from the Indus River valley to the more fertile Ganges valley, as the Aryans used iron tools to clear away the dense vegetation.

Most of what we know about this preclassical period in Indian history comes from literary epics developed by the Aryans, initially passed on orally. They were later written down in Sanskrit, which became the first literary language of the new culture. The initial part of this formative period, the Vedic Age, takes its name from the Sanskrit word *Veda,* or "knowledge." The first epic, the *Rig-Veda,* consists of 1028 hymns dedicated to the Aryan gods and composed by various priests. New stories, developed during the Epic Age between 1000 and 600 B.C.E., include the *Mahabharata,* India's greatest epic poem, and the *Ramayana,* both of which deal with real and mythical battles; these epics reflect a more settled agricultural society and better-organized political units than the *Rig-Veda.* The Epic Age also saw the creation of the *Upanishads,* epic poems with a more mystical religious flavor.

Aryan ideas and social and family forms also became increasingly influential. As the Aryans settled down to agriculture, they encouraged tight levels of village organization that came to be characteristic of Indian society and politics. Village chiefs, initially drawn from the leadership of one of the Aryan tribes, helped organize village defenses and also to regulate property relationships among families. Family structure emphasized patriarchal controls, and extended family relationships among grandparents, parents, and children were close.

The characteristic Indian caste system also began to take shape during the Vedic and Epic ages, as a means of establishing relationships between the Aryan conquerors and the indigenous people, whom the Aryans regarded as inferior. Aryan social classifications partly enforced divisions familiar in agricultural societies. Thus, a warrior or governing class, the *kshatriyas,* and the priestly caste, or *brahmins,* stood at the top of the social pyramid, followed by *vaisyas,* the traders and farmers, and *sudras,* or common laborers. Many of the sudras worked on the estates of large landowners. A fifth group gradually evolved, the untouchables, who were confined to a few jobs, such as transporting the bodies of the dead or hauling refuse. Handling leather hides was also in this category, because of Indian valuation of animals and disdain for people involved with killing them. It was widely believed that touching these people defiled anyone from a superior caste. Initially, the warrior group ranked highest, but during the Epic Age the brahmins replaced them, signaling the importance of religious links in Indian life. Thus, a law book stated, "When a brahmin springs to light he is born above the world, the chief of all creatures, assigned to guard the treasury of

duties, religious and civil." Gradually, the five social groups became hereditary, with marriage between castes forbidden and punishable by death; the basic castes divided into smaller subgroups, called *jati,* each with distinctive occupations and each tied to its social station by birth. India's caste system hardened with time, so what had been rather loose arrangements of social inequalities became life-determining. Only the highest three castes were directly authorized to read sacred texts. One of the heroes of Indian epics, Rama, was celebrated for cutting off the head of a peasant who read the Vedas while hanging upside down from a tree.

The *Rig-Veda,* the first Aryan epic, attributed the rise of the caste system to the gods:

> When they divided the original Man
> into how many parts did they divide him?
> What was his mouth, what were his arms,
> what were his thighs and his feet called?
> The brahmin was his mouth, of his
> arms was made the warrior.
> His thighs became the vaisya, of
> his feet the sudra was born.

The Aryans brought to India a religion of many gods and goddesses, who regulated natural forces and possessed human qualities. Thus, Indra, the god of thunder, was also the god of strength. Gods presided over fire, the Sun, death, and so on. This system bore some resemblances to the gods and goddesses of Greek myth or Scandinavian mythology, for the very good reason that they were derived from a common Indo-European oral heritage. However, India was to give this common tradition an important twist, ultimately constructing a vigorous, complex religion that, apart from the Indo-European polytheistic faiths, endures to this day. During the epic periods, the Aryans offered hymns and sacrifices to the gods. Certain animals were regarded as particularly sacred, embodying the divine spirit. Gradually, this religion became more elaborate. The epic poems reflect an idea of life after death and a religious approach to the world of nature. Nature was seen as informed not only by specific gods but also by a more basic divine force. These ideas, expressed in the mystical *Upanishads,* added greatly to the spiritual power of this early religion and served as the basis for later Hindu beliefs. By the end of the Epic Age, the dominant Indian belief system included a variety of convictions. Many people continued to emphasize rituals and sacrifices to the gods of nature; specific beliefs, as in the sacredness of monkeys and cattle, illustrated this ritualistic approach. The brahmin priestly caste specified and enforced prayers, ceremonies, and rituals. However, the religion also produced a more mystical strand through its belief in a unifying divine force and the desirability of seeking union with this force. Toward the end of the Epic period one religious leader, Gautama Buddha, built on this mysticism to create what became Buddhism, another major world religion.

PATTERNS IN CLASSICAL INDIA

By 600 B.C.E., India had passed through its formative phase. Regional political units grew in size, cities and trade expanded, and the development of the Sanskrit language, although dominated by the priestly brahmin caste, furthered an elaborate literary culture. A full, classical civilization could now build on the social and cultural themes first launched during the Vedic and Epic ages.

The rhythm of Indian political history was irregular and often consisted of landmark invasions that poured in through the mountain passes of the subcontinent's northwestern border. At first, patterns broadly resembled those of Zhou in China, though with a different cultural system. But India did not make China's move to a more decisive sequence of dynasties and attendant centralization.

Toward the end of the Epic Age and until the 4th century B.C.E., the Indian plains were divided among powerful regional states. Sixteen major states existed by 600 B.C.E. in the plains of northern India, some of them monarchies, others republics dominated by assemblies of priests and warriors. Warfare was not uncommon. One regional state, Magadha, established dominance over a considerable empire. In 327 B.C.E., Alexander the Great, having conquered Greece and much of the Middle East, pushed into northwestern India, establishing the small border state called Bactria.

Political reactions to this incursion produced the next major step in Indian political history, in 322 B.C.E., when a young soldier named Chandragupta seized power along the Ganges River. He became the first of the Maurya dynasty of Indian rulers, who in turn were the first rulers to unify much of the entire subcontinent. Borrowing from Persian political models and the example of Alexander the Great, Chandragupta and his successors maintained large armies, with thousands of chariots and elephant-borne troops. The Mauryan rulers also developed a substantial bureaucracy, even sponsoring a postal service.

Chandragupta's style of government was highly autocratic, relying on the ruler's personal and military power. This style surfaced periodically in Indian history, just as it did in the Middle East, a region with which India had important contacts. A Greek ambassador from one of the Hellenistic kingdoms described Chandragupta's life:

> Attendance on the king's person is the duty of women, who indeed are bought from their fathers. Outside the gates [of the palace] stand the bodyguards and the rest of the soldiers. . . . Nor does the king sleep during the day, and at night he is forced at various hours to change his bed because of those plotting against him. Of his nonmilitary departures [from the palace] one is to the courts, in which he passed the day hearing cases to the end. . . . [When he leaves to hunt,] he is thickly surrounded by a circle of

women, and on the outside by spear-carrying bodyguards. The road is fenced off with ropes, and to anyone who passes within the ropes as far as the women, death is the penalty.

Such drastic precautions paid off. Chandragupta finally designated his rule to a son and became a religious ascetic, dying peacefully at an advanced age.

Chandragupta's grandson, Ashoka (269–232 B.C.E.), was an even greater figure in India's history. First serving as a governor of two provinces, Ashoka enjoyed a lavish lifestyle, with frequent horseback riding and feasting. However, he also engaged in a study of nature and was strongly influenced by the intense spiritualism not only of the brahmin religion but also of Buddhism. Ashoka extended Mauryan conquests, gaining control of all but the southern tip of India through fierce fighting. His methods were bloodthirsty; in taking over one coastal area, Ashoka himself admitted that "one hundred and fifty thousand were killed (or maimed) and many times that number later died." But Ashoka could also be compassionate. He ultimately converted to Buddhism, seeing in the belief in *dharma,* or the law of moral consequences, a kind of ethical guide that might unite and discipline the diverse people under his rule. Ashoka vigorously propagated Buddhism throughout India, while also honoring Hinduism, sponsoring shrines for its worshippers. Ashoka even sent Buddhist missionaries to the Hellenistic kingdoms in the Middle East, and also to Sri Lanka to the south. The "new" Ashoka urged humane behavior on the part of his officials and insisted that they oversee the moral welfare of his empire. Like Chandragupta, Ashoka also worked to improve trade and communication, sponsoring an extensive road network dotted with wells and rest stops for travelers. Stability and the sheer expansion of the empire's territory encouraged growing commerce.

The Mauryan dynasty did not, however, succeed in establishing durable roots, and Ashoka's particular style of government did not

Column to Ashoka, 3rd century B.C.E.

have much later impact, although a strong Buddhist current persisted in India for some time. After Ashoka, the empire began to fall apart, and regional kingdoms surfaced once again. New invaders, the Kushans, pushed into central India from the northwest. The greatest Kushan king, Kanishka, converted to Buddhism but actually hurt this religion's popularity in India by associating it with foreign rule.

The collapse of the Kushan state, by 220 C.E., ushered in another hundred years of political instability. Then a new line of kings, the Guptas, established a large empire, beginning in 320 C.E. The Guptas produced no individual rulers as influential as the two great Mauryan rulers, but they may have had greater impact. One Gupta emperor proclaimed his virtues in an inscription on a ceremonial stone pillar:

His far-reaching fame, deep-rooted in peace, emanated from the restoration of the sovereignty of many fallen royal families. . . . He, who had no equal in power in the world, eclipsed the fame of the other kings by the radiance of his versatile virtues, adorned by innumerable good actions.

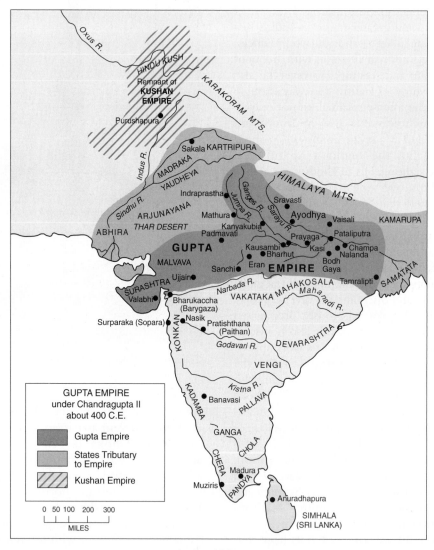

India, 400 C.E.

Bombast aside, Gupta rulers often preferred to negotiate with local princes and intermarry with their families, which expanded influence without constant fighting. Two centuries of Gupta rule gave classical India its greatest period of political stability, although the Guptas did not administer as large a territory as the Mauryan kings had. The Gupta empire was overturned in 535 C.E. by a new invasion of nomadic warriors, the Huns.

Classical India thus alternated between widespread empires and a network of smaller kingdoms. Periods of regional rule did not necessarily suggest great instability, and both economic and cultural life advanced in these periods as well as under the Mauryas and Guptas.

POLITICAL INSTITUTIONS

Classical India did not develop the solid political traditions and institutions of Chinese civilization, or the high level of political interest that characterized classical Greece and Rome. The most persistent political features of India, in the classical period and beyond, involved regionalism, plus considerable diversity in political forms. Autocratic kings and emperors dotted the history of classical India, but there were also aristocratic assemblies in some regional states with the power to consult and decide on major issues.

As a result of India's diversity and regionalism, even some of the great empires had a rather shaky base. Early Mauryan rulers depended heavily on the power of their large armies, and they often feared betrayal and attack. Early rulers in the Gupta dynasty used various devices to consolidate support. They claimed that they had been appointed by the gods to rule, and they favored the Hindu religion over Buddhism because the Hindus believed in such gods. The Guptas managed to create a demanding taxation system, seeking up to a sixth of all agricultural produce. However, they did not create an extensive bureaucracy, rather allowing local rulers whom they had defeated to maintain regional control so long as they deferred to Gupta dominance. The Guptas stationed a personal representative at each ruler's court to ensure loyalty. A final sign of the great empire's loose structure was the fact that no single language was imposed. The Guptas promoted Sanskrit, which became the language of educated people, but this made no dent in the diversity of popular, regional languages.

The Guptas did spread uniform law codes. Like the Mauryan rulers, they sponsored some general services, such as road building. They also served as patrons of much cultural activity, including university life as well as art and literature. These achievements were more than enough to qualify the Gupta period as a golden age in Indian history.

The fact remains, however, that the political culture of India was not very elaborate. There was little formal political theory and few institutions or values other than regionalism that carried through from one period to the next. Chandragupta's chief minister, Kautilya, wrote an important treatise on politics, but it was devoted to telling rulers what methods worked to maintain power—somewhat like the Legalists in China. Thinking of this sort encouraged efficient authority, but it did not very widely spread political values or a sense of the importance of political service, in contrast to Confucianism in China and also to the intense interest in political ethics in Greece and Rome. Ashoka saw in Buddhism a kind of ethic for good behavior as well as a spiritual beacon, but Buddhist leaders in the long run were not greatly interested in affairs of state. Indeed, Indian religion generally did not stress the importance of politics, even for religious purposes, but rather the preeminence of holy men and priests as sources of authority. It was true, however, that some brahmins served as advisors at royal courts and as administrators, though most brahmins served as priests to wealthy families or to peasant villages.

The limitations on the political traditions developed during this period of Indian history can be explained partly by the importance of local units of government—the tightly organized villages—and particularly by the essentially political qualities of social relationships under the caste system. Caste rules, interpreted by priests, regulated many social relationships and work roles. To a great extent, the caste system and religious encouragement in the faithful performance of caste duties did for Indian life what more conventional government structures did in many other cultures, in promoting public order.

India's caste system became steadily more complex after the Epic Age, as the five initial castes subdivided until ultimately almost 300 castes or jati subcastes were defined. Hereditary principles grew ever stronger, so that it became virtually impossible to rise above the caste in which a person was born or to marry someone from a higher caste. It was possible to fall to a lower caste by marrying outside one's caste or by taking on work deemed inappropriate for one's caste. Upward mobility could occur within castes, as individuals might gain greater wealth through success in the economic activities appropriate to the caste. The fact that brahmins replaced warriors as the top caste also indicates some flexibility. And rulers, like the Mauryans, might spring from the merchant caste, although most princes were warrior born. It is important not to characterize the caste system in an over-simplified way, for it did provide some flexibility. Nevertheless, the system gave India the most rigid overall framework for a social structure of any of the classical civilizations.

In its origins, the caste system provided a way for India's various races, the conquerors and the conquered, to live together without perpetual conflict and without full integration of cultures and values. Quite different kinds of people could live side by side in village or city,

separated by caste. In an odd way, castes promoted tolerance, and this was useful, given India's varied peoples and beliefs. The caste system also meant that extensive outright slavery was avoided. The lowest, untouchable caste was scorned, confined to poverty and degrading work, but its members were not directly owned by others. The system also did not prevent mobility within castes, for example by earning more money.

The political consequences of the caste system derived from the detailed rules for each caste. These rules governed marriages and permissible jobs, but also social habits such as eating and drinking. For example, a person from one caste could not eat or drink with someone from a lower caste or perform any service for that person. This kind of regulation of behavior made detailed political administration less necessary. Indeed, no state could command full loyalty from subjects, for their first loyalty was to caste. By the end of the classical period, a person's life was tightly defined by caste position. People who refused to perform the duties of their caste could face beatings by the community, or even ostracism. If thrown out of the community, most people died, because no one, even a family member, was allowed to offer support to an "outcaste." Religious and political leaders enforced the system as a primary duty, believing that it was supernaturally ordained.

More of the qualities of Indian civilization rested on widely shared cultural values than was the case in China. Religion, and particularly the evolving Hindu religion as it gained ground on Buddhism under the Guptas, was the clearest cultural cement of this society, cutting across political and language barriers and across the castes. Hinduism embraced considerable variety; it gave rise to important religious dissent, and it never displaced important minority religions and other intellectual and artistic interests. However, Hinduism has shown a remarkable capacity to survive and is the major system of belief in India even today.

HISTORY DEBATE

INTERPRETING CIVILIZATION, ROUND TWO

World historians have frequently debated the validity of the concept of civilization. We saw in Chapter 1 that civilizations differ from other societies but that the boundary lines are fuzzy, and also that societies that were not civilizations might be interesting and, in some cases, important historically. In dealing with the classical period, the initial definition of *civilization* is extended. The term still designates societies that have cities, organized governments, and usually writing. However, now it also designates some degree of coherence and distinctiveness within a given region—hence, Chinese civilization is different from Indian civilization.

Coherence, however, is not always easy to define. Except for Mesopotamia after Sumer, the river valley civilizations are not too problematic. Egypt, for example, usually had a single government and religion. By the classical centuries, however, civilizations covered large areas and embraced much diversity. South China differed from the north, even under the same government; there was much ethnic and linguistic tension. India, never entirely united by a single government (except briefly under foreign rule, well after the classical period) and with widely varied castes, is an even tougher case. Here, no single religion ever fully dominated, although Brahmanism and then Hinduism were the most characteristic. Even modern-day India does not control the whole subcontinent, in large part because of religious divisions. Here, the idea of a coherent, distinct civilization denotes predominant values (including the important overlap between Hinduism and Buddhism) and social structures, not full unity or identity.

Treating major civilizations as tendencies that include important internal divisions and tensions, as entities that must be defined rather than assumed, helps capture the reality of how people have acted and continue to act in world history. Examining a classical civilization such as India or China even helps frame the other major themes of world history, including the degree of openness to outside influences. Here too, however, some world historians differ, seeing common human impulses and global forces as the whole story, with civilizations merely an invention of scholars unable to shake off the arrogant claims of particular societies such as China or, more recently, western Europe. Here, it is important to establish one's own position as to how useful or misleading the concept of civilization is, while recognizing the main alternatives.

One other complication: the basic features of a given civilization do not stand still, nor do its boundaries. The transitions from river valley to classical civilizations illustrate this kind of passage. Each major period of world history requires a renewed definition, still with the basic goal of testing coherence and a certain degree of distinctiveness. India can still be labeled a civilization today. How do its characteristics and territory compare with those of its classical counterpart?

It also promotes other features in Indian culture. Thus, contemporary Indian children are encouraged to indulge their imaginations longer than Western children are, and they are confronted less sharply with outside reality. Some observers argue that even Indian adults, on average, are less interested in general, agreed-upon truths than in individually satisfying versions. A mind-set of this sort goes back to the religious patterns created more than 2000 years ago in classical India, where Hinduism encouraged imaginative links with a higher, divine reality. It is this kind of tradition that illustrates how classical India, although not the source of enduring political institutions beyond the local level, produced a continuous civilization that retained its cultural cohesiveness from this point on—even through centuries in which political control escaped Indian hands almost completely.

RELIGION AND CULTURE

Hinduism, the religion of India's majority, developed gradually over a period of many centuries. Its origins lie in the Vedic and Epic ages, as the Aryan religion gained greater sophistication, with concerns about an overarching divinity supplementing the rituals and polytheistic beliefs supervised by the brahmin caste of priests. The *Rig-Veda* expressed the growing interest in a higher divine principle in its Creation Hymn:

> Then even nothingness was not, nor existence. There was no air then, nor the heavens beyond it. Who covered it? Where was it? In whose keeping . . . ? The gods themselves are later than creation, so who knows truly whence it has arisen?

Unlike all the other world religions, Hinduism had no single founder, no central holy figure from whom the basic religious beliefs stemmed. This fact helps explain why the religion unfolded so gradually, sometimes in reaction to competing religions such as Buddhism or Islam. Moreover, Hinduism pursued a number of religious approaches, from the strictly ritualistic and ceremonial approach many brahmins preferred, to the high-soaring mysticism that sought to unite individual humans with an all-embracing divine principle. Unlike Western religions or Daoism (which it resembled in part), Hinduism could also encourage political and economic goals (called *artha*) and worldly pleasures (called *karma*)—and important textbooks of the time spelled out these pursuits. Part of Hinduism's success, indeed, was the result of its fluidity, its ability to adapt to the different needs of various groups and to change with circumstance. With a belief that there are many suitable paths of worship, Hinduism was also characteristically tolerant, coexisting with several offshoot religions that garnered minority acceptance in India.

Under brahmin leadership, Indian ideas about the gods gradually became more elaborate. Original gods of nature were altered to represent more abstract concepts. Thus, Varuna changed from

Painting of the god Ganesh from the Hindi pantheon.

a god of the sky to the guardian of ideas of right and wrong. The great poems of the Epic Age increasingly emphasized the importance of gentle and generous behavior and the validity of a life devoted to concentration on the Supreme Spirit. The *Upanishads,* particularly, stressed the shallowness of worldly concerns—riches and even health were not the main point of human existence—in favor of contemplation of the divine spirit. It was in the *Upanishads* that the Hindu idea of a divine force informing the whole universe, of which each individual creature's soul is thought to be part, first surfaced clearly, in passages such as the following:

> "Fetch me a fruit of the banyan tree."
> > "Here is one, sir."
> > "Break it."
> > "I have broken it, sir."
> > "What do you see?"
> > "Very tiny seeds, sir."
> > "Break one."
> > "I have broken it, sir."

"What do you see now?"

"Nothing, sir."

"My son, . . . what you do not per-
ceive is the essence, and in that essence the
mighty banyan tree exists. Believe me, my
son, in that essence is the self of all that is.
That is the True, that is the Self."

However, the *Upanishads* did more than
advance the idea of a mystical contact with a
divine essence. They also attacked the conventional
brahmin view of what religion should be, a set of
proper ceremonies that led to good things in this
life or rewards after death. From the Epic Age on,
Hinduism embraced this clear tension between a
religion of rituals, with fixed ceremonies and rules
of conduct, and the religion of mystical holy men,
seeking communion with the divine soul.

The mystics, often called *gurus* as they gathered disciples around them, and the brahmin
priests agreed on certain doctrines as Hinduism
became an increasingly formal religion by the first
centuries of the common era. The basic holy
essence, called *Brahma,* formed part of everything
in this world. Every living creature participates in
this divine principle. The spirit of Brahma enters
several gods or forms of gods, including Vishnu,
the preserver, and Siva, the destroyer, who could be
worshipped or placated as expressions of the holy
essence. The world of our senses is far less important than the world of the divine soul, and a proper
life is one devoted to seeking union with this soul.
However, this quest may take many lifetimes.
Hindus stressed the principle of reincarnation, in
which souls do not die when bodies do but pass
into other beings, either human or animal. Where
the soul goes, whether it rises to a higher-caste
person or falls perhaps to an animal, depends on
how good a life the person has led. The good life,
in turn, was defined primarily in terms of living up
to the duties of one's caste. Ultimately, after many
good lives, the soul reaches full union with the
soul of Brahma, and worldly suffering ceases.

Hinduism provided several channels for the
good life. For the holy men, there was the meditation and self-discipline of *yoga,* which means

"union," allowing the mind to be freed to
concentrate on the divine spirit. For others,
there were the rituals and rules of the brahmins.
These included proper ceremonies in the crema-
tion of bodies at death, appropriate prayers, and
obedience to injunctions such as treating cows as
sacred animals and refraining from the consumption of beef. Many Hindus also continued the
idea of lesser gods represented in the spirits of
nature, or purely local divinities, which could be
seen as expressions of Siva or Vishnu. Worship to
these divinities could aid the process of reincarnation to a higher state. Thus, many ordinary
Hindus placed a lot of importance on prayers,
sacrifices, and gifts to the gods that would bring
them through reincarnation into a higher caste.

Hinduism also provided a basic, if complex,
ethic that helped supply some unity amid the
various forms of worship. The epic poems, richly
symbolic, formed the key texts. They illustrated a
central emphasis on the moral law of *dharma* as a
guide to living in this world and simultaneously
pursuing higher, spiritual goals. The concept of
dharma directed attention to the moral consequences of action and at the same time the need
to act. Each person must meet the obligations of
life, serving the family, producing a livelihood
and even earning money, and serving in the
army when the need arises. These actions cannot
damage, certainly cannot destroy, the eternal
divine essence that underlies all creation. In the
Bhagavad Gita, a classic sacred hymn, a warrior is
sent to do battle against his own relatives. Fearful
of killing them, he is advised by a god that he
must carry out his duties. He will not really be
killing his victims because their divine spirit will
live on. This ethic urged that honorable behavior, even pleasure seeking, is compatible with
spirituality and can lead to a final release from
the life cycle and to unity with the divine
essence. The Hindu ethic explains how devout
Hindus could also be aggressive merchants or
eager warriors. In encouraging honorable
action, it could legitimize government and the
caste system as providing the frameworks in
which the duties of the world might be carried

out, without distracting from the ultimate spiritual goals common to all people.

The ethical concept of dharma was far less detailed and prescriptive than the ethical codes associated with most other world religions, including Christianity and Islam. Dharma stresses inner study and meditation, building from the divine essence within each creature, rather than adherence to a fixed set of moral rules. The key feature of dharma, however, was to live up to the duties and status attached to the caste in which one was born. Defying this dharma was one of the greatest sins, fulfilling it the key preparation for advancement through reincarnation.

The spread of Hinduism through India and, at least briefly, to some other parts of Asia had many sources. The religion accommodated extreme spirituality. It also provided satisfying rules of conduct for ordinary life, including rituals and a firm emphasis on the distinction between good and evil behavior. The religion allowed many people to retain older beliefs and ceremonies, derived from a more purely polytheistic religion. The religion reinforced the caste system, giving people in lower castes hope for a better time in lives to come and giving upper-caste people, including the brahmins, the satisfaction that if they behaved well, they might be rewarded by communion with the divine soul. Even though Hindu beliefs took shape only gradually and contained many ambiguities, the religion was sustained by a strong caste of priests and through the efforts of individual gurus and mystics.

At times, however, the tensions within Hinduism broke down for some individuals, producing rebellions against the dominant religion. One such rebellion, which occurred right after the Epic Age, led to a new religion closely related to Hinduism. This religion, Buddhism, provided one of classical India's greatest contributions to world history. Buddhism played an important role in classical India itself, sharing features with Hinduism but disagreeing on key points. In the longer run, as Hinduism ultimately triumphed, Buddhism's greatest impact was in other parts of Asia.

This beautifully detailed sandstone statue of the Buddha meditating in a standing position was carved in the 5th century C.E. Note the nimbus, or halo, which was common in later Buddhist iconography. The calm radiated by the Buddhist's facial expression suggests that he has already achieved enlightenment. As Buddhism spread throughout India and overseas, a wide variety of artistic styles developed to depict the Buddha and key incidents of his legendary life. The realism and stylized robes of the sculpture shown here indicate that it was carved by artists following the conventions of the Indo-Greek school of northwestern India.

Around 563 B.C.E., an Indian prince, Gautama, was born who came to question the fairness of earthly life in which so much poverty and misery abounded. Gautama, later called Buddha, or "the enlightened one," lived as a Hindu mystic, fasting and torturing his body. After six years, he felt that he had found truth, then spent his life traveling and gathering disciples to spread his ideas. Buddha accepted many Hindu beliefs, but he protested the brahmin emphasis on ceremonies. In a related sense, he downplayed the polytheistic element in Hinduism by focusing on the overall divine system over separate, lesser gods. Buddha believed in deeply spiritual rewards, seeing the ultimate goal as destruction of the self and union with the divine essence, a state that he called *nirvana.* Individuals could regulate their lives and aspirations toward this goal, without elaborate ceremonies. Great stress was placed on self-control: "Let a man overcome anger by love, let him overcome evil by good, let him overcome the greedy by liberality, the liar by the truth." A holy life could be achieved through individual effort from any level of society. Here, Buddhism attacked not only the priests but also the caste system; this was another sign of the complexity of Indian social life in practice. Consistently, Buddha and Buddhism focused on the problem of suffering, which was inevitably attached to things of this world, even those, indeed particularly those, that might seem pleasant. Escape from suffering could come only from ceasing to desire worldly goals. Enlightenment alone released one from suffering.

Buddhism spread and retained coherence through the example and teachings of groups of holy men, organized in monasteries but preaching throughout the world. Buddhism attracted many followers in India, and its growth was greatly spurred by the conversion of the Mauryan emperor Ashoka. Increasingly, Buddha was seen as divine. Prayer and contemplation at Buddhist holy places and works of charity and piety gave substance to the idea of a holy life on earth. Ironically, however, Buddhism did not witness a permanent following in India. Brahmin opposition was strong,

and it was ultimately aided by the influence of the Gupta emperors. Furthermore, Hinduism showed its adaptability by emphasizing its mystical side, thus retaining the loyalties of many Indians. Buddhism's greatest successes, aided by the missionary encouragement of Ashoka and later the Kushan emperors (particularly Kanishka), came in other parts of southeast Asia, including the island of Sri Lanka; off the south coast of India; and in China, Korea, and Japan. Still, pockets of Buddhists remained in India, particularly in the northeast. They were joined by other dissident groups who rejected aspects of Hinduism. Thus, Hinduism, although dominant, had to come to terms with the existence of other religions early on.

If Hinduism, along with the caste system, formed the most distinctive and durable products of the classical period of Indian history, they were certainly not the only ones. Even aside from dissident religions, Indian culture during this period was vibrant and diverse, and religion encompassed only part of its interests. Hinduism itself encouraged many wider pursuits.

Indian thinkers wrote actively about various aspects of human life. Although political theory was sparse, a great deal of legal writing occurred. The theme of love was important also. A manual of the "laws of love," the *Kama-sutra,* written in the 4th century C.E., is an unusually elaborate and expressive discussion of the sexual experience.

Indian literature, taking many themes from the great epic poems and their tales of military adventure, stressed lively story lines. The epics were recorded in final written form during the Gupta period, and other story collections, such as the *Panchatantra,* which includes Sinbad the Sailor, Jack the Giant Killer, and the Seven League Boots, produced adventurous yarns now known all over the world. Classical stories were often secular, but they sometimes included the gods and also shared with Hinduism an emphasis on imagination and excitement. Indian drama flourished also, again particularly under the Guptas, and stressed themes of romantic adventure in which lovers separated and then reunited after many perils. This literary tradition created a cultural framework that still survives in India. Even contemporary Indian movies reflect the tradition of swashbuckling romance and heroic action.

Classical India also produced important work in science and mathematics. The Guptas supported a vast university center—one of the world's first—in the town of Nalanda that attracted students from other parts of Asia as well as Indian brahmins. Nalanda had more than 100 lecture halls, three large libraries, an astronomical observatory, and a model dairy. Its curricula included religion, philosophy, medicine, architecture, and agriculture.

At the research level, Indian scientists, borrowing a bit from Greek learning after the conquests of Alexander the Great, made important strides in astronomy and medicine. The great astronomer Aryabhatta calculated the length of the solar year and improved mathematical measurements. Indian astronomers understood and calculated the daily rotation of the earth on its axis, predicted and explained eclipses, and developed a theory of gravity, and through telescopic observation they identified seven planets. Medical research was hampered by religious prohibitions on dissection, but Indian surgeons nevertheless made advances in bone setting and plastic surgery. Inoculation using cowpox serum against smallpox was introduced. Indian hospitals stressed cleanliness, including sterilization of wounds, while leading doctors promoted high ethical standards. As was the case with Indian discoveries in astronomy, many medical findings reached the Western world only in modern times.

Indian mathematicians produced still more important discoveries. The Indian numbering system is the one we use today, although we call it Arabic because Europeans imported it secondhand from the Arabs. Indians invented the concept of zero, and through it they were able to develop the decimal system. Indian advances in numbering rank with writing as key human inventions. Indian mathematicians also developed the concept of negative numbers, calculated square roots and a table of sines, and computed the value of "pi" more accurately than the Greeks did.

Finally, classical India produced lively art, although much of it perished under later invasions. Ashoka sponsored many spherical shrines to Buddha, called *stupas,* and statues honoring Buddha were also common. Under the Guptas, sculpture and painting moved away from realistic portrayals of the human form toward more stylized representation. Indian painters, working on the walls of buildings and caves, filled their work with forms of people and animals, captured in lively color. Indian art showed a keen appreciation of nature, and some of it also suggested several of the erotic themes expressed in works such as the *Kama-sutra.* This was an art that could pay homage to religious values, particularly during the period in which Buddhism briefly spread, but could also celebrate the joys of life.

Brahmin (early Hindu) sculpture: the god Siva Natarajah as the lord of dance.

There was, clearly, no full unity to this cultural outpouring. Achievements in religion, legalism, abstract mathematics, and a sensual and adventurous art and literature coexisted. The result, however, was a somewhat distinctive overall tone, different from the more rational approaches of the West or the Chinese concentration on political ethics. In various cultural expressions, Indians developed an interest in spontaneity and imagination, whether in fleshly pleasures or a mystical union with the divine essence.

ECONOMY AND SOCIETY

The caste system described many key features of Indian social and economic life, as it assigned people to occupations and regulated marriages. Low-caste individuals had few legal rights, and servants were often abused by their masters, who were restrained only by the ethical promptings of religion toward kindly treatment. A brahmin who killed a servant for misbehavior faced a penalty no more severe than if he had killed an animal. This extreme level of abuse was uncommon, but the caste system did unquestionably make its mark on daily life as well as on the formal structure of society. The majority of Indians living in peasant villages had less frequent contact with people of higher social castes, and village leaders were charged with trying to protect peasants from too much interference by landlords and rulers. The peasantry grew steadily as the Indo-Europeans settled down, though large sections of classical India were still dominated by dense tropical rain forests. Peasant productivity increased with the use of new tools, and the class formed the majority of the total population.

Family life also emphasized the theme of hierarchy and tight organization, as it evolved from the Vedic and Epic ages. The dominance of husbands and fathers remained strong. One Indian code of law recommended that a wife worship her husband as a god. Indeed, the rights of women became increasingly limited as Indian civilization took clearer shape. Although the great epics stressed the control of husband and father, they also recognized women's independent contributions. As agriculture became better organized and improved technology reduced (without eliminating) women's economic contributions, the stress on male authority expanded. This is a common pattern in agricultural societies, as a sphere of action women enjoyed in hunting cultures was gradually circumscribed. Hindu thinkers debated whether a woman could advance spiritually without first being reincarnated as a man, and there was no consensus. The limits imposed on women were reflected in laws and literary references. A system of arranged marriage evolved in which parents contracted unions for their children, particularly daughters, at quite early ages, to spouses they had never even met. The goal of these arrangements was to ensure solid economic links, with child brides contributing dowries of land or domestic animals to the ultimate family estates, but the result of such arrangements was that young people, especially girls, were drawn into a new family structure in which they had no voice.

Indian culture showed interesting ambiguities where women were concerned. On the one hand, they were often dismissed in the epics as weak and frivolous, often causing trouble. Good women were seen in terms of their service to fathers or husbands. But women were also described in the epics as strong willed and clever.

The rigidities of family life and male dominance over women were often greater in theory than they usually turned out to be in practice. The emphasis on loving relations and sexual pleasure in Indian culture modified family life, because husband and wife were supposed to provide mutual emotional support as a marriage developed. The *Mahabharata* epic called a man's wife his truest friend: "Even a man in the grip of rage will not be harsh to a woman, remembering that on her depend the joys of love, happiness, and virtue." Small children were often pampered.

SOLVING PROBLEMS

DEALING WITH INEQUALITY

Pronounced and well-defined social inequality was a striking feature of early and classical civilizations. Huge gaps developed between wealthy, landowning classes plus some state and religious officials and urban merchants, and the mass of the population. In the eyes of many classical philosophers, inequalities helped societies solve the crucial problem of generating sufficient agricultural and craft production to keep things going, while also supporting a higher group freed from manual labor, in some cases relatively well educated, and in principle capable of providing leadership to the whole endeavor. Confucius thus spoke of the need for ordinary people to meet their economic obligations and defer to their betters; Aristotle, in Greece, wrote of the necessity of slavery to sustain a ruling class. The assumption was that the upper group would govern wisely—the word *aristocracy* comes from the Greek "rule of the best"—but few people at the top questioned that pronounced inequality was a social necessity. From our vantage point today, with less firm ideas about how much inequality is justified, it is less easy to assume that inequality was the only response to the conditions of early civilizations. It obviously reflected constraints on agricultural production, which generated sufficient surplus only for a relatively small luxury class. At the same time, our contemporary world has experienced its own rapid increases in inequality, within societies like China, India, Europe, and the United States over the past two decades. Interpreting social inequality is not an easy task.

The inequality of early civilizations obviously created two ensuing problems. The first, on how to justify the situation, was met quite directly by philosophical and religious leaders. Hinduism built inequality into its larger view of existence, arguing that it was part of a divine order. The second, more intriguing, centered on the question of how inequality would be judged by those on the shorter end of the stick. Hinduism, again, provided explicit reasons for poor, low-caste people to accept the system in anticipation of advancement through reincarnation. As Confucian ideas spread beyond the elites, ordinary Chinese might agree that inequality could be accepted when the upper classes provided good, humane leadership. And the fact was the ordinary people, consumed by daily tasks, did not necessarily have much margin for thinking about abstract social issues. Still, the need to persuade ordinary people that inequality was legitimate was an important cultural task in early civilizations (and still, though in different circumstances, today). Obviously, all major civilizations addressed the problem, but with different specific social systems and patterns of belief.

QUESTIONS: *Which of the classical systems dealt best with issues of inequality (and how should best be defined)? What are the main differences and similarities between past and present patterns of inequality?*

"With their teeth half shown in causeless laughter, their efforts at talking so sweetly uncertain, when children ask to sit on his lap, a man is blessed." Families thus served an important and explicit emotional function as well as a role in supporting the structure of society and its institutions. They also, as in all agricultural societies, formed economic units. Children, after early years of indulgence, were expected to work hard. Adults were obligated to assist older relatives. The purpose of arranged marriages was to promote a family's economic well-being, and almost everyone lived in a family setting.

The Indian version of the patriarchal family was thus subtly different from that of China, although women were officially just as subordinate, and later trends—as in many patriarchal societies over time—brought new burdens. But Indian cultural allowance for resourceful women and goddesses contributed to women's status as wives and mothers. Stories also celebrated women's emotions and beauty. In the early part of the classical period, some women contributed directly to religious scholarship, though later they were banned from reading the sacred Vedic texts. Women also served as teachers, musicians, and artists, though the latter two activities were not highly esteemed. Generally, women had no respectable alternative to marriage, though groups of courtesans often surrounded the royal courts and, for Buddhists, monasteries provided opportunities for nuns. Women whose husbands died, particularly if they had not yet borne a son, were condemned to a difficult existence, often isolated in the compounds of the extended family.

The economy of India in the classical period became extremely vigorous, certainly rivaling China in technological sophistication and probably briefly surpassing China in the prosperity of its upper classes. In manufacturing, Indians invented new uses for chemistry, and their steel was the best in the world. Indian capacity in ironmaking outdistanced European levels until a few centuries ago. Indian techniques in textiles were also advanced, as the subcontinent became the first to manufacture cotton cloth, calico, and cashmere. Most manufacturing was done by artisans who formed guilds and sold their goods from shops.

Indian emphasis on trade and merchant activity was far greater than in China, and indeed greater than in the classical Mediterranean world. Indian merchants enjoyed relatively high-caste status and the flexibility of the Hindu ethic. And, they traveled widely, not only over the subcontinent but, by sea, to the Middle East and east Asia. The seafaring peoples along the southern coast, usually outside the large empires of northern India, were particularly active. These southern Indians, the Tamils, traded cotton and silks, dyes, drugs, gold, and ivory, often earning great fortunes. From the Middle East and the Roman Empire, they brought back pottery, wine, metals, some slaves, and above all gold. Their trade with southeast Asia was even more active, as Indian merchants transported not only sophisticated manufactured goods but also the trappings of India's active culture to places such as Malaysia and the larger islands of Indonesia. In addition, caravan trade developed with China. India became something of a hub for the interregional trade of the period.

Indeed, India played a central role in the interregional trading system of the classical period overall. Chinese rulers periodically sent voyages to India in search of specific goods. Under the Roman Empire, regular expeditions left the Red Sea for India, seeking valued products like pepper, and small groups of Roman merchants established themselves in India directly. All of this was in addition to the active role Indian merchants played through much of the Indian Ocean and in overland contacts with Persia and other parts of the Middle East.

At the same time, the Indian economy remained firmly agricultural at its base. The wealth of the upper classes and the splendor of cities such as Nalanda were confined to a small group, as most people lived near the margins of subsistence. But India was justly known by the time of the Guptas for its wealth as well as for its religion and intellectual life—always understanding that wealth was relative in the classical world and very unevenly divided. A Chinese Buddhist on a pilgrimage to India wrote:

> The people are many and happy. They do not have to register their households with the police. There is no death penalty. Religious sects have houses of charity where rooms, couches, beds, food, and drink are supplied to travelers.

INDIAN INFLUENCE

Classical India, from the Mauryan period on, had a considerable influence on other parts of the world. In many ways, the Indian Ocean, dominated at this point by Indian merchants and missionaries, was the most active linkage point among cultures, although admittedly the Mediterranean, which channeled contact from the Middle East to north Africa and Europe, was a close second. Indian dominance of the waters of southern Asia, and the impressive creativity of Indian civilization itself, carried goods and influence well beyond the subcontinent's borders. No previous civilization had developed in southeast Asia to compete with Indian influence. While India did not attempt political domination, dealing instead with the regional kingdoms of Burma, Thailand, parts of Indonesia, and Vietnam, Indian travelers or settlers brought to these locales a persuasive way of life. Many Indian merchants married into local royal families. Indian-style temples were constructed, and other forms of Indian art traveled widely. Buddhism spread from India to many parts of southeast Asia, and Hinduism converted many upper-class people, particularly in several of the Indonesian kingdoms. India thus serves as an early example of a major civilization expanding its influence well beyond its own regions.

Indian influence had affected China, through Buddhism and art, by the end of the classical period. Earlier, Buddhist emissaries to the Middle East stimulated new ethical thinking that informed Greek and Roman groups, such as the Stoics, and through them aspects of Christianity later on.

Within India itself, the classical period, starting a bit late after the Aryan invasions, lasted somewhat longer than that of China or Rome. Even when the period ended with the fall of the Guptas, an identifiable civilization remained in India, building on several key factors first established in the classical period: the religion, to be sure, but also the artistic and literary tradition and the complex social and family network. The ability of this civilization to survive, even under long periods of foreign domination, was testimony to the meaning and variety it offered to many Indians themselves.

CHINA AND INDIA

The thrusts of classical civilization in China and India reveal the diversity generated during the classical age. The restraint of Chinese art and poetry contrasted with the more dynamic, sensual styles of India. India ultimately settled on a primary religion, though with important minority expressions, that embodied diverse impulses within it. China opted for separate religious and philosophical systems that served different needs. China's political structures and values found little echo in India, whereas the Indian caste system involved a social rigidity considerably greater than that of China. India's cultural emphasis was, on balance, considerably more otherworldly than that of China, despite the impact of Daoism. Quite obviously, classical India and classical China created vastly different cultures. Even in science, where there was similar interest in pragmatic discoveries about how the world works, the Chinese placed greater stress on purely practical findings, whereas the Indians ventured further into the mathematical arena.

Beyond the realm of formal culture and the institutions of government, India and China may seem more similar. As agricultural societies, both civilizations relied on a large peasant class, organized in close-knit villages with much mutual cooperation. Cities and merchant activity, although vital, played a secondary role. Political power rested primarily with those who controlled the land, through ownership of large estates and the ability to tax the peasant class. On a more personal level, the power of husbands and fathers in the family—the basic fact of patriarchy—encompassed Indian and Chinese families alike.

However, Indian and Chinese societies differed in more than their religion, philosophy, art, and politics. Ordinary people had cultures along with elites. Hindu peasants saw their world differently from their Chinese counterparts. They placed less emphasis on personal emotional restraint and detailed etiquette; they expected different emotional interactions with family members. Indian peasants were less constrained than were the Chinese by recurrent efforts by large landlords to gain control of their land. Although there were wealthy landlords in India, the system of village control of most land was more firmly entrenched than in China. Indian merchants played a greater role than their Chinese counterparts. There was more sea trade, more commercial vitality. Revealingly, India's expanding cultural influence was due to merchant activity above all else, whereas Chinese expansion involved government initiatives in gaining new territory and sending proud emissaries to satellite states. These differences were less dramatic, certainly less easy to document, than those generated by elite thinkers and politicians, but they contributed to the shape of a civilization and to its particular vitality, its areas of stability and instability.

Because each classical civilization developed its own unique style, in social relationships as well as in formal politics and intellectual life, exchanges between two societies such as China and India involved specific borrowings, not wholesale imitation. India and China, the two giants of classical Asia, remain subjects of comparison to our own time, because they have continued to build distinctively on their particular traditions, established before 500 C.E. These characteristics, in turn, differed from those of yet another center of civilization, the societies that sprang up on the shores of the Mediterranean during this same classical age.

PATHS TO THE PRESENT

Contemporary India, like contemporary China, shows many vestiges of its classical past. The Hindu religion, professed by the majority, forms an active link between present and past. The Indian state is modern and effective, but its federal system reflects the strong regionalism established many centuries ago—as does the absence of a single national language. Rural India links strongly to earlier social and cultural traditions.

India also grapples with its classical heritage in other respects. The caste system has been outlawed for more than half a century, but its traces persist. Efforts to promote people of low-caste origins, for example, by providing special university scholarships, have been resisted by the former upper castes. And, women's inferiority is taken for granted still in many patriarchal families. As with racial issues in the United States and South Africa, it proves difficult to erase older, unequal social systems merely by implementing progressive laws.

Overall, the force of India's traditions, inherited in substantial part from the classical centuries, points in two directions. On the one hand, as a leading politician noted soon after India's independence, tradition forms a burden, limiting efforts at reform. On the other, tradition is a source of identity and pride, which many Indians successfully combine with fully contemporary activities in science and technology.

SUGGESTED WEB SITES

For more information on ancient India, see http://www.ancientindia.co.uk/, http://www.wsu.edu:8080/~dee/ANCINDIA/ANCINDIA.HTM; also http://www.mnsu.edu/emuseum/prehistory/india/ and http://www.hindubooks.org/sudheer_birodkar/hindu_history/landmaurya.html; on the ancient Indus Valley, see www.harappa.com/.

SUGGESTED READINGS

There are fewer provocative surveys of Indian history than are available about China, but several competent efforts exist: Romila Thapar, *Early India: From the Origins to 1300* (2002); P. Spear, *India* (1981); Stanley Wolpert, *A New History of India* (1994); Rhoads

Murphey, *A History of Asia* (1992); Jonardon Ganeri, *Philosophy in Classical India* (2001); Shankar Goyal, *Ancient India: A Multidisciplinary Approach* (2006); T. N. Madan, ed., *India's Religions: Perspectives from Sociology and History* (2004); and Milo Kearney, *The Indian Ocean in World History* (2004). See also Jennifer Howes, *The Courts of Pre-Colonial South India: Material Culture and Kingship* (2003); Suresh Ghosh, *The History of Education in Ancient India* (2001); and Romila Thapar, *History and Beyond* (2000). See also

Thomas McEvilley, *The Shape of Ancient Thought: Comparative Studies of Greek and Indian Philosophies* (New York, 2002); Thomas R. Traultmann, *The Aryan Debate* (2005); Thomas William Rhys Davids, *Buddhist India* (1999); Jennifer Howes, *The Courts of Pre-Colonial South India: Material Culture and Kingship* (2003); Alfred S. Bradford, *With Arrow, Sword, and Spear: A History of Warfare in the Ancient World* (2001); and Daud Ali, *Courtly Culture and Political Life in Early Medieval India* (2001).

6

Classical Civilization in the Mediterranean and Middle East: Persia, Greece, and Rome

The classical civilizations that sprang up in Persia and on the shores of the Mediterranean Sea from about 800 B.C.E. until the fall of the Roman Empire in 476 C.E. rivaled their counterparts in India and China in richness and impact. Two centers were involved, separately though in contact; briefly merged; then separate once more. Developments in the Middle East and the Mediterranean built directly on precedents established by the river valley civilizations not only in Mesopotamia but in Egypt. But different centers generated different emphases—the nature of Persian politics, for example, differed noticeably from that of Greece; and with Greece and Rome, civilization also extended westward, to other parts of Africa and to southern Europe. Both Persian and Mediterranean civilizations met the criteria of classical civilizations, in relying heavily on territorial expansion and empire and in founding institutions and cultural systems that would wield influence even after the classical period had ended.

A massive Persian empire developed, spurred initially by the kind of outside invasion that had earlier produced various Mesopotamian empires. But the Persian Empire grew far larger, illustrating the new capacities of the classical period. Durable political and cultural traditions were established that persisted in and around present-day Iran well beyond the classical period.

Centered first in the peninsula of Greece, then in Rome's burgeoning provinces, a new Mediterranean culture did not embrace most of the Middle East. Though less significant at the time, Greece rebuffed the advance of the mighty Persian Empire and established some colonies on the eastern shore of the Mediterranean, in what is now Turkey. Rome came closer to conquering the Middle East but even its empire had to contend with strong kingdoms in Persia. Nevertheless, Greece and Rome did not merely constitute a westward push of civilization from its earlier bases in the Middle East and along the Nile—although this is a part of their story. They also represent the formation of new institutions and values that reverberated in the later history of the Middle East and Europe alike.

For most Americans, and not only those who are descendants of European immigrants, classical Mediterranean culture constitutes "our own" classical past, or at least a goodly part of it. The framers of the American Constitution were extremely conscious of Greek and Roman precedents. Designers of public buildings in the United States, from the early days of the American republic to the present, have dutifully copied Greek and Roman models, as in the Lincoln Memorial and most state capitols. Plato and Aristotle continue to be thought of as the founders of our philosophical tradition, and skillful teachers still rely on some imitation of the Socratic method. Our sense of debt to Greece and Rome may inspire us to find in their history special meaning or links to our own world; the Western educational experience has long included elaborate explorations of the Greco-Roman past as part of the standard academic education. But from the standpoint of world history, greater balance is obviously necessary. Greco-Roman history is one of the several major classical civilizations, more dynamic than its Chinese and Indian counterparts in some respects but noticeably less successful in others. The challenge is to discern the leading features of Greek and Roman civilization and to next compare them with those of their counterparts elsewhere. We can then clearly recognize the connections and our own debt without adhering to the notion that the Mediterranean world somehow dominated the classical period.

Classical Mediterranean civilization is complicated by the fact that it passed through two centers during its centuries of vigor, as Greek political institutions rose and then declined and the legions of Rome assumed leadership. Roman interests were not identical to those of Greece, although the Romans carefully preserved most Greek achievements. Rome mastered engineering; Greece specialized in scientific thought.

Rome created a mighty empire, whereas the Greek city-states proved rather inept in forming an empire. It is possible, certainly, to see more than a change in emphases from Greece to Rome, and to talk about separate civilizations instead of a single basic pattern. And it is true that Greek influence was always stronger than Roman in the eastern Mediterranean, whereas western Europe encountered a fuller Greco-Roman mixture, with Roman influence predominating in language and law. However, Greek and Roman societies shared many political ideas; they had a common religion and artistic styles; they developed similar economic structures. Certainly, their classical heritage was used by successive civilizations without fine distinctions drawn between what was Greek and what was Roman.

■**KEY QUESTIONS**   *Three initial questions involve making sense out of variety. First, Persia established an important classical tradition; how can this also be seen in relationship to the Mediterranean? Second, on Mediterranean civilization itself: Greece and Rome tossed up a great mixture of political forms; what were the most important forms, and what was the political heritage of the classical Mediterranean for later societies? The third question: what did Greece, Hellenistic society, and Rome have in common that defined classical Mediterranean civilization? Were the changes from Greece to Rome any greater than those from Zhou China to Han China, during the same classical period? A fourth, crucial comparative question involves the end of the classical period: Classical civilization in the Mediterranean did not survive as well as its counterparts in India and China—why?*

THE PERSIAN TRADITION

After the fall of the great Egyptian and Hittite empires in the Middle East by 1200 B.C.E., much smaller states predominated the area. Then new powers stepped in, first the Assyrians and then an rulers developed a vital infrastructure for the whole empire. A major system of roads reduced travel time, though it still took 90 days to go from one end of the empire to the other. An east-west highway, largely paved, facilitated commerce and troop movement from the Indian border to the Mediterranean, and another highway reached Egypt. The Persians established the first regular postal service, and they built a network of inns along their roads to accommodate travelers. These achievements would help connect the Middle East to trade routes coming from central and eastern Asia, a vital step in the growth of new commercial connections.

Persian emperors, particularly Darius, who worked hard not only to expand but to integrate his vast territories, developed a substantial bureaucracy. This existed alongside an earlier, military nobility. The central government introduced several measures to control the activities of officials assigned to distant provinces. Tax collection was carefully regulated, and spies were sent out to make sure regional officials remained loyal to the central government, rather than allying with local political forces.

Persia was also the center of a major new religion. A Zoroastrian religious leader, Zoroaster (c. 630–550 B.C.E.), revised the polytheistic religious tradition of the Sumerians through the introduction of monotheism. He banned animal sacrifice and the use of intoxicants. He introduced the idea of individual salvation through the free choice of God over the spirit of evil. Zoroaster, and the growing group of Zoroastrian priests (the *Magi*) saw life as a battle between two divine forces: good and evil. Zoroastrianism emphasized the importance of personal moral choice in picking one side or the other, with a Last Judgment ultimately deciding the eternal fate of each person. The righteous would live on in a heaven, the "House of Song," while the evil would be condemned to eternal pain. Zoroastrianism influenced Persia's later emperors and spread widely in the population as a whole. A Greek traveler, Herodotus, noted that the

A relief of a procession decorates the ruins of a building at Persepolis, the capital of the Persian Empire.

influx of Iranians (Persians). A great conqueror emerged by 550 B.C.E. Cyrus the Great established a massive Persian Empire, which ran across the northern Middle East and into northwestern India. The new empire was the clearest successor to the great Mesopotamian states of the past, but it was far larger. The Iranians advanced iron technology in the Middle East.

Persian politics featured several characteristics, the first of which was tolerance. The Persian Empire embraced a host of languages and cultures, and the early Persian rulers were careful to grant considerable latitude for this diversity. Second, however, was a strong authoritarian streak. Darius, successor to Cyrus, worked hard to centralize laws and tax collection. The idea of wide participation in politics was rejected. Third, and related to the centralization process, Persian

Persian religion was much more spiritual than that of the Greeks, for the Persians did not believe in humanlike gods.

Indeed, the Persian religious influence would prove far greater than that of the Greeks, though Greek culture had wide impact in other respects. Only small groups of Zoroastrians survive in the world today, in Iran and through immigration in a few other places including the United States. But the religion retained a wide hold for a considerable period of time and its ideas and beliefs strongly affected Judaism, Christianity, and Islam.

Religion did not consume all of Persian cultural energies. An important artistic tradition also emerged with distinctive styles of painting and architecture.

Later kings expanded Persian holdings. They were unable to conquer Greece, but they long dominated much of the Middle East, providing an extensive period of peace and prosperity. Conquests also extended into North Africa and the Indian River valley. At its height, Persia embraced at least 14 million people. The population of Persia proper (present-day Iran), at 4 million people, had doubled under imperial rule. Ultimately, the Persian Empire was toppled by Alexander the Great, a Greek-educated conqueror. Persian language and culture survived in the northeastern portion of the Middle East, periodically affecting developments in the region as a whole. After the Hellenistic period, a series of Persian empires arose in the northeastern part of the Middle East, competing with Roman holdings and later states and reviving Persian identity in many ways.

Persian political institutions strongly impressed Alexander and his successors. Persian art would affect not only the region, but also India and the wider Middle East. Zoroastrianism, one of the major belief systems of the classical period, would ultimately fade in its competition with Islam, but its hold and influences continued well beyond the classical centuries.

PATTERNS OF GREEK AND ROMAN HISTORY

Greece

Even as Persia developed, a new civilization took shape to the west, building on a number of earlier precedents. The river valley civilizations of the Middle East and Africa had spread to some of the islands near the Greek peninsula, although less to the peninsula itself. The island of Crete, in particular, showed the results of Egyptian influence by 2000 B.C.E., and from this the Greeks were later able to develop a taste for monumental architecture. The Greeks were an Indo-European people, such as the Aryan conquerors of India, who took over the peninsula by 1700 B.C.E. An early kingdom in southern Greece, strongly influenced by Crete, developed by 1400 B.C.E. around the city of Mycenae. This was the kingdom later memorialized in Homer's epics about the Trojan War. Mycenae was then toppled by a subsequent wave of Indo-European invaders, whose incursions destroyed civilization on the peninsula until about 800 B.C.E.

The rapid rise of civilization in Greece between 800 and 600 B.C.E. was based on the creation of strong city-states, rather than a single political unit. Each city-state had its own government, typically either a tyranny of one ruler or an aristocratic council. The city-state served Greece well, for the peninsula was so divided by mountains that a unified government would have been difficult to establish. Trade developed rapidly under city-state sponsorship, and common cultural forms, including a rich written language with letters derived from the Phoenician alphabet, spread throughout the peninsula. The Greek city-states also joined in regular celebrations such as the athletic competitions of the Olympic games. Sparta and Athens came to be the two leading city-states. The first represented a strong military aristocracy dominating a slave population; the other was a more diverse commercial state, also including the extensive use of slaves, justly proud of its artistic and intellectual leadership. Between 500 and 449 B.C.E., the two states cooperated, along with smaller states, to defeat a huge Persian invasion. It was during and immediately after this period that Greek and particularly Athenian culture reached its highest point. Also during this period, several city-states, and again particularly Athens, developed more colonies in the eastern Mediterranean and southern Italy, as Greek culture fanned out to create a larger zone of civilization.

It was during the 5th century B.C.E. that the most famous Greek political figure, Pericles, dominated Athenian politics. Pericles was an aristocrat, but he was part of a democratic political structure in which each citizen could participate in city-state assemblies to select officials and pass laws. Pericles ruled not through official position, but by wise influence and negotiation. He helped restrain some of the more aggressive views of the Athenian democrats, who urged even further expansion of the empire to garner more wealth and build the economy. Ultimately, however, Pericles' guidance could not prevent the tragic war between Athens and Sparta, which depleted both sides.

Political decline soon set in, as Athens and Sparta vied for control of Greece during the bitter Peloponnesian Wars (431–404 B.C.E.). Ambitious kings from Macedonia, in the northern part of the peninsula, soon conquered the cities. Philip of Macedonia won the crucial battle in 338 B.C.E., and then his son Alexander extended the Macedonian Empire through the Middle East, across Persia to the border of India, and southward through Egypt. Alexander the Great's empire was short-lived, for its creator died at the age of 33 after a mere 13 years of breathtaking conquests. However, successor regional kingdoms continued to rule much of the eastern Mediterranean for several centuries. Under their aegis, Greek art and culture merged with other Middle Eastern forms during a period called *Hellenistic,* the name derived because of the influence of the Hellenes, as the Greeks were known. Although there was little

political activity under the autocratic Hellenistic kings, trade flourished and important scientific centers were established in such cities as Alexandria in Egypt. In sum, the Hellenistic period saw the consolidation of Greek civilization even after the political decline of the peninsula itself, as well as some important new cultural developments.

The Hellenistic period also provided an important opportunity for interregional contacts. Greek-Indian interactions in the kingdom of Bactria were unusual for the time. More significant was the further exchange between Greek and Persian traditions, and between Greek and Egyptian as well. Alexander himself, marrying a Persian princess, hoped for a fusion of Persian and Greek politics and culture. His political achievements highlighted an authoritarian strain that meshed with Persian precedents. Art and science benefited from creative exchanges among scholars in many parts of the eastern Mediterranean. The advances in science and philosophy that resulted provided a shared intellectual legacy for the whole region, even after the Hellenistic political kingdoms collapsed.

Rome

The rise of Rome formed the final phase of classical Mediterranean civilization, for by the 1st century B.C.E. Rome had subjugated Greece and the Hellenistic kingdoms alike. The Roman state began humbly enough, as a local monarchy in central Italy around 800 B.C.E. Roman aristocrats succeeded in driving out the monarchy around 509 B.C.E. and established more elaborate political institutions for their city-state. The new Roman republic gradually extended its influence over the rest of the Italian peninsula, among other things conquering the Greek colonies in the south. Thus, the Romans early acquired a strong military orientation, although initially they may have been driven simply by a desire to protect their own territory from possible rivals. Roman conquest spread more widely during the three Punic Wars, from 264 to 146 B.C.E., during which Rome

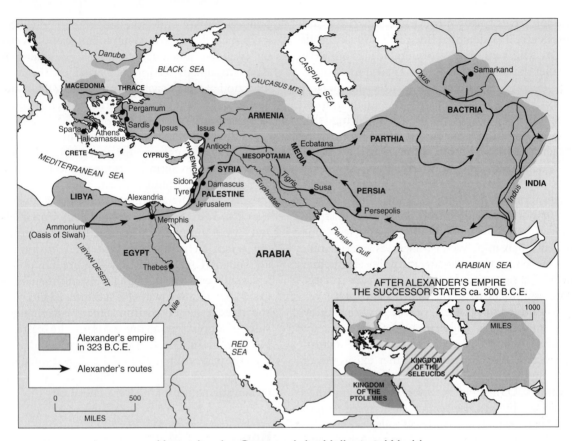

Alexander the Great and the Hellenistic World

fought the armies of the Phoenician city of Carthage, situated on the northern coast of Africa. These wars included a bloody defeat of the invading forces of the brilliant Carthaginian general Hannibal, whose troops were accompanied by pack-laden elephants. The war was so bitter that the Romans in a final act of destruction spread salt around Carthage to prevent agriculture from surviving there. Following the final destruction of Carthage, the Romans proceeded to seize the entire western Mediterranean along with Greece and Egypt.

The politics of the Roman republic grew increasingly unstable, however, as victorious generals sought even greater power while the poor of the city rebelled. Civil wars between two generals led to a victory by Julius Caesar, in

45 B.C.E., and the effective end of the traditional institutions of the Roman state. Caesar's grand-nephew, ultimately called Augustus Caesar, seized power in 27 B.C.E., following another period of rivalry after Julius Caesar's assassination, and established the basic structures of the Roman Empire. For 200 years, through the reign of the emperor Marcus Aurelius in 180 C.E., the empire maintained great vigor, bringing peace and prosperity to virtually the entire Mediterranean world, from Spain and north Africa in the west to the eastern shores of the great sea. The emperors also moved northward, conquering France and southern Britain and pushing into Germany. Here was a major, if somewhat tenuous, extension of the sway of Mediterranean civilization to western Europe.

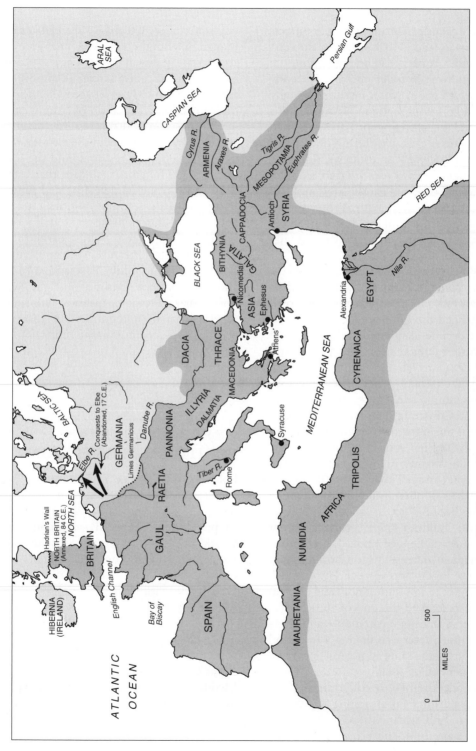

The Roman Empire at Its Greatest Extent, 98–117 C.E.

Roman expansion brought new contacts between Persian and Mediterranean society. A Persian empire, Parthia, had emerged from the fragmentation of Alexander the Great's conquests. Rome at various points, pushing strongly into the Middle East, sought to reconquer this territory. In 113 C.E., the emperor Trajan mounted the most ambitious campaign to invade Parthia, and his victories brought Rome into Mesopotamia and also Armenia. However, internal troubles forced him to pull back and Parthia soon regained considerable territory. Wars with Parthia and its successor, the Sassanid Empire, dotted the later history of the Roman Empire, with mutually inconclusive results.

After 180 C.E., the Roman Empire suffered a slow but decisive fall, which lasted more than 250 years, until invading peoples from the north finally overturned the government in Rome in 476 C.E. The decline manifested itself in terms of both economic deterioration and population loss: both the trade levels and the birth rate fell. Government also became generally less effective, although some strong later emperors, particularly Diocletian and Constantine, attempted to reverse the tide. It was the emperor Constantine who, in 313, adopted the then somewhat obscure religion called Christianity in an attempt to unite the empire in new ways. However, particularly in the western half of the empire, most effective government became local, as the imperial administration could no longer guarantee order or even provide a system of justice. The Roman armies depended increasingly on non-Roman recruits, whose loyalty was suspect. Then, in this deepening mire, the invasion of nomadic peoples from the north marked the end of the classical period of Mediterranean civilization—a civilization that, like its counterparts in Gupta India and Han China during the same approximate period, could no longer defend itself.

To conclude: the new Mediterranean civilization built on earlier cultures along the eastern Mediterranean and within the Greek islands, taking firm shape with the rise of the Greek city-states after 800 B.C.E. These states began as monarchies but then evolved into more complex and diverse political forms. They also developed a more varied commercial economy, moving away from a purely grain-growing agriculture; this spurred the formation of a number of colonial outposts around the eastern Mediterranean and in Italy. The decline of the city-states ushered in the Macedonian conquest and the formation of a wider Hellenistic culture that established deep roots in the Middle East and Egypt. Then Rome, initially a minor regional state distinguished by political virtue and stability, embarked on its great conquests, which earned it control of the Mediterranean, with important extensions into the Middle East and into western and southeastern Europe plus the whole of north Africa. Rome's expansion ultimately overwhelmed its own republic, but the successor empire developed important political institutions of its own and resulted in two centuries of peace and glory.

GREEK AND ROMAN POLITICAL INSTITUTIONS

Politics was very important in classical Mediterranean civilization, from the Greek city-states through the early part of the Roman Empire. Indeed, the word *politics* comes from the Greek word for city-state, *polis,* which correctly suggests that intense political interests were part of life in a city-state in both Greece and Rome. Greeks who visited Persia contrasted their political values with the more authoritarian structures of their neighbor. The "good life" for an upper-class Athenian or Roman included active participation in politics and frequent discussions about the affairs of state. The local character of Mediterranean politics, whereby the typical city-state governed a surrounding territory of several hundred square miles, contributed to this intense preoccupation with politics. Citizens believed that the state was theirs, that they had certain rights and obligations without which their government could not survive. In the Greek city-states and also under the Roman republic, citizens actively participated in the military, which further contributed to this sense of political interest and responsibility. Under the Roman Empire, of course, political concerns were restricted by the sheer power of the emperor and his officers. Even then, however, local city-states retained considerable autonomy in Italy, Greece, and the eastern Mediterranean—the empire did not try to administer most local regions in great detail. The minority of people throughout the empire who were Roman citizens were intensely proud of this privilege.

Strong political ideals and interests created some similarities between Greco-Roman society and the Confucian values of classical China, although the concept of active citizenship was distinctive in the Mediterranean cultures. However, Greece and Rome did not develop a single or cohesive set of political institutions to rival China's divinely sanctioned emperor or its elaborate bureaucracy. So in addition to political intensity and localism as characteristics of Mediterranean civilization, we must note great diversity in political forms. Here the comparison extends to India, where various political forms—including participation in governing councils—ran strong. Later societies, in reflecting on classical Mediterranean civilization, did select from a number of political precedents. Monarchy was not a preferred form; the Roman republic and most Greek city-states had abolished early monarchies as part of their prehistory. Rule by individual strongmen was more common, and the word *tyranny* comes from this experience in classical Greece. Many tyrants were effective rulers, particularly in promoting public works and protecting the common people against the abuses of the aristocracy. Some of the Roman generals who seized power in the later days of the republic had similar characteristics, as did the Hellenistic kings who succeeded Alexander in ruling regions of his empire.

Greece

Democracy (the word is derived from the Greek *demos,* "the people") was another important political alternative in classical Mediterranean society. The Athenian city-state traveled furthest in this direction, before and during the Peloponnesian Wars, after earlier experiences with aristocratic rule and with several tyrants. In 5th-century Athens, the major decisions of state were made by general assemblies in which all citizens could participate—although usually only a minority attended. This was direct democracy, not rule through elected representatives. The assembly met every 10 days. Executive officers, including judges, were chosen for brief terms to control their power, and they were subject to review by the assembly. Furthermore, they were chosen by lot, not elected—on the principle that any citizen could and should be able to serve. To be sure, only a minority of the Athenian population were active citizens: women had no rights of political participation, and half of all adult males were not citizens at all, being slaves or foreigners. This, then, was not exactly the kind of democracy we envision today. But it elicited widespread popular participation and devotion, and certainly embodied principles that we recognize as truly democratic. The Athenian leader Pericles, who led Athens during its decades of greatest glory between the final defeat of the Persians and the agony of war with Sparta, described the system this way:

> The administration is in the hands of the many and not of the few. But while the law secures equal justice to all alike in their private disputes, the claim of excellence is also recognized; and when a citizen is in any way distinguished he is preferred to the public service, not as a matter of privilege but as the reward of merit. Neither is poverty a bar, but a man may benefit his country whatever be the obscurity of his condition.

During the Peloponnesian Wars, Athens even demonstrated some of the potential drawbacks of democracy. Lower-class citizens, eager for

SOLVING PROBLEMS

CULTURAL ENCOUNTERS

One of the most interesting developments in world history involves points at which two quite different cultures encounter each other. The resultant problem centers on how to handle mutual differences but also to take advantage of new opportunities. Contact may result from trade, missionary activity, migration, or conquest. Its ramifications can be just as varied. The cultures involved may detest each other, or one might try (or be forced) to copy the other. However, the most common result, even when one culture is promoted by force, is a certain blending. This blending is called *syncretism*.

Alexander the Great hoped of course to establish a new cultural amalgam in his empire, but he did not live long enough to press the vision very far. His victories did however create genuinely new influences. When Alexander's conquests established a Hellenistic state for many decades in northwestern India, cultural contact ran high. Indians learned some additional mathematics from Greeks in the royal bureaucracy. They also admired Greek artistic styles. For some time, Buddhas in statues and other art forms were shown wearing Mediterranean-type hairdos and togas. Despite such displays, the Indians involved were not Hellenized. They maintained their own religion, for example, and their belief that art should serve this religion. Here was an early case of syncretism, which was a way to solve problems and take advantage of forced contact.

The impact on the Mediterranean was less clear. Indians grew more aware of the Middle East and sent Buddhist missionaries to the region. No major conversions resulted, but Buddhist ethical ideas may have influenced some Greek ethical systems and, through them, Christianity—it is simply not possible to be sure. Some obvious Indian developments, such as their superior numbering system, were ignored. Cultural borrowing is, among other things, oddly unpredictable.

■**QUESTIONS:**   *Why did Greek cultural forms apparently influence India more than the other way around? What are other examples of syncretism in world history?*

---

government jobs and the spoils of war, often encouraged reckless military actions that weakened the state in its central dispute with Sparta.

Neither tyranny nor democracy, however, was the most characteristic political form in the classical Mediterranean world. The most widely preferred political framework centered on the existence of aristocratic assemblies, whose deliberations established guidelines for state policy and served as a check on executive power. Thus, Sparta was governed by a singularly militaristic aristocracy, intent on retaining power over a large slave population. Other Greek city-states, although less bent on disciplining their elites for rigorous military service, also featured aristocratic assemblies.

Even Athens during much of its democratic phase found leadership in many aristocrats, including Pericles. The word *aristocracy,* which comes from Greek terms meaning "rule of the best," suggests where many Greeks—particularly, of course, aristocrats—thought real political virtue lay.

Rome

The constitution of the Roman republic, until the final decades of dissension in the 1st century B.C.E., which led to the establishment of the empire, tried to reconcile the various elements suggested by the Greek political experience, with primary reliance on the principle of aristocracy.

All Roman citizens in the republic could gather in periodic assemblies, the function of which was not to pass basic laws but rather to elect various magistrates, some of whom were specifically entrusted with the task of representing the interests of the common people. The most important legislative body was the Senate, composed mainly of aristocrats, whose members held virtually all executive offices in the Roman state. Two consuls shared primary executive power, but in times of crisis the Senate could choose a dictator to hold emergency authority until the crisis had passed. In the Roman Senate, as in the aristocratic assemblies of the Greek city-states, the ideal of public service, featuring eloquent public speaking and arguments that sought to identify the general good, came closest to realization.

The diversity of Greek and Roman political forms, as well as the importance ascribed to political participation, helped generate a significant body of political theory in classical Mediterranean civilization. True to the aristocratic tradition, much of this theory dealt with appropriate political ethics, the duties of citizens, the importance of incorruptible service, and key political skills such as oratory. Roman writers such as Cicero, an active senator, expounded eloquently on these subjects. Some of this political writing resembled Confucianism, although there was less emphasis on hierarchy and obedience or bureaucratic virtues, and more on participation in deliberative bodies that make laws and judge the actions of executive officers. Classical Mediterranean writers also paid great attention to the structure of the state itself, debating the virtues and vices of the various political forms. This kind of theory both expressed the political interests and diversity of the Mediterranean world and served as a key heritage to later societies.

The Roman Empire was a different sort of political system from the earlier city-states, although it preserved some older institutions, such as the Senate, which became a rather meaningless forum for debates. Of necessity, the empire developed organizational capacities on a far larger scale than the city-states; it is important to remember, however, that considerable local autonomy prevailed in many regions. Only in rare cases, such as the forced dissolution of the independent Jewish state in 63 C.E. after a major local rebellion, did the Romans take over distant areas completely. Careful organization was particularly evident in the vast hierarchy of the Roman army, whose officers wielded great political power even over the emperors.

In addition to considerable tolerance for local customs and religions, plus strong military organization, the Romans emphasized carefully crafted laws as the factor that would hold their vast territories together. Greek and Roman republican leaders had already developed an understanding of the importance of codified, equitable law. Aristocratic leaders in 8th-century Athens, for example, sponsored clear legal codes designed to balance the defense of private property with the protection of poor citizens, including access to courts of law administered by fellow citizens. The early Roman republic introduced its first code of law, the Twelve Tables, by 450 B.C.E. These early Roman laws were intended, among other things, to restrain the upper classes from arbitrary action and to subject them, as well as ordinary people, to some common legal principles. The Roman Empire carried these legal interests still further, in the belief that law should evolve to meet changing conditions without, however, fluctuating wildly. The idea of Roman law was that rules, objectively judged, rather than personal whim should govern social relationships; thus, the law steadily took over matters of judgment earlier reserved for fathers of families or for landlords. Roman law also promoted the importance of common-sense fairness. In one case cited in the law texts of the empire, a slave was being shaved by a barber in a public square; two men were playing ball nearby, and one accidentally hit the barber with the ball, causing him to cut the slave's throat. Who was responsible for the tragedy: the barber, catcher, or pitcher? According to Roman law, the slave—for anyone so foolish as to be shaved in a public place was asking for trouble and bore the responsibility himself.

Roman law codes spread widely through the empire, and with them came the notion of law as the regulator of social life. Many non-Romans were given the right of citizenship—although most ordinary people outside Rome itself pre-ferred to maintain their local allegiances. With citizenship, however, came full access to Rome-appointed judges and uniform laws. Imperial law codes also regulated property rights and com-merce, thus creating some economic unity in the vast empire. The idea of fair and reasoned law, to which officers of the state should themselves

WORLD PROFILES

JULIUS CAESAR
(100–44 B.C.E.)

Julius Caesar was, along with his grandnephew Augustus, the leading figure in transforming the Roman republic into an imperial form of government ruled by one dictator. Caesar had become a minor political official by the age of 40. Then, however, he began to attain greater power, serving as governor of southern Gaul and northern Italy, from where he went on to conquer most of the territory now covered by France, Belgium, part of the Netherlands, and part of Germany. Opening these territories to classi-cal Mediterranean civilization was his greatest and most lasting achievement. But his personal goals turned to ruling Rome itself, where he defied republi-can tradition, becoming Rome's dictator. He was killed by conservative members of the Senate for his ambi-tion. His death did not save the republic—the kind of government he planned, including wider citizenship for the empire, came about 14 years later. The statue pictured here conveys an image of Caesar that became popular long after his death: calm, soldierly, and statesmanlike. Why was Caesar so idealized, not only in Rome but also in later European history?

No representations of Julius Caesar survive from his lifetime. This statue was made 100 years after his death.

be subject, was a key political achievement of the Roman Empire, comparable in importance, although quite different in nature, to the Chinese elaboration of a complex bureaucratic structure.

The Greeks and Romans were less innovative in the functions they ascribed to government than in the political forms and theories they developed. Most governments concentrated on maintaining systems of law courts and military forces. Athens and, more durably and successfully, Rome placed great premium on the importance of military conquest. Mediterranean governments regulated some branches of commerce, particularly in the interest of securing vital supplies of grain. Rome, indeed, undertook vast public works in the form of roads and harbors to facilitate military transport as well as commerce. And the Roman state, especially under the empire, built countless stadiums and public baths to entertain and distract its subjects. The city of Rome itself, which at its peak contained more than a million inhabitants, provided cheap food as well as gladiator contests and other entertainment for the masses—the famous "bread and circuses" that were designed to prevent popular disorder. Colonies of Romans elsewhere were also given theaters and stadiums. This provided solace in otherwise strange lands such as England or Palestine. Governments also supported an official religion, sponsoring public ceremonies to honor the gods and goddesses; civic religious festivals were important events that both expressed and encouraged widespread loyalty to the state. However, there was little attempt to impose this religion on everyone, and other religious practices were tolerated so long as they did not conflict with loyalty to the state. Even the later Roman emperors, who advanced the idea that the emperor was a god as a means of strengthening authority, were normally tolerant of other religions. They only attacked Christianity, and then irregularly, because of the Christians' refusal to place the state first in their devotion.

Localism and fervent political interests, including a sense of intense loyalty to the state; a diversity of political systems together with the preference for

aristocratic rule; the importance of law and the development of an unusually elaborate and uniform set of legal principles—these were the chief political legacies of the classical Mediterranean world. The sheer accomplishment of the Roman Empire itself, which united a region never before or since brought together, still stands as one of the great political monuments of world history. This was a distinctive political mix. Although there was attention to careful legal procedures, no clear definition of individuals' rights existed. Indeed, the emphasis on duties to the state could lead, as in Sparta, to an essentially totalitarian framework in which the state controlled even the raising of children. Nor, until the peaceful centuries of the early Roman Empire, was it an entirely successful political structure, as wars and instability were common. Nonetheless, there can be no question of the richness of this political culture or of its central importance to the Greeks and Romans themselves.

RELIGION AND CULTURE

The Greeks and Romans did not create a significant, world-class religion; in this, they differed from India and to some extent from China and Persia. Christianity, which was to become one of the major world religions, did of course arise during the Roman Empire. It owed some of its rapid geographical spread to the ease of movement within the huge Roman Empire. However, Christianity was not really a product of Greek or Roman culture, although it was ultimately influenced by this culture. It took on serious historical importance only as the Roman Empire began its decline. The characteristic Greco-Roman religion was a much more primitive affair, derived from a belief in the spirits of nature elevated into a complex set of gods and goddesses who were seen as regulating human life. Greeks and Romans had different names for their pantheon, but the objects of worship were essentially the same: a creator or father god, Zeus or Jupiter, presided over an unruly assemblage of gods and goddesses whose functions ranged from regulating the daily passage of the sun (Apollo) or the oceans (Neptune) to inspiring war (Mars) or human love and beauty (Venus). Specific gods were the patrons of other human activities such as metalworking, the hunt, even literature and history. Regular ceremonies to the gods had real political importance, and many individuals sought the gods' aid in foretelling the future or in ensuring a good harvest or good health.

In addition to its political functions, Greco-Roman religion had certain other features. It tended to be rather human, of this world in its approach. The doings of the gods made for good storytelling; they read like soap operas on a superhuman scale. Thus, the classical Mediterranean religion early engendered an important literary tradition, as was also the case in India. (Indeed, Greco-Roman and Indian religious lore reflected the common heritage of Indo-European invaders.) The gods were often used to illustrate human passions and foibles, thus serving as symbols of a serious inquiry into human nature. Unlike the Indians, however, the Greeks and Romans became

Greek sculpture: the god Zeus. Compare this work to the more sensual Hindu religious art illustrated on page 87.

interested in their gods more in terms of what they could do for and reveal about humankind on this earth than the principles that could elevate people toward higher planes of spirituality.

This dominant religion also had a number of limitations. Its lack of spiritual passion failed to satisfy many ordinary workers and peasants, particularly in times of political chaos or economic distress. "Mystery" religions, often imported from the Middle East, periodically swept through Greece and Rome, providing secret rituals and fellowship and a greater sense of contact with unfathomable divine powers. Even more than in China, a considerable division arose between upper-class and popular belief.

The gods and goddesses of Greco-Roman religion left many upper-class people dissatisfied also. They provided stories about how the world came to be, but little basis for a systematic inquiry into nature or human society. And while the dominant religion promoted political loyalty, it did not provide a basis for ethical thought. Hence, many thinkers, both in Greece and Rome, sought a separate model for ethical behavior. Greek and Roman moral philosophy, as issued by philosophers such as Aristotle and Cicero, typically stressed the importance of moderation and balance in human behavior as opposed to the instability of much political life and the excesses of the gods. Other ethical systems were devised, particularly during the Hellenistic period. Stoics, for example, emphasized an inner moral independence, to be cultivated by strict discipline of the body and by personal bravery. These ethical systems, established largely apart from religious considerations, were major contributions in their own right; they also were blended with later religious thought, under Christianity.

The idea of a philosophy separate from the official religion, although not necessarily hostile to it, informed classical Mediterranean political theory, which made little reference to religious principles. It also considerably emphasized the powers of human thought. In Athens, Socrates (born in 469 B.C.E.) encouraged his pupils to question conventional wisdom, on the grounds that the chief human duty was "the improvement of the soul." Socrates ran afoul of the Athenian government,

Greek pottery. Depicting Greek soldiers (hoplites) fighting amid their chariots, this piece dates from 6th-century Athens.

which thought that he was undermining political loyalty; given the choice of suicide or exile, Socrates chose the former. However, the Socratic principle of rational inquiry by means of skeptical questioning became a recurrent strand in classical Greek thinking and in its heritage to later societies. Socrates' great pupil Plato accentuated the positive somewhat more strongly by suggesting that human reason could approach an understanding of the three perfect forms—the absolutely True, Good, and Beautiful—which he believed characterized nature. Thus, a philosophical tradition arose in Greece, although in very diverse individual expressions, which tended to deemphasize the importance of human spirituality in favor of a celebration of the human ability to think. The result bore some similarities to Chinese Confucianism, although with greater emphasis on skeptical questioning and abstract speculations about the basic nature of humanity and the universe.

Greek interest in rationality carried over an inquiry into the underlying order of physical nature. The Greeks were not outstanding empirical scientists. Relatively few new scientific findings emanated from Athens, or later from Rome, although philosophers such as Aristotle did collect large amounts of biological data. The Greek interest lay in speculations about nature's order, and many non–Westerners believe that this tradition continues to inform what they see as an excessive Western passion for seeking basic rationality in the universe. In practice, the Greek concern translated into a host of theories, some of which were wrong, about the motions of the planets and the organization of the elemental principles of earth, fire, air, and water, and into a considerable interest in mathematics as a means of rendering nature's patterns comprehensible. Greek and later Hellenistic work in geometry was particularly impressive, featuring among other achievements the basic theorems of Pythagoras. Scientists during the Hellenistic period made some important empirical contributions, especially in studies of anatomy; medical treatises by Galen were not improved on, in the

Western world, for many centuries. The mathematician Euclid produced what was long the world's most widely used compendium of geometry. Less fortunately, the Hellenistic astronomer Ptolemy produced an elaborate theory of the sun's motion around a stationary earth. This new Hellenistic theory contradicted much earlier Middle Eastern astronomy, which had recognized the earth's rotation; nonetheless, it was Ptolemy's theory that was long taken as fixed wisdom in Western thought.

Roman intellectuals, actively examining ethical and political theory, had nothing to add to Greek and Hellenistic science. They did help to preserve this tradition in the form of textbooks that were administered to upper-class schoolchildren. The Roman genius was more practical than the Greek and included engineering achievements such as the great roads and aqueducts that carried water to cities large and small. Roman ability to construct elaborate arches so that buildings could carry great structural weight was unsurpassed anywhere in the world. These feats, too, left their mark, as Rome's huge edifices long served as a reminder of ancient glories. But ultimately, it was the Greek and Hellenistic impulse to extend human reason to nature's principles that resulted in the most impressive legacy.

In classical Mediterranean civilization, however, science and mathematics loomed far less large than art and literature in conveying key cultural values. The official religion inspired themes for artistic expression and the justification for temples, statues, and plays devoted to the glories of the gods. Nonetheless, the human-centered qualities of the Greeks and Romans also registered, as artists emphasized the beauty of realistic portrayals of the human form and poets and playwrights used the gods as foils for inquiries into the human condition.

All the arts received some attention in classical Mediterranean civilization. Performances of music and dance were vital parts of religious festivals, but their precise styles have unfortunately not been preserved. Far more durable was the Greek

A great temple to Theseus, the legendary founder of Athens. This temple is an example of Doric architecture, the earliest Greek column style, in Athens during the 5th century B.C.E.

interest in drama, for plays, more than poetry, took a central role in this culture. Greek dramatists produced both comedy and tragedy, indeed making a formal division between the two approaches that is still part of the Western tradition, as in the labeling of current television shows as either form. On the whole, in contrast to Indian writers, the Greeks placed the greatest emphasis on tragedy. Their belief in human reason and balance also involved a sense that these virtues were precarious, so a person could easily become ensnared in situations of powerful emotion and uncontrollable consequences. The Athenian dramatist Sophocles, for example, so insightfully portrayed the psychological flaws of his hero Oedipus that modern psychology long used the term *Oedipus complex* to refer to a potentially unhealthy relationship between a man and his mother.

Greek literature contained a strong epic tradition as well, starting with the beautifully crafted tales of the *Iliad* and *Odyssey,* attributed to the poet Homer, who lived in the 8th century B.C.E. Roman authors, particularly the poet Vergil, also worked in the epic form, seeking to link Roman history and mythology with the Greek forerunner. Roman writers made significant contributions to poetry and to definitions of the poetic form that was long used in Western literature. The overall Roman literary contribution was less impressive than the Greek, but it was substantial enough both to provide important examples of how poetry should be written and to furnish abundant illustrations of the literary richness of the Latin language.

In the visual arts, the emphasis of classical Mediterranean civilization was sculpture and architecture. Greek artists also excelled in ceramic work, whereas Roman painters produced realistic (and sometimes pornographic) decorations for the homes of the wealthy. In the brilliant age of Athens' 5th century—the age of Pericles, Socrates, Sophocles, and so many other intensely creative figures—sculptors such as Phidias developed unprecedented skill rendering simultaneously realistic yet beautiful images of the human form, from lovely goddesses to muscled warriors and athletes. Roman sculptors, less innovative, continued this heroic-realistic tradition. They molded scenes of Roman conquests on triumphal columns and captured the power but also the human qualities of Augustus Caesar and his successors on busts and full-figure statues alike.

Greek architecture, from the 8th century B.C.E. onward, emphasized monumental construction, square or rectangular in shape, with columned porticos. The Greeks devised three embellishments for the tops of columns supporting their massive buildings, each more ornate than the next: the Doric, the Ionic, and the Corinthian. The Greeks, in short, invented what Westerners and others in the world today still regard as "classical" architecture, although the Greeks themselves were influenced by Egyptian models in their preferences. Greece, and later Italy, provided abundant stone for ambitious temples, markets, and other public buildings. Many of these same structures were filled with products of the sculptors' workshops. They were brightly painted, although over the centuries the paint faded, so that later imitators came to think of the classical style as involving unadorned (some might say drab) stone. Roman architects adopted the Greek themes quite readily. Their engineering skill allowed them to construct buildings of even greater size, as well as new forms such as the freestanding stadium. Under the empire, the Romans learned how to add domes to rectangular buildings, which resulted in some welcome architectural diversity. At the same time, the empire's taste for massive, heavily adorned monuments and public buildings, while a clear demonstration of Rome's sense of power and achievement, moved increasingly away from the simple lines of the early Greek temples.

Classical Mediterranean art and architecture were intimately linked with the society that produced them. There is a temptation, because of the formal role of classical styles in later societies, including our own, to attribute a stiffness to Greek and Roman art that was not present in the original. Greek and Roman structures were built to be used. Temples and marketplaces and the public baths that so

The Forum in Rome. In the ancient imperial city of Rome, the Colosseum was a triumph of Roman monumental architecture and a center for sports and ceremonies.

delighted the Roman upper classes were part of daily urban life. Classical art was also flexible, according to need. Villas or small palaces—built for the Roman upper classes and typically constructed around an open courtyard—had a light, even simple quality rather different from that of temple architecture. Classical dramas were not merely examples of high art, performed for the cultural elite. Indeed, Athens lives in the memory of many humanists today as much because of the large audiences that trooped to performances of plays by authors such as Sophocles as for the creativity of the writers and philosophers themselves. Literally thousands of people gathered in the large hillside theaters of Athens and other cities for the performance of new plays and for associated music and poetry competitions. Popular taste in Rome, to be sure, seemed less elevated. Republican Rome was not an important cultural center, and many Roman leaders indeed feared the more emotional qualities of Greek art. The Roman Empire is known more for monumental athletic performances—chariot races and gladiators—than for high-quality popular theater. However, the fact remains that, even in Rome, elements of classical art—the great monuments if nothing more—were part of daily urban life and the pursuit of pleasure.

ECONOMY AND SOCIETY IN THE MEDITERRANEAN

Politics and formal culture in Greece and Rome were mainly affairs of the cities—which means that they were of intense concern only to a minority of the population. Most Greeks and Romans were farmers, tied to the soil and often to local rituals and festivals that were rather different from urban forms. Many Greek farmers, for example, annually gathered for a spring passion play to celebrate the recovery of the goddess of fertility from the lower world, an event that was seen as a vital preparation for planting and that also suggested the possibility of an afterlife—a prospect important to many people who endured a life of hard labor and poverty. A substantial population of free farmers, who owned their own land, flourished in the early days of the Greek city-states and later around Rome. However, there was a constant tendency, most pronounced in Rome, for large landlords to squeeze these farmers, forcing them to become tenants or laborers or to join the swelling crowds of the urban lower class. Tensions between tyrants and aristocrats or democrats and aristocrats in Athens often revolved around free farmers' attempts to preserve their independence and shake off the heavy debts they had incurred. The Roman republic declined in part because too many farmers became dependent on the protection of large landlords, even when they did not work their estates outright, and so no longer could vote freely.

Farming in Greece and in much of Italy was complicated by the fact that soil conditions were not ideal for grain growing, and yet grain was the staple of life. First in Greece, then in central Italy, farmers were increasingly tempted to shift to the production of olives and grapes, which were used primarily for cooking and wine making. These products were well suited to the soil conditions, but they required an unusually extensive conversion of agriculture to a market basis. That is, farmers who produced grapes and olives had to buy some of the food they needed, and they had to sell most of their own product in order to do this. Furthermore, planting olive trees or grape vines required substantial capital, for they did not bear fruit for at least five years after planting. This was one reason so many farmers went into debt. It was also one of the reasons that large landlords gained increasing advantage over independent farmers, for they could enter into market production on a much larger scale if only because of their greater access to capital.

The rise of commercial agriculture in Greece and then around Rome was one of the prime forces leading to efforts to establish an empire. Greek city-states, with Athens usually in the lead, developed colonies in the Middle East and then in Sicily mainly to gain access to grain production; for this, they traded not only olive oil and wine but also manufactured products and silver. Rome pushed south, in part, to acquire the Sicilian grain fields and later used much of north Africa as its granary. Indeed, the Romans encouraged such heavy cultivation in north Africa that they promoted a soil depletion, which helps account for the region's reduced agricultural fertility in later centuries.

The importance of commercial farming obviously dictated extensive concern with trade. Private merchants operated most of the ships that carried agricultural products and other goods. Greek city-states and ultimately the Roman state supervised the grain trade, promoting public works and storage facilities and carefully regulating the vital supplies. Other kinds of trade were vital also. Luxury products from the shops of urban artists or craftspeople played a major role in the lifestyle of the upper classes. There was some trade also beyond the borders of Mediterranean civilization, for goods from India and China. In this trade, the Mediterranean peoples found themselves at some disadvantage, for their manufactured products were less sophisticated than those of eastern Asia; thus, they typically exported animal skins, precious metals, and even exotic African animals for Asian zoos in return for the spices and artistic products of the east.

For all the importance of trade, merchants enjoyed a somewhat ambiguous status in classical Mediterranean civilization. Leading Athenian merchants were usually foreigners, mostly from the trading peoples of the Middle East—the descendants of Lydians and Phoenicians. Merchants had a somewhat higher status in Rome, clearly forming the second most prestigious social class under the landed patricians, but here, too, the aristocracy frequently disputed the merchants' rights. Overall, merchants fared better in the Mediterranean than in China, in terms of official recognition, but worse than in India; classical Mediterranean society certainly did not set in motion a culture that distinctly valued capitalist money-making.

Slavery was another key ingredient of the classical economy. Philosophers such as Aristotle produced elaborate justifications for the necessity of slavery in a proper society. Athenians used slaves as household servants and also as workers in their vital silver mines, which provided the manpower for Athens' empire and commercial operations

HISTORY DEBATE

MEDITERRANEAN CIVILIZATION AND "WESTERN" CIVILIZATION

The impulse to regard Greece and Rome as the origins of what is now called Western civilization runs very deep. Rome's glory and the power of Greek culture obviously impressed thinkers and statesmen in western Europe, who looked back to these times for inspiration. This was a key theme in European history after the classical period. From western Europe, fascination with the classical Mediterranean world later spread to North America.

All the classical civilizations left strong imprints on later developments. At the same time, these imprints require careful assessment, because none of the civilizations remained static. The nature and impact of the legacy must be weighed against innovations. This general analytical requirement is doubly important when considering classical Mediterranean culture, for the simple reason that, after Rome, Mediterranean civilization split apart. Some common features remained, including cultural aspects such as a strong emphasis on the defense of personal honor plus social-economic institutions such as relatively large villages; however, no Mediterranean civilization continued to exist as a whole.

Some historians argue that regarding Greece and Rome as the origins of Western civilization is completely off the mark. Greece, particularly, was proud of its own uniqueness, and when it sought to expand, it looked to the lands of the Middle East, not the West; Rome also ended up placing special value on its eastern holdings. Not surprisingly, Greek-Roman heritage lived on more directly in southeastern Europe than in the West. Certainly, the West does not have sole claim to Mediterranean heritage.

Nonetheless, selective Greek-Roman values and institutions did affect western Europe, either immediately or in later revivals. So the debate continues about positioning the classical Mediterranean civilization in light of later developments.

The issue involves both the facts and judgment. What were the most important surviving characteristics of classical Mediterranean civilization? Were they taken out of context as they helped shape later civilizations? Take democracy, for example: to what extent did Mediterranean democracy "cause" later democracy in the West? (And, if it was responsible for causing this democracy, why did the process take so long?) Your evaluation may focus on cultural and political achievements, but it must also address the social and economic framework of this third major classical civilization.

alike. Sparta used slaves extensively for agricultural work. Slavery spread steadily in Rome from the final centuries of the republic. Because most slaves came from conquered territories, the need for slaves was another key element in military expansion. Here was a theme visible in earlier civilizations in the eastern Mediterranean, and within later societies in this region as well, which helps explain the greater importance of military forces and expansion in these areas than in India or China. Actual slave conditions varied greatly. Roman slaves performed household tasks—including the tutoring of upper-class children, for which cultured Greek slaves were highly valued. They also worked the mines, for precious metals and for iron; as in Greece, slave labor in the mines was particularly brutal, and few slaves survived more than a few years of such an existence. Roman estate owners used large numbers of slaves for agricultural work, along with paid laborers and tenant farmers. This practice was another source of the steady pressure placed upon free farmers who could not easily compete with unpaid forced labor.

Partly because of slavery, partly because of the overall orientation of upper-class culture, neither Greece nor Rome was especially interested in technological innovations applicable to agriculture or manufacturing. The Greeks made important advances in shipbuilding and navigation, which were vital for their trading economy. Romans, less adept on the water, developed their skill in engineering to provide greater urban amenities and good roads for the swift and easy movement of troops. But a technology designed to improve the production of food or manufactured goods did not figure largely in this civilization, which mainly relied on the earlier achievements of previous Mediterranean societies. Abundant slave labor probably discouraged concern for more efficient production methods. So did a sense that the true goals of humankind were artistic and political. One Hellenistic scholar, for example, refused to write a handbook on engineering because "the work of an engineer and everything that ministers to the needs of life is ignoble and vulgar." As a consequence of this outlook, Mediterranean society lagged behind both India and China in production technology, which was one reason for its resulting unfavorable balance of trade with eastern Asia.

Both Greek and Roman society emphasized the importance of a tight family structure, with a husband and father firmly in control. Women had vital economic functions, particularly in farming and artisan families. In the upper classes, especially in Rome, women often commanded great influence and power within a household. But in law and culture, women were held inferior. Families burdened with too many children sometimes put female infants to death because of their low status and their potential drain on the family economy. Pericles stated common beliefs about women when he noted, "For a woman not to show more weakness than is natural to her sex is a great glory, and not to be talked about for good or for evil among men." Early Roman law stipulated, "The husband is the judge of his wife. If she commits a fault, he punishes her; if she has drunk wine, he condemns her; if she has been guilty of adultery, he kills her." (Later, however, such customs were held in check by family courts composed of members of both families.) Here was a case where Roman legal ideas modified traditional family controls. If divorced because of adultery, a Roman woman lost a third of her property and had to wear a special garment that set her apart like a prostitute. On the other hand, the oppression of women was probably less severe in this civilization than in China. Many Greek and Roman women were active in business and controlled a portion, even if only the minority, of all urban property.

Because of the divisions within classical Mediterranean society, no easy generalizations about culture or achievement can be made. An 18th-century English historian called the high point of the Roman Empire, before 180 C.E., the period in human history "during which the condition of the human race was most happy or prosperous." This is doubtful, given the technological accomplishments of China and India. And certainly, many slaves, women, and ordinary farmers in the Mediterranean world might have disagreed with this viewpoint. Few farmers, for example, actively participated in the political structures or cultural opportunities that were the most obvious mark of this civilization. Many continued to work largely as their ancestors had done, with quite similar tools and in very similar poverty, untouched by the doings of the great or the bustle of the cities except when wars engulfed their lands.

We are tempted, of course, exclusively to remember the urban achievements, for they exerted the greatest influence on later ages that recalled the glories of Greece and Rome. The distinctive features of classical Mediterranean social and family structures had a less enduring impact, although ideas about slavery or women were revived in subsequent periods. However, the relatively unchanging face of ordinary life had an important influence as well, as many farmers and artisans long maintained the habits and outlook they developed during the great days of the Greek and Roman empires, and because their separation from much of the official culture posed both a challenge and opportunity for new cultural movements such as Christianity.

TOWARD THE FALL OF ROME

Classical Mediterranean society had one final impact on world history through its rather fragmentary collapse. Unlike China, classical civilization in the Mediterranean region was not simply disrupted only to revive. Unlike India, there was no central religion, derived from the civilization itself, to serve as link between the classical period and what followed. Furthermore, the fall of Rome was not uniform; in essence, Rome fell more in some parts of the Mediterranean than it did in others. The result, among other things, was that no single civilization ultimately rose to claim the mantle of Greece and Rome. At the same time, there was no across-the-board maintenance of the classical Mediterranean institutions and values in any of the civilizations that later claimed a

relationship to the Greek and Roman past. Greece and Rome lived on, in more than idle memory, but their heritage was unquestionably more complex and more selective than proved to be the case for India or China.

PATHS TO THE PRESENT

In contrast to India and China, no relatively straight line connects the classical period in Persia or the Mediterranean to the present day. A Persian tradition was established, in art, for example, but many aspects of Persian politics and culture, including the Zoroastrian religion, were disrupted or later replaced. Ultimately, both Persian and Mediterranean traditions added to the heritage but also the diversities and tensions in the Middle East.

As for the Mediterranean itself, its unity as a civilization ended with the fall of Rome. Certain cultural features remain, however, in southern Europe, North Africa, and the Middle East. For instance, these societies emphasize the importance of honor and the defense of honor, and relatively large peasant villages still exist, with a corresponding emphasis on market agriculture. These characteristics, however, although passed down from the classical period, are overshadowed by the current divisions in politics and religion.

If the classical Mediterranean world did not create a full heritage for the present, it did generate many features that were revived by later societies. Thus, when American leaders considered the styles for public buildings in the late 18th century, they could imagine no better model than the temples and theaters of Greece and Rome. Greek and Hellenistic emphasis on scientific and logical thinking also was later retrieved, as were the various Greek political forms, including democracy and the idea of a senate. We need to know about the classical Mediterranean to grasp the present, but less for reasons of literal survival than for the immense usefulness of selective revival.

Another factor complicates this classical–present relationship. Classical Mediterranean forms were revived not only in western Europe, but also—earlier and often more elaborately—in eastern Europe, including Russia, and in the Middle East and North Africa. This underscores the importance of the classical Mediterranean heritage, but its contribution to several later civilizations also complicates our understanding of it.

SUGGESTED WEB SITES

On the Roman Empire, see http://www.thebritishmuseum.ac.uk/world/rome/empire.html; on women in the ancient world, http://www.womenintheancientworld.com/index.htm and http://www.stoa.org/diotima/; for more on the ancient Greek world, see http://www.museum.upenn.edu/greek_world/Index.html. For a map of the Persian Empire, ca. 500 B.C.E., see http://www.lib.utexas.edu/maps/historical/shepherd/persian_empire.jpg

SUGGESTED READINGS

Important works include Xinru Liu and Lynda Norene Shaffer, *Connections Across Eurasia: Transportaiton, Communications and Cultural Exchange Across the Silk Roads* (2007); Lindsey Bell, *The Persian Empire* (2005); Richard A. Gabriel, *The Ancient World* (2007); Peter M. Edwell, *Between Rome and Persia: The Middle Euphrates, Mesopotamia, and Palmyra under Roman Control* (2008); George Cawkwell, *The Greek Wars: The Failure of Persia* (2005); Gene R. Garthwaite, *The Persians* (2004); Beate Dignas and Engelbert Winter, *Rome and Persia in Late Antiquity: Neighbours and Rivals* (2007); Peter Green, *The Greco-Persian Wars* (1996); John Curtis and Nigel Tallis, eds., *Forgottem Empire: The World of Ancient Persia* (2005); Nancy Demand, *A History of Ancient Greece* (1996), with a good bibliography; Waldemar Heckel, *Crossroads of History: The Age of Alexander* (2003); N. G. L. Hammond, *The Genius of Alexander the Great* (1997); Roger Brock, ed., *Alternatives to Athens: Varieties of Political Organization and Community in Ancient Greece* (2000); M. I. Finley, *Ancient Slavery and Modern Ideology* (expanded ed.,

1998). See also Thomas Benediktson, *Literature and the Visual Arts in Ancient Greece and Rome* (2001); George Cawkwell, *The Greek Wars: The Failure of Persia* (New York, 2005); Gary Forsythe, *A Critical History of Early Rome: From Prehistory to the First Punic War* (2005); Alain M. Gowing, *Empire and Memory: The Representation of the Roman Republic in Imperial Culture* (2005); Callie Williamson, *The Laws of the Roman People: Public Laws in the Expansion and Decline of the Roman Republic* (2005); Richard Holland, *Augustus: Godfather of Europe* (2004); Harriet I. Flower, *The Cambridge Companion to the Roman Republic* (2004); G. E. R. Lloyd, *Ancient Worlds, Modern Reflections: Philosophical Perspectives on Greek and Chinese Science and Culture* (2004); Marilynn B. Skinner, *Sexuality in Greek and Roman Culture* (2005); I. M. Plant, *Women Writers of Ancient Greece and Rome: An Anthology* (2004); Fiona McHardy and Eireann Marshall, eds., *Women's Influence on Classical Civilization* (2004); and James I. Porter, *Classical Pasts: The Classical Traditions of Greece and Rome* (2006).

There are a number of excellent sources on classical Greece and Rome, even aside from translations of the leading thinkers and writers. Florence Dupont's *Daily Life in Ancient Rome* (1999) examines Roman ideas of space and time and honor. See M. Crawford, ed., *Sources for Ancient History* (1983); C. Fornara, *Translated Documents of Greece and Rome* (1977); N. Lewis, *Greek Historical Documents: The Fifth Century B.C.* (1971); M. Crawford, *The Roman Republic* (1982); P. Green, *Alexander to Actium: The Historical Evolution of the Hellenistic Ages* (1990); and M. M. Austin, *The Hellenistic World from Alexander to the Roman Conquest* (1981). Important specialized works include R. Zewlnich-Abramovitz, *Not Wholly Free: The Concept of Manumission and the Status of Manumitted Slaves in the Ancient Greek World* (2005); Sarah Pomeroy, *Goddesses, Whores, Wives, and Slaves: Women in Classical Antiquity* (1975); and Renate Bridenthal and others, eds., *Becoming Visible: Women in European History* (1998). A recent book by Donald Kagan, *The Peloponnesian War* (2003), captures Greece's crisis moment. On Rome, see K. Christ, *The Romans: An Introduction to Their History and Civilization* (1984), which is eminently readable and provocative; J. Boardman et al., *Oxford History of the Classical World* (1986); and R. Saller, *The Roman Empire* (1987).

The Classical Period: Directions, Diversities, and Declines by 500 C.E.

The basic themes of the great classical civilizations involved expansion and integration. From localized beginnings in northern China, the Ganges region, or the Aegean Sea, commercial, political, and cultural outreach pushed civilization through the Middle Kingdom and beyond, through the Indian subcontinent, and into the western Mediterranean. The growth set in motion deliberate and also implicit attempts to pull the new civilizations together in more than name. Correspondingly, the most telling comparisons among the classical civilizations—identifying similarities as well as differences—involve this same process of integration and some of the problems it encountered.

Throughout the classical world, integration and expansion faltered between 200 and 500 C.E. Decline, even collapse, began to afflict civilization first in China, then in the Mediterranean, and finally in India. The position of Persia changed in this process as well. These developments signaled the end of the classical era and ushered in important new themes in world history that defined the next major period. The response of major religions to political decline formed a leading direction for world history to come.

KEY QUESTIONS   *Were there general causes and patterns in the decline of the classical civilizations? What was the relationship of religion to the process of decline, as cause or as effect? Finally, what were the key differences in patterns and what explains these differences?*

DECLINE IN CHINA AND INDIA

Between 200 and 600 C.E., most of the classical civilizations collapsed entirely or in part. During this four-century span, China, the Mediterranean, and India suffered from outside invasions, the result of growing incursions by groups from central Asia. This renewed wave of nomadic expansion was not as sweeping as the earlier Indo-European growth, which had spread over India and much of the Mediterranean region many centuries before, but it severely tested the civilized regimes. Rome, of course, fell directly to Germanic invaders, who fought on partly because they were, in turn, harassed by the fierce Asiatic Huns. The Huns swept once across Italy, invading the city of Rome amid great destruction. It was another Hun group from central Asia who overthrew the Guptas in India, and similar nomadic tribes had earlier toppled the Han dynasty in China. The central Asian nomads were certainly encouraged by a growing realization of the weakness of the classical regimes, for Han China as well as the later Roman Empire suffered from serious internal problems long before the invaders dealt the final blows. And, the Guptas in India had not permanently resolved that area's tendency to dissolve into political fragmentation.

By about 100 C.E., the Han dynasty in China began to enter a serious decline. Confucian intellectual activity gradually became less creative. Politically, the central government's control diminished, bureaucrats became more corrupt, and local landlords took up much of the slack, ruling their neighborhoods according to their own wishes. The free peasants, long heavily taxed, were burdened with new taxes and demands of service by these same landlords. Many lost their farms and became day laborers on the large estates. Some had to sell their children into service. Social unrest increased, producing a great revolutionary effort led by Daoists in 184 C.E. Daoism now gained new appeal, shifting toward a popular religion and adding healing practices and magic to earlier philosophical beliefs. The Daoist leaders, called the Yellow Turbans, promised a golden age that was to be brought about by divine magic. The Yellow Turbans attacked not only the weakness of the emperor but also the self-indulgence of the current bureaucracy. As many as 30,000 students demonstrated against the decline of government morality. However,

their protests failed, and Chinese population growth and prosperity both spiraled further downward. The imperial court was mired in intrigue and civil war.

This dramatic decline paralleled the slightly later collapse of Rome, as we shall see. It obviously explained China's inability to push back invasions from borderland nomads, who finally overthrew the Han dynasty outright. As in Rome, growing political ineffectiveness formed part of the decline. Another important factor was the spread of devastating new epidemics, which may have killed up to half of the population. These combined blows not only toppled the Han dynasty but also led to almost three centuries of chaos—an unusually long span of unrest in Chinese history. Regional rulers and weak dynasties rose and fell during this period. Even China's cultural unity was threatened as the wave of Buddhism spread—one of the only cases in which China imported a major idea from outside its borders until the 20th century. Northern China, particularly, seemed near collapse.

Nonetheless, China did revive itself near the end of the 6th century. Strong native rulers in the north drove out the nomadic invaders. The Sui dynasty briefly ruled, and then in 618 C.E. it was followed by the Tang, who sponsored one of the most glorious periods in Chinese history. Confucianism and the bureaucratic system were revived, and indeed the bureaucratic tradition became more elaborate. The period of chaos left its mark somewhat in the continued presence of a Buddhist minority and new styles in art and literature. But, unlike the case of Rome, there was no permanent disruption.

The structures of classical China were simply too strong to be permanently overturned. The bureaucracy declined in scope and quality, but it did not disappear during the troubled centuries. Confucian values and styles of life remained current among the upper class. Many of the nomadic invaders, seeing that they had nothing better to offer by way of government or culture, simply tried to assimilate the Chinese traditions.

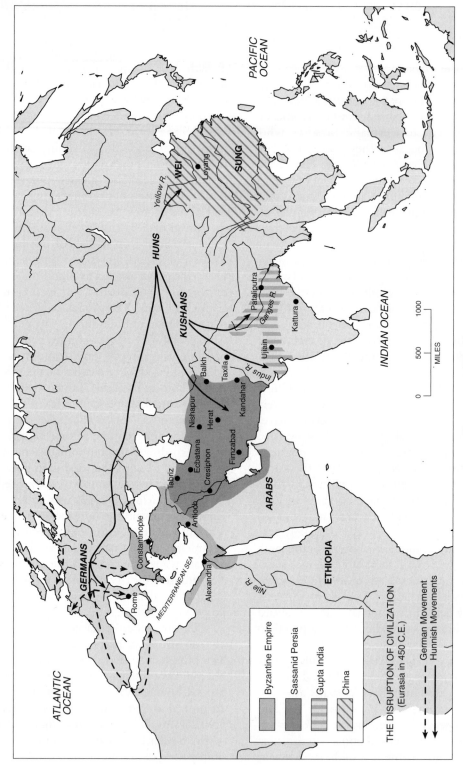

Eurasia in 450 C.E.

THE DISRUPTION OF CIVILIZATION
(Eurasia in 450 C.E.)

Byzantine Empire
Sassanid Persia
Gupta India
China

German Movement
Hunnish Movements

China thus had to recover from a serious setback, but it did not have to reinvent its civilization.

The decline of classical civilization in India was less drastic than the collapse of Han China. The ability of the Gupta emperors to control local princes was declining by the 5th century. Invasions by nomadic peoples, probably Hun tribes similar to those who were pressing into Europe, affected some northern portions of India as early as 500 C.E. During the next century, the invaders penetrated much deeper, destroying the Gupta empire in central India. Many of the invaders were integrated into the warrior caste of India, forming a new ruling group of regional princes. For several centuries, no native ruler attempted to build a large Indian state. The regional princes, collectively called *Rajput*, controlled the small states and emphasized military prowess. Few political events of more than local significance occurred.

Within this framework, Indian culture continued to evolve. Buddhism declined further in India proper. Hindu beliefs gained ground, among other things converting the Hun princes, who had originally worshipped gods of battle and had no sympathy for the Buddhist principles of calm and contemplation. Within Hinduism, the worship of a mother goddess, Devi, spread widely, encouraging a new popular emotionalism in religious ritual. Indian economic prosperity also continued at high levels.

Although Indian civilization substantially maintained its position, another challenge was to come, after 600 C.E., from the new Middle Eastern religion of Islam. Arab armies, fighting under the banners of their god Allah, reached India's porous northwestern frontier during the 7th century, and while there was initially little outright conquest on the subcontinent, Islam did win some converts in the northwest. Hindu leaders reacted to the arrival of this new faith by strengthening their emphasis on religious devotion, at the expense of some other intellectual interests. Hinduism also underwent further popularization; Hindu texts were written in vernacular languages such as Hindi, and use of the old classical language, Sanskrit, declined. These reactions were largely successful in preventing more than a minority of Indians from abandoning Hinduism, but they distracted from further achievements in science and mathematics. Islam also hit hard at India's international economic position and affected its larger impact throughout Asia. Arab traders soon wrested control of the Indian Ocean from Tamil merchants, and India, though still prosperous and productive, saw its commercial dynamism reduced. In politics, regionalism continued to prevail. Clearly, the glory days of the Guptas were long past, although classical traditions survived particularly in Hinduism and the caste system.

DECLINE AND FALL IN ROME

The Roman Empire exhibited a great many symptoms of decay after about 180 C.E. There was statistical evidence in the declining population in addition to growing difficulties in recruiting effective armies. There were also political manifestations in the greater brutality and arbitrariness of many Roman emperors—victims, according to one commentator at the time, of "lustful and cruel habits." Tax collection became increasingly difficult, as residents of the empire fell on hard times. The governor of Egypt complained that "the once numerous inhabitants of the aforesaid villages have now been reduced to a few, because some have fled in poverty and others have died . . . and for this reason we are in danger owing to impoverishment of having to abandon the tax-collectorship."

Above all, there were human symptoms. Inscriptions on Roman tombstones increasingly ended with the slogan, "I was not, I was, I am not, I have no more desires," suggesting a pervasive despondency over the futility of this life and despair at the absence of an afterlife.

The decline of Rome was more disruptive than the collapse of the classical dynasties in Asia. For this reason, and because memories of the collapse of this great empire became part of the Western tradition, the process of deterioration deserves particular attention. Every so often, Americans or western Europeans concerned about changes in their own society wonder if there might be lessons in Rome's fall that apply to the uncertain future of Western civilization today.

The quality of both political and economic life in the Roman Empire began to shift after about 180 C.E. Political confusion produced a series of weak emperors and many disputes over succession to the throne. Intervention by the army in the selection of emperors complicated political life and contributed to the deterioration of rule from the top. More important in initiating the process of decline was a series of plagues that swept over the empire. As in China, the plagues' source was growing international trade, which brought diseases endemic in southern Asia to new areas such as the Mediterranean, where no resistance had been established even to contagions such as the measles. The resulting diseases decimated the population. The population of Rome decreased from a million people to 250,000. Economic life worsened in consequence. Recruitment of troops became more difficult, so the empire was increasingly reduced to hiring Germanic soldiers to guard its frontiers. The need to pay troops added to the demands on the state's budget, just as declining production cut into tax revenues.

Here, perhaps, is the key to the process of decline: a set of general problems, triggered by a cycle of plagues that could not be prevented, resulting in a rather mechanistic spiral that steadily worsened. However, there is another side to Rome's downfall, although whether it is a cause or result of the initial difficulties is hard to say. Rome's upper classes became steadily more pleasure-seeking, turning away from the political devotion and economic vigor that had characterized the republic and early empire. Cultural life decayed. Aside from some truly creative Christian writers—the fathers of Western theology—there was very little sparkle to the art or literature of the later empire. Many Roman scholars contented themselves with writing textbooks that rather mechanically summarized earlier achievements in science, mathematics, and literary style. Writing textbooks is not, of course, proof of absolute intellectual incompetence—at least, not in all cases—but the point was that new knowledge or artistic styles were not being generated, and even the levels of previous accomplishment began to slip. The later Romans wrote textbooks about rhetoric instead of displaying rhetorical talent in actual political life; they wrote simple compendiums, for example, about animals or geometry, that barely captured the essentials of what earlier intellectuals had known, and they often added superstitious beliefs that previous generations would have scorned. This cultural decline, finally, was not clearly due to disease or economic collapse, for it began in some ways before these larger problems surfaced. Something was happening to the Roman elite, perhaps because of the deadening effect of authoritarian political rule, perhaps because of a new interest in luxuries and sensual indulgence. Revealingly, the upper classes no longer produced many offspring, for bearing and raising children seemed incompatible with a life of pleasure-seeking.

Rome's fall, in other words, can be blamed on large, impersonal forces that would have been hard for any society to control or a moral and political decay that reflected growing corruption among society's leaders. Probably elements of both were involved. Thus, the plagues would have weakened even a vigorous society, but they would not necessarily have produced an irreversible downward spiral had not the morale of the ruling classes already been sapped by an unproductive lifestyle and superficial values.

Regardless of precise causes, the course of Roman decay is quite clear. As the quality of imperial rule declined, as life became more dangerous and economic survival more precarious, many farmers clustered around the protection of large landlords, surrendering full control over their plots of land in the hope of military and judicial protection. The decentralization of political and economic authority, which was greatest in the western, or European, portions of the empire, foreshadowed the manorial system of Europe in the Middle Ages. The agricultural estates gave great political power to landlords and provided some local stability. But, in the long run, it weakened the power of the emperor and also tended to move the economy away from the elaborate and successful trade patterns of Mediterranean civilization in its heyday. Many estates tried to be self-sufficient. Trade and production declined further as a result, and cities shrank in size. The empire was locked in a vicious circle, in which responses to the initial deterioration merely lessened the chances of recovery.

Some later emperors tried vigorously to reverse the tide. Diocletian, who ruled from 284 C.E. to 305 C.E., tightened up the administration of the empire and tried to improve tax collection. Regulation of the dwindling economy increased. Diocletian also attempted to direct political loyalties to his own person, exerting pressure to worship the emperor as god. This was what prompted him to persecute Christians with particular viciousness, for they would not give Caesar preference over their God. The Emperor Constantine, who ruled from 312 to 337 C.E., experimented with other methods of control. He set up a second capital city, Constantinople, to regulate the eastern half of the empire more efficiently. He tried to use the religious force of Christianity to unify the empire spiritually, extending its toleration and adopting it as his own faith. These measures were not without result. The Eastern empire, ruled from Constantinople (now the Turkish city of Istanbul), remained an effective political and economic unit. Christianity spread under his official sponsorship, although there were some new problems linked to its success.

None of these measures, however, revived the empire as a whole. Division merely made the weakness of the western half worse. Attempts to regulate the economy reduced economic initiative and lowered production; ultimately, tax revenues declined once again. The army deteriorated further. When the Germanic invasions began in earnest in the 400s, there was scant basis to resist. Many peasants, burdened by the social and economic pressures of the decaying empire, actually welcomed the barbarians. A priest noted that "in all districts taken over by the Germans, there is one desire among all the Romans, that they should never again find it necessary to pass under Roman jurisdiction." German kingdoms were established in many parts of the empire by 425 C.E., and the last Roman emperor in the west was displaced in 476 C.E. The Germanic invaders numbered at most 5 percent of the population of the empire, but so great was the earlier Roman decline that this small, poorly organized force was able to put an end to one of the world's great political structures.

The collapse of Rome echoed mightily through the later history of Europe and the Middle East. Rome's fall split the unity of the Mediterranean lands that had been so arduously won through Hellenistic culture and then by the Roman Empire itself. This was one sign that the end of the Roman Empire was a more serious affair than the displacement of the last classical dynasties in India and China, for Greece and Rome had not produced the shared political culture and bureaucratic traditions of China that could allow revival after a period of chaos. Nor had Mediterranean civilization, for all its vitality, generated a common religion that appealed deeply enough, or satisfied enough needs, to maintain unity amid political fragmentation, as in India. Such religions reached the Mediterranean world as Rome fell, but they came too late to save the empire and produced a deep rift in this world—between Christian and Muslim—that has not been healed to this day.

However, Rome's collapse, although profound, was uneven. In effect, the fall of Rome divided the Mediterranean world into three

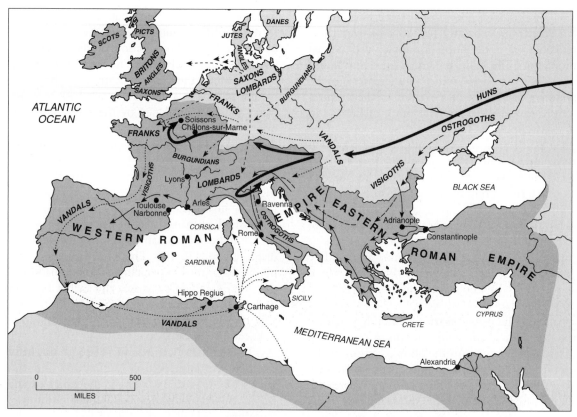

The Germanic Migrations, 4th Century to 6th Century

zones, which formed the starting points of three distinct civilizations that developed in later centuries. The revival of Persian traditions and a Persian (Sassanid) state factored into these developments as well.

In the eastern part of the empire, centered now on Constantinople, the empire in a sense did not fall. Civilization was more deeply entrenched here than in some of the western European portions of the empire, and there were fewer pressures from invaders. Emperors continued to rule Greece and other parts of southeast Europe, plus the northern Middle East. This Eastern empire—later to be known as the Byzantine Empire—was a product of late imperial Rome, rather than a balanced result of the entire span of classical Mediterranean civilization.

Thus, although its language was Greek, it maintained the authoritarian tone of the late Roman rulers. But the empire itself was vibrant, artistically creative, and active in trade. Briefly, especially under the Emperor Justinian (who ruled from 527 to 565 C.E.), the eastern emperors tried to recapture the whole heritage of Rome. However, Justinian was unable to maintain a hold in Italy and even lost the provinces of north Africa. He did issue one of the most famous compilations of Roman law, in the code that bore his name. But his was the last effort to restore Mediterranean unity.

The Byzantine Empire did not control the whole of the northern Middle East, even in its greatest days. During the late Hellenistic periods and into the early centuries of the Roman

This 1521 woodcut depicts the German King Theodoric exiling the Roman scholar Boethius from Rome to Padua.

Empire, a Parthian empire had flourished, centered in the Tigris–Euphrates region but spreading into northwestern India and to the borders of Rome's holdings along the Mediterranean. Parthian conquerors had taken over this portion of Alexander the Great's empire, reviving themes from Persia in the process. They produced little culture of their own, being content to rely on Persian styles, but they long maintained an effective military and bureaucratic apparatus. Then, around 227 C.E., a Persian rebellion displaced the Parthians and created a new Sassanid empire that more directly revived the glories of the earlier Persian empire. Zoroastrianism revived, although there was some conversion to Christianity. Persian styles in art and manufacturing experienced a brilliant resurgence.

Both the Parthian and the Sassanid empires served as bridges between the Mediterranean and the East, transmitting goods and some artistic and literary styles between the Greek-speaking world and India and China. As the Roman Empire weakened, the Sassanids joined the attack, at times pushing into parts of southeastern Europe. Ultimately, however, the Byzantine Empire managed to create a stable frontier. The Sassanid empire preserved the important strain of Persian culture in the eastern part of the Middle East, and this continued to influence this region as well as India. The Sassanids, however, were finally (in 651 C.E.) overthrown by the surge of Arab conquest that followed the rise of Islam, in the 7th century C.E.

Rome's fall, then, did not disrupt the northern Middle East—the original cradle of civilization—as much as might have been expected. Persian rule simply continued in one part of the region, until the Arab onslaught, which itself did not destroy Persian culture. Byzantium maintained many of the traditions of the later Roman Empire, plus Christianity, in the western part of the Middle East and in Greece and other parts of southeastern Europe.

The second zone that devolved from Rome's fall consisted of north Africa and the southeastern shores of the Mediterranean. Here, a number of regional kingdoms briefly succeeded the empire. While Christianity spread into the area—indeed, one of the greatest Christian theologians, Augustine, was a bishop in north Africa—its appearance was not so uniformly triumphant as in the Byzantine Empire or western Europe. Furthermore, separate beliefs and doctrines soon split north African Christianity from the larger branches, producing most notably the Coptic church in Egypt, which still survives as a Christian minority in that country. Soon this region was filled with the still newer doctrines of Islam and a new Arab empire.

Finally, there was the western part of the empire—Italy, Spain, and points north. Here is where Rome's fall not only shattered unities but also reduced the level of civilization itself. Crude, regional Germanic kingdoms developed in parts of Italy, France, and elsewhere. Cities shrank still further, and, especially outside Italy, trade almost disappeared. The only clearly vital forces in this region emanated not from Roman traditions but from the spread of Christianity. Even Christianity could not sustain a sophisticated culture of literature or art, however. In the mire of Rome's collapse, this part of the world forgot for several centuries what it had previously known.

In this western domain, what we call the fall of Rome was scarcely noted at the time, for decay had been progressing for so many decades that the failure to name a new emperor meant little. There was some comprehension of loss, some realization that the present could not rival the past. Thus,

Christian scholars were soon apologizing for their inability to write well or to understand some of the doctrines of the earlier theologians such as Augustine. This sense of inferiority to classical achievements long marked the culture of this western zone, even as times improved.

THE NEW RELIGIOUS MAP

The end of the classical period is not simply the story of decay and collapse. This same period, from 200 to 600 C.E., saw the effective rise of many of the world's major religions. The devastating plagues caused new interest in belief systems that could provide solace amid rising death rates. From Spain to China, growing political instability clearly prompted many people to seek solace in joys of the spirit, and while the religious surge was not entirely new, the resulting changes in the religious map of Europe and Asia and the nature and intensity of religious interests were significant new forces. Christianity, born two centuries before Rome's collapse began, became a widespread religion throughout the Mediterranean region as the empire's political strength weakened. Buddhism, although launched still earlier, saw its surge into eastern Asia furthered by the growing problems of classical China. Thus, two major faiths, different in many ways but similar in their emphasis on spiritual life and the importance of divine power, reshaped major portions of Europe and Asia precisely as the structures of the classical period declined or disappeared. Finally, shortly after 600 C.E., an entirely new religion, Islam, surfaced and became the most dynamic force in world history during the next several centuries. In sum, the religious map of the world, although by no means completed by 500 C.E., was beginning to take on dramatic new contours. This means that while civilization in many ways declined, it was also being altered, taking new directions as well as losing some older strengths. Never before had single religions spread so widely, crossing so many cultural and political boundaries.

HISTORY DEBATE

WHAT CAUSED DECLINE AND FALL?

Determining what causes major developments is never easy. Unlike laboratory science, repeated experiments, to narrow down the causes of a phenomenon, are not possible. It remains important to discuss causes as part of understanding what happened, and some plausible analysis is possible. However, debate is a vital part of the process.

In the case of the classical decline, particularly for Rome, debate has raged on and off for centuries. Even at the time, people wondered if perhaps the spread of Christianity was sapping Roman virtues and weakening the state (this is not a common explanation today). Other attempts to provide an appealing framework have included arguments that new patterns of sunspots reduced agricultural productivity (again, not widely believed now).

Current debates focus on inevitability and on external pressures versus internal decay. One of the great world historians of the 20th century, Arnold Toynbee, argued that civilizations inevitably undergo a life cycle in which prosperous middle age is followed by collapse. Loss of creativity, growing luxury, bureaucratic routine, and attacks from outside provide a law of history in which great empires finally shatter. Toynbee used Rome as one of his prime examples, and many historians concur with the approach. More recently, another well-known historian, David Kennedy, offered a slightly different interpretation: many societies, such as Rome, overexpanded, and they ended up reducing their internal strength by trying to support impossibly wide frontiers.

On the other hand, some historians disagree with such sweeping explanations. The Roman Empire, after all, did not decline across the board—the eastern part survived quite well. It is important, in this counterargument, to look for more specific factors, on a case-by-case basis.

The internal–external quarrel runs like this: many historians have long pointed to moral collapse as a key component of Rome's fall (and the argument can be applied to China and India too). Lower classes were sapped by bread and circuses, upper classes became greedy and pleasure-seeking, and the result was an inability to sustain vigorous institutions. There is evidence supporting this viewpoint, to be sure. But is the explanation necessary? The pressure of outside invasion plus the widespread impact of epidemic disease (particularly in Rome and China) may make the moral factors less salient. Some moral confusion may have resulted from growing death rates, rather than the other way around. The debate continues.

The newly expanding religions shared some general features. Christianity, Buddhism, and Hinduism, as well as Islam later on, all emphasized intense devotion and piety, stressing the importance of spiritual concerns beyond the daily cares of earthly life. All three offered the hope of a better existence after this life had ended, and each one responded to new political instability and to the growing poverty of people in various parts of the civilized world. They all came to believe in a missionary calling, to convert diverse peoples to a new faith.

The spread of the major religions meant that hundreds of thousands of people, in Asia, Europe, and Africa, underwent a conversion process as the classical period drew to a close. Radically changing beliefs is an unusual human experience, symptomatic in this case of the new pressures on established political structures and on ordinary life. At the same time, many people blended new beliefs with the old, in a process called *syncretism*. This meant that the religions changed too, sometimes taking on the features of individual civilizations even while maintaining larger religious claims.

Despite these important common features, the major religions were very different. Hinduism, as we have seen, retained its belief in reincarnation and its combination of spiritual interest in union with the divine essence and extensive rituals and ceremonies. The religion experienced greater popular appeal after the fall of the Guptas, associated with the expanded use of popular languages and with the worship of the mother goddess Devi. Buddhism was altered more substantially as it traveled beyond India's borders, becoming only a small minority faith in India itself.

Buddhism

The chief agents of Buddhist expansion and leadership were monks, for Buddhism tended to divide the faithful among a minority who abandoned earthly life in favor of spiritual dedication and the larger number who continued to work in the world while doing the best they could to meet their spiritual obligations. Some centuries after Buddha's death, a doctrine of *bodhisattvas* developed, which held that some people could attain nirvana through their own meditation while choosing to remain in the world as saints and to aid others by prayer and example. Buddhism increasingly shifted from an original emphasis on ethics to become a more emotional cult stressing the possibility of popular salvation. The role of the bodhisattvas was crucial in this transformation, because it broadened the prospect of salvation for ordinary people by leading them in prayer and advising them on spiritual matters.

Buddhism evolved further as the religion spread seriously to China after the fall of the

Spread of Buddhism: a Buddhist grotto in China.

Han dynasty, when the idea of a celestial afterlife proved almost irresistible. Monasteries in India and the Himalaya mountains continued to serve as spiritual centers for Chinese Buddhism, but the religion developed strong roots in east Asia directly, spreading through China and from there to Korea and Japan. The east Asian form of Buddhism, called *Mahayana*, or the Greater Vehicle, retained basic Buddhist beliefs. However, the emphasis on Buddha himself as god and savior increased in the Mahayana version. Statues devoted to Buddha as god countered the earlier Buddhist hostility to religious images. The religion improved its organization, with priests, temples, creeds, and rituals. Buddhist holy men, or bodhisattvas, remained important. Their souls after death resided in a kind of super heaven, where they could receive prayers and aid people. Intense spirituality continued to inform Buddhist faith as well. But prayers and rituals could now help ordinary people to become holy. Buddha himself became a god to whom one could appeal for solace, "the great physician for a sick and impure world." East Asian Buddhism also spurred new artistic interests in China and, later, in Japan, including the pagoda style of temple design and the statues devoted to Buddha.

Buddhism had a complex impact on women in China, largely among families who converted. On the face of things, Buddhism should have disrupted China's firm belief in patriarchal power, because Buddhists believed that women, like men, had souls. Indeed, some individual women in China captured great attention because of their spiritual accomplishments. But Chinese culture generated changes in Buddhism within the empire. Buddhist phrases such as "husband supports wife" were changed to "husband controls his wife," whereas "the wife comforts the husband"—another Buddhist phrase from India—became "the wife reveres her husband." Here was a vital case of cultural blending, or syncretism. Finally, many men valued pious Buddhist wives, because they might benefit the family's salvation and because Buddhist activity

kept their wives busy, calm, and out of mischief. Buddhism was perhaps appealing to Chinese women because it led to a more meaningful life, but it did not really challenge patriarchy. A biography of one Buddhist wife put it this way: "At times of crisis she could be tranquil and satisfied with her fate, not letting outside things agitate her mind."

Buddhism was not popular with all Chinese. Confucian leaders, particularly, found in Buddhist beliefs in an afterlife a diversion from appropriate political interests. They disliked the notion of such intense spirituality and also found ideas of the holy life incompatible with proper family obligations. More important, Buddhism was seen as a threat that might distract ordinary people from loyalty to the emperor. When imperial dynasties revived in China, they showed some interest in Buddhist piety for a time, but ultimately they attacked the Buddhist faith, driving out many missionaries. Buddhism remained a minority current in China, and many villages worshipped in Buddhist shrines. Thus, China's religious composition became increasingly complex, but without overturning earlier cultural directions. Daoism reacted to Buddhism as well, by improving its organization and emphasizing practical benefits obtainable through magic. It was at this point that Daoism developed a clear hold on many peasants, incorporating many of their beliefs in the process. Buddhism had a greater lasting influence in the religious experience of other parts of east Asia, notably Japan, Korea, and Vietnam, than in China itself. And, of course, Buddhism had also spread to significant parts of southeast Asia, where it remained somewhat truer to earlier Buddhist concepts of individual meditation and ethics.

In the world today, some 255 million people count themselves as Buddhists. Most live in the areas of east and southeast Asia, where the religion had taken root by 500 C.E. Buddhism did not, by itself, dominate any whole civilization; rather, it lived alongside other faiths. However, it provided major additions to Asia's religious map and an important response to changing conditions in the troubled centuries after the classical period had ended.

Christianity

Christianity moved westward, from its original center in the Middle East, as Buddhism was spreading toward east from India. Although initially less significant than Buddhism in terms of the number of converts, Christianity ultimately proved to be one of the two largest faiths worldwide. And it played a direct role in the formation of two postclassical civilizations, those of eastern and western Europe. Despite important similarities to Buddhism in its emphasis on salvation and the guidance of saints, Christianity differed in crucial ways. It came to place more emphasis on church organization and structure, copying from the example of the Roman Empire. Even more than Buddhism, it placed a premium on missionary activity and widespread conversions. More, perhaps, than any other major religion, Christianity stressed the exclusive nature of its truth and was intolerant of competing beliefs. Such fierce confidence was not the least of the reasons for the new religion's success.

Christianity began in reaction to rigidities that had developed in the Jewish priesthood during the two centuries before the birth of Jesus Christ. A host of reform movements sprang up, some of them preaching the coming of a Messiah, or savior, who would bring about a Last Judgment on humankind. Many of these movements also stressed the possibility of life after death for the virtuous, which was a new element in Judaism. Jesus of Nazareth, believed by Christians to be the son of God sent to earth to redeem human sin, crystallized this radical reform movement. Combining extraordinary gentleness of spirit and great charisma, Jesus preached widely in Israel and gathered a group of loyal disciples around him. Initially, there seems to have been no intent on his or his followers' part to found a new religion. After Jesus'

crucifixion, the disciples expected his imminent return and with it the end of the world. Only gradually, when the Second Coming did not transpire, did the disciples begin to fan out and, through their preaching, attract growing numbers of supporters in various parts of the Roman Empire.

The message of Jesus and his disciples seemed clear: there was a single God who loved humankind despite earthly sin. A virtuous life was one dedicated to the worship of God and fellowship among other believers; worldly concerns were secondary, and a life of poverty might be most conducive to holiness. God sent Jesus (called *Christ* from the Greek word *christos*, for "God's anointed") to preach his holy word and through his sacrifice to prepare his followers for the widespread possibility of an afterlife and heavenly communion with God. Belief, good works, and the discipline of fleshly concerns led to heaven; rituals, such as commemorating Christ's Last Supper with wine and bread, promoted the same goal.

Christianity's message spread at an opportune time. The official religion of the Greeks and Romans had long seemed rather sterile, particularly to many of the poor. The Christian emphasis on the beauty of a simple life and the spiritual equality of all people, plus the fervor of the early Christians and the satisfying rituals they created, captured growing attention. The great reach of the Roman Empire made it relatively easy for Christian missionaries to travel widely in Europe and the Middle East, to spread the new word, although as we have seen, they also reached beyond, to Persia, Axum, and Ethiopia. Then when conditions began to deteriorate in the empire, the solace this otherworldly religion provided resulted in its even wider appeal. Early Christian leaders made several important adjustments to maximize their conversions. Under the guidance of Paul, not one of the original disciples but an early convert, Christians began to see themselves as part of a new religion, rather than part of a Jewish reform movement, and they

WORLD PROFILES

SAINT PAUL
(PAUL OF TARSUS)

Paul was a prominent Jewish official when early Christians were organizing their religion after the death of Christ. He was also a Roman citizen and proud of his connection to the empire. Paul was a member of a Jewish group called *Pharisees*, which organized around individual rabbis rather than the Jewish priesthood. Originally hostile to Christianity, he organized persecutions of Christians. But, presumably on the road to the city of Damascus, Paul had an intense conversion experience and began to assume a leadership role in this new religion. Against the opposition of some Christian leaders, Paul went on missions to convert non-Jews in what is now Greece and Turkey (between 48 and 55 C.E.), and Paul is credited with making the changes that began to move the religion from a Jewish reform movement to a world religion. He argued that non-Jews could be good Christians without conforming to Jewish law, and he emphasized baptism as the entry to religious faith. Paul also softened some of the radical stances of early Christians, for example, placing more emphasis on the submission of women. And he worked on church organization, using Roman principles. He organized communities with overseers (bishops) and appointed ministers under them. Some of Paul's writings became part of the New Testament, as it was formulated, confirming his role in converting a passionate religious movement to an organized church.

Saint Paul (Paul of Tarsus).

welcomed non-Jews. Paul also encouraged more formal organization within the new church, with local groups selecting elders to govern them; soon, a single leader, or bishop, was appointed for each city. This structure paralleled the provincial government of the empire. Finally, Christian doctrine became increasingly organized, as the writings of several disciples and others were collected into what became known as the New Testament of the Bible.

During the first three centuries after Christ, the new religion competed among a number of eastern mystical religions. It also faced, as we have seen, periodic persecution from the normally tolerant imperial government. Even so, by the time Constantine converted to Christianity and accepted it as the one true legitimate faith, perhaps 10 percent of the empire's population had accepted the new religion. Constantine's conversion brought new problems to Christianity, particularly some interference by the state in matters of doctrine. However, it became much easier to spread Christianity with official favor, and the continued deterioration of the empire added to the impetus to join this amazingly successful new church. In the eastern Mediterranean, where imperial rule remained strong from its center in Constantinople, state control of the church became a way of life. But in the West, where conditions were far more chaotic, bishops had a freer hand. A centralized church organization under the leadership of the bishop of Rome, called *Pope* from the word *papa*, or "father," gave the Western church unusual strength and independence.

By the time Rome collapsed, Christianity had thus demonstrated immense spiritual power and developed a solid organization, although one that differed from east to west. The new church faced a number of controversies over doctrine but managed to promote certain standard beliefs as against several heresies. A key tenet involved a complex doctrine of the Trinity, which held that the one God had three persons—the Father, the Son (Christ), and the Holy Ghost. Experience in fighting heresies promoted Christian interest in defending a single belief and strengthened its intolerance for any competing doctrine or faith. Early Christianity also produced an important formal theology, through formative writers such as Augustine. This theology incorporated many elements of classical philosophy with Christian belief and aided the church in its attempts to gain respectability among intellectuals. Theologians such as Augustine grappled with problems such as freedom of the will: if God is all-powerful, can mere human beings have free will? And if not, how can human beings be justly punished for sin? By working out these issues in elaborate doctrine, the early theologians, or church fathers, provided an important role for formal,

rational thought in a religion that continued to emphasize the primary importance of faith. Finally, Christianity was willing to accommodate some earlier polytheistic traditions among the common people. The celebration of Christ's birth was thus moved to coincide with winter solstice, a classic example of syncretism, which allowed the new faith to benefit from the power of selective older rituals.

Like all successful religions, Christianity combined a number of appeals. It offered devotion to an all-powerful God, stressing absolute faith. However, Christianity also developed its own complex intellectual system, or theology. Mystical holy men and women flourished under Christian banners, particularly in the Middle East. In the West, soon after the empire's collapse, this impulse was partially disciplined through the institution of monasticism, first developed in Italy under Benedict, who started a monastery among Italian peasants whom he lured away from the worship of the Sun god Apollo. The Benedictine Rule, which soon spread to many other monasteries and convents, urged a disciplined life, with prayer and spiritual fulfillment alternating with hard work in agriculture and study. Thus, Christianity attempted not only to encourage but also to discipline intense piety, and to avoid a complete gulf between the lives of saintly men and women and the spiritual concerns of ordinary people. Christianity's success and organizational strength obviously appealed to political leaders. But the new religion never became the creature of the upper classes alone. Its popular message of salvation and satisfying rituals continued to draw the poor, more than most of the great classical belief systems; in this regard, it was somewhat like Hinduism in India. Christianity also provided some religious unity among different social groups. It even held special appeal for women. Christianity did not create equality among men and women, but it did preach the equal importance of male and female souls. And it encouraged men and women to worship together, unlike many other faiths.

Early Christian art: figure of Christ on a carved ivory box.

Christianity promoted a new culture among its followers. The rituals, the otherworldly emphasis, the interest in spiritual equality—these central themes were far different from those of classical Mediterranean civilizations. Christianity modified classical beliefs in the central importance of the state and of political loyalties. Although Christians accepted the state, they did not put it first. Christianity also worked against other classical institutions, such as slavery, in the name of brotherhood (although later Christians accepted slavery in other contexts). Christianity

may have fostered greater respectability for disciplined work than had been the case in the Mediterranean civilization, where an aristocratic ethic dominated. Western monasteries, for example, set forth rigid work routines for monks. Certainly, Christianity sought some changes in classical culture beyond its central religious message, including greater emphasis on sexual restraint. But Christianity preserved important classical values as well, in addition to an interest in solid organization and some of the themes of classical philosophy. Church buildings retained

Roman architectural styles, although often with greater simplicity if only because of the poverty of the later empire and subsequent states. Latin remained the language of the church in the West, Greek the language of most Christians in the eastern Mediterranean. Through the patient librarianship of monks, monasticism played an immensely valuable role in preserving classical as well as Christian learning.

When the Roman Empire fell, Christian history was still in its infancy. The Western church soon spread its missionary zeal to northern Europe, and the Eastern church reached into the Slavic lands of the Balkans and Russia. By then, Christianity was already established as a significant world religion—one of the few ever generated. A world religion is defined as a faith of unusual durability and drawing power, one whose complexity wins the devotion of many different kinds of people. Major world religions, such as Christianity and Buddhism, are able to cut across different cultures, to win converts in a wide geographic area and amid considerable diversity.

The spread of Hinduism in India, Buddhism in east and southeast Asia, a more popular Daoism in China, Christianity in Europe and parts of the Mediterranean world, and ultimately Islam (after 600 C.E.) was a vital result of the changes in classical civilizations brought on by attack and decay. Despite the important diversity among these great religions, their overall development suggests the way important currents could run through the civilized world, crossing political and cultural borders—thanks in part to the integrations and contacts built by the classical civilizations. Common difficulties, including invading forces that journeyed from central Asia and contagious epidemics that knew no boundaries, help explain parallel changes in separate civilizations. Trade and travel also provided common bonds. Chinese travelers learned of Buddhism through trading expeditions to India, whereas Ethiopians learned about Christianity from Middle Eastern traders. The new religions

Table 7.1

MAJOR RELIGIONS AND THEIR DISTRIBUTION IN THE WORLD TODAY*

Religion	Distribution
Christianity	2 billion
Islam	1.3 billion
Hinduism	780 million
Buddhism	350 million
Shintoism	3 million
Daoism	31 million
Judaism	18 million

*Figures for several religions have been reduced, over the past 50 years, by the impact of communism in eastern Europe and parts of Asia.

spurred a greater interest in spiritual matters and resulted in a greater tendency to focus on a single basic divinity instead of a multitude of gods. Polytheistic beliefs and practices continued to flourish as part of popular Hinduism and popular Daoism, and they were not entirely displaced among ordinary people who converted to Christianity, Buddhism, or Islam. But the new religious surge reduced the hold of literal animism in much of Asia and Europe, and this too was an important development across boundaries. Table 7.1 summarizes the distribution of major religions in the world today.

PATHS TO THE PRESENT

The decline of the great empires most obviously signaled the end of an era, rather than the launching of new themes that might survive to the present. The legacies of China, India, Persia, and the Mediterranean, discussed earlier, obviously had to survive the declines in order to participate in framing later world history.

The decline phenomenon itself connects to the present in three ways. First, alterations in the world's map, set in motion by the fall of the Roman Empire, proved durable. A few efforts to reconstitute a unified Mediterranean—by an eastern Roman emperor, and later, to an extent, by Arab leaders—failed. The Mediterranean world remains divided to this day.

Second, the promotion of greater religious interest and new conversions that resulted in part from the failure of earthly empires helped set a religious map for Asia, north Africa, and Europe that has lasted, with a few modifications, to the present day (see Table 7.1). This religious configuration had not been achieved by the end of the classical decline period, but the process of its formation was in motion.

Third, the fact of collapse—particularly for people aware of the Roman legacy—added to humans' recurrent anxieties. If such great achievements could fail, what were the prospects of more recent gains? People in various parts of Europe and the Mediterranean might wonder whether their societies would follow the path of Rome, seeing a period of success followed by disintegration and collapse. Some observers in western Europe and the United States during the past century have noted the analogy between weaknesses in their societies, for example, the overextension of finances and natural resources, the moral decay, and Rome—and wondered about the ultimate implications of that analogy. It is sometimes hard to avoid and shake off the thought—and this is a legacy of the collapse period in its own right.

SUGGESTED WEB SITES

On the invention of antiquity, see http://www .brynmawr.edu/library/exhibits/antiquity/ index2.htm; on the decline of the Roman Empire, see http://www.roman-empire.net/ decline/decl-index.html; on the Silk Roads, see http://www.ess.uci.edu/~oliver/silk.html; on the origins of Germany, see http://mars.wnec .edu/~grempel/courses/germany/lectures/ 01origins.html; on the history of Christianity,

see http://history-world.org/world%20religions% 20development_of.htm.

SUGGESTED READINGS

On the decline process, see Jared Diamond, *Collapse: How Societies Choose to Fail or Succeed* (2005), and J. H. G. W. Liebeschuetz, *Decline and Change in Late Antiquity: Relition, Barbarians and Their Historiography* (2006).

The fall of the Roman Empire has generated rich and interesting debate. For interpretations and discussion of earlier views, see James W. Ermatinger, *The Decline and Fall of the Roman Empire* (2004); A. H. M. Jones, *The Decline of the Ancient World* (1966); J. Vogt, *The Decline of Rome* (1965); and F. W. Walbank, *The Awful Revolution—the Decline of the Roman Empire in the West* (1960). On India and China in decline, worthwhile sources include R. Thaper, *History of India*, Vol. 1 (1966); R. C. Majumdar, ed., *The Classical Age* (1966); Raymond Dawson, *Imperial China* (1972); J. A. Harrison, *The Chinese Empire* (1972); and Denis Twitchett and John K. Fairbank, eds., *The Cambridge History of China*, Vol. 3, Part 1 (1979). On Africa, see K. Shillington, *History of Africa* (1989), and Graham Connal, *African Civilizations: Precolonial Cities and States in Tropical Africa, an Archeological Perspective* (1987). On the role of disease, W. McNeill, *Plagues and Peoples* (1977), is useful. For the rise or spread of new religions, consult N. C. Chandhuri, *Hinduism: A Religion to Live By* (1979); S. Renko, *Pagan Rome and the Early Christians* (1986); M. Hengel, *Acts and the History of Earliest Christianity* (1986); A. Sharma, ed., *Women in World Religions* (1987); D. Carmody, *Women and World Religions* (1985); G. Clark, *Women in Late Antiquity: Pagan and Christian* (1993); and B. Witherington, *Women in the Earliest Churches* (1988). Peter N. Stearns, *Gender in World History* (2001), deals with women and world religions. The new edition by Peter Brown, *The Rise of Western Christendom* (2003), is a vital contribution, as is K. Jamanadas, *Decline and Fall of Buddhism: A Tragedy in Ancient India* (2004).

Other work includes Joseph A. Tainter, *The Collapse of Complex Societies* (1988); Norman Yoffee and George L. Cowgill, *The Collapse of Ancient States and Civilizations* (1991); and J. H. W. G. Liebeschuetz, *Decline and Fall of the Roman City* (2001). For an overview of the development of Christianity and the spread of world religions, see David Shotter, *The Fall of the Roman Empire* (2005); Noel Lenski, ed., *The Cambridge Companion to the Age of Constantine* (2006); Dale B. Martin and Patricia Cox Miller, *The Cultural Turn in Late Ancient Studies: Gender, Asceticism, and Historiography* (2005); P. J. Heather, *The Fall of the Roman Empire: A New History of Rome and the Barbarians* (2006); Bryan Ward-Perkins, *The Fall of Rome: And the End of Civilization* (2005); A. H. Merrils, *History and Geography in Late Antiquity* (2005); Charles Freeman, *The Closing of the Western Mind: The Rise of Faith and the Fall of Reason* (2002); and Andrew Bell-Fialkoff, *The Role of Migration in the History of the Eurasian Steppe: Sedentary Civilization vs. "Barbarian" and Nomad* (2000).

The Classical Period, 1000 B.C.E. to 500 C.E.

CONTACTS AND IDENTITIES

The most obvious change in the tension between local identities and the advantages or inevitabilities of contact came with the formation of the classical civilizations themselves, because of the stress the integration efforts caused for smaller cultural and institutional systems. As the Chinese included southern China, for example, leaders from the north put forth massive efforts to reduce the separateness of southern Chinese ethnic groups, including sending many settler groups from north China to reduce local attachments. The conquering leaders insisted on common education and that elites speak Mandarin. Finally, something of a larger Chinese identity was forged. This did not mean that all local identities were lost—southerners continued to speak a different form of Chinese, even when they learned Mandarin to use for certain purposes—but they were modified. Only on the frontiers, particularly in the west, did Chinese leaders face ongoing problems of locals vigorously retaining non-Chinese identities.

Similar tensions arose in the Mediterranean, though Greek and Roman leaders were somewhat more tolerant of local variations, including religious variations. Roman military settlers were posted to different parts of the empire, where they helped keep order; the lifestyles they established, including entertainments and the classic Roman public baths, attracted some locals, but there was usually no effort to break down local identities entirely. Romans themselves remained conscious of their own identity within the larger empire. They worried, for example, about corruption by Greek influences, because the Greeks were held to be softer and less manly and military, even as Greek artistic styles and intellectual practices spread. A few local identities were perceived as

subversive because they loudly refused to place loyalty to the Roman state first: the Jews, particularly, were uprooted from Jerusalem and its surroundings because of this clash of identities.

Identity issues surfaced in India as Indian civilization spread to the whole subcontinent. They were modified, however, by great tolerance of local variants, including languages. Even the caste system protected separate identities within the discrete castes.

Still, the tension between previously established languages, beliefs, and customs, and the new power of integrating civilizations, was real. This meant a considerable extension of the tension itself throughout the world, compared to the previous period when smaller river valley societies had predominated.

A larger tension, however, than that of the friction between local identity and assimilation into a larger culture existed in the classical period, although less clearly so. To some degree, particularly among elite social groups, the major civilizations themselves formed identities: Chinese had some sense of what was "Chinese," Greeks of what was "Greek." Leaders celebrated these identities by contending that people outside the civilizations were "barbarians"—a clear sense of difference from, and superiority to, the rest of the known world.

These new civilizational identities were not, however, severely tested by the contacts among civilizations. Silk Roads trade and commerce in the Indian Ocean continued to exchange goods, but not with the intensity that brought a wider sense of outside influence against which established identities had to be more sharply defined. Even when Greeks and Indians encountered each other, there is little record of the contact having generated identity issues. Indians briefly borrowed a few Greek styles, which modified their artistic identity for some decades, but there was little sense of a deep clash between the cultures.

Relationships between Greeks and Persians were another matter, something of an exception in the classical period. These two societies frequently interacted and fought. Greeks formed definite prejudices about the Persians. They tended to argue, particularly, that Persian government was more arbitrary, its rulers more unrestrained, than was true in Greece—and that the Persian system was decidedly inferior. Here was a rare case in which identity was sharpened by larger regional contacts. Alexander, of course, hoped to fuse Greeks, Persians, and other cultures in the larger Middle East, which was another response to the tension between identity and contact, but his effort fell short. Indeed, some Greek companions tried to insult Alexander by calling him a "Persian"—a clear sign that identities had not been significantly modified.

Identity was tested, again, at the end of the classical period when Buddhism moved into China. Here was a case, for several centuries, in which the attractions of an outside influence—a religion—outweighed Chinese insistence on preserving their own identity. Even here, however, as we have seen, the Chinese quickly modified Buddhism to make it more compatible with their view of what was proper. Only later, under a subsequent dynasty, did leadership largely turn against the religion on the grounds it was incompatible with Chinese values.

The classical period produced signs, in other words, that distinct civilizations were forging identities that might clash with other cultural identities as a result of contact. But, as we have seen, not all civilizations framed the tensions around identity in the same way: Chinese values insisted more fiercely on identity preservation than did the more tolerant Indian approach. For the most part, however, contacts among the civilizations were light enough that identity issues did not surface too harshly. Also, many merchants and consumers found the advantages of interregional trade, particularly along the Silk Roads, too great to sacrifice to relatively minor identity concerns. Starker tests of civilizational identities awaited the future.

PART III

The Postclassical Period, 500–1450 C.E.

INTRODUCTION: MARKING THE NEW ERA

The postclassical period of world history runs from roughly 500 C.E. to about 1450 C.E. Its beginning was marked by the final stages of decline of the classical empires and their aftermath. With this came the spread of world religions—including Islam after 600 C.E.— the definition of a strong remnant of the Roman Empire in the east (the Byzantine Empire), and, soon, the rise of the Arabs.

The end of the period saw a decline of Arab political and commercial power, despite the continued importance of Arab peoples and culture; the end of the Byzantine Empire; and the end of a series of post-Arab frameworks for interregional trade. By 1450 western Europeans were well launched in a series of explorations and trading expeditions that propelled them into a new role in world history, while China had developed production capacities that long affected world trade.

THEMES: RELIGION AND LONG-DISTANCE TRADE

The postclassical period was defined, internally, by two major themes. The first involved the ongoing consequences of the expansion of the world religions, plus the vital addition of Islam to the religious roster. Thanks to unprecedented missionary fervor from Buddhist, Christian, and Islamic leaders, hundreds of thousands of people changed their beliefs in fundamental ways. Polytheistic religions continued to decline; the expanding monotheistic faiths showed the capacity to cut across religious and political boundaries. New religious emphasis tended to eclipse political interest; there were fewer bold political ventures, certainly fewer empires, in this period than in the preceding classical centuries, in part because more resources and talent went into religious than into political ideas and institutions. World religions also affected social structure, tempering continued inequality with new ideas about the religious value of poverty and the universality of souls.

The period's second main theme was the acceleration of interregional trade and the establishment of new, regular commercial routes. The key trade axis now ran east–west, from the Middle East through the Indian Ocean to southeast Asia and China. In addition, seaborne trade moved along Africa's eastern coast. Overland trade ran from north to south from northern Europe through western Russia, reaching the Middle East, and also from south to north in west Africa. Japan began trading regularly with Korea and China. A final regular route, established a bit later, brought western European merchants into the Mediterranean, again linking up with the Arab routes. Travel increased: by the 13th century venturesome individuals might go widely into Africa and Asia; the most tireless example, Ibn Battuta from north Africa, journeyed more than 75,000 miles. Accounts of distant places, along with better maps, both reflected and encouraged the new emphasis on long-distance commerce.

New technologies did not cause the expanding trade, but they did support it. Arabs improved ship design. The Chinese introduced the compass, which by the 13th century was being widely adopted in southeast Asia, the Middle East, and Europe. Trade also promoted the spread of other technologies and ideas. Arabs learned of papermaking from China, of a more efficient numbering system from India. Other groups, trading with the Arabs, later adopted these gains in turn.

The twin themes of the period, religion and trade, were an odd pairing in some ways. Religious leaders worried about too much devotion to commerce and moneymaking, and some merchants repented of their careers, turning to religion at the end of life. But the themes supported each other as well. The spread of major religions created larger cultural zones, while beliefs in a single divine framework or plan made long-distance trade seem less risky. Merchants often brought religion with them, as when Islam accompanied Arab commerce to the islands of present-day Indonesia or through the Sahara to west Africa. And commercial success helped persuade many people that religious change was worthwhile, linking conversion with worldly success as well as spiritual gain.

The two themes might also have had additional, diverse impacts. The three major world religions taught that women had souls, along with men. All provided new opportunities for religious expression, even some religious leadership, for women. But women's conditions also deteriorated in several places during the postclassical period. The practice of footbinding spread in China and women in India and the Middle East became more secluded. Many societies used growing prosperity—the result of new trade—to place women in a more purely ornamental role, particularly women in the upper classes. The complexity of gender trends in several regions shows the unexpected impact of religion and commerce.

The world religions and trade both also supported the theme of growing contacts. The world religions all promoted wide interactions. Buddhist scholars traveled extensively in Asia, seeking enlightenment in different locations from India to Vietnam. Muhammad urged his followers to "seek knowledge, even unto China," and pilgrimages maintained wide connections through the expanding Islamic world. Christian pilgrims moved across borders within Europe, and some also sought to visit the Holy Land. The religions also, of course, set up new separations among religious zones—unlike trade, in this respect—but the spur to contact was substantial, as well.

A NEW GEOGRAPHY

The postclassical period was marked by another important theme: the number of civilizations and the geographical areas they covered, both expanded. The four initial centers of civilization continued to exert impact: Mediterranean values and institutions showed up both in Byzantium and in the Arab world, and the Indian and Chinese legacies also played a major role in these regions. Persian traditions persisted as well, though modified by Arab conquest and widespread conversion to Islam. But civilization, as a form of human organization, now spread to additional parts of Africa, to the eastern and western portions of northern Europe, to Japan, and to further sections of southeast Asia. Expansion occurred in the Americas as well, from centers in Central America and the Andes.

With these extensions, and the division of the Mediterranean world, the tally of civilizations changed as well, from the original four (east Asia, south Asia, the Middle East, and north Africa) to seven, with the addition of sub-Saharan Africa, eastern Europe, Western Europe, and the Americas. Different definitions—for example, were Japan and China part of the same civilization?—could further expand the list.

Against this complexity, however, it is important to remember that most of these civilizations, whether old or new, were affected by the major themes of religious and commercial change. These themes linked the various cultures, even if each society reacted to the influences in different ways. Furthermore, as we will see, many new regions began actively to imitate some of the older civilizational centers. Here was a vital result of the increase in contacts and connections, and a spur to further links as well. This final key process in the postclassical period provides a framework in which several otherwise disparate societies can be coherently analyzed and compared.

Chapters in this part deal first with the rise of Islam in the Middle East and north Africa, then with the two other societies most affected by Islam and by Muslim trade: south Asia and Africa. The two European regions, explored next, were less deeply touched by Islam, though trade links with Islamic cultures were vital. The later chapters cover another major, though more regional, set of interactions within the new world network, with the spread of east Asian culture, and the growth of Chinese trading power. Finally, chapters deal with the separate development of the Americas and with the impact of the Mongol period in providing additional links between east Asia and other parts of Eurasia. The last chapter also examines developments around 1450, in transition from the postclassical period to the next era in world history.

The postclassical period was a busy one in world history. Key changes during this time, especially in commerce and culture—particularly the cultural impacts of the world religions—organized much of the experience of many societies.

GLOBAL CONNECTIONS

Both of the dominant themes of the postclassical period generated new connections among different regions. The world religions are so called precisely because they spread over geographic and cultural barriers. Missionaries fanned out from the Middle East to India and Africa, from Constantinople to east-central Europe and Russia. Ultimately, of course, the religions created barriers of their own. While Muslims and Christians often coexisted peacefully, collaborating actively in places such as preconquest Spain, the two religions also experienced new hostilities. Buddhism was less confrontational, but it too created divisions with other belief systems.

Trade cut across boundaries even more thoroughly than the new religions did. Muslims, Buddhists, and Confucianists interacted via trade in China, southeast Asia, and the Middle East. Sometimes warily, Christians and Muslims traded as well.

Thanks to religion, but even more so to the new trade routes, it was during the postclassical period that the balance of world history shifted from separateness to convergence. Individual societies' local values and institutions still shaped many aspects of human experience, but increasingly, contacts among societies helped forge binding economic and cultural relationships.

Take, for example, the role of Islam. Islam and Arab politics and trade were the most dynamic set of forces during the early centuries of the postclassical period. Here was, in many ways, the first world power. The results touched literally every civilization in Africa, Europe, and Asia. Europe, including Russia, largely rejected Islam, but Europeans had to decide what to do about Islam's power and how to trade with Arab merchants despite rejecting the merchants' religion. Islamic invasions and commerce helped create a new and important Islamic minority in India. Conversions in central Asia were even more widespread. Chinese and Islamic armies fought in western China, where another Islamic minority was planted, which created a complicating factor for China that still affects Chinese policies today. Islam became a predominant force in the Middle East/north Africa and in parts of southeast Asia, a significant force in several other societies, and a challenging force for contact more widely still. Islam's role as cultural connector is clear.

The new importance of contact showed also in the decision by leaders in many societies to imitate features of their neighbors' cultures. Many leaders sent delegations into neighboring provinces to further this process. Japan decided to copy China. Russia, slightly less formally, learned from the Byzantine Empire. Sub-Saharan Africa culled characteristics from Islam and the Arab world. Western Europe imported ideas and technologies from several sources, including Islam. And direct borrowing was practiced among the older civilization centers, as when Arabs adopted Chinese technology and Indian mathematics. Connections counted. What had been gradual and informal processes of cultural diffusion now shifted gears with this deliberate interaction, becoming relatively rapid.

By around 1000, a world network was being created that drew in societies from Africa to Russia, England to Japan. To be sure, the key interactions still occurred in stages. For instance, although England and Japan were involved in the network, they had neither mutual knowledge nor mutual contact. Trade between distant societies occurred through intermediaries, particularly Arab and other merchants in the Indian Ocean, and the English and Japanese focused on relations with neighbors such as France and China, respectively, rather than on the larger exchange routes or each other.

It is revealing, however, that when one framework for interregional contact faltered, another sprang up in its stead. By the 13th century, Arab political power was declining, Arab merchants faced increasing challenges, and the organization of the east-west trade routes became less clear-cut. But it was also in the 13th century that the Mongol conquests in central Asia created an alternative network. Interlocking Mongol empires, or *khanates*, developed from China to east-central Europe, directly affecting trade in the Middle East, southeast Asia, Europe, and Japan. The organization of this huge territory, combined with the Mongol's tolerance of outsiders, allowed unprecedented travel and exchange among various parts of Asia and with Europe, using both overland and Indian Ocean routes.

When the Mongol structure began to collapse by the later 14th century, another alternative briefly surfaced to spearhead international trade: a new pattern of Chinese sea routes emerged during the first half of the 15th century. Clearly, by the latter part of the postclassical period, the advantages of wide trade and contact had become so obvious that the world network no longer depended on a single set of trade routes. When one pattern of routes faltered, another soon took its place—and this proved true again, after 1450, when Chinese policy changed in favor of more domestic focus.

The acceleration of contacts among disparate cultures was the most significant feature of the postclassical period, but despite this fact, the contact was not yet global. Several major societies operated in effective isolation outside the world network. The American civilizations, particularly, proved creative in generating complex economies and elaborate political structures; they had no need to participate in the network to achieve impressive results. But isolation inevitably creates vulnerability, and this too became visible soon after 1450—providing another illustration, though a negative one, of how important contacts had become to the rest of the world.

The Rise of Islam: Civilization in the Middle East

We begin with what became the center of the postclassical world: the Islamic Middle East and north Africa. Military conquests and a new empire, the caliphate, were one key ingredient. More important were an explosion of trade activity and the new religion of Islam. "There is no God but Allah, and Muhammad is his prophet." This prophet, an Arab born in the city of Mecca, intended to perfect a religion that focused on the power of a single god more clearly than any other religion—and by many measures he succeeded. The new faith of Islam sought to place its believers under the tutelage of an all-powerful divinity. Common Islamic names still reflect this orientation; many names include the Arabic word *Abd*, meaning *slave*, to indicate subjugation to God. The religion's name, Islam, means "submission to the will of God." Islam quickly became the fastest-growing religion in the world, maintaining this pace throughout the postclassical period.

Islam was born among the Arab people and served to carry their influence over much of the Middle East. This Semitic people had long existed on the southern fringes of Middle Eastern civilization, from their center in and around the Arabian desert. They had considerable experience in trade because of their proximity to the main routes between the Mediterranean and the wealth of India. They had undertaken agriculture, although some (called *bedouins*) remained nomadic herders with a tribal organization under their warrior chiefs, or *shaykhs*. The Arabs had developed writing and a literature. They had also produced great works of art. Their religion was polytheistic, with priests organizing prayers and sacrifices to the various gods.

The rise of Islam and the Arabs supported major changes in Middle Eastern civilization from the 6th century on. A vital new religion spread over this region and beyond, although minorities of Christians and Jews remained. While Islam ultimately pushed beyond the Arabs, it initially served as a vehicle for Arab assertion against states such as Persia and Christian Byzantium that had long dominated the region. Arabs brought a new language as well, although again, pockets of other languages persisted. However, there was important continuity. Muhammad, Islam's founder, viewed himself as a prophet who spoke in God's voice. He deliberately built on other religions in the Middle East, notably Judaism and Christianity. Furthermore, older traditions survived in other respects. Middle Eastern culture, although altered by Islam, retained some of the traditions of Hellenistic philosophy and science. Arab merchants extended Middle Eastern commercial patterns, but they built on the trading practices that had already made the Middle East a vital commercial link between the Mediterranean and Asia. The Middle East, in sum, displayed new powers with the rise of Islam and the Arabs, but it relied heavily on the earlier achievements of civilization in the region.

KEY QUESTIONS   *Comparing Islam with the other world religions is a vital starting point: what was distinctive about Islam? Keeping religion in perspective is another challenge: what developments in Middle Eastern civilization during the postclassical period are not primarily explained by Islam? Finally, why did the vigor of Arab society begin to lag somewhat by the 13th century?*

THE ADVENT OF ISLAM

The Arabs burst into larger Middle Eastern history started with the life of Muhammad, who around 570 C.E. was born of poor parents in Mecca, a trading city that already had some religious significance for the Arabs. First a camel driver, then a businessman happily married to a wealthy woman, Muhammad increasingly turned his thoughts to religious subjects. He experienced a conversion that brought him a sense of immediate understanding of Allah. He was fascinated by the Christian and Jewish faiths, both of which had many followers in Mecca, but he sought a purer statement of God's divinity—one uncluttered, for example, by complex doctrines such as the Christian Trinity—and a statement that was uniquely Arab. Writing what he believed were God's words, he argued that Allah, previously a rather vague Arab divinity, was the one true God and that Jewish and Christian leaders had merely been earlier prophets of Allah's truth. In Muhammad's view, the Jewish Old Testament and the work of Jesus, seen as a preacher but not as divine, provided a basis for the true religion. A series of ecstatic revelations convinced Muhammad that he had been called upon to organize this religion and to persuade others. He began attracting converts, whom he called *Muslims* ("surrendered to God").

Chased from Mecca by authorities who feared that he was organizing insurrection against them, Muhammad fled in 622 to Medina, whose citizens looked to him for religious and political leadership. His flight to Medina, called the *Hejira*, is regarded as the year 1 in the Islamic calendar. In Medina, Muhammad built a mosque for Muslim worship, while also attempting to join Muslims, Christians, and Jews in a single community. This early example of Muslim tolerance for peoples sharing religious traditions also brought frustrations at incomplete conversions to Islam. Muhammad also led Medina's government in a war with Mecca. Medina won, and many Arab tribesmen began to then negotiate peace with Muhammad. In one such negotiation, Mecca yielded to Islam but retained its status as the chief holy place. Muhammad, who had first ordered his followers to pray in the direction of Jerusalem, now told the supplicants to face toward Mecca. His decision was eased by the fact that most Jews, whom he had hoped to convert, rejected the new faith.

Muhammad died in 632. The revelations he received from Allah, via the intermediary of the archangel Gabriel, formed the Muslim holy book, called the *Qur'an* (or Koran). To loyal

WORLD PROFILES

MUHAMMAD
(570–632 C.E.)

Muhammad is a fascinating historical figure. He was born into a poor family but later served as camel driver to a wealthy widow, whom he eventually married. No official portrait exists, but he was described as a handsome man with piercing black eyes and a full beard. Not an active businessman, Muhammad spent 15 years happily married and, in the eyes of local merchants, was regarded as somewhat indolent. Despite a lack of formal learning, he contemplated religious matters, experiencing a conversion that brought him an immediate understanding of Allah, a rather shadowy divinity in Arab tradition, as sole God. Future visions impelled Muhammad to convert others to his faith. These efforts culminated in the conversion of most of the Arabian peninsula by his death in 632. Muhammad and the Qur'an continued to be central reference points in Islam in life and law. Today, Muhammad is the most common male name in the world.

Islam's disapproval of representational art limited attempts to depict Muhammad even in an idealized fashion. But this miniature, in the Persian artistic tradition, shows the prophet building a mosque in Medina with his disciples.

Muslims from this time on, the Qur'an has stood as the direct word of God, brooking no contradiction. It is God's "full and complete" statement of a perfect religion, including the "pillars of faith," or basic religious obligations. These provided further guidance for a proper life. After his death, Muhammad's disciples also began to

assemble the Hadith, based on multiple recollections of the prophet's sayings and other rules and regulations for the Islamic community. These provided further guidance for an upright life.

Muhammad's death thus did not disrupt his religious message. As one of his disciples said, "Whoso worshippeth Muhammad, let him know that Muhammad is dead. But whoso worshippeth God, let him know that God liveth and dieth not." However, the new religion, and the political organization Muhammad had formed in Medina, needed new leadership. One of Muhammad's closest followers, Abu Bakr, was selected as *caliph*, or successor. Abu Bakr restructured his regional state and what was still a regional religion into a war machine, using small but brilliantly led armies to vanquish a series of rebellions against the rule of the Muslim states. The Arab people became firmly converted as a result. A rift developed, however, during the conversion process. A minority group, the Shiites, favored a direct descendant of Muhammad over Abu Bakr, whose followers formed the majority of Sunni tradition. Shiite Muslims generally contended that they followed Muhammad's teachings more closely than their Sunni rivals. The real split between Sunni and Shiites remained important in many parts of the Middle East, though it did not affect the spread of Islam to other regions, which occurred under Sunni auspices.

Even with this important split, conversion seemed to galvanize the Arabs into several generations of conquest. Religion and a desire for material gain, through conquest, made for a powerful mixture. Muhammad had encouraged military effort in the name of Islam, claiming that anyone killed in a *jihad*, or holy war in defense of the faith, automatically attained an afterlife in heaven. Most historians believe that the economic desire of a poor people to gain access to the wealth of their neighbors provided a more important motive. Indeed, for most Muslims, the concept of Jihad came to emphasize an internal struggle for religious purity. The Arab armies were not particularly large, nor did they benefit from advanced weaponry. They were ably led, however, by the generals who served under Abu Bakr and several subsequent caliphs. And they profited from the weakness of their neighbors, who had been ineffectually ruled from Constantinople since the fall of Rome. Egypt and north Africa lacked strong governments. To the north, the Byzantine Empire and the Persians had exhausted each other by repeated wars. As a result, there was territory ripe for the plucking.

PATTERNS OF ISLAMIC HISTORY

During the decades following Muhammad's death and the creation of a government by his successors, called the *caliphate*, swift expansion continued. The speed and extent of Arab victories rivaled the earlier sweep of Alexander the Great. Islamic forces first turned northward to the heart of the Middle East. In 635, they defeated a larger Byzantine army and conquered Syria and Palestine. The Muslims also defeated the Persians after a three-day battle during which Arab poets chanted war songs and pious Muslims recited the Qur'an. This victory pushed the borders of the Islamic caliphate north to the Caucasus mountains and east to the frontiers of India. The Arabs also turned west, attacking Egypt and establishing a new capital on the Nile. Then, later in the 7th century, the Arabs invaded the rest of north Africa, conquering or assimilating the native Berber peoples. Berber opposition, at first fierce, eased as the people converted to Islam and gradually accepted the Arab language. Finally, aided by Berber troops, the Muslims invaded Spain in 711, defeating a weak Germanic kingdom there.

Only beyond the Pyrenees were the Muslims stopped—Frankish leader Charles Martel defeated their forces in 732—although it was the strain on Muslim troops and supplies, not Frankish power, that turned the tide. Most of Europe thus remained outside the Islamic orbit, although Spain and parts of southern Italy were Muslim-ruled for several centuries. The Muslims also failed to conquer Byzantium and began to encounter new resistance in northwestern India. These various setbacks ended the period of Arab conquest by the second quarter of the 8th century.

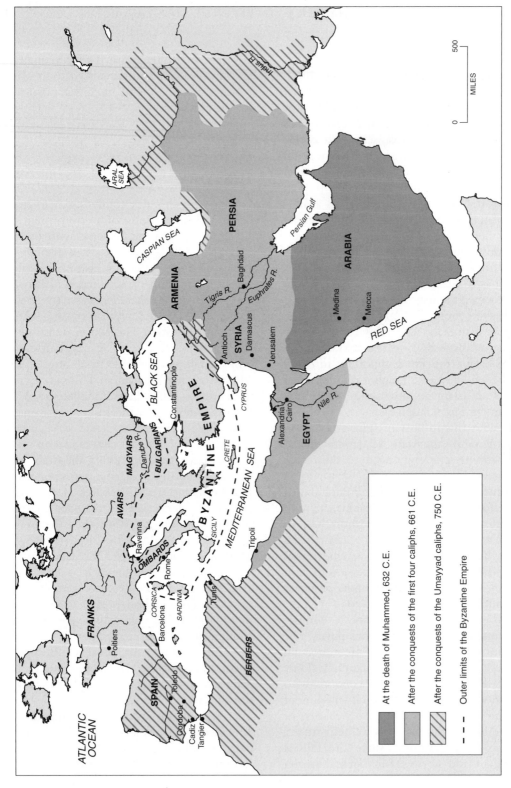

The Expansion of Islam

Nevertheless, even as it settled into a period of consolidation after the conquests, the Islamic caliphate ruled a larger territory and more people than the Romans had. The orders of the caliph were obeyed from Spain to the western borders of India and China. Organizing this huge area was no small matter. The second caliph, Umar, who spearheaded early Arab conquests, began the process of forming a larger government apparatus.

One source of control was the leadership of the Arab military. As leaders fanned out in conquest, they acquired considerable wealth and became something of a local ruling class. Islamic belief, holding that all land belonged to Allah, justified their seizure of property, but in fact most Arabs were content to leave the land in the hands of the original owners, collecting a tax instead. This tax became the main financial support for not only the new Arab ruling class, but also the government of the caliphate.

The Islamic conquerors were also tolerant of other religions. They believed that Judaism and Christianity were kindred faiths, just not aware or accepting of the complete truth. This policy of tolerance facilitated Islamic rule, resembling earlier Roman policies. However, Islam did win many new converts because of the purity of its doctrine and admiration for Arab success in conquest. Most converts, such as the north African Berbers, learned Arabic, for Islamic leaders were reluctant to see the Qur'an translated into other languages. Thus, not only a process of conversion to Islam but also the development of a larger common culture began throughout much of the Middle East and north Africa. This, too, consolidated Arab rule.

The actual government of the caliphate was not strikingly original. Under Umar, the caliph claimed great authority, down to the amount of pension each soldier was to receive. However, the assertions of authority were not backed up with solid power. Many caliphs were assassinated; others proved to lack political talents. A recurrent difficulty was the lack of agreement, in Arab custom, over procedures for succession to the throne after a ruler died. Umar established an election process, but it was soon ignored in favor of heredity. Throughout the history of Middle Eastern civilization in the postclassical period, assassinations and plots frequently disrupted political tranquility.

One dynasty did establish power over the caliphate for about a century (661–750). This dynasty, under the Umayyad family, transferred the caliph's government to Damascus, Syria, where greater prosperity allowed a more luxurious court. But another family, the Abbasids, seized power in 750, although a few regions including Spain remained in Umayyad hands. The Abbasid dynasty moved the capital still farther east, to Baghdad. It also began the use of professional soldiers and slaves for troops, a sign that the military zeal of the Arabs was beginning to falter. This policy, like that of Rome before it, was risky in the long run. The use of mercenary troops from a central Asian people called the *Turks* proved particularly questionable, as Turkish influence in the Middle East gradually began to increase.

But Abbasid power remained solid for several centuries, despite some important rebellions and even though the dynasty was often severely troubled by plots and counterplots. The Abbasids continued the process of broadening Islam's base in the Middle East beyond the Arab peoples alone. Abbasid rulers held that all Muslims, Arabs or not, were equal in the sight of God and roughly equal in law as well. Further, any Muslim who spoke Arabic was regarded as Arab—a move that solidified the hold of the Arab language over most of the Middle East and north Africa. Only in Persia did conversion to Islam not bring acceptance of Arabic; Persia, now Iran, remains one of the only non–Arab-speaking parts of the region even today.

The Abbasids not only extended Islam and the Arab language as unifying elements in their vast empire, but they also served as sponsors of art and literature. The greatest flowering of

Islamic creativity took place under their auspices, with Baghdad as its center.

Politically, however, Abbasid rule began to decline before the year 1000, although the dynasty officially lasted until 1258. A number of internal revolts rocked the royal family. The hold of mercenary troops and Turkish advisors became increasingly important. As more non-Arab people converted to Islam, the special tax revenues levied on nonbelievers declined—an ironic effect of Muslim success. Several key provinces broke away, including Egypt and Spain. European troops reconquered southern Italy (in 1061) and began to push back the Muslim rulers of Spain. The weakness of the Abbasid government allowed Christian crusaders in the 11th and 12th centuries to conquer parts of the Holy Land, establishing the short-lived kingdom of Jerusalem. More ominous still, Turkish nomads, already converted to Islam, began to move in from central Asia, causing Abbasid power to erode further.

The long and painful decline of the Abbasids did not, initially, signal a decline in the larger Islamic-Arab culture. Creative works in art, literature, and theology survived into the 13th century. Gradually, however, political difficulties had a severe impact. Islam still reigned. Indeed, political chaos served to extend its hold on the common people, particularly those in the countryside, some of whom had been only superficially touched by the new religion previously. But religious devotion increasingly monopolized Arab culture, to the detriment of other outlets. After 1200, a new movement, Sufism, gained growing influence; it expanded Islam's spiritual power while narrowing other interests in the name of piety. The Sufi leaders were holy men who experienced mystical visions of God. They gathered followers and inspired them by their holiness, using highly emotional rituals, including elaborate dances. The spread of the Sufi movement signaled important changes in Middle Eastern civilization, especially in Arab culture, even as it deepened the hold of Islam in the countryside and inspired missionary movements in other parts of the world.

The decline of the Abbasids did not signify a permanent disruption of the Middle East. A few areas were lost. The last Muslims were driven from Spain in 1492, but Christianity had won back most of this country beforehand. The northwestern tip of North Africa, the kingdom of Morocco, although firmly Islamic, became independent. But the rise of Turkish military power soon brought new and in some ways more effective government to most of the Islamic Middle East. What the Abbasid decline did result in, however, was a prolonged political eclipse of the Arab world. The caliphate was toppled by a brutal invasion of Mongol troops in 1258. From that point until after World War II, most Arabs were governed by others. Initially, the rulers were Turks and Muslims, but even they looked down on their Arab subjects because of their political and military fall from power.

The story of Arab civilization is thus one of swift rise and expansion ultimately followed by an incomplete decline. Despite these sudden changes, the civilization that was partially redefined by the Islamic religion and Arab leaders produced durable institutions and values in the Middle East. Other regions were affected as well. By 1300, Islam was spreading to parts of Africa south of the Sahara, to India, and to southeast Asia. Here, the agents of diffusion were not military conquerors, but traders who brought religion and a sophisticated lifestyle along with their wares and fervent missionaries, including those inspired by the new Sufi movement. Military conquest played little role in Islam's surge beyond the borders of the Middle East. But Islam's entry into other civilizations, while creating some similarities to Middle Eastern society, is, in part, a separate story to be taken up in later chapters. Before 1300, the greatest impact of Islam lay in reshaping Middle Eastern civilization itself.

ISLAMIC POLITICAL INSTITUTIONS

Muhammad and his immediate followers generated significant political ideals. In their view, shaped in part by Muhammad's own experience in running the city of Medina, a perfect state should be governed by a religious leader—there was no differentiation between secular aims and religious goals. The state and its leader should put the faith first and serve as agents of Allah.

Islam was born connected to the state, in contrast to Christianity, and the difference mattered. Political ideals were an important and durable vision in the new Middle Eastern civilization. Political movements even during the 20th century returned to the idea that state and religion are one. In practice, however, the ideal did not usually prove feasible. Umayyad and Abbasid rulers did not always keep the interest of the faith foremost, particularly as their taste for luxury and for cultural patronage increased. But Islam did not formulate clear principles to guide a state that fell short of the ideal. Should Muslims obey any government, regardless of quality? Muhammad had declared this for the sake of emphasizing attention to religion. Or should Muslims try to work toward a government more attuned to Islamic ideals? These are questions still debated in Islam.

Officially, of course, the caliphs continued a tradition of combining political rule with the enforcement of religious law. Many Abbasid caliphs were indeed personally pious, which aided their popularity. Cultural achievements occurred in a variety of fields, from art to leisure. However, Abbasid governments, in fact, depended heavily on the whims of an individual ruler. A number of caliphs were cruel and arbitrary, often ordering the execution of not only potential rivals for the throne but also chief ministers. A leading Abbasid caliph, the pious

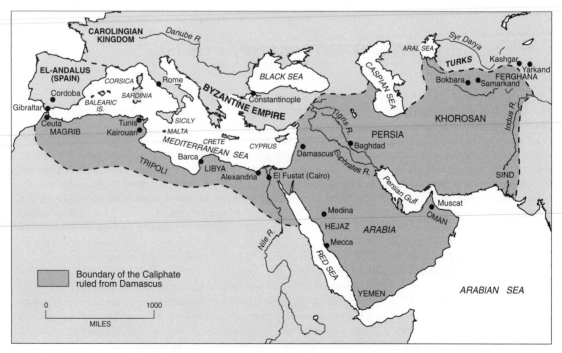

The Caliphate at Its Greatest Extent, About 750 C.E.

Harun al-Rashid, provided an important period of peace and stability for much of the Middle East, but a study of his regime also reveals the use of arbitrary power. He is reported to have ordered the execution of his favorite minister on sudden impulse. Then, overcome with remorse, he put the executioner to death because he could not bear to look on the man who had slain his favorite. Many caliphs impressed their subjects as much with their luxury—traveling in public surrounded by an escort of parasol carriers, flag bearers, and musicians—as by their religious fervor or political acumen. Harun al-Rashid won a great reputation by frequent acts of generosity, including his support to writers. An Arab admirer wrote: "No Caliph had been so profusely liberal to poets, lawyers, and divines, though as the years advanced he wept over his extravagance among his other sins."

The caliphate could provide effective rule. Harun was an able soldier, conquering rebellions and maintaining the upper hand in warfare with the Byzantine Empire. The absence of a strong titled aristocracy, with claims on political power, facilitated central administration. However, the Abbasid caliphs did suffer for their reliance on slaves and foreigners as chief bureaucrats. Many bureaucratic positions became virtually hereditary, unless their occupants were unseated by assassination. Thus, it was small wonder that the Abbasid dynasty lost effective control of its own government and that important new groups, particularly the Turks, established regional administrations of their own.

In fact, the caliphate, especially under the later Abbasids, became increasingly remote, not even very actively commanding its provincial bureaucracy. Local administrators, although appointed by

HISTORY DEBATE

POLITICAL IMPLICATIONS OF ISLAM

Historians find various messages in the political ideals and early experience of Islam. There is no question that the ideals differed from those in Christian western Europe, where a separate church institution reduced the theoretical importance of the state. In asking for a state that pursued religious goals first and foremost, Islam set a high standard. The real debate involves what Islam should encourage if the standard is not met. Muhammad specifically urged obedience to the state no matter what, for the goals of a religious person transcended political problems. Some historians have argued that this stance, plus the development of a separate system of religious law and increasing popular piety, produced a political passiveness among Muslims. This, it is argued, accounts for the frequent authoritarian governments in the Middle East, the common use of non-Muslims in the bureaucracy, and (some contend, by extension) the difficulties for modern democracy to take root. However, other leading historians try to show that Islam suggested two paths, not one. Passivity might be replaced by an eager desire to make the state better, to bring it closer to the religious ideal—and this, in a modern context, could even generate support for the goal of democratic political participation, so that the true Muslim voice can be heard.

Comparison with Christianity usefully supplements the debate, for despite their frequent mutual hostility, Christianity and Islam shared a host of features. Christianity, like Islam, might be involved in political movements against a state regarded as evil. But Christianity also urged obedience, and the Catholic church established a model of authority, not participation. Zealous Christians could ignore political life. Thus, the complexity of Islam is not unique, and attempts to use the religion to explain current political practices may be risky or overly simplistic. All three world religions generated complex political impulses, and Islam needs to be assessed within this framework.

the central court, had substantial autonomy, so long as they returned satisfactory tax revenues to the caliph in Baghdad. Reliance on mercenary troops and slave soldiers reduced the need to recruit directly from the Arab population. The caliph's growing use of Turkish, Persian, and even Christian advisors, although designed to limit the power of upper-class Arabs, underscored the remoteness of the government from most people. To be sure, all governments in agricultural societies, even in China, were remote by modern standards: they had little contact with most peoples' day-to-day lives. But the caliphate, and the lack of political ideals in Islam that helped legitimize an "imperfect" or not simply religious state, intensified this remoteness. The combination hastened Abbasid decline after several centuries of splendor.

However, the limitations of the government established by the caliphate were not the whole story of Islamic politics. Islamic political ideals were far more closely realized in the religiously run legal system that spread throughout the Middle East. Islam did not establish an elaborate, centralized organization outside the state. But local religious leaders, schooled in Islamic law, did more than lead prayers. Building on the Qur'an and the Hadith, Islamic leaders gradually developed an elaborate body of law known as the *Sharia*, or straight path. This law reflected a mixture of Qur'anic principles with interpretations offered in the Hadith. Sharia law regulated many aspects of social behavior, including family relations, economic contacts, and outright crimes. It was interpreted and extended by groups of Islamic scholars and religious leaders known as the *ulema*. The ulema, which initially arose spontaneously and was then encouraged by the caliphate, consisted of local experts in Islamic law and doctrine—and Islam was a highly legalistic religion, generating a wide array of rules of conduct. The ulema were knowledgeable about the Qur'an and skilled in interpreting the deeds of the prophet Muhammad and other precedents so they might be able to determine God's will in

any matter of conduct. The result, after generations of expertise following Muhammad's death, was an elaborate system of rules and laws, built by the learned men of Islam and regarded as sacred and unchangeable. This was no generalized code of behavior to be captured in a few, powerful commandments, but a very detailed set of laws.

By the time of the Abbasids, Islamic experts existed in every town and marketplace, passing judgment on all matters of conscience brought before them. A good deal of the work of government and law was handled by village authorities—called *imams*—and the regional ulema. And here, surely, is a partial reflection of Muhammad's belief that state and faith were one and the same—there was no need for two court systems, for the ulema alone could carry out God's will for the community by enforcing the Sharia.

Religious minorities, particularly Jews and Christians, were not covered by the Sharia. They were often shown considerable tolerance and allowed to run their own community affairs. This was the final ingredient in the political system developed by the Arab dynasties, and one that helps explain their success in maintaining authority over a wide and diverse region amid the fluctuations of the caliphate.

ISLAM AND MIDDLE EASTERN CULTURE

Not surprisingly, the Islamic religion formed the core of the new culture of Middle Eastern civilization, but although the Arabic word for religion means "way of life," it was not the only ingredient during several centuries of remarkable artistic creativity. It was Islam, however, that survived most successfully among the various elements of the new Middle Eastern civilization at its height. Islam also helped organize various other cultural features or movements, particularly in the visual arts.

Dome of the Rock. Built by Muhammad's second successor, Caliph Omar, on the site of a Jewish temple torn down by the Romans, this was the first Islamic building constructed in Jerusalem after the conquest of Palestine. Note the geometrical design, which follows Muslim rules on art.

As in politics, the intellectual impact of the Islamic religion was an emphasis on Allah's great power and the pervasive legalism. The power of Allah and the clarity of Islam as a perfect religion rested on five "pillars of Islam," as stipulated in the Qur'an. Observance of these five basic obligations was central to religious life, for Islam offered no special avenues to divine grace or sacraments: obedience was central. The first pillar was faith itself; there was no God but Allah, and Muhammad was his final prophet. The second pillar required all Muslims to pray at five different times of the day, facing in the direction of Mecca. The prayers did not have to occur in a mosque, except for the midday prayer on Friday, the holy day. Callers from the mosque's tower, or minaret, issued the five daily calls to prayer, with the faithful observing wherever they might be. The third pillar was the fast of Ramadan, the month in

which God revealed himself to Muhammad. In this month, Muslims were not supposed to eat or drink during daylight hours. The fourth pillar involved charity. Islam held that all faithful Muslims were brothers, but they were not equally wealthy. It was therefore essential that charity be extended to the Muslim poor. Finally, as the fifth pillar, the faithful were required if possible to make at least one pilgrimage to the holy city of Mecca during a lifetime—the *hadj*. The pilgrimage reminded all Muslims of their essential unity, and it also involved a number of rituals in Mecca itself. The five pillars of Islam spelled out the central observances of a good Muslim life. They formed a bridge between lowly humans and the all-powerful Allah, otherwise awe-inspiring in his omnipotence. Collectively, the pillars reinforced a sense of shared community obligation for Muslims.

This photograph shows pilgrims during the holy night of Ramadan at the Kabaa in Mecca in Saudi Arabia.

However, the emphasis on legalistic observance extended beyond the five pillars to a host of other regulations that were not required for a holy life but were enjoined for proper social relations and even personal hygiene. Muhammad and other Islamic leaders were interested in disciplining certain traditional habits of the Arabs. Thus, the religion forbade alcoholic drink, for Arabs had earlier acquired a reputation for excess in this regard. Several rules related directly to health; prohibitions against eating pork, for example, followed from the diseased state of hogs in the Middle East. Sexual behavior was also strictly regulated; women, particularly, were enjoined to remain pure before marriage and faithful to their husbands within marriage. But while Islam displayed much sensual restraint, it was more open than Christianity about the importance of sexual pleasure in marriage. The tendency to see in Islam an elaborate legal code, beyond the five pillars, was reinforced by Islamic support for harsh earthly punishments for misbehavior, although careful rules of evidence and a belief in mercy set important limits. Thus, the Qur'an on theft:

> Male or female, cut off his or her hands: a punishment by way of example, from God, for their crime; and God is Exalted in Power. But if the thief repents after his crime, and amends his conduct, God turneth to him in forgiveness; for God is Oft-forgiving. Most Merciful.

On a larger scale, belief in a day of judgment—"when the World on High is unveiled; when the Blazing Fire is kindled to fierce heat; and when the Garden is brought near;—Then shall each soul know what it has put forward"—and belief in life after death were central to Islamic teaching. The Muslim heaven featured boundless delight of mind, body, and soul. In contrast, the Muslim hell was full of the darkest pain and torture, surpassing most Christians' visions of Satan's torments.

Islam was not a constant, although its basic principles persisted. As the Sufi movement gained ground, from 1200 on, mystical leaders, called dervishes, played a growing role in inspiring the faithful. Their activities bore some resemblance to those of monks in Christianity, but there was no general discipline of the Benedictine sort. Spiritual and emotional example gave new force to Islam. It also helped inspire missionary activity.

The religious fervor Islam could generate, plus the local quality of much of the religious organization, guaranteed religious division. The Sunni–Shiite split continues from the 7th century, with the Shiite Muslims revering the memory of Muhammad's son-in-law, Ali, and lamenting the martyrdom of his son Huseyn. They also believed that they were truer to Islamic law than the majority group, called the *Sunni*. Shiites continued to expect additional prophecies. And they formed a clearer religious structure than the majority group, identifying religious leaders, such as the ayatollahs in Persia, who could direct the faithful and select and instruct local religious officials. The Shiite

minority gained particular strength in the north, in the present-day countries of Iran and Iraq, but elements of Shiite culture may be found in many parts of the region. Their special religious fervor remains an important factor in Middle Eastern life in the early 21st century. The Sunni–Shiite split frequently encouraged political disunity in the Middle East, including periodic assassinations and other acts of violence. This penchant, too, recurred in modern times, with each side viewing the other as heretical.

Islamic leaders often delighted in discussing the meaning of a virtuous life. Arab religious thinkers also detailed their ideas about heaven, coming up with a seven-stage scheme often represented in art. However, here were fewer discussions about the nature of God or problems of free will than in Christianity. Islamic theology was mainly confined to the search for truths in the Qur'an and to the study of the traditions of Muhammad and his early followers. Simply keeping track of the various traditions and laws of the Sharia was no easy task. By the time of the Abbasid dynasty, Muslim scholars found it necessary to collect the traditions that had developed. One scholar spent 16 years touring the Middle East, gathering 600,000 customs and beliefs, which he reduced to 7275 regarded as authentic religious truths. This code helped promote the Islamic emphasis on charity and the importance of God's rules for humankind, one of the important attractions of Islamic faith. But the task of interpreting the traditions of Islam remained a challenging assignment. Strict Muslims believed that no other intellectual enterprise was valid, for faith alone was all that Allah required.

Nevertheless, a wider philosophy persisted in Middle Eastern civilization, inspired in part by knowledge of older Greek and Persian learning still available in the region. By the 9th century, a host of scholars were busy translating Greek and Persian sources into Arabic. Huge libraries were erected in cities such as Baghdad. This bustling cultural life was aided by the introduction of paper from China, which made book production more extensive and cheaper.

Arab calligraphy: a leaf from the Qur'an, dating from the 8th or 9th century, illustrates the Kufic form of Arabic calligraphy.

Greek tradition, of course, contradicted the strictest Islamic belief system, for it held that people could understand a great deal through the use of reason. Arab philosophers grappled with this schism for several centuries, and many urged a rationalistic approach without breaking with Islam. A similar disparity arose later in the Christian West, in part because of the Arab precedent. By the 1100s, many Arab philosophers were trying to build a rationalistic framework for all knowledge, mixing religious truth, science, mathematics, and rational speculation. This work both preserved and extended the Hellenistic heritage.

As in philosophy, the fine arts were strongly influenced by Islamic rules—but not entirely constrained by them. Muhammad, eager to develop the purest possible focus on Allah, forbade idols, and later the ulema extended prohibitions against all representation of human or animal forms. The goal was to purge Muslims of any impulse to worship lesser images. As a result, most Islamic art centered on the nonrepresentational. Only a few artists, particularly those in Persia, continued to create sculpture or painting involving human or animal figures. Muslim artists instead placed distinctive geometric designs and the flowing patterns of Arab script on pottery, metalware, textiles, and leather and on buildings' tile and stucco. Mosques, which are the Muslim houses of prayer, and palaces were especially covered with glazed tile and stucco relief in intricate designs. This powerful artistic style spread beyond the Middle East to influence art in Spain and Portugal, even after the expulsion of the Muslims, and in India. In the Middle East itself, concern for rich decorative images on buildings and in the form of a host of artifacts remained central to the arts.

Middle Eastern architects learned much from the earlier classical styles of the Mediterranean. Palaces often reflected a Roman influence, with an open courtyard and fountain surrounded by

WORLD PROFILES

OMAR KHAYYAM
(C. 11TH–12TH CENTURY)

The vitality of Islamic intellectual life shows in the career of the Persian Omar Khayyam, the type of person who in Western culture might be known as a Renaissance man. Omar's early life is obscure; his last name means *tentmaker*, which may suggest his father's occupation. He obtained an extensive education and came to the attention of the Turkish sultan then ruling the region (despite the continuance of the Abbasid caliphate). The sultan sponsored his scientific work. Omar became a royal astronomer and helped reform the Islamic calendar. His books on algebra were particularly notable, as he classified equations of the first degree. He is best known in the world at large for his poems, which were collected in *The Rubaiyat* and translated into English during the 19th century. These quatrains feature complex, multiple rhymes in the first, second, and fourth lines. Their subject matter emphasized the pleasures of this life. Omar was at times humble toward Allah, at other times defiant; he was also very critical of Islamic extremists, such as the Sufis, who nonetheless adapted his work. The main theme of *The Rubaiyat* was the beauty of earthly existence; God created humans as he is, so he will not punish; a person should enjoy the only life we can be sure of. How does Omar Khayyam fit the main themes of Middle Eastern culture during the postclassical period?

This representation of Omar Khayyam is based on an English painting by H. M. Burton. It reflects a later Western interpretation of the great poet and scientist and his setting. Omar Khayyam is shown working out a calendar, surrounded by samples of his philosophic aphorisms and astronomical work.

separate rooms. For mosques, Muslim architects created a distinctive kind of tower, the minaret, from which the faithful were called to prayer at the appointed hours. Most mosques were domed buildings, preceded by a hall of columns with distinctive, horseshoe-shaped arches. These innovations in arches and towers helped inspire the Gothic style that later emerged in western Europe. Both Muslims and Christians sought structures that directed the eye toward heaven.

Music also received considerable attention. Muhammad and his followers frowned on the frivolity of music, which was not part of Islamic prayer services. However, most people in the Middle East did not take this particular prohibition too seriously. As one writer put it, "Wine is as the body, music as the soul, and joy is their offspring." Musicians, and particularly singers, gained in respect. The singer Tways, who lived from 632 to 710, was the originator of the high-pitched, nasal singing style popular in the Arab world. He introduced new rhythms and was the first to sing with accompaniment—a tambourine. Other instruments commonly used were the lute and guitar. Arab rhythm and instrumentation influenced Spanish musical styles, which in turn influenced the styles later developed in Latin America.

Middle Eastern literature emphasized poetry above all. Most cultivated Arabs and Persians have rated poetry as the highest achievement of their civilization after Islam itself. Arab poetry predated Muhammad. But, as the Arabs came into contact with other peoples in the Middle East, their literary efforts became more polished. Abbasid caliphs patronized scores of poets, and the knowledge of poetry and ability to express oneself in verse became the mark of a cultivated person—as in Confucian China.

Poets wrote on many themes, most of them nonreligious, as in Omar Khayyam's *The Rubaiyat*. A black ex-slave in Baghdad gained great popularity with poems that poked fun at the traditional Arab emphasis on heroism. Many Persian poets, writing in Arabic, used sensual themes, praising the joys of hunting and drinking, but also expressing some religious sentiments.

Overall, Arabic poetry showed a growing concern for polished manners and a life of refinement, characteristic of an aristocracy that was becoming more devoted to culture and the good life than to military prowess. The poetry also revealed an unusual interest in pure style, as poets strove for perfection in each individual line and, by Western literary standards, seemed more preoccupied with their stylistic devices than content. Frequent changes of subject, word associations, and images were the hallmarks of this poetry, which focused on both nature and human experience. Thus, one

poet praised the lion-mouthed fountain at an Arab palace in Grenada, Spain (a palace that still exists). His description served as a trigger for all sorts of word associations:

> And lions people this official wood
> encompass the pools with thunder
> and profuse over aureate-banded
> bodies their skulls gush glass . . . .
> Sun is tinder to the stirred
> colors, is light to long tongues,
> is a hand to unsheathe the lunging
> blades that shiver out in a splash.

However, Arab poetry could also be terse and humorous, as in this verse, "The Radish":

> The radish is a good
> And doubtless wholesome food,
> But proves, to vex the eater,
> A powerful repeater.
> This only fault I find:
> What should be left behind
> Comes issuing instead
> Right from the eater's head.

Science, including history and geography, provided the final outlet for the high culture of the Middle East. A scientific interest followed, of course, from the rationalistic concerns of the leading philosophers and from the Hellenistic heritage. Arabs found a practical application for it in the study of medicine, astronomy, and geography. Medicine could cure. Knowledge of the stars, it was believed, might help predict the future—hence, interest in astrology ran high. And geography served the direct needs of Arab trade. Abbasid caliphs supported considerable scientific study in all these areas, in addition to the translation of earlier Greek and Persian scholarship.

Arab astronomers made no major advances, in part because they relied heavily on the theories of the Hellenistic astronomer Ptolemy and his claim that the earth was the center of the universe. However, observatories checked the accuracy of various Greek measurements, and scientists acquired more precise knowledge of eclipses and the length of the solar year. Arab scientists, aware that the earth was a sphere, also calculated the planet's circumference. In medicine, a host of empirical observations were recorded. Doctors in Baghdad chose the location for the central hospital by carefully studying environmental conditions. Although in medical science, too, there were no new general theories, the idea of contagion was strongly suggested as a practical finding. As one doctor wrote: "The result of my long experience is that if a person comes into contact with a patient, he is immediately attacked by the disease with the same symptoms." In a similar pragmatic spirit, doctors described the symptoms of a variety of common diseases and the properties of hundreds of therapeutic drugs. Finally, some advances were made in the study of chemical elements, and Greek and Indian discoveries in chemistry and physics were assimilated within this body of knowledge. Without question, Arab science predominated in the world by 1200, with only Chinese scholarship a near rival.

SOLVING PROBLEMS

RELIGION AND TRADE

The relationship between the two major themes of the postclassical period was complex. The growth of trade posed a major problem for many religious leaders, far too much devotion to material gain could easily distract from piety and the goals of salvation or spiritual advancement. Many early Christian leaders worried about the distraction of wealth, and of course key monastic movements in Christianity and Buddhism advocated poverty. Well into the postclassical period Christian writers such as Thomas Aquinas urged attention to a just price—as opposed to seeking profits by taking advantage of scarcities—and argued against taking interest on loans (usury). Individual Christian merchants not uncommonly worried about the state of their souls. Some gave large gifts to charity or to religious art. Not a few abandoned trade in later life, retreating into a monastery to better assure their salvation. The tension was real, and different people sought to solve the problem in different ways.

In principle, the trade–religion connections were somewhat less problematic for Islam. Muhammad praised merchants. Islam provided clear paths for merchants to seek profit while also sincerely fulfilling religious duties. Giving to charity was a vital requirement, but regular prayer and the pilgrimage provided linkages as well. Still, Muslim thinkers did come to worry about excessive merchant zeal. The great north African historian and philosopher Ibn Khaldun, writing in the 14th century, argued that "flattery, and evasiveness, litigation and disputation" are "characteristic" of merchants: "And these qualities lead to a decrease and weakening in virtue . . . for acts inevitably affect the soul." Ibn Khaldun admitted that trade was essential, but Islamic law did try to set some limits to greed—for example, by banning usury in lending.

Solutions to the trade–religion problem were not only varied; they could change. By the later postclassical period, for example, as the European economy became more vigorous, many Christian leaders softened their stance about profit-making and even charging interest. And for many religions, headed in this period by Islam, advances in trade and religion went hand in hand. Venturesome merchants, sincerely pious, brought religion with them—for example, helping to establish Islam in regions in the eastern Indian Ocean. Missionaries could blaze trails that merchants would follow.

■**QUESTIONS:**   *What key problems might merchant life pose for religious values? What kinds of compromise solutions help explain why religion and commerce both spread widely during the postclassical period?*

Arab scholars also showed some interest in mathematics, taking over the Indian numbering system. Particular advances were made in algebra, which is an Arab-derived word. The text written by the greatest Arab mathematician, al-Khwarismi, was translated and used in European universities until the 16th century. It established new territory in algebraic multiplication and division and in equations of the second degree.

Because of their extensive travels, Arab merchants and missionaries produced more abundant geographical knowledge than the world had ever known—or was to know again until the age of European exploration began in the 15th century. In history, the north African Ibn Khaldun, writing in the 14th century and building on a long tradition of narrative accounts of the past, achieved an understanding of the dynamics of social behavior that has had few rivals before or since.

Overall, Arab scientists were not as adept at formulating general theories as they were at recording careful observation and preserving the learning of their own scholars and scholars of the past. Nonetheless, they contributed to a flourishing intellectual life, in which not only scholars but also aristocrats and other wealthy urbanites gained an extensive education that combined the Muslim faith with a healthy enjoyment of secular culture. In this spirit, an unusually large elite became literate and a series of major universities were founded, as in Egypt in the 10th century and in Baghdad in 1065. Schools and universities taught religion, poetry, philosophy, the sciences, and history—a fair sampling of the cultural knowledge Middle Eastern civilization had created.

ECONOMY AND SOCIETY IN THE MIDDLE EAST

A lively economy was a vital part of the new Middle Eastern civilization, and it built on earlier traditions of agriculture and trade. Economic activity served as a key element in the spread of Islam to Africa and southeast Asia. It also set the stage for the bustling cities, the educated elite, and the luxurious court life of the caliphate.

Agriculture, long established in this area, remained highly productive. The Abbasid caliphate drained swamps, extended systems of irrigation, and otherwise supported agricultural development. Wheat, barley, and rice were the main crops, whereas dates and olives constituted important secondary goods. A free peasant class did most of the farming, and under the early Abbasids the conditions of the peasants improved somewhat. Most peasants remained poor, however, and they owed heavy taxes to the state and local landlords. The Abbasid caliphate provided more equitable treatment by assessing a percentage of the crops produced, rather than a fixed fee, as taxes, so that peasants would not suffer unduly when harvests were bad.

The Islamic empire had substantial mineral holdings, including iron and precious metals. Some large private mining operations arose; one, in the 10th century, employed 10,000 miners. Manufacturing was extensive and, like agriculture, won encouragement from the state. Textile production, including carpets and other luxury items, gained ground steadily. Persian rugs became particularly famous. City centers were crowded with artisans who manufactured in and sold from their own homes. The bustle of a Middle Eastern marketplace, or bazaar, reflected the abundant production of craft goods and vigorous trade.

There were, however, few basic technological improvements in Middle Eastern agriculture or manufacturing. The Arabs did import papermaking from China. The manufacture of fine iron products, particularly of swords, made Damascus famous. But careful organization and vigorous activity, not innovation in techniques, served as the hallmarks for this economy.

Commerce, nevertheless, flourished, and a strong merchant spirit was a central feature of this renewed civilization. To be sure, governments often seemed to consider merchants mainly as subjects for taxation and did little to encourage transportation or trade. However, a large merchant class evolved, both for the local trade at bazaars and for international operations. Most overseas trade centered on luxury products, but some basic goods, such as timber from India and slaves from Africa and Europe, were also involved. Merchants brought silks, spices, and tin from India, China, and southeast Asia, for use at home and for sale to Europe and Africa. One source lists the goods brought from China: perfumes, silks, crockery, paper, ink, peacocks, swift horses, saddles, felt, cinnamon, and rhubarb; from the Byzantine Empire: gold and silver, drugs, slave girls, engineers, marble workers, locks, and trinkets; and from India: tigers, panthers, elephants, skins, rubies, sandalwood, ebony, and coconuts.

Islamic sailors were quite at home in all the Asian waters from the 8th century on, aided by good mapmaking. Improved sailing ships facilitated commerce also, particularly in the Indian Ocean; Arab dhows had both speed and considerable capacity. By sailing into the Black and Caspian seas, Muslims traded with Russians and Scandinavians. Thousands of Muslim coins have been found in Sweden, brought back from this trade; indeed, the first Swedish coins copied Muslim models. Active trade developed with Africa. Overland expeditions imported gold, salt, and slaves. Slave marches were brutal affairs, with many thousands perishing. Islamic ships also traded with ports farther down the east African coast. Trade with western Europe was less active, because the Europeans had few goods of interest to the more sophisticated Middle East. However, there was some exchange, often undertaken by Jewish entrepreneurs, through which the Middle East obtained cloth, furs, and slaves. Here, technology did play a role. Mapmaking and navigational instruments changed as well.

Far-flung trade led to improvements in banking. Some Baghdad banks had branch offices in other cities. It was thus possible, for example, to draw a check in Baghdad and cash it in Morocco.

Islamic culture gave merchants considerable esteem—more than in any other civilization at that time. The Islamic religion did not see profitmaking as a contradiction of spirituality

or honor, so long as active charity ensued. Muhammad, with merchant experience of his own, proclaimed merchants to be models of a virtuous life: "On the day of judgment, the honest, truthful Islamic merchant will take rank with the martyrs of the faith," and "Merchants are the couriers of the world and the trusted servants of God upon earth." One caliph supposedly said: "There is no place where I would be more gladly overtaken by death than in the marketplace, buying and selling for my family." Manuals were written to encourage good commercial and investment practices.

The commercial zeal of Islam, along with the religion itself, made the new Middle Eastern civilization the most significant force in the world for many centuries. Although India, southeast Asia, and east Africa were most closely affected, more remote parts of Europe and Africa also experienced the impact of this unusual dynamism. Economic life solidified important values in the Middle East and brought luxury and wealth to the upper classes. The attractiveness of the urban marketplaces, as evidenced in the vital role that trade came to play in city life, survives to the present day. Even more than artistic achievement, trade expressed a central quality of the Middle East.

Socially, Middle Eastern civilization displayed many of the features expected in a prosperous agricultural region. A landlord class flourished, as had long been the case in the Mediterranean world. Arab conquerors, some of them former merchants, assumed the landlord role in many areas. Urban artisans, as well as the merchants, were numerous and well organized. Although some peasants worked entirely for landlords, we have seen that, in the most prosperous centuries before the Abbasid decline, a significant free peasant class existed.

The social order was complicated by three factors. First, the mixture of racial groups and minority religions added to the region's diversity. Even among Muslims, tensions often surfaced between Arabs and non-Arabs. Second, Islam maintained a strong egalitarian theme. Muslims believed that all people were basically equal under God. Such a doctrine made some adherents uncomfortable with existing social inequality, and it spurred some lower-class elements to revolt in the name of religion itself. But Muhammad had not intended to preach social equality. His insistence on the importance of charity acknowledged, in fact, that there would always be the rich and the poor in this life. However, the spiritual equality that Muhammad avowed sometimes added bitterness and confusion to the society shaped by Islam.

The third complicating factor in the civilization of the Middle East was the substantial presence of slavery. Islamic civilization during this period depended more heavily on slave labor than did any of the other major civilizations except Central America. In India, slavery had been largely displaced by the caste system, whereas in east Asia and Europe, slavery, although it did exist, was confined primarily to occasional household service. The existence of slavery was, to be sure, less important in the Islamic Middle East than it had been under the Roman Empire. Agriculture, for example, did not rely on slave labor. But slaves provided domestic service, manual labor for many of the mines and sailing vessels, and above all, troops for military operations. As we have seen, the Abbasids also used elite slaves as soldiers and bureaucrats. Furthermore, Islam developed an extensive slave trade. Initially, most slaves in the Middle East had been taken in conquest, as had been the case in most other slaveholding societies. However, the need for slaves did not cease when Arab conquests stopped, and the active trading impulse of the Arabs provided a clear alternative. Slaves formed the most sought-after goods in sub-Saharan Africa and parts of Europe. Their use, particularly in the armies of the caliphate, made them virtually indispensable. Some slaveholding survived in the Middle East until quite recent times.

In principle, slaves could not be Muslims; their being so contradicted the spiritual equality of all believers. But slaves who converted to Islam were not promised their liberty—although the freeing of slaves was considered a pious act that could win rewards in heaven.

Slave uprisings were rare, but they did occur. Black slaves revolted between 869 and 889. Inspired by a leader aware of Islamic values, the slaves claimed that "God would save them" and "make them masters of slaves and wealth and dwellings." Their leader was executed, his head brought to Baghdad on a pole as a warning against similar uprisings. This was, to be sure, an unusual rising. Slaves used for other functions, including palace service and the army, were better positioned to exert pressure. Periodic revolts involved military troops who were legally slaves.

Peasant revolts also occurred in the name of greater equality. Some of these had racial overtones, with non-Arab Muslims protesting Arab control. One of the goals of the rebellions was the sharing of property; the peasants argued that social equality should match religious equality. A poet thus captured the spirit of peasant rebellions in the 10th century:

> By God, I shall not pray to God while I am
>   bankrupt . . .
> Why should I pray—where are my wealth,
>   my mansion
> And where are my horses, trappings, golden
>   belts?
> Were I to pray, when I do not own
> An inch of earth, then I would be a hypocrite.

Peasant uprisings were always vanquished, but they cropped up recurrently.

Families served as a basic institution for the upper class, merchants, and peasants alike. Family discipline was tight, although often tempered by affection. One caliph described how he wanted a tutor to treat his son:

> Be not strict to the point of stiffening his faculties nor lenient to the point of making him enjoy idleness. Treat him as much as thou canst through kindness and gentleness. Fail not to resort to force and severity should he not respond.

The position of women was particularly noteworthy in the Muslim family. Muhammad carefully stated the spiritual importance of women, noting that they had souls just the same as men. And he introduced some rules designed to protect women. For example, he granted women the right to divorce men and not simply the reverse. He tried to prevent the killing of female babies, a common practice in many agricultural societies where women were regarded as less useful than men and female infanticide was a means of population control. Women could also own property, and their property rights within marriage were carefully defined. Despite Muhammad's attention to certain conditions of women, Islam helped maintain the pronounced inferiority of females within the Islamic family. Women worshipped separately, and the Hadith characterized them as particularly likely to become sinners. As in Christianity, spiritual equality warred with disdain in its views of women.

One sign of the subjugation of women was polygamy. A woman could take but one spouse, whereas a man could have up to four wives. In fact, only the very wealthy could contemplate more than one wife, because Islamic law insisted that a man support his children, so polygamy was never widely practiced. Other rules were more important. A man could divorce his wife far more easily than the other way around. A woman typically married early, at the age of 13 or 14, according to an arrangement made by her father. Once she was married, the duty of a wife was "the service of the husband, care of the children, and the management of the household." In public life, the segregation of the sexes increased steadily, for as in many advanced agricultural societies, inequalities increased over time. By the 10th century, urban women rarely left their household compound. In the 11th century, a caliph decreed that women had to wear a veil when mixing with men and in all public places, extending the pre-Muslim Arab and Middle Eastern custom. Many people came to believe that veiling was part of Islam.

In this segregated situation, Muslim women established intricate social contacts with each other, particularly among other women in the same extended household. Furthermore, the severest limitations on women were not always strictly imposed. Especially in peasant households, where women's work was vital, the total seclusion and veiling of women were often ignored. Nevertheless, a strict differentiation between men and women, in the family and beyond, developed during this formative period and persisted as a basic feature of Middle Eastern civilization.

Even as women's public position deteriorated, however, complexity remained. Many individual women were highly educated. With their property rights, they often ran businesses, though hampered by constraints on their appearing in public. Political roles were limited. A young wife of Muhammad, Aisha, had led armies in battle, but she ultimately failed and her example was widely questioned.

THE DECLINE OF MIDDLE EASTERN CIVILIZATION

After about the year 1200, Middle Eastern civilization began to display a number of symptoms of decline. We have seen that, at the top, the Abbasid caliphate was already in a compromised position, losing control over its provinces and about to collapse completely. However, disintegration ran even deeper than this. At the same time, the decline of Arab civilization was never complete—not like the fall of Rome. What was occurring involved a loss of vitality and diversity, and political problems were only one symptom.

By 1300, a shift in intellectual life was noteworthy. Increasingly, religious leaders gained the upper hand over poets, philosophers, and scientists. The earlier tension among diverse cultural elements yielded to the predominance of the faith. The new piety associated with the rising Sufi movement was both the cause and the result of this development. In literature, an emphasis on secular themes, such as the joys of feasting and hunting, gave way to more strictly religious ideas. Persian poets, writing now in their own language instead of Arabic, led the way. Religious poetry, and not poetry in general, became part of the education of upper-class children. In philosophy, the rationalistic current encountered new attack. In Islamic Spain, the philosopher Ibn Rushd (known as *Averroës* in Europe) espoused Greek rationalism, but his efforts were largely ignored in the Middle East. European scholars were, in fact, more heavily influenced by his teachings. In the Middle East proper, a more typical philosopher now claimed to use Aristotle's logic to show that it was impossible to discover religious truth by human reason—in a book revealingly, if not subtly, titled *The Destruction of Philosophy*.

The Sufi movement was a reaction to both the secularism and corruption of the declining caliphate and the formalism of Islam. The movement emphasized individual contact with God, and at first it surfaced in purely personal formulations. Sufi groups began to form in the 12th and 13th centuries, often among outlying peoples such as the Turks. They reflected an interesting cultural syncretism, borrowing several features from the Christian monastic movement and others from Buddhism. Some Sufi groups stressed works of charity, but others practiced autohypnotism that could allow people to swallow burning embers or pass knives through their bodies; these groups also featured impassioned dances. Sufism contradicted traditional Islam in emphasizing saints or holy men, but in so doing, it provided an outlet for a vital religious impulse. It not only furthered the Islamic missionary effort but also increased the piety of ordinary people.

Increasingly, then, Middle Eastern scholarship focused on religion and the Islamic legal tradition. Some interest in science remained, although it too began to fade. In its place, many Sufi scholars wrote excitingly of their mystical contacts with God and the stages of their religious transformation. This narrowing of Middle Eastern cultural life had less impact on the arts. Artisans' production continued to flourish in many centers, maintaining the Middle East's distinctive commitment to richly decorated rugs, leather goods, and other wares.

Changes in society and the economy were still more subtle, but in many ways at least as ominous as the shifts in politics and intellectual life. As the authority of the caliphate declined, landlords seized greater power over the peasantry. From about 1100 on, peasants increasingly lost their freedom, becoming serfs on large estates. This loss was not the peasants' alone, for agricultural productivity suffered as a result. Landlords turned to draining whatever profit they could from their estates, rather than trying to develop a more vital agriculture; peasants had little incentive and no means to do better, as they were tied to the land and obligatory labor and production output for the landlords. With this gradual social deterioration came fewer tax revenues for the state and less of a basis for flourishing trade. Indeed, Arab traders began to lose ground. Few Arab coins have been found in Europe dating from later than 1100; European merchants were beginning to control their own turf and soon began to challenge the Arabs in other parts of the Mediterranean. Arab commerce remained active in the Indian Ocean, but the time fast approached when it faced new competition there as well, from Chinese and southeast Asian merchants, many of whom had converted to Islam.

The main point is clear, however. Between 600 and 1400, a significant new culture arose in the Middle East. It was unquestionably the most dynamic in the world during most of the period. Important ingredients of this culture remained dominant in the region even after 1400, for this was a durable new society. Even after 1400, the region's role in a complex set of international relationships continued, for Middle Eastern society galvanized a new set of contacts that ran from China in the east to Spain in the west.

PATHS
TO THE PRESENT

Many aspects of present-day Middle Eastern and north African culture trace back to developments in the postclassical period—including the fact that most people in the region, for all their diversity, regard themselves as Arabs and Muslims. Traditionalists in the region maintain styles of dress developed or revived in this period, including veiling for women. Lively commercial traditions, including bustling markets and price bargaining, persist as well. Islamic law remains a vital factor in business relations and family conduct. The Sunni–Shiite split remains vivid, deeply affecting current political prospects in places in Iraq.

The vigor of the Islamic heritage is undeniable, but it is also complex. Islam—as do other religions—contains profound internal tensions. The Qur'an emphasizes peace and the humane treatment of others. Yet the concept of jihad sometimes is used to justify militancy in the name of Allah, in the postclassical centuries and today. Under Islam, women gained important protections—to such a degree that some contemporary Muslim feminists argue that true Islam provides an appropriate basis for gender equity. But other traditions from the postclassical period seem to enforce the inferiority of women. It is also vital to remember that Islam is not the only legacy from this period of the region's history. Vigorous commerce and sophisticated urban life also link present to past in many parts of Middle Eastern/north African civilization.

SUGGESTED WEB SITES

For more on medieval Islamic cultures, see http://www.sfusd.k12.ca.us/schwww/sch618/Islam_New_Main.html, http://www.fordham .edu/halsall/sbook1d.html, and http://www.wsu .edu:8080/~dee/ISLAM/MED.HTM. For more on the history, religion, and civilization of Islam, see http://magde.info/religious/Islam? IslamReligHistCivil.htm.

SUGGESTED READINGS

Two important works are Charles Lindholm, *The Islamic Middle East* (2002), and Mahmoud Ayoub, *Islam: Faith and History* (2004), on issues in the early history of Islam and its outreach. General texts include Francis Robinson, ed., *The Cambridge Illustrated History of the Islamic World* (1998); Sheldon Watts, *Disease and Medicine in World History* (2003); and Leila Ahmed, *Women and Gender in Islam* (1992). A splendid interpretation is M. Hodgson, *The Venture of Islam* (1975). On the development of Islam, see Matthew S. Gordon, *The Rise of Islam* (2005); T. Andrae, *Mohammed: The Man and His Faith* (1970), and W. M. Watt, *What Is Islam?* (1968). Good sources for other topics include Patricia Crone, *From Arabian Tribes to Islamic Empire: Army, State and Society in the Near East c. 600 – 850* (2008); Hugh Kennedy, *When Baghdad Ruled the Muslim World: The Rise and Fall of Islam's Greatest Dynasty* (2005); G. E. Von Grunebaum, *Medieval Islam* (1961); Roman Ghirshman, *Iran from the Earliest Times to the Islamic Conquest* (1961); and Seyyed H. Nasr, *Science and Civilization in Islam* (1968). Ira M. Lapidus, *A History of Islamic Societies* (2002), is a masterful survey. See also M. M. Ahsan, *Social Life Under the Abbasids* (1979); Bernard Lewis, *Race and Slavery in the Middle East* (1990); Lois Beck and Nikki Keddi, eds., *Women in the Muslim World* (1978); and F. Mermiss, *The Veil and the Male Elite: A Feminist Interpretation of Women's Rights in Islam* (1992). Two useful source collections are Eric Schroeder, *Muhammad's People* (1955), with Arabic poetry, and W. M. Watt, trans., *The Faith and Practice of Al-Ghazali* (1953). The Qur'an has also been widely translated. See also Jonathan P. Berkey, *The Formation of Islam: Religion and Society in the Near East* (2003), and Donna Lee Bowen, ed., *Everyday Life in the Muslim Middle East* (2002).

India and Southeast Asia Under the Impact of Islam

The impact of Islam extended to many areas besides the Middle East and north Africa. Some military activity, plus trade and missionary outreach, installed Islam in central Asia, as far as western China. Sub-Saharan Africa was another important case, where trade and missionary endeavor were largely responsible for Islamic success; we turn to the African experience in chapter 10. This chapter deals with two other areas of Islamic impact: India and southeast Asia. Islam provided a key new ingredient in these regions, along with growing participation in trans-regional trade. The results persist to the present day.

The force of Islam and growing involvement in the world network did not result in the exact replication of Middle Eastern patterns in these other locations. Africa and southeast Asia, for instance, retained distinctive characteristics. The real challenge is to understand how change combined with the patterns of still-separate civilizations during the postclassical period.

Such a combination is even more central to the experience of postclassical India, where Islam provided a new political force and a new religious minority, but in a civilization already well established. Key features of classical India, including the Hinduism of the majority, the caste system, high levels of trade, and regional politics, all continued. Hinduism adjusted somewhat, in order to remain a vital force in the face of Islamic competition. Many new Hindu temples were built in the postclassical period, particularly in the south. Indian traders also adapted to the growing dominance of Arab commerce in the Indian Ocean. Significant trade and manufacturing survived, and India was a key participant in the world network as the Indian Ocean became the most important center for world commerce.

Developments in southeast Asia partially paralleled those on the Indian subcontinent. This was no accident, for Indian trade and culture left a strong mark on several parts of this extensive region as Indian influence radiated before the arrival of Islam. Hinduism receded in Indonesia, but the Buddhist influence that had spread out from India established deep roots in Burma (present-day Myanmar) and in Thailand and on the island of Sri Lanka. Like India, southeast Asia operated under decentralized or regional governments—there was no overarching empire. Like India, southeast Asia participated actively in Indian Ocean trade, producing spices and other goods for a wide market.

The dynamic impact of Islam began to be felt from the 7th century on. Neither India nor southeast Asia completely fell under Islam's sway, although a minority of Indians converted and several areas in southeast Asia became fervently Muslim—indeed, the largest single Islamic nation in the world today, Indonesia, began its conversion process during this period. The elaboration of a new and rather complex religious map in India and southeast Asia was a major development in the centuries between 600 and 1400. Through Islamic contacts and growing trade links, parts of southeast Asia were drawn more fully into the mainstream of world history than ever before, another specific illustration of civilization's general spread during the centuries after the classical age. Thus, this period holds a significant place in southern Asian history.

KEY QUESTIONS   *There are two main challenges. Why is it obvious that India remained a separate civilization despite growing Muslim impact? How can the vast region of southeast Asia, never unified in a single political or religious unit, best be defined in world history?*

THE DEVELOPMENT OF INDIAN CULTURE

Even during the classical age, India had never functioned as a single political unit. Unity came closest during the Maurya dynasty, but even then it was incomplete. After the Hun invasions, regional political units characteristically prevailed for many centuries. In northern India, a

few vigorous states were formed. One military leader in the north, Harsha, conquered a number of territories early in the 7th century. A Buddhist, Harsha through his conquests helped extend this religion to Tibet. However, although Harsha was an able administrator, he was unable to extend his bureaucracy throughout the empire, and after his death, regional units resurfaced. In general, northern India was dotted with small states ruled from capital cities by princes, called *Rajput* when they came from the dominant military caste. The princes maintained few paid officials, rewarding their administrators with land grants instead. This system produced limited governments with few functions. Frequent wars pitted these feeble states against one another, for in conquest the princes sought new lands with which to reward new followers.

The political situation in southern India was somewhat different. This area had not been a center of Indian culture previously. During the classical age, most attention, and the most vigorous political forms, focused on the great river valleys of the north. After about 600 C.E., however, stronger kingdoms arose in southern India, particularly among Tamil-speaking peoples. Less subject to invasion than northern India, this region also maintained more active trading contracts with other societies, especially parts of southeast Asia. Trade, and the merchant wealth it produced, provided the financial basis for the new southern kingdoms. Here, too, regional units prevailed; there was no single southern Indian state. Few of the governments developed tightly centralized systems even within their own boundaries, and local autonomy for landlords and peasant villages remained considerable. A few kingdoms had regional assemblies of landlords, merchants, and even artisans to provide advice; assemblies took place also at the village level. Taxes, which in theory ranged from one-tenth to one-sixth of all agricultural produce, in fact provided only a limited income. Hence, southern kingdoms were also likely to engage in warfare to secure the means to support their armies and administrators. Some of the southern states also maintained navies and occasionally fought with states of southeast Asia, including one empire that developed on several islands in present-day Indonesia.

Ironically, during the very period when regional politics predominated, greater cultural unity emerged than ever before. As in the West, cultural unity, based on religion, spread even amid divided, sometimes chaotic, politics. Buddhism, already a fading religion in India, was virtually eliminated after the 7th century. In the north, Hun invaders disliked the contemplative emphasis of Buddhism, preferring the more varied approach provided by Hinduism. Hinduism also spread to the south with increasing force, after some earlier interest in Buddhism within this region. The spread of Hindu temples often included administration of landed estates, frequently backed by local political leaders. In addition, the caste system gained acceptance in the south; many of the new regional kings saw it as a good means of organizing society and providing greater stability. With the caste system came greater influence from the brahmin or priestly caste, which further encouraged Hinduism. Hindu leaders controlled a flourishing educational system. Schools and colleges were attached to the Hindu temples. Some minority religions, including Buddhism, still survived in India, but before the Muslim challenge the influence of Hinduism became increasingly pervasive.

Hinduism also tended to reach out, more clearly than before, to the ordinary Indian. Although Sanskrit remained the literary language of the brahmins, a substantial literature—not all of it religious—also arose in more popular languages such as Hindi and Tamil. This ensured that India was not unified linguistically, but it increased the service of Hinduism as a cultural bond across linguistic and political boundaries. Various Hindu thinkers worked within the basic tradition of the Vedas. The philosopher Shankara argued that the world is an illusion, or *maya,* which obstructs pure perception. He established

a number of centers to promote his teachings. Another philosopher, Ramanuja, emphasized devotion rather than pure intellect as the path to God. Writing in the 11th century, he inspired devotional groups all over the subcontinent.

Religion guided important artistic activity. A number of temples were constructed, with painted walls depicting religious stories and legends. Around the temples clustered not only schools but also centers for dance and music, and a host of stores and banks. Ornate designs and statues adorned many temple complexes.

Along with the religion-centered culture, characteristic economic and social forms predominated throughout the subcontinent, supported of course by the pervasive caste system. Urban society, although open only to a minority of the whole population, continued to flourish during this period of Indian history. Many merchants worried about their religious lives, often contributing to temples to help cleanse themselves, but their status were higher in India than in early Christian Europe. Indian merchants exchanged goods with southeast Asia and participated in caravan trade with China and the Middle East. Indian cities harbored artisans and small shopkeepers. Some artisans were of a low caste. Leatherworkers, for example, because they handled the skins of dead animals, were members of the untouchable caste, even though their products were essential. Artisans such as carpenters and brick makers enjoyed higher status.

Throughout most of India, the caste system solidified into the form that was to persist into our own century. The four major groups, brahmins, warriors, peasants, and untouchables, had subdivided, in part according to precise occupation, so that more than 3000 castes and *jati* subcastes had come into existence. Each caste had a governing body to enforce caste rules and make sure no caste member was "polluted" by inappropriate contact with other caste members. Caste organization also provided some mutual assistance to its members. Even more than before, this

A chariot pulled by elephants, carved from the stone of the Hindu Vittalaraya Temple at Hampi, from postclassical India.

system in many ways replaced government in regulating relations among Indians.

For those at the bottom of the caste system—the untouchables—life in some ways differed little from that of menial slaves or serfs in other societies. For them, there was perhaps a more varied routine and a greater sense of belonging to a partly separate society, but a similar vulnerability to great poverty and harsh treatment by superiors existed. Overall, however, the caste system produced a distinctive society, by differentiating social rules and contacts for all groups and so providing a clear identity at all social levels. Even aside from the sheer number of castes, the system was complex. A class system coexisted within castes, so that in some cases people who

were brahmins could be found not serving as priests but as peasants tilling the soil. Inherited status protected their caste membership but did not prevent confusing occupational differentiation and mobility within a caste. Wealth could vary greatly for families within a single caste.

Family ties continued to serve as a focal point for Indians of all castes. Considerable loving attention was lavished on children, particularly boys. Literacy was fairly widespread in wealthier groups, so that even the children of prosperous farming families could often read and write. Increasingly, Indian parents arranged marriages for their children at an early age, in part to ensure that girls were virgins on their wedding night. Thus, most girls were legally married before they reached

HISTORY DEBATE

THE CASTE SYSTEM

Two features of India's caste system, spreading and solidifying during the postclassical period, continue to draw debate. Both reflect the extent to which the system seems strange in modern eyes. First, historians argue over the system's precise definition. Many now argue that the basic castes were not as important, in actually regulating relations among peoples, as the subcastes or *jati*. These units, it is argued, played a greater role in defining who could eat or socialize with whom, and how tasks were divided. Even the untouchables were divided, with sweepers looking down on manure handlers, who in turn despised leatherworkers.

The second debate involves the "livability" of a system that differs from the way most modern people, officially at least, think society should be organized. Some Indian historians, while not defending the system, urge that it allowed different groups some autonomy and cultural identity, through separate caste structure and rituals. This limited outright prejudice, they suggest, or the direct imposition of one group's authority over others that slavery, for example, entailed. Castes are now illegal in India, but caste background still counts, to the advantage of some groups or the disadvantage of others. Figuring out and evaluating the system's past is not just a historical exercise. How do the caste system and slavery compare?

puberty, often to men they had never seen. The actual wedding, however, was delayed until after puberty, when the wife could start a family of her own. Despite the arranged marriage practice, it was assumed that husbands and wives could learn to love each other. Hindu law recommended that couples forgo sex for the first three nights of their marriage so they could get to know each other and form an emotional bond before a physical union was attempted. As wives, women were expected to obey their husbands and were usually confined to household activities. Within the warrior caste, a practice called *sati* developed in these centuries, whereby wives were expected to throw themselves on the funeral pyre of their husbands, confirming in death that the two could have no life apart. This practice was never widespread, and some argue that it developed to protect widows against rape or imprisonment by invaders. It nevertheless indicates some intensification of India's particular version of a patriarchal system.

In practice, however, many Indian women developed a strong role in the family based on

their household authority. One Indian poem showed the power of a vigorous wife:

> But when she has him [her husband] in her clutches, it's all housework and errands. Fetch a knife to cut this gourd. Get me some fresh fruit. We want wood to boil the greens, and for a fire in the evening. Now paint my feet. Come and massage my back.

THE MUSLIM CHALLENGE IN INDIA

The weakness of Indian political structures after the Hun invasions left the subcontinent a tempting target for subsequent attack. Arab forces approached northwestern India during their great military campaigns following Muhammad's death. Arab and Turkish armies pushed into the Indus valley. The purpose combined religious zeal, as against Hindus regarded as idolaters, and desire for plunder. There was no durable conquest at this point. However, conversions to Islam took place in the northwestern region, which, because of its proximity to the Islamic Middle East, was to be the center of Islam in India proper. This first threat helped convince Hindu leaders that they needed to develop clearer popular ties in their own religion, thus encouraging some of the cultural changes that affected India more generally.

A second wave of Islamic invasion occurred toward the end of the 10th century. Again, the path lay through the valleys of northwestern India. But the Muslim armies this time were composed of Turks, not Arabs. While some Turks had been moving from their original home in

Carving in the Palitana Jain Temple, Gujarat, India. Some of the 863 temples of Palitana were built in the 11th century. The sensual aspect of Indian art is evident here.

central Asia into the Middle East, influencing the caliphate and, as we will see, also attacking the Byzantine Empire, others remained in the East, although they too had converted to Islam from their earlier animist beliefs. A Turkish kingdom in present-day Afghanistan provided the starting point for the invasions into India. A Turkish chieftain named Sabuktigin, a devout Muslim, raided as far as the Ganges valley, attacking many Hindu shrines and statues because they represented false gods.

Once again, invasion did not lead to conquest. But then, in 1192, a new line of Turkish kings in Afghanistan mounted an attack, this time with plans to annex the conquered territory rather than simply raiding it. Turkish forces seized the city of Delhi, in the Ganges valley, and extended their control throughout most of northern India. Again, Hindu shrines and statues were destroyed, and Buddhist centers were also demolished. Tens of thousands of monks were killed at the Buddhist university center in Nalanda, effectively ending Buddhism in India, while Hindu centers were also attacked. A Turkish general established a new regional kingdom, called the Delhi sultanate, that produced additional territory in central and southern India. This Islamic kingdom represented a deliberate imposition of minority rule over the Hindu majority. Most administrators were brought in from the Middle East. Mosques were constructed in many places, changing the face of Indian architecture.

Under the encouragement of the Delhi sultanate, Islam gained a solid hold on northwestern India—what is now Pakistan. Here, Islam had the appeal of a conquering force. It also won Indian converts from the lower castes, for Islamic belief had no place for the caste system. Elsewhere in India, though, Hinduism largely prevailed, even though divided political units could muster no unity against Islamic armies. Most Indians viewed the Delhi sultans as merely another outside force that could be largely endured. Governed by the regulations of the separate castes, Indians could ignore foreign rule more readily than other people. Later Delhi sultans also were more tolerant. Furthermore, Hinduism had deep roots that were not easily shaken.

Hindus objected to Islam on many grounds. Its rituals conflicted with Hindu practice. Muslims shunned pork, which Hindus sometimes enjoyed, whereas Muslims saw no reason to avoid beef. Hindus also saw no virtue in avoiding religious music or statues created to honor the gods. Turkish attacks on Hindu religious centers obviously added to the clash between the two religions. Finally, Hindus disagreed with the Muslim practice of veiling and secluding women, though, over time, Ilsamic influence encouraged wider tendencies to keep women in India within the household.

The Delhi sultanate did not consistently attack the Hindu faith, although the destruction of leading Hindu shrines during their invasions could not be reversed. (One result was that present-day India has few remaining examples of earlier Hindu monumental architecture.) Islamic rulers, while not viewing Hinduism as embodying as much of the true faith as Christianity or Judaism, did see some religious validity in Hindu spirituality. Hence, the Muslim impulse of religious tolerance was given some sway. Increasing Hindu emphasis on popular devotion to key Hindu gods encouraged intense religious piety among the masses of Hindu faithful, which helped solidify the religion among about 70 percent of the subcontinent's population.

The Delhi sultanate encountered the characteristic problems of any regime seeking control over India, for smaller political units soon reemerged. Southern kingdoms arose by the 1330s, confining the sultanate once more to the north. A new Turkish raid in 1398 weakened the sultanate in the north, and by 1400 India was again politically divided, with the Delhi sultanate merely a regional kingdom.

The first waves of Islamic invasions thus brought no permanent political change to India.

Moreover, although they created a new religious minority, of great importance to India's future, they encouraged the hold of Hinduism on the majority and actually stimulated a growing piety among the general population.

SOUTHEAST ASIA

Even before the end of India's classical age, civilization in southeast Asia had developed under considerable stimulus from the subcontinent. Hindu traders brought Indian artistic as well as religious forms to several centers in the islands of Indonesia. Buddhism had already begun to spread overland, to other parts of southeast Asia. Furthermore, the southeast Asian form of Buddhism, with its emphasis on personal devotion and meditation, remained truer to the Buddhist ideal than the Buddhist variants adopted in China and Japan. However, southeast Asia was not purely and simply an extension of Indian culture. Hinduism did not gain a durable hold in the region. Nor did the caste system develop, because among other factors, Buddhists were always hostile to this brahmin-devised structure.

Indian influences did penetrate more widely in southeast Asia between about 650 and 1250, nonetheless. Buddhist missionaries and Indian (particularly Tamil) merchants played a leading role in this movement. Indian emissaries in many places encountered new peoples moving into the region from the north. Their relations with most of these peoples were peaceful, but there were some important wars between southern Indian kingdoms and local states on the Malay Peninsula and the islands of the Indian Ocean.

In one part of the region, tribes of Thai people pushed southward in the 8th century, establishing the Buddhist kingdom of Thailand. Their language was related to Chinese, but they adopted an Indian-derived writing system. Another people, the Burmese, set up a kingdom in the 9th century. Yet another people, the Khmers, established a Cambodian empire in 782, which long served as the largest political unit on the southeast Asian mainland. This empire, again largely Buddhist and heavily influenced by India, began to decline around 1200. Buddhist leaders did sponsor the massive temple complex of Angkor Wat in this country. Cambodian kings adapted Hindu ideas about divine sources for political power, using the temple building to consolidate their authority. In the process, religious leadership passed from priests to Buddhist monks.

On the main Indonesian islands of Borneo, Sumatra, and Java, another empire took shape, the Srivijaya. At its height, this empire also controlled the southern part of the Malay Peninsula.

The empire was weakened in the 11th century by attacks from a leading kingdom in southern India. During the 13th century, traders from China began to exert influence in the region as well, crippling the power of the local merchant group. By the 14th century, local kingdoms governed most parts of Indonesia.

Thus, diverse and largely regional kingdoms became characteristic of southeast Asia during the centuries of civilization's expansion. In contrast to India, there was never even a brief tradition of political unity. Cultural unity was somewhat greater, although it was affected by competing influences from India and China. Indian artistic forms helped inspire a number of great temples, particularly in Cambodia and Indonesia. Indian literature and

The great temple at Angkor Wat, in Cambodia.

legends spread widely. Southeast Asian monarchs, greatly attracted to Indian culture, passed it along to their subjects.

Buddhism was the clearest winner in this process of cultural diffusion during most of the postclassical period. Buddhist emphasis on direct contact with ordinary people, its strong missionary impulse, and its intense focus on religious devotion and ethical behavior gave it a clear edge over Hinduism in southeast Asia. Many southeast Asians made pilgrimages to Buddhist centers in India and on the island of Sri Lanka, which further confirmed the religion's influence. Many rulers, inspired by Buddhist promptings toward an ethical life as preparation for nirvana, offered humane government to their subjects.

Indian influence also surfaced in the area of economics. Indian merchants, many of them Muslims, encouraged the considerable production of spices and other goods for a wider market, which brought southeast Asia firmly into contact with the central routes of world trade. From this point on, southeast Asian goods played a vital role in world trade. Merchants from the region became increasingly active in east–west trade in the Indian Ocean, quickly adapting advances such as the canpos. The region also sponsored considerable piracy against Chinese, Arab, and even Japanese shippers.

Then, by about 1300, a third influence added new complexity to the southeast Asian mix. By this point, Arab traders had gained increasing significance in southeast Asian trade, displacing many Indian merchants. Southeast Asian spices and teas were brought to the Middle East and even Europe in Arab vessels or through Arab intermediaries. This merchant influence was particularly strong in the Indonesian islands, as well as in the southern part of the Philippine islands and on the Malay Peninsula. The reduction of Indian independence, during the Delhi sultanate, added to the possibility of growing Islamic activity in this region. Then the new missionary spirit that arose in the Middle East with the Sufi movement sent another vigorous signal

to southeast Asia. Increasing numbers of Malays, Indonesians, and Filipinos converted to Islam. By 1400, Buddhism had been almost entirely eliminated in these places, while Hinduism was displaced except on a few islands, such as Bali, where it continues to be practiced.

By this point, the diverse religious map of southeast Asia had become established fact. Hinduism was a minor strand, but Buddhism held great importance in most of the regional kingdoms of the mainland. On the islands, however, as on the Malay Peninsula, Islam was becoming dominant. Written forms were similarly diverse. Writing for many of the southeast Asian languages derived from scripts used in India, including Sanskrit. However, Malay writing developed under Arabic influence, whereas in Vietnam, writing derived from Chinese ideographs. In essence, many features of southeast Asian culture were derivative, but they came from no one center, despite the special importance of Indian influences. At the same time the area played a vital role in the world network. Its goods were highly valued and its merchants provided increasing competition for the Arabs in the Indian Ocean.

PATHS TO THE PRESENT

As with other parts of Afro–Eurasia, south and southeast Asia experienced enduring religious changes during this period. Buddhism and Islam predominated in different parts of southeast Asia, blending with diverse local cultures. Indonesian Muslims, for example, did not adopt Middle Eastern styles of women's dress as they converted to Islam, reserving the wearing of a veil for strictly religious occasions. Regional identities formed during this period, in places such as Thailand and many parts of Indonesia, have persisted to the present.

The creation of a Muslim minority in India, and the alternation of tolerance and tension in its relationship with the Hindu majority, set an important framework for the future. Political divisions on the subcontinent today, particularly between India and Pakistan, form the latest product of several centuries of jockeying. A great deal of India's artistic heritage, which is today regarded as traditional, stems from this period and its blending of Hindu, Islamic, and Persian styles.

SUGGESTED WEB SITES

On Muslim mysticism in India (the poet Kabir), see http://goto.bilkent.edu.tr/gunes/KabirPoems .htm. On the spread of Islam in south and southeast Asia, see http://users.erols.com/ zenithco/indiamus.htm and http://www.ucalgary .ca/applied_history/tutor/islam/fractured/ SAEsai.html. On Sufism, refer to http://www .geocities.com/Athens/5738/intro.htm.

SUGGESTED READINGS

For Indian history in this period, see Romila Thapar, *A History of India* (1990), and the relevant chapters of Rhoads Murphy's *History of Asia* (4th ed., 2002).

India's wider influence is examined in H. B. Q. Wales, *The Indianization of China and Southeast Asia* (1967). An excellent summary on southeast Asia is D. G. E. Hall, *A History of Southeast Asia* (1981). On Indian Ocean trade patterns, see J. L. Abu-Lughod, *Before European Hegemony: The World System A.D. 1250–1350* (1988). For good recent works, see *Paul Michel Munoz, Early Kingdoms of the Indonesian Archipelago and the Malay Peninsula* (2006); Sunil Kumar, *The Emergence of the Delhi Sultanate, 1192–1286* (2007); Richard M. Eaton, *India's Islamic Traditions* (2003) and Catherine Asher and Cynthia Talbot, *India Before Europe* (2006).. See also Sukhdev Singh, *The Muslims of Indian Origin: During the Delhi Sultanate: Emergence, Attitudes and Role, 1192–1526 A.D.*(2005); Richard C. Martin, *Approaches to Islam in Religious Studies* (2001); and Bruce B. Lawrence, ed., *Beyond Turk and Hindu: Rethinking Religious Identities in Islamic South Asia* (2000). See also, Peter Jackson, *The Delhi Sultanate* (Cambridge, 1999); Andre Wink, *Al-Hind: The Making of the Indo-Islamic World* (1990); Milton Osborne, *Southeast Asia: An Illustrated Introductory History* (2005); and D. R. Sar Desai, *Southeast Asia Past and Present* (2003).

10 Africa and Islam

During the postclassical period, Africa actively participated in the expansion of civilization and in creating new contacts with the developing world network. Islam's sweep across north Africa effectively joined this region to the Middle East in a single, if sometimes politically fragmented, civilization. Below the Sahara desert, Islam also gained important influence although, as in southern Asia, it competed with other beliefs. Sub-Saharan Africa remained an area of independent civilization, even as it participated in the radiation of religion, commerce, and politics from Islam. A distinct set of African identities persisted. At the same time, portions of sub-Saharan Africa borrowed more than from Islam than India did, importing not only religion but also Arabic writing. Africa in this sense imitated the more established centers of civilization, as did Russia, Japan, and western Europe during this same postclassical period. Parts of the African economy were more closely tied to the Arab world than was true in India, as Africans sent gold, raw materials, and slaves in return for horses and some luxury craft items.

■KEY QUESTIONS *There are three main challenges in approaching this vital period in African history. The first involves any lingering stereotypes that Africa was uncivilized or that no developments of significance occurred before European penetration. In contrast, African developments rivaled or surpassed those in western Europe at this point. The second challenge involves the need to combine an appreciation of great diversity with some shared features in African civilization. What did (many) Africans have in common, and where do generalizations break down in the face of distinctive local societies? Finally, how does this case of Islamic influence compare with those in India and southeast Asia, and in the Middle East itself? How can the African place in the Islamic world best be defined?*

SUB-SAHARAN AFRICA AND THE WORLD NETWORK

Because of its diverse sources and the vast territory involved, sub-Saharan African history, before the modern centuries, is not easy to grasp. Because most African societies did not develop writing, the formal historical record is sparse, gleaned from accounts of non-African travelers (notably the Muslims), archeological remains, and the detailed stories and family histories that many African peoples transmitted by word of mouth. Technology, although benefiting from the extensive use of iron—introduced below the Sahara by 1000 B.C.E.—lagged behind Asian standards. Animal diseases, including that spread by the dreaded tsetse fly, limited livestock and animal transportation. Although political organization featured monarchies in many parts of Africa—emerging at about the same time and in some of the same ways that monarchies arose in western Europe—there were more African societies without formal politics beyond villages and tribes than was the case in Asia and Europe.

Furthermore, African societies were diverse. The continent, even below the Sahara, is vast. It includes huge deserts such as the southern Sahara and, in the south, the Kalahari; extensive mountains in the east; grasslands below the Sahara and again in the south; and the dense tropical jungle in the center. Large African empires developed, but none ever embraced more than a fraction of the sub-Saharan region. Fragmentation produced considerable diversity. No religion has ever swept over the whole of sub-Saharan Africa, nor has any language provided unified communication.

However, diversity was not absolute. Although there are more than 1000 languages in use in sub-Saharan Africa, they derive from no more than four or five basic tongues, which means that many of the languages are closely related to one another. While political unity was never achieved, there were some recurring political trends in many parts of the continent. Although a single religion never

flourished, a strong polytheistic leaning resulted in some basic common ground where the African religious experience was concerned. Similarities of this sort, while they cannot be pressed too far, highlight certain tendencies in African civilization—tendencies that reached fuller expression when civilization itself began to spread widely, although not universally, from about the year 600 C.E.

The impetus for this spreading civilization was twofold, involving prior achievements and new connections. As with other early civilizations, several African societies built on foundations already established. Civilization had flourished in the northeast for more than a millennium. Agriculture had been well entrenched in the northern and western regions of sub-Saharan Africa even longer. It had not, by 500 C.E., reached into or through the equatorial jungles, where small hunting-and-gathering groups persisted. Thus, the southern part of the continent, ultimately a fertile agricultural region, remained untouched. But in the north and west, long centuries of agriculture had provided a solid economic base. Ironworking was also well established. Village organization was tightly knit, and the local communities, along with firm ties among kinship or extended family groups, provided a durable political base for further cultural achievements. In some African societies, the stable local units and tight links among family members sufficed to ensure order. Family or lineage bonds were a distinctive feature, and Africans devoted great attention to memorizing elaborate family trees so that relatives could be identified even in fairly distant regions. In many kinship groups, or clans, certain vocations were inherited, such as the work of traders, peasants, political officials, and even slaves. The importance of clans explains the often unstructured quality of African government.

Finally, religion, although varying widely in specific local forms, gave Africans an explanation of the workings of nature, including rites and beliefs to deal with illness and natural disasters, and also a firm sense of their own identity. Each clan had its own sacred animal that expressed a divine spirit and could not be killed by clan members. Because most African religions included both the worship of spirits in nature and a veneration of ancestors, they served a social as well as mystical function.

In sum, the first context for expanding civilization in Africa was the solid foundation formed by an agricultural economy many centuries old and a supportive religious and political culture. Stronger kingdoms, such as Ghana in west Africa, began to emerge as early as 300 C.E. on these bases. The expansion of civilization in Africa started even before the postclassical period.

A crucial development, beginning before the postclassical period but continuing through it, involved the great Bantu migration. Bantu peoples, from west-central Africa, gradually moved south and southeast, spreading agriculture through these parts of the continent. They also brought the use of iron. Most African languages are Bantu in origin, reflecting this huge movement. The word *Bantu* means "many peoples." Civilization areas that emerged in the south in this period, notably Zimbabwe, reflected the Bantu impact, as did later societies.

The second stimulus for the spread of civilization resulted from trading contacts that developed between the 7th and the 10th centuries. New levels of interregional exchange established two principal channels. On Africa's east coast, Islamic sailors from southern Arabia set up urban centers. Trade to and from these centers, across the Indian Ocean, became extensive. Ivory and gold, plus some slaves, were exported to the Middle East, India, and even China, in return for manufactured products including Chinese porcelain. Although this commerce remained largely in non-African hands, the Arab traders settled in the east African cities, intermarried extensively, and provided the foundation for a number of city-states and local kingdoms. They even developed a language, Swahili, that combined Arab and African features to promote wider communication. East African cities did not have extensive contacts with the interior, which limited their impact in Africa, but they were also a noteworthy development.

More significant was the second trade channel, across the Sahara from Muslim north Africa. Here, caravans traveled, by camel and by foot, on arduous journeys. Although the domestication of camels occurred earlier, widespread African use of camels began about 200 C.E. and revolutionized trading opportunities. By 700, Muslim traders were seeking gold, ivory, salt, and some slaves from sub-Saharan Africa. They also traded for the cola nut, a stimulant not mentioned in the Qur'an and therefore permitted to the faithful. The wealth that resulted permitted the development of thriving African cities. Timbuktu, in the southern Sahara, was the greatest center, boasting a large military force, a huge treasury, and—in the words of an early European visitor—"many magistrates, learned doctors, and men of religion." The city became an integral part of the Islamic intellectual world. More broadly, west African–Arab interaction stimulated growing trade, the manufacture of cloth and precious metals, and new social and political patterns in a wide stretch of Africa below the Sahara. African merchants expanded their operations through many parts of west Africa. Social divisions began to form, between rich and poor, between soldiers, artisans, and farmers, some of which cut across traditional kinship lines.

Africa was thus part of the Islamic orbit and a growing participant in international trade. It was also one of the first societies to imitate other civilizations, using its trade contacts and selective borrowings from Islam to accelerate aspects of its historical development. The postclassical period saw distinctive characteristics persist in Africa, but also the increasing influence of larger world trends.

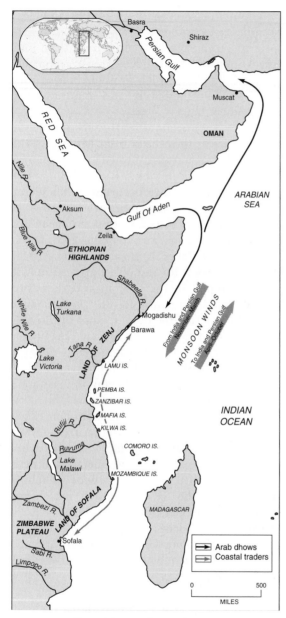

East African Trade Routes

THE GREAT KINGDOMS

Not surprisingly, the first great African kingdoms—not counting the states in the upper Nile—arose in the region of the southern Sahara and the grasslands below. This area is called the Sudan (from the Arab word for "black"); in these centuries, however, it stretched all along the southern Sahara rather than the upper Nile area that is now the nation of Sudan. The Sudanese kingdoms exacted some tribute from merchants, which provided considerable wealth without an extensive taxation of the peasant class.

Ghana was the earliest of a series of Sudanic kingdoms. Its origins extended to the classical period, but its clearer development from about 800 related to the growth of cross-Saharan trade and the expansion of salt and gold mining in the region. The kingdom, built around several cities that have since vanished, served as a crossroads between north Africa and the gold and ivory producers of the grassland and forest areas to the south. Kings of Ghana imposed taxes on the trade that crossed their region. According to one Arab writer, "All pieces of gold that are found in this empire belong to the king." This monopoly carefully protected against the unauthorized production of gold that might flood the market and supplemented the direct tax (also to be paid in gold) levied on every donkey or camel bearing salt. With these resources, the Ghanese king sustained a lavish court, offering banquets to thousands of guests and surrounding himself with luxurious trappings. Ceremony and ritual helped the king express his power; so did the related belief that the king was in some sense divine, descended from and protected by the gods. The features of divine kingship, as it has been called, became common in African political organization during this period and beyond.

Ghana developed a complex relationship with the Islamic world. Its kings hired Arabs to keep records, which helped them develop the bureaucracy necessary for the expansion of the state. Trade with Islamic north Africa was needed not only for tax revenues but also as a source for horses, on which military activities, notably the cavalry, depended (local horse breeding was limited by the presence of the

SOLVING PROBLEMS

TECHNOLOGY AND TRADE

An appealing pattern of historical explanation involves a genius inventor coming up with a dramatic new technology that in turn changes the world, for better or worse. Creative technology comes first, in this sequence of causes, and then produces varied effects. In fact, technology more often flows from clearly established needs, resulting from changes in situation and then (undeniably) causing further changes in turn—technology solves newly perceived problems. Trade patterns in the postclassical period illustrate this process clearly. Muslim merchants, as Arabs gained access to the mature trading centers of the Middle East (including Persia), began to increase their interest in seagoing trade, particularly from the eastern and southern ports of the region into the Indian Ocean. They were spurred by knowledge of the profits that could be made from commerce in gold, spices and other products. Technology did not cause these new interests, but technological changes were vital to help take advantage of the links possibly among the Middle East, east Africa, and southern Asia.

The relevant devices came from various sources. Already the Hellenistic period in the Mediterranean had seen the invention of the astrolabe, an instrument that enabled shippers to calculate latitude. This was now taken up by Arab and Persian merchants. The merchants also gained knowledge of the compass from China, where it had first been introduced, and this provided vital guidance on the high seas. From India and Southeast Asia, Arabs also adopted a triangular sail, the lateen sail, which increased a ship's maneuverability. These devices were crucial in expanding the range and volume of trade in the Indian Ocean, particularly helping Middle Eastern merchants take advantage of seasonal trade winds to and from the south, along the east African coast.

Later in the postclassical period new needs and interests spurred another round of technological changes, in this case in China. Chinese merchants had long stuck close to coastlines, trading mainly with Korea and Japan but leaving longer-distance trade to Middle Easterners and south Asians. By the 10th century, however, new tastes developed from spices and other products from Southeast Asia, and the Chinese wanted to reach out directly. Again, they had a new problem to be solved. Obviously, they took advantage of the compass for their new ventures. They also learned how to build increasingly large ships, fastened with nails and waterproofed with oils, which could be steered through new types of rudders. The result was another round of trade expansion in the latter centuries of the postclassical period. Causation in all this is definable but complex. Trade and new trade interests spurred technology, which of course then led to further trade.

■**QUESTIONS:** *Why was there more change in trade technologies than in manufacturing technologies in the postclassical period? Are there cases where a dramatic invention springs from a creative genius unexpectedly and then leads to huge change?*

tsetse fly). The cavalry allowed the state to expand into the plains of the Sudan, to exact tribute and acquire slaves. However, these contacts with Islam and a growing dependence on trade also made Ghana vulnerable to nomadic raiders and invasions from states to the north. The kingdom's wealth inevitably drew attention from north Africa, while local Islamic residents may have invited the presence of fellow Muslims. The kingdom of Ghana, always loosely organized through alliances between king and local leaders, lacked the ability to survive this situation. Although its wealth was great, Ghana's defense depended on arrangements with local military groups, rather than professional soldiers. And the kingdom maintained only a rudimentary bureaucracy, understandably focused on tax collection. Weakened by military raids from outside its borders, the kingdom collapsed around 1200.

A number of other kingdoms had already formed in the Sudan region, some of them organized with councils as well as kings. Copper production and textiles flourished in several of these kingdoms, a few of which endured into the 19th century. A number of African trading companies developed, sometimes organized along hereditary lines so that their administration remained within the same extended family across generations. Some of these companies, too, survived into present times. Thriving market centers assumed a major place in the life of west Africa, in portions of contemporary nations such as Nigeria.

The clearest successor state to Ghana, however, emerged during the 13th century. Its regional basis was slightly different from that of Ghana, and its political organization was better developed. It too, however, relied on cavalry, trade, and contact with Islam. The kingdom of Mali was established under the leadership of an able general named Sundiata, who defeated a number of smaller states and ruled for about a quarter century until his death in 1260. Sundiata's state rested on the wealth derived from trade with north Africa, and also on the unusual fertility of the Gambia River valley, where rice and several other crops thrived. Sundiata and his successors were regarded as divine monarchs, similar to the pattern in Ghana, where a ruler's religious authority and magical power were emphasized. They also formed alliances with a variety of local leaders. But Sundiata converted to Islam, partly as a gesture of goodwill toward his north African trading partners. Although he did not force Islam on his subjects, he and his successors employed Islamic bureaucrats and popularized the use of Arabic script. As a

religion of the elite, Islam provided a sense of coherence and also skills in law and writing that allowed the development of a more extensive bureaucracy and legal system than had prevailed in Ghana.

The rulers of Mali also accrued great wealth. One successor to Sundiata, Mansa Musa, making a pilgrimage to Mecca in 1334–35, dazzled Egyptians and other Arabs with the gold and ornaments of his entourage. His staff loaded 90 camels with gold dust, each load weighing 300 pounds, to provide spending money for the trip. Several thousand subjects accompanied Mansa Musa on the pilgrimage. He offered substantial gifts to people he met along the way and to the holy cities of Mecca and Medina. Not surprisingly, his reputation spread widely. (Also not surprisingly, he ran out of gold and had to borrow in Egypt; the size of the loan, quickly repaid, threw Egyptian banks into some confusion.) A French map, some decades later, recalled Mansa Musa's name, adding provocatively that "so abundant is the gold that is found in his land that he is the richest and most noble king of all the area." But Mansa Musa was more than a big-spending pilgrim. He organized a pool of many Muslim scholars, from as far away as Egypt, in his capital city; his government engaged in diplomacy, including the exchange of ambassadors, with other north African countries and possibly other even more distant nations.

Mali became one of the great nations of the Islamic world, extending from the Atlantic deep into the interior of the Sudan. Mali emperors promoted active trade and also patronized Islamic learning; Timbuktu served as a major center of Islamic scholarship, where books, it was said, were valued above gold. Regular scholarly exchange connected Timbuktu with centers in Morocco and Egypt, linking west Africa more firmly with the Mediterranean and Islamic world. Laws were strictly enforced, and the Mali empire enjoyed a long period of peace and prosperity. The great trading families extended their commercial skills. An Arab visitor noted,

WORLD PROFILES

SUNDIATA

One of the greatest postclassical kingdoms in west Africa, Mali, was formed when the Malinke people broke away from the state of Ghana in the 13th century. Its leader was Sundiata, a brilliant warrior and statesman. His exploits launched a great oral tradition. The griots, professional oral historians who advised kings and kept their traditions, began their histories of Mali with this "Lion Prince."

> Listen then sons of Mali, children of the black people, listen to my word, for I am going to tell you of Sundiata, the father of the Bright Country, of the savanna land, the ancestor of those who draw the bow, the master of a hundred vanquished kings. . . . He was great among kings, he was perfect among men; he was beloved of God because he was the last of the great conquerors.

Sundiata had a difficult childhood, amid great family feuds. He created a unified state, setting basic rules for Malinke society and outlining the government of Mali. He established groups of freemen who could bear arms, another group of priests, and several classes of artisans, including the historian griots. These divisions were not new, but Sundiata won credit for them. He allowed for regional and ethnic differences but also set up garrisons to keep order in his large kingdom. He worked to protect travelers and punish crime—both important in a society that depended on secure trade. Sundiata died about 1260, but his successors carried his achievements still further.

Mansa Musa was a later ruler of Mali, when the kingdom's resources had developed beyond even Sundiata's time. The representation of royal power, however, suggests the ruling structure that Sundiata helped establish.

"Neither the man who travels nor he who stays at home has anything to fear from robbers or men of violence."

Mali began to decline, however, by about 1400. Its place was taken by a third great Sudanese kingdom, Songhai, which flourished from the late 15th century to 1591. Songhai, although somewhat smaller than Mali, continued the development of a civil service to supplement the personal authority of the king. This state, too, was Islamic, though again most of the inhabitants remained true to their polytheistic traditions and to the considerable freedom granted women in public. Rather than depending on alliances with local lords, the kings of Songhai built armies that owed loyalty only to them; some of their soldiers were slaves, the personal possessions of the monarchy. Many new territories were gained by conquest.

The spread of Islam in Africa is represented by the great mosque at Jenne on the Niger River in what is now the Republic of Mali. Jenne was a major center of ironworking and trade. Along with Timbuktu, 200 miles to the north, it was also a center of Islamic learning and scholarship.

The kingdom of Songhai collapsed only as a result of new attacks from north Africa, notably from a rival state based in present-day Morocco, and internal rebellion. With its downfall, the great period of the Sudanic kingdoms came to an end, although in fact a variety of new kingdoms formed in subsequent centuries. Basic west African political patterns proved quite durable.

Partly through the example of the Sudanic kingdoms, by the 14th century a number of other states formed in northern and western sub-Saharan Africa. Most were monarchies, with kings claiming the authority and trappings of divine right. Characteristically, such divine claims were balanced by rather weak control over most subjects and by councils of local leaders and townspeople that provided, although informally, something of the same pattern of government existing in the early parliamentary institutions of Europe during the same period. The kingdoms that spread into the forested areas of west Africa, in parts of present-day Nigeria and other states, also benefited from the trading and craft skills of the Sudanic peoples. Particularly in the loosely organized kingdom of Benin, an important artistic tradition developed in woodcarving and metal sculpture, featuring powerful portrayals of divine spirits and human forms alike.

By about 1400, then, much of northern and central Africa south of the Sahara was organized

Bust of a king from Benin, west Africa, center of some of the most imaginative African art. Gold-braided hair and necklace show the man's royal status.

into regional kingdoms, with an especially potent imperial tradition in the Sudan. Most states were not tightly organized. Some were Muslim in leadership, others strictly polytheistic. Boundaries among states were not firmly set, in part because bureaucracies were too small to enforce them, in part because political rule still depended heavily on personal loyalties and alliances. And there were areas, including many active trading centers and artistic cultures, organized on a purely local basis in addition to the city-states of east Africa. The forested regions of west Africa contrasted with the large states of the Sudan, in part because their geography prevented the travel and operation of any cavalry. These were stateless societies in terms of structures beyond village and family levels. Clearly,

however, agriculture and advances in crafts, manufacturing, and trade were spreading ever more widely into the tropical forests, and with this came a tendency toward more formal and effective political administration.

Even more widely, the Bantu migrations continued. As early as 860 C.E., some Bantu farmers had reached territory in what is now the nation of South Africa. Bantus also spread into the rich agricultural plateaus of eastern Africa, in present-day Kenya and Uganda. This was a gradual migration, spurred by recurring land shortages. Until 1500, many of the Bantu settlements were short-lived, as farming problems or conflicts with local hunting groups forced periodic movement. As a result, not many large political units developed until a later point. A few kingdoms

HISTORY DEBATE

HANDLES FOR AFRICAN HISTORY

Until fairly recently, most Westerners viewed Africa as a land of considerable mystery and backwardness, the "dark continent," and assumed that most of it had little history until the arrival of Europeans. Important research and scholarly work on African history has proved this imperialistic attitude wrong. More recently, some scholars have blasted what they see as consistent efforts to belittle the African past, arguing that the continent's great achievements, beginning with ancient Egypt, need far more emphasis and that Western criteria for measuring a society's success are distorted and narrow.

In between some of these debates, a number of historians seek explanations for some general features of African civilization in the postclassical period and beyond. Comparison can help. One scholar has noted how similar African and western European societies were around 1200. Both imitated more advanced centers in the Mediterranean. Both had fairly loose political organizations, although African kingdoms were larger than their European counterparts; tribal loyalties were important in both regions. Both saw the rapid advance of trade and merchants. Of course, differences exist, particularly in the degree of impact world religions have had and in the extent of writing, but the similarities are revealing. Two hundred years later, the comparison changes shape: Europe was beginning to explore more widely, whereas Africa maintained established patterns to a greater extent. Africa had never emphasized oceangoing activity, in part because (particularly on the Atlantic coast) it did not have a rich network of navigable rivers. Its relations with Islam were smooth, in contrast to Christian Europe, where a dependence on Islam for trade was viewed negatively. Unlike Europe, Africa gained little from new knowledge of Asian technologies. This represents a complex mix of factors, reflecting some African limitations by European standards, but also an absence of some of the problems that beset postclassical Europe. Does a society largely content with its substantial achievements—as African leaders were by 1400—require special explanation?

arose, often with Bantu overlords ruling a subject local people; two such kingdoms, Rwanda and Burundi, have survived into the 21st century.

One great empire flourished for a time in Zimbabwe. This was a gold-producing region, with links to the trading cities of east Africa. Powerful kings built a huge stone-walled city, the ruins of which fascinated archeologists in later ages. The sheer size of the stone monuments of Zimbabwe rivals the buildings of ancient Egypt and the Mayans. Concepts of divine kingship prevailed in this great state, which at its height around 1300 ruled a vast territory in southeastern Africa. Zimbabwe declined, as mysteriously as it rose, after about 1400. Although unique in its monument-building capacity, it serves as additional evidence of the

spread, however uneven, of new political organization across much of Africa.

FEATURES OF AFRICAN CIVILIZATION

African civilization, as it had developed by the 15th century, was characterized by obvious diversity and disunity on the one hand, and common general themes on the other. In politics, the tendency to embrace a divine monarch, but to temper this form of government with some kind of advisory councils, set a clear—although again far from uniform—political pattern. Africans in many regions were acquiring skills in the art of state-building. In the Sudanic kingdoms, increasingly sophisticated forms of organization were devised, and, on the whole, African political development shows a progression much like that of western Europe during the Middle Ages.

Africans were also creating a significant commercial tradition, particularly, of course, on the east coast and in the Sudan. There were no institutional innovations, such as banking networks, but the family-based trading companies had genuine cohesion. Landowning lords emerged in many parts of Africa, and in some cases one tribal group was controlled by an upper class from another tribe; this was true in some areas settled by the Bantu. In general, however, African farmers were freer than their counterparts in western Europe during most of the Middle Ages; there was no manorial system to dispute peasants' control of property. At the same time, slavery was practiced in a number of areas. Many slaves were taken in the frequent wars that occurred during early African history. Some families, however, were enslaved on a hereditary basis. Slaves were used for a variety of tasks, ranging from personal service to mining and soldiering.

The African economy was bounded by limitations on technology. Despite the displays of great wealth in some states, there was less wealth overall than in the civilizations of Asia, and populations were smaller as a result. African farmers established irrigation systems and developed considerable knowledge of a variety of crops. Mining techniques improved steadily, as Africans discovered ways to sink deeper shafts and refine gold more efficiently. By the 15th century, west African miners had produced a total of perhaps 5500 tons of gold, and they produced as much again during the next four centuries. Copper and ironworking also had developed extensively, although overall, by 1400, manufacturing technology (as opposed to artistic creativity) was lagging behind Eurasian standards, in part because Africans imported fewer technologies from Asia.

African society characteristically featured tight family structures. The links among extended kin, even in different villages, formed one of the key bonds of African society even when political structures, in a more formal sense, were weak. African families, moreover, devoted considerable time to children. Mothers typically carried infants while at work, in contrast to the Western tendency to separate mother and child as early as possible. Women were officially inferior in the African family, and some African groups controlled women's behavior rigorously. In general, however, women had considerable status in not only the family but also public functions such as operating shops in the open market. Their diverse roles in agriculture and commerce stood in contrast to their place in most Asian societies.

Women's public freedom and colorful dress, as we have seen, differed from the Islamic traditions of north Africa and the Middle East. The famous 14th-century Arab traveler, Ibn Battuta, an admirer of African wealth, political power, and piety, was nonetheless shocked by what he saw among women. "With regard to their women, they are not modest in the presence of men, they do not veil themselves in spite of their perseverance in the prayers. . . . The women there have friends and companions among men." Here was another case where contact and even imitation did not erase regional traditions. Although Africans participated in the spread of Islam, and such involvements resulted in real change, they did so in their own way.

By 1400, religious divisions were important in sub-Saharan Africa. Ethiopia maintained its Christianity. Islam had spread to various parts of the Sudan and to the port cities on the Indian Ocean. Islam was not yet a mass religion in Africa, but its hold over a substantial portion of the north and west was already established.

Africans converted to Islam for several reasons, including personal piety and engagement with Islamic intellectual life. Some leaders saw political benefits in Islam, using Muslims for their skills in writing and in bureaucracy. Some leaders, however pious, also maintained older commitments to "divine kingship" to supplement

Islamic political principles. Many Africans were attracted to Islam through its role in trade. Some men found benefits in Islam's espousal of polygamy. Some African women valued the protection of property rights in the dowry that was established in Islamic law.

Most Africans, even in the sub-Saharan Islamic states, remained polytheists. As in many other agricultural societies, Africans relied heavily on magical explanations of natural occurrences that they could not otherwise explain. African polytheism was elaborate and comprehensive in its scope, which helps account for its durability even when competing against monotheistic religions such as Islam. It involved belief in a supreme being, who was responsible for creating the universe and a corresponding set of beliefs, and subsidiary gods and spirits, good and evil, who actually managed daily affairs such as crops and wars. These lesser gods, who had the greatest influence on people's lives, received the most attention. Religious rituals, organized by medicine men, played an important role in treating illness. At the same time, Africans had a certain sense of skepticism; too much religious fervor was regarded with suspicion. A Nigerian proverb held that when a person displayed excessive religious belief, "people can tell him the wood he is made of"—that is, they can remind him that he is only mortal.

Religion played a significant role in directing African artistic achievements. Work in wood, ivory, and terra-cotta had advanced steadily by 1400, particularly in west Africa. Many masks and statues had religious significance and were used in dances of worship and other ceremonies. African art emphasized strong, stark portrayals, without intricate detail. Artists had an important place in urban society, along with most other artisans. In certain areas, such as the Bantu regions, African art displayed a particular interest in the circle, rather than in other shapes, as the basic geometric unit for art and architecture. Many homes and great temples—in Zimbabwe, for instance—were built in a circular form. Even today, many African children readily draw perfect circles, in contrast to the great reliance on squares and angles characteristic of European and Asian education.

African development was proceeding actively by 1400. New kingdoms endured for many centuries, as did artistic, religious, and family traditions. European contacts altered the face of some regions in Africa increasingly after about 1500, but without the overwhelming disruption of an entire society that occurred in the Americas. Among other things, Africans had maintained sufficient ties with other cultures to develop adequate immunity to some of the great diseases of Europe and Asia; hence, the population was not decimated through plagues, as happened among the native peoples of the Americas. The arrival of Europeans by the late 15th century thus represents a partial break in African history. However, European explorers and settlers interacted with a highly developed African society, and for many centuries basic trends established during the formative period of civilization south of the Sahara continued.

PATHS TO THE PRESENT

Sub-Saharan Africa did not establish a single "great tradition," in contrast to key civilizations in Asia and Europe. Most notably, it adapted world religions from other regions, rather than establishing its own. This complicates African legacies as they affect the contemporary world. Furthermore, European imperialism in modern Africa overran many African institutions, including political boundaries, disrupting Africans' connection with their past.

Still, African developments during the postclassical period have continuing impact. They provided monuments with which contemporary Africans can identify—hence the use of older names such as *Ghana* and *Mali* for modern nations. They provided enduring political themes. Many observers note an ongoing African penchant for the leadership of "big men" in government and believe it may link to older ideas and symbols associated with divine kingship. The creative art forms pioneered in west Africa survive in African art today and have influenced artistic styles in other places as well, including Europe and North America. Patriarchal ideas about gender persist, though their complexity resists facile description. Some African feminists praise the strong role some women have achieved in traditional Africa, while also believing in the validity of the protections provided by solid community life and family ties. Some male-dominated African courts, in places such as Zimbabwe, have recently evoked African traditions that gave men the ownership of all family property—which includes women and children. Finally, Islam continues to play a vigorous role in sub-Saharan African culture, building from the basis established in the postclassical centuries.

SUGGESTED WEB SITES

On medieval African kingdoms, see http://score.rims.k12.ca.us/score_lessons/medieval_african_kingdoms/; on Africa during the Middle Ages, see http://www.medieval-life.net/africa.htm; on Africa to ca. 1500 C.E., see http://hercules.gcsu.edu/~dvess/africa.htm; on African heritage, see http://whc.unesco.org/exhibits/afr_rev/toc.htm.

SUGGESTED READINGS

On sub-Saharan Africa, several source collections are interesting reading: G. S. P. Freeman-Greenville, *The East African Coast: Select Documents from the First to the Earlier Nineteenth Century* (1962); D. T. Niane, *Sundiata: An Epic of Old Mali* (1986); and Ross Dunn, *Adventures of Ibn Battuta, A Muslim Traveler of the Fourteenth Century* (2005). Recent works include Graham Connah, *African Civilizations: An Archaeological Perspective* (2001); Philip Curtin et al., *African History from Earliest Times to Independence* (1995). See also B. Davidson, *Africa in History* (1974); J. D. Fage, *Africa Discovers Her Past* (1970); Richard Olaniyan, *African History and Culture* (1982); R. S. Smith, *Warfare and Diplomacy in Pre-Colonial West Africa* (1969); N. Levtzion and Hopkins, eds., *Ancient Ghana* (1981); Anne Hilton, *The Kingdom of the Kongo* (1985); David Birmingham and Phyllis Martin, *History of Central Africa*, 2 vols. (1983); Derek Nurse and Thomas Spear, *The Swahili: Reconstructing the History and Language of an African Society* (1985); and J. Middleton, *The World of the Swahili and African Mercantile Civilization* (1992). On Africa and Islam, see Uthman Sayyid Ahmad Ismail Al-Bili, *Some Apsects of Islam in Africa* (2008) and Nehemia Levtzion, *Islam in Africa and the Middle East: Studies on Conversion and Renewal* (2007). On women, refer to N. Hafkin and E. Bay, *Women in Africa* (1976), and H. Loth, *Women in Ancient Africa* (1992). See also A. H. M. Jones and Elizabeth Monroe, *A History of Ethiopia* (1955), and two studies by one of the pioneers in using new sources to reexamine early African history, J. Vansina, *The Children of Woot: A History of the Kuba People* (1978), and *Art History in Africa* (1984). On trade patterns, see Richard W. Bulliet, *The Camel and the Wheel* (1975). An interesting recent work is Christopher Ehret, *The Civilizations of Africa: A History to 1800* (2002). See also Eva Evers Rosander, ed., *African Islam and Islam in Africa* (1997); Timothy Insoll, *The Archeology of Islam in sub-Saharan Africa* (2002); and Ahmend S. Bangura, *Islam and the West African Novel* (2000).

CHAPTER 11

East European Civilization: Byzantium and Russia

Important civilizations expanded in Europe during the postclassical period. They linked actively with the world trade network, while interacting with Islam even as they developed different world religions. Eastern Europe initially led the way. The existence, in Byzantium, of a successor empire to Rome, in the northeastern Mediterranean, served as a beacon to emerging kingdoms in eastern Europe, particularly among many Slavic groups.

Two major Christian zones arose in Europe during the postclassical centuries. Each represented a distinctive version of that faith, symbolized by the formal split between the Eastern Orthodox and Western Catholic churches in the 11th century. Similar beliefs, some shared memories of classical Greece and Rome, and their geographical position as neighbors produced some common features in east and west European civilizations. On the whole, however, the two societies took different forms, and the centuries after 500 saw these differences develop and then solidify.

Indeed, Byzantium had much the same kind of outreach that India and China demonstrated during the postclassical period, as it helped shape other parts of eastern Europe in establishing basic cultural and political patterns. Byzantium, at its height, approximated the economic and political sophistication of the Asian civilizations, as evidenced by its great capital city, Constantinople. Like its purely Asian counterparts, Byzantium built on classical foundations while responding to new religious fervor. East European civilization, initially centered in the Byzantine Empire, had the closest contacts with the traditions of the classical Mediterranean world. As a result, for many centuries this east European civilization greatly surpassed the West in political sophistication, culture, and economic vitality. Like its neighbor to the west, however, it had one important feature: a strong desire to expand, particularly through the Christian religion. Blocked from expansion to the east and south by the rise of the Islamic caliphate, the Byzantine emperors and church patriarchs turned their eyes to the northern peoples. The spread of Orthodox Christianity in eastern Europe rivaled that of Roman Catholicism in the West, with key contacts running south to north in each case.

KEY QUESTIONS   *This chapter presents east European society as a different civilization from that of western Europe, despite the spread of Christianity in both regions. Is this framework more accurate than dealing with a single Christian Europe? What were the main differences between East and West? (Answering this question involves this chapter and the next.) How did each society use its Greco-Roman heritage? Another juxtaposition is useful: how did Russia's imitation of the Byzantine Empire compare to African imitation of the Middle East (or Japanese use of Chinese models)? What was copied, and what was not? Finally, what were the causes and results of east European decline toward the end of the postclassical period?*

THE BYZANTINE PHASE

The development of the Byzantine Empire effectively began in the 4th century C.E. It was at this point that the Roman Empire established its eastern capital in Constantinople, which quickly became the most vigorous center of the otherwise fading empire. The Emperor Constantine ordered the construction of many elegant buildings, including Christian churches, in his new city, which was built on the foundations of a previously modest town called Byzantium. Soon, separate eastern emperors ruled from this city, even before the western portion of the empire fell to Germanic invaders. Constantinople was responsible for the Balkan Peninsula, the northern Middle East, the Mediterranean coast, and north Africa. Although for several centuries Latin served as the court language of the Eastern empire, Greek was the common tongue and,

after the Emperor Justinian, it became the official language as well. Indeed, in the eyes of Easterners, Latin became an inferior, barbaric means of communication. Knowledge of Greek enabled educated people in the Eastern empire to read the philosophical and literary classics of ancient Athens and the Hellenistic culture.

As the Eastern empire took shape, Christianity also began its split between East and West. In the West, the Roman pope controlled basic church organization. But there was no comparable leader in the Eastern church. The patriarch, or bishop, of Constantinople held top prestige, but there were three other patriarchs in the East, none of whom had political control over the church. For several centuries, the Eastern church in principle acknowledged the authority of the pope, but in practice papal directives had no hold over the Byzantine church. Rather, the Eastern emperors regulated church organization, creating a pattern of state control over church structure quite different from the tradition that developed in the West, where the church insisted, although not always successfully, on its independence. Disputes over doctrine, including such issues as the recipe used to make bread for the *eucharist,* the sacramental celebration of Christ's sacrifice in the mass, further divided the two churches. Even the two churches' monastic movements differed, following separate rules.

The early history of the Eastern empire, which came to be known as *Byzantine* after the capital city's name, was marked by the constant threat of invasion. The Eastern emperors vanquished Sassanid Persian and Germanic attacks. Early emperors developed a solid military base, recruiting local soldiers in addition to hiring some mercenaries. Upper-class Greeks, recapturing their lapsed military tradition, provided a series of able generals. The Emperor Justinian tried, of course, to regain Roman territories in western Europe and north Africa, but despite brief successes, his effort left the Eastern empire exhausted and financially drained. The empire was successful, however, in expanding a bit to the north. A major fort in the Crimea, for example, north of the

WORLD PROFILES

THE EMPEROR JUSTINIAN
(527–565 C.E.)

The Emperor Justinian attempted to revive the Roman Empire; he achieved considerable although short-term success. He also served, somewhat unintentionally, as a founding figure in the Byzantine Empire that long survived. Justinian and his generals briefly succeeded in regaining Roman territories in western Europe and north Africa. The law code compiled during his reign assembled and reconciled the laws and legal precedents of the later Roman Empire, thus preserving and clarifying Roman law for all of Europe. Justinian also oversaw the construction of Saint Sophia, the great church of Constantinople that influenced Byzantine and Islamic architecture for centuries. Despite his desire to restore Roman culture, it is interesting to note the revealing differences between his image in art and the more traditional portrayal of the Roman Caesars (see Chapter 6). In the mosaic shown here, Justinian's costume, and the surrounding group of church and court officials, indicated the unity of the Byzantine state and the Orthodox church, as the emperor is portrayed as both king and priest. How does this depiction compare with the Roman political tradition?

This mosaic of Justinian is from San Vitale in Ravenna, Italy. Ravenna was one of the many cities Justinian recaptured in western Europe, a city that also served at times as the capital of the Western empire.

Black Sea, helped prevent Germanic invasions. Justinian's monumental law code, assembling and reconciling the law and legal precedents of the later Roman Empire, was of vital service in preserving and clarifying Roman law for both eastern and western Europe. However, Justinian's ideas on territorial expansion were less fortunate. He was a somber personality, autocratic by nature, and prone to grandiose conceptions. A contemporary historian named Procopius, no friend of the emperor, described him as "at once villainous and amenable; as people say colloquially, a moron. He was never truthful with anyone, but always guileful in what he said and did, yet easily hoodwinked by any who wanted to deceive him." The emperor was also heavily influenced by his wife, Theodora, of humble origin but willful and eager for power. Justinian, urged on by Theodora, contended successfully with massive popular unrest at one point by putting 30,000 rebels to death.

Later emperors were eager to consolidate the Eastern territories alone, recognizing that grander visions were unrealistic. The Persians were defeated early in the 7th century, and the newer threat, from the Arabs, was also averted, although not without the loss of most of the Mediterranean portions of the empire south of Constantinople. Arab armies besieged the capital city, but they were repelled in part through the use of a flammable weapon called "Greek fire," a mixture of petroleum, quicklime, and sulfur. Greek fire was shot through long copper tubes and could, among other things, burn enemy ships. The result of these battles was an empire about half the size of the previous eastern half of the Roman Empire, united around its Greek and Balkan populations. Once more, carefully organized military recruitment served the embattled empire well, because strong army officers were often able to control weak emperors. After a final invasion attempt, in 718 C.E., the Arabs never seriously threatened Constantinople again.

Soon after this, the Byzantine Empire began to seek new territories and cultural allies in the vast stretches of eastern Europe. The attractions of

Hellenistic culture remained strong. Many regional rulers in southeastern Europe, such as the kings of Bulgaria, admired its accomplishments and often were educated at Constantinople. They were not easy neighbors, however, sometimes seeking territory at the empire's expense and, during the many disputes over legitimate ascendancy to the Byzantine throne, occasionally claiming imperial rule directly. A Bulgarian king in the 10th century took the title of *tsar*, a Slavic version of *caesar*. However, diplomacy, intermarriage, and, above all, war eroded regional kingdoms such as Bulgaria. In the 11th century, the Byzantine emperor Basil II, known appropriately enough as Bulgaroktonos, or slayer of the Bulgarians, used the empire's wealth to bribe many Bulgarian nobles and generals. He defeated the Bulgarian army in 1014 and blinded as many as 15,000 captive soldiers—the sight of whom later brought on the Bulgarian king's death. Thus, Bulgaria became part of the empire, its aristocracy settling in Constantinople and merging with the leading Greek families.

Even more important than Byzantine expansion into the Balkans—an area stretching between the present-day nations of Slovenia in the west and Bulgaria and Romania in the east—was the extension of Eastern, or orthodox, Christianity to these regions and beyond. A major missionary effort was mounted to convert the Slavic and other peoples in the Balkans and points north to Eastern, or Orthodox, Christianity. In 864, the government sent the missionaries Cyril and Methodius to the territory that is now the Czech Republic and Slovakia. The conversion attempt failed in this region, where Roman Catholic missionaries were more successful. But the Byzantine missionaries did pull back into the Balkans and southern Russia, where their ability to speak the Slavic language greatly aided their efforts. They devised a written script for this language, derived from Greek letters; to this day, the Slavic alphabet is known as *Cyrillic*.

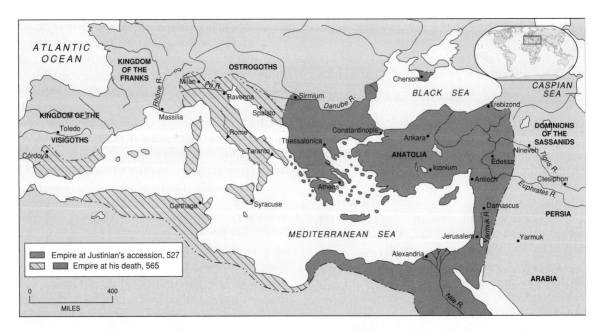

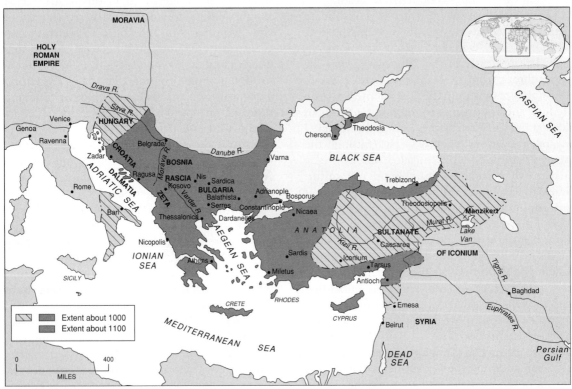

The Byzantine Empire and Its Decline

Use of "Greek fire" by a 9th-century Byzantine fleet against an invader.

The Byzantine Empire entered a particularly stable period during the 9th and 10th centuries under a family dynasty from Macedonia. This dynasty managed to avoid the quarrels over succession that had beset earlier ruling families. The result was growing prosperity as well as solid political rule. The luxury of the court and its buildings steadily increased. Elaborate ceremonies and rich imperial processions created a magnificence designed to dazzle the empire's subjects. The Macedonian dynasty also extended the empire's territories in central Asia and the Balkans. Substantial trade with Asia developed, along with a thriving production of silk. Constantinople, in the northeastern corner of the Mediterranean and at the entrance to the Black Sea, was an ideal location for trade, both from east to west and from south to north. The empire became the hub of a new trade northward, through Russia to Scandinavia. Not only silk but also other luxury products such as gold and jewelry gave the empire a favorable trading position with less sophisticated lands. Briefly, at the end of the 10th century, the Byzantine emperor may have been the most powerful single monarch on earth, with a capital city whose rich buildings and abundant popular entertainments awed visitors from western Europe.

It was at the end of this vigorous period that Byzantium broke fully with Western Catholicism. There had been no serious contact between the two branches of Christianity for several centuries, but neither side had cared to make a definitive statement on this fact. In 1054, however, an ambitious patriarch in Constantinople raised a host of old disputes, including the quarrel over what kind of bread to use for Mass. He also attacked the Roman Catholic practice of insisting on celibacy for its priests; Eastern Orthodox priests could marry. Delegations of the two churches discussed the disputes, but this led only to renewed bitterness. The Roman pope finally excommunicated the patriarch and his followers; the patriarch, in turn, excommunicated all Roman Catholics. Thus, the split between the Roman Catholic Church and Eastern Orthodoxy, which came to include several Orthodox churches—the Greek, the Russian, and the Serbian, among others—became formal; it endured until 1965 when the Pope and the Eastern Patriarch finally cancelled the mutual excommunication. The schism was not, despite the drama, a total break. But there was growing estrangement between the two branches of Christianity.

Shortly thereafter, the Byzantine Empire entered a long period of decline. Having already gained increasing influence in the Islamic caliphate, Turkish invaders began to attack the eastern borders. In the later 11th century, Turkish troops seized almost all the Asiatic provinces of the empire, thus cutting off the most prosperous

Saint Sophia, the great church in Constantinople built under Justinian. It was converted to a mosque by the Turks after their successful conquest. At that point, the minarets were added.

sources of tax revenue as well as the territories that had supplied most of the empire's food. The empire eked by for another four centuries, but its doom was virtually sealed. At one point, a force of crusaders from Italy and other west European territories even captured Constantinople, on the pretext that they were seeking reconquest of the Holy Land. This fourth crusade, in 1204, destroyed three-quarters of the city and also furthered a process by which Western, particularly Italian, merchants came to dominate trade with the Middle East, reinforcing the economic decline of Byzantium. Then a new group of Turks, the Ottomans, invaded, closing in on Constantinople by the early 15th century. The Turks finally laid siege to the city in 1453, using the largest cannon

ever constructed up until that point. Byzantine efforts to obtain help from western Europe failed, because the Western and Eastern churches could not agree on religious terms. The city fell, becoming the capital of a new Ottoman Empire. The great cathedral built by Justinian, St. Sophia, was converted to a magnificent Islamic mosque. As the Turks took control of the final remnants of the empire in the Balkans, in the eight years after 1453, the long history of Byzantium finally closed.

Elements of its heritage, however, lived on. If Byzantium achieved nothing else, its contribution to forming a new civilization among many of the Slavic peoples of eastern Europe alone justifies its place in history. With the decline and fall of the Byzantine Empire, the focus of east European civilization passed northward, particularly to Russia.

THE EARLY RUSSIAN PHASE: KIEVAN RUS'

Slavic peoples had moved into the sweeping plains of Russia and eastern Europe during the time of the Roman Empire. They were already familiar with the use of iron, and they extended agriculture in the rich soils of what is now western Russia. Their political organization long rested in family tribes and villages; they maintained a polytheistic religion with gods for the sun, thunder, wind, and fire. Gradually, some loose regional kingdoms formed among the Slavs.

During the 6th and 7th centuries, traders from Scandinavia began to journey to the Slavic lands, moving along the great rivers of western Russia, particularly the Dnieper. Through this route they were able to reach the Byzantine Empire, and a flourishing trade developed between Scandinavia and Constantinople. The Scandinavian traders, who were militarily superior to the Slavs, gradually established some governments along their trade route. A monarchy emerged, and according to legend, Rurik, a native of Denmark, became the first king of Russia, ascending to the throne around 855. This kingdom soon established its center in the city of Kiev, which remained the capital of Russia until the 12th century. Kievan Rus' centered in what is now Ukraine, but its contacts affected Russia proper as well. It was the Scandinavian traders, indeed, who coined the term *Russia*—possibly from a Greek word for *red*, referring to the hair color of many of the northern people. The Scandinavians gradually mingled with the larger Slavic population.

Contacts between Kievan Russia and Byzantium extended steadily. Russia became one of the several societies during the period that freely imitated Byzantine civilization. Kiev, because of its central location, became a

The Cathedral of St. Dmitry was built from 1194 through 1197, during the reign of Prince Vsevolod III. Its famous white stone carvings celebrate the myths and heroes of many cultures as well as the beauty of the biblical God's creation through the portrayal of numerous plants and animals.

prosperous trading center, channeling goods, from the Muslim lands as well as from Byzantium, that had first passed through Constantinople. Many Russians visited Constantinople. These exchanges led to a growing knowledge of Christianity. King Vladimir I (980–1015) finally took the step of converting to Christianity, not only in his own name but in that of all his people. Vladimir was eager to avoid the influence of Roman Catholicism, because he feared papal control as being competitive with his own power; he was also influenced by rivalries with his neighbor, the king of Poland, who had recently converted to Catholicism.

In addition, Russian awe at the splendor of religious services in Constantinople may have played a role. Vladimir certainly wanted the link to the Byzantine Empire. Rebuffed when he asked to marry the emperor's daughter, he conquered Byzantine territory in the Crimea, promising to give it back if he could marry the princess. And the court obliged. Once converted to Christianity, Vladimir proceeded to organize mass baptisms for his subjects, forcing conversions by military pressure when necessary. Remnants of the old religion were incorporated into Russian Orthodoxy, as when gods of nature were made into Christian saints.

An early Russian chronicle described the conversion of Vladimir and his subjects to Christianity as follows:

> For at this time the Russes were ignorant pagans. The devil rejoiced thereat, for he did not know that his ruin was approaching. He was so eager to destroy the Christian people, yet he was expelled by the true cross even from these very lands. . . . Vladimir was visited by Bulgars of the Mohammedan faith. . . . [He] listened to them for he was fond of women and indulgence, regarding which he heard with pleasure. But . . . abstinence from pork and wine were disagreeable to him. "Drinking," said he, "is the joy of the Russes. We cannot exist without that pleasure." [Russian envoys sent to Constantinople] were astonished [by the beauty of the churches and the chanting], and in their wonder praised the Greek ceremonial. . . .
>
> [Later, Vladimir was suffering from blindness; a Byzantine bishop baptized him] and as the bishop laid his hand upon him, he straightway recovered his sight. Upon experiencing this miraculous cure, Vladimir glorified God, saying, "I have now perceived the one true God." When his followers beheld this miracle, many of them were also baptized. Thereafter Vladimir sent heralds throughout the whole city to proclaim that if any inhabitant, rich or poor, did not betake himself to the river

> [for mass baptism] he would risk the Prince's displeasure. When the people heard these words, they wept for joy and exclaimed in their enthusiasm, "If this were not good, the Prince and his nobles would not have accepted it." . . . There was joy in heaven and upon earth to behold so many souls saved. But the devil groaned, lamenting, "Woe is me. How am I driven out hence . . . my reign in these regions is at an end."

By this point, Kievan Russia was the largest state in Europe, although it remained loosely organized. Rurik's descendants tried to avoid damaging fights over succession to the throne. The Russian kings were able to issue a formal law code, borrowed in part from Byzantium; this code among other things reduced the severity of traditional punishments in Russia and replaced personal vendettas with state-run courts.

The Kievan kingdom began to decline from about 1100 on. Rival princes established their own regional governments. Invaders from Asia whittled away at Russian territory. The eclipse of Byzantium reduced Russia's wealth, for the kingdom had always depended heavily on the greater prosperity and sophisticated manufacturing of its southern neighbor. A new kingdom was briefly established around a city near present-day Moscow, but by 1200, Russia was weak and disunited. The final blow, in this stage of Russian history, came in 1236, when a large force of Mongols from central Asia moved through Russia, hoping to add not only this country but also the whole of Europe to their growing empire. The Mongols, or *Tatars* as they are called in Russian history, easily captured the major Russian cities and moved into other parts of eastern Europe, including Poland, ending their invasions only because of political difficulties in their own homeland. For more than two centuries, Russia remained under Tatar control, although regional differences increased as both the Baltic peoples and Ukrainians began to emancipate themselves from Mongol-dominated Russia proper.

HISTORY DEBATE

A RUSSIAN CIVILIZATION?

Russia in the postclassical period was just beginning to shape an identity. It was not, by itself, a major player in world history. Many historians treat Russia as a part—often, a minor part—of Europe as a whole. Certainly Russia's distinctive features, compared to other parts of Europe, have changed over time. In the postclassical period, differences in religious and political styles, and trade routes, predominated. East European art, though similar in Christian subject matter, was also different. Later, social differences in distinguishing Europe east and west loomed larger, along with politics. Today, just to add a final complication, many Russians (though not all) hope to become more Western, and earlier distinctions may fade. Decisions about characterizing Russia have never been easy. This is not a self-evident case of civilization coherence, unlike that represented by China.

Discussions about Russia, finally, spill over to neighboring parts of east central Europe, where patterns have sometimes resembled those in Russia, sometimes more those of the West. Without much doubt, the boundary between eastern and western Europe has changed with time—the past 15 years included.

EAST EUROPEAN POLITICAL INSTITUTIONS

The postclassical period was a formative one for what proved to be a durable east European civilization, particularly in Russia. Even the era of Mongol rule did not displace basic characteristics established in Russia in part through Byzantine influence, including, of course, Orthodox Christianity. Obviously, much was yet to happen in the development of east European civilization, as Russia came into its own again in the late 1400s. Furthermore, as in other cases of cultural diffusion during the postclassical period, the great influence Byzantium exerted on Russia did not result in complete assimilation. Nevertheless, especially in politics and culture, some customs and traditions dating from Byzantine and early Russian history still echo in east European civilization to the present day.

The Byzantine and early Russian political system emphasized authoritarian rule under an emperor or king. A key ingredient of this authoritarianism involved the state's control over the

Orthodox churches. Unlike the West, where the church remained partly separate from the state, and unlike the Muslim lands, where the ulema maintained separate religious institutions, east European rulers expected to be able to regulate church organization and even intervene in doctrinal disputes. This did not lessen the intense piety of Orthodox Christianity, but it unquestionably enhanced the power of the state.

In Byzantium, that power was also exemplified by the elaborate ceremonies and luxury of the imperial court. The functions of government were also extensive. As a state almost constantly at war, the Byzantine Empire naturally stressed strong military organization and recruitment. It also attended to economic affairs. The state directly operated an immense silk factory and was active in regulating trade. An elaborate bureaucracy supported the various state functions. Its efficiency was sometimes questionable, as complex deals had to be struck to conduct new policies or even to make simple arrangements. In the English language, the term *byzantine* came to suggest a pattern of bargaining and bribing rather than straightforward procedures.

The early Russian monarchy, ruling over a less prosperous area, could not rival Byzantine splendor or the functions that the imperial government maintained. Yet Russian rulers, too, were attracted to luxurious ceremonies and to the idea, if not yet the reality, that the state should have widespread duties and a sweeping range of activity. The Russian bureaucracy remained small, as regional rulers owing allegiance to the king performed most administrative duties, but some features of Byzantine bureaucratic procedures later surfaced in Russia.

Russian authoritarianism was more directly enhanced by the Byzantine example through a sense of special mission. Byzantine rulers understandably claimed their imperial mantle as the heritage of the great Roman Empire. Early Russian kings acknowledged this, calling the Byzantine ruler tsar, or caesar. But when Byzantium fell, and when the Russian monarchy extricated itself from Tatar rule after 1450, Russian rulers took on the title tsar for themselves and claimed a new sense of imperial mission.

EAST EUROPEAN RELIGION AND CULTURE

The dominant feature of east European culture, in this early period, was of course Orthodox Christianity—the Greek Orthodox church established under the patriarch of Constantinople and the Russian and other Slavic Orthodox churches formed as a result of missionary efforts and state-led conversions.

Organizationally, the Orthodox churches, under some direction by the state, established bishoprics, and they assigned priests to conduct worship and maintain the faith. Many early Russian bishops were appointed by the patriarch in Constantinople, but the Russian church acquired increasing independence. Leading bishops were characteristically appointed by the king or a regional prince; this was a chief mechanism of state control even though the bishops then maintained considerable powers through appointments and the administration of church property and church law in their own right.

Orthodox Christianity conveyed a vivid sense of the power of God. A large number of saints, holy men and women whom the church recognized for their religious example, also commanded the attention of the faithful, becoming objects of prayer and veneration. Orthodox Christianity emphasized the importance of ritual. Churches were usually ornate, filled with the pungent smell of incense. Icons—pictures of religious figures, including the saints—helped direct religious devotion. Some Orthodox leaders attacked the use of icons, fearing that they would become religious objects in and of themselves, but their creation and use persisted.

In addition to ritual and the adoration of holy figures, Orthodox religion stressed Christian morality and charity toward the poor and unfortunate. Rulers as well as ordinary people were encouraged to behave ethically. Traditional practices, such as polygamy among the early Russians, gradually yielded to the Christian family ethic, which held that a man should take only one wife. Almsgiving to the poor and aid to institutions that comforted the sick received great emphasis, in Kiev as well as in Constantinople. Good works of this sort were seen as a vital component of faith and worship. The strong tradition of personal almsgiving as a means of gaining God's grace actually delayed the development of more formal charitable and welfare organizations in imperial Russia.

Orthodox Christianity did not encourage an elaborate theology—that is, an intricate examination of the nature of God and the universe. Even in Byzantium, despite the accessibility of Greek philosophical texts, no extensive tradition of rational speculation or scientific inquiry developed. The importance of faith and good works seemed to preclude this kind of activity. Certainly in Russia, which remained intellectually more backward than its Byzantine exemplar, most religious writing continued to be strictly devotional, full of praises to the saints and invocations of the power of God. Disasters, according to Russian writers, came as just expressions of the wrath of God against the wickedness of humanity; success in war involved the aid of God and the saints, in the name jointly of Russia and the Orthodox faith. Beliefs of this sort were common in western Europe as well as in the east European zone, but the absence of other kinds of philosophical and scientific inquiry proved to be a distinctively Eastern trait.

The special cultural attributes of Eastern Orthodoxy showed clearly in the monastic movement, both in the Byzantine Empire and in Kievan Russia. Monasteries received large grants of property from charitable donors. Some monks, to be sure, maintained an existence as hermits, an Eastern tradition of mortification of the flesh that was not so widely adopted in the West. But most monks lived in congregations, under rules established by St. Basil of Cappadocia in the 4th century. Orthodox monks lived their lives performing useful works, presiding over hospitals, orphanages, and homes for the aged, and administering extensive charity to the poor. Unlike Western monks, they did not devote much attention to intellectual activities, seeing a life of zealous faith and good works as sufficient service to God.

The spread of Christianity to Russia and the development of the Cyrillic alphabet facilitated the creation of Russian literature. A strong tradition of oral history existed already, although many sagas were not recorded until later. Early Russian literature consisted primarily of chronicles by members of the clergy, who sought to record the histories of their region and what they perceived as God's work in the world. The first of these narratives dates from the 12th century. Some secular poetry also described wars and the activities of the princes.

Byzantine art and architecture, brought to Russia along with Christianity, established a rich decorative tradition. Orthodox churches were typically built in the form of a cross, surmounted by a dome. Many early Russian churches were wooden and have not survived, but some stone buildings were also constructed. For decoration, the Byzantines and early Russians used elaborate mosaics, depicting religious figures and scenes from the lives of the saints. Some paintings were created, particularly in the form of frescoes (wall paintings), and there were abundant icons, usually picturing the heads of saints. Following the Byzantine example, a Russian tradition of icon painting arose in Kiev, along with some fine work in illuminated manuscripts; this technique featured attention to detail and miniature figures.

Music also played a vital role in Russian culture, and Russian kings and princes maintained court musicians. In Orthodox religious services, chants helped move the spirits of the faithful.

Along with the religiously oriented art and literature, a vigorous popular oral tradition continued, combining music, street entertainments, and some theater. The Russian church constantly tried to suppress these forms, because they contained pre-Christian elements, but it was not entirely successful in this regard.

Overall, this formative period in east European civilization saw the development of a powerful religious sentiment. Religion and art alike developed quite separately from the forms of west European culture during the same time period. Cultural distance long supplemented geographical distance in keeping east European religious and intellectual life on its own wavelength. During much of the period from 500 to 1400, the fact that Byzantium so clearly outshone the West in art and some branches of literature only enhanced east European indifference to available Western models. Then, the long period of Tatar rule, while it did great harm to levels of cultural life in Russia, added to the differentiation of East and West in Europe, for the West was spared this kind of invasion and control.

A partition featuring the Russian icons of St. Olga, as Russians assimilated and then advanced this Byzantine art form.

EAST EUROPEAN ECONOMY AND SOCIETY

During most of the postclassical centuries, eastern Europe was well ahead of the West in technology and commerce; even Russia and the Balkans dominated iron manufacturing and other key processes. However, from about the 12th century on, the balance began to shift—as western European dominance over Constantinople in the Mediterranean amply signified. After centuries of Mongol rule, Russia emerged as distinctly inferior to the West in terms of levels of manufacturing and commercial skills. Thus, the leading economic achievements of this period did not create a significant legacy for east European society later on.

There were, however, some features worthy of note in the economy and social patterns of eastern Europe at this point. In both the Byzantine Empire and Russia, a large free peasantry was the dominant social class. This contrasted with the serfdom of many west European peasants and contributed to the productive agriculture of eastern Europe. Both Byzantium and Russia tolerated some slavery, a practice that was rarer in the West at this time. Widespread slavery persisted in Russia through the 17th century, although the Orthodox church tried to curtail it.

An important aristocracy developed in eastern Europe as well. Aristocrats in Russia, called *boyars,* had less political power than their counterparts in western Europe, except when kings were weak. Nevertheless, the nobility exerted some authority. Along with the church, aristocrats controlled considerable land, and their hold over the land only increased in later centuries, thus reducing the holdings of the free peasantry. Unlike the feudal pattern of western Europe (or Japan), aristocrats did not join together in bonds of mutual loyalty.

Socially and economically, as in other ways, eastern Europe developed according to its own dynamic; it was not simply a distant echo of western European civilization. Even when east European social trends later shifted, this characteristic, on the whole, remained.

EAST EUROPEAN CIVILIZATION IN ECLIPSE

The period that had seen an early east European civilization raise and extend its borders ended with that same civilization in apparent disarray. The collapse of the Byzantine bastion and Tatar control of Russia might well have destroyed the civilization outright. It is certainly true that the active south–north trade that had linked the various centers of eastern Europe never reoccurred. Even within Russia, commerce fell off and the levels of manufacturing deteriorated. Cultural activity withered as well. Some chronicles continued to be written, but literacy declined; many priests did not know how to read. In this respect as well as in economics, eastern Europe emerged after 1400 with a great deal of catching up to do.

Although Byzantine society was never restored, the decline of east European civilization overall proved only temporary. In Russia, key political traditions, major social groups including the boyar aristocracy, and religious and artistic traditions emerged virtually unscathed. In this sense, Tatar domination, although frightening to Russians, was fairly superficial in its effects. There were also some benefits, such as the introduction of a postal system and paper money. Russia also gained new trade contacts with Asia.

One final point requires clarification, as it relates to both the formative east European centuries and more recent developments. East European civilization initially developed within the context of large empires: first the Byzantine, then the Russian. However, the civilization, both before 1400 and since, also spilled over to other parts of eastern Europe that never formed durable empires. Orthodox Christianity and a Cyrillic rather than Latin alphabet thus spread to Bulgaria and Serbia as well as to Russia. Yet other east European territories, such as Poland and Bohemia (now the Czech Republic and Slovakia), had more contacts with the West than the East. Although Slavic, these countries used a Latin alphabet and largely adopted Roman Catholicism. Their regional kingdoms, at points quite extensive, long existed as a sometimes uncomfortable buffer between Russia and the monarchies of western Europe. In other words, the boundary between west and east European civilizations was somewhat fluid, and it has shifted at different points over the centuries. The existence of a "border region" between Russia and the West was itself an important product of the spread of civilization northward in Europe from distinct Eastern and Western bases during the postclassical period.

PATHS TO THE PRESENT

Even though the Byzantine Empire is a thing of the past, east European postclassical history leaves traces in today's world apart from the splendid existing examples of Byzantine art.

Postclassical eastern Europe was defined in terms of Christianity, but the dominance of religion has faded in some parts of the region during the past century. Areas, such as Russia, that were Orthodox Christian developed a tight link between church and state that, many historians believe, has encouraged an authoritarian approach to government. Current differences between Russia and the West were hardly predetermined by the east–west European split in the postclassical period, but they are affected by it.

Russia was shaped by its contacts with Byzantium in other ways as well. Russian territorial expansion—which ultimately motivated the creation of one of the world's great landed empires—might have occurred without Byzantine example. But there is no doubt that Russian leaders were impressed with Byzantium's imperial claims and its legacy from the Roman Empire. The results of this are visible today in a country that stretches across 11 time zones.

The postclassical period also contributed to defining a fluid zone in east-central Europe, with potential ties both eastward and westward. The region was divided between Roman Catholicism and Orthodoxy, and between the Cyrillic and the Latin alphabets. This, along with the area's geographical position between Russia and western Europe, which has made it something of a borderland from the postclassical period on, helps explain the fluctuations in the region's orientation in recent decades. Currently, its alignments seem decidedly Western, with participation in the movements toward European unity; but the long-standing divisions have not been entirely mended, and questions of east-central Europe's orientation might reopen.

SUGGESTED WEB SITES

On Byzantine studies, see http://www.fordham. edu/halsall/byzantium/, http://www.doaks. org/research/Byzantine/, and http://www. byzantium1200.com/; on Kievan Rus', see http:// www.mnsu.edu/emuseum/history/russia/ kievanrus.html.

SUGGESTED READINGS

Recent work includes Michael Maas, *The Cambridge Companion to the Age of Justinian* (2005); Timothy Gregory, *A History of Byzantium* (2005); Averil Cameron, *The Byzantines* (2006); Helen C. Evans, ed., *Byzantium: Faith and Power (1261–1557)* (2004); Rowena Loverance, *Byzantium* (2004); Carolyn L. Connor, *Women of Byzantium* (2004); Ioli Kalavrezou, *Byzantine Women and Their World* (2003); Gilbert Dagron, *Emperor and Priest: The Imperical Office in Byzantium* (2003); Jonathan Harris, *Byzantium and the Crusades* (2003); Lucy-Anne Hunt, *Byzantium, Eastern Christendom and Islam: Art at the Crossroads of the Medieval Mediterranean* (1998); Anthony Cutler, *Byzantium, Italy and the North* (2000); and Robert Geraci, *Of Religion and Empire: Missions, Conversions and Tolerance in Tsarist Russia* (2001).

For studies on the Byzantine Empire, see Jonathan Shepard, ed., *The Expansion of Orthodox Europe: Byzantium, the Balkans and Russia* (2007); J. Hussey, *The Byzantine World* (1982); A. A. Vasiliev, *History of the Byzantine Empire* (1968); S. Runciman, *Byzantine Civilization* (1956); Norman Baynes and H. St. L. B. Moss, eds., *Byzantium* (1961); G. Every, *The Byzantine Patriarchate, 451–1204* (1978); D. M. Nicol, *Church and Society in the Last Centuries of Byzantium* (1979); E. Kitzinger, *Byzantine Art in the Making* (1977); and H. J. Magoulia, *Byzantine Christianity: Emperor, Church and the West* (1982). An excellent analysis of Byzantine influence in Eastern Europe is D. Obolensky's *The Byzantine Commonwealth: Eastern Europe, 500–1453* (1971). See also S. Runciman, *A History of the First Bulgarian Empire* (1930). On Russian history, the best survey is Nicholas Riasanovsky and Mark Steinberg, *A History of Russia*, 7th ed. (2005); it also includes a good bibliography. See also J. H. Billington, *The Icon and the Axe: An Interpretive History of Russian Culture* (1966); Wladyslaw, *Viking Rus: Studies on the Presence of Scandinavians in Eastern Europe* (2004); Valerie A. Kivelson and Robert H. Greene, *Orthodox Russia: Belief and Practice under the Tsars* (2003); and Sergei M. Soloviev, ed., *Russian Society: 1389–1425* (2001).

CHAPTER

12 Western Civilization: The Middle Ages

In contrast to eastern Europe, conditions deteriorated markedly in western Europe after Rome's fall. The deterioration of political forms, trade, city life, and intellectual endeavor reduced the achievements of classical Mediterranean civilization to only a faint memory. Between 700 and 1400 C.E., however, western Europe revived, creating new institutions and styles to accompany the selective adoption of earlier Roman and Greek traditions. Active interchange both with Byzantium and with the Arab world was a crucial part of this process. During most of this period, the area remained backward by standards of the great civilizations of the world. But, with the advantage of hindsight, we see that Western civilization was not only taking shape but also beginning to develop growing dynamism, particularly from the 11th century on.

Like other societies on the borders of the former classical world—Japan, Russia, the Sudanic kingdoms, and southeast Asia—western Europe borrowed actively during the postclassical period, although in ways that preserved a distinctive identity. There was no single source for imitation in this case, however, as west Europeans looked to Islam and Byzantium as well as the earlier traditions of Greece and Rome for guidance. The availability of several models may have been an advantage. Certainly, it helped open west Europeans to the importance of maintaining international contacts, even as they experienced fierce rivalries with many neighboring civilizations. In certain respects, however, western Europe resembled other borrowing societies, not only in its eagerness to imitate but also in its relatively loose political framework and the limitations (compared to the most advanced centers) on urban and manufacturing forms.

The postclassical period in western Europe thus saw the establishment of a largely new civilization and its extension northward. During much of the time, the leading centers of activity were in France, the Low Countries, Germany, and England—areas at best peripheral to civilization in Roman days. Spain lay in Muslim hands; Italy, although the center of the Catholic church and usually active in trade, was somewhat outside the Western mainstream in other respects. The usual label for this era of Western history is *medieval,* or the *Middle Ages.* The term is, in some sense, misleading; it suggests a way station between classical times and the more modern versions of Western civilization that took shape only after 1300 or 1400. Rather than being "between" two grander eras, the Middle Ages, in fact, witnessed the development of a largely new civilization and its presence in parts of Europe that had previously been isolated. But it is true that some of the institutions and values developed in the Middle Ages were unique to the period. Thus, in viewing these centuries as formative for a new Western civilization, we must also distinguish between important but peculiar features of medieval life on the one hand and, on the other, significant customs and traditions created by medieval people that shaped Western society even in later periods of development.

▮**KEY QUESTIONS**   *It is often hard to sort out a dominant theme from other important developments. Christian culture was western Europe's unifying feature as it emerged in this period as a civilization. Did it shape all the main features of society and politics? Change is another central point: how did this phase of European history differ from the Greco-Roman (classical) past? What were the most important changes within the period itself, including its last two centuries? Finally, what are the most revealing comparisons with other postclassical societies? How did western Europe resemble, and how did it differ from the other imitative societies of the period?*

EARLY PATTERNS IN WESTERN CIVILIZATION

From 500 to almost 1000, major events in western Europe were few and far between. Effective political organization was largely local, although Germanic kings ruled some territories, such as a portion of present-day France. Most people lived on self-sufficient agricultural estates called *manors.* They received some protection from their landlords, including the administration of justice, and in return they were obligated to turn over part of the goods they produced and to remain on the land. The manorial system had originated in the later Roman Empire; it was strengthened by the decline of trade and the lack of larger political structures.

Landlords themselves formed some alliances. Greater lords provided protection and aid to lesser lords, called *vassals,* who in turn owed their lords military service, some goods or payments, and advice. This system formed the beginnings of the European version of feudalism. However, early feudalism did not prevent a great deal of disorder. Many local wars occurred. In addition, western Europe was often raided by Viking pirates from Scandinavia and other groups. Because of the disarray, poverty, and general educational decline from the late Roman Empire on, few cultural developments of any note took place. The scattered intellectuals who existed, all members of the clergy, were busy trying to preserve and understand older Christian and classical learning.

During these centuries, the Catholic church provided the only extensive example of solid organization. Roman popes built a careful hierarchy through their control over local bishops. The popes did not always appoint the bishops, for monarchs and local lords often claimed this right, but they did nonetheless issue directives and receive important information. The popes also regulated doctrine, successfully undermining several heresies that threatened a unified

Christian faith. Moreover, they sponsored extensive missionary activity. Papal missionaries converted the English and Irish to Christianity. They brought the religion to northern and eastern Germany, beyond the borders of the previous Roman Empire, and ultimately, by the 10th century, to Scandinavia. They were active, of course, in the border regions of eastern Europe, sometimes competing directly with Orthodox missionaries. The solid structure of the church, which gave it a vital organizational edge over what secular government there was in the West, and the spread of Christianity constituted significant developments in the history of the West. Christian values increasingly became the essential cement of the newly developed civilization that covered virtually the whole of western Europe.

One significant political development occurred during these difficult centuries, sometimes called the Dark Ages. The royal house of a Germanic people, the Franks, grew in strength during the 8th century. A new family, the Carolingians, assumed the monarchy of these people, which was based in northern France, Belgium, and western Germany. One founder of the Carolingian line—Charles Martel, or Charles the Hammer—was responsible for defeating the Muslims in the Battle of Tours in 732. This defeat helped confine the Muslims to Spain and, along with the Byzantine defeat of the Arabs during the same period, preserved Europe for Christianity.

A later ruler in this same royal line, Charles the Great, known as Charlemagne, established a substantial empire in France, the Low Countries, and Germany around the year 800. Briefly, it looked as if a new Roman Empire might revive in the West, and indeed the term *Holy Roman Empire* ("Holy" denoted that it was firmly Christian) was later used by Charlemagne's successors in Germany. Charlemagne helped to restore some church-based education in western Europe, and the level of intellectual activity began a slow recovery, in part due to these efforts. When Charlemagne died in 814, however, his empire did not survive him. Rather, it was split into three geographic sectors—the outlines of modern France, Germany, and a middle strip consisting of the Low Countries, Switzerland, and northern Italy. Several of Charlemagne's successors, with nicknames such as "the Bald" or "the Fat," were not models of political dynamism even in their regional kingdoms.

From this point on, the essential political history of western Europe consisted of the gradual emergence of national monarchies. This was to be a civilization with strong cultural unity, initially centered in Catholic Christianity, but with pronounced political division.

The royal houses of several lands gained new power soon after Charlemagne's empire split. At first, the emperors who reigned over Germany and northern Italy were in the strongest position. It was they who claimed the title Holy Roman Emperor, beginning around the 12th century. By this time, however, their rule had become increasingly shallow, precisely because they relied too much on their imperial claims and did not build a solid monarchy from regional foundations. The future lay elsewhere, with the rise of monarchies in individual states—states that ultimately became nations.

From the 900s on, the kings of France began to assume growing authority. They amassed territory around their base in Paris, directly under their control; they formed feudal alliances with great lords in other parts of France, creating what is called a feudal monarchy. Regional monarchies began to form in Spain as Christian lords were able to push back the Muslims, from 1018 on, but a national royal house was formed only in the 15th century with the marriage of Ferdinand and Isabella. In England, an invasion from the French province of Normandy occurred in 1066. The Duke of Normandy, who was of Viking descent, had already built a strong feudal domain in northwestern France, and he now extended this system to England. William the Conqueror and his successors thus tied the great lords of England to the royal court by bonds of feudal loyalty, giving them estates in return for their military service.

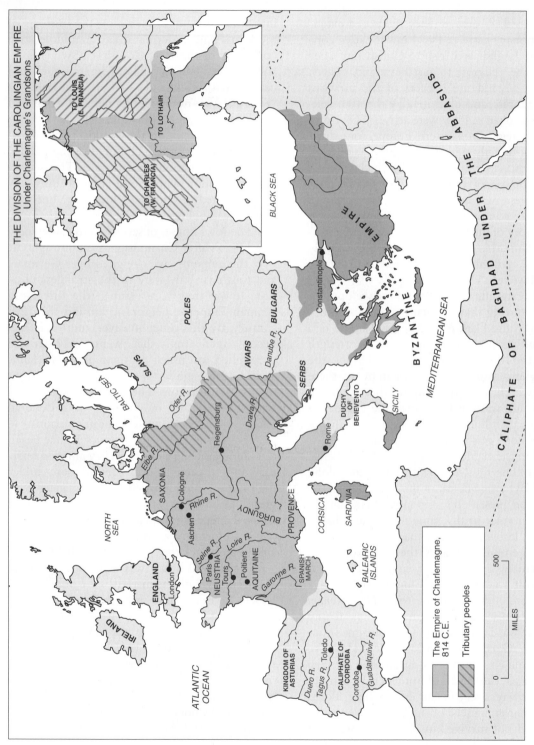

THE DIVISION OF THE CAROLINGIAN EMPIRE
Under Charlemagne's Grandsons

TO LOUIS (E. FRANCIA)

TO LOTHAIR

TO CHARLES (W. FRANCIA)

BLACK SEA

EMPIRE

Constantinople

POLES

BULGARS

Danube R.

AVARS

SERBS

SLAVS

BALTIC SEA

Oder R.

Drava R.

BYZANTINE

MEDITERRANEAN SEA

SICILY

DUCHY OF BENEVENTO

Rome

Elbe R.

Regensburg

SAXONIA

Cologne

Rhine R.

Aachen

BURGUNDY

PROVENCE

CORSICA

SARDINIA

BALEARIC ISLANDS

NORTH SEA

Seine R.

Paris

NEUSTRIA

Loire R.

Tours

Poitiers

AQUITAINE

Garonne R.

SPANISH MARCH

ENGLAND

London

IRELAND

ATLANTIC OCEAN

KINGDOM OF ASTURIAS

Duero R.

Tagus R.

Toledo

CALIPHATE OF CORDOBA

Cordoba

Guadalquivir R.

THE ABBASIDS

CALIPHATE   OF   BAGHDAD   UNDER   THE

The Empire of Charlemagne, 814 C.E.

The Empire of Charlemagne, 814 C.E.

Tributary peoples

0   500

MILES

The development of stronger feudal units and some powerful monarchies increased the orderliness of European life, starting in the 10th century. Invasions by the Vikings ceased; both trade and intellectual pursuits began to revive rapidly. The growth in the west European population reflected the new stability and encouraged improvements in agriculture and commerce. City life perked up gradually, as metropolitan areas became the centers for economic and cultural activity. Medieval Europe blossomed, and the centuries between 1000 and 1300 form the high point of this early version of Western civilization. It was during this period that the West began to show its muscle beyond its borders; a series of Crusades set out, from 1096 until the early 14th century, to reconquer and defend the Holy Land from the Muslims. The Crusades had only limited success in achieving their explicit goal, as a Kingdom of Jerusalem was established for about two centuries; even this success did not demonstrate real Western superiority against Muslim civilization, for the West remained backward. But as an expression of a combination of religious zeal—the Crusades were initiated by the pope—and growing commercial and military vigor on the part of the knights and merchants who organized the largest efforts, the Crusades unquestionably showed the distinctive spirit of the Western Middle Ages at their height. They also helped open the West to new cultural and economic influences from the Middle East, a major spur to further change.

As medieval society developed, the Catholic church went through several periods of decline and renewal. At times, church officials and the leading monastic groups became preoccupied with their holdings in land and their political interests. Reform-minded popes, such as Gregory VII (1073–1085), sought to purify the church more generally. They began to insist that all priests remain unmarried, to separate the priesthood from the ordinary world of the flesh. Gregory also endeavored to free the church from any vestige of state control. He quarreled vigorously with the Holy Roman Emperor, Henry IV, over the practice of state appointment, or investiture, of bishops in Germany. Ultimately, by excommunicating the emperor from the church, Gregory won his point. Gregory and several later popes made clear their beliefs that the church was to be not only free from state interference but also superior to the state in its function as the direct communicator of God's word. These claims were not entirely accurate, as governments influenced religious affairs still, but they were not altogether untrue. It was this sort of affirmation, indeed, that enabled the church to inspire kings and warriors to fight in the Crusades and also to war against several heresies that arose during the same centuries.

Monasteries and convents played a vital role in postclassical Europe. They served as centers of piety, and they provided men and women an alternative to ordinary life in the world. They also controlled much land and wealth. This sometimes led to corruption, which could in turn cause movements of reform and renewal, with the formation of new monastic orders. Some orders worked in the growing cities, or joined in attacks on heresy. Overall, monastic movements helped preserve and further learning and also provided examples of best available practices in agriculture. These functions might relate quite directly. As monks used parchment made from sheepskin, they had to raise or acquire as many as 500 sheep simply to produce a single copy of the Christian Bible.

Even in the centuries of its greatest strength, the church was by no means the only institution of importance during the High Middle Ages. As feudal monarchs extended their power, particularly in France and England, they became increasingly involved in the administration of justice and, through taxation, in the economic affairs of their subjects. Growing military strength made it possible for the royal families to assert their power against the claims of the church. Early in the 14th century, the French king actually imprisoned the pope in a dispute over taxation rights. Finally, the raising of armies by the national monarchs led to the beginning of a long series of wars in Europe.

The chief rivals were the kings of France and England. The English throne claimed large sections of French territory, from the days when they also had been dukes of Normandy; French kings steadily pressed against these territories. This rivalry evolved during the 14th and 15th centuries into a long, intermittent struggle called the Hundred Years War, in which France ultimately triumphed. From this point on, no century was to pass without major warfare among the leading nations of western Europe.

MEDIEVAL POLITICAL INSTITUTIONS

The characteristic political structure of the High Middle Ages, and the one of greatest importance for the later history of Western civilization, was the feudal monarchy. This was not, of course, the only political form in existence. Territories such as Germany and Italy remained more loosely organized, despite the grandiose claims of the Holy Roman Emperors. Feudal monarchy itself was a gradual development, not a carefully planned institution. It reflected a balance between the principles of feudalism pure and simple and the growing claims of the leading royal families. The result was an effective but distinctly limited government.

The monarchies of France, England, and ultimately Spain acquired several key functions during and after the 11th century, in addition to a general if vague recognition that kings and queens deserved some special loyalty. Medieval royal families, from the 10th and 11th centuries on, used the lands under their direct control to pay for armies and a small central bureaucracy. Often, they chose urban business or professional people to serve in this bureaucracy, partly because such people had expertise in financial matters and partly because, unlike the aristocracy, they owed allegiance to the crown alone. French and English monarchs began to introduce bureaucratic

specialties, so that some of their ministers handled justice, others finance, still others military matters. They found ways to send centrally appointed emissaries to the provinces, to supervise tax collection and the administration of justice. In England, from the Norman Conquest on, kings appointed local sheriffs to oversee the administration of justice. None of these activities gave the monarchs extensive contacts with ordinary subjects; for most people, effective governments were still local. But once the principle of central control was established, a steady growth of state-sponsored rule followed. By the end of the Middle Ages, monarchs were gaining the right to tax their subjects directly. And they were beginning to recruit professional armies, instead of relying solely on an aristocratic cavalry, whose loyalties depended on feudal bonds or alliances. Several medieval kings also gained a solid reputation as lawgivers, which allowed the gradual centralization of legal codes and court systems. Rediscovery of Roman law, in countries such as France, encouraged this centralization effort.

However, feudal monarchy was a delicately balanced institution, of which the central government formed only one of the key ingredients. The power of the church served to check royal ambitions. As we have seen, the church could often win in a clash with the state by excommunicating rulers and thus threatening to turn the loyalties of the population against them. Although the church entered a period of decline at the end of the Middle Ages, the principle was rather clearly established, as part of feudal monarchy, that there were areas of belief and morality that were not open to manipulation by the state.

The second limitation on the royal families came from the traditions of feudalism and from the landed aristocracy as a powerful class. Aristocrats tended to resist too much monarchical control in the West. And they had the strength to make their objections heard, for these aristocrats, even when they were vassals of the king, had their own economic base and their own military force—sometimes, in the case of certain powerful nobles, an army greater than that of the king. The growth of the monarchy reduced aristocratic power, but this led to new limits on kings. In 1215, an unpopular English king, John, faced opposition to his taxation measures from an alliance of nobles, townspeople, and church officials. Defeated in battle, John was forced to sign the Great Charter, or Magna Carta, which confirmed basically feudal rights against monarchical claims. John promised to observe restraint in his dealings with the nobles and the church. The few references to the general rights of the English people against the state that were included in the Magna Carta largely served to show where the feudal concept of mutual limits and obligations between rulers and the ruled could later lead.

This same feudal balance led, late in the 13th century, to the creation of parliaments, as bodies representing not individual voters but privileged groups such as the nobles and the church. The first full English parliament convened in 1265, with the House of Lords representing the nobles and the church hierarchy and the Commons made up of elected representatives from wealthy citizens of the towns. The parliament institutionalized the feudal principle that monarchs should consult with their vassals. In particular, parliaments gained the right to rule on any proposed changes in taxation; through this power, they could also advise the crown on other policy issues. While the parliamentary tradition became strongest in England, similar institutions arose in France, Spain, and several of the regional governments in Germany. Other countries, as we have seen, used councils in government. However, it was Western feudalism alone that led to the more formal institutions of parliament.

Medieval government was not modern government. People had rights according to the estate into which they were born; there was no general concept of citizenship. Thus, parliaments represented only a minority, and even this

minority only in terms of three or four estates (nobles, clergy, urban merchants, sometimes wealthy peasants), not some generalized group of voters. But by creating a concept of limited government and some hint of representative institutions, Western feudal monarchy produced the beginnings of a distinctive political tradition. This tradition differed from the political results of Japanese feudalism discussed in chapter 13, which emphasized group loyalty more than checks on a central power. Nonetheless, remnants of medieval traditions, embodied in institutions such as parliaments and ideas such as the separation between God's authority and state power, defined a basic thread in the Western political process even into the 21st century.

One other feature of medieval politics deserves note: its unusual focus on war. Although feudal monarchies created increasing internal order within individual countries, the idea of the state as an institution for warfare remained strong. Given the failure to develop any lasting political unity in Europe, this penchant ensured recurrent conflict within Western civilization. It is true that, during the Middle Ages, warfare continued to be a fairly limited activity. The basic military force was composed of the landed nobility, who alone could afford horses, weapons, and armor and the training needed for skill in battle. However, this interest in war sparked attention in improved weaponry. During the Hundred Years War, states learned to use archery and, particularly, the longbow, which opened the way to larger armies and began to limit the effectiveness of the aristocratic cavalry. At about the same time, the introduction of gunpowder stimulated still more portentous developments, as Europeans by the 14th century improved cannons so they could project firepower over considerable distances. Now, not only cavalry but also the fortified castles of the aristocracy became increasingly vulnerable. Warfare thus stimulated technological advances in Western society, which ultimately

HISTORY DEBATE

HOMOSEXUALITY AND RELIGION

The advent of Christianity brought new concerns about homosexuality, different from the ideas that had applied, at least to elite male behavior, during the Greek and Roman centuries. There is no question that concern about and hostility to homosexuality increased. The pattern of relationships between adult men and boys in the upper classes disappeared or (sometimes perhaps) went underground. What historians have debated, during the last two decades, involves issues of timing, in the first place, and following this, issues of causation.

Some authorities have argued that Christianity turned against homosexuality early on, viewing it as one of several unnatural and sinful sexual practices. This was presumably part of a larger concern about sensuality and sexual temptation, seen as dangerous to spiritual goals. After all, Western Catholicism would come to regard chastity as the surest path to salvation, required in monastic orders and the priesthood alike. Efforts to define unnatural sexuality were extensions of this general approach. Several early Christian law codes threatened harsh penalties for homosexual behavior. But actual church practice seemed to have emphasized the possibility of confession of sin and penance, rather than legal punishments. For this reason other historians have argued that while Christianity set a framework for greater condemnation, the real attack on homosexuality came later, during the middle of the postclassical period. Catholic rules began to urge more vigorous prosecution of sexual vices during the 12th century, and by the 13th century church law called for the death penalty (though it is not clear how often this was administered). Town governments began to enforce penalties, mainly in terms of fines and banishment, by this point as well. Popular preachers began to associate religious heresy and sexual deviation. Indeed, growing concern about religious purity may help explain the new level of hostility.

Debates about homosexuality also apply to gender. In terms of law and formal religious discussion, lesbian practices were long viewed more fiercely than homosexuality among men. But in fact, because many Christian leaders viewed women as naturally more sinful than men in any event, actual lesbian contacts may have encountered less attention than male behaviors. Again, historians try to figure out, despite a lack of abundant evidence, what attitudes developed; why they developed; and how they related to actual behavior and practice. Their inquiry is complicated by the fact that modern ideas about homosexuality, tending to see homosexuals as a definable group, differed from more traditional notions that focused on behaviors rather than rigid categories.

There is little question, however, that Christian, or at least postclassical Christian, approaches differed not only from classical precedents but also from other societies. Islam attacked homosexual practices as acts of adultery, a serious moral crime, but actual prosecutions were rare and there was considerable tolerance in practice. And in east Asia, firm rules against male homosexual acts did not develop until encounters with Western society in the 19th century. As interest in homosexuality, and tensions about contemporary issues increase, efforts to figure out the historical record, and its comparative dimensions, inspire growing research and new kinds of debate.

enhanced the power of the state and increased the means available for destruction. The inclination to rely on the battlefield to settle disputes also proved a durable part of the Western political tradition. It contrasted particularly with the lower level of interest of civilizations such as China in matters of military goals and technologies.

MEDIEVAL RELIGION AND CULTURE

As in eastern Europe and Islam during these centuries, religion was the focal point of medieval cultural life. But Western Christianity spawned a

11th century, however, a new style termed *gothic* took hold, which was far more original (although it benefited from the knowledge of Muslim arches). Gothic architects, taking advantage of growing engineering expertise, built soaring church spires and massive, arched windows. Although their work focused on the creation of large churches and great cathedrals, some gothic architects created civic buildings and palaces, using the same design motifs. The gothic was one of the three main architectural styles ever developed in Western culture (the others being the earlier classical and the later modern). Music for church use also flourished during the Middle Ages.

The cathedral of Notre-Dame (Our Lady) at Amiens, France, is a grand example of gothic architecture, which flourished during the later Middle Ages in western Europe. The cathedral, which dwarfs the surrounding buildings, was built between 1220 and 1402 and was the tallest building in Europe at the time of its completion.

Medieval literature reflected strong religious interests. Most Latin writing dealt with points of philosophy, law, or political theory. There was little concern with style for its own sake. But alongside writing in Latin came the development of a growing literature in the spoken languages, or vernaculars, of western Europe. A number of oral sagas were written down, dealing with the deeds of great knights and mythic figures from the past. From this tradition evolved the first known writing in early English, *Beowulf,* and in French, the *Song of Roland*. Late in the Middle Ages, a number of writers created adventure stories, comic tales, and poetry in the vernacular tongues, such as Chaucer's *Canterbury Tales*. Much of this work, and also a number of plays written for performance in the growing cities, reflected a tension between Christian values and a desire to portray the harshness of life on this earth. Chaucer's narrative, in its colorful language, thus shows a willingness to poke fun at the hypocrisy of many Christians as well as an ability to capture some of the tragedies of human existence. In France, a long poem called the *Story of the Rose* wove together various kinds of sexual imagery, while the poet Villon wrote, in largely secular terms, of the terror and poignancy of death. Finally, again in vernacular language, a series of courtly poets (troubadours), based primarily in southern France, wrote hymns to the love that could flourish between men and women. Although such verses stressed platonic devotion rather than sexual love, and paid homage to courtly ceremonies and polite behavior, the troubadours' concern with love was the first sign of the new value this emotional experience had taken on in the Western tradition.

Medieval intellectual and artistic life, in sum, created a host of important themes. Religion served as the centerpiece, but it did not curtail a growing range of interests from science to romantic poetry. Medieval culture was a rich intellectual achievement in its own right. It also set in motion a series of developments—in rationalist philosophy, science, artistic representations of nature, and vernacular literature—that served as building blocks for later Western thought and art.

ECONOMY AND SOCIETY

Medieval thinkers liked to picture their society in rather simple terms, not unlike the metaphors of classical India. Borrowing from classical Greek and Roman concepts, John of Salisbury, an English churchman, likened society to the human body. Peasants were the feet, without which society could not function. Knightly warriors were the hands, to defend. Priests provided heart and soul, the king the head. Each part was essential, but each fit into a clear hierarchy in which subordinates were properly ruled by their superiors.

In fact, medieval society was far more complicated, and it evolved toward ever-greater complexity. In the early Middle Ages, and to some extent throughout the period, the key social relationship, as far as most people were concerned, was that between landlord and serf. Just as feudal relationships described contacts among the landlords, so manorialism described contacts between those who ruled the landed estates and those who performed the manual labor of farming. There were a few free farmers in the early Middle Ages, but most peasants were serfs, clustered in villages on the lords' estates. From the lords, the peasant-serfs received some military and judicial protection, and some aid, where possible, during periods of poor harvest. To the lords, they owed a portion of their harvests and considerable work service. Serfs were not free to leave their land, but they were not outright slaves, because in normal circumstances they could not be evicted from their land. Most land was, in this sense, jointly owned, with both the serf and lord having some control over it—although the lords and church owned some estates outright, which they worked mainly through the serfs' labor.

This agricultural society was quite primitive. Tools were simple. Peasants had to leave a third

Peasants and lords work near a fictional late-medieval castle in the Loire valley of France. (Illuminated manuscript from the *Très Riches Heures du duc de Berry*.)

or more of their land fallow each year, to replenish the soil. Most estates produced mainly for their own subsistence, and there was little market activity.

By the 9th and 10th centuries, partly because of the restoration of order, the agricultural economy began to improve. New techniques developed through contacts with eastern Europe and Asia. A heavier plow was devised, the moldboard, which made it much easier to till the heavy soils of Europe. The horse collar, first invented in Asia but now finally introduced in the West, allowed for the use of horses as well as oxen to pull plows and carts. Advances of this sort increased agricultural productivity and promoted a steady growth of population, which lasted until the 14th century. This rising population, in turn, encouraged the settlement of new lands in various parts of Europe, as forests were cleared and swamps drained. To attract farmers to the new lands, the conditions of serfdom were relaxed. There was great variety in this process; in many parts of western Europe, a strict manorial system lasted well beyond the Middle Ages. However, by the 12th and 13th centuries, many peasants retained very few obligations to their lords, often little more than rent (which also reflected the fact that many peasants were now able to directly sell part of their produce to the market). Some peasants owned their land outright and could sell it if they wished. Compared to east European and most Asian civilizations by 1400, the west European peasantry was unusually free, and although its agricultural techniques were not as advanced as those in some areas, such as east Asia, there had nonetheless been considerable improvement in this regard.

Shifts in agriculture promoted and reflected changes in commerce. With rising agricultural productivity, from about 1000 C.E. on, a minority of people were able to concentrate on other economic activities. In parts of Italy, the Low Countries, England, and northern Germany, about 20 percent of the population could now be supported away from the farms. This meant new possibilities for trade and for the expansion of cities. New commercial opportunities, in turn, inspired some peasants and landlords to turn more fully to the market, rather than concentrate on subsistence agriculture. The use of money spread steadily, to the dismay of many Christian moralists and many ordinary people who preferred the more direct, personal methods of traditional society.

Rising trade took a number of forms. Western Europe exchanged goods with other parts of the known world and became an active part of the world network, which allowed the cultural borrowings from Byzantium and Islam and stimulated commerce. Wealthy Europeans developed a taste for some of the spices and luxury goods of Asia; the Crusades played a role in bringing these products to wider attention. A Mediterranean trade redeveloped, mainly in the hands of Italian merchants dealing with Arab traders, in which European cloth and some other products were exchanged for the higher-quality goods of the East. Commerce within Europe involved exchanges of timber and grain from the Baltic regions for cloth and metal products manufactured in Italy and the Low Countries. England, at first an exporter of raw wool, developed some manufactured goods for exchange by the later Middle Ages. Huge fairs in northern France and the Low Countries brought together merchants from various parts of Europe. Commercial alliances developed. Cities in northern Germany and southern Scandinavia united in the Hanseatic League to encourage trade. Banking facilities spread, particularly through the efforts of the Italians. It thus became possible to organize commercial transactions throughout much of western Europe. Bankers, including a number of Jewish businessmen, were valued for their service in lending money to monarchs and to the papacy. The growth of trade and banking in the Middle Ages served as the genesis of capitalism in Western civilization. The greater Italian and German bankers, the long-distance merchants of the Hanseatic cities, were clearly capitalistic in their

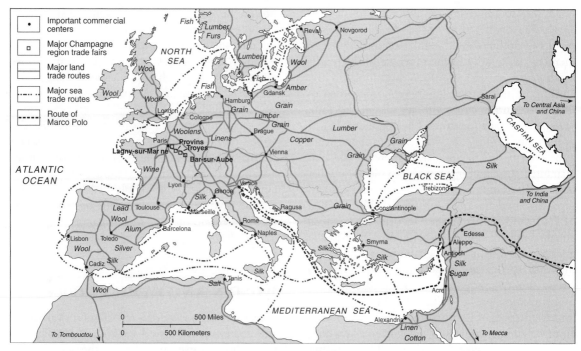

European–Middle Eastern Trade Connections

willingness to invest considerable sums of money in trading ventures with the expectation of substantial profit.

This was not, by world standards, a totally unprecedented merchant spirit. European traders were still less venturesome and less wealthy than some of their Muslim counterparts. Nor was Western society any more tolerant of merchants than Muslim or Indian societies. But Western commercial endeavors were clearly gaining in dynamism. Because Western governments were weak, with few economic functions, merchants had a freer hand than in many other civilizations. Many of the growing cities, in particular, were ruled by commercial leagues. Monarchs liked to encourage the cities as a counterbalance to the power of the landed aristocracy, and in the later Middle Ages and beyond, traders and kings were typically allied. But aside from taxing merchants

and using them as sources of loans, royal governments did not interfere extensively with trading activities. Merchants even developed their own codes of commercial law, administered by city courts. Thus, the rising merchant class, although not unusual in strength or its adventurous spirit, was staking out an unusually powerful and independent role in European society. Christian concerns about profit-making began to decline.

However, capitalism was not yet typical of the Western economy. Most peasants and landlords had not become enmeshed in a market system. In the cities, the dominant economic ethic stressed group protection, not unlimited profit-seeking. The characteristic institution was not the international trading firm but the merchant or artisan guild. These organizations, new in western Europe but similar to guilds in various parts of Asia, stressed security and mutual control. Merchant guilds thus sought to ensure all members a share in any endeavor. If a ship docked with a cargo of wool, the clothiers' guild of the city insisted that all members participate in the purchase of that commodity, so no one member monopolized the ensuing profits. Artisan guilds were composed of the people in the cities who actually made cloth, bread, jewelry, or furniture. These guilds tried to limit membership, so that all members were assured of work. They regulated apprenticeships to guarantee good training, but also to make sure that no member employed too many apprentices and thus garnered undue wealth. They discouraged new methods, again because security and general equality, not maximum individual profit, was the goal. Guilds also tried to guarantee good workmanship, so that consumers would not have to worry about shoddy quality on the part of some unscrupulous profit seeker. Guilds played an important political and social role in the cities, ensuring their members of recognized status and, often, a voice in city government. Their statutes were, in turn, upheld by municipal law and often backed by the royal government as well.

Despite the traditionalism and security-mindedness of the guilds, manufacturing as well as commercial methods did improve in medieval Europe. Western Europe was not yet as advanced as Asia in ironmaking or textile manufacture, but it was beginning to catch up. In a few areas, such as clock making—which reflected both sophisticated technology and an interest in precise time—and heavy metallurgical casting for monumental church bells, European artisans had, in fact, forged a world lead. Furthermore, some manufacturing spilled beyond the bounds of guild control. Particularly in the Low Countries and parts of Italy, groups of workers were employed by capitalists to produce for a wide market, working with simple equipment in their homes.

The plain fact was that, by the later Middle Ages, western Europe's economy and society embraced a number of contradictory groups and principles. Commercial and capitalist elements coexisted alongside the slower pace of economic life in the countryside and even the dominant group protectionism of most urban guilds. Most people remained peasants, but a minority had escaped to the cities, where they found more excitement, although also increased danger and higher rates of disease. A few prosperous capitalists flourished, but most people operated according to quite different economic values. At the same time, the conditions of serfdom were easing for many in rural life. This was not, in sum, either a static society or an early model of a modern commercial society. It simply had its own flavor and its own tensions—the fruit of several centuries of economic and social change.

WOMEN AND FAMILY LIFE

The increasing complexity of medieval social and economic life may have had one final effect that is familiar from patterns in other agricultural societies: setting new limits on the conditions of women. Women's work remained, of course, vital in most families. Christian emphasis on the equality of all souls and the practical importance of monastic groups organized for women, offering some an alternative to marriage, continued to lend distinctive features to women's lives in Western society. The popular veneration of Mary and other female religious figures gave women real cultural prestige, counterbalancing the biblical emphasis on Eve as the source of human sin. In some respects, women in the West had higher status than their sisters under Islam: they were less segregated at religious services (although they could not lead them) and less confined to the household. Still, women's effective voice in the family may have declined during the Middle Ages. Urban women often played important roles in local commerce and even operated some craft guilds, but they found themselves increasingly constrained by male-dominated organizations. By the late Middle Ages, a literature arose that stressed women's subordinate role to men,

SOLVING PROBLEMS

POPULATION GROWTH

Significant population growth has always been a dynamic, and sometimes a troubling, force in world history. By the postclassical era several regions of the world had reached a maximum population capacity that would not be exceeded until the 19th century. Egypt, for example, with a population of about 5 million did not surpass this figure until after 1800. Middle Eastern population grew a bit in the early part of the Arab conquest, but then soil exhaustion and high taxes cut into population levels.

China and western Europe, however, experienced significant population growth in the postclassical period, after the decreases that resulted from plagues and political instability as the great classical empires had collapsed. Better government in Tang China, which promoted economic growth, and the opening of new agricultural land in south China, generated expansion. In Europe, the opening of new lands in northern France and Germany, by cutting down forests, plus use of a heavy wheeled plow expanded food production and enabled population growth.

This growth soon (by the 11th century) caused problems that required further solution. Population pressure helped push German settlements eastward, not only cutting back the forests but also displacing Slavic and other peoples in east-central Europe. This was a major settlement change. Population growth also pushed a minority of people off the land entirely, to seek jobs in growing cities; and it helped relax serfdom in favor of motivating peasants to increase their agricultural production and sell to urban markets.

By the 14th century, however, the problem of population growth began to defy solution, particularly in Europe. Agriculture could no longer keep up, and population levels dropped back. Then the new round of plagues, called the Black Death, affected both China and Europe, pushing population down still further, by as much as 50 percent. But both regions began to recover in less than two centuries, which was a much more rapid rebound than in earlier points in world history—suggesting that the changes in the agricultural economy that responded to postclassical population growth had dynamic implications for the future.

■ QUESTIONS: *When does population growth cause creative innovations, and when does it become excessive? What were the main ways postclassical societies could respond to rapid population growth?*

listing supplemental household tasks and extolling docile behaviors as women's distinct destiny. Patriarchal structures seemed to be taking deeper root.

TENSIONS IN THE LATER MIDDLE AGES

Medieval society reached its apogee in the 12th and 13th centuries. Beginning about 1300 and continuing for about 150 years, it exhibited a number of symptoms of stagnation and decline.

This was not a collapse of Western civilization or even a deterioration of the long-term sort that began to affect Muslim civilization during the same period. Rather, western Europe encountered a number of short-term difficulties. These, in turn, prompted the society to shed part of its medieval skin, like a snake, only to emerge with renewed dynamism in somewhat different garb toward the middle of the 15th century.

Item. By the early 1300s, medieval population had clearly surpassed the limits that the existing economy could sustain. Growing food crises caused widespread starvation through severe periodic famines. Then, massive plague, sweeping through city and countryside alike, took its deadly toll. The Black Death, the bubonic plague, killed more than a quarter of the population during the late 14th century. Population loss of this sort both reflected and caused economic dislocation.

Item.   During the 14th century, the ruling class of medieval society, the landowning aristocracy, began to show signs of confusion about its function. It had long staked its claim to power on its control of much of the land and also on its military prowess. However, its skill in warfare was now open to question. The growth of professional armies and particularly the new weaponry of crossbow and cannon made traditional fighting methods increasingly irrelevant. The aristocracy did not, as a result, simply disappear. Rather, the nobility chose to emphasize a rich ceremonial lifestyle, featuring tournaments in which military expertise could be employed in competitive games. The spread of courtly love poems signaled another new focus, an interest in a more refined culture. The idea of chivalry—carefully controlled, polite behavior, especially toward women—gained ground. This was a potentially fruitful development in indicating increased cultivation among the upper class. We have seen similar transformations in considering earlier changes in the Chinese and Muslim aristocracy. But at the time of transition in the West, some of the elaborate ceremonies of chivalry seemed rather shallow, even a bit silly—a sign that medieval values were losing hold without being replaced by a new set of beliefs.

Item.   The balance between church and state, which had characterized medieval life, began to shift decisively after 1300. For several decades, French kings controlled the papacy, which they relocated from Rome to a town in France; then rival claimants to the papacy confused the issue further. Ultimately, a single pope was returned to Rome, but the church was clearly weakened. Moreover, the church began to lose some of its grip over Western religious life. Church leaders were so preoccupied with their political quarrels that they tended to neglect the spiritual side of their faith. Religion did not decline as a result. Indeed, signs of intense popular piety blossomed, along with the formation of new religious groups. But devotion became partially separate from the institution of the church. One result, again starting in the 14th century, was a series of popular heresies, with leaders in places such as England and Bohemia preaching against the hierarchical structure of the church in favor of a more direct experience of God.

Item.   The medieval intellectual and even artistic movements started to falter. After the work of Aquinas, later rationalists engaged in petty debates over such topics as how many angels could dance on the head of a pin. Church officials became less tolerant of intellectual pursuit, as they even declared some of Aquinas's writings heretical. In art, a growing interest in realistic portrayals of nature suggested the beginnings of a shift away from medieval artistic standards. Some medieval artistic styles became trite; gothic design, for example, soon exhibited great detail, in a style called *flamboyant gothic*—a symptom of waning creativity.

Item.   Social unrest increased in the 14th and 15th centuries, spurred in part by the new economic problems and popular religious heresies. Many peasants and townspeople joined in egalitarian protests against the control of guild masters or landlords. Sometimes, they spoke out for greater equality. As an English rioter put it, "When Adam delved and Eve span, Who was then a gentleman?" In the Italian city of Florence, a democratic government was briefly installed after an artisan revolt in 1378. These revolts had little lasting success, although they did set in motion a new current of protest that, in certain respects, lasted for several centuries. Peasants were beginning to seek greater freedom from what was left of serfdom, and lower-level artisans wondered if the guild system was working equitably. At times, these groups revolted in a violent manner. One English observer wrote of peasant attacks on manorial lords and records:

> These myschevous people thus assembled without capitayne or armoure, robbed, brent and slewe all gentylmen that they coude lay handes one, and forced and ravysshed ladyes and dawmosels and dyd such shameful dedes that no hymayne creature ought to think on any such.

Elements of this protest tradition lasted well beyond the period of medieval decline and ultimately help reshape political and social relationships in the West. At the time, popular uprisings served as one final indication that the medieval version of a social and economic structure was losing its validity.

PATHS TO THE PRESENT

The postclassical period established several enduring features of western European civilization, adding to elements revived from the classical Mediterranean. Many historians believe, in fact, that the core of Western civilization took shape during this period.

The civilization was defined in part by a shared version of Christianity, including the important separation between the institutional church and the state. Even though Christianity has changed and, in many cases, declined in western Europe since that time, the common intellectual legacy remains. The sense of religious limits on the state later helped generate distinctive statements about political power.

The European version of feudalism, with its emphasis on contract and consultation, also

helped shape the region's political tradition. The emergence of parliaments during this era, though not yet modern in form, suggests the emerging notion of legislative checks on executive power. This balance was not always preserved in later Western political history, but it has always recurred.

Western society, from its postclassical roots, was also warlike and open to technologies that could aid in the art of war. Many argue that this characteristic persists in Western civilization, helping to define its later approach to the wider world.

The postclassical period also saw the rise of merchant activity in the West. This was not in itself distinctive: Islamic, Indian, Chinese, and African merchants rivaled or surpassed Western levels of trade. But merchants in the West faced fewer political controls than those in some other regions, because of the weakness of the feudal state. This provided a backdrop for later interest in relatively unregulated merchant activity.

Many aspects of the postclassical West were confined to the period: religious art, for example, though still treasured in museums, is not an active force in Western art today. But in at least four respects—and further analysis might suggest more—important precedents were created for Western society later on, not only in Europe, but also in areas unusually open to Western influence.

SUGGESTED WEB SITES

For more on the Middle Ages, see http://www.byu.edu/ipt/projects/middleages/; visit the Arador Amour Library at http://www.arador.com/main/index.html; on Medieval European history, see http://www.medieval-life.net/history_main.htm; a good gateway to resources for Medieval studies can be found at http://www.georgetown.edu/departments/medieval/labyrinth/labyrinth-home.html; visit the Early Middle Ages Museum at http://www.roma2000.it/zmumedio.html.

SUGGESTED READINGS

Recent work includes Julia Smith, *Europe after Rome* (2005); Peter N. Stearns, *Western Civilization in World History* (2003); Richard Landes, ed., *The Apocalyptic Year 1000* (2003); Richard F. Gyug, *Medieval Cultures in Contact* (2003); Charles Freeman, *The Closing of the Western Mind: The Rise of Faith and the Fall of Reason* (2003); Christopher Dyer, *An Age of Transition? Economy and Society in England in the Later Middle Ages* (2005); John H. Arnold, *Belief and Unbelief in Medieval Europe* (2005); Paul Maurice Clogan, ed., *Studies in Medieval and Renaissance Culture: Reengaging History* (2005); Roger French, *Medicine Before Science: The Rational and Learned Doctor from the Middle Ages to the Enlightenment* (2003); Lawrence Besserman, ed., *Sacred and Secular in Medieval and Early Modern Cultures: New Essays* (2006); Chiara Frugoni, *A Day in a Medieval City* (2005); Rosalynn Voaden and Diane Wolfthal, *Framing the Family: Narrative and Representation in the Medieval and Early Modern Periods* (2005). See also Georges Duby's *Art and Society in the Middle Ages* (2000) and Tom Chippey, ed., *Appropriating the Middle Ages: Scholarship, Politics, Fraud* (2001). B. Tierney's *The Middle Ages* (1978) provides useful source material. See also Michael D. Bailey's *Battling Demons: Witchcraft, Heresy, and Reform in the Late Middle Ages* (2003). For unusual insight into medieval society, also with considerable source material, see the highly readable E. Leroy-Ladurie's *Montaillou: The Promised Land of Error* (1979). Excellent studies on more specialized topics include J. R. Strayer, *On the Medieval Origins of the Modern State* (1972); C. Brooke, *The 12th Century Renaissance* (1970); H. Rashdall, *The Universities of Europe in the Middle Ages* (1936); H. Berman, *Law and Revolution: The Formation of the Western Legal Tradition* (1983); R. Bridenthal and C. Koonz, *Becoming Visible: Women in European History* (1977); and N. Pevsner, *An Outline of European Architecture* (1963).

On the medieval economy, consult J. Gimpel, *The Medieval Machine: Tthe Industrial Revolution of the Middle Ages* (1977), and David Landes, *Revolution in Time: Clocks and the Making of the Modern World* (1985). Social history has dominated much recent research on the period; see P. Ariès and G. Duby, eds., *A History of Private Life*, Vol. 2 (1984), and Barbara Hanawalt, *The Ties That Bound: Peasant Families in Medieval England* (1986), for important findings in this area. David Herlihy's *Medieval Households* (1985) is a vital contribution, as is J. Chapelot and R. Fossier's *The Village and House in the Middle Ages* (1985). J. Kirshner and S. F. Wemple, eds., *Women of the Medieval World* (1985), is a good collection. On tensions in popular religion, see C. Bynum, *Jesus as Mother: Studies in the Spirituality of the High Middle Ages* (1982), and L. Little, *Religious Poverty and the Profit Economy in Medieval Europe* (1978).

China's Impact and the Spread of East Asian Civilization

This chapter returns to the subject of the world network and deals with a second set of connections within it: those radiating from China. These connections were partially separated from the Islam-generated network and operated within a somewhat smaller orbit than the one Islam had forged. They primarily affected east Asia and to some extent southeast Asia. Trade and some technology exchange linked China to the rest of Asia however, and through this, to Europe and Africa. China and its outreach formed the second great regional story in the postclassical period, after that of the Isamic Middle East.

Although the Islamic network was much larger than the connective web generated by China, developments in east Asia during this period were crucial in their own right. Japan, for example, formed some of its key characteristics during this period. Several specific innovations, for instance, advances in Chinese and Korean technology, gained worldwide importance. And, despite the massive changes in religious affiliations and trading patterns that erupted throughout the Middle East and southern Asia after 600 C.E., these cultural currents had little impact on China and its east Asian neighbors. The Chinese briefly encountered Arab soldiers on their western borders and had some interaction with Turkish converts to Islam, but, although the western Chinese population at times included an Islamic minority, China did not become Islamic. Similarly, trade in Chinese goods, toward points west, passed increasingly into Arab hands. But these developments were peripheral to Chinese history in the period. After the year 500 C.E., however, the Chinese did react to the one serious outside influence that had reached deeply into their population: Buddhism. Apart from this interchange, however, the Chinese proceeded, as they long had done, as if there was little to learn from beyond their borders.

Without question, the postclassical centuries between 600 and 1400 C.E. were a vigorous and important period in Chinese history and in China's relations with other parts of east Asia. China introduced innovations in bureaucracy, art, foreign policy, and technology. Indeed, during this time, the Chinese were responsible for more fundamental improvements in technology than any other civilization.

Any student of world history, after mastering an understanding of the basic patterns of individual civilizations, is tempted to look for larger themes or lessons. Do civilizations, for example, follow some general law of rise and fall? There certainly seems to be a common scenario in which a culture starts to grow with unusual vigor—such as the Arabs in the 7th century—and then, some centuries later, begins to wane. But one should not make too much of this rise-and-fall pattern. For, while some civilizations decline or stagnate, others go through temporary periods of readjustment only to reemerge with equal or greater strength. China clearly illustrates this latter process and may still be exemplifying it in our own day as the nation revives after more than a century of partial eclipse.

Furthermore, China radiated a vigorous regional influence during this period, serving as a model to many other societies in east Asia. Vietnam, Korea, and Japan did not become smaller versions of China; each had distinctive features that long differentiated it from its giant neighbor. But important elements of Chinese society were exported to these cultures, and a larger east Asian zone of civilization took shape. The spread of civilization in east Asia on the basis of a significant Chinese example forms one of the key illustrations of the general phenomenon of civilization's extension and the new process of borrowing during the postclassical centuries.

The period opens soon after the year 500, when the sequence of China's ruling dynasties was renewed, ending the long period of disruption that followed the collapse of the Han dynasty. Also around 500 C.E., Japan began to import techniques from China, including writing, enabling it to become a clear domain of east Asian civilization—although during this entire period, Japan played a far less commanding part in Asian civilization than China.

The era did not end smoothly, reflecting the fact that east Asian patterns of civilization remained somewhat separate from those in other parts of the Eurasian world. In 1278, Mongol invaders toppled the reigning Chinese dynasty; the invaders were expelled 90 years later. These decades serve as something of a transition in Chinese history. During the 1330s, Japan entered a new period of political instability. Thus, there was a sense of change in Japan and China, although for different reasons, during the 14th and early 15th centuries.

■**KEY QUESTIONS**   *The China that emerged in the postclassical period revived many basic features of classical China. Two questions emerge: Why was there so much continuity? And what did, nevertheless, change? ("How did postclassical China differ from China during the Han dynasty?" is another way to ask the second question.) The next question involves the larger east Asian region, including Korea and Japan: were these societies, given their partial imitation of China, part of a common east Asian civilization?*

POLITICAL AND CULTURAL DEVELOPMENTS IN CHINA

Because Chinese civilization was not new, or even reformulated during the centuries after 500, there is no need to describe its most familiar features. Following China's recovery from the nomadic invasions, during the 6th century, the dynastic cycle resumed and served to express and organize much of the nation's political structure. The first postclassical dynasty, the Sui, formed in 589 and was short-lived, although it reestablished a centralized state and repaired the Great Wall. The Sui dynasty also undertook a series of new conquests, pressing into Vietnam and the island of Taiwan and also extending westward, into Turkish lands of central Asia. A period of popular unrest against high taxes brought an end to the Sui ruling family, however, and the Tang dynasty emerged in its place. The reign of this dynasty, along with the earlier Han, is regarded as one of the two golden eras of Chinese history.

The Tang dynasty continued the policy of expansion. Its conquest of Turkish areas in central Asia helped push the Turks westward, thus setting in motion their advance toward the Middle East. The Tang regime also formed protectorates over Tibet, Vietnam, and Korea, which helped spread Chinese institutions without directly annexing these areas to the empire. Japan paid tribute to the Tang. In effect, the Chinese now controlled the entire world, as they knew it. The Tang did lose a key battle with the Arabs, at Talas in 754, which reduced their influence in central Asia, where conversions to Islam increased. But the results did not show immediately.

WORLD PROFILES

TAIZONG
(626–649 C.E.)

The Tang emperor Taizong was a brilliant general and an astute administrator. He set the stage for one of China's major dynasties by restoring the imperialist bureaucratic system of the Han and increasing the emphasis on education. He was a tolerant and cosmopolitan emperor as well, unperturbed by the continued spread of Buddhism. Finally, Taizong masterminded Chinese military gains in Vietnam, Tibet, Mongolia, and Korea, where Chinese influence combined with continued political autonomy. Through his immense personal abilities, Taizong was responsible for the revival and dissemination of basic trends in Chinese political history. How does his role as an individual compare to that of his near contemporary in the Middle East—Muhammad?

This image of Tang emperor Taizong was created by a Song dynasty court painter several centuries after the emperor's death.

Under rulers such as the Empress Wu (690–705), one of the few women to reign over China, the Tang reestablished the power of the central government. Like earlier dynasties, notably the Qin and Han, the Tang government reduced the power of independent landlords. Their taxing power was abolished, in favor of direct payment by peasants to the state. The government required the free peasants to submit to military training, which greatly increased the power of the state and its role in individual lives. Finally, the government established comprehensive, accurate censuses of people and property, as the means for imposing fair but also reliable taxation. A growing bureaucracy accompanied these new measures, and the civil service examinations, based on political knowledge but also Chinese philosophy and literature, were revived. As before, this examination system provided relatively able bureaucrats, although drawn mainly from the upper classes, and also promoted cultural unity within the empire. Indeed, the bureaucratic system was greatly elaborated under the Tang. Examinations became stricter, and education counted far more than birthright as the aristocratic role faded in favor of a scholar-bureaucrat ideal. Bureaucrats even amassed the authority to correct the emperor by citing relevant Confucian wisdom or historical examples.

The Tang dynasty resumed the tradition of extensive government functions, regulating trade, building roads and canals, and organizing justice and defense. A new agency, the Board of Censors, was created to supervise the bureaucracy and guard against misconduct.

The Tang program ultimately included a vigorous attack on Buddhism as a potentially subversive element. Although early Tang emperors had favored Buddhism, the religion was finally officially rejected, as alien and subversive. Thousands of shrines and monasteries were destroyed. Buddhism remained an important minority religion in China, but its period of growth was forcibly brought to a halt. The Tang, even more than their Han predecessors, clearly felt that they had both the right and the duty to regulate the beliefs of their subjects in the interests of political loyalty.

The dynastic decline of the Tang began in the late 700s. Government became less effective. Earlier population growth, the result of Tang prosperity, had increased poverty; there was not enough land to go around. The Tang policy of direct taxation on peasants drove the latter to seek landlord protection and spurred a series of major popular protests. Attacks by nomads from central Asia increased. The Tang dynasty was finally displaced by civil war in 906. However, this time chaos did not last long, for the traditions of centralized rule were too powerful to lapse. The dynasty might fade, but the bureaucratic state was virtually indestructible.

A new dynasty, the Song, came into power in 960. Again, it broke the power of local military leaders, encouraging them to enter civilian life. The Song dynasty did not regain all the territory the Tang had held; indeed, northern China, along the Huanghe River, remained in the hands of nomadic invaders, including some Mongol groups. The founder of the Song dynasty, a northern general named Zhao Kuangyin, realized that he could not take on all enemies simultaneously, so he was willing to allow the continued presence of the nomadic warriors in the north. But he developed an excellent strategy for assuming control of the prosperous southern states, and he extended his influence into Indochina. Despite sporadic warfare, the Song dynasty was economically dynamic, with abundant tax revenues and a tight central administration. Commercial and urban life expanded notably, including heightened consumerism. Population growth and the expansion of cities followed from improved agricultural productivity and advances in the output of coal and iron. The use of commodities such as tea, previously an upper-class luxury, spread more widely. Trade within China increased, and although mainly in the hands of foreign merchants, exports to India and the Middle East grew as well. Song taxation relieved the peasantry by

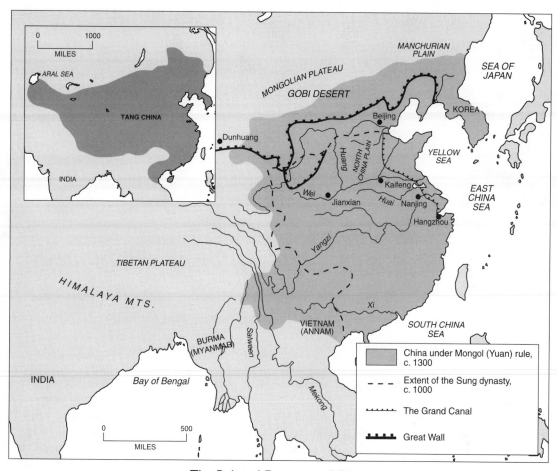

The Political Divisions of China

focusing on merchants instead, and peasant revolts subsided for centuries.

Nonetheless, the Song, too, ultimately faded, in part because they never definitively resolved the problem of nomadic warriors in the north. Although the economy remained prosperous, including the large manufacturing sector, administrative inefficiency reduced tax revenues. One Song emperor tried to introduce reforms to relieve the hard-pressed peasantry, but he was undermined by the powerful, conservative bureaucracy. Invasions by nomadic peoples, particularly the Mongols, became harder to contain. Finally by 1278,

under brilliant new generalship, the Mongols conquered the entire Song Empire.

During the Sui, Tang, and Song dynasties, Chinese culture enjoyed a brilliant period. Confucianism remained the dominant philosophy. The challenge of Buddhism led Confucian thinkers to expand their range of philosophical concerns. The philosopher Zhu Xi (1120–1200) played a major role in drawing together some Buddhist themes and orthodox Confucianism, to discuss the nature of the universe and its basic patterns as well as the more familiar issues of ethics and political loyalty. Zhu Xi emphasized family rule, under the benevolence of the father,

Guo Xi (Chinese, c. 1020–1075). *Old Trees, Level Distance,* 11th century, Northern/Song dynasty (960–1127). Handscroll, ink and color on silk.

and the state as a family system applied to the whole empire. He demonstrated how Confucian traditions could be confirmed but also taken in new directions. Giving Confucianism a scope it previously lacked, he also opened a dialogue on basic philosophical issues that had been monopolized earlier by Buddhist thinkers and urged meditation. Such was Zhu Xi's creativity that his own work became part of the Chinese classics, read and relied on for centuries along with the Confucian *Analects* and the Five Classics. While confirming basic features of the Confucian ethic, with emphasis on moral teaching and self-restraint, Zhu Xi added depth to the Chinese philosophical tradition, extending it to areas that Buddhist beliefs, urging meditative union with some basic essence, had opened to new consideration. However, Zhu Xi's success had some drawbacks. Its breathtaking range, from philosophy through history, encouraged the perception that a final synthesis had been achieved; further speculation was discouraged. In the long run,

this promoted a growing sterility in Chinese intellectual life, but the accomplishments of Zhu Xi himself illustrate the creativity of the Tang and Song periods of Chinese history.

Daoism and Buddhism continued to be important popular religions. Also, the Chinese introduced several variants of the Mahayana Buddhist faith. The most famous of these, known now as Zen, its later Japanese name, stressed meditation and spiritual growth. Chinese Buddhism continued, however, to be less otherworldly than its southeast Asian counterpart. Chinese Buddhists stressed the value of hard work and a love of nature, and not simply contemplation. For its part, Daoism continued its development as a religion, integrating popular beliefs in magical healing as it spread more widely.

The incorporation of Buddhism in popular culture, particularly before the Tang persecutions, led to new developments in literature and especially art. Chinese sculptors copied some Indian styles of statuary. The pagoda was introduced as a new architectural form and spread from China to other parts of Asia, including Japan and Thailand. Buddhist artists painted religious scenes and also acquired a new interest in nature. Even after Buddhism declined as a cultural force in China, the reliance on natural subjects remained. Chinese artists stressed simple statements of nature, carefully arranged and with muted colors. An emperor issued a guide to painters: "Depict objects as they exist. Simplicity and nobility of line is to be the aim." A small object from nature, such as a spray of bamboo, was held to represent the whole universe.

Other arts flourished under the Tang and the Song, and many artists became well known by name, not simply as anonymous craftworkers. Pottery took on a more sophisticated style. The emperors built elaborate palaces, including pagodas with glazed roofs and upturned eaves at the end, designed to withstand windstorms. Urban architecture became something of an art itself. Cities were planned rationally, in a checkerboard pattern. The Tang capital of Changan was a rectangular city, contained by walls, which held a population of almost 2 million people. Neighborhoods were laid out in blocks, and a central boulevard led to the government headquarters.

In sum, Chinese art combined growing sophistication in technology and orderly planning with a love of nature inspired by Daoist and Buddhist thought. Chinese art showed the diversity of a civilization that, although traditionalist, remained creative.

In literature, the traditional pursuits of compiling the classics and writing histories combined with new styles. In poetry, a five-syllable meter, called the *shi*, became increasingly popular. Both Daoist and Confucian poets flourished. Li Bo (701–762) was a Daoist who wrote of his love of wine; legend has it that he drowned while reaching out in drunken ecstasy for the reflection of the moon in the water. The popularity of poetry as an art for educated gentlemen led to the composition of hundreds of thousands of poems during this period, with themes ranging from Confucian morality to the beauties of nature. Many verses had a slightly melancholy ring, such as these lines from the Song poet Meng Zhao:

> Man's life is like morning dew,
> A flame eating up the oil night by night.
> Why should I strain my ears
> Listening to the squeaks of this autumn
>   insect?
> Better lay aside the book
> And drink my cup of jade-white wine.

During the Song period, finally, more urban literary forms appeared, particularly through the rise of popular romantic stories and an active theater.

Chinese science retained its vitality. The government sponsored mapmaking and astronomical observation. Chemistry advanced, and biologists accumulated new information on the pharmaceutical uses of plants and minerals. Texts were written on forensic medicine; in fact, the Chinese were the first to develop a science of crime detection. Hosts of encyclopedias summed up available scientific knowledge ranging from mathematics to the principles of magnetism. As before, the Chinese did not emphasize sweeping scientific theories but, rather, placed value on precise and practical observations. Their scientists knew a great deal about the actual working of the physical universe, and their grasp increased steadily through research and compilation.

Science, in this Chinese tradition, was linked closely to technology, and here the mastery of this civilization remained unmatched. Experiments led to new procedures in insect control. Engineers developed the first suspension bridges, the first locks on canals, the first gear systems to be applied to the milling of grain. The invention of the magnetic compass served as a great aid to navigation. The abacus came into use in calculating commercial transactions. Even the invention of the simple wheelbarrow, not known in other societies for many centuries, was a great boost to agriculture and construction. Porcelain manufacture arose under the Tang, creating a new artistic and production specialty.

The most significant inventions of the Tang–Song period were explosive powder and the printing press. Explosive powder, first used for fireworks, was applied to weaponry by the Song dynasty, which developed land mines, hand grenades, and other projectiles. Printing (first introduced in Korea) resulted from the desire to circulate authentic versions of important books, such as the Buddhist sutras. By the 7th century, the Chinese could rub paper over inked, carved stone in a primitive form of the block press. Woodblocks were soon in use. By the middle of the 10th century, every classic was in print, and books of all types became common under the Song. Paper currency and playing cards were other resulting uses of print. The technology of printing, like explosive powder, spread to the West by the 15th century, via central Asia and the Middle East.

ECONOMY AND SOCIETY IN CHINA

Chinese politics and culture depended on a flourishing economy, and many of the new inventions directly spurred agricultural production and manufacturing. The state continued to encourage economic development, particularly by extending the transportation network. The Chinese genius for practical organization led to standardized measurements for grain, silk, and other goods, an innovation that facilitated both taxation and commerce.

In the vigorous periods of the Tang and Song dynasties, China became the most prosperous agricultural society in the world. As a result of prosperity, the empire's population tripled, passing the 100 million mark even in the restricted territory of the Song dynasty.

Chinese agriculture benefited from the introduction of quick-growing strains of rice and an increasing use of fertilizers. Production of commercial crops such as tea and cotton expanded. In the manufacturing sector, such enterprises as food processing, ceramic making, shipbuilding, and papermaking all improved in technique. A major iron and steel industry developed, with coal heated to make coke, which was then used to fire blast furnaces for iron smelting. Iron was used mainly for weapons but also for farming and construction tools. In technology and output alike, Chinese manufacturing led the world.

An expanding commerce followed from the growth of agriculture and manufacturing. China underwent something of a commercial revolution between 700 and 1200. Marketplaces and shops cropped up throughout the cities, and commercial cities, rather than urban areas serving primarily as political centers, came into being for the first time. Canal building encouraged trade, particularly between the rice-growing regions and the north. Private merchants proliferated, and merchant associations, called *hang*, coordinated their efforts and aided in banking and long-distance transactions. The use of money spread rapidly, with paper currency making its debut in 811.

Foreign trade flourished, although overseas operations remained mainly in the hands of Muslim merchants who exported Chinese goods as far as east Africa. Koreans dominated China's trade with Japan. But under the Song, Chinese merchants took a more active role in oceangoing trade. Overall, China was the most commercial society in the world by 1300, with the most highly developed manufacturing sector. Clear evidence of China's economic power lay in its ability to export finished manufactured goods and import mainly cheaper raw materials, including horses, leather, and precious stones.

Despite all its accomplishments, China did not break the basic mold of an agricultural economy. Some scholars have speculated that it could have done so in this period by parlaying its extensive natural resources, excellent technology, and

Yan Ciyu, *Hostelry in the Mountains,* late 12th century, Southern Song dynasty.

sheer wealth into an industrial revolution. The advancement of Chinese society was restricted by at least three factors. First, population growth often outstripped available resources, making it difficult for the economy to keep up, much less to evolve into radically new forms. Periods of stability encouraged population increases, which put pressure on the available land, making subsistence, not change, the main goal. Second, the government bureaucracy remained conservative, eager for abundant tax revenues but not interested in

pioneering commercial ventures. Government taxation and regulation, indeed, often interfered with economic growth. Finally, Chinese society retained its adherence to values that stressed the importance of scholarship and bureaucratic achievement. Merchants, for all their gains, were still frowned upon, and many traders used their wealth not to establish the basis for further economic gains but to seek entry into the educated, bureaucratic, landowning elite. So China did not fundamentally alter its course, and indeed, by the later Song period, the pace of economic growth began to slow.

Nevertheless, China remained a world economic leader, particularly in manufacturing. Many women were involved in production, especially in silks. Under the Song, new encouragement promoted oceangoing trade, from which the dynasty hoped for further tax revenues. A maritime trade commission in nine coastal cities pushed for more commerce while improving harbors. By 1150, China had the most sophisticated ships in the world, guided by compasses and sailing regularly along southeast Asia and in the Indian Ocean to the Persian Gulf.

Economic change also produced social change. Cities did spring up, and an important urban culture developed. Urban entertainments, including houses of prostitution, and theaters and gambling establishments, proliferated for a wealthy minority. But the landlord-bureaucratic class continued to command peak prestige. Many in this group, in fact, resided in the growing cities and scorned the backwardness of rural ways. Upper-class society increasingly turned away from military pursuits, devoting itself instead to a life of ceremony and cultivated amusements.

Some interest in what we today call consumerism developed in the urban upper classes. New luxuries in food and clothing spread among the rich. Previously, drinks such as tea had not been available, and even though China produced silk, most wealthy people in north China wore coarse hemp cloth. Under the Tang dynasty (618–907), however, things changed. Tea and sugar (this last imported from southeast Asia), and rituals and objects associated with their use, gained great attention among the wealthy. Wu Tzu-mu noted that "the things that people cannot do without every day are firewood, rice, oil, salt, soybean sauce and tea." The idea of fashion—clear but also changing standards of dress—appeared at the imperial court. One royal consort, Yang Guifei, exerted particular influence through a taste for exotic fads and fancies. Tang fashions spread elsewhere. A tall

lady's hat made its way to Europe, where it was called the *bennin* in the French court. Wealthy merchants in China also picked up a taste for fashion, and sections of cities such as Hangzhou mixed stores selling novelty items with new kinds of entertainments. Marco Polo described Hangzhou as a pleasure city, with just a bit of overgeneralization:

> For the people of this city think of nothing else, once they have done the work of their craft and their trade, but to spend a part of the day with their womenfolk, or with hired women, in enjoying themselves either in their barges or in riding about the city in carriages. . . . For their minds and thoughts are intent upon nothing but bodily pleasure and the delights of society.

A full consumer society, devoted to acquisition and new styles, did not develop, however. These interests clashed with Confucian emphases on devotion to the public good and to clear social hierarchy. Confucianism, not hostile to wealth, was hostile to excessive display and novelty. Later Tang emperors passed laws confirming established fashions in clothing and banning innovations. A few style leaders were put to death, a clear warning to others not to press new values too far.

The masses of people in China did not find the rhythms of their life greatly interrupted, even when new crops and tools were introduced. Village life did not change significantly for most peasants. The growth of cities did create a burgeoning class of urban poor, who were aided, inadequately, by private and government charity efforts.

The position of women deteriorated somewhat during the Tang dynasty, ironically as a result of rising prosperity. Chinese family life had long been strictly patriarchal. In upper-class life, women had fewer functions than they had maintained before, particularly in the cities. As a result, they were increasingly treated as mere ornaments. Officials and some merchants often

Going Up the River at the Spring Festival: Life in the city of Kaifeng. This painting illustrates China's development of a larger urban culture.

took more than one wife. The upper class introduced the custom of binding women's feet: while still young, girls had their feet tightly wrapped until the arch was broken and the toes bent under. The practice resulted in permanent crippling but produced small, delicate feet and a shuffling walk that were considered to be the marks of great beauty. The custom of footbinding gradually spread to the masses mainly between 1500 and 1900, except in a few parts of south China, and it persisted among wealthier

groups into the 20th century. Women's conditions improved somewhat during the Song. Some conducted businesses; others gained education. But public opportunities remained limited for respectable women, and the patriarchal system persisted.

Developments in Chinese society, although significant, displayed on the whole less vitality than parallel alterations in economic and cultural life. Basic values did not shift, and stability was cherished. To most Chinese, or at least to the civilization's leaders, it seemed that a satisfying balance had been achieved, in which prosperity and cultivated diversions were compatible with continuities in political and intellectual life. Increasingly, China's upper class began to think in terms of protecting this rich tradition from outside forces. The 90 years of Mongol rule enhanced the perception that the world outside China was a hostile, dangerous, but inferior place from which China was wise to isolate itself. This adherence to tradition and suspicion of outside forces persisted into modern times, providing the Chinese with great and understandable pride in their own culture but compromising their ability to respond to changes in other parts of the world.

CIVILIZATION IN KOREA, VIETNAM, AND JAPAN

China's power and prestige during the Tang and Song dynasties guided the spread of civilization to other parts of east Asia. Korea and Vietnam adapted Chinese ideographs to their local languages, resulting in the first writing in these languages. Chinese artistic styles, the bureaucratic examination system, and Confucian learning were assimilated in these areas as well, along with the Buddhist religion as it had passed through China. Chinese influence in Korea peaked between the 7th and 9th centuries, during which time Korean rulers imitated Chinese city planning, imported Confucianism, and copied Chinese artistic styles. The Korean economy was less advanced than China's, however, and depended on virtual slave labor for work in the mines to produce raw materials for export. The aristocracy oppressed the Korean masses, although for several centuries Buddhism was shared across class lines. A social revolt in the 14th century resulted in a new dynasty, the Yi, who ruled until the 20th century and quickly restored aristocratic rule. This dynasty also enforced a rigorous Confucianism, emphasizing the gap between elites

and commoners and attacking Buddhism. Confucian ceremonies around the royal court replaced religious ones, particularly within the new capital of Seoul.

Chinese influence in Vietnam also affected the upper classes more than the common people, whose culture, including the enjoyment of cockfights, was more like that of other parts of southeast Asia. Vietnamese rulers, after periods of Chinese occupation, realized they needed to emulate Chinese strengths simply to protect their region, and Chinese bureaucracy and agricultural technology were widely imitated. After the fall of the Tang dynasty in China, Vietnamese rulers gained their independence and began a process of expansion southward. Unlike in Korea, political unity was rare, and internal warfare frequently consumed Vietnamese energies.

Japan was the third geographic area to enter the Chinese orbit. Even more than Korea and Vietnam, however, Japan remained distinct in important respects, in part because, as an island network, the Chinese never conquered it. Thus, the Japanese produced a unique variant of east Asian civilization, akin to Chinese but sufficiently different as to make Japan, ultimately, a major separate force in the world.

As Japan became aware of Chinese achievements, by about the year 400, it developed the habit of selective borrowing—a practice the Chinese had never seen fit to adopt. The custom remained in Japan's collective memory, promoting, much later, a response to Western influences that bore some resemblance to Japan's acceptance of Chinese ways. In the centuries after the year 500, the Japanese proved willing to learn from a superior culture—the Chinese—while retaining a vigorous sense of their own traditions. Particularly in social and political structure, however, the Japanese ultimately did not imitate the Chinese model.

Before Chinese influences happened upon the scene, the Japanese had already developed strong regional political units; the Shinto religion, which worshipped the spirits of nature in local shrines and regarded the emperor as divine; and a prosperous agriculture based on the cultivation of rice. The fragmentation of politics was fostered by the mountains that divide the major islands of Japan, making communication difficult. Shintoism provided a simple, satisfying ritual in which priests led ceremonies and offerings to the gods. The religion also emphasized rituals of cleanliness and discouraged popular festivals featuring games and drinking. Shintoism, like the regional political pattern, long survived influences from the outside, indeed coexisting with them; thus, Japanese Confucianists, Buddhists, and, more recently, dynamic business leaders combine newer values with older Shinto practices.

Japan began copying China in earnest around the year 600. Students and envoys traveled to China and were impressed with the economic and political achievements there. In 604 C.E., the Japanese ruler, Prince Shotoku, issued a constitution establishing a centralized government and bureaucracy and urging reverence for Buddhism and Confucian virtues. Chinese-style architecture and urban planning were introduced, along with Chinese ideographs. Regular exchanges with China, organized by the Japanese government, brought back increasing knowledge, as well as the artistic products of the neighboring giant. Under Chinese influence, a new calendar was adopted. A significant result of Japan's assimilation of Chinese culture was that the position of Japanese women deteriorated. Japanese families had long been tightly knit, but with important public and workplace roles for women. Confucian values led to women being considered inferior, and although the Japanese never went as far as their Chinese mentors did in proscribing women's roles, they did confine women's authority to household and child-rearing. In the arts, too, Japan mirrored its neighbor. Chinese dance and musical forms were introduced to court ceremonies and remain the basis for traditional Japanese culture in these areas even today.

Scroll with Depictions of the Night Attack on the Sanjo Palace (Sanjo-den youchi no emaki). Illustrated scrolls on the events of the Heiji Era, Japan, second half of the 13th century, Kamakura period. Handscroll; ink and colors on paper.

As noted, however, complete imitation did not take place, in part because the Japanese economy remained more backward and less commercial than China's. The centralized Japanese bureaucracy did not succeed in displacing local landowning aristocrats. In politics, particularly, the Chinese model soon began to pall. The Japanese aristocracy was quite comfortable with numerous aspects of Chinese culture, but it did not hesitate to diverge from China in terms of political style. In any event, the decline of the Tang dynasty made the Chinese model less attractive for a time. The short-lived Japanese experiment with centralized government soon faded. The emperor remained, but chiefly as a religious figure, rather than an effective political ruler. Real government lay in the hands of regional military leaders.

Japanese rule was, by the year 800, a full-blown feudal system, quite similar to that which developed separately in western Europe during roughly the same period. Powerful regional aristocrats grouped local landowners under their banners, providing protection and courts of law in return for economic aid and military service. The result was a pyramid, with the peasant masses at the bottom of this power structure. The great lords, called *daimyo,* or "great names," used their revenues to hire professional soldiers, called *samurai.* This feudal system was, obviously, a step backward from centralized rule. It brought frequent periods of warfare to the islands and a considerably greater emphasis on military virtues than prevailed in China. Major wars occurred between 1051 and 1088, and again in the following centuries. Nonetheless, the feudal system blended with Confucian values learned from China. Samurai soldiers had a powerful code of honor and bravery and were expected to commit ritual suicide if they dishonored this code. At the same time, the samurai valued literary accomplishments, such as the writing of poetry, and important ceremonies, such as the tea ceremony. In this respect, Japanese feudal lords were different from their rougher-hewn European counterparts. Other distinctions existed between Eastern and Western feudalism. Because Confucianism encouraged the Japanese lords to

believe that good government required absolute loyalty, Japanese feudalism did not give way to institutions designed to check the power of the greater lords, like the parliaments that arose from European feudalism. According to the Japanese, admirable personal conduct, the loyalty of the lesser lords, and the mutual devotion of the daimyo to their servants produced proper government. Japanese feudalism involved tight group cohesion, whereas the western European version was characterized by a greater sense of contract between individuals. These differences between Japanese and Western society, translated today into business organizations, are a key example of how successful features of a civilization survive and adapt.

Japanese feudalism was used to build a somewhat stronger government structure after 1185. A single aristocratic family, the Minamoto, gained military dominance over the whole of Japan, establishing a central office called the *shogunate.* Each shogun served officially as chief officer to the emperor, but in fact the shogun was the real ruler of the country and commanded the fidelity of the regional lords. Faithful generals were rewarded with estates scattered throughout the country, which helped convert feudal loyalties into effective national politics. The new shogunate took its name from its capital city of Kamakura. Under the Kamakura shogunate, which lasted until 1333, Japan experienced greater peace than ever before. The new government was strong enough, among other things, to resist two attempts by Mongol invaders from China to conquer their country. In the second invasion effort, the Mongols massed the largest overseas expedition the world had ever known, with 140,000 men. However, a typhoon destroyed the fleet, and this "divine wind" was long remembered by the Japanese, who believed that their country was uniquely blessed by the gods.

Japanese politics, as it had developed by the end of the Kamakura period, provided a unique mix of Chinese and local ingredients. Confucian loyalty and ceremony blended with military skills, including elaborate exercises in horsemanship, archery, and fencing, and with intense devotion to

EAST ASIAN CIVILIZATION?

The spread of civilizations in the postclassical world increased the number of existing civilizations. It also raised questions about how to define particular societies—whether to subsume them under larger civilization headings or to treat them as separate entities.

Japan's pattern of imitating China produced binding connections between the two countries (Vietnam and particularly Korea also were linked to these two cultures). Many historians, as a result, have talked of a larger east Asian civilization, strongly based in Chinese power and precedent. This civilization used Chinese characters, even when other writing systems were introduced. It shared the Chinese version of Buddhism, though some of the smaller countries did so with greater intensity than China itself. It developed common artistic forms, for example, in painting and gardening. It shared social and family ideas, though did not directly copy specific Chinese forms such as footbinding. It was strongly influenced by Confucianism beginning in the postclassical period, and even more so later. It emphasized intricate social etiquette and careful manners. These shared features took on and were compatible with local variations and innovations, but they arguably provided a framework for a larger common culture.

But Japan was not China, even aside from variations and incomplete imitations. The very fact of imitation created potential differences, for China lacked Japan's experience with borrowing from outsiders. Most obviously, Japanese feudalism created a significantly different set of political and military traditions from China's, which permanently shaped Japanese history.

The question of whether the differences among China and its smaller, imitative neighbors outweighed their similarities affects analysis of the region's history, not least because of the sheer number of civilizations that must be considered. This issue is not merely academic. China's economy is joining Japan's as one of the modern world's leading forces, and Korea has begun to participate more on the world stage. Thus, it is important to consider whether a distinctive set of east Asian political and economic approaches is defining the world's future—or whether the differences among the region's countries will modify or dilute this impact.

one's lord. The bureaucratic element of Chinese culture played little role as yet. The feudal code, imposing mutual bonds between leaders and followers, served instead as the principal political link. Even today, the feudal heritage of Japan manifests itself in the close connection between government, business managers, and workers. The Kamakura shoguns translated the dominant sense of group loyalty into a series of committees to oversee their administration. The tradition of collective rule, rather than individual or purely bureaucratic control, also maintains a strong hold on Japanese society; it is, in part, responsible for the unusual skill of the Japanese in group leadership and for the economic surge of their nation in the contemporary world.

CULTURE, SOCIETY, AND ECONOMY IN JAPAN

The Japanese economy developed steadily under the feudal system and the Kamakura shogunate. Even periods of internal warfare did not permanently retard economic growth. Farming became increasingly productive. The aristocracy was conscious of the importance of good agricultural administration, and village leaders instilled the same goals among ordinary peasants. Japanese agriculture, supported by careful systems of irrigation for the rice crop, sustained a far larger population than most areas of comparable size elsewhere in the world.

Commercial ties spread among the islands. By the 12th century, trading cities dotted the nation; manufacturing increased, with a focus on metallurgy, paper, and pottery as well as textiles. Japan still depended on China for most luxury products, including silks, but it offered some manufactured goods in exchange. Moreover, trade and manufacturing produced a growing group of townspeople and merchants. Japanese society, like Chinese society, was originally centered on divisions between aristocratic landlords and peasants, and of course the feudal system tended to reinforce this hierarchy. A small number of slaves also existed, confined to menial occupations. The rise of an aggressive merchant group, skilled in seafaring and navigation through the use of instruments invented in China, jostled the foundations of an agricultural society. Japan did not officially value the merchant middle class highly, but it never developed the intense prejudice against moneymaking characteristic of Chinese elites.

The Japanese borrowed more heavily from China in culture than in politics or social structure. A Japanese system of writing developed, after an initial attempt to use Chinese characters to express the quite different spoken language of Japan; the new system was still based on Chinese ideographs. As in China, poetry was the preferred literary form, although some novels and adventure stories were also produced during the Kamakura period. A collection of some 4500 poems appeared around the year 700. Japanese poetry emphasized form, particularly short poems written in a careful sequence of syllables. For example, the *tanka* form required 31 syllables written in 5 lines, in a 5–7–5–7–7 syllable sequence. Japanese poetry often involved the use of words with multiple meanings. The phrase *Senkata naku* means "there is nothing to be done," with the word *naku* making the sentence negative, but the same word also means *to cry*, allowing a poet to suggest futility and sorrow in the same phrase. Like Chinese poetry, although with different specific forms, Japanese poetry stressed elegance, technical virtuosity, and a pervasive melancholy.

Thus, one poet expressed his sorrow over the death of his wife:

Suddenly there came a messenger
Who told me she was dead—
Was gone like a yellow leaf of autumn,
Dead as the day dies with the setting sun,
Lost as the bright moon is lost behind the
    clouds,
Alas, she is no more, whose soul
Was bent to mine like bending seaweed.

As in China, finally, the growth of cities added new literary interests to the Japanese repertoire, particularly through the development of theater. The *No* plays, dramatic poems enacted by dancers, became an especially popular and symbolic form, alternating ritualistic gestures and slapstick comedy.

Japanese literature was, even apart from specific differences in form, no mere imitation of Chinese styles. A delight in war stories provided a distinctive element. But the strong similarities between Japanese and Chinese literary styles brought complexity to Japanese life. The warlords and samurai differed greatly from their Chinese counterparts in political relationships and military ardor, but they shared an interest in appreciating and even writing poetry and drama.

Japanese art derived much from China as well. Buddhist temples, often using the pagoda form, were sometimes built by Chinese architects. Buddhist statuary developed widely. Many Buddhist painters and sculptors created both frightening images to ward off hell and temple decorations representing spiritual joys. Japanese painters featured landscape scenes as well as religious subjects, using bold strokes to capture mountains, waterfalls, and forests. Gardening and flower arrangement, or *ikebana,* became an important art form in Japan as well as in China. Emphasis was placed on small, carefully constructed courtyard gardens, often with one or two artificial hills and a pond with an island and bridge.

Japanese culture during this period did not involve elaborate philosophical speculations or significant scientific work. In this respect, Japan simply omitted some important aspects of Chinese intellectual life. Confucian ethics, as well as a sense of ceremony, did spread widely. Many Japanese combined Buddhism with Shintoism, seeing Shintoism as a set of comforting rituals and Buddhist ceremonies as an avenue to salvation. Buddhist scholars provided detailed descriptions of the horrors of hell and the bliss of paradise. Adherents of the Buddhist faith ranged from the emperor down to many common people, whose religious fervor tended to strengthen in times of political strife. This religious mix was considerably different from that in China and included not only a greater Buddhist element, but also an emphasis on popular congregations and the doctrines of salvation that made Japanese Buddhism increasingly distinctive.

Japanese society was still in the process of development when the Kamakura shogunate fell in 1333, bringing a new period of internal warfare. Further developments in Japanese culture evolved only in later centuries. Yet the Japanese had already created a distinctive variant of east Asian civilization, combining Chinese forms with local religious, political, and social traditions. The result was a society with more contradictory ingredients than in China—which may have been a source of creativity in the long run.

Despite their burgeoning culture, the Japanese did not do what many other newly civilized people have done: embark on an effort of conquest. There was an exception to this: during the 16th century, they tried to capture Korea, but failed. Logically, the Japanese, increasingly skilled in seafaring, might have moved toward the Philippines, or even North America. But at this point, the Japanese orbit was so firmly set by China that expansion made little sense. Like the Chinese, the Japanese considered real civilization to exist only in their world, so they were not tempted to stray widely from its path. And, although Japanese sea trade expanded, it was not yet a match for Muslim fleets or for the navies from Christian Europe that followed later.

Russia and Japan as Imitators

The fact of widespread, reasonably explicit imitation during the postclassical period raises obvious comparisons of various world civilizations. Japan and Russia, for instance, developed in ways so unlike each other because they were in contact with very different models—China and the Byzantine Empire, respectively. Further, Japan was much more imitative than Russia was.

Yet, interesting commonalities existed between Japan and Russia. Both strongly emphasized important cultural forms and cultural apparatus, including writing systems and religion. Both were interested in the political achievements of their "mentors" but were unable to import more sophisticated and centralized political forms at this point. Why cultural imitation seemed more significant and feasible than political imitation is worth pondering: is the same thing true in imitation situations today?

Despite these similarities, differences between the two cultures loomed large again at the end of the postclassical period. With the decline of the Byzantine Empire and a myriad of internal problems, Russia found itself on the cusp of a difficult time that was capped by the Mongol invasion. Japan was spared invasion and, proud of its new Chinese-augmented culture, began to believe that it had surpassed its model, especially when China fell to the Mongols. Its experience, like Russia's, was about to change, but in vastly different ways.

EAST ASIAN SELF-CONFIDENCE

The Japanese, like the Chinese, concentrated mainly on their own development. They even came to believe in their own peculiar destiny.

WORLD PROFILES

MUGAI NYODAI

On the surface, and in many ways in fact, patriarchalism deepened in Japan because of Chinese influence. Women's property and inheritance rights declined, for example, though Japan never pressed women's inferiority as far as China did with footbinding. There were two ways, however, in which certain upper-class women found new opportunities in postclassical Japan. The first was writing. Precisely because Chinese models were so prestigious, educated women who wrote in Japanese had a relatively free hand. It was a woman, Murasaki Shikibu, 978–c. 1016, who wrote the world's first novel, *The Tale of Genji*.

Buddhism was another channel. Mugai Nyodai, in the 13th century, served as director of more than 15 temples and Zen convents. Born to an aristocratic family, she had been trained by a Chinese Buddhist priest invited to Japan by a regional leader. Mugai became the priest's successor. Buddhism was ambivalent about women, sometimes holding them to be impure. But they did acknowledge women's spirituality and provided convent life as an alternative to marriage. Mugai was a leading beneficiary of this kind of interest. And some male Zen leaders provided remarkable statements of principle along the same lines. The leader Dogen thus noted, "When we talk of noble persons, these surely include women. Learning the Law of Buddha and achieving release from illusion have nothing to do with whether one happens to be a man or a woman. . . . The four elements of the human body are the same for a man as for a woman. . . . You should not waste your time in futile discussions of the superiority of one sex over the other."

Mugai Nyodai.

When China was overrun by the Mongols, Japan found itself—by its own standards—the only real civilization it knew about. Thus, the Japanese became accustomed to thinking in terms of their superiority. This confidence remained part of Japanese culture, characterizing the Japanese even during the past century as they have freely imitated Western society. It also served, ironically, to limit Japanese influence in the wider world for many centuries, for the Japanese, like the

Chinese, were accustomed to the isolation of their civilization and not eager to participate in exchanges with other cultures. And so, east Asian civilization entered the next period of world history in many ways the best developed of any of the major world cultures, but among the least eager to investigate what was happening outside its own orbit. Thus, without intending to, the civilization left the door open for expansionary forces from other areas, regions in many ways less developed than east Asia itself.

PATHS TO THE PRESENT

The postclassical period was important in shaping China. More active international trade provided connections and precedents that later Chinese commerce built upon. The creation of significant urban traditions, even some definable consumerism, generated dynamics that, arguably, still influence China today. The further establishment of traditions of bureaucracy and bureaucratic education resurfaced in contemporary China, though with different specific forms.

This period was more obviously formative for Japan. Many cultural elements borrowed by Japan from China, including painting techniques and styles, still partially define Japanese culture. Japan's ability to successfully imitate its giant neighbor without losing its identity, undoubtedly encouraged the country's active interest in similarly selective cultural borrowing in modern times. (This precedent helps explain some differences between Chine and Japanese reactions to outside influence during the past century or so.) Japanese feudalism, with its special emphasis on group loyalty, generated features that show up in Japanese politics and business even now, differentiating the specifics of Japanese economic success from those of the West. Here, quite clearly, experiences accumulated many centuries ago echo in the contemporary world. Some commentators even find strong traces of samurai self-discipline and team loyalty in the success of current Japanese baseball players—the past can reach far beyond itself.

SUGGESTED WEB SITES

For more information on Asia during the Middle Ages, see http://www.medieval-life.net/asia.htm; on the dynasties of classical imperial China, see http://www.mnsu.edu/emuseum/prehistory/china/classical_imperial_china/fivedynasties.html; refer to both http://age.easia.columbia.edu/Song/ and http://hercules.gcsu.edu/~dvess/china.htm for information on China and east Asia; and on Chinese studies, see http://www.chinaknowledge.de/index.html

SUGGESTED READINGS

Recent work includes Bruce Cumings, *Korea's Place in the Sun: A Modern History* (2005); Roger Des Forges and John S. Major, *The Asian World, 600–1500* (2005); Martin Stuart-Fox, *A Short History of China and Southeast Asia: Tribute, Trade and Influence* (2003). Wang Ping, *Aching for Beauty: Footbinding in China* (2002); Charles Benn, *China's Golden Age: Everyday Life in the Tang Dynasty* (2004); S. A. M. Adshead, *Tang Ching: The Rise of the East in World History* (2004); David R. Knechtges and Eugene Vance, eds., *Rhetoric and the Discourses of Power in Court Culture: China, Europe, and Japan* (2005); Charles D. Benn, *Daily Life in Traditional China: The Tang Dynasty* (2002); Tonia Eckfeld, *Imperial Tombs in Tang China, 618–907: The Politics of Paradise* (2005); Linda Walton, *Academics and Society in Southern Sung China* (1999); Heng Chye Kiang, *Cities of Aristocrats and Bureaucrats: The Development of Medieval Chinese Cityscapes* (1999); and Tansen Sen, *Buddhism, Diplomacy and Trade: The Realignment of Sino-Indian Relations, 600–1400* (2003).

For information specific to Japan, see Richard Bowring, *The Religious Traditions of Japan, 500–1600* (2005); William E. Deal, *Handbook to Life in Medieval and Early Modern Japan* (2006); and Mikael Adolphson, Edward Kamens, and Stacie Matsumoto, eds., *Heian Japan, Centers and Peripheries* (2007). On

Korea, see Kang Jae-un, *The Land of Scholars: Two Thousand Years of Korean Confucianism* (2006).

Several studies deal with special features of Chinese history during this period (but see also the general surveys mentioned in Chapter 2): Arthur Wright and Denis Twitchett, eds., *Perspectives on the T'ang* (1973); Mark Elvin, *The Pattern of the Chinese Past* (1973); Jacques Gernet, *Daily Life in China on the Eve of the Mongol Invasion, 1250–1276* (1962); Patricia Ebrey, *The Inner Question: The Lives of Chinese Women in the Sung Period* (1993); and J. Dardess, *Conquerors and Confucians: Aspects of Political Change in Late Yuan China* (1973). On Chinese consumerism (and consumerism's later history), see Peter N. Stearns, *Consumerism in World History* (2002).

14 Centers of Civilization in the Americas

Far from the world trading network and the missionary religions, two centers in the Western Hemisphere experienced a significant expansion of civilization in the postclassical period and slightly beyond: Central America and the Andes region. Civilization was not, of course, new to either of these areas. The Olmecs and others had already established a basis for solid political organization, an elaborate religion whose followers worshipped at massive monuments, and extensive agriculture and trade.

The centers of civilization in the Americas had no link with the international network taking shape in Asia, Africa, and Europe. At most, they serve, by negative example, to highlight how important that network was. The Americas formed a separate system in the history of world civilizations, although the two major American centers of civilization had no regular contact even with each other. For this reason, as well as the paucity of domesticated animals, American Indian civilizations, though impressive in many ways, lagged behind other societies in the level of technology available. While groups in the Andes used the llama for carrying light cargo, Central Americans had no animals to use for transport or for plowing. Furthermore, American Indian civilizations did not utilize the wheel, save for children's toys, and ironworking was not practiced. Nevertheless, these civilizations developed a complex agriculture, capable of sustaining large populations. The leading Aztec city was far bigger than European cities of the time and awed the first Spanish invaders.

In some respects, the flourishing of impressive civilizations in the Americas resembled a somewhat earlier stage in civilization's rise elsewhere. The growth of civilization in the Americas is more similar to that in Egypt and Mesopotamia than in classical China or the Islamic Middle East and north Africa. The resulting differences in religion and technology between the Americas and the European-Asian axis guaranteed massive problems in later

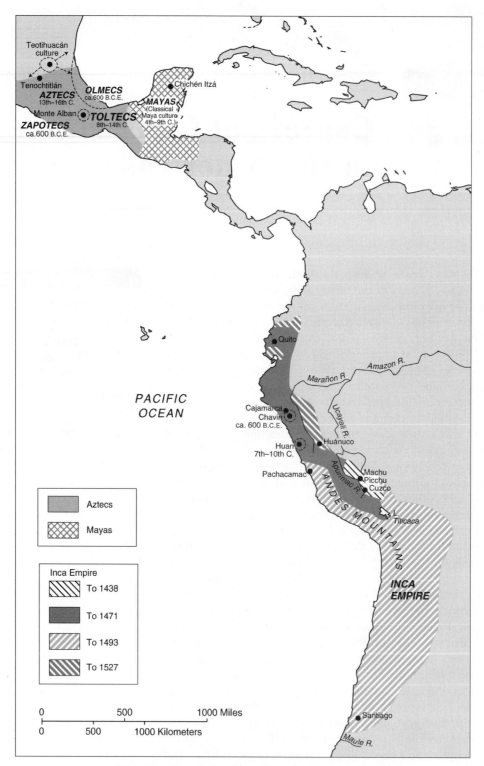

The Americas Before the Spanish Conquest

encounters, when the Americas were drawn into worldwide contacts for the first time.

Note that, because American patterns developed separately, Afro-Eurasian chronology does not fit them tidily: key developments in the Americas began before the postclassical period, while Aztec and Inca achievements crested between 1450 and the early 16th century; 1500, not 1450, was the key break in American history.

KEY QUESTIONS *Central American and Andes centers were quite different. What comparisons best highlight the values and institutions of each center? How did both manage to flourish without many of the standard features of civilizations in Afro-Eurasia?*

THE MAYAS AND AZTECS

The disappearance of the first agricultural societies in Central America, those of the Olmecs and their immediate successors, is shrouded in considerable mystery. Direct traces of these civilizations, except for the monumental ruins that still remain, vanished by the 7th century. Probably one factor in their decline involved invasion by peoples farther north, in the valley that runs through present-day central Mexico. Several of these peoples, in turn, were able to build on the earlier civilizations, creating still more elaborate cultures of their own. The most important of these societies were the Mayas, who established their initial civilization by about 100 C.E. (when they still relied on hunting and gathering) and emerged as the dominant group in the middle region of Central America by the year 600, as they turned increasingly to agriculture. From this point, Maya history divided into three stages: the first phase of particular creativity, from 600 to about 900, centered in the northern portion of present-day Guatemala; then a decline and move northward to the Yucatán Peninsula in Mexico, where the Mayas intermingled with other American Indian groups from the north, notably the Toltecs; and then the definitive collapse of this

mixed culture, from about 1200 on, culminating in the virtual destruction of formal Maya society, including its written language, during the Spanish conquest of the 16th century.

Maya civilization sprang from a tropical rain forest, in areas of great fertility that required immense efforts to maintain. The difficulty of preserving agricultural land from animals, insects, and lush vegetation helps explain the intensity of Maya polytheistic religion, bent on placating a host of savage gods. Central American civilization practiced bloodletting through self-mutilation and human sacrifice, which Mayas believed kept the universe going. Body piercing was also common.

It was religion that gave the clearest structure to Maya society. Huge temples and pyramids were erected to honor the gods. The Mayas did not construct cities in the usual sense, where a variety of activities could take place, though there were some trading centers at intersections of road networks. Instead, Mayans emphasized enormous ceremonial complexes, such as Chichén Itzá. Here, priests conducted rituals to honor the gods. Religious festivals in these centers stimulated intense involvement among ordinary men and women, who produced richly decorated costumes and performed elaborate dances. Games were conducted in the religious centers as well, again to honor the gods. In one game, played in a rectangular courtyard, opposing teams tried to throw a ball through a small circular hoop attached to the side wall, with particular religious significance attached to winning—although it is important to note that scoring was so difficult that most games ended in a tie. Political organization, too, seems to have been dominated by the priestly caste, which organized secret societies to preserve their aura of power and mystery.

Science was also oriented toward the service of religion. Along with the massive monuments the Mayas constructed, the development of a detailed calendar, based on careful astronomical studies made from observatories in the religious centers, rates as their highest achievement. More than any other people at this point, the Mayas had an extraordinary sense of time. The calendar

Mayan temple, Cancun, Mexico: ruins of pyramic and opulent Mayan palace at the ancient site of a ruined city dating back to 300 C.E.

was used particularly to regulate the cycle of religious celebrations and coordinate them with the cycle of the agricultural year. However, the Mayas also used their calendar to calculate back by hundreds of thousands of years, perhaps realizing that time had no beginning. Maya culture also predicted future upheavals based on calendar formulas. Associated with calendar development came unusually accurate measurements of the length of the year (which Mayas figured out to within two hours) and sophisticated mathematics; the Mayas were one of only three civilizations to independently devise the concept of zero.

Religion dominated art. The great pyramids, normally uninhabited except for priests, were designed to impress observers with the remoteness of the gods and the power of those who climbed the steps to commune with them. Statues portrayed gods, often in semi-animal form, with emphasis on the feline grace and ferocity of the jaguar; other statues, particularly in female form, celebrated more benign deities of fertility. Finally, the Mayas developed a hieroglyphic writing, which they used for decorating temples, composing books, and establishing markers for the passage of time.

Maya society was hierarchical. Upper-class families set themselves apart visually. They used a kind of press to distort the skulls of their children, before the skulls hardened. This gave the heads an elongated appearance and was presumably regarded with respect.

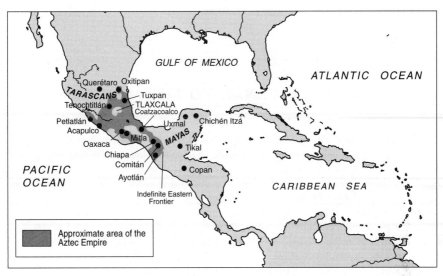

Aztec and Maya Civilizations

Several features of Maya civilization remain unknown. The jungle now claims many religious centers. Few books have survived, for the Spanish tried zealously to destroy all traces of Maya culture in their thirst to Christianize the heathen. Somewhat more extensive evidence of the Maya-Toltec culture exists on the Yucatán Peninsula than for classical Maya achievements. Through the Toltecs, the Mayas added to their religion some human sacrifice, chiefly involving prisoners of war. Secular rulers seem to have gained increasing prominence. Invasions by other American Indian groups proved to be a growing problem; in the 13th century, the great center of Chichén Itzá was sacked by invaders. The Mayas then constructed another capital defended by five miles of walls. This too was conquered, apparently by an uprising of Maya peasants, in about 1460. By this point, Maya civilization was virtually extinguished, although the last Maya stronghold surrendered to the Spanish only in 1699.

Because of technological limitations, particularly the absence of extensive ironworking and the lack of a usable wheel, but also because of the failure to develop arches as a means of support for their buildings, Maya culture depended on immense human labor. At the same time, the extensive religious activity, especially in the ceremonial complexes, required a great deal of human effort. Perhaps it was for this reason that the Mayas proved so vulnerable to invasion and that their art and political skills deteriorated relatively quickly after the high point of the civilization—in some contrast to the more complex ebb and flow of most civilizations in Asia and the Mediterranean. A related explanation of the dramatic declines of American civilizations such as the Maya emphasizes the problems of maintaining adequate agriculture. With no metal tools and few fertilizers, it was hard to maintain the land, keep weeds at bay, and expand acreage. Periods of Maya decline remain hard to interpret. A recent theory suggests that Maya political structure may have permitted families to simply move away when the ruling class became too oppressive.

The Aztec Empire

The Aztecs entered the central valley of Mexico from the north, prior to 1350. They displaced the Toltecs, who had already dispersed, and extended the Aztec Empire into other parts of

HISTORY DEBATE

WHAT HAPPENED TO THE MAYAS?

Figuring out why a people fade from power after centuries of creative achievement is always fascinating. In the case of the Mayas, debate is heightened by the absence of abundant sources. We have no records of anyone musing about what was going wrong. Among historians, warfare was an early favorite as an explanation because of what we know of its destructive power. But on the whole, archeological evidence does not support this, and in fact wars, by themselves, seldom have ended a civilization outright. Soil exhaustion or degradation of the land is another possibility. Some experts now argue that changes in the water supply—or what is called the "Great Maya Drought"—played a major role. The problem with this theory is that declines occurred in different times and places, and while there is evidence of water shortage, the dates do not correlate perfectly with the Maya withdrawal. So far, in other words, no one explanation is perfect. This may mean that a more complex combination of factors was in play. Would this correspond to the causes of decline in other world history cases?

Despite decline, elements of Maya culture survived, combining with that of later peoples such as the Toltecs. Maya villages remain to this day in the Yucatán Peninsula of Mexico and in Guatemala. And Maya people may still go to church to pray to a saint who is also one of the old gods. But the apparatus of the civilization unquestionably disintegrated.

Central America. Their capital was a new city constructed on the marshes around Lake Texcoco, where they built an elaborate network of bridges and causeways to support their great center, Tenochtitlán. With over a hundred thousand inhabitants, based on intensive agriculture, it was one of the largest population concentrations in the world at the time. The Aztec Empire as a whole was a military establishment, controlled by a warrior people who allowed subordinate groups, including the Mayas, to run their own regions so long as they paid regular, high tribute in the form of gold and slaves. Aztec religion, featuring gods of war as well as gods of nature, blended fairly readily with the religions already current in the region, and the Aztecs devoted considerable attention to works of art and pyramidal monuments in honor of the gods.

The Aztec Empire displayed great magnificence. Tenochtitlán, which was the forerunner to the Spanish capital Mexico City, featured ornate palaces, statuary, and temples. The most intensive agriculture in the world developed to support a population of perhaps 20 million in the central Mexican plateau as a whole. Extensive regional trade included vibrant markets, and the Aztecs used merchants as spies. Central America traded widely with Indian societies in what is now the United States southwest. Culturally, Aztecs relied on the earlier stylistic achievements of the Mayas and Toltecs. More important, they depended on extensive slave labor and, as noted, exacted tributes to maintain their luxury. Thus, although their wealth and engineering accomplishments awed the first Spanish settlers, who claimed that the Aztecs' cities surpassed the glories of Rome or Constantinople, they failed to create any basis other than force for their political regime. Government was centralized, under a king who claimed divine authority, and the level of violence was high.

To glorify their gods, the Aztecs extended earlier practices of human sacrifice, killing no less than 20,000 people at the dedication of one of the great pyramids. The Aztecs believed that the gods themselves had been sacrificed in order to create the sun, which needed human blood as food, and their worship reenacted this drama. As a result, not only the economy but also the religion required a steady flow of victims, mainly drawn from persistent warfare. This was an inherently fragile period in Central American history, for the subjects of Aztec rule had no reason to revere their masters. In fact, many American Indian groups initially welcomed the arrival of the Spanish explorers as liberators from their harsh tyranny. Ironically, the Aztecs were hampered in their response to Spanish incursions, not only by their inferior weaponry—for they lacked guns or iron weapons of any sort—but also by their own uncertainty about the future of their rule. Their empire, built on the greater creativity of earlier civilizations in the region, proved to have scant impact beyond its own time.

The Inca Empire

A second and quite separate center of American Indian civilization developed, during the centuries of Maya and Aztec ascendancy, in the Andes mountains of present-day Peru and Bolivia. Here, building on the earlier culture that had extended carefully terraced agriculture in the region and constructed substantial monuments to the gods, an Inca Empire arose from the 12th century on.

The American Indian civilization in Central America, particularly before the final Aztec period, in certain features resembled the earlier river valley civilization of Mesopotamia. The emphasis on regional states, the creativity in science, the interest in art and active trade in luxury goods, even the pessimistic tone of the religion all offer vague echoes of Sumer and its successors. In contrast, the Inca Empire reflects, again in very general terms, the styles of ancient Egypt, especially in its focus on the sun god and the establishment of a highly centralized state led by a ruler regarded as divine.

A large Inca earthenware *aryballos* with polychrome painted figural and geometric decoration, from 1400 through 1532 C.E.

The Incas, centered initially in a small area in what is now Peru, began expanding their authority over other civilized peoples in the region, learning more elaborate political and artistic forms as they went. By the late 1400s, their empire extended from Ecuador to central Chile, constituting the largest governmental unit ever created up until that time in the Americas. The empire included a network of roads over 10,000 miles of mountain terrain. On these roads, runners regularly carried messages, both carefully memorized oral communications—for the Incas never developed writing—and records coded by knots in colored ropes (a system called *quipu*). The Inca people themselves served as a ruling caste in their empire. They were led by a man called *Sapa Inca*, or "only Inca." This ruler governed despotically, regulating marriage and movement and officially controlling all produce. The government, in other words, monitored the labor force closely. Exchanges, carried by llama transport, provided food for craftsworkers and cloth for the farmers. There was no trade in the sense of a money economy, and local self-sufficiency was emphasized. Many areas traded mainly among various levels in the same region, from mountain to valley, each producing what was best suited and exchanging for the rest. Copper tools were manufactured, and gold and silver were used for luxurious ornamentation in the royal palaces. The government regulated the education of local elite among the conquered peoples to ensure their allegiance. Protest was dealt with by military force, followed by the resettlement of disaffected peoples to reduce the potential for further trouble.

The Inca system, far less brutal than that of the Aztecs, was extremely tolerant of local beliefs and religion, although the Incas themselves worshipped a sun deity from whom the royal family was presumably descended. The Incan religion highlighted separate lines of gods and goddesses. Like the ancient Egyptians, the Incas mummified their dead to preserve them for an afterlife.

By the 1400s, the Incas had probably overextended their territory. Without writing, their recordkeeping ability was limited, which meant substantial dependence on local leadership. Conquered peoples were not always content, and technology lagged, which further limited the economic and political links that could be sustained. Thus, the Inca Empire was already receding somewhat even before the Spanish conquest, and in any event the methods and weapons of war the Incas had developed were no match for the guns of the Spaniards.

THE ISSUE OF ISOLATION

The achievements of the American civilizations were impressive by any standard, but particularly when viewed within the context of unusually stark isolation from any other civilized areas. All societies in Asia, Africa, Europe, and even China had benefited from ideas and techniques they borrowed from others, and as we have seen in previous chapters, the importance of borrowing increased during the postclassical period for several areas of new civilization. The Americas had no part in this or in the shared disease pool that resulted from international contacts.

Several other major areas sponsored important new developments in isolation during the postclassical centuries. Polynesian contacts with Hawaii became more extensive, and the settlement of New Zealand began. Polynesians adapted an essentially Neolithic technology in their new settings, utilizing local resources for foods while importing certain animals. As in Central America, a rigid social structure helped compensate for technological limitations; it included an important priestly caste and was geared for frequent warfare. Polynesian society was able to maintain its isolated development until the 18th century, when European contacts brought many of the same results, in terms of conquest and disease, that the Americas had earlier experienced. Here, too, isolation became a historical issue—and a very grave one—when it was ended.

PATHS TO THE PRESENT

The high cultures of the Mayas and Incas left few traces for later civilization in the Americas to build on, in part because of their internal limitations but especially because of their conquest by Europeans, beginning in the 16th century. Tragically, the Europeans brought with them not only greater firepower but also a host of diseases against which the original Americans had not developed immunity; 80 percent of the Indian population was stricken, without the benefit of available treatment. The civilizations that did arise in the Americas after European conquest owed little to previous indigenous patterns at the level of formal religion or politics. Had the Europeans not come, with their superior technology, civilization might well have spread or diversified. Even as the Incas declined, new centers of advanced culture developed in places such as present-day Colombia. In North America, although many Indian groups followed a hunting-and-gathering economy combined with seasonal farming, settled agriculture had spread not only to the southwest, from the more advanced centers in Mexico, but also along the Atlantic coast. Pueblo Indians reflected Central American civilization, whereas slash-and-burn farming enhanced Indian societies in the Mississippi and New England regions. Loose political alliances had formed among certain peoples, such as the five Iroquois tribes around the eastern Great Lakes, which might ultimately have developed into a tighter form of administration. This future was undone, however, by European control and the spread of certain diseases.

However, in important respects, the history of American Indian civilizations did reverberate in later periods, even aside from the fact that surviving Indian groups in both North and South America preserved an important sense of language and heritage. There were two clear links to the present. First, the crops so creatively developed during centuries of agriculture, particularly in Central America and the Andes, were a vital contribution to the nutrition of peoples worldwide when they were more widely disseminated. European settlers in the Americas, as well as Africans, Asians, and Europeans, found their diets and thus their lives substantially altered by corn, squash, and the potato, whose cultivation had been developed by the Incas and Mayas and their ancestors. The spread of important new

foods from the Americas from the 16th and 17th centuries on was a major factor in world history.

Second, beneath the surface, where American Indian civilizations had taken deepest root, significant traces of their societies remained long after official European conquest. Thus, in Central America and the Andes, American Indians long preserved elements of older religious beliefs, even under a facade of Christianity. Communal festivals as well as some secret rituals allowed traditional dances, games, and other recreations to survive. More important still, many American Indian groups preserved certain artistic patterns in their geometrically designed pottery and jewelry and their brightly colored clothing that became characteristic of the new civilization formed by a merger between Spanish and American Indian heritages. Finally, American Indians in these areas maintained distinctive local customs and economic and political styles into the 21st century. The very appearance of Indian villages, notably in Central America, resembled that of traditional communities, with a Christian church and perhaps an official government building merely supplementing earlier housing patterns and a characteristic market square.

Many villages also preserved a communal system of agriculture that had supported the larger American Indian civilization. In the Andes, villagers frequently held land in common, rather than through individual ownership, and stressed the production of most goods essential to village life. Elaborate market systems and a profitmaking motive long remained foreign to this village tradition. Important segments of the indigenous population thus long resisted fully embracing the habits and institutions of the conquering Europeans. This fact encouraged a distinctive, sometimes uncomfortable fusion of European and American Indian ways, beneath the levels of official government and religion, toward forming a Latin American culture that was neither purely American Indian nor purely European in nature. The surviving traditions also ensured future conflicts when, as in recent decades, customary economic values encountered much more direct challenges than initial Spanish conquest and administration had compelled. It is overly simplistic to claim that popular culture in the areas of Latin America where American Indian populations remained largest—notably, those areas that had previously been civilized and so possessed a vigorous agricultural base—merely combined European and American Indian customs to produce a new culture. Such a statement ignores the fact that the governing institutions of American Indian civilization really were destroyed; therefore, there were great differences in the bargaining power of the conqueror and the conquered. But important popular forms did persist alongside new or imported patterns brought by the Spaniards and their heirs, and they continue to influence the lives of Latin Americans in Mexico, Peru, Bolivia (where an Indian was elected president for the first time in 2006), and other countries of these regions even in the present day.

SUGGESTED WEB SITES

On the ancient Maya history, see http://www.digitalmeesh.com/maya/history.htm and http://www.mnh.si.edu/anthro/maya/; on Inca civilization, see http://www.crystalinks.com/incan.html; on the Ancient Aztecs, see http://library.thinkquest.org/27981/; on the culture and history of the Americas, see http://www.loc.gov/exhibits/kislak/. Also see the National Museum of the American Indian, http://www.nmai.si.edu/; and http://www.allempires.com/article/index.php?q=americas_history for an extensive list of links concerning the pre-Columbian Americas.

SUGGESTED READINGS

Recent work includes Robert Sharer, *The Ancient Maya* (2006); Adam Herring, *Art and Writing in the Maya Cities* (2005); Michael D. Coe, *The Maya* (2005); Peter G.

Tsouras, *Montezuma: Warlord of the Aztecs* (2005); Prudence M. Rice, *Maya Political Sceince: Time, Astronomy and the Cosmos* (2004); Karen Vieira Powers, *Women in the Crucible of Conquest: The Gendered Genesis of Spanish American Society, 1500–1600* (2005); Frances F. Berdan, *The Aztecs of Central Mexico: An Imperial Society* (2005); David Carrasco et al., *Montezuma's Mexico: Visions of the Aztec World* (2003); Michael E. Moseley, *The Incas and Their Ancestors: The Archaeology of Peru* (2001); Rosemary A. Joyce, *Gender and Power in Prehispanic Mesoamerica* (2000); Michael E. Smith and Marilyn A. Masson, *The Ancient Civilizations of Mesoamerica: A Reader* (2000); Stuart Stirling, *The Last Conquistador* (1999); Catherine Julien, *Reading Inca History* (2000); Hugh Thomson, *The White Rock: An Exploration of the Inca Heartland* (2003); and Ian Graham, *Alfred Maudslay and the Maya: A Biography* (2002).

On Indian civilization in the Americas, see also Charles C. Mann, *1491: New Revelations of the Americas Before Columbus* (2005); J. Eric Thompson, *Mexico Before Cortez—An Account of the Daily Life, Religion and Ritual of the Aztecs and Kindred Peoples* (2007); Ignacio Bernard, *Mexico Before Cortez: Art, History, Legend* (1975); M. D. Coe, *Mexico* (1984); Frances Berdan, *The Aztecs of Central Mexico: An Imperial Society* (1982); M. P. Weaver, *The Aztec, Maya and Their Predecessors* (1981); and Eric R. Wolf, ed., *The Valley of Mexico: Studies in Pre-Hispanic Ecology and Society* (1976). Inga Clendinnen's *The Aztecs* (1991) is splendid.

On the Incas, consult Brian S. Bauer, *Ancient Cuzco: Heartland of the Inca* (2004); titu cusi Yupanqui, translated by Ralph Bauer, *An Inca Account of the Conquest of Peru* (2005); and David Cahill, ed., *New World, First Nations: Native Peoples of Mesoamerica and the Andes Under Colonial Rule* (2006); John Murra, *The Economic Organization of the Inca State* (1980); Irene Silverblatt, *Moon, Sun, and Witches: Gender Ideologies and Class in Inca and Colonial Peru* (1987); and John V. Murra, Nathan Wachtel, and Jacques Revel, eds., *Anthropological History of Andean Politics* (1986).

CHAPTER 15

The Mongol Interlude and the End of the Postclassical Period

This chapter focuses on the huge changes that occurred between 1250 and 1450, including the decline of Arab leadership and the rise of new frameworks for global interactions in Afro-Eurasia. Contacts among cultures increased. Both east Asia and western Europe became more involved in the world network of interactions. Africa, partly because it worked through the Middle East as an intermediary, was less affected. In addition to these societal shifts, key technologies also changed, establishing the groundwork for further developments. The result was a different world balance by 1450 from that which prevailed two centuries before.

Not surprisingly, social and cultural trends among major societies varied greatly as the postclassical period drew to a close. Peasants in western Europe gained some freedom from serfdom, while their counterparts in the Middle East encountered new landlord demands. Russia began to lose vitality, even before the Mongol invasions, as Japan and western Europe gained momentum. A few trends, however, were generally similar across diverse cultures, in much of Asia, Africa, and Europe. For example, many aristocracies shifted from their emphasis on warfare to focus on gaining greater cultural sophistication. Conditions for women deteriorated as agricultural economies yielded larger surpluses, permitting families to treat women as mere ornaments. And, the great world religions continued to gain ground. Furthermore, because the interregional trading network had intensified during the postclassical period, several major developments caused changes that brought the period itself to a close while setting the stage for the initial dynamics of the period to come. Isolated civilizations were not affected by these changes, however, and Africa was less touched by them than were Asia and Europe.

The first of these developments was the decline of Arab political strength and the narrowing of Middle-Eastern culture and economy. The Arabs had played such a strong leadership role in forming the international network that their problems inevitably reverberated beyond their borders. African trading, although still vigorous, was constrained by the shifts in Arab society, with which African merchants most closely interacted. Western Europe, although heartened by Arab decline, grew anxious as the second of these developments took place: the Turks' vigorous invasions of the Middle East and their establishment of a new Muslim empire. The Turks succeeded in capturing Constantinople in 1453 and assumed control of Byzantine holdings in the Balkans, as well as in much of the Arab Middle East, acts that reconfigured this region. They also provoked major reactions, particularly on the part of nervous Europeans, who redoubled their efforts to find trade routes that would allow them to bypass the Muslim heartland.

The ramifications of Arab decline and Turkish invasion were amplified by an even greater event—the Mongol conquests in Asia and eastern Europe.

■**KEY QUESTIONS**   *Mongols were once often regarded as fierce, brutal invaders; most world historians now emphasize constructive features of their rule, including the new connections they promoted. Which is the correct judgment, and why do such polarized views exist? What happened when the Mongol emperors declined? How was the world different in 1400 from what it had been in 1200, as a result of the Mongol era?*

MONGOL EMPIRES

The Mongol conquests in this period—the last of their kind, in which nomadic warriors overturned the governments of agricultural societies—contributed to important changes in east Asia,

southern Asia, the Middle East, and Russia. Even more, they enhanced the international network, facilitating new exchanges and whetting appetites for greater international involvements.

Mongol herders had been pressing at the northern frontiers of China for some time. They were superb equestrians and archers, using an iron stirrup that allowed them to fire their bows while riding; peasant foot soldiers could not compete with such military prowess. Organized in family clans by leaders who advanced because of their military abilities, the Mongols formed a tightly knit fighting unit, highly trained and able to ride in close formation. Europeans called this fighting force a "horde." The Mongol cavalry ultimately included between 50,000 and 70,000 horsemen, all adept at avoiding head-on clashes with larger forces and skilled at organizing ambushes and cutting off supply routes.

The great Mongol conqueror Chinggis (or Genghis) Khan was born about 1147. His first task was to unify the tribal groups of Mongols; his name, which meant "universal ruler," was adopted at the end of this process, in 1206. Chinggis was a superb general and also an able administrator who used Turkish writing or script to facilitate his bureaucracy. Chinggis Khan invaded China early in the 13th century; he also conquered a Turkish kingdom in south central Asia. Each conquest fed Mongol wealth and increased the size of the armies. Successors to Chinggis Khan swept through the Middle East, toppling the Abbasid caliphate. An Egyptian army pushed the Mongols back to Persia in 1260 with a victory in present-day Israel, but a Mongol-controlled Persia persisted for decades. The Mongols' impact on the eastern Islamic lands, including the terror they generated, had long reverberated. They also seized all of Russia and pressed into the smaller kingdoms of eastern Europe. They might have continued farther west, but they were called back by a domestic political crisis.

Mongol forces completed the conquest of China, unseating the Song dynasty in 1279.

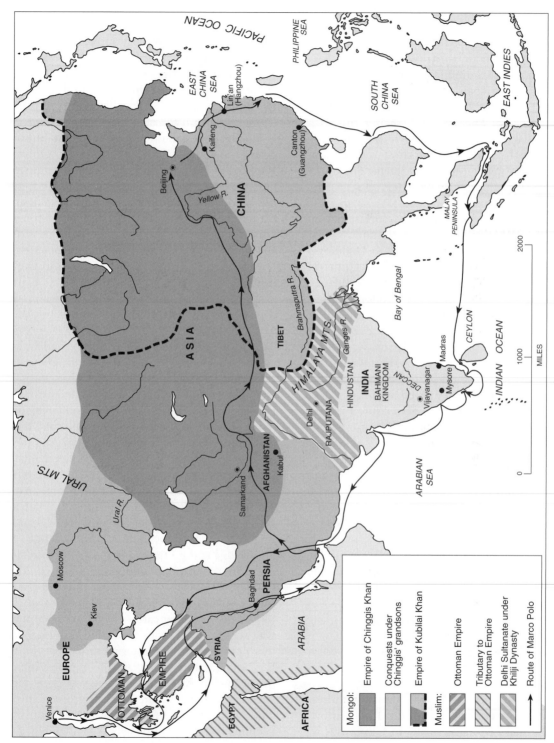

Mongol and Muslim Empires, c. 1000–1500 C.E.

Mongol:
- Empire of Chinggis Khan
- Conquests under Chinggis' grandsons
- Empire of Kubilai Khan

Muslim:
- Ottoman Empire
- Tributary to Ottoman Empire
- Delhi Sultanate under Khilji Dynasty
- Route of Marco Polo

From the Chinese base, the greatest Mongol emperor, Chinggis Khan's grandson Kubilai Khan, organized invasions into southeast Asia and India. He also attempted seaborne attacks on Indonesia and Japan, although these ended in failure. The first effort against Japan was undone by a typhoon. The Japanese, seeing this as a "divine wind," thought they were specially protected by the gods. Despite these setbacks, by 1300 the Mongols ruled or influenced most of the Eurasian civilized world. Their own territories stretched about 6000 miles.

The Mongol period produced fascinating interactions between personalities and history. Various Mongol rulers converted to Buddhism or Islam. Kubilai Khan himself ruled China in grand style. Of necessity, he preserved the Chinese bureaucratic system but used foreigners—Turks and other Muslims and even a handful of Europeans—as his chief ministers because he distrusted the Chinese Mandarins, who were assigned to lower bureaucratic ranks. Repressive laws that prevented the Chinese from assembling or traveling by night bred resentment. But for some decades, Kubilai Khan ruled as few Chinese dynasts had ever done before him, operating a splendid court that was completely open to foreign visitors. Among these were members of an Italian family—Marco Polo, and his father and uncle—who had traveled across Asia to serve at the Great Khan's court. Encouraged by Khan's friendly curiosity, Marco Polo was able to learn a great deal about China. However, given his European background, he could not understand some items, including the use of coal to smelt iron. However, his travel account was widely read; at first regarded as fantasy, it contributed greatly to acquainting Europeans with the East.

But the Mongol empire was short-lived. It was weakened by protests and banditry in places such as China. Disputes over leadership succession also plagued the Mongols. China withdrew from Mongol control later in the 14th century, and the main Mongol legacy in China was an enhanced distaste for foreigners, for the Mongols had been bitterly resented as barbarians. Mongol impact in the Middle East was also short-lived, for the Turks increasingly held power in this region. Direct Mongol influence in India was also slight, although a later Mongol-Turkish force, pressing into India early in the 1500s, established another great Muslim empire in much of the subcontinent. Only in Russia did Mongol control leave an enduring legacy, perhaps setting back economic and cultural levels but also stimulating an intense desire, on the part of the Russians, to imitate Mongol conquests. Russia gained full freedom from Mongol domination in 1480 and began a pattern of expansion of great importance in world history.

The Mongol impact on world history, however brief, was significant in several respects. Mongols provided safe passage for travelers over land routes, and they were tolerant and interested in learning from newcomers. Overland trade and travel linking western China, through central Asia, to Persia and the Middle East, were not of course new; the silk roads had developed during the classical centuries. But silk road trade had involved mainly regional travel, with traders passing goods on to another set of merchants at various intervals; and it had crossed a variety of political boundaries and nomadic territories. This now changed under the Mongols. The vast stretch of territory under Mongol control made possible an unprecedented interchange of knowledge and products among the various civilizations of Europe and Asia. In particular, Chinese discoveries—explosive powder, paper money, printing, porcelain, and medical techniques, even playing cards—began to make their way westward. Mongol-facilitated diffusion was of special benefit to western Europe, previously backward, and helps explain this region's subsequent rise, as Asian technology was combined with a territorially ambitious, aggressive spirit. The Mongol presence was also significant in keeping western Europe, albeit accidentally, out

WORLD PROFILES

CHABI KHAN

Chabi, wife of the great Mongol emperor Kubilai Khan (who ruled from 1260 to 1294), was an important historical personage in her own right. Obviously, in patriarchal societies, a woman most commonly gained access to power (even on a very local level) through the position of her husband. Chabi advised Kubilai actively, guiding counterstrategies against his ambitious brothers and promoting Buddhist interests in the highest government circles. Chabi also urged tolerance for the defeated Chinese rulers, arguing that leniency would best reconcile the Chinese to Mongol rule; she influenced her husband to abandon a plan to turn farmland near the capital into pastures for the Mongols' horses. At the same time, Chabi and other Mongol women resisted integration with Chinese customs concerning women, from Confucian doctrines to footbinding. They moved freely in public, and they hunted on horseback with their husbands and in parties of their own. These women had no enduring impact on Chinese gender patterns, however. Does this suggest some distinctive limitations on the historical role of even great women in the postclassical era? Or do great people in general have limited power to change the directions of a society?

Chabi, wife of Kubilai Khan, the 13th-century Mongol ruler of China.

of the hands of foreign powers. For a century (and more than that in Russia), most major civilizations in eastern Europe and Asia were preoccupied with invasion, the threat of invasion, or foreign control. Western society enjoyed the fruits of new contacts with Asia without the attendant hardships and distractions. This, too, helps us understand why Western nations displayed such surprising vigor on the world scene by the late 15th century.

The Mongols also affected the conduct of war. They helped teach both the Turks and Europeans the effective use of explosive powder. By the early 15th century, both groups were utilizing the cannon in warfare, to great effect.

New intercontinental contacts also promoted new contagions, an unhappy by-product of the increased level of Eurasian commerce by the end of the postclassical period. Bubonic plague broke out early in the 14th century. It may have been started in China, but a more likely initial site was central Asia around the Caspian Sea. It spread unprecedentedly rapidly, reflecting the new range and intensity of trade contacts. Carried probably by fleas on pack animals, it reached the Middle East by the mid-14th century, hitting north African ports by the 1340s. From there, it spread quickly to Italian ports (by 1347–1350) and then to the rest of western Europe. The overall result was one of the most deadly world epidemics in all of human history, with mortality rates more than 25 percent in parts of China, the Middle East, and Europe. Only the plagues of the late classical period and the later European-borne diseases in the Americas and Pacific island areas rival this international plague in known consequences.

The Mongol period was finite, of course. By the 14th century, China had expelled the great Khans, and soon after Russia would do the same. With the revival of separate civilizations, some barriers to interregional exchange were restored. European contacts with China, for example, were reduced for some time. Overland travel became more difficult, placing a new premium on sea routes. Nevertheless, the knowledge of new techniques, products, and trade routes could not be reversed. The interregional network was poised for further definition.

Although the Mongols disappeared from the world stage, they continued to hold significant territory for several centuries. A Mongol, or Tatar, khanate ruled the Crimea (now part of Ukraine) under Turkish patronage until the Russians conquered it in the late 18th century. Though they were Muslims, the Mongols tolerated their Christian subjects. Taxes were low, as the Khans raised money by selling salt and other services. Tatar Khans regularly conducted council meetings, and council approval was necessary for any decisions made by the Khan. Here is a reminder that legislative traditions existed outside the West. Several older women from the harem sat with the council, for the Tatars preserved Mongol respect for women's opinion. The Crimean Khan also periodically raided Russia, once, in 1550, reaching as far as Moscow.

CHINA AND THE WEST AS NEW WORLD POWERS

The decline of the Mongols posed an implicit challenge to the many societies that now depended on extensive intercontinental trade among Asia, Africa, and Europe: who could now organize new contacts? Both China and Europe quickly responded, though by stressing oceanic trade now that overland contacts across Asia were complicated by the decline of political connections. Both responses occurred despite the ravages of the bubonic plague and attendant population loss and dislocation.

The revived Chinese empire, under its new Ming dynasty, provided the first response. The Ming dynasty marked a period of unusual stability in Chinese history, but it began with an unaccustomed display of expansionist behavior. It was as if a release from Mongol control awakened a desire to push outward—as happened later, with more durable results, in Russia. The first Ming emperor rather naturally expanded China's land boundaries by pushing the Mongols to the north. The Ming also reestablished influence over neighboring governments, as in the earlier Tang period, winning tribute from states in Korea, Vietnam, and Tibet. What was more unusual was a new policy, adopted in the early 1400s, of mounting huge, state-sponsored trading expeditions to southern Asia. A first fleet, under a Muslim Chinese admiral, Zheng He, sailed in 1405 to India, with 62 ships carrying 28,000 men. Later voyages reached the Middle East and the eastern coast of Africa, bringing chinaware and copper coins in exchange for local goods. Chinese shipping at its height consisted of 2700 coast guard vessels, 400 armed naval ships, and at least as many long-distance ships. Nine great "treasure ships" were the

HISTORY DEBATE

CAUSES OF GLOBAL CHANGE BY 1450

It is easy to see that world conditions were changing rapidly by the 15th century. Western Europe, although still backward in many respects, was beginning to extend its reach toward new power—a long process that lasted into the 19th century. What were the key causes of such global change? Here is where the debate lies.

Several explanations focus on various features of Europe. Christianity provided a missionary spirit. Feudal wars accustomed Europeans to fighting and schooled them in the importance of gaining an advantage over rivals. The new Renaissance, a cultural movement, gave Europeans greater confidence in the powers of individual effort and generated more interest in secular, rather than purely religious, goals (see Chapter 16).

These explanations may be supplemented by focusing on the traditionalism of societies outside Europe. Carlo Cipolla, writing about European expansion, notes that the Chinese, for example, simply refused to follow Europe's technological gains, because innovation would threaten the established social structure, with scholar-gentry on top, and anticommercial Confucian values. Again, Europe can be seen as unique.

A different argument focuses on changes in world conditions that almost accidentally gave western Europe an advantage. The Mongol era provided western Europe with a chance to imitate Chinese technology without actually experiencing invasion (an obvious contrast with eastern Europe or even the Middle East). After the Mongol era, new barriers to overland international trade shifted attention to ocean routes—another boon for western Europe. Europe was motivated to seek change not necessarily because of a distinctive culture, but rather because of certain acute economic liabilities. It simply did not have the goods to exchange for the spices and other Asian products it had come to cherish, so it needed to find sources of gold. It also feared dependence on Muslim merchants, particularly as Ottoman power showed a revival of Muslim political strength, so it looked for alternative sea routes. According to this worldview, changing world forces, not special European qualities or strange Asian blind spots, were the primary reason for increasing European power.

Which historical approach seems most plausible? Are there ways to combine them?

biggest in the world, capable of carrying a year's supply of grain and equipped with tubs to grow garden vegetables. Ships of this sort, the most sophisticated in the world at the time in their size and provisions and also in the improved compasses they used for navigation, explored not only the Indian Ocean but also the Persian Gulf and the Red Sea, establishing regular trade with all parts of southern Asia and the Middle East.

Historians have debated the reasons for these expeditions. There was no desire to conquer, though Chinese forces engaged in some battles in southeast Asia. Trade was probably an indirect motive. What the Chinese emperors probably

intended was an expanded system of tribute, as already occurred with neighboring states such as Vietnam and Japan. Certainly many of the gifts brought back, for example giraffes from Africa (which created a sensation), intrigued the Chinese elite. The expeditions also built on the trade patterns that the earlier Song dynasty had established.

There is no question that, had the Chinese thrust continued, the course of world history would have been immeasurably altered, for the tiny European expeditions that began to venture down the western coast of Africa at about the same time would have been no match for China's combination of merchant and military organization. But the emperors called the expeditions to a halt in 1433. The costs seemed unacceptable, given the continuing expenses of the campaigns against the Mongols and the desire to build a luxurious new capital city in Beijing. The government was rebuilding the Great Wall, at huge expense. Confucian suspicion concerning merchants surfaced as well. This decision left the door open for a new west European surge, which began to take clear shape by the mid-15th century.

West Europeans had several bases for this unprecedented advance, despite their backwardness during the postclassical period. They had merchant skills and a vigorous iron industry. They had a missionary Christian religion, an active military tradition, and a host of internal rivalries that could propel traders and kings alike to seek advantageous gains by successful ventures abroad. They also had some problems. They feared the new Turkish Empire. Their upper classes had a taste for Asian luxuries and spices that the European economy could not easily afford. During the postclassical period, this trade lay largely in Muslim hands, with Europeans transporting the goods only in the Mediterranean region. Now it seemed desirable to find more direct access, without the Muslim intermediary. Europe's economy, furthermore, generated few goods that Asians wanted. They supplied some tin, wool, and salt, but the balance had to be paid for in gold. Europe had no real gold supply; this was another reason to push into new territories, in the hope of finding rich holdings. Finally, by the 15th century, Europeans were able to assimilate some of the technologies that had passed their way, thanks to the Mongol empire, and even to improve on them. They had cannons and gunpowder; they possessed the compass; they were advancing in the design of sailing ships.

Initial European attempts to find routes to Asia and gold began earlier in the postclassical period. As early as 1291, an expedition from the Italian port city of Genoa sailed into the Atlantic seeking a westward route to the Indies, but the expedition was never heard from again. During the 14th century, Italian sailors reached islands in the Atlantic—the Canaries, the Madeiras, and possibly the Azores. There they established sugar plantations, importing African slaves to do the work—a sign of the system Europeans soon developed into worldwide traffic of human beings.

Spanish expeditions also ventured as far as the northwest Atlantic coast of Africa. However, such voyages were limited by the small, oar-propelled ships used in Mediterranean trade, for they could not press far into the oceans. During the 15th century, however, round-hulled ships were developed for the Atlantic, and the Europeans also began to use a compass for navigation—an instrument that they copied from the Arabs, who in turn had learned of it from the Chinese. Mapmaking and other navigational devices improved as well. Western Europe was ready for its big push.

THE END OF TRANSITION: POSTCLASSICAL TO EARLY MODERN

By 1450, the world had changed in many ways from just three centuries before. The Arabs, who had provided the first global civilization, were in partial eclipse. Major empires in the Americas were tottering. The reverberations of Mongol conquests continued, particularly in central Asia, Russia, and India, although the Mongols themselves were in retreat. New players in the game of international influence were beginning to emerge. The powerful influence of world religions continued, but this theme was no longer center stage. The clearest constant, aside from regional continuities in China and elsewhere, was the importance of international contacts. The greatest contribution of the postclassical period to world history was the creation of a regular international network affecting most of Asia, Africa, and Europe. The definition of the network changed, as Arabs yielded to Mongols and Mongols to Chinese as effective chief administrators of the network. However, its importance steadily intensified. What was about to happen, after the postclassical period closed, was a reformulation of the network, which broadened to include the entire world for the first time in history.

The Mongol period generated different effects in various parts of the world network. Even direct Mongol control, for example, affected Russia differently from China. Japan, spared invasion, gained in self-confidence in relation to the rest of the world. Mongol incursions added to instability in the Middle East. Western Europe benefited from new contacts, as learning opportunities, without facing a direct threat. Sub-Saharan Africa continued its international interactions—Mongol leaders wore headdresses made from monkey skins imported from east Africa—but was not directly affected by the Mongols, in terms of new contacts or new threats. Its stability contrasted with other regions in the network. These variations had obvious impact in the next stages of international contact, after the Mongol era passed.

The Mongol conquests, and the even briefer flurry of Chinese expeditions, were anchored in the past. China's decision to end its expeditions, opening the way for other international traders, may seem more important than the ventures themselves. The modern nation of Mongolia, meanwhile, has been under Soviet Russian control since 1991. In an attempt to reclaim some of its postclassical glory, it has renewed its celebration of heroes such as Chinggis Khan, but it remains on the benches, rather than being a world player.

PATHS TO THE PRESENT

The most obvious legacy of the postclassical transition period is the world's heightened realization of the importance of interregional trade and exchange. At the end of this period, China decided to reduce its involvement in this network—though not to end it—for its role in world trade remained vital. This did not slow the pace of global commerce, however, that accelerated due to other nations' efforts. New European access to Asian technologies, another result of the Mongol period, helps explain Europe's increasingly active role in a world network that was about to be redefined.

SUGGESTED WEB SITES

On the Mongols in world history, see http://afe.easia.columbia.edu/mongols/, http://www.mongolianculture.com/mhisotyr.html, and http://www.coldsiberia.org/. For more information on Chinggis Khan and the Mongols, see http://www.fsmitha.com/h3/h11mon.htm and http://www.lacma.org/khan/index_flash.htm.

SUGGESTED READINGS

Recent work includes Lynn A. Struve, ed., *Time, Temporality, and Imperial Transition: East Asia from Ming to Qing* (2005); Gerard Chaliand, *Nomadic Empires: From Mongolia to the Danube* (2004); Jean-Paul Roux, *Genghis Khan and the Mongol Empire* (2003); Stephen Turnbull, *Genghis Khan & the Mongol Conquests, 1190–1400* (2004); Paul D. Buell, *Historical Dictionary of the Mongol World Empire* (2003); Sarah Schneewind, *Community Schools and the State in Ming China* (2006); Frances Wood, *The Silk Road: Two Thousand Years in the Heart of Asia* (2002); Peter C. Perdue, *China Marches West: The Qing Conquest of Central Eurasia* (2005); Stephen G. Haw, *Marco Polo's China: A Venetian in the Realm of Khubilai Khan* (2006); David R. Knechtges and Eugene Vance, eds., *Rhetoric and the Discourses of Power in Court Culture: China, Europe, and Japan* (2005); Jack Weatherford, *Genghis Khan and the Making of the Modern World* (2004); David Wang Der-wei and Shang Wei, eds., *Dynastic Crisis and Cultural Innovation: From the Late Ming to the Late Qing and Beyond* (2005); Thomas Allsen, *Culture and Conquest in Mongol Eurasia* (2001); Linda Komaroff, *The Legacy of Genghis Khan: Courtly Art and Culture in*

Western Asia (2002); Bat-Orchid Bold, *Mongol Nomadic Society: A Reconstruction of the Medieval History of Mongolia* (2001); and Uradyn E. Bulag, *Mongols at China's Edge: History and the Politics of National Unity* (2002).

The fullest and most accessible summary of the links between Mongol expansion and the spread of the Black Death can be found in Ole J. Benedictow, *The Black Death 1346–1353: The Complete History* (2004). On international contacts, see Jerry H. Bentley, *Old World Encounters: Cross-Cultural Contacts and Exchanges in Pre-Modern Times* (1993), and J. L. Abu-Lughod, *Before European Hegemony: The World System A.D. 1250–1350* (1989).

The Postclassical Period, 500–1450 C.E.

CONTACTS AND IDENTITIES

The growing importance of interregional contacts raised vital issues of regional identity during the postclassical period. More and more societies modified their previously separate patterns of development through mutual influence and even outright imitation. The postclassical period was a crucial turning point in the balance between localized and global perspectives.

The two great trends of the postclassical period, affecting all major societies in Africa, Asia and Europe, both had huge implicaitons for identities. The new religious map brought different regions and peoples together under the banners of Buddhism, Christianity, or Islam. The religions provided their own new identities, but they might not overcome some regional definitions. Even more obviously, increasing trading contacts raised questions about how societies would balance growing reliance on goods and even fashions produced elsewhere, at least for elite clienteles, and more regional patterns. The emergence of increasingly explicit imitation of other societies, another great trend in the period related both to religious dissemination and trading connections alike, created issues as well, particularly for the new range of imitators from southeast to northeast Asia, and from northern Europe (east and west) to sub-Saharan Africa.

Not all contacts had huge impacts on identity, of course. Europe's growing taste for Asian spices, for example, was fairly neutral in terms of its affect on European identity—though it did signal a softening of the military aristocracy in favor of greater consumerism.

But the new level of tension among world societies at the end of this period was real and measurable. The spread of the world religions shifted identities in favor of outside influences. While great ethnic and linguistic diversity persisted in the Middle East and north Africa, more and more people in these regions modified their identities not only to become Muslim but also to become assimilated into an Arab identity. Of course, distinctions persisted even amid religious conversions. Persians became Muslim in the main, and Zoroastrianism faded, but they maintained a separate language and a more representational artistic tradition despite Muslim precepts. Similarly, Arab travelers to west Africa noted how the local elites had become truly pious Muslims while also, however, retaining local customs concerning the dress and behavior of women. Even today, Muslims in some of the mountainous regions of central Asia continue to combine Islam with the worship of nature spirits. Scandinavians converted to Christianity but also retained traditions such as burning large pine trees during summer solstice ceremonies to honor the Sun and keep it in the heavens. All of these were compromises that allowed citizens of a given region to retain a sense of local identity amid growing cultural convergence.

Explicit efforts at imitation obviously challenged identity. In the 7th century, many Japanese leaders wanted Japan to become as Chinese as possible. This goal misfired, as we have seen in previous chapters: even as the Japanese became more like the Chinese, the Japanese identity persisted, especially in high culture and in politics. This convergence, however, involved a different and more subtle balance of cultures than the ones mentioned earlier.

Identity issues also showed clearly in Europeans' love-hate relationship with the Middle East. Middle Eastern goods and ideas were greatly valued by Europeans, and they deliberately and extensively borrowed these entities from Arab culture. But Christians' hostility to Islam as a false religion maintained clearly separate identities between Europeans and Arabs. Many Europeans, in fact, downplayed the extent of their imitation of the Middle East in favor of claiming an assertive Christianity.

The tension between identity and interaction became steadily more complex during the postclassical period. One result was an unpredictable intersection between abrupt insistence on identity and considerable intercultural tolerance. China's Tang dynasty thus moved from acceptance of Buddhism to an assertion of a separate Chinese identity against Buddhist influence. Christians and Muslims interacted creatively and peacefully in Muslim Spain, but the Christian crusading spirit, which included "reconquering" Spain, defined Christian identity as being quite different from that of Muslims.

PART IV

A New World Economy, 1450–1750

THE EARLY MODERN PERIOD, 1450–1750

Several major developments altered the framework of world history during the three centuries after 1450. As its label suggests, the early modern period generated changes that we recognize in the world today—this is the "modern" part; several patterns were distinctive to the period itself, however, and subject to significant later change—this is the "early" aspect.

The period opened, between 1450 and the early 1500s, with the end of the Byzantine Empire and the rise of a new Ottoman Empire in much of the Middle East and also parts of southeastern Europe and north Africa; with the increasing independence of Russia from Mongol control; and with the growing role of Europe in global seafaring, signaled in the 1490s both by the "discovery" of the Americas and by the navigation around southern Africa and the consequent ability to reach India directly. Several of these developments also deployed significant new technologies in the design of ships, the use of improved navigational devices, and the availability of cannon and gunpowder.

The end of the period hinges on no single event. By the later 18th century, however, Europe's economic power in the world was shifting from considerable to near-dominant. This shift was both expressed and furthered by Europe's leadership in the Industrial Revolution, launched by the 1770s with inventions such as the steam engine in Britain.

During the period itself, three major themes predominated. First, the Americas were brought into the full global economic system (and at the end of the period, Australia and Pacific Oceania also were). This helped intensify interregional

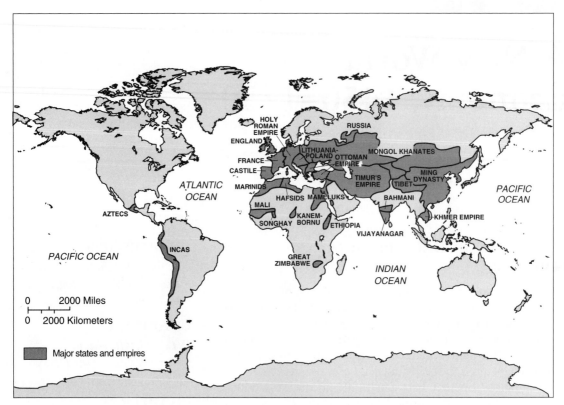

The Postclassical World in Transition, about 1400 C.E.

trade—theme #2—but it also propelled a series of biological exchanges between the Americas and the rest of the world that are called the *Columbian exchange.* American foods were adopted in many other places, with corn and the potato being particularly important; Afro-Eurasian animals, diseases, and people (including many African slaves) were brought to the Americas in turn. The result changed lives in both the old world and the new. American and African populations were considerably disrupted for an extended period of time. In the Americas, and later in the Pacific, population loss to disease opened territories to outside conquest and settlement. In the long run, however, the main result of the Columbian exchange was to improve global food supplies by diversifying available crops, and thereby to encourage rapid

population growth—first in Asia, then in Europe, then more generally.

The increase in interregional trade had many facets. The variety of goods in commerce expanded. Sugar became the first globally traded product that was a mass consumer staple. Many societies also became increasingly dependent on the import of silver. Trade routes shifted: the Atlantic became a major artery; trade within the Mediterranean became less important. Above all, trade levels became substantial enough to feed new levels of global inequality. A few societies, mainly in western Europe, began to dominate world trade, earning disproportionate profits in the process. Other societies, such as China, managed to profit considerably as well; merchants and money became more important not only in

Europe but in many Asian societies. A number of societies, however, initially in Latin America and the Caribbean, found themselves increasingly locked into an inferior position in the same trading system. These dependent societies could not escape participation in world trade, but they did so at considerable disadvantage.

Finally, the period's third major theme was the use of gunpowder and other military assets to construct a new series of empires. Empire formation during the period was striking, showing new political and military capabilities. Five great European cultures—first the Portuguese and the Spanish, then the British, Dutch, and French—formed numerous overseas empires. These holdings included territories in the Caribbean and the Americas, but also various ports and islands in Africa and Asia. But new land-based empires also sprung up during the first half of the early modern period and were at least as significant as the empires created overseas by European countries. These land-based empires included the unprecedented expansion of Russia; the Ottoman Empire, which revived political strength in the Middle East; one of the great empires in Indian history; and a new Persian–centered empire—all of which were in addition to the established empire in China. In central Asia, the spread of several new empires steadily reduced the operation of nomadic societies, a tremendous change in this aspect of Eurasian history.

The three themes interrelated, of course. Biological exchanges and population growth affected trade and vice versa; all the new empires had to develop policies concerning their role in international trade, and several built on global trade directly.

The early modern period did not see the emergence of clearly global patterns of cultural change, though major developments occurred in individual societies. Nor, aside from gunnery and navigation, were there global technological surges. Many historians have argued that early modern global change produced one other striking pattern: increased pressure on human labor. In many societies, including those dependent on new forms of slave labor, the importance of production increased, as a means of both handling population growth and winning profits for merchants and landowners, including those engaged in global trade. The results were an increased exploitation of child labor, greater difficulty in reducing work later in life, a heightened pace of work, and in some instances a reduction of traditional leisure time and outlets. Here was a crucial change in the human experience just beneath the surface of the leading events.

Chapters in this part deal first with the transformation of the world economy; then with changes within western Europe and Russia; and finally with new empires in Asia, Asian participation in world trade, and significant political developments in Japan. For the first time in human history, all parts of the world now interacted with the leading patterns of change, albeit in very different ways.

GLOBAL CONNECTIONS

Connections formed the framework of the early modern period. Most dramatic of these were the links forged by European traders across the Atlantic and Pacific oceans. The inclusion of the Americas in global linkages was a critical development both for the Americas and for the rest of the world: the impact of the Columbian exchange demonstrates the speed and significance of seaborne connections. China and Africa adopted American crops within a century of Columbus' voyages—China, particularly, learned of them through contact with European merchants in the Philippines, where Spaniards were experimenting with corn and the potato in hopes of increasing the local food supply. European adoption of new foods was slower, as Europeans feared to use crops not mentioned in the Bible. Perhaps most strikingly, the new nature and speed of linkage were demonstrated, more than symbolically, by Magellan's circumnavigation of the globe in 1519–1521.

Other kinds of connection, some old, some new, occurred during this period as well. Russian expansion brought parts of central and particularly northeastern Asia into regular interaction with larger trade routes for the first time. China continued its active trade with southeast Asia, where Chinese commercial minorities set up shop to supply China with the only products, such as certain kinds of tea, that China needed from the outside world. Japan, though more isolated than before, maintained some regular exchange with Korea and China.

Africa had long been involved in interregional connections. Trade between eastern Africa and the Middle East continued, and the products included slaves. Europeans conducted some activities along the east African coast, but this trading did not displace Europe's other links. In west Africa, however, the European-run slave trade significantly altered earlier routes, reducing the importance of connections across the Sahara in favor of the new Atlantic channels.

Some links involved more than trade and the movement of peoples. Catholic missionaries fanned out from Europe. Their main impact was in Latin America and the Caribbean, but they won a few conversions in parts of Asia and concretely changed the religious landscape of the Philippines. By the 18th century, these same cultural channels enabled new scientific exchanges between Europe and the Americas as well. Also by this point, cultural exchange connected Russia and western Europe in new ways. Globally, the early modern period was not as defined by missionary activity and religious conversion as were

the postclassical centuries, but some new patterns were created.

Connections—and particularly the clashing ambitions of the European powers—also now meant war. The Seven Years War, 1756–1763, was in a real sense the first world war. The key confrontation was between Britain and France, but it involved several other powers, as well, and local groups took sides. Europeans faced each other in North America and India, as well as on the seas. Correspondingly, the results of war initiated changes on three continents and realigned and redefined European activities in India, in the Americas, and on many islands. The Treaty of Paris, which settled the war, shows the sweep of European-led world conflict: Britain acquired Canada from France and Florida from Spain, and it won French territory on the African west coast; holdings in India were redivided between France and Britain, laying the foundation of increasing British control of the subcontinent. The French regained several crucial sugar-producing islands in the West Indies, which they regarded as far more important economically than Canada, and they gave the Louisiana territory to Spain to compensate for the loss of Florida. Obviously, this settlement did not affect the whole world. Never before, however, had a single treaty touched so much territory, never before had any power claimed the right to dispose of other lands as confidently as the European leaders did.

Contacts and their importance increased steadily during the early modern period. They did not all fall within a European-dominated orbit. The contacts highlighted trade more than cultural or technological exchange, but some of the latter inevitably occurred. The world was effectively smaller by 1750 than it had been three centuries before.

CHAPTER 16

The West and the World: Discovery, Colonization, and Trade

W hy does a civilization begin to ascend within the ranks of the various societies of the world, gaining new power and importance? The question is hardly less complex than the issue of why civilizations decline. In the case of the West, in its rise to greater world prominence after 1450, the problem was enhanced by some of the civilization's overall drawbacks: here was a society still politically divided, often locked in internal wars and intense social unrest, with a relatively small total population. How could it, in the space of a few centuries, seize control of the world's oceans and some of its richest lands?

The answer to this question involves two kinds of factors: those that are measurable and material, and those deriving from culture and outlook. On the material side, the West, even as it launched its systematic explorations of the Atlantic in the 15th century, was gaining in technological sophistication. It was not yet the world's most advanced society in overall technology, but it was fast moving in that direction. It certainly had superiority over sub-Saharan African and American Indian cultures in manufacturing and agricultural know-how. More specifically, Western skills in shipbuilding and navigation, aided by refinements in the compass and other directional devices, were at a high level and would improve steadily to the point that, by the 16th century, they surpassed those of east Asia. More specifically, west Europeans had been quickest to develop high-quality gunnery, using the knowledge they gained of Chinese explosive powder to forge weaponry that was awesome by the standards of the time (and more than a bit terrifying to many Europeans, who had reason to fear the new destructive power of their own armies and navies). The West maintained its weapons advantage over all other civilizations in the world into the 20th century, and even today its arms technology remains among the most highly developed. A crude but possibly accurate explanation of the West's rise, then, focuses simply on its technological edge in the art of war and intimidation.

However, sophisticated weaponry and other technological superiority may not have been the whole story. We have seen that Europe's problems, including an unfavorable balance of trade with Asia and the fear of Muslim power, created some special motives for Western leaders. East Asia had some comparable technological leads, surpassing the West not in weaponry but in navigation during the 15th century, but it chose not to exploit these advantages in a quest for new power in the wider world. Outlook, as well as material means, had to play an important role in the West's rise. Earlier civilizations that had influenced wide sectors of the world beyond their borders, notably classical India and then Islam, had usually possessed an active merchant spirit, and certainly the West had this in abundance from its medieval heritage. In Christianity, the West also had a religion eager to spread the truth to nonbelievers, even by force. Trade and Christianity typically went hand in hand in the West's new rise. The specific culture of the Renaissance may have contributed as well. We will see in Chapter 17 that a new set of beliefs developed in Europe. This change, called the Renaissance, brought new interest in worldly affairs and a new sense of confidence and individualism to key leaders. Certainly, it was no accident that the first discoveries in the Atlantic occurred during the Renaissance, when some Europeans were experiencing a new thirst for achievement and knowledge. The zeal of a Henry the Navigator to penetrate the unknown and the sheer adventurism of a Christopher Columbus related closely to other Renaissance enthusiasms. Finally, even the divisions within Europe pushed all the many vying civilizations toward a new world role. National monarchies soon competed for discoveries and colonies, as part of their overall rivalry.

The period of discovery and early colonization was an exciting example of Western power and daring. It also changed some key patterns of world history, which means that it must be assessed not only from the standpoint of European efforts but also in terms of impact on the cultures it affected. Here, several zones developed, ranging from the Americas—where the European arrival began quickly to change basic cultural patterns toward creation of new civilizations or outright assimilation with the West—to east Asia, where European activities made little difference to the historical patterns of the next several centuries. Between these two extremes were several societies: Africa, where European contact caused important alterations in some regions but had little impact on others; India and the Middle East, where Western pressure grew but without undermining earlier traditions; and Russia, whose own new quest for power was colored by knowledge that the West had forged ahead.

■**KEY QUESTIONS**   *Try to decide what caused the West's rise, and then figure out its differential impact on the rest of the world. How did the West and the world economy it engendered affect Africa compared to Latin America, or Asia compared to either of these? How were superiority and inferiority in the world economy defined? How did the world economy affect political and labor systems? What were the characteristics of the new civilization that began to emerge in Latin America?*

PATTERNS OF EXPLORATION AND TRADE

When west Europeans began to venture forward into the wider world, their knowledge of where they were going was surprisingly scanty. Significant debate focused on the size of the earth's sphere. To be sure, Viking adventurers from Scandinavia had crossed the Atlantic in the 10th century, reaching Greenland and then North America, which they named "Vinland." But they quickly lost interest, in part because they encountered Indian warriors whose weaponry was good enough to vanquish the intruders.

HISTORY DEBATE

EARLY MODERN STEREOTYPES

The early modern period generates vivid but inaccurate images that world historians work hard to dispel. At the same time, these images often embrace a grain of truth. So, there is an unresolved debate: how can the falsehoods be retired without also losing their kernel of reality?

The most obvious challenge regarding these images involves the position of western Europe during the period. Many U.S. high schools' curricula, having sketched world history with some accuracy before the early modern period, turn after 1450 to an almost exclusive emphasis on Western power and achievements. The implicit suggestion is that the rest of the world so declined in independent potential that there is no reason to pay attention to it, at least until new Western contacts revived some spark in it.

The reality, however, is that societies in most of Asia and parts of Africa preserved substantial independence of action through the 17th century and often beyond. Asian manufacturing superiority persisted as well, at least until after 1700. What the West did was not of primary importance to the regions. So, it is crucial to see early modern world history in terms of a number of centers of development, each of which was important in its own right.

But, it is true that the West accumulated new economic and military power at a faster rate than other societies. It is at least arguable that changes within the West were more dramatic and, ultimately, more globally influential than changes in most other societies. So, the debate: how do we view world changes in relative balance without converting early modern history into a story of the West and its global activities?

China has often been portrayed as isolated and declining in the early modern period. Again, this is untrue. China in some ways profited from world trade more than the West did, and this meant it was actively involved in contacts. The isolationist label is just plain wrong. But, Chinese merchants were less globally venturesome than Europeans were. There was hesitation about opening to too many contacts. There was a degree of obliviousness to Western gains that might have been profitably imitated, most obviously in technology—20th-century Chinese leaders themselves noted that this period was marked, in part, by missed opportunities. So, the debate: how do we acknowledge a distinctive position without invoking a greater assumption of isolation than actually existed?

Similarly, Ottoman and Mughal empires are duly noted in world history as bringing important new developments to the Middle East and India. But they did not, ultimately, sustain their initial vigor, and by the 18th century the Mughals, at least, were in obvious decline, while European opinion of the Ottomans was increasingly one of a corrupt and weak society. It is tempting to concentrate on the deterioration of these empires and to forget their achievements. So, the debate: how do we generate the proper balance in our view of these cultures, lest again we move too quickly to a story of Western gain at Asian expense?

As we have seen, scattered expeditions from Spain and Italy into the Atlantic dotted the later Middle Ages, but they had no specific results. It took new technical knowledge, particularly the navigational devices imported from Asia, and growing problems, in the form of new needs to reach Asia directly and to seek gold as payment for the desired Asian products, to permit a more systematic effort in the 15th century.

The initiative began in the small kingdom of Portugal. The rulers of this country had just finished driving out the Muslims, who still threatened from north Africa. This threat, and the surge of energy that sometimes accompanies the expulsion of an occupation force, prompted the Portuguese during the 15th century to look for conquests in Africa. Portugal's rulers were drawn by the excitement of discovery, the harm they might cause to the Muslim world, and a thirst for wealth—for European legends of gold in Africa and elsewhere were abundant. This was not a matter of mere greed; Europe's lack of gold for its trade with Asia was becoming a serious problem. A Portuguese prince, Henry the Navigator, directed a series of expeditions down the African coast and outward to islands such as the Azores. Beginning in 1434, the Portuguese began to journey down the African coast, each expedition going a little farther than its predecessor. They brought back some slaves and perpetuated the tales of gold that they had not yet been able to find.

Later in the 15th century, Portuguese sailors ventured around the Cape of Good Hope, planning to find India and also the African east coast, which was thought to be the source of gold. They rounded the Cape in 1488, but weary sailors forced the expedition back before it could reach India. Then, after news of Columbus' discovery of America for Spain in 1492, Portugal redoubled its efforts, hoping to stave off the new Spanish competition. In 1497, Vasco da Gama's fleet of four ships reached India, with the aid of a Muslim pilot picked up in east Africa. The Portuguese mistakenly believed that the Indians were Christians, for they assumed the Hindu temples they encountered to be churches. Although they faced the hostility of Muslim merchants, who had long dominated trade in this part of the world, the Portuguese nonetheless managed to return home with a small load of spices.

This success set in motion an annual series of Portuguese voyages to the Indian Ocean. Da Gama went back to India, this time heavily armed. He killed a number of Indians, eager to intimidate the region into greater trade. Another expedition, blown off course, reached Brazil, where it proclaimed Portuguese sovereignty. With growing experience, both Portuguese and Spanish expeditions became increasingly comfortable with voyages in the South Atlantic and the Indian Ocean. Portugal began to establish forts on the African coast and also in India—the forerunners of such Portuguese colonies as Mozambique, in east Africa, and Goa, in India. By 1514, the Portuguese had reached the islands of Indonesia, the center of spice production, and also China. By 1542, a Portuguese expedition also arrived in Japan, where a Christian missionary effort was launched that met with some success for several decades.

Meanwhile, only a short time after the Portuguese quest began, the Spanish reached out with even greater force. Here, too, was a country only recently freed from Muslim rule, full of missionary zeal and a desire for riches. The Spanish had traveled into the Atlantic during the 14th century. Then in 1492, in the same year that the final Muslim fortress was captured in Spain, the Italian navigator Christopher Columbus, sailing in the name of the new Spanish monarchy and its rulers, Ferdinand and Isabella, set off on a westward route to India. As is well known, he failed, reaching the Americas instead and mistakenly naming their inhabitants "Indians." Although Columbus believed to his death that he had sailed to India, later Spanish expeditions indicated that he had voyaged to a region to which Europeans and Asians had not traveled before. One expedition, led again by an Italian initially in Spanish service, Amerigo Vespucci, gave the New World its name. Spain, eager to claim this American land, won papal approval for Spanish dominion over most of what is now Latin America, although a later treaty awarded Brazil to Portugal.

Finally, a Spanish expedition under Ferdinand Magellan set sail westward in 1519, passing the southern tip of South America and sailing across the Pacific, reaching the Indonesian islands in 1521 after incredible hardships. It was on the basis of this voyage, ultimately the first trip around the world, that Spain claimed the Philippines, which remained Spanish territory until 1898.

Portugal emerged from this first round of exploration with coastal holdings in various parts

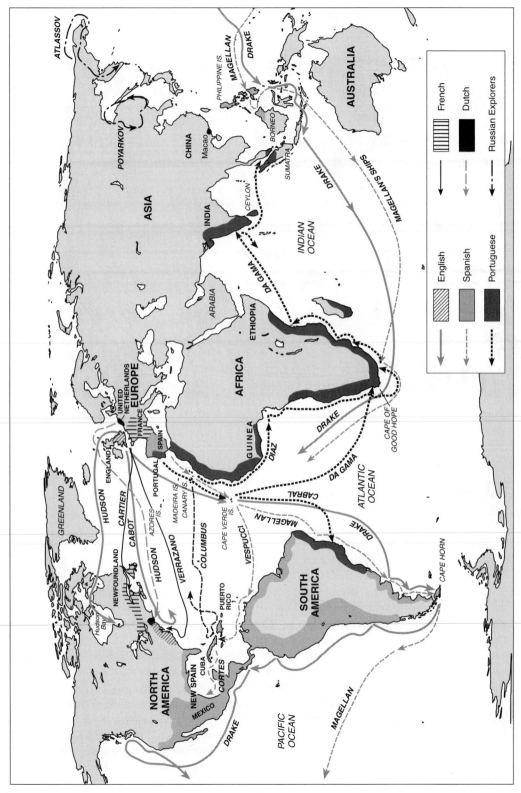

"Discoveries" in the 15th and 16th Centuries

Ship technology in the expanding West. This is the *Vittoria,* the only one of Magellan's five ships that completed the first circumnavigation of the globe in 1522.

of Africa and the Indian port of Goa; a lease on a Chinese port, Macao; short-lived interests in trade with Japan; and, finally, the claim on Brazil. Spain asserted its hold on the Philippines and various Pacific islands, and on the bulk of the Americas. (The Pope helped to rule which Catholic power held which American territory.) During the 16th century, the Spanish attempted to assert its American claims through military expeditions to Mexico and South America. The Spanish also held Florida in North America, and they ultimately launched expeditions northward from Mexico into California and other parts of what later became the southwestern United States.

Later in the 16th century, the lead in further exploration passed to northern Europe. In part, this resulted because Spain and Portugal were now busy ruling their new territories; in part, it was because northern Europeans, particularly

the Dutch and the British, improved the design of oceanic vessels, producing lighter, faster ships than those of their Catholic adversaries. Britain won a historic sea battle with Spain in 1588, in which the British navy and adverse weather routed a massive Spanish armada. From this point on, the British and Dutch, and to an extent the French, vied for dominance on the seas.

French explorers first crossed the Atlantic in 1534, reaching Canada, which was claimed in France's name. French voyages increased during the 17th century, as various expeditions pressed down from Canada into the Great Lakes region and the Mississippi valley.

The British also turned their attention particularly to North America, starting with a brief expedition as early as 1497. The English hoped, in vain, to discover a northwest passage to India, but in fact they accomplished little beyond an exploration of the Hudson Bay area of Canada during the 16th century. England's serious expeditions commenced in the 17th century, with the colonization of the east coast of North America.

The Dutch entered the picture after winning independence from Spain and quickly became a major competitor with Portugal in southeast Asia. The Dutch sent a significant number of sailors and ships to the region, ousting the Portuguese from the Indonesian islands by the early 17th century. Voyagers from Holland explored the coast of Australia, although without much immediate result. Finally, toward the middle of the 17th century, Holland established a settlement on the southern tip of Africa, mainly to provide a relay station for its ships bound for the East Indies.

Dutch and British exploration and trade were government-sponsored, but unlike the Spanish and Portuguese expeditions, and to some extent the French, they owed much to the private initiative of merchant groups. Holland, Britain, and France all chartered great trading companies, such as the Dutch East India Company or the British firm of similar name. These companies were given government monopolies of trade in the regions designated, but they were not rigorously supervised by their own states. Thus, semiprivate companies, formed by pooling merchant capital and amassing great fortunes in commerce, long acted almost like independent governments in the regions they claimed. For some time, a Dutch trading company virtually ruled the island of Taiwan, off the coast of China; the British East India Company played a similar role in parts of India during much of the 18th century.

TOWARD A WORLD ECONOMY

By the 16th century, west Europeans had gained control of most of the world's seas. They were moving freely across the Atlantic Ocean and with some regularity across the vast Pacific as well—the first time in world history that an endeavor of this magnitude had ever occurred. The Europeans did not displace all Asian shipping from the coastal waters of China and Japan, nor did they completely monopolize the Indian Ocean; in east Africa, Muslim merchants remained active. But Muslim and Hindu traders now focused on regional specialties; they did not command the chief routes. In the Mediterranean, finally, where European power had been growing even earlier, the Spaniards inflicted a decisive defeat on the navy of the Ottoman Empire, in the battle of Lepanto in 1571. Although Ottoman forces won some later battles, they could not systematically rival European naval power. By this time, the greatest competitors Europeans faced were other European states, and their battles peppered world history from this point until the mid-20th century. By the 16th century, European traders even shipped products from one part of Asia to another, making profits by handling goods with which Europe had no direct involvement at all. World trade and its expansion lay largely in Western hands.

Into the 18th century, however, the Europeans' power, although astonishing by their own or anyone else's previous standards, was a sea power, and sea power had limits. Only in rare special circumstances were the Europeans able to penetrate inland, far from the protection of their ever-improving ship's cannon. The major exception, of course, was in the Americas, where the Spanish gained continental control and the English and Portuguese important regional centers. Elsewhere, the European grasp extended mainly to islands—with the control of major parts of the Indonesian islands the most significant achievement—and scattered port cities. Even in Africa, where the Europeans had greater influence than they did in most parts of Asia, European control was mainly coastal until after 1800. In the Middle East and eastern Europe, Westerners seized no territory at all, although their trading influence was actively felt; in east Asia, even their commercial efforts were kept to a minimum after a brief initial flurry.

Hence, outside the Americas, the Europeans affected but did not dominate major civilizations. We will examine their influence and its limitations in subsequent chapters. Even in India, until the 18th century, European presence and the seizure of a few coastal cities were fairly minor incidents, hardly rivaling the ongoing presence of a Muslim government in a largely Hindu population.

It is important, then, not to exaggerate the significance for world history of what the Europeans liked to call their age of exploration. There was no question of their new strength, but until about 1800, when the situation changed, they were not yet directing the world stage.

Nonetheless, western Europe was beginning to shape new global economic contracts, which brought them great advantage and affected economic activity in many other parts of the world. Europe's wealth increased rapidly because of profits drawn from the Americas, Africa, and even Asia. The Europeans never uncovered the golden treasures they had hoped for, but they did gain access to vast supplies of silver in the New World. Spain was the chief initial beneficiary of this wealth within Europe, but bankers and merchants in northern Europe soon profited even more substantially. With the new supply of precious metals and resulting control of shipping, the Europeans were able to improve the balance of world trade for the first time. Spice and tea plantations in southern Asia began to produce for the growing European market on terms of trade that were no longer set by the rarity of their products but by the buying power of the West—expressed particularly through its use of New World silver.

Awareness and use of silver spread rapidly in the 16th century. Europeans utilized silver in the Americas, particularly in the great mines of Potosi in the Andes, and they quickly learned how to increase production. They traded silver for the goods they sought in Asia, leading to new accumulations in places such as China. Indeed, the West's service as broker between the Americas and Asia—rather than as a Western economic power in its own right—accounts for much of the dynamics of the world economy in the early modern countries. Huge amounts of silver went through the Western-controlled port in Macao; by the end of the century, the Ming dynasty could require that taxes be paid in silver. For a time, Japan also participated actively in silver production, which linked the nation to world trade until greater isolation was imposed after about 1600. The extent of the silver trade and its results showed the dimensions of the world economy, and how quickly it could promote change.

By the 17th century, as Europeans used some of their wealth to improve their own manufacturing base, they increasingly offered manufactured products to the world market—guns, cloth, and metal wares—instead of precious metals alone. The division was deliberately fostered by the policies of the Europeans, whether as governments or as giant trading companies. The reigning theories of mercantilism urged 17th- and 18th-century Europe to monopolize as much manufacturing as possible, leaving other parts of the world to specialize in agricultural production or mining. By the 18th century, several parts of the world were producing raw materials or foodstuffs for a Western market and receiving more sophisticated and expensive manufactured goods in return. Russia and Poland sold grain; Africa, slaves; and the Americas, sugar, silver, and tobacco. These goods, because they involved less processing, tended to command lower prices than did Europe's own products. So a global economy was being shaped in which much of the world sold goods (generated by cheap labor) to the West, which sold more expensive items and in whose ships the goods were exchanged. Here was the beginning of a division in the world economy between haves and have-nots, which echoes to the present day.

The impact of this division could run deep. Basic labor systems increasingly responded to economic position. Western Europe required labor flexible enough to participate in growing manufacturing; hence, it increasingly developed a wage-labor force, often ill-paid. Areas dependent on producing raw materials, particularly where workers were in short supply because of disease, relied on compulsory labor systems, such as slavery or extensive serfdom, that could keep costs down for unskilled work. Gender was affected. In many areas, men were responsible for an increasing amount of production for sale, relegating women to domestic tasks. New slave traders preferred men: two-thirds of all African slaves sent to the Americas were male, and this extended systems of polygamy in Africa as a means of dealing with an overpopulation of females.

However, this was only the beginning of an international economy dominated by the West. Most people were not deeply affected by the new patterns of trade. The Chinese were far more heavily influenced by new foodstuffs brought by European traders, by the seeds and tubers they introduced from the Americas, than by Europe's economic position within the world community. Indeed, as we will see, China still did very well in the world economy. Most Asians, Russians, Africans, and even many American Indians were not drawn into production for the world market as yet, although it is true that Europe's financial influence reached farther than their ships. Here is another factor, along with outright European contacts, to be considered in contemplating the development of major civilizations between 1450 and 1800.

In three major cases, however, European influence did penetrate farther, even in the early modern centuries, so that major alterations in historical patterns resulted. Developments in sub-Saharan Africa, Spanish or Latin America, and North America revealed the extent of Western penetration and an emerging New World economy to reshape politics, culture, and individual lives.

AFRICA

It was long assumed, by prideful Westerners, that African history did not really begin until the coming of the Europeans. This, of course, is nonsense;

African culture had evolved to a significant extent before Europeans journeyed down the Atlantic, and more to the point, it continued into the 19th century to develop apart from European influence. However, Europeans did have profound effects on a number of regions, and this new factor must be linked with other trends to describe African diversity after about 1500.

European exploration of Africa was limited by several factors. Transportation barriers were as great for them as for Africans; it was hard to move inland from the coast, particularly in the thickly forested areas. Moreover, the main rivers were not navigable for any distance. Disease also hit the Europeans hard, for they lacked the immunity to tropical diseases that Africans had developed over time. Most importantly, the political powers of most African kingdoms were sufficient to block European entry until the 19th century. To be sure, the great African empires ended with the fall of Songhai late in the 16th century; in the south, there was nothing to match the earlier Zimbabwe. But regional kingdoms flourished, some old, some rising for the first time. This meant that in most instances, Europeans had to negotiate carefully with African leaders, offering real value in exchange for value received; with a few exceptions, they could not seize territory.

Here, for example, is how a Dutch representative described the king of the west African kingdom of Benin (where the Dutch traded actively during the 17th century, replacing the Portuguese as principal European contacts):

> I saw and spoke to the king of Benin, in the presence of his great counselors. He was seated on an ivory throne under a canopy of Indian silk. He was about forty years old and of lively expression. According to custom I stood about thirty feet away from him. So as to see him better I asked permission to draw closer. He laughingly agreed.

The representative was also awed by the splendor of the palace, as big as the stock exchange in

Amsterdam, supported by "wooden pillars encased in copper, where the victories of the kingdom are recorded."

European activity, however, did make a difference in Africa. The Portuguese and then other Europeans, particularly the French, established forts and urban settlements along the western coast, usually leased or made available by other arrangement with local rulers. With this base, the Europeans altered west African trading patterns. They encountered many valuable goods in Africa—cloth and iron items—but their main interests lay in gold, ivory, and slaves. They found African merchants as well as political rulers to be demanding negotiators, but they did have goods to offer in return: cloth, iron tools, and above all muskets. European imports reduced African craft production, which disrupted the economy severely. Dependence on weapons imports also brought change. Not infrequently, Europeans participated as allies in wars among African kingdoms, where their firepower could spell the difference in outcome. These trading activities brought new contacts to west Africa, drawing the region into a European-dominated world economic network and away from traditional trade routes across the Sahara to north Africa. The presence of Western trading stations on the coast also had an effect on some urban Africans, leading to a limited number of conversions to Christianity.

West Africa was more specifically and deeply affected by the growing Atlantic slave trade, which began in the 16th century but intensified greatly after about 1650. West African slaves were purchased by sea captains from Holland, Britain, and particularly France, to be sold in the North and South American colonies and the West Indies. Slavery was not new to this region of Africa, as many states had held troops captured in battle as slaves. But the European demand transformed a traditional practice beyond recognition. Between 1500 and the end of the slave trade in the 19th century, as many as 12 million Africans may have been taken away as slaves. This exodus, one of the greatest and most terrible forced

movements of peoples in human history, devastated some regions of west Africa, which lost population rapidly and found it difficult, in the absence of sufficient younger workers, to maintain traditional economic levels. Nonetheless, some west African states profited from the slave trade, at least in the short run. The actual capture and sale of slaves to European merchant sailors was almost always handled by African agents, who traded slaves for guns, gold, and other goods. One new, unusually centralized state, the Fon kingdom of the 18th century, organized all its dealings with Europeans in a single location, to minimize contact between Europeans and inland Africans. The state carefully regulated and taxed the slave trade, controlling the import of firearms and ammunition.

Thus, the impact of the massive slave trade on west Africa was mixed and not simply the result of unchallenged European profiteering (although there were huge profits to be made from the exchange, even after the African agents were paid; this was one source of rising merchant wealth in western Europe). Many parts of west Africa came to depend on the slave trade for their own economies. However, the long-term damage overshadowed any gains. African birth rates grew more slowly than those of most other societies throughout the 19th century, in part as a result of sheer population loss. Economic development was surely slowed, but it is hard to say exactly how much change would have resulted had the slave trade not interfered. In addition, relations among west African kingdoms grew more warlike and chaotic, as various states clashed to gain slaves, and others armed to prevent raids. Destabilization was not complete, and again there was variety, depending on how a given kingdom handled negotiations. Indeed, some west African kingdoms deliberately stayed out of the slave trade altogether. But there is no question about the serious impact this practice had on west African history for more than two centuries.

There was also no question about the harsh life slaves were soon forced to endure, and the

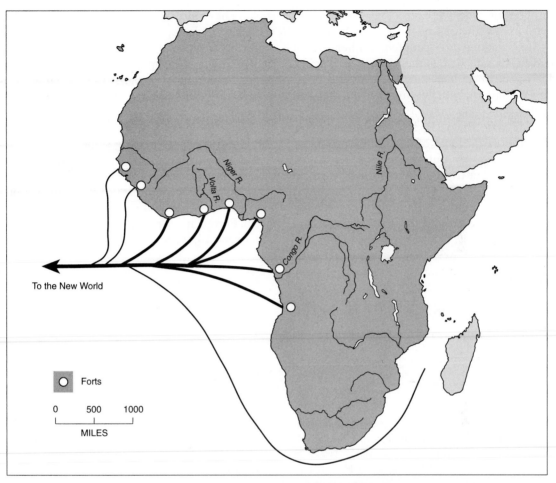

Patterns of the 18th-Century Slave Trade

inhuman circumstances to which they were often subjected upon capture:

As the slaves come down . . . from the inland country, they are put into a booth or prison, built for that purpose near the beach, all of them together; and when the Europeans are to receive them, they are brought out into a large plain, where the ships' surgeons examine every part of every one of them . . . Such as are allowed good and sound are set on one side, and the others by themselves; these rejected slaves are called Makrons, being above 35 years of age, or defective in their lips, eyes or teeth, or grown grey . . . Each of the others passed as good is marked on the breast with a red-hot iron, imprinting the mark of the French, English, or Dutch companies so that each nation may distinguish their own property.

Typically, a week after capture, the voyage across the Atlantic began, a terrifying, foul experience during which as many as half the slaves died. The survivors were rewarded with a life of servitude in a strange land.

Slave trading also disrupted another part of the west African coast, in the territory of Angola, which came under increasing Portuguese control. The Portuguese, initially interested in precious metals, soon concentrated on capturing slaves for trade with Brazil. Ruling Angola outright, through corrupt local officials, they produced growing chaos in this region for centuries. Here, in contrast to the picture farther north in present-day countries such as Nigeria, there was no question of some compensatory benefits from the European quest for slaves; Angola simply suffered.

The southern end of Africa was greatly affected by European exploration. Holland established a small colony on the Cape of Good Hope in 1652, to help supply its ships bound for Asia. This community of *Boers* (the Dutch word for farmers) soon escaped Dutch control, fanning out on large farms in a region still lightly populated by Africans. The Boers clashed with local hunting groups, enslaving some of them. Later, after 1770, they came into increasing contact with Bantu farmers, initiating a long struggle for control of the region that still affects the nation of South Africa today.

European influence on African history between 1450 and 1800 was thus intense but, for

WORLD PROFILES

OLANDAH EQUIANO

Olandah Equiano was one of the few enslaved Africans able to later write about his experiences. He was born in a Nigerian village, Isseke, in 1745, to a wealthy, slaveholding family. He was kidnapped by slave traders and in 1756 taken to Barbados and then Virginia. Finally able to buy his freedom from a Quaker master, he went to England in 1767. By this point, he was both literate and well read. He became active in the antislavery movement, publishing his memoirs in 1788 as a protest against the entire institution of slavery. Equiano poignantly described his desperate feelings when he and his sister were tied up and put in sacks, and then separated from each other. He detailed the greater brutality of European slave shippers, compared to his initial African captors, and the ordeal of imprisonment among strangers and the frightening voyage to an unknown land with little hope of return. Though there is some historical debate about whether Equiano personally experienced all he claimed, his account was one of the first in a wave of memoirs by former slaves and part of a growing movement against the system on both sides of the Atlantic. What kind of antislavery arguments might have worked best in the context of 18th-century Europe?

Olandah Equiano.

the most part, regional. It set new forces in motion in southern Africa and Angola, and strongly affected the economic and political life of west Africa without, however, overturning all previous patterns.

Other parts of Africa were scarcely affected by the West during these centuries. Ethiopia, although Christian and in some contact with Portuguese missionaries, remained aloof. East Africa had little to do with Europeans; here, trading patterns were still oriented toward the Middle East, and both Africans and Arab traders pushed into the eastern interior in search of agricultural products and slaves. The slave trade to the Middle East and north Africa also expanded in the early modern period; totaling perhaps 3 million people, it remained more modest than its Atlantic counterpart.

Overall, the patterns of African culture remained much as before. Politically, most of the continent was organized in regional kingdoms, with rulers who allied with local leaders and operated as divine monarchies. Most Africans remained polytheistic, although Islam was a potent force in the Sudan region. Late in the 18th century, conversions to Islam began to increase in this area, as the religion became a popular force and not simply an elitist movement. Scholars such as Usuman dan Fodio (1754–1818) argued against the traditional policy of living tolerantly alongside nonbelievers. Usuman and his followers, active in Muslim scholarship and law, conducted several holy wars in the western Sudan, winning over many ordinary people and producing a number of well-organized new states.

In another continuing trend, Bantu penetration southward persisted. This movement, as noted, brought Bantus into conflict with Dutch settlers. The severe crowding it produced in Bantu lands by around 1800 prompted Bantus to begin organizing into more coherent political units.

Finally, although African economic life was deeply affected by European trade at least in some key regions, there was no massive change in economic forms or technologies on the continent overall. Europeans did import corn seeds from the New World, which were adopted by many African farmers and thereafter used as a food staple. But because of the slave trade and the loss of so many men of childbearing age, the crop did not result in a significant population increase at this point; indeed, relative to world population growth, the African share actually decreased.

In sum, major changes occurred in Africa between 1450 and 1800. Some of these changes were of European origin or represented African reaction to European contacts, but others were quite distinct, resulting from Islam or Bantu migration. No single force mobilized more than individual regions of the continent; beneath the surface, important traditional patterns of politics, art, belief, and social organization largely persisted.

COLONIZATION IN LATIN AMERICA: THE BIRTH OF A NEW CIVILIZATION

European impact in the Americas was far more significant than that in Africa: here, the Europeans began to alter basic patterns as early as the 16th and 17th centuries, creating a new civilization in Latin America and extending Western civilization to the eastern seaboard colonies of North America. The natives' lack of iron weapons and their vulnerability to disease, often with devastating consequences, created a context far different from that in Africa. African independence long contrasted with the growing European colonies in the Americas. The colonization process, of course, also brought the Americas into mainstream world history and linked the two continents to the emerging world economy on conditions set mainly by the Europeans.

In Central and South America and the West Indies, Spanish efforts to follow exploration with outright conquests began early in the 16th century. The chief goals were God and gold. The Spanish hoped to tap what they believed was the vast wealth of the new lands—their appetites having been whetted by the rich ornaments they encountered among groups such as the Aztecs and by a taste for myth. And, as the most powerful Catholic state, soon heavily influenced by the active Jesuit order, Spain planned to win new converts to Christianity. Expeditions led to the occupation of leading West Indian islands, including Cuba, starting in 1512. Soon after this, a small army under Hernán Cortés conquered Mexico from the Aztecs. Although pockets of American Indian resistance remained in parts of Central America until the later 17th century, Spanish control was essentially complete by 1550. By this point, the empire extended loosely into parts of what are now the southern and southwestern United States.

From their colony in Panama, the Spanish moved into South America. They took over the northern part of the continent fairly easily, conquering loosely organized American Indian cultures. In 1531, an expedition attacked the Inca empire, inspired by tales of its many treasures. Intense combat was necessary to seize Peru, but the Spanish commander, Pizarro, ultimately prevailed. From this base, other missions extended along the Andes mountain chain, finding the Amazon River and seeking the silver mines of Bolivia. Spanish expeditions also moved into Argentina, founding a settlement in Buenos Aires in 1536. Only at the end of the 16th century, however, did the Spanish really begin to colonize Argentina, introducing cattle raising and other forms of agriculture once the thirst for

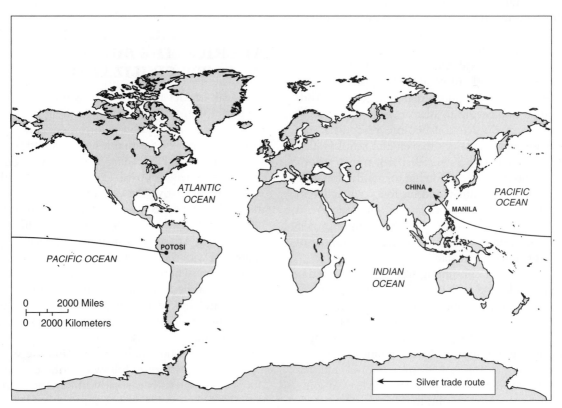

The Silver Trade Route: Potosi, Bolivia, to Manila, Philippines, to China

quick riches had somewhat diminished. Finally, early in the 17th century, the Portuguese began to journey inward from small coastal settlements in Brazil, taking effective hold of much of the vast interior territory.

The conquest of Latin America, complete in outline during the 17th century, was amazingly swift. This was no well-coordinated, carefully planned venture. Many expeditions, such as Pizarro's against Peru, were essentially

The Americas by the 18th Century

mounted by groups of adventurers or private merchants. All the campaigns, even those sponsored by the Spanish government, were small. How did they conquer such a vast territory so easily?

Superior technology was, of course, a key. The American Indians lacked not only guns and cannons but also horses and metal weapons of any sort. The Europeans also profited from civil wars and dissent within American Indian ranks. Hostility to the Aztecs provided Cortés with many American Indian allies at first. The Inca empire was weakened by internal warfare shortly before Pizarro's arrival. Trickery played a role: many Spanish commanders initially negotiated treaties with Inca, Aztec, and other leaders, only to violate the agreements at the earliest opportunity, often putting their erstwhile allies to death. But the hold of the Europeans was not at first thorough. Many villages were untouched by a Spanish or Portuguese presence for decades; many local American Indian leaders were given considerable autonomy so long as they pledged loyalty to the new colonial government.

However, in scarcely more than a century, the Spanish had leveled the leading American Indian civilizations, destroying their political structures and obliterating their formal cultures. Their task was aided not only by their desire to impose "civilization" on non-Christian peoples, but also by the diseases, particularly smallpox, that they brought with them. American Indians, so long isolated, had no resistance to these scourges. The result was plagues that resembled those at the end of the classical and postclassical periods in Eurasia, but even worse. Within less than a century, 90 percent of the Mexican population had been wiped out; entire populations on the West Indian islands vanished. Overall, as has been noted, 80 percent of the previous American Indian population of North and South America died as a result of disease. Europeans increasingly tried to fill this vacuum.

LATIN AMERICAN CIVILIZATION

After the conquest period, the Spanish and Portuguese settled down to the construction of new political and religious institutions and a new economic framework for their vast colonies. The result, during the 17th and 18th centuries, was essentially a formative period for a new, Latin American civilization, closely tied to Europe but also distinct in significant ways.

Politically, this new civilization was characterized by the rule imposed from the outside by the monarchies of Spain and Portugal. European-born men held virtually all of the administrative positions, in what became significant bureaucracies. Two main provinces were created, called *viceroyalties*—one administered from Mexico, the other from Peru. Later, the huge South American holding was further divided, with new centers in Argentina and Colombia. In theory, this governmental system was highly centralized. In fact, the territories were much too vast for effective central control, which meant that church leaders, estate owners, and villagers had considerable latitude. Latin America was long characterized by a gap between seemingly strong political authority and the actual weakness of the state in relation to local regions and to institutions such as the village and hacienda.

One result of the gap between government claims and the reality of very lax state control was a sense that government power ought to be increased, that this was the chief problem in Latin American society. Even in the 18th century, Spanish colonial administration tried to expand its authority, and the quest continued into the 19th and 20th centuries as well. A second result was that the centralized system, however superficial in reality, prevented any wide participation in the new society, as most colonials were firmly barred from governmental activity. Spain further tightened the monopoly of Spanish-born

St. Augustine, Florida. As the oldest city in the United States (founded in 1565), it was established to guard the Spanish sea route from the Caribbean that the silver fleets used to travel back to Spain.

appointees in the later 18th century, resulting in new grievances among the native-born Creoles.

Culturally, the leading feature of the new society was a fervent and pervasive Catholicism. Far more than the Spanish and Portuguese governments, the Jesuits and other missionaries moved actively among the common people, working hard to undermine the influence of indigenous religions and replace them with Christianity. Many American Indian groups long remained isolated from this effort, but there was steady change. Mission schools, an extensive network of local churches, and the destruction of American Indian culture soon produced measurable results. The power and success of the new conquerors helped make the missionaries persuasive. But they also offered a gentler religion with greater compassion for ordinary people than many of the religions the American Indian civilizations of South and Central America had developed. Although American Indians resented the abolition of many ceremonies and even maintained some in secret, the elimination of human sacrifice and the power of the earlier priestly castes may have been welcomed by many. And there were numerous opportunities for syncretism. Many American Indians combined the notions of certain earlier gods or goddesses with Catholic saints, thus helping to transition while producing a lively and distinctive religious art.

The Europeans also sought to introduce some features of their own wider culture. Major cathedrals were built in the Spanish baroque style, and public buildings also followed European architectural models. Cities were established as islands of European order, building on the traditional belief in urban life that the Spanish inherited from the Romans and Arabs. Grid-like streets radiated from a central plaza, which was graced by a major church and a government building and jail. However, westernized artistic culture was not yet advanced. Spanish-style religious paintings were attempted, but they did not match the vigor of Christianized Indian or mestizo designs. Literature was virtually nonexistent, as the Spanish authorities discouraged printing save in a few centers. Furthermore, American Indian artistic forms continued to survive, in pottery and textile design. This was not high art, but it was responsible for an important diversity in Latin American culture that had important effects in the future. Outside of the extension of Catholicism, then, Latin American culture was clearly in a formative stage but showed signs of some differentiation from purely European models.

Two kinds of economic activity coexisted in this early period of Latin American history. First, many American Indians and *mestizos*—people of mixed Spanish and Indian ancestry—operated in a village or a small-town economy, producing corn and other foods for largely local needs. The economic life of many American Indian villages, even their communal ownership of the land, was left virtually undisturbed—although the Spanish eliminated the leading institutions of American Indian society, they did not eliminate all traces of this culture.

Along with this local village structure was an economy geared for export, and specifically for the profit of the Spanish and Portuguese. This economy involved mining operations, particularly in the Andes region, where 16,000 tons of silver were produced for Europe by the year 1650.

The market economy also promoted large landed estates established by the Spaniards or

The Portuguese baroque style of architecture was used frequently in South America: San Francisco Church in Salvador de Bahia, Brazil.

Creoles—Europeans born in the new land. The Spanish did not attempt to enslave many American Indians, partly because of fierce resistance and partly because Catholic leaders, eager to protect their new converts, opposed such a policy. But they did set up a network of large estates. As American Indians died of European diseases, land was left vacant and often seized by mestizos or Spaniards, who benefited from the government authorization of such ownership. At first, it seemed that the original Spanish conquerors might become a feudal nobility, but the Spanish government, aware of the importance of more central control, resisted this pattern save in a few areas. Nevertheless, many large estates resulted from land grants and seizures, particularly when a brief effort at the direct governmental distribution of American Indian labor failed. Estate owners worked hard to command labor resources, increasingly scarce as the Indian population shrank. An early form of labor control, not necessarily corresponding to a single estate, was the *encomienda*, where the Spanish or Creole grantee was given rights over a certain percentage of American Indian labor. This was one source of the labor used in silver and mercury mines in the Andes region; at its height, labor drafts generated 13,000 workers a year for the leading mine. More common still was the *hacienda*, a large estate on which a number of American Indian villages were granted to a Spaniard, often one of the initial conquerors. Village inhabitants on the hacienda were required to pay tribute in goods (food and textiles) plus providing labor service. This system, which after a generation or two turned into effective ownership of the village lands, closely resembled the harsher forms of earlier European serfdom; the landlord provided some protection and a court system for his villagers, in return for payments in kind and almost absolute control over the farmers. In a few cases, estate owners hired low-paid American Indian or mestizo laborers, who were encouraged to go into debt and officially forbidden to leave until often impossible sums were paid off—again, a means of attempting to reduce rural freedom in order to address the twin realities of labor shortage and market opportunity.

Haciendas and the other estate forms did not, for the most part, produce for the export trade directly. But they did yield grains and meats that were sold to mining centers and the growing populations of port cities and administrative capitals such as Mexico City. Thus, a vigorous Latin American market agriculture developed, but on the basis of low-paid or servile labor under effective landlord control.

A somewhat different version of estate agriculture arose in the West Indies and some parts of the South American continent, particularly Brazil. Here the crops produced—tobacco and especially sugar—were intended for sale in Europe. These estates used hundreds of thousands of black slaves imported from Africa, initially in part because local labor was so scarce as a result of disease. Three times as many Africans were brought to Latin America and the Caribbean as to North America. Not only Spanish and Portuguese holdings, but also British, French, and Dutch West Indian islands, developed this slave-holding system. This was a slave-based economy on a scale never before known, the result of the commercial opportunities and appetites of the new global economy.

Latin America thus quickly developed an economy dependent on a world market, for which it produced agricultural and mining products; additional specialized commercial farming led to the development of mining and governmental centers. Relatively little manufacturing was undertaken, save for local needs; sophisticated manufactured products and craft items were imported from Europe. Here was the most acute case of a European intrusion producing a dependent economy. Latin American landowners could reap tidy profits from their market sales, but for their success they relied on a low-paid, fully or partially enslaved, labor force.

Clear social divisions followed from this economic pattern, and they were enhanced by racial divisions. Spanish and Portuguese settlers were much less firmly racist than their English counterparts to the north. However, Latin American society was rather firmly split between a minority of political officials, mine owners, and landlords, and the majority of impoverished workers. The privileged classes were European-born or Creole; the masses were American Indian, black, and—the largest group overall—mestizo. There were, of course, some local merchants and shopkeepers, but the size of this middling group was small. Almost all European trade was conducted by Europeans themselves.

Colonization and economic change inevitably affected gender relations. Although European officials tried to discourage intermarriage, the fact that most colonists and imported slaves were male inevitably encouraged sexual unions with American Indian women. American Indian family arrangements were often disrupted, and the growth of the mestizo population accelerated. Marriage among African slaves was often forbidden—for example, in Brazil—which led to an additional set of sexual patterns.

As agriculture spread, based on local crops and also crops and animals introduced from Europe (cattle, sheep, rice, wheat), the Latin American population began to grow, despite the staggering effects of disease among the American Indians. Prosperity increased also, during the 18th century, and many Creole owners became wealthy. However, resentment grew as well. Spanish and Portuguese policies were designed to keep Latin America subservient, and in the 18th century, would-be enlightened despots in both countries tightened controls over the colonies. The colonial administrations imposed heavy taxes on Latin American trade and limited it to a few ports and a handful of privileged companies. Contact with the more advanced economies of northern Europe was banned, although in fact some illegal trade developed, particularly with Britain, which was allowed to import slaves. Latin Americans grew increasingly restless under these limitations and also because of their exclusion from political rule. Many Creoles traveled in Europe and learned of the new political theories of the Enlightenment. In Colombia and other centers, new kinds of intellectual activity arose, as scientific discoveries and

WORLD PROFILES

SOR JUANA INÉS DE LA CRUZ
(1651–1695)

Sor Juana Inés de la Cruz was one woman in premodern times who rose to public prominence on the basis of her intellectual qualities and piety. An author, poet, musician, and social thinker, she was welcome at the viceroy's court in Mexico City. She represented the growing attempt to produce a European-style and predominantly Catholic culture in the new Latin American civilization. Like many Christian thinkers before her, she ultimately abandoned her wider interests, at the urging of her religious superiors, to concentrate on purely spiritual matters. Why did religion give some women a chance to rise in early modern world history? Were colonial conditions in the Americas more or less favorable to women in public life than were conditions in most established societies?

Sor Juana Inés de la Cruz.

reform ideas were discussed. This intellectual ferment was modest, confined mainly to cities and Creoles, but combined with the other, more widespread grievances, it was the basis for a series of wars of independence that produced the first massive slave revolt in Haiti, in 1798, and then swept across virtually the entire society between 1808 and 1820.

By the 18th century, a Latin American civilization was taking shape on the basis of ongoing popular traditions among many American Indian peoples; new political, cultural, and technological influences from Europe; and the special conditions of the colonial economy and government. The civilization depended heavily on European models, but it was not identical to Europe. Racial diversity, slavery and the estate systems, the nature of the export economy, and a popular culture combined with Catholicism set it apart; so did the combination of wide governmental claims with limited actual authority over local conditions. Latin American civilization, still new, was also capable of important change. New cultural products, a more vigorous internal economy, and Creole contacts with the European Enlightenment all exhibited the spirit of innovation characteristic of the 18th century itself. In a different sense, a series of American Indian risings in the Andes region, toward the end of the century, performed a similar function, with leaders combining novel political demands with references to Inca heritage.

WESTERN CIVILIZATION IN NORTH AMERICA

French colonial holdings in Canada and along the Mississippi River, although vast on paper, were only lightly administered. Important French settlements were established only in parts of Canada. The French were far more interested in their West Indian islands, which produced so profitably for the European market. From North America, they gained only some fur trade and some leverage against Britain's growing empire.

The British colonies along the eastern seaboard, however, were another matter. By the 18th century, 3 million Europeans had settled in these colonies, and a large number of African slaves had been imported as well. In the southern colonies, a slaveholding estate system developed—producing rice, sugar, tobacco, and dyes—that in many ways resembled that of the West Indies and Brazil. Britain imposed some of the same limitations on all the colonies that Spain established for its Latin American holdings. Governors were appointed from Britain; taxes were high; manufacturing was discouraged as the British sought to protect their markets in the colonies and procure cheap raw materials and foodstuffs.

Nonetheless, the society that developed in the British colonies was far closer to western European forms than was that of Latin America. The colonies operated their own assemblies, which provided considerable political experience; local town governments were also active. Despite British regulations, a substantial manufacturing economy developed, and the North Americans ran extensive trading companies and merchant shipping. North American products were less interesting to western Europe than were those of Latin America and the West Indies. The southern colonies, to be sure, produced tobacco and later cotton, using slave labor, which served as the leading exports. And southern planters imported expensive craft products from Europe. Here was a dependent economy quite similar to that of Latin America. But in New England and the Middle Atlantic colonies, aside from some furs and woods, there were no natural resources of great interest in the early modern world economy. These colonies were therefore left free to develop their own localized agriculture and also their own trading patterns, including merchant shipping and local manufacturing based on family businesses and wage labor. Britain did try to impose more characteristic dependency with new regulations and taxes in the 1760s, but by this point such attempts to control the colonies were too late.

The colonial economy was not as advanced as that of western Europe, but it demonstrated a somewhat similar range of activities, including growing merchant zeal.

The North American colonists' intellectual contacts with Europe were also vigorous. North America was closer to Europe than Latin America was. The tie with Britain gave North Americans access to one of the most dynamic centers of political theory and scientific inquiry in the Western world. Hundreds of North Americans during the 18th century contributed scientific findings to the British Royal Society, and discussion groups among American intellectuals were active as well. North American literacy rates were quite high, which encouraged participation in a European-derived intellectual life. In contrast, Latin America's ties to Spain, where Enlightenment activity was more modest, limited its access to the new intellectual currents of Western civilization.

British, and to an extent French, North America thus evolved less as a separate culture than as part of Western civilization. There were vital differences, of course. The North American colonies did not produce a full aristocracy, of the sort that still dominated west European society; this fact gave the values of merchant groups and free farmers freer rein. Colonial governments were also weak, by European standards, with few functions beyond defense and a rudimentary system of law courts. In addition, North American family patterns were somewhat distinctive. Blessed with more abundant land, North Americans had higher birth rates than their European counterparts during the 17th and 18th centuries. They treated children with greater care; thus, the practice of swaddling children was less common in British North America. Americans also placed somewhat greater emphasis on the family as the center of emotional stability, perhaps because of the strangeness of their surroundings. Most importantly of all, the North American colonies did establish a slaveholding system that, although concentrated particularly in the South, strongly affected the history of the whole region—even after slavery was finally abolished.

North Americans were conscious of their distinctiveness. They lacked Europe's elaborate art and great cities, although by the 18th century, the imitation of European artistic forms was well underway. Americans felt somewhat inferior to Europe but rejoiced in what they perceived as their greater freedom (slavery aside) and a more youthful vigor. But the habit of imitating Europe remained strong as well. In fact, the British colonies were so similar to Europe that the course of their history closely resembled that of the rest of the expanded Western world. Even when the colonies rebelled, in 1776, they did so in the name of Western political ideals and proceeded to establish a government that, although it maintained certain distinctive features, remained clearly within the range of Western political values.

NORTH AND SOUTH AMERICA: REASONS FOR THE DIFFERENCES

Western penetration of the Americas from 1450 to 1800 had two leading results. It created an important although distinctive version of Western civilization in North America. It created an essentially new civilization, albeit one with unusually close ties to Western patterns, in South and Central America and Mexico. Because of its size and economic role, Latin American civilization was by far the more important in world history during the early modern period.

How and why did these two outcomes differ? Part of the distinction rests with differences between Spain and Portugal on the one hand, and Britain and northern Europe on the other. Spain was an intensely Catholic country, with a fervent missionary movement, but it was somewhat removed, particularly after 1600, from the mainstream of European intellectual life. Spain lacked a substantial merchant class of its own, which contributed to the Latin American emphasis on landed estates rather than elaborate commerce. Spain's tendency toward centralized

Spanish scene of soldiers confronting South American Indians.

control, at least in principle, discouraged extensive political life in the new colonies. Latin American civilization, although still not fully formed, thus emerged with a political tradition, an economy, and a social structure quite different from what came to characterize its northern neighbor.

Latin America also developed a different racial balance from that of the English colonies. Disease decimated the American Indian population everywhere, but because of its prior size, substantial concentrations persisted in Latin America. North American Indians were also less fully organized into agricultural societies, and they were more easily forced to move. The American Indian role in the ultimate culture and social structure of North America was not great. In Latin America, in contrast, particularly in Central America and the Andes region, the values and labor contributions of a sizable American Indian population played an ongoing role. The rise of a large mestizo population, virtually unknown in the more racially conscious English colonies, added to the differentiation. Latin American civilization resulted, in part, from a fusion of Western and American Indian peoples and social forms; it also had a much

larger African slave contingent. North America saw a much more straightforward extension of Western values over small, often badly treated and segregated, American Indian and African minorities.

From these early differentiations, Latin America and what became the United States and Canada were to follow substantially different historical rhythms. To be sure, struggles for independence occurred almost simultaneously. The North American colonies (apart from Canada) rose first, and most of Latin America, inspired in part by this very example, soon followed. But from these wars came quite different results, in the political features of the new nations and in their economic base, as the new United States quickly joined western Europe in industrialization, whereas Latin America remained in a more dependent position in the world economy.

THE WORLD ECONOMY REVISITED

Like all major developments in human history, the rise of the world economy resulted in both gains and losses. It increased economic inequalities among civilizations. Latin America and major parts of Africa, for instance, were drawn into the world economy as producers of largely unprocessed goods that depended on cheap or free (slave) labor, and thus were losers, overall, in the world economy, although individuals in these societies profited along with the Europeans. Furthermore, the inequalities of the world economy tended to be self-perpetuating. Only the English colonies of North America, on the fringe of dependency into the 18th century, managed to break free fairly easily, to become part of the dominant economy of the West.

The world economy also unleashed a new profit motive, through the spread of commercial capitalism. This motive, although capable of generating large-scale exploitation, also supported technological innovation as another means of

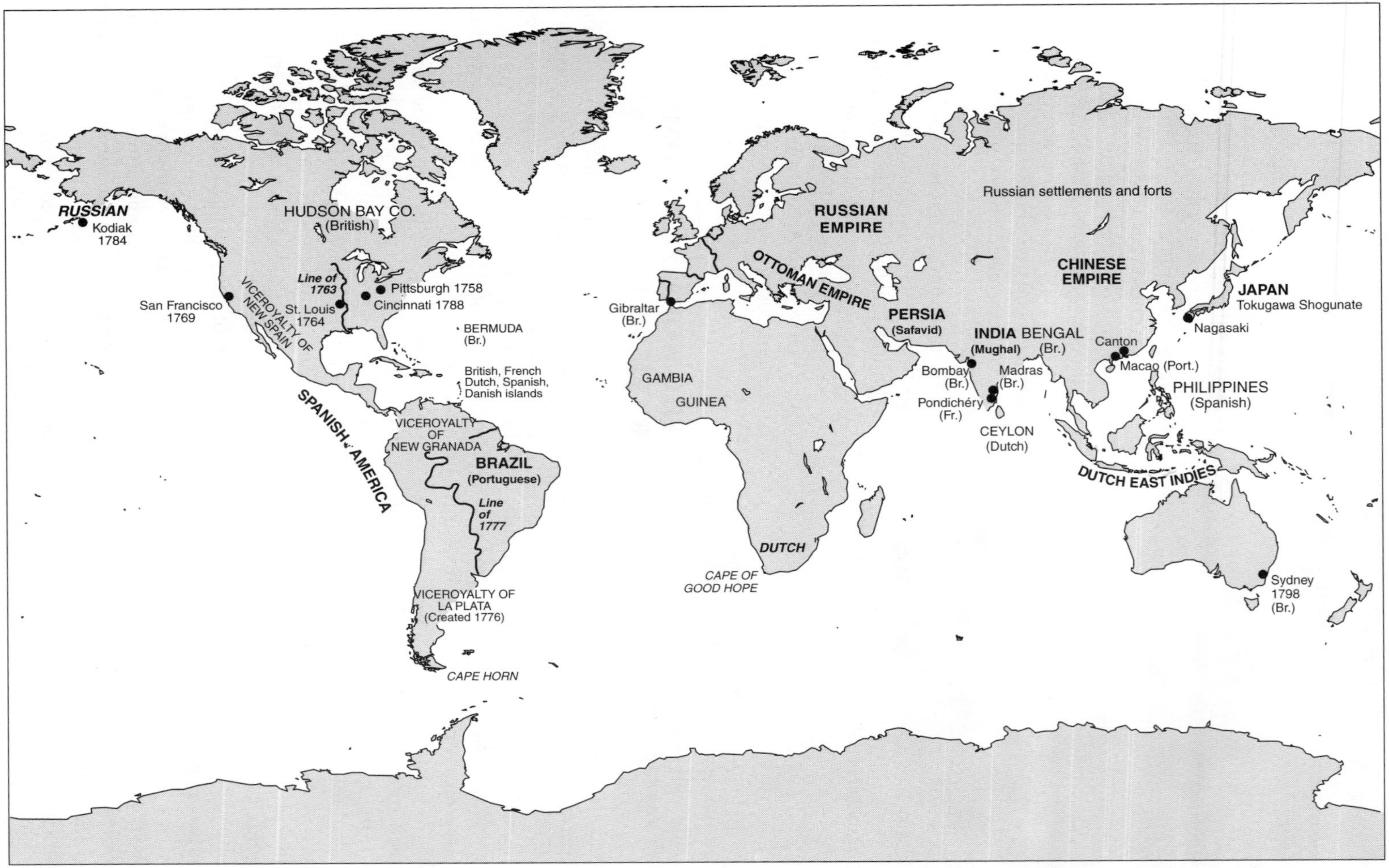

The World By 1763

RUSSIAN
Kodiak
1784

HUDSON BAY CO.
(British)

Pittsburgh 1758
Cincinnati 1788

Line of 1763
St. Louis 1764
VICEROYALTY OF
NEW SPAIN

San Francisco
1769

BERMUDA
(Br.)

British, French,
Dutch, Spanish,
Danish islands

VICEROYALTY
OF
NEW GRANADA

BRAZIL
(Portuguese)

Line
of
1777

VICEROYALTY
OF
LA PLATA
(Created 1776)

SPANISH AMERICA

CAPE HORN

Gibraltar
(Br.)

GAMBIA

GUINEA

OTTOMAN EMPIRE

PERSIA
(Safavid)

RUSSIAN
EMPIRE

Russian settlements and forts

CHINESE
EMPIRE

JAPAN
Tokugawa Shogunate

Nagasaki

Macao (Port.)

Canton

PHILIPPINES
(Spanish)

DUTCH EAST INDIES

INDIA
(Mughal)

BENGAL
(Br.)

Madras
(Br.)

Bombay
(Br.)

Pondichéry
(Fr.)

CEYLON
(Dutch)

DUTCH

CAPE OF
GOOD HOPE

Sydney
1798
(Br.)

increasing production at low cost. Before long this thirst, backed by the capital already earned in world trade, produced vast changes in manufacturing methods, which in turn yielded measurable benefits even beyond Western society.

Before this occurred, however, other civilizations in the world, not fully caught up in the world economy but nonetheless affected by it, had to define their own relationship to the West and the new patterns of trade. Some, such as China and the Middle East, were not strangers to commercial capitalism, although they had not before encountered it on such a scale. Because of previous economic and technological strength, and strong political structures and distinctive values, most of Asia and eastern Europe held their own in to the world economy well into the 18th century, participating to a degree but not engulfed by it. However, such civilizations, too, faced the prospect of change, even if they intended otherwise.

The world economy, with its inclusion of the Americas, also had significant environmental impact. Europeans were eager to introduce plants native to one region to as many other areas as possible, to increase production and profit. American forests began to be cut back in favor of crops such as sugar. The importance of new animals such as horses challenged the American environment as well. The Spanish actively experimented with American crops such as corn and the potato in the Philippines, from where they spread to other parts of Asia.

PATHS TO THE PRESENT

Three categories describe the relationships between the recasting of the world economy in the early modern period and the world today. The first is defined by a number of the period's major developments that simply played themselves out. The population devastation in the Americas, a result of the Columbian exchange, gravely wounded Native American societies and paved the way for massive immigration and new interbreeding. But, we no longer live with the exchange, and population levels in the Americas began to rebound as early as the 18th century. Japan's considerable isolation was reversed a century and a half ago, and while a few vestiges of it persist—the Japanese allow less immigration than other industrial societies—the main effects of early modern policy have long since vanished.

The second category involves developments that also have ended, but that left stronger traces. The slave trade is gone, but its devastating consequences linger. People of African origin in the Americas remember slavery, and the fact of prior enslavement continues to affect their position in society, feeding ongoing racism. Two United States presidents have visited slave-trade sites in Africa during the past 15 years, both of whom apologized for America's atrocities to African slaves—a clear sign of the ongoing need to deal with this memory. Strong vestiges of the treatment of Native Americans also persist, both in minority and in majority populations.

The third category contains more direct connections. The importance of Atlantic trade, established in the early modern period, obviously continues today. Most significant of all is the durability—some argue, the tragic durability—of the unequal economic relationships established five centuries ago. The West continues to enjoy a dominant position in global trade, though it now shares that position with other societies. Its profits have become, to some degree, self-perpetuating. Societies that were guided to focus on the production of raw materials and its attendant cheap labor have found it difficult, if not impossible, to escape economic dependency on the economies for which they supplied those materials. For example, a straight line connects the global economic relationships established in early modern centuries and the poverty and lack of economic control characteristic of nations in the Andean region of Latin America today. Here, despite all that has happened since, is a truly living legacy.

SUGGESTED WEB SITES

For more information on transatlantic slavery, see http://www.liverpoolmuseums.org.uk/maritime/slavery/; on colonial America, see http://members.aol.com/TeacherNet/Colonial.html and http://www.americaslibrary.gov/cgi-bin/page.cgi/jb/colonial; on Africans in America, see http://www.pbs.org/wgbh/aia/part1/map1.html; on Latin American studies, see http://www.latinamericanstudies.org/. A very good bilingual, multiformat English-Spanish digital library site that explores interactions between Spain and the United States in America from the 15th to the early 19th centuries can be found at http://international.loc.gov/intldl/eshtml/eshome.html.

SUGGESTED READINGS

Recent work includes Martha Keber, *Seas of Gold, Seas of Cotton* (2002); Cathy Matson, *The Economy of Early America: Historical Perspectives & New Directions* (2006); Stephen J. Hornsby, *British Atlantic, American Frontier: Spaces of Power in Early Modern British America* (2005); Michael D. Bordo, Alan M. Taylor, and Jeffrey G. Williamson, *Globalization in Historical Perspective* (2003); Londa Schiebinger and Claudia Swan, eds., *Colonial Botany: Science, Commerce, and Politics in the Early Modern World* (2005); William Jankowiak and Daniel Bradburd, eds., *Drugs, Labor, and Colonial Expansion* (2003); Sanjay Subrahmanyam, *The Career and Legend of Vasco da Gama* (1997); Merry Wiesner Hanks, *Christianity and Sexuality in the Early Modern World* (2000); and, especially, Kenneth Pomeranz's *The Great Divergence: China, Europe, and the Making of the Modern World Economy* (2000), an important world history study.

Excellent discussions of Western exploration and expansion are C. M. Cippolla's *Guns, Sails, and Empires* (1985) and J. H. Parry's *The Discovery of South America* (1979). Additional important recent work includes Alan K. Smith, *Creating a World Economy: Merchant Capital Colonization and World Trade, 1400–1825* (1991); Michael Pearson, *Port Cities and Intruders: The Swahili Coast, India, and Portugal in the Early Modern Era* (1998); and James Tracy, ed., *The Rise of Merchant Empires* (1990) and *The Political Economy of Merchant Empires* (1991). See also C. R. Boxer, *Four Centuries of Portuguese Expansion* (1969); W. Dorn, *The Competition for Empire* (1963); Alfred Crosby, *The Columbian Exchange: Biological and Cultural Consequences of 1492* (1972); C. A. Bayh, *Indian Society and the Making of the British Empire* (1988); and D. K. Fieldhouse, *The Colonial Empires* (1971). See also J. H. Elliott, *The Old World and the New, 1492–1650* (1970) and J. K. Thornton, *Africa and the Africans in the Making of the Atlantic World, 1400–1800* (1997).

On Latin America, consult Christopher Schmidt-Nowara and John M. Nieto-Phillips, eds., *Interpreting Spanish Colonialism: Empires, Nations, and Legends* (2005); Susan Kellog, *Weaving the Past: A History of Latin America's Indigenous Women from the Prehispanic Period to the Present* (2005); John Fisher, *Bourbon Peru 1750–1824* (2003); Stanley J. Stein and Barbara H. Stein, *Silver, Trade, and War* [electronic resource]: *Spain and the America in the Making of Early Modern Europe* (2000); James Lockhart and Stuart B. Schwartz, *Early Latin America* (1982); Lyle N. Macalister, *Spain and Portugal in the New World* (1984); Eric Williams, *Capitalism and Slavery* (1964); J. Fagg, *Latin America* (1969); S. J. Stein and B. H. Stein, *The Colonial Heritage of Latin America* (1970); and A. Lavin, ed., *Sexuality and Marriage in Colonial Latin America* (1989). See also John H. Elliott, *Empires of the Atlantic World: Britain and Spain in America 1492–1830* (2007); and Antonio Barrera-Osorio, *Experiencing Nature: the Spanish American Empire and the Early Scientific Revolution* (2006).

Useful sources on the slave system are David K. O'Rourke, *How America's First Settlers Invented Chattel Slavery: Dehumanizing Native Americans and Africans with Language, Laws, Guns, and Religion* (2005); Peter H. Wood, *Strange New Land: Africans in Colonial America* (2003); David Eltis et al., eds., *Slavery in the Development of the Americas* (2004); Robert Blackburn, *The Making of New World Slavery* (1997); O. Patterson, *Slavery and Social Death: A Comparative Study* (1982); and D. B. Davis, *Slavery and Human Progress* (1984).

On the slave trade, see Marcus Rediker, *The Slave Ship: A Human Story* (2007); James Rawley, *The Transatlantic Slave Trade* (1981); Roger Anstey, *The Atlantic Slave Trade and British Abolition* (1975); Paul Lovejoy, *Transformations in Slavery: A History of Slavery in Africa* (1983); Patrick Manning, *Slavery and African Life* (1990); and Joseph Miller, *Way of Death* (1989). On other key topics, including discovery and interaction, see Alfred W. Crosby, Jr., *Columbian Exchange: Biological and Cultural Consequences of 1492* (2003); David Abulafia, *The Discovery of Mankind: Atlantic Encounters in the Age of Columbus* (2008); John E. Kicza, *Resilient Cultures: America's Native Peoples Confront European Colonization, 1500–1800* (2003). Also consult Nancy Farriss, *Maya Society under Colonial Rule* (1984); Louisa Schell Hoberman and Susan Migden Socolow, eds., *Cities and Society in Colonial Latin America* (1986); and Stuart Schwartz, *Sugar Plantations and the Formation of Brazilian Society* (1985).

Readable texts on the West and Asia and Africa include Paul Bohannan and Philip Curtin, *Africa and Africans*, 3rd ed., (1988); Martin Hall, *The Changing Past: Farmers, Kings, and Traders in Southern Africa* (1987); Leonard Thompson, *A History of South Africa* (1990); A. Hyma, *The Dutch in the Far East: A History of the Dutch Commercial and Colonial Empire* (1942); and S. D. Pen, *The French in India* (1958). See also K. N. N. Chaudori, *Trade and Civilization in the Indian Ocean* (1985). A provocative, although controversial, overview of the development of a new global economy is Immanuel Wallerstein's *The Modern World System*, 2 vols. (1980). For source reading, see P. Curtin, ed., *Africa Remembered: Narratives by West Africans from the Era of the Slave Trade* (1967). On colonial North America, see Jack Greene and J. R. Pole, eds., *Colonial British America: Essays on the New History of the Early Modern Era* (1984). See also Paul Ahluwalia, *White and Deadly: Sugar and Colonialism* (1999).

Western Civilization Changes Shape in the Early Modern Centuries

Developments in early modern western Europe reflected the region's gains in the world economy, adding up to new revenue and power. Europe's world role encouraged dynamic internal patterns, which in turn affected its global activities. Western Europe changed in many ways during the early modern period: compare a summary of the year 1750 with that for 1450. Europe's world position, its political structures, its social structures, and its culture had all shifted profoundly. Big changes in this period include the replacement of feudalism with national monarchies, greatly increased commercialization and the shift away from serfdom to wage labor, and a decline of traditional popular beliefs plus the rise of science.

Between 1450 and 1750, west European society went through a series of profound transformations. Each century produced at least one major new current. The 15th century featured the Renaissance, which began indeed a bit earlier in Italy and then spread to northern Europe. In the 16th century, the Protestant Reformation upstaged the continuing impact of the Renaissance, breaking the unity of Western Christendom; the Catholic Reformation, in turn, responded. Political turmoil dominated the first half of the 17th century, but still more profound change resulted from the Scientific Revolution, which was one of the most basic reorientations of intellectual life in the history of any civilization. Finally, during the first half of the 18th century, the Enlightenment extended the principles of the Scientific Revolution to generate new views of politics and society, indeed new views of human nature itself.

Thinkers during the Enlightenment professed embarrassment at the very existence of the medieval period, which seemed to them remote and backward in contrast to their own sophisticated world. Such a view was, in fact, too extreme, as well as unfairly demeaning to the achievements of medieval society: the heritage of the Middle Ages was still visible in political, intellectual, and economic life. There was no question, however, that Western civilization showed a marked ability to change its focus.

So much seemed to be changing that it is sometimes difficult to identify coherent directions in the period as a whole. Transformation was not neat and tidy: different movements overlapped, such as the Renaissance and the Reformation. Some events represented a resurgence of earlier values. The Reformation, for example, stemmed in part from a very medieval piety, although it had quite nonmedieval results. Although it is important to gain a sense of specific developments, it is also possible to observe general trends. Various movements tended to strengthen the central state in European monarchies, but for different reasons. Historical processes led, even more clearly, to a significant transformation of Western intellectual and artistic life. This ultimately resulted in a decline in the religious approach to understanding the world in favor of a rational, scientific framework. Trends of this sort were gradual, often complex, and usually incomplete. But they gave shape to a vibrant period in Western history.

This was also a time of fundamental change in Western economic and social life. Developments in these areas were just as important as the overall intellectual revolution and, indeed, more important than political change. The Western economy became commercialized in an unprecedented way, and technologically—for the first time—the most advanced in the world. The European family took on unusual dimensions, and its importance in certain aspects of Western life grew.

Between 1450 and 1750, political, cultural, and economic shifts involved Western civilization increasingly in the larger world. Traders and explorers in overseas colonies brought back new techniques and cultural values. Even more obvious, from 1500 on, Western society drew increasing wealth from its global contacts. In turn, based on its new internal dynamism, western Europe began to influence other civilizations in a variety of ways.

■**KEY QUESTIONS**   *How did specific events, such as the Reformation, relate to the big changes of the early modern period as a whole in the West? It is important to capture the specific currents, each with its own character, but not lose sight of the big picture. Why did western Europe change so much in these centuries? Finally, what continuities accompanied change? In what ways were earlier features of Western civilization still present by 1750?*

PATTERNS OF EARLY MODERN WESTERN HISTORY

The Renaissance

The spotlight in Western history, around 1400, was on Italy. This region had never fully embraced medieval customs, especially feudalism. The peninsula was largely organized in terms of city-states, some ruled by kings, others by aristocratic or merchant councils, still others by military tyrants. Many city-states had extensive trade and cultural contacts with other parts of the Mediterranean. From these exchanges, especially with Byzantium, Italian scholars gained a new appreciation of Greek and Latin literature. At the same time, growing commercial wealth encouraged cities such as Florence and Venice to create new artistic styles to celebrate their exciting achievements.

From Italy's mixture of trade and scholarly and artistic endeavor arose the movement known as the Renaissance, which took shape in the 1300s. It started most clearly as a literary and artistic movement. Writers such as Dante, Petrarch, and Boccacio—all three writing in Italian as well as the traditional Latin—began to address more strictly secular subjects than had been popular in the Middle Ages. Petrarch wrote

WORLD PROFILES

MARIA PORTINARI

Maria Portinari (b. 1456) was the wife of a Florentine banker (Tommaso, c. 1432–1501) who made a fortune as a representative of the Medici banking family in Bruges, Flanders (now Belgium). The image here shows her richly but somberly dressed. Her slightly melancholy expression may have been appropriately pious, for the Renaissance in northern Europe set a strong spiritual tone for laypeople. Historians have also realized that the Renaissance, striking as it was in terms of cultural innovation, may have led to a deterioration in the position of upper-class women, who were treated increasingly as ornaments and excluded from most of the new sources of learning. How might a woman such as Maria Portinari have reacted to the changes sweeping through western Europe during the 15th century?

This portrait of Maria Portinari is by the Flemish master Hans Memling.

love sonnets to his Laura; other poems praised his own valor in climbing mountains—a new sign of individualism and pride in human achievement. Boccacio wrote earthy stories of love and lust, and although he later recanted, professing his devotion to religious faith, his earlier writings won a wide audience. In art, Giotto developed a new sense of perspective, allowing three-dimensional portrayals of nature. Both writers and artists began to copy classical styles, writing of and painting gods and goddesses and human scenes, rather than strictly Christian motifs; their work thus reflected increasing realism.

Seldom has an age produced as many cultural greats as did the Renaissance in Italy. A host of architects designed churches and public buildings in classical styles, renouncing the Gothic aesthetic. Leonardo da Vinci advanced the realistic portrayal of the human body in art, even painting pictures of medical dissections. Michelangelo's statues offered graphic displays of human musculature. Overall, Italian Renaissance art, developed from the 14th through the early 16th century,

Classical themes and styles in the Italian Renaissance: *Birth of Venus* by Botticelli.

stressed themes of humanism—a focus on humankind as the center of intellectual and artistic endeavor. The humanistic concerns spread also to music, where elegant choruses sang of love, drink, and the beauties of nature. A new interest in human history also emerged, and several Renaissance historians, using a newly critical approach to past documents, challenged traditional church claims in areas such as the origins of the papacy.

The new spirit extended also to political theory. Writing around 1500, the Florentine Niccolò Machiavelli described what a ruler must do to gain and maintain power: how to use cruelty, how to sway public opinion. Machiavelli combined a detailed knowledge of Italian politics of his time with the use of Greek and Roman examples—a characteristic Renaissance mixture.

The Italian Renaissance had flourished in part because Italy was free from the medieval political forms that continued to influence much of the rest of Europe. During a good deal of the Italian Renaissance, France and England were locked in their Hundred Years War. Then, late in the 15th century, the larger monarchies started to gain strength. France and Spain looked greedily upon the weak Italian city-states and embarked on wars of conquest in the 1490s. Italian trade also began to decline as interest shifted away from the Mediterranean to the Atlantic trade routes that France, Spain, and England soon dominated.

However, as Renaissance creativity faded in its Italian birthplace, it passed northward. Northern artists directly copied the new themes and styles of the Italians. Palaces in the classical style became the rage among northern rulers such as Francis I of France, who increasingly fancied themselves patrons of the arts. Northern humanists gained growing knowledge of Latin and Greek literary and philosophical sources; soon they turned to writing in their own languages. Typical northern humanists, such as Erasmus in the Netherlands, were more religious than some of their Italian counterparts but shared their interest in human affairs and a pure style.

The Renaissance spirit also prevailed in 16th-century writers such as England's Shakespeare and France's Rabelais; they addressed a wide variety of earthly subjects, with an emphasis on human passions and drama. Their works, and those of Spain's Cervantes, developed new literary traditions in their respective nations.

The northern Renaissance had political implications as well. Renaissance kings increased the pomp and ceremony within their courts and tried to expand their power. Francis I claimed new authority over the operations of the Catholic church in France. Leading monarchs from the Tudor dynasty in England, particularly Henry VIII and Elizabeth I, ruled with firm hands. They encouraged trading companies and colonial enterprises, and they even passed laws on how to deal with the poor. During the Renaissance, monarchs also cultivated a more open interest in wars of conquest than their medieval predecessors. England engaged in a lengthy effort to conquer Ireland; France invaded Italy and tried to construct alliance systems to counter the power of Spain and the Holy Roman Empire, both ruled for a time by a single royal family, the Habsburgs. Francis I even allied briefly with the sultan of the Ottoman Empire; the alliance meant little in practical terms but showed that political interests had gained ascendancy over traditional Christian hostility to Islam.

The Religious Upheaval

Political and economic patterns in Renaissance Europe were soon embroiled in the currents of the next major change—the Reformation. In 1517, a German monk named Martin Luther published a document containing 95 thesis, or major arguments. He was specifically protesting claims made by a papal representative that paying money to the Church by buying indulgences advanced one's salvation. For Luther, the idea of indulgences became an utter perversity; according to his reading of the Bible, salvation could come only through faith, not through works and certainly not through the money that the Renaissance popes sought for the upkeep of their own expensive court. Luther's protest, rebuffed by the papacy, soon led him to challenge most of the traditional Catholic sacraments and the authority of the pope himself.

The stand taken by the German monk gained wide support. Many Christians believed that the Catholic church had become too corrupt and many of its practices meaningless. Some Renaissance intellectuals welcomed Luther's use of original documents, such as the Bible, and also his nationalistic defiance, as a German, against religious rule from Rome. A number of individual rulers liked Lutheranism because it broadened their authority; they could direct Lutheran churches without the interference of still powerful popes. Some ordinary people, finally, saw in Lutheranism an opportunity to speak out against their poverty and the landlords who dominated their lives, although Luther did renounce the idea of popular protest. As Luther firmly rejected Catholic attempts to undermine his influence, Lutheranism spread widely in Germany and also in Scandinavia.

Once Christian unity was breached, other Protestant groups evolved. In England, Henry VIII established the Anglican church, initially to challenge papal attempts to enforce his first marriage, which had failed to produce a male heir. (Henry ultimately had six wives in sequence; he had two of them executed.) Henry was also attracted to some Lutheran doctrines. His son and his daughter, who later became Queen Elizabeth I, were Protestants outright, so the Anglican church became increasingly Protestant in doctrine as well as a separate form of church government. Still more important were the churches inspired by Jean Calvin, a Frenchman who established his base in the city of Geneva. Calvinism insisted on God's predestination, or prior determination, of those who would be saved; nothing humans did, and certainly no sacraments, could win

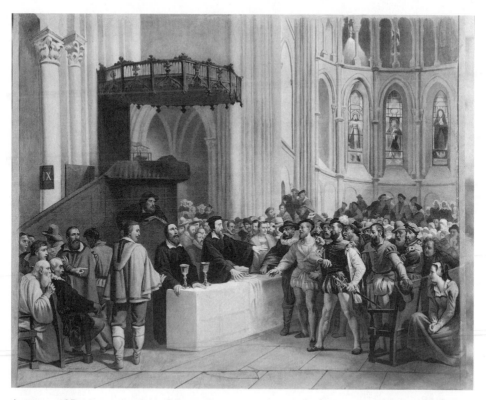

An image of Protestantism: John Calvin refuses sacraments to the libertines. In this representation of the Geneva (Switzerland) Cathedral in the 16th century, a soberly dressed John Calvin denies Christian sacraments to a high-living crowd, because he did not find them morally worthy.

God's favor. At the same time, those elected to God's grace had the obligation to encourage others to behave morally and seek knowledge of the Bible. Calvinist ministers became moral guardians and preachers of God's word, not special sacramental representatives of the deity. Like other Protestant ministers, they could marry. Calvinism sought the participation of other believers in local church government; it also promoted wider popular education, so that more people could have direct access to the Bible (which various Protestant groups now translated into the vernacular languages). Calvinism was accepted not only in parts of Switzerland but also in Germany and France, where it produced strong minority groups, and in the Netherlands, England, and Scotland.

Beginning about 1550, the Catholic church, although unable to restore religious unity, reacted to Protestantism. Church councils not only condemned Protestant doctrine but also communicated a message of greater religious concern to the pope. A new order of monks, the Jesuits, became active in politics, education, and missionary work, helping to strengthen the faith of most Catholics in Italy and Spain and to regain some territories initially open to Protestantism, such as Hungary. The result was a revivified Catholic church.

The rise of the Protestant churches triggered a long period of religious war in Europe. During the second half of the 16th century, France was the scene of major battles between Protestant and Catholic groups. The conflict ended only with

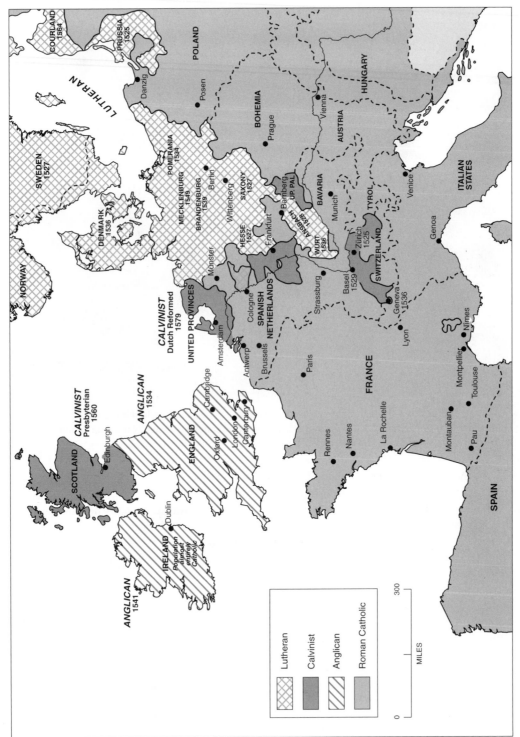

Established Churches, About 1600

Legend:
- Lutheran
- Calvinist
- Anglican
- Roman Catholic

MILES
0 — 300

LUTHERAN

COURLAND 1564
PRUSSIA 1525
POLAND
Danzig
Posen
SWEDEN 1527
NORWAY
DENMARK 1536
POMERANIA 1534
MECKLENBURG 1549
BRANDENBURG 1539
Berlin
Wittenberg
SAXONY 1527
BOHEMIA
Prague
Vienna
AUSTRIA
HUNGARY
ITALIAN STATES
Venice
BAVARIA
Munich
Bamberg UP. PAL.
ANSBACH 1528
HESSE 1527
Frankfurt
WÜRT. 1536
TYROL
SWITZERLAND
Zürich 1525
Basel 1529
Genoa
Münster
Cologne
SPANISH NETHERLANDS
Strassburg
Geneva 1536
CALVINIST
Dutch Reformed 1579
UNITED PROVINCES
Amsterdam
Antwerp
Brussels
Paris
Lyon
Nîmes
FRANCE
Montpellier
Toulouse
Montauban
Pau
Rennes
Nantes
La Rochelle
SPAIN
CALVINIST
Presbyterian 1560
SCOTLAND
Edinburgh
ANGLICAN 1534
ENGLAND
Cambridge
Oxford
London
Canterbury
ANGLICAN 1541
IRELAND
Population almost entirely Catholic
Dublin
ANGLICAN

the granting of tolerance to Protestants in 1598. Catholics and Protestants waged war recurrently in Germany, although several negotiations were held in the hope of dividing Germany among Catholic and Protestant states. In 1618, the Thirty Years War broke out, in which foreign powers as well as Germans fought over their religious beliefs. The Spanish monarchy, self-appointed chief defender of the Catholic faith, tried to aid its coreligionists, whereas Swedish armies assisted the Protestant cause in a war so bloody that it reduced Germany's economic activity and its population level for many decades. The war ended with Spain's power reduced and a reluctant agreement to permit religious division among the German states. Religious passions helped fuel a war between the Netherlands and Spain, in which the former ultimately won its independence. Religious strife simmered in England during parts of the 16th century, until Queen Elizabeth I imposed a peace under a rather tolerant Anglican church; strife erupted again in the 1640s, contributing to a civil war in which Calvinists fought Catholic sympathizers. Eventually, the Anglican church was restored, but with tolerance for other Protestant groups. The English Civil War ended formally in 1660, but the full settlement, including limited religious toleration, was reached only in 1688–1689.

For the most part, the Reformation, which had dominated Western political as well as religious history during the greater part of the 16th century, was assimilated in Europe by the first half of the 17th century. Even the Thirty Years War in Germany was as much a battle among national monarchies as it was a religious dispute. Thus, France during that war sided with Protestant forces in order to weaken its enemy Spain. Although Protestantism and revived Catholicism had a lasting impact on not only the religious map but also social and economic life, the battles among Christian groups no longer set the agenda for events in Europe itself. By 1650, it was becoming clear that Western Christianity was permanently divided, and unintentional repercussions of the Reformation began surfacing in business and family life.

In this context, during most of the 1600s, attention shifted to culture and politics. In culture, the leading development was the spate of new scientific discoveries, culminating in the great physical laws as advanced by Isaac Newton. Scientists learned how gravity works; they determined that Earth was not the center of the universe but, rather, rotated around the sun; they discovered how blood circulates in the human body. Perhaps most importantly, they developed a coherent understanding of how the scientific method functions, through a combination of rational hypothesis, empirical testing through observation or experiment, and final generalization in theory or law. Far more than the Renaissance, the Scientific Revolution of the 17th century produced a fundamental reorientation of Western intellectual life.

The Rise of the Monarchies

During the same period, leading Western monarchies gained new organizational power. With Spain in growing eclipse, after a century of glory in defense of the church and as Europe's major colonizer in the New World, France emerged as the bellwether nation. The French monarchy decisively defeated the remnants of feudal political forces during the 17th century. After 1614, the kings stopped summoning the national parliament. The greatest French monarch of this period, Louis XIV, also rescinded the toleration of Protestants. No group was allowed officially to limit the monarch's power. This political system, perfected under Louis XIV, was called, appropriately enough, *absolute monarchy*. Louis, dubbing himself the Sun King, extended his patronage of the arts. He built sumptuous palaces, where the nobles competed for royal favor instead of cultivating their independent power base in the provinces. Military administration improved, as Louis's advisors built better forts and established ways to supply provisions to troops in the field.

Louis set up military hospitals and even a military pension plan. Absolute monarchy also meant increasing attention to economic controls, mainly in the interest of securing greater tax revenue. The state tried to encourage exports and regulated manufacturing within France.

Absolutism was copied in a number of other countries. Particularly noteworthy was the rise of monarchies in central Europe along absolutist lines. Prussia, long a backward regional state in eastern Germany, began to strengthen its administration and expand its armies, gaining new power among the various German states. The Habsburg monarchs, although still claiming to be Holy Roman Emperors, worked to develop a solid monarchy in Austria. After Habsburg forces managed to repel the armies of the Ottoman Empire, by 1700 their rule extended to Hungary as well.

One of the clear purposes of the new absolute monarchs was to wage war. Louis XIV conducted several major wars, extending France's boundaries in the north and east. It took a coalition of other powers, including England, Holland, and some of the German states, to keep his ambitions in check. In the 18th century, France and England fought several times, although mainly in their colonies in North America and India. Prussia and Austria also fought, with Prussia winning important new territory. The idea of recurrent battle among the national monarchies and alliance systems designed to prevent any one European power from becoming dominant gained increasing ground.

The pattern of absolute monarchy continued into the 18th century. The French monarchy, exhausted by the wars and ruinous taxation of Louis XIV, was weaker than before. But despite numerous reform movements, no new political system emerged. Prussian administration became more efficient. The Prussian kings, led by the able Frederick the Great, tried to improve agricultural production and extend education while maintaining absolute political power and emphasizing military strength. Rulers such as Frederick, because of

their reform interests and their fascination with new political ideas, liked to call themselves *enlightened despots* rather than absolute monarchs, but the difference was not substantial.

Absolutism, enlightened or otherwise, was not the only political form to surface in Europe during the 17th and 18th centuries. In Britain and the Netherlands, parliamentary monarchies developed that built more clearly on older post-classical traditions through which kings were checked by some kind of assembly. In England, the power of Parliament had been curbed during the reign of the strong Tudor kings of the 16th century, but the institution had not disappeared. Then, when less able monarchs in the 17th century tried to introduce taxes without parliamentary consent, supporters of Parliament joined religious dissidents in attacking royal power. One king, Charles I, was executed during the English civil wars of the 1640s, and for a time England was ruled by a military dictatorship. The monarchy, restored in 1660, again tried to defy Parliament while flirting with Catholicism. It was this combination that resulted in a final settlement, the so-called Glorious Revolution of 1688–1689. A new king was crowned, under parliamentary authority, establishing the principle that Parliament, not the king, had supreme power in the realm, although royal power remained considerable through the 18th century. The crown could not suspend laws, levy taxes without parliamentary consent, or maintain a standing army in times of peace. The assembly was to meet regularly rather than depending on the king's summons. Parliament itself remained a largely medieval body, with a hereditary House of Lords and a House of Commons, whose members were elected by small numbers of voters. Campaigns for parliamentary office after the Glorious Revolution involved few questions of principle and a great deal of bribery. But Parliament had unquestioned authority, and no English king's power could be considered absolute, although it remained extensive throughout the century.

Thus, Western civilization, now divided by religion, was for a time divided by political systems as well. Absolute monarchs not only ruled without parliaments but also created governments with larger bureaucracies and greater functions than the government of England (united with Scotland in 1700 to form Great Britain). At the same time, absolute monarchies were in some ways less flexible than the parliamentary states. They depended on efficient rulers, not always produced by heredity, and they tended to provoke discontent if their wars were unsuccessful or their taxes too high. Popular dissatisfaction mounted particularly in France during the 18th century and resulted in massive revolution in 1789. Ultimately, through this revolutionary current, a greater degree of political unity returned to Western society. Until then, the absolutist and parliamentary impulses were largely separate, and both were important in expressing significant aspects of the evolving Western political tradition.

After the turmoil of the religious wars, it was the development of the new political systems and the recurrent military conflicts that gave the clearest superficial shape to Western history from the early 1600s until the 1750s. Ironically, the new divisions within Europe only spurred Western influence in other parts of the world. Catholics and Protestants, not content with their internal rivalry, spilled over into rival missionary efforts in Asia and the Americas. National monarchies battled overseas as well. Prussia and the Habsburg monarchy fought in Europe alone, but by the 18th century, Britain and France were prepared to wage war on virtually a worldwide basis. Thus, the last of the strictly monarchical wars in Western history, called the Seven Years War in Europe for the good reason that it lasted from 1756 to 1763, saw Prussia defeat an effort by Austria to restrict its growing power, while Britain and France battled on three continents. Even earlier, English–Dutch, English–Spanish, and French–Spanish conflicts over territory and control of the seas had encouraged the formation of new European colonies in various parts of the

world. Seemingly endemic tensions in Western society were now affecting the wider course of world history.

POLITICAL INSTITUTIONS AND IDEAS

The growth of the power and efficiency of the national state was the key political trend in early modern Europe. The Renaissance encouraged the greater splendor and ceremony, including artistic patronage, of the ruler's court. Renaissance interests also tended to weaken religious restraints on political power; even the Renaissance papacy acted more like a secular government, concerned with amassing wealth and acquiring art objects, than like a religious institution. Except in the Italian city-states, new government structures were not developed during the Renaissance, but there was a change in tone and motivation.

The Reformation enhanced the power of the state quite simply by weakening that of the church. Even Catholic monarchies, such as those of France or Spain, gained because the Catholic papacy during the Reformation depended on them for support. Jesuit advisors, although devoted to the Catholic cause, also helped secular rulers increase their power base. In the Protestant camp, Lutheran kings and princes and the English monarch as head of the Anglican church took over control of church government directly.

Still, before 1600, important traditional patterns persisted in politics. In particular, the aristocracy retained considerable power. Many church disputes, such as the religious wars in France, found some aristocrats using the Protestant cause to support their claims against the monarchy. Revolts by nobles occurred again in France in the 1660s, when Louis XIV was a child, but this was a last gasp. The English civil wars featured landowning gentry backing the parliamentary cause against the king—whose main defenders were also landowning aristocrats.

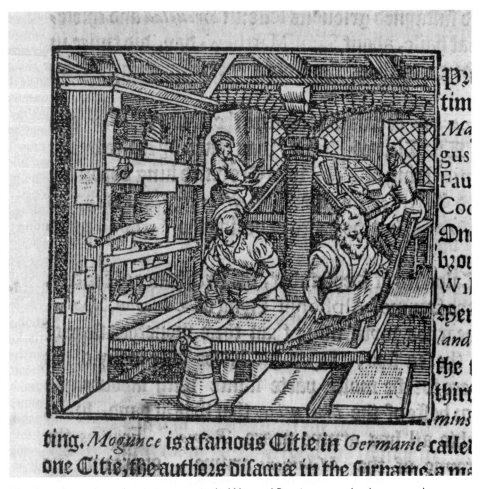

This shop shows the early printing press in the West and Renaissance technology at work.

and others began to generate theories about the impact of gravity, proving experimentally that Aristotle was incorrect in claiming that heavy bodies fell more quickly than light ones. Here was another blow to the dominance of traditional wisdom. Scientists shifted to an emphasis on what new truths they could discover.

Although work of this sort greatly advanced the knowledge of physics, biology also gained ground. Better instrumentation and observation led to a more accurate understanding of the human anatomy. The Englishman William Harvey showed how blood circulates through the body. Other scientists studied the behavior of

gases. Thus, by the mid-17th century, the Western world was responsible for a veritable explosion of knowledge about the physical universe. As part of this process, many intellectuals came to challenge the idea that learning was best approached through a reverence for tradition, for experiment was seen as an alternative, and sometimes more accurate, path to truth.

The Scientific Revolution also applied to science much of the rationalism that had informed Greek and then medieval scholastic thinking. Here was a crucial link in Western intellectual life, even amid great change. Most scientists believed that they could do more than disprove old theories and

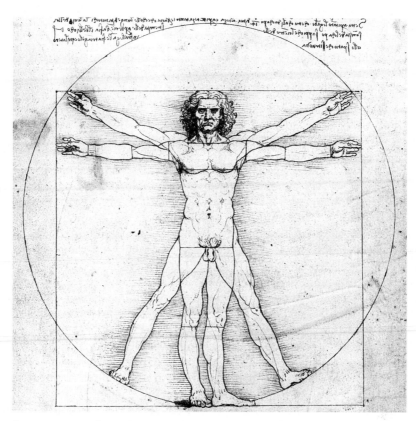

Renaissance art often reflected the emerging Scientific Revolution: anatomical sketches by Leonardo da Vinci.

discover new data. They believed that they could formulate general laws of natural behavior—that there was a correlation between human reason and the orderliness of the universe. Here, the physics of Isaac Newton late in the 17th century seemed to culminate a long quest. In three basic laws, Newton established how physical motion operated on Earth and throughout the universe: a physical body preserves its momentum in a straight line unless forced by outside pressure to deviate; change of motion is proportional to the impressed force and takes place in the direction to which the force is applied; and to every action there is always an equal reaction. Additional work on the law of gravity showed why the planets remain in orbit and explained why objects fall at the same speed. Laws of this sort could be mathematically expressed, and Newton

and others added to not only scientific theory but also mathematical knowledge, particularly in the area of calculus.

What had occurred, by 1700, was a real intellectual revolution in the West, and the establishment of a central scientific approach that no civilization had ever before ventured. The importance of a scientific outlook in Western history after the late 16th century therefore raises the obvious comparative question: why the West? Several other civilizations had produced significant scientific achievement. Byzantium preserved Hellenistic science, although it did not greatly advance it or encourage scientific work elsewhere in eastern Europe. Important science in India and the Middle East was ultimately limited by the rise of narrower religious concerns and, at key points, by political instability. Western science benefitted, even during the early modern period, from contact with Arab and Indian research and theory. China poses another interesting case, for the Chinese preserved a long tradition of elaborate empirical work. Unlike the West, of course, China had little contact with scientific discoveries outside its borders; its intellectual pursuits lacked the exciting challenge of mastering Greek and Arab learning. Chinese thought also tended to stress ethical knowledge over elaborate inquiry. Zhu Xi's emphasis on knowledge might have encouraged scientific inquiry, but it was modified by traditional Confucian stress on the individual's values. Chinese science itself differed from the Western approach in its more complete empiricism—its lack of large-scale, rationalistic attempts to fathom general laws of nature. Thus, despite extensive biological and physical data, the Chinese did not promote an overall belief that science was key to a basic understanding of the universe. Finally, we will see that at the time Western science began to surge, Chinese intellectual life was becoming more stagnant, a fact that would, ironically, encourage Chinese scholars to ignore Western scientific achievements for some time.

Western science involved popularization as well as basic discoveries. Information about the new science spread widely among the educated public. Scientific societies were founded to promote research. Many business and professional people began to dabble in science, finding new species of plants and animals and participating, however humbly, in this exciting expansion of knowledge. Popularized tracts explained scientific laws and advanced the idea that knowledge was progressing and reason, not faith, was the key to understanding how the physical world works.

Through scientific ferment, which simply grew as time passed, religion declined in importance in providing a basic intellectual framework. Rationalistic science became more vital in shaping habits of thought than ever before, in any civilization. Without necessarily eroding the importance of art, it did supersede creative expression as the foremost cultural influence; as one result, the late 17th and 18th centuries were not particularly significant in terms of stylistic developments, except in music. Scientific thought was heralded as the path to knowledge. And rationalism generated steady progress in the development of such knowledge, as intellectual leaders gradually turned away from a belief that classical learning was the basic path to truth. It was thought that rationalism might have other beneficial effects as well. Scientific writers such as Francis Bacon, in England, argued that further discoveries would lead to technological improvements, making life easier and more rewarding.

These ideas gained ground during the 18th century. Scientific work continued. Chemists discovered much about the functions of oxygen. Biologists acquired increasing knowledge of a variety of animal and plant species. The science of psychology began to take shape, as scholars studied the workings of the human mind.

Another important development involved the effort to apply the principles of the Scientific Revolution to discussions of human nature and human affairs. Enlightenment thinkers, centered in France but operating in many countries, continued to popularize science and to attack errors of faith and superstition. They also developed a number of social sciences by writing of political and economic systems. The basic idea was that rational laws could be applied to social as well as physical behavior, producing an understanding of how humankind throughout the world operates. The Scottish philosopher Adam Smith, in his *Wealth of Nations*, thus posited a number of clear principles of economic behavior, based on the notion that people act according to self-interest and, through competition, would work to promote economic advancement if they are not distracted by government interference. This was a compelling statement of the doctrine of laissez-faire, that private initiative rather than state intervention promotes economic progress. Smith's work was also a groundbreaking treatise on social science, as it suggested that general models of human behavior could be rationally derived.

In addition, Enlightenment thinkers believed in the inherent goodness and rationality of human beings. Progress in knowledge convinced them that more general human progress was also possible. Children can improve through education; old-fashioned methods of discipline were ridiculed. Criminals can become useful members of society if treated humanely; traditional methods of punishment were replaced or outlawed. Political life can improve if people are free, and the state does not try to force religious conformity and pays some attention to popular demands. The Enlightenment did not, in fact, produce a single political theory. Many writers were attracted to the idea of enlightened despotism, believing that a reform-minded ruler could produce social progress. Others talked of the importance of constitutions and parliaments. But they all agreed that political life, like other aspects of life, could be reformed, through rational calculations and a belief in the essential goodness of human nature. Late in the Enlightenment, during the 1780s and 1790s, this thinking even produced statements of socialism, arguing that property laws should be reformed in the name of equality, and of feminism, asserting that women as well as men should participate in political life and benefit from legal reforms.

The Enlightenment, then, served as the intellectual origin of a number of modern impulses in Western society. It set the stage for modern political movements, from liberalism through socialism. In emphasizing secular rather than religious thinking, it outlined a rationalistic approach rooted in social science that continues to describe this part of the Western intellectual world even today. It promoted a host of humanitarian reform movements. Most basically, by extending and translating the results of the Scientific Revolution, it established the framework for modern Western intellectual life. There were changes to come, to be sure. Most Westerners no longer think in precisely the same terms as those of the Enlightenment. However,

many of the issues and fundamental approaches of the Enlightenment remain current. Simply put, the modern way of thinking, in Western society, took shape between about 1680 and 1750.

The Enlightenment hardly resulted in unanimous approval of its basic beliefs. A broader dissemination of some of the basic ideas was still to come. Numerous Christian writers objected vigorously to Enlightenment thinking, and they had many followers. Nonetheless, the Enlightenment was a popularizing movement. Leading writers, such as the Frenchman Voltaire, who argued for human freedom and against church domination, became wealthy through the widespread sale of their works. From the aristocracy to the urban artisanry, many people were aware of at least some of the Enlightenment claims. Huge publishing ventures, such as the *Encyclopédie* in France and later the *Encyclopaedia Britannica* in England, tried to summarize all relevant human knowledge in Enlightenment terms, with an emphasis on science and social science and a pronounced interest in technological improvements. Furthermore, the Enlightenment was essentially a Western-wide movement, striking chords in not only France and Britain but also Italy, Germany, Scandinavia, and the British colonies of North America. In this sense, it rivaled the earlier spread of Christianity in providing a common cultural framework for Western civilization.

TRANSFORMATIONS IN ECONOMIC AND SOCIAL LIFE

The Role of Commerce

During the early modern period, a steady expansion of commerce, along with significant changes in culture, helped transform Western life. Renaissance leaders were proud of the commercial bustle in their cities. Reformation thinkers also tended to favor trade. Luther and Calvin actually influenced the public to discard the traditional belief that merchants might be pursuing false values. Because ordinary people could have direct links with God, the duties and tasks of everyday life were not seen as contradicting religious purposes. Of course, God came first, but commercial success could be construed as proof that God's favor had been won. Not all Protestants became fervent entrepreneurs, however, and Catholic business activities grew as well. But there was some relationship between the spread of Protestantism and the increasing interest in commerce. Finally, the expanding monarchies encouraged merchants to form powerful trading alliances. State backing helped organize great merchant companies to trade with Russia, India, southeast Asia, and the Americas.

SOLVING PROBLEMS

DEALING WITH THE ASIAN ADVANTAGE

As European explorers and traders reached out to the world, they obviously learned more about the manufacturing levels attained in key Asian societies such as China and India, as well as the size and magnificence of many Asian cities. They wanted to take advantage of their new trade contacts, but they also knew they were in many ways operating at a disadvantage.

Several strategies emerged to deal with this problem of relative economic strength. Europeans often used force—their naval strengths backed by gunnery—to compensate for trade deficiencies. This was how Vasco da Gama responded on his second trip to India, and it was an approach used to gain trading footholds along coastlines. Cultural scorn was another response. While many European travelers admired Asia, an attitude quickly developed that called attention to real or imagined Asian sluggishness in technology. Europeans noted and exaggerated Chinese traditionalism, for example, in contrast to their own eagerness to try new methods. A basis emerged, in other words, for claiming European superiority.

For much of the early modern period, the key tactical response involved European transmission of silver mined in Latin America as a means of paying for desired Asian spices and manufactured goods. This compensated for the trading inferiority where European goods alone were involved.

But there was active rivalry, as well, that would ultimately boost European manufacturing. Printed cotton cloth from India was, early on, noted as a desirable consumer good in Europe. It was colorful and relatively inexpensive. European trading companies made strong profits importing cloth for a growing consumer market back home. Gradually, however, European businessmen tried to rival India's output themselves, by setting up production operations. It was hard to compete with the skill and low wages of Indian craftsmen, but by the 18th century, in centers in France and Britain, technologies were introduced to print cloth mechanically in ways that competed with Indian quality and price. Several governments enhanced this gain by slapping high tariffs on Indian goods, helping to nurture a cotton industry that would in turn prove fundamental to the European industrial revolution.

■QUESTIONS: *In what kinds of industries did Asian centers have particular advantages in the early modern period? How did Europeans gradually move from becoming transmitters to producers in the world economy? How much of early modern world history can be explained in terms of European reactions to economic inferiorities?*

Commerce was also stimulated by the new supplies of gold and silver brought back from the New World, particularly from Spain's American colonies. During the 16th century, these precious metals produced a price revolution in Europe. As the supply of money rose on its traditional gold-and-silver base, the production of foods and manufactured goods could not keep pace, and the result was rapid inflation. Rising prices encouraged merchants to take greater risks, because they could borrow money with the understanding that it would be worth less when they had to pay it back. Capitalists also saw the profits to be made in trade with far-flung parts of the world. Asian spices commanded handsome prices. From the late 16th century on, grain from Poland and Russia and furs, sugar, and tobacco from the Americas were imported at increasingly rapid rates, all through trade organized by European merchants.

Commercial expansion began to focus greater attention on Europe's manufacturing base. Growing wealth at home produced new markets for goods, and there was also a need to produce goods to sell to foreign markets. Although most production remained in artisan hands, a significant expansion of domestic manufacturing took place under capitalist auspices. Merchants in this system provided raw materials, particularly textile fibers, to workers scattered in rural settings, who spun and wove the fibers into cloth on simple machines; their products were then collected and paid for, and sold by the merchants on a wide market. Even in the artisan system, commercial expansion created a growing gap between guild masters and their journeymen; as masters pressured their workers to produce more, many journeymen became a permanent paid labor force, manufacturing items such as books, guns, and metal tools for wide market sales.

European technology steadily improved in this climate of economic expansion. Better mining techniques allowed the increased production of iron and coal. Better mill wheels facilitated the processing of grains. Textile equipment,

although still manually guided, was also becoming more sophisticated. By the 17th century, European technology had no peer in the world in most branches of production, and the pace of change continued to be high. Early in the 18th century, the first steam engine was devised in England to pump water out of deep mine shafts. In 1733, the Englishman James Kay invented the flying shuttle, which automatically interwove fibers to make cloth; with this new system, one weaver could now complete the work of two, although the looms were still powered by hand.

Improvements in agriculture were somewhat slower in coming, but the expansion of commerce and the growth of cities encouraged increasing numbers of farmers to produce for the market. Late in the 17th century, Dutch farmers began to experiment with new crops that replenished the fertility of the soil without necessitating periods of fallow, in which nothing could be grown. The Dutch, hard-pressed to support a large population in a small land, also developed new methods of draining swamps and constructing dikes to keep out ocean tides. Interest in agricultural improvement spread further in the 18th century, and many societies were organized to disseminate knowledge of new crops and fertilizers and new machines to sow seeds.

The tide of economic change must not be exaggerated, however. Most people continued to use rather traditional methods, in both agriculture and manufacturing. Most people still did not depend heavily on market sales for their livelihood. The merchant class expanded, but it did not yet command the highest social levels. Many, indeed, still aspired to become aristocrats in their own right, for moneymaking alone did not provide adequate prestige. Nonetheless, western Europe became more substantially commercialized than ever before. Enlightenment thinkers, generally hostile to the aristocracy, which they saw as an idle class, praised hard work and profitmaking, a sign that social values were changing even before the social structure had been revolutionized.

One clear effect of commercial expansion was that Europe's wealth increased. An Englishman, writing in the late 1580s about village life, noted "three things to be marvelously altered in England within his own sound remembrance." First, farmers' cottages had more chimneys, which meant they were bigger and better heated. Second, beds and pillows had replaced straw mats for sleeping. Third, pewterware, instead of wooden utensils, was used for eating. With time, the list of advances in the standard of living continued to expand. By the early 1600s, French peasants began to consume wine fairly regularly with their meals. This was a sign of greater wealth, and also of the growing market production of wines, which could not be effected in every area of France. A frenzy of tulip buying occurred in the Netherlands in the early 17th century, one of Europe's first great consumer fads. People invested in tulip bulbs, tried to be the first to have a new flower, and even bought pictures of tulips. By 1700, ordinary people in western Europe were consuming coffee, tea, and sugar—all imported goods that they had to buy on the market and that they therefore had to have enough money to afford. By this time, European farmers and artisans had far more objects in their possession—tools, furnishings, and the like—than any other people in the world. Consumerism advanced still further in the 18th century.

However, new wealth was by no means evenly distributed. Some parts of the Western world were richer than others. Material standards lagged in Germany, in part because of the devastation of the Thirty Years War. They also lagged in Spain, where merchant activity remained rather low despite the influx of wealth from the colonies; most Spanish gold passed to the vigorous merchants and banks of northern Europe. Social disparities also intensified. As a core group of farmers or peasants increased in size—the people who could sell to urban markets and whose standard of living thus rose—the poverty of those without property also grew. Western Europe by the 17th century faced significant problems of poor relief. Almshouses and other institutions designed to aid the poor, but also to isolate them, were one common result. The existence of growing pockets of poverty amid rising wealth represented another important theme for European society; it is a social contradiction with which Westerners are still grappling today.

Social and economic change also produced recurrent unrest. Many journeymen resented the growing power of guild masters and formed associations to promote their own interests. The first strikes in Western history occurred during the Renaissance. Riots were even more common, continuing a theme from the later Middle Ages. Peasants periodically rebelled against ever steeper exactions from landlords. Both rural and urban riots commonly arose when grain and bread were in short supply. Considerable popular unrest accompanied the tensions of the Reformation. French peasants rose in many regions during the 1590s, in the aftermath of the religious wars. They attacked their landlords, who "had reduced them to starvation, violated their wives and daughters, stolen their cattle and wasted their land," while urban merchants with whom they had to trade sought "only the ruin of the poor people, for our ruin is their wealth." Popular unrest also surfaced during the English civil wars, with farmers and urban workers organizing to demand political rights and economic reforms. These uprisings produced an amazing series of revolts around 1648, in not only England but also southern Italy and elsewhere. Protest declined somewhat during the next decades, partly because population growth, which had been substantial during the 16th century, leveled off. But the early modern period was not a peaceful time in Western society, even aside from the recurrent wars.

The Role of the Family

Social change also involved the Western family. During the 15th and 16th centuries, the characteristic structure of the family began to shift, producing a "European-style" family that was quite different from the patterns of most other agricultural societies. The contributing factors were simple. First, common people began to marry at a rather late age—about 27 or 28 (members of the aristocracy, in contrast, married much earlier). A rather sizable minority of ordinary people never married at all. The reason for these developments was a desire to protect family property against the demands of too many children. Late marriages led to reduced birth rates, so that a given family did not have more than three or four children living to adulthood. While understandable, such a system required considerable self-control and family supervision, for it meant that young people passed many years between puberty and the point at which heterosexual activity was generally permissible—in marriage. Tensions increased between young adults and older parents, for economic independence and marriage normally depended on the death or retirement of the elderly. Suspicion and fear led many older people to prepare careful contracts to spell out what support they would receive from their children if they turned over their land. The new family pattern also promoted greater interaction between men and women. Men remained officially and legally the heads of their families. But with the emphasis now on rather small units, a husband and wife and their children, economic cooperation between men and women increased. Generally, the new family structure shielded Europeans from the population density that had long been a fact of life in east Asian and Indian society.

During the 17th century and beyond, changes in the quality of family life contributed to earlier structural shifts. Europeans began to spend more leisure time within the family environment. Meals at home became more elaborate than before. This was partly the result of growing wealth, but it also involved some explicit choices. Women became the family agents who regulated its social life, preparing more intricate dishes and presiding over mealtime ceremonies and conversation. Here was a new aspect of Western family life that continued to gain in importance until very recently.

Family affection was also increasingly encouraged. Seventeenth-century Protestant writers stressed the importance of love as an ingredient of family life. As one English minister put it, "Keep up your Conjugal Love in a constant heat and vigor." This growing emphasis on the family as a center of emotional pleasure, which spread to Catholic areas by the 18th century, resulted in significant transformation. Fostered by religious developments, it may also have been a reaction to rapid social and economic change in the wider environment; families were seen as a comfortable and reliable refuge. Here, too, themes were set in motion that perpetuated to recent times. There were implications, finally, for the treatment of children within this new family environment. By the late 17th century, many writers were advocating love, rather than harsh physical discipline, as the means of raising children. They developed the revolutionary idea that parents owed children certain rights and protections, rather than espousing the traditional belief that children were obliged to accept whatever their parents might impose. The implications for women of all this change were not so clear. Their role in the family other than as bearers of children improved, but opportunities narrowed; in Protestant areas, the abolition of religious orders made marriage even more important for women.

Overall, changes for women pointed in conflicting directions. Their family status improved, but they were more tied to it. Skilled urban jobs became harder to get, as male guilds pushed women out. The interdependence of men and women in Europe's nuclear families might encourage joint decision-making, but it could promote dispute. Some women gained new education, but the Reformation stressed the father as the family's Bible-reader and moral guide. During times of ferment, such as the English civil wars, women petitioned for political attention, but they were turned away. Even the freedom-loving

Enlightenment mainly ignored women or ridiculed their intellectual powers. But some upper-class women gained prestige by sponsoring *salons*—receptions—for male artists and philosophers. Finally, the emergence of greater consumerism emphasized attractive clothing for women, as if the gender had a particular obligation to be pretty.

Changes in family life, along with the shifts in broader economic and social structure, reveal a society that was beginning to alter some very basic patterns. Fundamental features of daily existence, even human emotion or at least its recommended expression, were taking new forms. Here was a potential source of further change as well. As an example, if parents began to change the way they treated their children, spanking them less often, drawing them more actively into an orbit of parental affection, these children might mature into somewhat different kinds of adults. During the 18th century, child-rearing practices changed still further. Widespread Western practices of swaddling young children—wrapping them tightly so that parents could work without worrying about their coming to harm—began to disappear. Children grew up a bit freer, receiving more active adult care in place of physical restraints. These changes, widely urged by Enlightenment writers, who believed that children improved through better treatment, had significant implications for Western adults. If child-rearing became freer, might adults not also seek greater liberty?

HOW EARLY MODERN TRENDS IN THE WEST INTERRELATED

The various trends of early modern Western society did not neatly mesh. There was overlap, to be sure. Commercial development and economic expansion were encouraged by some of the ideas of the Renaissance and Reformation, although not always intentionally; economic change also was the catalyst for some of the key values of the Enlightenment. Increased interest in carefully planned organization showed in business ventures, publishing, and government bureaucracy. Even more amorphous values, such as greater individualism, related cultural and religious movements to capitalism and possibly to family organization—the family was seen less as an economic institution, more as an emotional bond among individuals.

On the other hand, different currents had varied results, and many key shifts were slow and uneven. Changes in beliefs and the economy, however, added up to a major strain on people at various levels. One key symptom was a wave of witchcraft trials that occurred in many parts of western Europe, and ultimately New England, from the late 15th century until the middle of the 17th century. Europeans had long believed in witches and magical powers, but they had never considered these forces to be such ominous threats as they did during these decades, when witchcraft trials sent hundreds of accused people to death and involved many thousands in mounting hysteria. Many factors were behind this sweeping fear. New anxieties about the poor were one cause, because many of the accused were among those bypassed by the growing prosperity. Protestant–Catholic divisions, shaking convictions about where religious truth lay, contributed to the fear. So did uncertainties about the changing roles of women and the elderly in the family (most accused witches were female, said to be "used by the devil," and a disproportionate number were elderly). There were also new confusions about how to respond to sickness (whether through doctors or by superstitious remedies). A new belief system was taking shape in Western society, but its early stages left many people insecure and fearful.

Just as the witchcraft hysteria stemmed from a variety of intense concerns generated by change, so the end of the witchcraft trials signified the continuing spread of new ideas about how to understand the world. Growing numbers of officials and ordinary people simply stopped believing that witchcraft was a real phenomenon, capable of disrupting the laws of nature. Although beliefs in witchcraft persisted and a few trials continued into the 18th century, the craze ended in most places by the 1680s. The spread of Enlightenment ideas in later decades, although again not universal in a society in which most people still could not read, was a further sign that the Western outlook was shifting in some common directions.

For all its tensions and confusions, the fact remained that by the 18th century, western Europe had created a distinctive kind of agricultural society, compared to the traditions of the other great civilizations of the world. Its unusual qualities stemmed primarily from the changes that had been occurring since the late 15th century at almost all levels of social activity. The West was unusually commercial, unusually scientific, and shaped by family structures that encouraged property control and considerable individualism. Not accidentally, Western society was simultaneously extending its influence to the rest of the world, despite political organizations that were in many ways inferior to the world's great empires of the time.

PATHS TO THE PRESENT

Many features of modern Western civilization were born in the transformations of the early modern period. The most obvious legacy of this time is the importance of science and its ramifications in other intellectual domains and in popular culture. In addition, people of means now expected to profit from activities in the world economy. Assumptions about the logic of the nation-state as a unit of political organization are another legacy. They

have dimmed with the growing importance of supranational collaborations, but continue to influence Western society.

Developments of the 18th century have continued and amplified. The new emphasis on romance as the basis for marriage and the assumptions about the educability of children are two important examples of this. Modern consumerism clearly emerged 300 years ago, and even though it has exploded, it still exists within a framework already definable by 1750.

Eighteenth-century attitudes toward poverty, redefined from the 16th century, continue to crop up in Western discourse. The notion that poverty results from the faults of the poor is challenged in contemporary social policies in the West, but it endures.

Still more major changes were to come, of course: the West of 1750 was not the West of today. For instance, the Industrial Revolution was a profound intervening development. But even these changes were shaped by the values and institutions launched in early modern times.

SUGGESTED WEB SITES

On the Renaissance, see http://renaissance.dm .net/ and http://www.ibiblio.org/wm/paint/ glo/renaissance/; on the Renaissance and baroque architecture, see http://www.lib .virginia.edu/dic/colls/arh102/; on the Protestant Reformation, see http://www.mun. ca/rels/reform/reform.html and http://www .newgenevacenter.org/west/reformation.htm; on printing during the Renaissance and Reformation, see http://www.sc.edu/library/ spcoll/sccoll/renprint/renprint.html; and on exploring the early Americas, see http://www .loc.gov/exhibits/.

SUGGESTED READINGS

For an overview of developments in Western society during this period, including extensive bibliographies, see Sheldon Watt, *A Social History of Western Europe,*

1450–1720 (1984), and John Merriman, *History of Modern European Civilization*, Vol. 1 (1996). Charles Tilly's *Big Structures, Large Processes, Huge Comparisons* (1985) offers an analytical framework based on major change; see also Tilly's edited volume, *The Formation of National States in Western Europe* (1975), and Fernand Braudel, *Civilization and Capitalization*, 3 vols. (1952). Coverage of the Renaissance and the religious transformations can be found in J. F. New, *The Renaissance and Reformation: A Short History* (1977); K. H. Kannenfeldt, ed., *The Renaissance: Medieval or Modern* (1959); J. Atkinson, *Martin Luther and the Birth of Protestantism* (1981); J. H. Plumb, *The Italian Renaissance* (1986); O. Chadwick, *The Reformation* (1983); Steven Ozment, *The Age of Reform, 1520–1550* (1980); and Hubert Jedin and John Dolan, eds., *Reformation and Counter Reformation* (1980). On the important changes in science, consult H. Butterfield, *Origins of Modern Science* (1965), and A. R. Hall, *From Galileo to Newton, 1630–1720* (1982). On important transformations in popular life and behavior during the period, see Peter Burke, *Popular Culture in Early Modern Europe* (1978); P. Stearns, ed., *The Other Side of Western Civilization*, Vol. 2, 6th ed. (1999); Jeffrey Pilcher, *Food in World History* (2006); and Merry Wiesner Hanks, *Women and Gender in Early Modern Europe* (1993). See also Robert Duplessis, *Transitions to Capitalism in Early Modern Europe* (1997).

For additional recent work, see Samuel Cohn, *The Black Death Transformed* (2002); Andrew Zega, *Palaces of the Sun King: Versailles, Trianon, Marly* (2002); Elizabeth Cohen, *Daily Life in Renaissance Italy* (2001); Alina Payne, *Antiquity and Its Interpreters* (2000); George L. Hersey, *Architecture and Geometry in the Age of the Baroque* (2000); John J. Hurt, *Louis XIV and the Parlements: The Assertion of Royal Authority* (2002); Katherine A. Lynch, *Individuals, Families and Communities in Europe, 1200–1800: The Urban Foundations of Western Society* (2003); Charles R. Mack, *Looking at the Renaissance: Essays Toward a Contextual Appreciation* (2005); Julia Crick and Alexandra Walsham, eds., *The Uses of Script and Print, 1300–1700* (2004); Wilbur Applebaum, *The Scientific Revolution and the Foundations of Modern Science* (2005); Peter Robert Dear, *Revolutionizing the Sciences: European Knowledge and Its Ambitions, 1500–1700* (2001); Andrew Pettegree, *Reformation and the Culture of Persuasion* (2005); Ulinka Rublack, *Reformation Europe* (2005); David Bagchi and David C. Steinmetz, eds., *The Cambridge Companion to Reformation Theology* (2004); and Peter A. Coclanis, ed., *The Atlantic Economy During the Seventeenth and Eighteenth Centuries: Organization, Operation, Practice and Personnel* (2005).

18 The Rise of Russia

Along with Africa and the Americas, eastern and east central Europe were dramatically affected by the rise of the West during the early modern period. By the 18th century, some smaller regions, such as Poland, produced cheap grains for export to the West, using serf labor in a fashion not unlike the estate systems in Latin America. The Russian story was more complex, however, Russian dynamism involved many factors, and not just contact with the West, as if formed a great empire of its own. Yet, in contrast to the Americas, where local populations had little choice, Russian leaders deliberately chose to imitate certain Western ways. This pattern began haltingly in the 16th century and then accelerated during the 18th century. Explicit choice did not preclude important tensions as the Russian economy experienced still more Western influence and cultural reactions formed against too much imitation. Nonetheless, Russia's relation to the West remained unique.

One reason for the distinctiveness lay in the new trend toward expansion, initiated in the 15th century, that to begin with had nothing to do with the West. Russia's dynamism increased long before it had significant contacts with the West. Western techniques were later courted, although very selectively, to help maintain the surge of expansion.

What causes a civilization to rise? The question, now a familiar one, remains complex. Western civilization expanded on the basis of a diverse but distinctive culture, which produced an aggressive, conquering spirit, plus, a rapidly improving technology. Russia's case, coincident in time, was different. Shaking off Mongol domination, the Russians embarked on a policy of conquest without a major technological impetus.

Russia shared some expansionist thinking with the West. Both could look back to the precedent of the Roman Empire as an example of what societies could do when they were truly great. Both were Christian, and although the Russian missionary spirit was perhaps less active than that of the West, Christianity may help explain a common desire to achieve new victories. However, Russia long lagged behind the West technologically; it remained backward by Western standards into the 20th century. It lacked the merchant tradition or commercial expertise of the West; indeed, Russia during the early modern period depended considerably on Western-directed trade patterns. In these respects, Russian differences from the West increased in the early modern period.

Russia did have a large and gradually growing population. It occupied a strategic geographical location, hovering between Europe and Asia, surrounded, except in the north, by few natural barriers. This position made it vulnerable to invasion, as the Mongols had proved, but it also facilitated expansion when the Russians decided to follow the Mongol example. Russia also had the advantage of excellent natural resources, although its climate placed certain limits on agriculture. Russia's iron ore spurred manufacturing and weaponry. Furs and timber could be traded not only with the West but also with Asia, which helped fuel expansion.

The early modern period saw an elaboration of characteristic Russian social and political institutions. Earlier, Russian civilization had been barely defined. Now, building on many precedents, it was more fully formed. It became increasingly important as the Russians constructed one of the world's great empires.

KEY QUESTIONS   *Russia proved to be the most successful of the land-based "gunpowder empires" formed in the early modern period. How does it compare to the other empires, such as the Ottoman or Mughal? How, also, did it change, when its characteristics of 1750 are compared with those of 1450? Russia's contacts with the West set the final main questions: what did Russia westernize, and why, and what did it shelter from westernization?*

PATTERNS OF EARLY MODERN RUSSIAN HISTORY

Russia's emergence as a new power, first in eastern Europe and western Asia and ultimately on a still larger scale, depended initially on its winning freedom from Mongol (Tatar) control. Mongol influence had not reshaped Russian institutions significantly, although many Russians had adopted Mongol styles of dress and social habits. Most Russians remained Orthodox Christians; most maintained a separate identity from that of the Mongols. Moreover, local Russian princes had continued to rule, although paying tribute to their Mongol military overlords. It was the duchy of Moscow that served as the center for the Russian liberation effort, beginning in the 14th century. Under Ivan III, or Ivan the Great, who claimed succession from the Rurik dynasty, a large part of Russia was finally freed after 1462. Ivan organized a strong army—giving the new government a military emphasis it long retained. He also capitalized on Russian and Orthodox loyalties—that is, a kind of nationalism along with religion—to win support for his campaigns. By 1480, Moscow had been freed from Mongol control and acquired a vast territory running from the borders of Poland, in the west, to the Ural Mountains.

It was under Ivan that Russian beliefs in an imperial mission took on a new shape. Ivan's marriage to the niece of the last Byzantine emperor prompted him to proclaim himself the protector of all Orthodox churches and also to insist that Russia had succeeded Byzantium as the "third Rome." Accordingly, Ivan entitled himself *tsar*, or Caesar—the "autocrat of all the Russians." The next important tsar, Ivan IV, or Ivan the Terrible, attacked the Russian nobles whom he suspected of conspiracy; many were killed. But Russian expansion continued nevertheless. Ivan III and Ivan IV encouraged some peasants to migrate to the lands seized from the Mongols and other groups, particularly in the south, along the Caspian Sea, and in the Urals. These peasant-adventurers, called *cossacks*, were true Russian pioneers, combining agricultural skills with impressive military prowess on horseback. During the 16th century, the cossacks not only completed their conquest of the Caspian Sea area but also, early in the century, moved across the Ural Mountains into Siberia, beginning the gradual takeover and settlement of these vast plains.

Russian expansion occurred despite the setbacks the Russian economy and culture had suffered under Mongol rule. Russia had become almost entirely agricultural, its earlier urban and merchant past largely forgotten. There was little trade and only localized manufacturing; although some commerce developed with central Asia, creating regional economic ties, subsistence agriculture predominated. Not only peasants but also many landlords lived under poor material conditions. Rates of illiteracy were unusually high for an agricultural society, and artistic and literary production had almost ceased. In this situation, Russia was open to new influences from western Europe, with its expanding commercial powers. Ivan III had been eager to launch diplomatic missions to leading Western states as a symbol of Russia's renewed independence and a sign that it wanted contact with the Western network of international relations. During the reign of Ivan IV, British merchants established trading relations with Russia, selling manufactured products in exchange for furs and raw materials. Soon, outposts of Western merchants were established in Moscow and other centers.

Ivan IV's death without an heir set off the Time of Troubles, early in the 17th century, in which Russian nobles, the boyars, attacked tsarist power; several neighboring states, including Sweden and Poland, captured Russian territory. However, in 1613, a noble assembly chose a member of the Romanov family as tsar; this family ruled Russia until the great revolution of 1917. Michael Romanov drove out foreign invaders and restored order, although the power of the nobles limited the tsarist government until late in the 17th century. Even amid some confusion, however, Russian military efforts continued; successful wars against Poland resulted in the annexation of the Ukraine, including Kiev, and extended Russian boundaries in southeastern Europe to the Ottoman Empire. Russian settlers moved into some of these areas, forming new minorities, and use of the Russian language gradually spread.

A second Romanov, Alexis, restored tsarist autocracy by abolishing the assemblies of nobles and claiming new authority over the Russian church. Alexis was eager not only to gain power, but also to purge the Orthodox church of many of the superstitions that had developed during Mongol rule. His reform movement, however, antagonized some Russians, who were known as Old Believers; their resistance to church reforms caused thousands of them to be exiled to Siberia or southern Russia, where they extended Russia's colonizing activities. Alexis also developed cultural as well as economic contacts with Western nations.

Alexis's son, Peter I, or Peter the Great (1689–1725), greatly expanded his father's work. He was an energetic leader of exceptional intelligence. A giant himself, standing 6 feet, 8 inches tall, he was eager to reform his giant nation still further. He traveled widely in the West, incognito, seeking Western allies for a crusade against Turkish power in Europe. He even worked as a ship's carpenter in Holland, gaining an interest in Western science and technology and bringing back scores of Western artisans with him to Russia. Politically, Peter defended tsarist autocracy firmly, vanquishing revolts with great cruelty. In foreign policy, Peter attacked the Ottoman Empire without significant results, then warred with Sweden, winning extensive Russian territory on the eastern coast of the Baltic Sea and reducing Sweden to the status of a second-rate power.

Russia now had a "window on the Baltic," including an ice-free port, and from this time on became a major player in European diplomatic and military conflict. Peter the Great, in accordance with his desire to reform Russia in some Western directions, commemorated Russia's emergence into the European diplomatic orbit by moving his capital from Moscow to a new Baltic city that he named St. Petersburg.

Internally, Peter's reforms concentrated mainly on streamlining Russia's bureaucratic and military apparatus and increasing central control under the tsar. He improved the organization and weaponry of the army and, with help from Western advisors, created the first Russian navy. New munitions factories and shipyards facilitated this effort, and a substantial iron industry developed: Russia did not depend on the West for weapons production. Peter eliminated former noble councils, establishing a set of advisors under his control and a specialized set of ministries in their stead. The central government appointed provincial governors, and although town councils were elected, here too a tsar-appointed magistrate served as the final authority. The church was placed still more firmly under state control, with the tsar as head of the church and a committee of bishops, under his direction, responsible for running religious affairs. Peter's regime rationalized law codes and extended them throughout the empire. The tax system was reformed, and taxes on ordinary Russian peasants steadily increased. Finally, the bureaucrats who ran the government were given special training, and Peter relied on non-nobles as well as nobles in his search for the best possible talents.

Peter the Great thus sought to create a state and military force that could compete with those of his rivals and peers in western Europe. He also introduced some additional reforms designed to make Russian manners—particularly those of the aristocracy—more westernized. Edicts were issued requiring nobles to shave off their beards and wear Western dress; in symbolic ceremonies, Peter removed the Mongol features, for instance, long sleeves, of nobles' garments. Women in the upper classes were encouraged to become less isolated. Upper-class women could attend theater and ballet, as in the West. Peter abolished a wedding tradition whereby the bride's father handed a whip to the groom, symbolizing the transfer of male power. Russia even imported the custom of Christmas trees, from Germany. These reforms were more than cosmetic. They were designed to enhance Russia in Western eyes and to jolt the noble class out of their established routine.

This was, however, a very selective process of westernization. Although the education and culture of the aristocracy were profoundly altered (enhancing the tsar's control along with westernizing much of the ruling class), the conditions of the masses were not significantly changed. Peter had no desire to initiate wage labor, as opposed to serfdom, in western Europe. Nor was he interested in the parliamentary monarchies of the

Tsar Peter the Great cutting off the beard of an Orthodox Old Believer. This 18th-century cartoon shows the westernization of hair styles.

West. Nor, finally, did he wish to fully imitate the Western economy. His technological borrowing focused on heavy industry and munitions. He did not encourage a massive merchant class or a major role in the world economy. Westernization increased Russia's economic contacts with the West, as not only technology but artistic items had to be imported, paid for by growing raw materials and grain exports. Russia was an unequal partner in this trade, which was handled for the most part by Western trading companies. But the bulk of the Russian economy remained outside this orbit, focusing on agriculture and limited trade with central Asia; it remained far different from its counterpart in the West.

Peter's death in 1724 was followed by several decades of weak rule, dominated by various power plays among army officers who guided the selection of several ineffective emperors and empresses. Peter III, the nephew of Peter the Great's youngest daughter, reached the throne in 1762. He himself was retarded, but his wife, a German-born princess who changed her name to Catherine, soon took matters in hand and continued to rule as empress after Peter III's death. Catherine—later, Catherine the Great—flirted with the ideas of the French Enlightenment, summoning various reform commissions that did very little. In fact, her goals continued to be those of her illustrious predecessors: to centralize power under the crown and enlarge Russia's territory. She put down a vigorous peasant uprising, led by Emelian Pugachev, who was subsequently executed. She used the Pugachev rebellion as an excuse to extend the powers of the central government in regional affairs, while confirming the nobles' control over most of the land. Catherine resumed Peter the Great's campaigns against the Ottoman Empire, with much greater success; she won new territories, including the Crimea, bordering the Black Sea. Catherine also accelerated Russian interference in Polish affairs, finally agreeing with Austria and Prussia to divide, or partition, this once vigorous state. Three partitions of Poland, in 1772, 1793, and 1795, finally eliminated Poland as an independent state,

giving Russia the lion's share of the spoils. Finally, Catherine speeded the colonization of Russia's holdings in Siberia and encouraged further exploration, claiming the territory of Alaska. Russian explorers even moved down the Pacific coast of North America into what is now northern California, while tens of thousands of pioneers spread over Siberia.

By the time of Catherine's death in 1796, Russia had passed through slightly more than three centuries of extraordinary development. It had freed itself from all traces of foreign rule, had constructed a strong central state, and perhaps most importantly of all, had extended its control over the largest land empire in the world at that point.

Russia's expansion had followed three basic directions. First, it had moved eastward, into the vast stretches of Siberia, most of which had previously been inhabited by hunting-and-gathering peoples. This expansion had brought Russia to China's borders, which were regulated by the 18th-century Amur River agreement. Russia's thrust into east Asia was bolstered by vigorous, sometimes forced, colonization; being "sent to Siberia" was no 20th-century invention, as thousands of Old Believers and other dissidents could attest. Siberia also offered new lands for agriculture; colonization not only added to Russian resources but also benefited some of the colonizers.

The second direction of Russia's expansion was toward the south, into central Asia. This expansion brought Russia to the borders of the Ottoman Empire, and Russia's increasingly successful rivalry with this empire was a key factor in Ottoman decline. Russia's central Asian holdings resulted in Russian control over a number of diverse ethnic groups, mostly Muslim. This control was again enhanced by vigorous colonization by the cossacks, bringing not only Russian rule but also a strong ethnic Russian presence into this region. Russian occupation of central Asia eliminated once and for all this region's long-standing role as a center of periodic invasions directed at other parts of Europe and Asia.

Finally, Russia moved westward along the Baltic and into Poland. By 1796, Russian borders

WORLD PROFILES

CATHERINE THE GREAT
(1762–1796)

Catherine the Great was one of the most important rulers in Russian history and the only
woman in their number. A German-born princess,
she married Peter III, who was mentally impaired, and
soon took over effective control of the government.
She continued to rule as tsarina after Peter III's
death. True to her own origins and the legacy of
Peter the Great, Catherine continued a program of
westernization. In the 1762 portrait shown here, she
appears dressed in Western fashion—although with a
military emphasis that was no accident. Catherine
also maintained more distinctive Russian traditions
and was not willing to allow Western influences to
weaken her autocratic power. Many of her reform
moves, as a result, were mere facades. Catherine was
also responsible for laws that gave nobles more
power over their serfs and, at the end of her life, for
banning Western contacts and Western-inspired
writings during the French Revolution. In addition to
her impact on Russian history, which included successful expansion, Catherine was one of the liveliest
personalities of world history, her person inspiring
numerous stories and myths of great and varied sexual appetites. Even with the advantages of noble birth
and marriage, what qualities does a woman need to
make this kind of mark in history?

Catherine the Great, woman of uncommon power.

met those of Prussia and Habsburg Austria; most
of the smaller nations of eastern Europe had
been eliminated. Here, too, Russia assumed control
over the government of many minority peoples,
including various Slavic groups, some Germans,
and many Jews. The Russian empire propelled
itself into the mainstream of European diplomacy, winning alliances at various points with a
number of Scandinavian and central European

nations and increasing both naval and overland
access further into Europe.

Russian expansion was by no means complete by 1800. Further efforts to expand extended
in all three directions. The Russian government
had established a clear and successful tradition of
careful military aggrandizement. Segments of the
Russian people had demonstrated a vigorous
pioneering spirit, which took them into new,

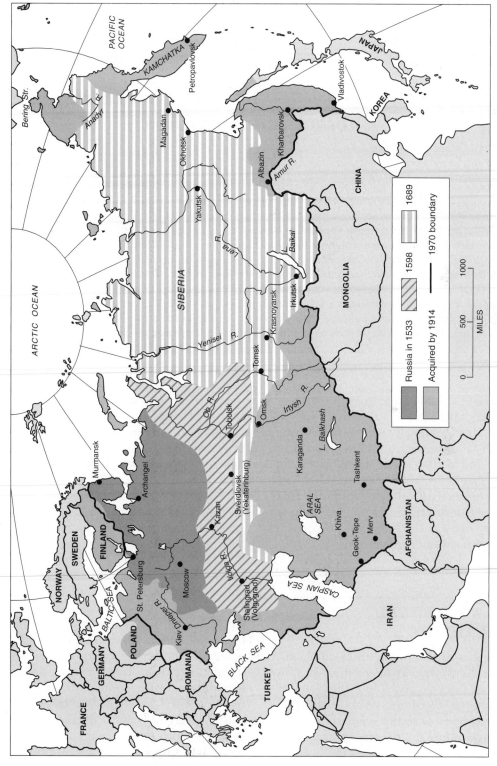

Russian Expansion in Europe and Asia

HISTORY DEBATE

A RUSSIAN CIVILIZATION?

Historians continue to wonder how best to fit Russia into the larger patterns of world history. A traditional impulse among Western historians was to include Russia as part of overall European history from the 15th century on. In the 1970s, even at the height of the cold war, a French leader said that Russia was at least as European as England was. However, Russia has never been fully Western (although, of course, it may become so in the future, as many Russians currently hope and as others fear). In the 15th and 16th centuries, even as Italian artists and technical advisors were brought in, Moscow's high culture remained Byzantine; libraries, although still small, were filled with Byzantine books, mainly religious. Social structures remained dramatically different from those in the West. Russia was also heavily influenced by central Asia. The tsar called himself the khan of the north, to impress central Asian peoples, and individuals from this region took oaths of loyalty on the Qur'an. Central Asian models long guided the bureaucracy. Clearly, Russia emerged as a civilization under mixed influences, which it continued to blend when more extensive, although selective, westernization began. The issue of how European Russia was, aside from geography, depends on what factors we use to determine the basic nature of a society.

---

sometimes hostile lands, quite like the settlers of North America during the same period. Not too long after 1800, a French aristocrat, Alexis de Tocqueville, commenting on the dynamism of the new United States, compared American growth to that of the world's "sleeping giant"—Russia. He predicted that these two pioneering nations would someday emerge even more strongly in world affairs, and that they resembled each other, in their exuberant growth, more than anyone yet realized. His foresight was impressive.

RUSSIAN POLITICAL INSTITUTIONS

Russia's political structure was firmly autocratic, a centralized government under the tsar. This structure had been suggested in earlier Russian history, through Byzantine example and the Orthodox tradition of church–state unity; it was further enhanced by the military government's need to expel the Mongols and by the example of the khans. Russia's steady territorial expansion was aided by such a strong central government and, in turn, served to bolster the regime.

Russian tsars did not, to be sure, develop extensive direct contacts with ordinary Russian subjects, although they claimed to be "fathers" to their people. Newly acquired territories were often run for a time rather separately from tsarist control, by freedom-minded cossacks. Only gradually did the tsarist government regularize all their holdings. Most peasants were ruled by noble landlords, particularly during the 17th and 18th centuries. They had scant access to tsarist courts but, rather, were confined to a judicial system directed by their own landlords. Peasants on a given estate regulated their own mutual relations through village governments, which tried to settle land disputes and other matters on the basis of communal tradition. Because of the power of landlords and the importance of village, or *mir*, governments, Russia was in some ways quite decentralized, as Latin America was becoming, although without the colonial overlay. At this point, the Russian empire could not compare to its Chinese counterpart in size or the varied functions of its bureaucracy.

However, the tsars did wield great power, and by the 18th century there was no formal institution to check their power. Like China, for example, but unlike the Western monarchies, the tsars established a secret police to prevent dissent and to supervise the bureaucracy. The Chancery of Secret Police was initially established by Peter the Great and survived, although under different names and with changing functions, until the late 20th century.

One key to the tsars' great power rested in their special relationship with the nobility—the Russian boyars. At the end of the period of Mongol rule, the boyars possessed extensive landholdings and hereditary titles. There was potential here for significant aristocratic defiance of the tsars' wishes. Periodically, as during the Time of Troubles, this kind of opposition did develop; it had some institutional base, for a time, in the councils of nobles called to determine tsarist succession. But Russians had no tradition of feudalism to compare with that of the West. Furthermore, Russia's rapid expansion allowed tsars to grant additional lands to new nobles, whose loyalties were more firmly tied to the crown. Here was a key way in which military expansion strengthened tsarist rule and encouraged the tsars to continue seeking more territory. From Ivan III on, tsars steadily pressed both new and old nobles to serve the state as military commanders and bureaucrats; they were not allowed to develop separate political loyalties. Thus, Russia's aristocracy differed crucially from its counterpart in the West, because it viewed itself as an extension of the state rather than as a force of partial opposition. Later tsars, such as Peter the Great, in promoting new bureaucrats to aristocratic ranks, reinforced this state-service orientation. They could not tamper with social structure, lest they offend their aristocratic allies.

In many ways, the expansion of the tsarist state resembled the rise of the absolute monarchy in western Europe. Indeed, Peter the Great deliberately copied some of the organizational and military structures of states such as Prussia. In the West, as in Russia, aristocratic power declined in relation to that of the central state. The collapse of the nobles' councils in Russia was reminiscent of the long period in which the French Parliament was not convened. The seeming resemblance between their government and that of much of the West encouraged rulers such as Catherine the Great to dabble in the Western theories of enlightened despotism. Nonetheless, similarity was not identity. Russia lacked the church–state division and the feudal and parliamentary traditions that still flourished in the West. It did not generate the constitutional political theories that developed in the West during this period, and indeed Russian rulers were at pains to censor literature incorporating this kind of Western thought. It was not astonishing, then, that when political revolution rekindled the idea of limiting monarchical power in the West, from 1789 on, Russia stayed resolutely apart.

Russia's efforts at partial westernization, not surprisingly, confirmed the empire's autocratic tradition. Under Peter the Great and Catherine the Great, change came from the top down. It increased the hold of the tsar over the nobles, while genuinely seeking to retrain them. No Western monarch treated the aristocracy in such a superior manner, as Peter did in patronizingly and publicly ridiculing the traditional costumes of his boyars. None tried to impose education on them, as Peter did in requiring that all nobles and other bureaucrats learn mathematics. Russian bureaucratic procedures and culture may indeed have benefited from this forced dose of westernization, in the form of better schools, increased literacy, and more science. But it was clear that this kind of reform movement reflected and enhanced the special place of an autocratic central government in Russian political life.

RUSSIAN CULTURE

For most Russian people, culture during the early modern period meant the Orthodox religion and traditional forms of oral expression—the heroic epics, the rich musical life, the often witty proverbs designed to explain life's vagaries. The carefully structured rituals of the Orthodox church and the worship of many saints allowed ordinary Russians to pray for victories or for protection from disease and famine. They represented the focal point of an elaborate system of festivals, more numerous in Russia than in the West, in which feasting and celebration contrasted with the ordinary, often harsh, routine of work. Early modern Russia did not experience the change in popular culture that was occurring in the West.

Russian cultural traditions revived in many ways after the Mongol period. From the 15th to the 17th century, icon painting became increasingly distinctive as a Russian art form. From individual heads of saints and the Holy Family, Russian painters moved to more abstract and complex religious scenes. In literature, the tradition of narrative histories and chronicles written by monks resumed. Church building picked up

again, not only in Moscow but also in regional centers such as Kiev.

During the early modern period as a whole, however, Russian culture was marked by important tensions—between popular tradition and elite tastes and between westernizing tendencies and a desire to define special Russian characteristics. Under Ivan the Great and Ivan the Terrible, Italian architects were summoned to design church buildings and the magnificent tsarist palace in the Kremlin in Moscow. These architects did not introduce Western styles without modification. They generated some fusion between Renaissance classicism and Russian building traditions, producing the ornate, onion-shaped domes that became characteristic of Russian (and other east European) churches.

With Peter the Great and Catherine the Great, the desire to westernize went even further.

Miracle of St. George and the Dragon, early 16th century.

Russian religious art: Icon of the Annunciation, Moscow school.

however, before 1800, elite culture was largely imitative.

Furthermore, Western influence was by no means uniformly welcomed. Ordinary Russian peasants, even the provincial nobility, were largely unaffected by these developments. A growing cultural gap between the upper class and the masses developed that was resolved only through revolution in the 20th century. Some literate priests and nobles protested westernization in the name of an often vaguely defined Russian soul. One wrote to the tsar Alexis: "You feed the foreigners too well, instead of bidding your folk to cling to the old customs." A number of cultural leaders tried to articulate traditional or "patriotic" forms opposed to the new influences.

Russian culture during the early modern period thus saw important improvements represented by revitalized art forms and some fruitful mergers with Western styles. Literacy and schooling advanced, although only a minority of Russians benefited; few Russians entered an essentially Western intellectual orbit. But this was not yet an integrated culture. While a revived interest in science and new forms of painting and architecture were significant influences in Russian intellectual life, the most enduring single legacy was a heritage of ambivalence about Russia's relationship to the West. Collectively, after a period of stagnation in their own nation's artistic development, Russia's cultural representatives were torn between a desire to imitate the West and a desire to define Russian values as different from and superior to those of the West. In one form or another, this ambivalence continues to characterize Russian cultural development.

Russia's most enduring image is probably St. Basil's Cathedral, located in Red Square, west of the historic district of Kitay Gorod.

The leading aristocrats almost entirely embraced Western cultural influences. Many nobles during the 18th century spoke only French, and some did not know Russian at all. European artistic styles began to displace the icon-painting tradition; cultural forms such as the ballet were embraced so fervently that they became part of Russia's own heritage. Western-style schools encouraged a new interest in science and secular philosophy. The public buildings of St. Petersburg were carefully constructed in Western classical styles. Russia was at this juncture still absorbing Western culture; later, in the 19th century, Russians made powerful contributions to the Western pool of literature, science, and music. At this point,

ECONOMY AND SOCIETY IN RUSSIA

As Russia moved partially into a Western diplomatic orbit and appropriated a number of Western cultural forms, the empire's economy and society pushed in rather different directions. Here was one of the key signs that Russia remained a separate civilization, although with special ties to the West.

As the Western economy became increasingly commercial, Russia continued to be resolutely agricultural, save for the iron-manufacturing sector and the continuation of active trade in central Asia. Its economic growth, although considerable, rested on the extension of its agricultural lands as the empire expanded, as well as on the increasingly effective use of vast mineral resources. Russia developed only a small merchant class. Indeed, aristocrats deliberately discouraged local merchants, who were seen as potential rivals. Growing trade with the West was handled by the communities of British, Dutch, and other Western traders from their enclaves in Moscow and St. Petersburg, although Russian merchants were more active in the overland commerce with Asia. Russian cities, as a result, were small, less than 5 percent of the total population.

Most Russian agriculture was designed for local consumption; few peasants were engaged in a market economy, and few handled much money. Village artisans supplied most of the manufactured goods that the masses required and could not make themselves. Luxury items and more complex equipment were largely imported from the West. Village-level technology did not change rapidly.

Russia did, however, enter the world economy, and on somewhat better terms than areas such as Latin America or even sub-Saharan Africa, despite the empire's rather backward economic condition after the period of Mongol rule. In exchange for Western goods and commercial services, including merchant shipping, Russia initially offered furs, along with timber supplies from its vast northern forests. Then, in the 18th century, the empire began to sell grain to the West, from the rich lands of the Ukraine and, later, Poland. Furthermore, Peter the Great used government officials to help organize a growing mining industry, so that Russia sold considerable quantities of iron ore to the West as well. Government-sponsored improvements in Russia's network of rivers and the development of St. Petersburg as a major Baltic port facilitated this process.

The government in Russia essentially took the place of merchant capitalists in organizing mining exports, just as it assumed the lead in sponsoring munitions factories and related iron-processing works. Here was an important extension of government functions under the tsars, from Peter the Great on, that helped Russia maintain some balance with the more commercially developed West. Russia used government regulation and unusually rich natural resources to avoid falling hopelessly behind in the world economy.

However, the key to Russia's economic advances lay in its reliance on unfree labor. Some slaves were used, into the 18th century, as war brought many captives. More important, however, was the pervasive and rigorous system of serfdom. As serfdom increasingly unraveled in the West, it became more rigid in Russia and other parts of eastern Europe. By using cheap servile labor, eastern Europe sought to participate in the world market, taking advantage of the West's growing demand for grains and minerals. Serfs worked most of the land, and the government also assigned serfs to the iron mines and metallurgical factories.

The initial intensification of Russian serfdom involved internal political and economic issues. Over time, however, growing reliance on the exploitation of serf labor reflected increased Russian involvement in the world economy and the need for low production costs for agricultural goods sold to Western nations. This joined Russia to trends not only in other parts of eastern Europe, but also in the Americas, where reliance on slavery and unfree peasant labor reflected similar world market pressures.

Ironically, prior to the Mongol conquest, Russian peasants had been mainly free farmers, with their legal position superior to that of their Western counterparts. But after the expulsion of the Tatars, increasing numbers of Russian peasants fell into debt and had to accept servile status under the noble landowners when they could not repay their debt. From the 16th century on, the Russian government actively encouraged this process. Essentially, the government offered the support of serfdom to the aristocracy, in exchange for loyalty. As new territories were added to the empire, this system of serfdom extended to areas where it had not been known before. By 1800, half of Russia's peasantry was enserfed to the landlords, and much of the other half owed comparable obligations to the state. Various laws passed during the 17th century tied serfs to the land; a 1649 act proclaimed the status of serfs to be hereditary, so that people born to this station could not legally escape it.

On landed estates, serfs were taxed and policed through their landlords and even bought and sold like ordinary property. Although the earnings of peasants varied somewhat and they sometimes used village governments for community regulation, most remained impoverished and ill educated. And the legal servitude of most peasants only increased with time. Although Catherine the Great sponsored a few model villages to exhibit an enlightened form of serfdom, she, in fact, turned over the rule of serfs to the landlords more completely than ever before. A law of 1785 allowed landlords to administer harsh penalties to any of their serfs convicted of major crimes or rebellion. Serfdom spread to new regions, with nobles granted other new rights. Here was proof positive of the vital political basis of serfdom, as Catherine garnered the loyalty of the nobles by giving them, in effect, rule over half of the Russian masses.

In Russian serfdom, not only on the landed estates but also in the mines, the key obligation was not payment in cash or payment in kind, although taxes were high and rising as the government needs for revenue increased. Labor service was the obligation that made economic sense of this system. Peasants owed up to a tenth of their yearly labor to their landlords or the state. This was the labor that produced the grain available for export and serviced the mines and factories.

Russia's distinctive social and economic system worked well in many respects. It produced

enough revenue to support an expanding state and empire. It underwrote a wealthy upper aristocracy and its glittering, westernized culture. It supported a far larger number of gentry, who lived more modestly and often resented the Western ways of the imperial court but who were nonetheless secure in their position and loyalty to the tsar. The system also promoted considerable population growth. Population nearly doubled in the 18th century, to 36 million people, and although some of this growth was the result of territorial expansion, most was due to a natural increase. For an empire that contained few regions of great fertility and where the climate was harsh, this was no small achievement, although periodic famines and epidemics continued to plague Russia into the 20th century, for this was a poor land in many ways. But there could be no question that the economy had advanced.

However, the Russian system suffered from important limitations. There was little incentive for agricultural improvements; most methods remained rather primitive. Peasants certainly lacked the motivation, for whatever surplus they produced was not theirs. Landlords, inspired by Western advances in the 18th century, did form associations to exchange information on new crops and methods, but little was done to improve production on a large scale. Given the secure base in servile labor, there seemed little need for change. Indeed, pressure from landlords caused the government to enact measures against a growing system of peasant-run domestic manufacturing and trade in the 18th century, for the aristocracy feared that growing peasant wealth might challenge its rule. Thus, Russia did not experience a significant increase in internal commerce or consumer-directed production comparable to that occurring in the West.

Most importantly, the system generated recurring peasant unrest. Russian peasants, although mainly loyal to the tsar, harbored bitter resentments against their landlords, who were seen as having taken lands that rightfully belonged to the peasants. Periodic rebellions attacked manorial records, seized land directly, and sometimes resulted in the deaths of landlords and their officials. The Pugachev uprising was the leading 18th-century example of this kind of outburst: at its height the rebellion had three million participants and controlled a third of Russia's territory, before it was put down. But there were later riots, and popular unrest continued to swell into the 19th century. Peasants had more than a sense of grievance; they also had tight links to each other through village governments and traditions of communal support. They maintained strong family ties, extending among many relatives; the network of the Russian family was thus larger than that of the West, with less stress on a purely nuclear unit. Community and family bonds provided a political basis for action, and although the peasants were never successful against the power of the landlords or the military strength of the state, they could not be permanently repressed.

Not surprisingly, by the early 1800s, it was clear that Russia had a major "peasant problem." Not only by Western standards, but also in terms of economic advance and political order, it seemed increasingly clear that something had to be done about Russia's unfree masses. Also not surprisingly, it was very difficult for those in a position of authority or oppression to decide what to do.

THE WORLD'S FIRST EFFORT AT WESTERNIZATION

Russia, particularly during Peter the Great's rule and on, was the first non-Western civilization to attempt a partial "westernization." The country was geographically close to the West and shared some of the same religious traditions. It had emerged from the Mongol period aware of its backwardness and eager to employ Western models as a partial remedy. What Russian leaders had attempted, in westernization from the top down, was tried to some extent in other societies and is still being tested today. The Russians sought to adapt key Western forms, not to make their society entirely Western but to modify it in

such a way that it could compete with the West militarily. Thus, the emphasis was on bureaucratic training and military organization and armament. However, there was some sense within Russia that yet more should be done, that cultural styles and even personal manners should move in Western directions; hence, the changes, among the upper classes, in styles of dress as well as art.

Nonetheless, westernization represented a limited effort. It served to enhance the distinctive Russian autocracy, not to import the full, complex political culture of the contemporary West, and certainly not to change the beliefs of the masses. Russia's leaders—like many later cultures in their attempts to westernize—did not want to reproduce Western civilization wholesale. Small wonder that by the late 18th century, some intellectual dissidents, attracted by the West, pressed for further change—although other writers continued to urge the sanctity of Russian traditions.

Rather, the current of westernization fed into the more general growth of the Russian state and empire. Limited changes were sufficient, in combination with Russia's vast size, population, and resources, to maintain the country's growing role in world diplomacy, challenging smaller nations in eastern and central Europe plus China and the Ottoman Empire in Asia. In strictly economic terms, Russia's relationship to the Western-dominated world economy was not vastly superior to that of Latin America; in both cases, the terms of trade were not advantageous, and any success depended on an unfree labor force. But in the military and political sphere, the story was quite different. Russia carved out one of the great landed empires in world history.

PATHS TO THE PRESENT

The early modern period was a defining era for Russia in several respects, as it was for the West. The establishment of a huge, multinational empire created the territorial base for modern Russia, though the empire further expanded during the 19th century. Though Russia surrendered some key regions in the 1990s, it remains one of the great empires of the world, clearly the most successful—at least in terms of durability—of all the gunpowder empires created in the early modern period.

Russian's emphasis on authoritarian government, though prefigured by developments in the postclassical period and under Mongol control, is another legacy. The tsars are long gone, victims of a massive modern revolution. But assumptions about the importance of firm state control and the need for order continue to influence Russian politics, affecting leaders' reactions and popular expectations alike.

Finally, the debate about Russia's relationship with the West continues as well. Russia is torn between the temptation to accept Western models and standards and the countervailing impulse to insist on a separate and desirable Russian alternative, and this internal conflict affects Russian life in many ways. The specifics of the debate have changed—the focus has shifted to whether Russia will accept Western patterns of consumerism or political democracy—but the basic terms and tensions are recognizable as stemming from Peter the Great's initiatives.

SUGGESTED WEB SITES

For more information on Russia, see http://countrystudies.us/russia/ and http://russia.nypl.org/level1.html; on Catherine the Great, see http://www.petersburg-russia.org/catherine-the-great/Default.htm; on the State Russian Museum, visit http://www.rusmuseum.ru/eng/; on the Russian Empire, see http://www.loc.gov/exhibits/empire/; for more on the Romanovs, see http://www.nypl.org/research/chss/slv/exhibit/roman.html.

SUGGESTED READINGS

Two important source collections about this period of Russian history are T. Riha, ed., *Readings in Russian Civilization*, Vol. 2: *Imperial Russia 1700–1917* (1969),

and Basil Dmytryshyn, *Imperial Russia: A Sourcebook, 1700–1917* (1967). Excellent general coverage is provided in N. Riasanovsky, *A History of Russia*, 4th ed. (1993); see also Otto Hoetzsch, *The Evolution of Russia* (1966), and Greta Bucher, *Daily Life in Imperial Russia* (2008). On more specialized topics, consult H. Kohn, *The Mind of Modern Russia* (1955); M. Raeff, *Peter the Great, Reformer or Revolutionary?* (1963); H. Rogger, *National Consciousness in Eighteenth Century Russia* (1963); and A. Kahan, *The Knout and the Plowshare: Economic History of Russia in the 18th Century* (1985). Peter Kolchin, *Unfree Labor: American Slavery and Russian Serfdom* (1987), is an important comparative study.

Additional work includes Lindsey Hughes, *Peter the Great and the West: New Perspectives* (2001); Paul Bushkovich, *Peter the Great: The Struggle for Power* (2007); Michael Khodarkovsky, *Russia's Steppe Frontier: The Making of a Colonial Empire, 1500–1800* (2002); Alexander Chubarov, *The Fragile Empire: A History of Imperial Russia* (1999); Geoffrey Hosking, *Russia: People and Empire* (1997); Lee A. Farrow, *Between Clan and Crown: The Struggle to Define Noble Property Rights in Imperial Russia* (2004); Bruce W. Menning and David Schimmelpenninck van der Oye, eds., *Reforming the Tsar's Army: Military Innovation in Imperial Russia from Peter the Great to the Revolution* (2004); John Paxton, *Leaders of Russia and the Soviet Union: From the Romanov Dynasty to Vladimir Putin* (2004); Richard Stites, *Serfdom, Society, and the Arts in Imperial Russia: The Pleasure and the Power* (2006); Mark Cruse and Hilde Hoogenboom, *The Memoirs of Catherine the Great* (2005); Isabel Madariaga, *Russia in the Age of Catherine the Great* (2002); Ernest A Zitser, *The Transfigured Kingdom: Sacred Parody and Charismatic Authority at the Court of Peter the Great* (2004); James Cracraft, *The Revolution of Peter the Great* (2003); Nicholas V. Riasanovsky, *Russian Identities: A Historical Survey* (2005); Valerie A. Kivelson and Robbert H. Greene, eds., *Orthodox Russia: Belief and Practice Under the Tsars* (2003); and James Cracraft and Daniel Rowland, eds., *Architectures of Russian Identity: 1500 to the Present* (2003).

CHAPTER

19 The Ottoman and Mughal Empires

Two great Islamic states were created during the early modern period, one covering much of the Middle East and the Balkans, the other much of India. A somewhat smaller Islamic Empire, the Safavids, introduced important changes into present day Iran. Both the Ottomans and the Mughals brought new influences to these regions, including great political and military strength. The two empires resembled Russia in establishing large landed holdings with new boundaries during the early modern period. They also, like Russia, included a host of different linguistic, ethnic, and religious groups. Neither empire, however, attempted westernization during this period, even selectively. Early Mughal emperors had a tolerant interest in Western culture, including its religion, but there were few real attempts to imitate it; the Western intrusion into India later on was a matter of conquest and economic exploitation. Ottoman rulers, with minor exceptions, explicitly avoided borrowing from the West.

Both Islamic empires followed their own paths during most of the early modern period, introducing important changes that had little to do with the West or the world economy. Contacts with the West did increase with time, so that in contrast to east Asia, a more substantial Western presence began to affect internal developments by the late 17th to early 18th century.

The evolution of the Middle East and India after 1450 revolved around the rise of the two new empires, one brought by the Turks to the Middle East, the other by Turkish-Mongol conquerors who ruled over the Hindu majority in India. (The third Islamic empire, the Safavids, developed for a time in Persia.) The Muslim empires provided new political and military solidity to their Asian territories. Under the Ottomans, the previous political decline of the Arab caliphs was reversed. Under the early Mughals, India achieved a degree of political unity rarely before attained. Both empires created great cities and diversified economies long envied by European visitors.

The Ottoman and particularly the Mughal empires were not, however, as solidly based as those of China and Russia. The Mughals represented a minority religion as well as a foreign political force. The Ottomans, though sharing religion with the Arab majority of their empire, were also outsiders who looked down on the Arab population for their political and military weakness. Finally, both empires began to decline well before 1800. In India, this resulted in direct European penetration during the 18th century. The Ottoman Empire remained intact, but by 1800, it was becoming a weaker force in regional and world affairs.

KEY QUESTIONS *What were the durable contributions of the Mughals and Ottomans to their regions? How did the new empires manage the diverse ethnicities and religions of the regions they controlled? Why did the Mughals decline more rapidly than the Ottomans?*

THE EXPANDING FORCE OF THE OTTOMAN EMPIRE

The Ottoman Empire had taken shape during the several centuries before the early modern period, although its complete development followed the Turkish conquest of Constantinople in 1453. Turkish groups had been moving into the Middle East, from their original lands in central Asia, for some time. They served in the armies of the caliphs and as advisors. This interaction spread Islamic belief and knowledge of urban cultural styles and government even to those Turks still in central Asia.

The Osmanli group of Turks, or Ottomans as Europeans knew them, were not one of the original Turkish peoples involved in Middle Eastern affairs. Their movement into the region came later, stimulated in part by the rise of the Mongol empire in Asia during the 13th and 14th centuries. Large numbers of migrants took over lands at the northern rim of the Middle East, in the country that is now Turkey—the only part of the Middle East that was heavily populated by Turks—where they became an agricultural people. Regional Osmanli leaders, exhibiting their military abilities, began to challenge both the Arabs and the Byzantines. The Ottomans were fervent warriors, spurred by intense Islamic beliefs and a tightly knit military. By the 14th century, their leaders began to call themselves sultans, as they settled in the plains of Anatolia, the heartland of present-day Turkey. The first sultan, Orkhan, established a new army of soldiers called *janissaries* in order to fight remnants of the Byzantine Empire in southeastern Europe. He had already conquered some European territory by 1400. The Ottomans viewed this conquest of Christian lands as a virtual crusade, and during the 1390s they captured Serbia, Bulgaria, and Greece. Already, the Ottoman Empire was the strongest state in the Middle East in the wake of the collapse of the Abbasid caliphate.

Nonetheless, the chief prize was Constantinople, the capital city of eastern Christendom. Several Turkish sieges failed before Sultan Mehmet II, known as "the Conqueror," finally succeeded in 1453, aided by the use of a huge cannon and the strict discipline he imposed on his troops. The Turks set up their imperial capital in what was now a Muslim city, renamed Istanbul. Soon after this, the Turks conquered Arab Syria and also took control of the Greek islands and the last Byzantine settlements around the Black Sea. By 1517, Egypt was vanquished, the last of the regional Arab kingdoms that had survived the fall of the caliphate. A major victory for Egyptian forces opened much of north Africa to the Ottomans. The Ottoman Empire was thus heir to both Arab and Byzantine lands, establishing one of the largest empires the Middle East had ever known; it was the last great attempt at unification in the region, to the present day.

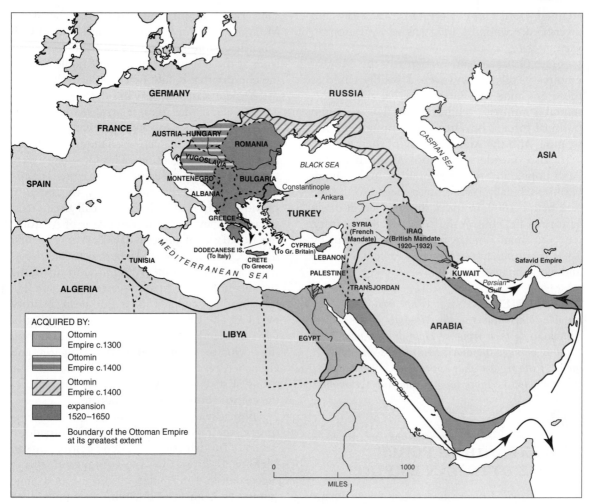

ACQUIRED BY:

Ottomin
Empire c.1300

Ottomin
Empire c.1400

Ottomin
Empire c.1400

expansion
1520–1650

Boundary of the Ottoman Empire
at its greatest extent

0   1000

MILES

The Expansion of the Ottoman Empire 1300–mid-1600

During the 16th century, Ottoman conquests continued. The sultans conquered part of Persia and much of the southern Arabian peninsula. They pursued territories in Europe, attacking several Italian cities and conquering Hungary after a victory in 1526. In 1529, they besieged the Habsburg capital city of Vienna, in Austria, although this effort failed. They also captured islands in the Mediterranean. The conquest of the island of Cyprus in 1571 led to the establishment

of a Turkish settlement that coexisted uneasily with the Greek majority, a tense situation that persists to this day. Minor conquests continued until 1715, although in most respects the high-water mark of the empire as a conquering force was reached in the late 16th and early 17th centuries.

By this point, the Ottoman Empire embraced the whole of southeastern Europe to the Danube River. It included a protectorate over Tatar provinces in the Crimea as the Ottoman Empire stretched around virtually the entire circumference of the Black Sea. It encompassed most of the Middle East, with some Arab settlements in desert regions and the smaller Safavid empire in Persia alone escaping its grasp; it also controlled most of north Africa. Ottoman rule over the holy cities of Mecca and Medina gave the empire new religious force, and the sultans assumed the title of caliph of Islam, implying a direct link to the Muslim faith. As caliphs, the sultans required that their names be used in the prayers of the faithful in the mosques.

The Ottoman Empire, although of greatest importance in the Islamic world, played a crucial role in European history as well. In its hold over the Balkan lands of southeastern Europe, the Ottomans preserved this region from direct Western control; a minority of Balkan people converted to Islam.

The Ottoman Empire's success rested on two leading factors. The first, visible from the early Osmanlis on, involved strong military organization and conquest. The Ottomans, like many other imperial conquerors, depended heavily on a fairly steady course of expansion, which gave military leaders rewards in the form of new territories, plus slaves to serve as troops. When conquests largely ceased, the empire became increasingly troubled.

The second factor was Ottoman leaders' considerable tolerance for the various peoples in their vast realms, like that of Arab conquerors before them. Mehmet II did not attack the Greek Orthodox church; indeed, he appointed a new patriarch to provide separate religious government for this people. Christians were taxed more heavily than Muslims, and in the provinces of southeastern Europe, they were forced to perform labor duties and allow the conscription of some of their youth as soldiers. For the most part, Christianity remained strong in southeastern Europe and, as a minority religion, in parts of the Middle East, and individual Christians

rose high in the Ottoman government. Jews were also widely tolerated, as the Turks again demonstrated their willingness to accept a multiracial and multireligious society. The Turks did harbor some disdain for their fellow Arab Muslims and decidedly favored Sunni beliefs over the Shiite minority. But on the whole, Arab Muslims, from ulema scholars to the ordinary faithful, were not disturbed in their religious practices. Many Ottoman sultans were personally pious, interested in religion and culture as well as military affairs.

The greatest of the Ottoman sultans, near the height of the empire's power, was Suleiman, who ruled from 1520 to 1566. Known as "the Magnificent" to European traders, who marveled at the wealth of his court, he was called "the Legislator" by the Turks themselves because of his interest in just and disciplined rule. Although not a joyful warrior—indeed, his portraits reveal a rather gloomy man burdened by the cares of his state—Suleiman did pursue a policy of conquest. It was under his rule that the kingdom of Hungary was conquered and new portions of the Middle East, particularly present-day Iraq, were won from the Persians. Suleiman also constructed a major Mediterranean fleet, hoping in this way to extend his challenge of the Christian West. He strengthened Ottoman control of north Africa, especially Algeria, and frequently raided Italian and Spanish ports. In his later years, Suleiman grew less interested in battle and concentrated on the building of new mosques. However, his life remained troubled, as he had to put to death one son to please his favorite wife, leaving her incompetent son as his heir.

Under Suleiman, the institutions of the Ottoman Empire assumed their fullest shape, forming a successful political system long capable of administering vast and diverse territories. In theory, this was an absolute state, claiming control over all wealth and property in the empire. Annual tax revenue was massive by the standards of Western kingdoms. Although all power officially rested in the sultan, he, in fact, delegated much authority to his chief minister, the grand *wazir*. The wazir and other leading ministers were able to accumulate their own considerable fortunes through bribery and graft, although they had to struggle against rivals and the sultan's power to retire—and often execute— them at any given moment.

The provinces of the empire were ruled by governors called *pashas*, who paid for their office with an annual fee. A pasha of Cairo was said to have bribed the grand wazir with a large yearly payment in order to preserve his lucrative position. Under the pashas, most land outside the cities was parceled out in fiefs to Turkish and other Muslim landlords, who collected revenues and enforced the laws on a local basis. Under a levy, or conscription, system, each landlord was obligated to furnish soldiers to the sultan. Under this decentralized system, regional rulers and landlords were encouraged to milk their holdings for as much revenue as they could. There was no hereditary nobility, because in theory the sultan owned all the land. This fact initially gave sultans control over regional officials who owed their position to the central court, but it also promoted short-term exploitation of the provinces by officials eager to turn a profit while they could still enjoy it. Suleiman did prepare a centralized law code, which served as a unifying legal force throughout the empire until the 19th century.

The Ottomans expanded the earlier Arab use of slaves in the army and administration. Using slaves of Christian origin in the central bureaucracy, from the wazirs on down, bypassed the Qur'an's prohibition on enslaving Muslims and also integrated non-Muslims, who formed a majority in the empire for its first 200 years. Government slaves were carefully educated, alongside the sultans' own sons, and promoted according to merit and seniority. Here was another solution to the government of an agricultural society, different from both Chinese bureaucracy and feudalism. It made the Ottoman

Empire the best-governed state in the world well into the 16th century.

The army was the main unifying element throughout the empire. In addition to the landlord levies, sultans such as Suleiman directly controlled the force of *janissaries*, who were recruited from the families of Christians, particularly in southeastern Europe, in what amounted to an annual slave tax. These young men were taken from their homes at an early age, converted to Islam, and trained to become fierce and able soldiers. They seldom numbered more than 15,000, because the sultans feared that they might otherwise grow too powerful; indeed, janissary revolts troubled the empire periodically even so. Forbidden to marry, the janissaries were expected to remain loyal to the sultan alone, from whom they received good pay and many other benefits. Until the 18th century, when their fighting spirit declined and their interference in internal politics increased, they did indeed serve the empire well. The janissaries were normally well disciplined and remained an excellent fighting force, particularly in battles with European Christians, which were still seen to an extent as holy wars.

The Ottoman navy, on the other hand, was somewhat limited. Although it operated in the eastern Mediterranean, it could not wrest control of the bulk of the Mediterranean from Italian and Spanish forces. Ottoman ships also lost ground to Portuguese competition in the Indian Ocean. The empire lacked a large merchant marine, a fact that weakened its efforts on the seas. It used slaves as oarsmen; they had little interest in battle save as a chance to escape. Although the navy gained brief prominence under Suleiman, it suffered a defeat at European hands in the battle of Lepanto in 1571. Some naval activity continued, however, not only along the eastern coast of the Mediterranean, where the navy protected existing Ottoman provinces, but also in extending Ottoman control over parts of north Africa.

Even at its height, the Ottoman Empire displayed some important limitations. It ruled over the oldest commercial economy in the world, but it did not sponsor significant economic advance. As the focus of world trade moved away from the Mediterranean, the empire was obviously at a disadvantage. Great efforts were exerted to sustain the magnificent city of Istanbul. Most farming was done by serfs, who were routinely exploited by greedy landlords and regional governors. This system did not encourage agricultural productivity. The Turks were not greatly interested in commerce. Most regional trade was conducted by Arabs, Greeks, and Jews, who maintained an active urban economy and a strong manufacturing base. The empire's role in the larger world economy declined. Once Europeans learned to sail around Africa directly to Asia, the position of the Middle East as an intermediary between Asia and Europe became less important. Trade between the Middle East and Europe lay largely in Western hands, and a growing colony of Western traders emerged in Istanbul.

The empire embraced and encouraged a lively religious life, although the most renowned Islamic scholars were more often Arab than Turk. The building of mosques and palaces stimulated architecture and crafts, which maintained earlier Arabic styles for the most part, although to some extent Persian influences were also evident. Decorative arts, including rich carpets and fine metalwork, flourished. But there was little new literature, particularly in Turkish; Arab poetry continued, but as in the later days of the caliphate, mainly in a religious vein. Arab schools and universities concentrated primarily on religious instruction and the complicated scholarship of Islamic law. Egypt served as the cultural center for Arab intellectual life, but most Egyptian writers devoted their efforts to compiling older works and commenting on them, or preparing biographies of ancient Muslim holy men. The rich and diverse cultural traditions of the earlier Arab civilization at its height were not revived. In the 16th century, Turkish literature began to develop, as sultans encouraged the writing of state histories highly favorable to those in power and as Turkish poets and songwriters copied Persian and Arabic verse. Much Turkish writing was devoted to accounts of the life of the prophet Muhammad and leading dervishes, confirming the heavily religious orientation of Middle Eastern culture.

Conditions for Ottoman women maintained Middle Eastern patterns. Many urban women were veiled and secluded. Leaders maintained several wives and, often, additional concubines. But an active social life could develop among women in extended households, including opportunities for private enjoyment of consumer goods. Because upper-class boys were raised in the harems for their first seven years, the informal influence of mothers could be considerable. Women could also own property, a key source of bargaining power within families.

Major innovations in popular culture, however, favored men. The most important was the development of coffee consumption. Coffee had first been cultivated in southern Arabia in the 14th century, from wild plants brought in from Ethiopia. It was popularized for Sufi religious ceremonies, because it encouraged wakefulness for nighttime rituals. But by the 16th century, coffee's social functions were spreading, and coffeehouses began to spring up in Egypt and in Istanbul. Arab and Turkish men now used coffeehouses for social purposes, and all sorts of serving equipment developed. By 1560, there were more than 600 coffeehouses in Istanbul, some with elaborate gardens, others very simple. Arab merchants and growers in Africa and southern Arabia controlled the coffee trade.

The Ottoman Empire remained, in part, a military movement. Turkish leaders continued to esteem military virtues above all, although they often tempered their commitment to warfare by pursuing religious concerns and the enjoyment of art. The Turks had little interest in the dull work of the bureaucracy. Most administrative posts under the sultans were held not by Turks, but by east Europeans—mainly Slavs and Greeks—and by Jews. Only a minority of the wazirs were Turkish. Most of the literate bureaucrats were Europeans,

The Blue Mosque, so called thanks to the blue Izkin tile work that decorates its interior, features large domes and six tall minarets. It was originally the Mosque of Ottoman Sultan Ahmet I.

Christian Armenians, and Jews. Decentralized rule combined with strong military power held this empire together, although high taxes, forced labor, and military recruitment caused discontent, particularly in southeastern Europe, where the Turks became cordially detested.

Despite its limitations, however, the Ottoman Empire enjoyed more than three centuries of clear success, from its dynamic beginnings in the 14th century until well after the defeat at Lepanto. The Ottomans' record compares favorably with the glory days of other military empires such as that of Rome.

THE OTTOMAN EMPIRE IN DECLINE

A certain degree of Ottoman decline began late in the 17th century. The quality of individual sultans deteriorated after Suleiman. Many ruled for only brief periods; a few were mentally incapacitated. Many devoted themselves to sensual pleasures, surrounded by large harems of concubines. Palace intrigues and military interference increasingly dominated the Ottoman state, which perhaps helps account for the poor political performance of those who became sultans. Periodic reform efforts, to tighten central control and reduce the corruption of regional governors, had no permanent effects, although they helped sustain the regime. Religious and local institutions supplemented the government by providing courts, charity, education, and public works—another reason the system survived. The government also tried to defend against unrest by limiting certain innovations. Printing, for example, was fully banned until the 18th century.

During most of the 17th century, the empire held onto its territory. Its control over north Africa (aside from Egypt) weakened, in part because of the declining navy. North African states became small principalities and were the source of considerable piracy until the 19th century. However, Western powers, caught up in their own colonial expansion, had no interest in a direct attack on Ottoman lands.

The Ottoman Empire made one last attempt at conquest in 1683, in a new assault on Vienna. For three months, a huge Turkish army laid siege to this city, until a mixed German and Polish force drove them back. Soon after this, the Austrian Habsburg emperor, in a loose alliance with the Russian tsar Peter the Great, attacked the Ottomans. Austrian troops drove the Turks from Hungary, inflicting the worst defeat the Turks had suffered since the early days of the Osmanlis. From this point, the Ottomans were on the defensive in southeastern Europe and central Asia. In the 18th century, Russian attacks pushed them from the northern coast of the Black Sea, while Austria also gained some territory in Serbia.

During the 18th century, the quality of internal government deteriorated further. Control over provincial governors declined; a few governors even rebelled against Constantinople. Many governors became increasingly corrupt, using their rule as a means of acquiring vast personal fortunes. Taxation, earlier restrained by some central regulations, grew heavier. Popular discontent increased, although there were no vast uprisings. Arab involvement with intense Muslim piety, under the leadership of Sufi mystics, helped limit the impact of protest, expressing hostility to the existing order but through attention to religious rather than political goals. On the southern borders of the empire, however, a puritanical version of Islam developed in the Wahabi movement. This formed partly in protest against the secular tone of Ottoman rulers. The Wahabis developed military forces and later in the 18th century, for a time, seized Mecca from the Ottomans.

As the power of the empire faltered, Europe's economic penetration of the Middle East began to intensify. Even before, Western traders, led by the French, had won special privileges from the sultans, establishing merchant colonies that were exempt from Ottoman law. French, British, and Dutch groups thrived in not only Constantinople but Syria and Egypt as well. The West also had some cultural impact, as Middle Eastern Christians, particularly those in Lebanon, sought new ties with the Catholic church. Christian printing presses were set up in Arabic, although presses were banned by the Turks for Muslims until 1729.

For the most part, Turkish political leaders and Arab cultural leaders remained uncertain in reacting to the declining strength of their civilization, although officials were aware of the specific problems this decline posed. There was no successful effort at political reform until after 1800. Muslim cultural figures were convinced of their superiority over their European neighbors. No attempts were made, again until after 1800, to translate European scientific or technological works, for this intellectual current seemed irrelevant in Muslim eyes. A few Western doctors were imported by the sultans—which was ironic, because medicine was one area where Muslim science was just as good as its Western counterpart—but the larger disparities with western Europe were simply ignored. Many Ottoman merchants were quite familiar with the West, but they had little impact back home. The cultural blanket of Islamic legalism and faith, plus the army and bureaucracy, continued to protect this important civilization, even as both Western and Russian interests in the region increased.

THE SAFAVID CHALLENGE

During most of the early modern period, another Islamic empire, taking shape between the Caspian Sea and the Persian Gulf, not only consolidated territory, aided by the use of guns and field cannon, but formed a durable rivalry with the Ottoman lands. The Safavid Empire

HISTORY DEBATE

GUNS AND THEIR IMPACT

It is easy to write early modern world history as if guns were European. Without question, Europe's advance in world trade and colonialism owed much to European advances in gunnery, particularly on ships. Guns also had massive effects within early modern Europe, making feudal warfare and strongholds such as castles less effective. Siege cannon could reduce noble castles to ruin; this forced the nobility into new behaviors and clearly weakened feudal politics and the feudal ethic.

Increasingly, however, historians examine the use of guns in other cultures. Obviously, explosive powder was Chinese in origin. But nomadic peoples quickly picked up the implications. Siege cannon did not cause the rise of the Mongols, which was based on cavalry, but they were added to the Mongol arsenal as the armies began to attack cities in China, Russia, and Islamic areas. The Ottomans used janissaries as their artillery corps, and this became a driving force behind Ottoman expansion. Babur, in forming the Mughal empire in India, used cannon as well. There is no question that guns played a major role in the formation of Asian as well as European empires. One key result was the decline of nomadic attacks. Even though Mongols and other nomads were initially adept with cannon, in the long run developing an armament industry and improving weaponry depended on a large tax base, that is, on established governments. Here was a key component in the nomadic decline in the early modern period.

Guns also complicated the later development of many of the land-based gunpowder empires as well. Guns allowed expansion of territory in advance of effective communication or government. In both the Ottoman and the Mughal empires, a key result of such expansion was weak central control and great power in the hands of regional military leaders. This in turn weakened the empires still further. Western European states, smaller, managed a more effective bureaucratic and taxation system, which Russia was able to copy to some extent. This increased the Western or Russian competitive edge against the Islamic empires. Ultimately, the story of guns tips the global balance of power in favor of Europe—which brings the story back to more familiar contours. But there is important complexity in the middle of the process—the 14th- to 17th-century transition period in the relationship of guns and empires—that needs attention as well.

emerged from invasions by rival Turkic nomadic groups in the 14th and 15th centuries. Conquest of the city of Tabriz, in 1501, opened Persia to the Safavids and led to the proclamation of the victorious general as shah, or emperor. The Safavid rulers, fervently pious Muslims, espoused the Shiite version of Islam. This added to the territorial tensions with the Ottomans to the west, who were equally vigorous defenders of the Sunni faith. Attacks on the rival sects occurred in both empires. While the Ottomans won some decisive victories over the Safavids, beginning with Chaldiran in northwest Persia in 1514, they could not seize the new empire itself.

Safavid rule relied on a combination of military and religious strength, with growing utilization of Persian officials and religious scholars. Under the regime, the bulk of the Iranian population converted to Shiism during the early modern centuries, setting the region off from its Arab and Turkish neighbors. The Safavids also established Farsi as the Iranian language, while promoting Persian artistic and architectural forms. The Safavid Empire fell to factional disputes and rebellions by the early 18th century, creating something of a power vacuum in the region; but its cultural achievements proved durable.

THE MUGHAL EMPIRE: INVASION, CONSOLIDATION, AND DECLINE

India during the 15th century was locked in its recurrent pattern of regional states. The Delhi sultanate, which earlier had provided Muslim rule for much of northern India, was now merely one among many principalities, most of them headed by Hindu princes.

This situation changed as a result of another invasion early in the 16th century, the last echo, in a way, of the great period of Mongol conquests. Babur, a regional chieftain in Afghanistan and a Muslim, was of mixed Turkish and Mongol ancestry. Beginning in 1526, he used the familiar passes through the mountains of northwestern India to mount a war of conquest, within four years bringing a large part of the northern plains under his control.

Babur's conquests benefited obviously from India's political division, as regional states could not join forces effectively. But Babur was no ordinary raider. His vision was a new empire, for himself and his descendants, not plunder. He was a bold, often cruel general, but a lover of gardening and poetry who wrote a long memoir that showed real sensitivity for the rest of humankind. He cherished books and liked to select prize volumes from the libraries that came under his dominion. The dynasty he established was called *Mughal*, from the Persian word for Mongol; from the wealth of Babur and his successors came the English word *mogul*. At the outset, however, this was a regime with serious political purposes, not simply a luxury-loving enterprise. To solidify his new dynasty, Babur carefully avoided acts of intolerance against Hindus, whose customs he studied closely.

Babur's chief heir, after a brief period of confusion under a weak son, was his grandson Akbar, who took charge in 1555. Initially winning only a portion of Babur's empire, Akbar soon conquered one of the largest empires ever established in India, recalling the former days of the Maurya dynasty. Akbar's awe-inspiring achievements gained him the respect of many Europeans, who named him the "Great Mughal." Akbar was brave almost to the point of foolhardiness. As a boy, he liked to ride his own fighting elephants; he reveled in the hunt, once killing a tiger with his sword in single combat. He was also an excellent marksman—and guns spread to India initially through Muslim influence. But Akbar was also a cultivated man, a book collector, and patron of painting and architecture. Mughal culture reached its peak under his rule. Furthermore, Akbar carried the tolerance of Hinduism to an unusual extreme, marrying a Hindu princess and allowing Hindu women in his court to practice their religion openly, an unprecedented act for a Muslim ruler. He even listened to Portuguese Jesuit missionaries who reached the west coast under his regime, although he himself never converted. Akbar seems to have had a vague notion of sponsoring a new religion that would blend Hinduism and Islam, although it never had much of a significant following.

Akbar's empire built on a combination of great military force and careful administration. His army numbered 140,000 troops at its height, a massive number for the age, far greater than the forces of the leading European powers. At the same time, he established a clearly defined bureaucracy, divided into specialized ministries to deal with finance, law, and military affairs. Akbar's administrative reform drew on practices in Afghanistan that were refined by his Hindu chief minister. Eighteen provincial governors, called *subahdars*, administered the major regions of his empire. Akbar united virtually the whole of northern India and began the conquest of the Deccan region in the south. His legal system sought to moderate what he saw as some excesses in Hindu customs; thus, he attempted to ban sati, the practice of suicide by widows, and he forbade child marriage by insisting on a marriage age of 16 for boys and 13 for girls. Akbar also endeavored

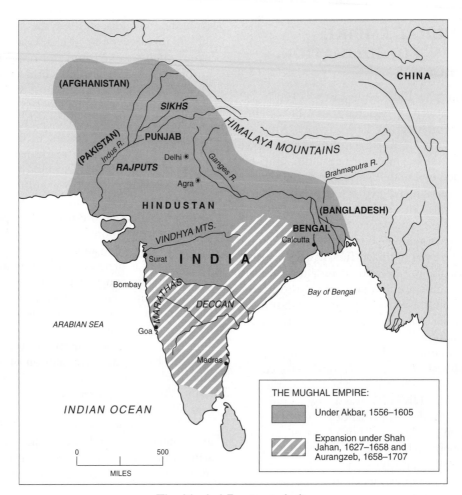

The Mughal Empire in India

to create a common language for his empire, enabling his scholars to produce the synthetic mixture called *Urdu*, or Hindustani, which provided a vehicle of communication for his bureaucrats and ultimately spread to a large minority of his subjects, particularly Muslims. The language combined Persian with elements of Turkish and Hindi. Urdu forms one of three major languages, along with English, on the subcontinent today, and it is the official language of Pakistan.

Above all, Akbar and his subordinates developed an efficient system of military recruitment and taxation, the latter based on landed property.

This along with massive support for Mughal success in relying on appointed provincial authorities provided a political model used in India for many centuries. Even with the huge demands of Akbar's government for revenue, prosperity increased in northern India. Muslim rule provided India with not only stable government but also new products such as paper. India continued an active regional trade with southeast Asia in spices and other products, even as Western shipping spread.

Akbar's reign was the high point of Mughal rule in India, yet the empire survived until the

19th century. Akbar's immediate successors, although less able than he, maintained the policy of conquest; during the first half of the 17th century, the empire reached its greatest size through gains in the south. Patronage of the arts continued. Mughal portrait painters flourished, and some influences from Western art crept into their works—as in the halos painted around the heads of the emperors. Mughal art had a distinctive style, different from Middle Eastern tradition, as the use of portraits demonstrates. In architecture, the Muslim heritage, including the use of decorative motifs, loomed larger. Under the Emperor Shah Jehan I, who ruled from 1627 to 1658, the great tomb called the *Taj Mahal* was built. Designed by a Turkish architect, it required 14 years to construct. Initially intended for Jehan's favorite wife, Mumtaz Mahal, it also served as a shrine for Jehan himself and is still rated one of the two or three most beautiful buildings in the world. Thus, in painting and architecture, as in the development of Urdu, the Mughals contributed greatly to India's artistic and cultural legacy. European Catholic missionaries to India encountered a solid culture. Except in Portuguese Goa, they effected few conversions. Several missionaries, in fact, picked up Hindu values and styles.

Indian economic prosperity also advanced, at least until the later 17th century. European traders flocked to the subcontinent to seek Indian goods, including brightly colored cotton cloth and other manufactured products. They brought items from other parts of Asia, including spices, as well as American silver in exchange—few European goods were attractive as yet in Asian markets.

The political structure of the Mughal empire, however, began to unravel during the mid-17th century. Jehan departed from the tradition of toleration for Hindus. Hindu officials still served in his bureaucracy, and the emperor patronized Hindu poets and musicians, but many Hindu temples were demolished. Jehan also attacked Portuguese settlements in the east (Kolkata in present-day India), although his huge army had great difficulty subduing a force of merely 1000 troops, whose superior weaponry foreshadowed later Western power on the subcontinent. Many Christian churches were destroyed, and thousands of Christian converts were killed. Taxes were increased to cover the growing expenses of the luxurious court. Many peasants were forced off the land because of escalating taxes, and rural crime became a growing problem.

Tensions increased under Jehan's son Aurangzeb, the last important Mughal ruler (1658–1707). Aurangzeb, who seized power by imprisoning his father, did manage to reduce taxation. But he intensified the attacks on the Hindu majority in the name of Islamic law. More temples were destroyed, and taxes on Hindus were raised. Hindus who sought bureaucratic service normally had to convert to the Muslim faith. Hindu resistance, not a major factor in most of the empire previously, now increased. This helped to rally regional princes in the south, who prevented the further conquest of the Deccan region. A new Hindu leader in the south, Shivaji, generated something akin to Hindu nationalism in forming a new Deccan state against which Aurangzeb battled in vain until his death.

Another important center of resistance arose in the northwest. Here, a new religion had evolved in the 16th century, in part as a reaction to earlier Muslim influence. This Sikh religion was closely related to Hinduism, although it was held by its leaders to be inspired directly by God. The Sikh faith combined Hindu practices and beliefs with a more activist approach. Sikhs abolished the caste system in their religion, creating a military brotherhood dedicated to a vigorous role in the affairs of this world, including something like a holy war. The contemplative side of Hinduism was played down, although Sikh temples maintained many Hindu rituals, and a belief in reincarnation persisted. As the Mughal empire weakened, Sikhs established a regional realm of their own that lasted until 1849. Not only fierce fighters but also the turbaned Sikhs were active

Perhaps no single building has come to symbolize Indian civilization more than the Taj Mahal. The grace and elegance of the tomb that Shah Jehan built in his wife's honor provide an enduring source of aesthetic delight. The white marble of the tomb is inlaid with flowers and geometric designs cut from semiprecious stones. The windows of the central chamber, which houses the tombs of Shah Jehan and Mumtaz Mahal, are decorated with carved marble screens, which add a sense of lightness and delicacy to the structure.

in business and agricultural improvements. They formed an important religious minority in India from the 17th century on, along with the larger Muslim group.

By the time of Aurangzeb's death, India was divided into essentially three major states: the Mughal empire (the largest), the new Deccan state, and the Sikh empire. Several smaller states survived in the south, while European settlements—Portuguese Goa, but also British and French ports—dotted both the east and the west coasts. Within the Mughal empire, Hindus and Muslims were increasingly in conflict. Many Hindus withdrew into their own communities, fervently embracing their religious rituals in order to preserve their identity in a state they could no longer actively accept. Under Aurangzeb's 18th-century

successors, Mughal administration became increasingly conservative and inefficient. Not only did political control become more lax, but India's educational system also declined as a result of Hindu isolation and Mughal inattention, and the economy deteriorated. Merchants suffered under the taxation of the later Mughals, who had no love for commerce. Indian technology—like that of much of Asia by the 17th and 18th centuries—stagnated.

In sum, an empire that had commenced with great brilliance and promise declined with extraordinary rapidity. Intolerance seems to have been a key to the downfall, along with the continued ability of most Hindus to retain their faith. In this situation, Mughal rulers became increasingly beleaguered and ineffective.

WESTERN INTRUSION INTO THE MUGHAL EMPIRE

Growing weakness and division in 18th-century India provided an unintended invitation to more active European intervention. Western merchant companies were drawn increasingly into Indian political affairs, to provide what they saw as necessary stability for their commercial operations. This was the most important impact of the new world economy on Asia in the early modern period. This motive for intervention was enhanced by conflicts among the European groups for influence on the subcontinent and particularly by the recurrent battles between England and France. Although European forces were small, their superiority in weapons gave them centralizing power in a divided region.

By the 18th century, Portugal's role in India was minor; the colony at Goa remained, but Portugal was too weak to reestablish other centers after the Mughal attacks. Dutch power was also declining, as the Dutch were preoccupied with administering their important holdings in the Indonesian islands. France and Britain had both established toeholds on the subcontinent during the 17th century, winning port rights by bargaining with local princes. The British East India Company operated a station at Calcutta, which gave them some access to the great wealth of the Ganges valley. The company had enormous influence over the British government and, through Britain's superior navy, excellent communication on the ocean routes. Their French rivals, in contrast, had less political clout at home, where the government was often distracted by purely European wars. The French were also more interested in missionary work than the British, who were long content to leave Hindu customs alone and devote themselves to commercial profits.

French–British rivalry raged bitterly through the middle decades of the 18th century. Each side recruited Indian princes as allies. Outright warfare erupted in 1744, and then again during the Seven Years War. British officials had become alarmed at growing French influence with local princes. They were also roused in 1756 by the capture of Calcutta, by an Indian official, who imprisoned British captives in a "Black Hole"—an underground chamber originally used as a jail by the British themselves; many British officials suffocated. The East India Company's army recaptured Calcutta and then seized additional French and Indian territory, aided by generous bribes distributed to many regional princes. French power in India was decimated, and Britain was committed, without plan or clear intent, to the administration of Bengal, which stretched inland from Calcutta. Soon after this, the British also gained the island of Sri Lanka (Ceylon) from the Dutch. Although the British military force remained small, its superior weaponry, including field artillery, proved decisive in battles with Indian rulers. At the same time, more sophisticated naval power allowed Britain to outdistance its European rivals. Thus, from 1764 on, a British empire in India was truly launched. Along with Indonesia and the Americas, India became one of the great territorial acquisitions of the West prior to 1800.

The complete history of British India did not begin until late in the 18th century, when the British government took a more active hand in Indian administration, supplementing the quasi-government of the East India Company. Indeed, before 1800, British control of the subcontinent was incomplete. The Mughal empire survived, although it was increasingly powerless, as did other regional kingdoms, including the Sikh state. Britain gained some new territories by force of arms but was also content to ally with local princes without disturbing their internal administration, again until after 1800.

However, British, and to an extent French and Dutch, commercial activities in India had an important effect even before the full implications of India's new colonial status were clear. Throughout the 18th century, much of India was increasingly drawn into the world trading patterns dominated by the West. Like Indonesia, but unlike the Americas, India offered a well-developed manufacturing economy along with a vast population and solid agricultural base. European merchants were eager to exploit India's wealth but were concerned that India not compete with their own manufacturing capabilities. Early in the 18th century, Britain began to levy high tariffs on the import of cotton cloth. This was one of India's chief industries, but it was just getting started in Britain. By limiting Indian access to a British market, London effectively reduced India's opportunities in world trade. British-made goods, including textiles, were widely sold on the subcontinent, while hundreds of thousands of Indian textile workers began to lose their jobs. In turn, the Indians exported gold and also agricultural products, such as tea, which were grown on commercial estates staffed by low-paid wage laborers. British agents also assumed growing command over Indian textile production, dictating wages and conditions to the workers, while the British East India Company claimed Indian gold as payment for their costs of administration.

These exploitative economic policies were not Britain's final statement on Indian affairs. As the British Empire matured after 1800—and particularly after 1830—economic relations with India became less one-sided. In this early period, however, India was clearly added to the list of world territories that helped feed European wealth. An 18th-century Indian account described the climate of exploitation:

> But such is the little regard which they [the British] show to the people of this kingdom, and such their apathy and indifference for their welfare, that the people under their dominion groan everywhere, and are reduced to poverty and distress.

To be sure, some Indians welcomed British rule as an alternative to intolerant Muslim control. And many, particularly those in the independent kingdoms that still, in 1800, governed more than half of the subcontinent in loose alliance with British administration, were scarcely aware of the British presence as yet. But the initial impact of European, especially British, operations deepened India's decline from the high point of Mughal rule. The Hindu religion, still the fundamental cultural resource for the majority, had ceased to spark vigorous philosophical and artistic statements. India's schools and universities were inactive. Manufacturing stagnated, and the level of prosperity reached under Akbar was not regained.

Basic structures—the family, the village, and the caste system—still organized daily life effectively. However, the subcontinent had suffered yet another foreign-imposed regime, the Mughals, whose ultimate political legacy involved the embittered relations between Hindus and Muslims and its own decline. As the 18th century drew to a close, India experienced yet another administration imposed from the outside. British rule relied on superior military technology rather than the sheer numbers of its forces, as earlier Muslim rulers had. The British concentrated more on commercial purposes, in contrast to the Muslim tendency, at least ultimately, to focus on religious gain. But in many ways, the British occupation confirmed what was now a well-established Indian tradition of long-suffering subjugation and control by outside forces, secure in the belief that basic local and religious structures could be preserved and were unable, in any event, to offer an effective political or military alternative. It could not be predicted, in 1800, whether British rule would finally overturn this aspect of the Indian tradition.

THE RISE AND DECLINE OF ASIAN EMPIRES

The rise of the great early modern empires in India, in Persia, and in the Middle East, dazzling though they were, did not prevent the relative decline of these regions in the face of the rapid change and expansion of Western civilization. Partly because of the persistence of cultural and political traditions, partly because of the institutions of foreign military rule, neither Indian nor Middle Eastern civilization remained actively innovative, in their technology or intellectual life, between 1700 and 1800. The conditions of most ordinary people, the bulk of them peasants, changed little. Taxes rose, especially under rapacious Ottoman governors, and economic conditions deteriorated somewhat—most obviously in India—but the basic framework remained the same.

This pattern was not totally different from that of China during the same period. Here, too, we will discuss a growing stagnation, even as the West continued to develop rapidly. Here, too, there was relative decline as a result. But in the Middle East and particularly in Persia and India, the outcome of relative decline was more quickly visible. None of the Muslim empires was able to mount a policy of strict isolation, and European merchants began entering in growing numbers. Also unlike the Chinese, the Ottomans were unable to establish any durable agreement with expanding Russian forces, in part because the Russian heartland was closer, and in part because Russian appetites for warm-water ports and contact with Middle Eastern Orthodox Christians were more vigorous than vaguer interests concerning expansion against China. Despite outside pressures and the example of imaginative individual leaders such as Suleiman and Akbar, the Ottoman and Mughal empires were no more eager than the Chinese to undertake significant internal reform. For Muslims, a reluctance to copy the West, so long viewed as culturally barbarian, was at least as great as resistance to imitation in China.

The results of first relative, then absolute, decline began to emerge after 1700. The growing British hold over much of India was the most dramatic sign that internal weakness plus Western ambition was a powerful combination. But the Middle East was vulnerable as well. In 1798, a small naval expedition under a discontented French revolutionary general, Napoleon Bonaparte, sailed to Egypt and conquered the province after brief fighting. This was a minor episode in the European history of the time, and the French were indeed soon routed by British naval forces as Napoleon returned to France to pursue grander scenarios. But to Muslims, the shock waves were profound; they came to realize that even a minor European excursion could now topple a proud Ottoman province. The question of a Western threat for the Turks and Arabs and of Western domination for the Indians was becoming paramount by 1800, despite the important political strengths that had surfaced in the 16th and 17th centuries. Indian and Middle Eastern responses, after 1800, differed widely. However, for a moment, both civilizations seemed caught in a similar position between the expansive rise of the West and Russia and the proud isolation of east Asia.

PATHS TO THE PRESENT

The Mughal empire perished by the early 19th century, the Ottoman by the early 20th. It is important to remember the empires' long success—particularly in the case of the Ottomans, the duration of whose empire surpassed that of the Romans—but political and military achievements lessened with imperial decline.

Mughal legacies to the present include the solidification of the Muslim position in the subcontinent, including the creation of Urdu as the new common language, and a host of artistic achievements. Many of the art forms seen as characteristically Indian date from Mughal patronage and the mixture of influences the emperors sponsored; the same applies to the enduring Mughal contributions to Indian cuisine.

The Safavid role in reviving and amplifying a Persian cultural and political identity had durable consequences as well, along with the establishment of a new and vigorous base for the Shiite version of Islam. Key elements of this legacy show vividly in the characteristics of present-day Iran.

As for the Ottomans' legacy, their empire consolidated Turkish peoples in the northern Middle East and created a Muslim minority in the Balkan region—part of the complex mixture of traditions and tensions that continues to fuel conflict in that area. The Ottomans also contributed greatly to the artistic and craft traditions that still exist in the region: not only did the Ottoman sultans build lasting monuments, particularly the great mosques, but the Ottoman style also influenced the making of rugs, fine metal designs, and leather work that continue to express the region's tastes and inspire considerable economic activity.

SUGGESTED WEB SITES

On the Ottomans, see http://www.theottomans .org/english/index.asp; on the history of the Ottoman Empire, its decline and fall, refer to http://www.turizm.net/turkey/history/ ottoman3.html; on the art of the Ottoman Empire, see http://www.artmuseums.harvard .edu/exhibitions/featured/GL/index.html and http://www.metmuseum.org/toah/hd/grot/ hd_grot.htm. For an extensive history of Mughal India, see http://www.sscnet.ucla.edu/ southasia/History/Mughals/mughals.html.

SUGGESTED READINGS

Recent work includes Gulru Necipoglu, *The Age of Sinan: Architectural Culture in the Ottoman Empire* (2005); Donald Quataert, *Consumption Studies and the History of the Ottoman Empire* (2000); Rifa'at Ali Abou-El-Haj, *Formation of the Modern State: The Ottoman Empire Sixteenth to Eighteenth Centuries*

(2005); Nabil Matar, *Turks, Moors & Englishmen in the Age of Discovery* (1999) and *In the Lands of the Christians: Arabic Travel Writing in the Seventeenth Century* (2003) (his two good works); Colin Imber, *The Ottoman Empire, 1300–1650: The Structure of Power* (2002); Elisabeth Ozdalga, ed., *Late Ottoman Society: The Intellectual Legacy* (2005); Nancy Bisaha, *Creating East and West: Renaissance Humanists and the Ottoman Turks* (2004); Daniel Goffman, *The Ottoman Empire and Early Modern Europe* (2002); and Eunjeong Yi, *Guild Dynamics in Seventeenth-Century Istanbul: Fluidity and Leverage* (2004). Other references include Suraiya Faroqhi, *The Ottoman Empire and the World Around It* (2004); Gábor Ágoston, *Guns for the Sultan: Military Power and the Weapons Industry in the Ottoman Empire* (2005); and *The Ottoman Empire Sixteenth to Eighteenth Centuries* (2005).

On the Mughals, see Catherine Asher and Cynthia Talbot, *India Before Europe* (2006); Farhat Hasa, *State and Locality in Mughal India: Power Relations in Western India, c. 1572–1730* (2004); Ruby Lal, *Domesticity and Power in the Early Mughal World* (2005); Kalindi Kumari, *Status of Hindus in Mughal India* (2006); M. Athar Ali, *Mughal India: Studies in Polity, Ideas, Society and Culture* (2006); Daniel Goffman, *Britons on the Ottoman Empire* (1998); Asli Curakman, *From the "Terror of the Word" to the "Sick Man of Europe": European Images of Ottoman Empire and Society from the Sixteenth Century to the Nineteenth* (2002); and Lynda Carroll, ed., *Historical Archaeology of the Ottoman Empire: Breaking New Ground* (2000).

On the Middle East generally, L. S. Stavrianos, *The Ottoman Empire: Was It the Sick Man of Europe?* (1957), offers cohesive interpretations of key issues. For comprehensive surveys, see Stanford Shaw, *History of the Ottoman Empire and Modern Turkey*, Vol. 1, *1280–1808* (1976), and Peter F. Sugar, *Southeastern Europe Under Ottoman Rule, 1354–1804* (1977). For information about India, see M. Prawdin, *The Builders of the Mogul Empire* (1963); P. Spear, *Twilight of the Mughals* (1951), provides additional insight. On Mughal cultural development, consult Gavin Hambly, *Mughal Cities* (1968). For an excellent overview, see Ira Lapidus, *A History of Islamic Societies*, 2nd ed. (2002).

20 East Asia: Vital Trends in Politics and Trade

The response of east Asia to the West and the new world economy differed greatly from the reactions that developed in Russia during the early modern period. The east Asian situation differed from that of the Muslim empires as well. China, Japan, and Korea made absolutely no attempt at westernization, although Japan briefly flirted with the idea. Geographically most distant from the West, operating in a culture much more accustomed to highly selective reactions to outside influence, east Asia stood apart from the rest of the continent. At the same time, different sets of trends took root in China and Japan. China participated heavily in the world economy from its solid manufacturing base. Japan stood apart, nurturing important internal changes in culture and politics.

Both China and Japan adopted new policies in response to the growing level of global contacts under Western auspices after the 15th century. Japan decided on substantial isolation quite explicitly, after more than a half century of intense interaction with Western influence and participation in the silver trade. China's decisions were more complex. The active commercial outreach of the Song and early Ming dynasties was not resumed. Chinese merchants remained active in the Philippines and southeast Asia, but not beyond. World trade came to China, not the other way around. But it did come, with significant profits for China because of its unrivaled manufacturing of silks and other luxury products. Westerners were not entirely banned, but they were treated as an insignificant and decidedly inferior group. These policies succeeded during the early modern period itself. But the policy of partial isolation raised problems for the more distant future, for by the 18th century, east Asian civilization was no longer maintaining the pace set by other areas of the world, particularly the West.

■KEY QUESTIONS   *What was China's position in the world economy? How did Chinese and Japanese responses to the West and the world economy compare? What were the most important changes in Japan during the early modern period?*

CHINA: THE RESUMPTION OF THE DYNASTIES

Mongol rule in China turned out to be no more than a painful but passing episode, lasting from the later part of the 13th century until 1368. Chinese resentment of the Mongols as barbarians confirmed their suspicions of the world outside their boundaries. In fact, the Mongol episode paid tribute once again to the historic assimilating power of Chinese culture. The Mongol rulers used the bureaucracy, rather than destroying it, for the simple reason that they, like earlier invaders, could think of no better administrative system. Kubilai Khan, himself a Buddhist, supported Confucian scholarship, although Confucianists did not return his affection. Trade actually increased, as contacts with Islamic merchants expanded. Chinese culture continued to experiment with new forms, particularly new dramatic and musical styles for urban audiences.

Although Chinese vitality seemed unaffected by Mongol rule, resentment increased, especially when serious flooding pushed the peasantry to revolt. Revolutionary forces drove out the Mongols, to the northern plains of Mongolia, in 1368. A rebel leader, born of peasant stock, seized the Mongol capital of Beijing and proclaimed a new *Ming*, meaning "brilliant," dynasty, which was to last until 1644.

The Ming dynasty early on experimented with the great trading expeditions through the Indian Ocean and then, in 1433, suspended these voyages, on the grounds that the effort was too costly for what it yielded to China. The growth in Chinese maritime activity that had begun around 1000 was noteworthy, but the decision to limit

international initiatives was in many ways more important to China's course during the early modern period. Other expenses, for a dynasty bent on building a splendid capital while protecting China from any Mongol resurgence, helped prompt the decision. However, the withdrawal reflected other, more important factors, beginning with a preference for traditional expenditures rather than distant foreign involvements. Chinese merchant activity continued to be extensive in southeast Asia. Chinese trading groups established permanent settlements in the Philippines, Malaysia, and Indonesia, where they contributed to the cultural diversity of the area and maintained a disproportionate role in local and regional trading activities into the 20th century.

To Western eyes, accustomed to judging a society's dynamism by its ability to reach out and acquire new territories or trading advantages, China's decision may seem hard to understand, the precursor to some inevitable decline, but in fact China did not obviously suffer from its decision to pull back. The government carefully regulated contacts with the West, permitting trade only through the Portuguese-controlled port of Macao. Ming emperors consolidated their rule over the empire's vast territory, although there was more factional fighting in the imperial court than had been true in earlier dynasties. The bureaucracy functioned well, as the Ming sent out representatives to guard against corruption by local officials. Internal economic development continued as well. Industry expanded, with growth in the production of textiles and porcelain. Ongoing trade with southeast Asia enriched the port cities. Agricultural production and the general population both increased. There was one striking economic change. Because Chinese goods were so widely sought abroad—Europeans began calling porcelain tableware *china* in the 17th century—the country gained new profits in world trade. In particular, it imported more New World silver (brought in Western ships either to China directly or to the Philippines) than any other country in the world. (India was second, and for similar reasons in terms of balance of trade.) Silver provided new tax resources for the state.

Historians of China have characterized the Ming period in terms of the importance of "change within tradition." The phrase aptly summed up developments under Ming rule, after the trading expeditions ceased. Chinese society evolved within frameworks previously established. There were no intellectual breakthroughs, no basic alterations in social structure, with the continued preeminence of the educated gentry-bureaucrat group. The expansion of trade, and the rise of a group of "overseas Chinese" merchants in southeast Asian cities with close ties to the homeland, did not shake the earlier social priorities. Cultural activity focused on summarizing expanding knowledge in medicine, agriculture, and technology; on maintaining the interest in drama and poetry; and on pursuing philosophical training in Confucianism. Family structure remained similarly stable, with an emphasis on patriarchal control, reverence for elders and ancestors, and the provision of male heirs.

The Ming dynasty began to decline early in the 1600s. Emperors grew weaker, the bureaucracy more corrupt, while peasant unrest increased under the impact of population pressure. Rebellions and roving gangs of bandits became widespread. A popular rebellion caused the last Ming emperor to hang himself. This internal disorder attracted invaders from southern Manchuria, who in 1644 established a new dynasty, the Qing (sometimes called *Manchu*), which lasted until 1912—the last royal house to rule China.

Again traditionally, the Qing (or Pure) dynasty started out with a flourish. The Manchurian emperors were foreigners in the eyes of most Chinese, and they maintained a separate military establishment to support their regime. But on the whole, their rule quickly took on familiar patterns, with a substantial reliance on the bureaucracy, which remained in Chinese hands, dominated by the educated scholar-gentry. The emperors also encouraged Confucianism. Like

From the Qing Dynasty, an ornamental pottery figure on a horse, showing continuity in Chinese ceramic styles.

most early dynasties, the Qing initially expanded the empire's territory. They pushed the Mongols still farther north and extended the empire into Muslim central Asia; they also took over the supervision of Tibet. Finally, they conquered the offshore island of Taiwan, which had previously been ruled by trading officials from the Dutch East India Company. This expansion, directed by the able Emperor Kangxi from 1662 to 1722, revealed the successful merger of Manchurian military skill and Chinese administrative expertise. Kangxi himself mastered the Confucian classics and sponsored important cultural competitions, endearing him to the Chinese scholar-gentry class.

Kangxi and his 18th-century successors also worked on increasing government centralization—another common impulse of vigorous early dynasties in the Chinese tradition. Central schools for training would-be bureaucrats expanded, and a Grand Council was established to direct the bureaucracy and process the mountain of paperwork resulting from the regular reports of local and provincial administrators. Carefully formulated regulations specified the punishments for local rebellions. Village leaders were held responsible for individuals within their community who committed crimes or tried to evade legitimate debts. Chinese society remained the most closely regulated and the most centralized in the world. Local and central administrations intertwined, and there was no real separation, as in the Western tradition, between public and private concerns.

During this vigorous period, the Qing dynasty continued to regulate European contacts with China. Kangxi negotiated an agreement with the expanding Russian empire that set their mutual border along the Amur River and that

SOLVING PROBLEMS

TRYING TO MANAGE FOOD SUPPLIES

Supplying food was hardly a new issue in the early modern period. However, rising populations in many places, plus some changes in popular outlook that began to look to the state for protection against starvation, created new tensions and new experiments.

In France, from the late 17th century onward, food shortages and increases in food prices often occasioned riots. Ordinary people, often headed by militant women who were responsible for feeding their families, frequently believed that merchants were making unfair profits and that the state should regulate them. They also resisted exports of food from their regions, arguing that their hunger came first. A great sense of moral righteousness accompanied these popular riots.

The Chinese state, with more elaborate traditions of activism, worked hard to try to prevent shortages. The Qing dynasty was eager to demonstrate its competence. During the early 18th century, the state supplemented merchant activity by setting up grain storage facilities. This allowed it to lend food to poor farmers in the spring, to be repaid at harvest time. Officials could also use these reserves to ship grain to famine-stricken regions. These activities did not, however, prevent food riots. In a crisis in 1742–1743, crowds seized grain from rich landowners and merchants, whom they accused of cheating on prices. By the end of the 18th century, furthermore, the Qing granary system began to falter, another sign of the decline of government effectiveness. Many local officials became corrupt, while growing effort was required to supply military forces needed to suppress popular unrest.

In the Ottoman Empire, government efforts focused on supply grain to the cities (including the holy cities of Mecca and Medina). Here too, functions deteriorated by the later 18th century. Many officials and elements of the military sold food for their own profit. Governments decreed price controls but could not enforce them. Popular riots resulted, put down by force.

Both ordinary people and governments tried to solve problems of food supply. Periodic bad harvests were simply part of life in agricultural economies, but pressures from cities and population growth had newer features. In several cases, food became a political issue as never before.

QUESTIONS: *What might ordinary people expect the state to do to resolve food problems? What caused the growing similarities in the perception of food as a political issue in early modern China and France?*

lasted until 1850. This checked Russian expansion into Chinese territory, although the Russians continued to move eastward into Siberia. Small numbers of Jesuit missionaries had been allowed into China since the 16th century, from western Europe, mainly because they brought useful scientific and technical knowledge, including superior clocks. For their part, the missionaries were careful to adopt many Chinese ways, approving ancestor worship and wearing Confucian clothing. In the 18th century, the government, growing less secure, began to persecute the small number of Christians in China.

The Chinese outlook toward limited Western contacts was symbolized by its reaction to the Portuguese community set up on Macao. Although some officials wanted to force the Portuguese out, the dominant view was that it was safe to leave them there because they could be so closely supervised. Indeed, it was easier to control them in this single center than to try to monitor their activities on the high seas. As one viceroy put it:

> Our military forces can watch over the foreigners by just guarding the surrounding sea. We shall know how to put them at death's door as soon as they cherish any disloyal design. Now if we move them to the open sea, by what means could we punish the foreign evildoers and how could we keep them in submission and defend ourselves against them?

Cultural contacts with the West, or indeed with any other civilizations outside the traditional Chinese orbit, thus reached only modest levels by 1800. The explicit policy of regulating foreign merchants and missionaries combined with great confidence in the superiority of Chinese ways to produce this result. Efforts by Britain and other Western countries to open further trading contacts were consistently rebuffed. An English representative in 1793 was treated as if he brought tribute from an inferior state. The emperor, rejecting the representative's request for more trade, wrote a long, patronizing letter to King George III explaining that China had no need of English goods.

Christian missionary (a Bajan Jesuit) in China, 17th century. Jesuits proceeded cautiously, respecting Chinese culture.

CULTURAL AND SOCIAL TRENDS: NEW ISSUES

There was no reason to suspect in 1800 that China was on the eve of some unprecedented difficulties going beyond the usual decline of a dynasty. However, significant problems in the empire occurred under the Qing even before this point. These problems were not initially political; the institutions of government remained secure. Nevertheless, they raised important issues.

First, Chinese culture even under the early Qing seemed to stagnate. The Qing, as foreign rulers, favored traditional styles of Chinese expression as a means of proving their sympathy with Chinese ways. Thus, the already strong emphasis on the classics of Chinese literature and philosophy increased. By the 18th century, most educated Chinese turned to collecting antique art and expounding literary criticisms of ancient works, rather than seeking to create new styles and new compositions. The amount of cultural effort was great; many bureaucrats and other educated people painted nature scenes or dabbled in calligraphy and poetry writing. But the goal was decidedly uninspired, with trivial themes emphasized and traditional styles rigidly defended. Similarly in philosophy, attention focused on expounding past principles and offering extended commentary on what had been written in earlier periods. Thus,

the earlier Chinese ability to blend a reverence for tradition with an interest in promoting new styles and stimulating new thinking seemed somewhat stultified.

The Chinese economy, for its part, did not break fundamental new ground either. Revealingly, after the early Ming advances in navigational devices, the Chinese produced no significant technologies during the Ming and Qing dynasties. This was not a matter of general decline, however: Chinese levels of achievement remained high in the arts and in the production of Chinese crafts.

One key symptom of the new outlook toward technology showed in the Chinese reaction to European superiority in weapons. The Chinese were perfectly capable, in the 16th and 17th centuries, of building cannons as good as the Europeans had, even though they had not pioneered their design. But, in fact, they did not care to; the subject did not interest them greatly, and

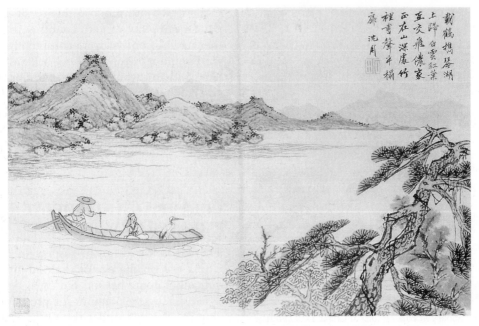

Shen Zhou (Chinese), *Scholar and Crane Returning Home*, Ming Dynasty (1368–1644).

they were content to assemble inferior muskets and small guns, confident that their strength on the land was sufficient to keep any European threat at bay. To be sure, the Chinese had never been as interested in military advances as in manufacturing technology, but their earlier creativity in the whole area was demonstrably slipping.

The interruption of China's tradition of innovation in basic technology did not, indeed, prevent continued internal economic development, supported by both the government and private business interests. During the late Ming and early Qing dynasties, manufacturing, city growth, and internal trade surpassed all previous levels. China's strong production base and extensive market activities help explain why, well into the 19th century, the nation could largely ignore Western goods, leaving Western merchants casting about for items to trade for sought-after Chinese

products such as silk and porcelain. Much production lay in the hands of rural cottage artisans whose low wages discouraged more elaborate capitalist arrangements. And by the mid-18th century, the economy began to stagnate, bringing renewed poverty and distress. Why did China not make a fuller turn to new economic forms?

The Chinese upper class had, of course, always esteemed traditionalism and looked rather scornfully at purely economic activity; such a viewpoint, nonetheless, had not prevented earlier technological or commercial advance. The increasing centralization of the government under Qing rulers, who were more cautious than their Han or Tang forebears, may have been a factor as well.

The influx of New World silver had both exhilarating and disruptive effects on Chinese society. As early as 1600, officials worried about

HISTORY DEBATE

CHINESE AND WESTERN ECONOMIES

By 1750, western Europe's economy was on the verge of a major transformation, the Industrial Revolution. China's was not. Most historians acknowledge China's great prowess in manufacturing, its skilled workers, and important natural resources. Some, eager to expand this recognition and to avoid overvaluing the West, argue that the difference between China and the West was trivial. Britain, faced with shrinking forests, had to develop a more coal-based economy to compensate, and by chance, it had well-located coal deposits; Spain had discovered the Americas by accident. But there were no deep gaps involved, no huge Western plus or Chinese minus.

Other historians stress the importance of key Western values in promoting technological change, such as a desire to dominate nature. They note greater Chinese conservatism, including the suspicion of merchant values. Europeans, by the 17th century, commented on how the Chinese tended to prefer old ways and scorn technological change, in contrast to eager European interest. (By this point, Europeans were prone to judge other societies by their technological prowess, which usually left Europeans feeling good about themselves.)

This debate has contemporary implications. China is now growing fast industrially. Some historians see this as a big change, others as a resumption of more traditional manufacturing prowess, though with new machines.

Which point of view—China and the West running neck and neck, or traditional China as flawed in industrial potential compared to the West—makes most sense?

growing income inequality. One wrote, "One man in a hundred is rich, while nine out of ten are impoverished. The poor cannot stand up to the rich who, though few in number, are able to control the majority. The lord of silver rules heaven and the god of copper cash reigns over the earth." Even Europeans noted price inflation in China, thanks to the silver influx. In China itself, Confucian traditionalists were troubled by flashy new wealth along with new signs of dire poverty.

A more fundamental problem was a rapid increase in population levels, from the late Ming dynasty on. Between 1600 and 1800, the Chinese population more than doubled, from 150 million to more than 300 million people. China's well-organized agriculture and the strong cultural emphasis on high birth rates, in order to produce male heirs in the family, had long encouraged population growth. Many dynasties had previously declined when such growth outstripped available resources, creating greater poverty. Usually, however, population rates then leveled off, but this did not happen during the late Ming and early Qing periods. Agricultural techniques were advanced enough to maintain a large but impoverished population. Cultivation of some crops brought in from the Americas by European traders and missionaries, particularly corn and the sweet potato, added to the agricultural production that could support high population levels. New strains of rice, which grew more rapidly than older varieties, achieved the same end. As a result of these crop changes, China began to shift from a society in which population sometimes outstripped resources to a society chronically challenged by its population levels.

Population pressure, in turn, had two clear effects, quite apart from the great poverty of many Chinese peasants and urban workers. First, it made political unrest a greater threat than had usually been the case except when dynasties were losing their grip. Second, it diverted resources that might have been used to encourage further

manufacturing or trade to a desperate effort to sustain the vast population. The empire's economic flexibility was reduced by the need to devote so much labor and land to agricultural subsistence. This may be the clearest cause of the lack of innovation in the economy and possibly even in the culture.

By the late 18th century, massive poverty and slow economic growth began to surface as clear political problems. The Qing government found it increasingly difficult to collect adequate taxes. Collection efforts, along with grinding misery, also began to produce a new series of popular revolts. Peasants in many regions formed secret societies. An uprising by one such society in the 1790s, the White Lotus, was vanquished only with great difficulty. At the same time, the Qing dynasty was showing signs of internal decay: military virtues waned among the Manchu generals, who preferred more luxurious living, and court officials became more corrupt, siphoning off money from the state. This kind of decline normally prefaced a period of growing instability and, ultimately, the rise of a new dynasty. Greater disorder came, without question, in the 19th century, but for once in China's long history, a new regime, not a new dynasty, was the ultimate result.

Stagnation and political problems were not the only feature of Chinese society under the Qing. Some interesting changes occurred in popular culture, as Confucian leaders managed to persuade more and more peasants to abandon older beliefs in magic and superstition and to use doctors instead of shamans in cases of illness. This shift in outlook, somewhat similar to changes occurring in the West during the same period, differentiated China from most agricultural societies, where popular religion had yet to be disturbed. The scholar-bureaucrats also pressed peasants and city dwellers to standardize the worship of local gods and goddesses. The practice of celebrating various deities and building temples to them had persisted from the classical period or before, along with other belief systems, and the government long tried to bend this popular faith toward loyalty to the state. Certainly, in 1800, the Chinese government remained easily able to regulate China's contacts with other cultures. European influence, most notably, remained no greater than it had been two centuries before, and European traders were powerless to escape government supervision. Only developments after 1800 broke this stalemate, to China's disadvantage.

JAPAN AND THE ORIGINS OF ISOLATION

Japanese social forms were less firmly set around 1450 than those of China, so it is not surprising that Japanese history shows more movement, more basic change, than the evolution of its giant neighbor. However, the Japanese shared one basic concept with the Chinese: the belief that the outside world was a risky and inferior place, best kept at bay.

Japan was touched only indirectly by the Mongol invasions. The failure of the two great Mongol attacks on Japan bolstered Japanese confidence in the god-protected superiority of their own society even over that of China, which now lay under foreign thrall. But the defense effort was costly to the ruling government of the shogun; it contributed to the fall of this essentially feudal monarchy in 1338. Japan returned to a stage of regional feudal governments, of the warlike *daimyos* and their samurai supporters. A central government remained in form only. In fact, disorder and warfare, punctuated by some peasant rebellions, continued until 1573. A host of classic campaigns, celebrated in legend and more recently in Japanese films, dotted this period, in which samurai fighting techniques and codes of honor were perfected.

Despite disorder, the Japanese economy continued to progress. Because the daimyos were well aware of the importance of prosperous agriculture

for their own tax revenues, they promoted irrigation efforts and improved methods of farming. Trade also grew, and the use of banking and money expanded. Daimyo supervision of trade established a pattern of government–business collaboration that in many ways has remained to the present day.

Japanese culture continued to develop as well, again creating durable new forms. The Zen strain of Buddhism, stressing calm meditation and a love of nature, predominated in religion, although there were many Buddhist sects, and Shintoism still guided family ceremonies as well. Zen Buddhism encouraged an interest in rituals, as demonstrations of the simplicity of true beauty and as signs of self-control. Tea ceremonies and flower arrangements were important parts of family and social life. The Zen spirit also influenced art, leading to a focus on simple but dramatic representations of nature.

In literature, adventure stories and poetry continued to dominate. Soon after 1600, a new poetic form, the *haiku*, a 17-syllable verse in a 5-7-5 pattern, became popular. Although this was a new style, it maintained the east Asian tradition of carefully enunciated rules of poetry and an interest in the clever play on words. Composing haiku became a favored pastime among all social classes.

By the mid-1500s, however, the Japanese combination of feudal warfare and economic and cultural creativity was eroding. Feudalism could no longer contain the forces at work in Japanese society. A rising merchant class complicated the feudal pattern. Armies of peasant soldiers were sometimes able to beat samurai swordsmen—just as common bowmen in Europe had ultimately dislodged the feudal cavalry. Furthermore, Portuguese traders reached Japanese shores in 1542, and although they were initially welcomed by a people who had once before learned from others, their presence encouraged a desire among more conservative cultural and political leaders to develop a stronger government that could regulate foreign

The arrival of Francis Xavier and his entourage in Japan is depicted in this 16th-century screen painting. The painting wonderfully conveys Japanese perceptions of these strangers from distant lands as exotic, awkward, and curiously dressed. Other than differences in skin color, to which the Japanese were highly sensitive, all have rather similar facial features, perhaps because the Japanese thought that all Westerners looked alike.

intrusion. And the guns and cannons the Portuguese brought obviously threatened the fighting traditions of the samurai. Many regional daimyos tried to ally with the foreigners to gain a weapons advantage; the result, for a time, was simply further disorder. In the long run, however, the advent of gunpowder increased the possibility of greater governmental centralization. As the Japanese quickly learned to manufacture their own muskets, the fate of the undiluted feudal system was sealed.

The end of pure feudalism came in the form of several brutal wars at the conclusion of the 16th century in which a successful general, Hideyoshi, emerged victorious. Hideyoshi was able to reestablish centralized rule by using the allegiance of the daimyos. Thus, the feudal classes remained in Japan but were once again overseen by a national administration. After Hideyoshi's death, a general from the Tokugawa family took over the office of shogun and completed the process of centralization. A "great peace" settled on Japan, after more than two centuries of internal warfare.

This new centralization caused a reassessment of Japan's contacts with the outside world.

The Portuguese come to Japan, 16th century.

Hideyoshi contemplated a policy of foreign conquest to keep the warlike samurai busy—a policy later renewed by Japan after 1890. However, an attempt to invade Korea failed, as Chinese armies supported their vassal government there, and this convinced the new Japanese government to concentrate instead on its own unique territories.

Hideyoshi and the early Tokugawa shoguns thus turned to what they saw as the problem of Western influence. Initial Western contacts had been welcomed not only for the guns and navigation technology the Westerners brought but also, among some Japanese, for the religious message of Christianity. Interested in learning from foreign example and impressed by a religion that seemed to accompany military and trading success, several thousand Japanese converted to Catholicism in the port cities where Europeans clustered, during the late 16th century. But Japan's new rulers looked harshly on this development. They feared European power and thought that where Western religion went, political control might not be far behind. When the Spanish government established military outposts in the Philippines, to enhance the missionary effort there, Hideyoshi's fears deepened. In 1597, he banned all foreign missionaries, crucifying 9 of them and 17 of their Japanese followers.

Western weapons seemed at least as great a threat as Christianity. The new central rulers feared the results of independent daimyo access to Western firearms. Rather, they sought state control over guns, while also protecting samurai warrior values. To do this, they needed to restrict foreign trade.

The Tokugawa shogunate completed the destruction of Christianity in Japan. It severely curtailed Western trade as well. Only merchants from the Netherlands were allowed in Japan— Holland was feared less than Spain or Portugal because, being Protestant, it was not linked to what seemed to the Japanese an ambitious and powerful papacy. Dutch traders were confined to one isolated, carefully controlled port (Nagasaki). Even Chinese merchants were supervised. In 1635, the Japanese themselves were forbidden to travel abroad, and those already overseas were not allowed to return home. Finally, the government prohibited the construction of large, seagoing ships; only vessels for coastal trade were permitted. Japan, far more than China, was substantially cut off from the outside world. A nation that had once eagerly imitated foreign example, and would do so again in the 19th century, pulled back on this occasion. European ways seemed too foreign, and too inferior, to be allowed free play,

WORLD PROFILES

TOYOTOMI HIDEYOSHI
(R. 1536–1548)

Toyotomi Hideyoshi was an outstanding military leader who extended earlier 16th-century efforts to tame the power struggles among the daimyos in favor of more centralized, orderly rule. The son of a peasant, Hideyoshi used his military acumen to rise to power in Japan; he then parlayed even greater diplomatic talents into the creation of a string of alliances with the daimyos that resulted in a central state by 1590. Hideyoshi, unlike most Japanese leaders before or after, dreamed of wider achievements as he contemplated ruling China and even India (despite, or perhaps because of, knowing little about either place). He did launch two abortive attacks on Korea, the last still in progress when he died. More importantly, Hideyoshi also launched the campaign to limit European and Christian influence in Japan. Hideyoshi's hopes to pass power to his son were dashed as the Tokugawa family seized control and his plans of overseas expansion were dropped. Nevertheless, he had contributed greatly to changing the course of Japanese history. How does Hideyoshi compare, in achievements and goals, to other great military leaders in world history who rose from the ranks?

This portrait reflects the military might and confidence that spurred Toyotomi Hideyoshi's achievements.

and attacking outside influence was a useful way of cementing new national loyalties after the long period of disunity.

The policy of isolation combined with the regulation of military technology, now that foreign items could not be imported. The shogunate deliberately turned against guns, preferring to preserve the Japanese social structure. Only a few could be manufactured each year—sometimes no more than nine for the whole country. Even more than in the Ottoman Empire, where printing was long shunned, Japan decisively rejected the idea that new technology is always good technology.

In isolation, Japan proceeded to construct effective political forms and completed the development of a national culture, sponsoring considerable social change while seeming to maintain older values. Unlike the earlier Kamakura shogunate, the Tokugawa rulers depended less on personal ties with feudal lords and more on an efficient bureaucracy imbued with Confucian values. The warrior aristocracy was given great social prestige, including

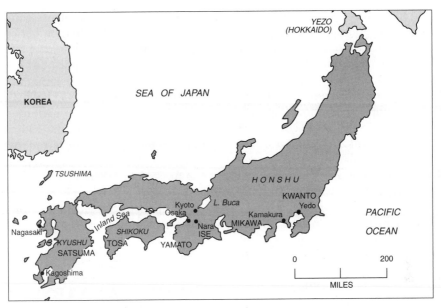

Feudal Japan Under the Shogunate, 16th Century

special privileges in law, and special costumes, although in fact there was no fighting to be done. Although warrior values and military training continued to describe the samurai ethic, upper-class bureaucrats learned the importance of administrative efficiency and training—Confucian principles that gained ground during the 17th and 18th centuries. This was an important period of cultural change in Japan, as Confucianism, and therefore secular interests, increasingly dominated intellectual life. The rapid spread of Confucian education and literacy disseminated the new cultural interests by the 19th century. The Japanese interpretation of Confucianism involved far wider access to schools than in China, and Buddhist schools contributed as well. Thanks to extensive schooling, literacy (at 25 percent among adult men) was far higher than in any society outside western Europe and North America.

Although largely confined to internal trading, merchant activity flourished during the Tokugawa period. The government favored commerce but was somewhat scornful of the merchant class. Great

trading houses emerged, selling rice, textile goods, metals, and liquor all over Japan; some of these big family firms still operate in Japan today. This was a key period for the development of banking and merchant experience in Japan. Some trade with China and the West (through Dutch merchants) continued, and even grew during the 17th century. Japanese agriculture advanced, becoming more technologically sophisticated than any other system in Asia. Japanese farmers learned about crop specialization and the better use of fertilization; they also became increasingly accustomed to producing for sale on the market. Although economic growth slowed somewhat after 1700, Japan had the most advanced commercial economy in the world after that of Western society. In another important development, population size was controlled in the 18th century, in contrast to the situation in China. Many peasants practiced infanticide of unwanted—and particularly female—children.

Japanese literature and art remained vigorous under the Tokugawa, who supervised cultural life to prevent disorder. Enthusiasm for

haiku poetry and the stylized *No* theater continued. Literacy and book publishing spread. As in
China, the growth of cities—particularly the
capital city, Edo, which had a million inhabitants
by 1700—encouraged a flourishing entertainment industry. Professional women entertainers,
called *geisha*, or "accomplished persons," specialized in singing and dancing for male clientele. A
new form of drama, Kabuki, developed in the
18th century, more popular in its portrayals
than the No forms; Kabuki theater remains
active in Japan today. Not surprisingly, the varied artistic endeavors and continuing isolation
of Japan produced a heavy emphasis on the
nation's uniqueness and superiority, the forerunner of a cultural nationalism that still runs
strong in Japan.

Japan thus emerged, by the 18th century, as
an unusually diverse society, tolerating more
internal tensions than China. Feudal and
Confucian elements coexisted. An official lack of
interest in commerce belied rapid commercial
expansion; Buddhist spiritual fervor could survive in the face of a national emphasis on controlled expression and secular education. These
tensions contributed to the dynamism of
Japanese society, which had unquestionably
advanced under the policy of isolation.

Indeed, by the 18th century, the policy of
isolation was slightly relaxed. Some Japanese
were allowed greater contact with Dutch
traders in the port of Nagasaki; a few scholars
learned Dutch and became familiar with
Western advances in military technology and
medicine. These early exchanges helped prepare the way for the fuller adaptation of
Western ways in the 19th century. At the same
time, they whetted the appetites of those few
Japanese aware of the gap between their society and the West; Japanese backwardness in
scientific and medical knowledge seemed particularly galling.

There were problems by 1800. Japan did
not experience the kind of population pressure
that burdened China, although its islands were
severely crowded. But Japan's commercial agriculture resulted in a division between landowning peasants and landless paid laborers, whose
discontent produced periodic revolts. On the
whole, however, Japan's strengths, generated by
the important developments of the early modern
period, help explain the nation's extraordinary
reaction to challenges in the 19th century, when
isolation finally had to be abandoned completely.
The contrast with the looming crisis in China
was marked, but there were some new concerns,
and these too help explain why Japan became
more open to the possibility of more radical
transformations.

VITALITY AND TENSION IN EAST ASIA

East Asian history between 1400 and 1800
involved a complex interplay between change
and continuity. Change involved new political
dynasties but also new cultural and economic
forms, particularly in Japan. It also meant some
new problems, such as the overpopulation that
surged in China. The role of tradition was strong
as well, in Japanese culture and its sense of
national identity, in Chinese politics and society
more generally.

East Asia's deliberate distancing from
Western innovations in technology and military
organization during these centuries left the civilization vulnerable after 1800. This choice was so
clearly disastrous for China that it inspired
China's communist leader in 1984 to claim that
the Ming–Qing period of isolation—as well as a
more recent, brief attempt to insulate China
from foreign contact—was a mistake.

During the early modern period, China's
success in participating in the world economy
on its own terms, and Japan's success in generating effective political and cultural changes, easily
overshadowed any sense of future problems,
however.

PATHS
TO THE PRESENT

Several trends of the early modern period contributed to the framework of contemporary east Asia. China's population growth eventually intensified to such an extreme that it generated dramatic government measures at the end of the 20th century. China's position as a world manufacturing center, though interrupted during the late 19th to early 20th century, resumed by the 21st century, and some officials regarded this as a return to traditional normalcy. Japan's growing interest in Confucianism, and its increasing interest in spreading Confucian education, helped explain later Japanese secularism and educational enthusiasm—though Confucianism itself was somewhat modified in Japan.

Distinctions between Japan and China also shifted between. In the postclassical period, Japan differed from China mainly by failing to imitate its neighbor completely. During this period, the two societies made different choices about population, participation in world trade, and the extent of available education. Today, Japan and China continue to share many features but still follow rather different political and cultural paths. Much of the distinction between the two societies stems from more recent historical experiences, including lingering hostilities from 20th-century wars, but certain distinctions were generated by the greater separation that occurred during the early modern centuries.

SUGGESTED WEB SITES

Asia resources, including gateways to information on China, Japan, Korea, and Vietnam, may be found at http://www.aasianst.org/links/asiawww.htm. Information for educators on Asia can be found at http://afe.easia.columbia.edu/ and at http://afe.easia.columbia.edu/webcourse/key_points/kp_8.htm; the latter has an excellent link to information on China, Japan, and Korea. For students, information on later imperial China can be found at http://www.mnsu.edu/emuseum/prehistory/china/later_imperial_china/yuan.html. Students can visit the National Museum of Japanese History at http://www.rekihaku.ac.jp/index_ne.html.

SUGGESTED READINGS

An excellent collection of sources is W. T. de Bary, ed., *Sources of Chinese Tradition*, 2nd ed. (2000); close to source reading and offering fascinating insight into Chinese provincial life is Jonathan Spence, *The Death of Woman Wang* (1979). Larger studies of China include Edward L. Dryer, *Zheng He: China and the Oceans in the Early Ming Dynasty 1405–1433* (2006); Catherine Jami, Peter M. Engelfriet, and Gregory Blue, eds., *Statecraft and Intellectual Renewal in Late Ming China: The Cross-Cultural Synthesis of Xu Guangqu* (2001); J. D. Spence and J. E. Wills Jr., eds., *From Ming to Qing: Conquest, Religion and Continuity in Seventeenth Century China* (1979); Pei-kai Cheng and Michael Lestz, with Jonathan D. Spence, eds., *The Search for Modern China: A Documentary Collection* (1999); Albert Chan, *The Glory and Fall of the Ming Dynasty* (1982); Roy Huang, *1587: A Year of No Significance; The Ming Dynasty in Decline* (1981); Lynn A. Struve, ed., *The Qing Formation in World-Historical Time* (2004); and Jonathan Spence, *The Memory Palace of Matteo Ricci* (1984) and *The Search for Modern China* (1990).

On Japan, consult Constantine Nomikos Vaporis, *Tour of Duty: Samurai, Military Service in Edo, and the Culture of Early Modern Japan* (2008); Lee Butler, *Emperor and Aristocracy in Japan, 1467–1680* (2002); Peter Duus, *Feudalism in Japan* (1976); H. D. Harootunian, *Toward Restoration: The Growth of Political Consciousness in Tokugawa Japan* (1970); and E. O. Reischauer, *Japan: The Study of a Nation*, 3rd ed. (1981). Noel Perrin, *Giving Up the Gun* (1979), is a fascinating account of shogun policies on weapons and trade. On the much debated, important topic of peasant conditions in the Tokugawa shogunate, see H. Bix, *Peasant Protest in Japan, 1590–1884* (1986).

Recent work includes Anthony Reid, *Sojourners and Settlers: Histories of Southeast Asia and the Chinese* (2001); Paul Varley, *Japanese Culture* (2001); Kenneth Pomeranz, *The Great Divergence: China, Europe, and the Making of the Modern World Economy* (2000); Zvi Ben-Dor Benite, *The Dao of Muhammad: A Cultural History of Muslims in Late Imperial China* (2005); Sarah Schneewind, *Community Schools and the State in Ming China* (2006); D. E. Mungello, *The Great Encounter of China and the West, 1500–1800* (2005); Peter C. Perdue, *China Marches West: The Qing Conquest of Central Eurasia* (2005); Roger V. Des Forges, *Cultural Centrality and Political Change in Chinese History: Northeast Henan in the Fall of the Ming* (2003); Michael Marmé, *Suzhou: Where the Goods of All the Provinces Converge* (2005); Michael Szonyi, *Practicing Kinship: Lineage and Descent in Late Imperial China* (2002); Kurt Singer, ed., *The Life of Ancient Japan: Selected Contemporary Texts Illustrating Social Life and Ideals Before the Era of Seclusion* (2002); William E. Deal, *Handbook to Life in Medieval and Early Modern Japan* (2006); and Bert Edstrom, ed., *Turning Points in Japanese History* (2002).

A New World Economy, 1450–1750

CONTACTS AND IDENTITIES

The early modern period is an intriguing chapter in the world history of contacts and identities. Contacts changed and accelerated. More societies were more strongly affected by world trade than ever before—some profited, others experienced loss. The intensification of global contacts was greeted by unusual efforts to preserve identities—which is one reason that it is difficult to point to truly global cultural trends during this period.

The expansion of new landed empires raises questions similar to those generated by earlier patterns in world history. To what extent would new rulers, initially from central Asia, integrate their holdings? For instance, Ottoman expansion might unsettle Arabs, who were under unfamiliar rule. Mughal operations in India raised issues for Hindus, particularly when tolerance declined. The rise of the Safavids added to Persian or Iranian identity. Russia embraced new minorities, some of whom, such as most Muslims in the empire, maintained largely separate identities. But what about Ukrainians now under the rule of Russians, who had kindred religions and languages—could a larger common Russian identity be forged?

Broader identity issues arose in other places: American Indian identities were deeply affected by new contacts with Europeans and with Christian missionaries. Europeans pressed not only new religious loyalties but also new gender standards on native peoples, arguing for example that many Native American women had too much independence and should be more acquiescent to their husbands' authority. This is a major case of contact-induced transformation. As in other historical episodes of this sort, however, native groups managed to retain some identity. In Latin America,

particularly, Indians managed to combine traditional art forms and religious beliefs with Christianity, while often maintaining traditional village community structures. Gradually, a new Latin American culture emerged that combined European and native influences in a major case of syncretism, often with substantial African contribution.

Russia's westernization process is another case of identity modification due to imitation of other cultures. Russian leaders selected their models carefully and retained many badges of traditional identity, including the Orthodox version of Christianity. Common people, far less affected by encounters with foreign influences, faced less identity challenge. Even members of the elite soon argued that resistance to certain Western influence was vital, preferring to maintain as pure a Russian identity as possible. This launched within Russian a debate about identity and westernization that has continued, in various forms, to the present day.

Far more cases of identity alteration, however, suggest that the vigorous increase in international trade contacts caused an almost deliberate resistance to modification of traditional identity. Japan, to take an obvious example, decided that having more than very limited outside contacts would jeopardize political and cultural independence—Japanese leaders saw the Philippines, which was now controlled by the Spanish and extensively influenced by Catholicism, as a case in point. Japan was also concerned about preserving its social identity: the decision to largely abandon guns and cannon was motivated, above all, by the desire to maintain samurai values and social prestige. Japan did not abandon all contact, however, and opened the doors a bit wider in the

18th century, when it realized that Western scientific and medical knowledge might be useful. For the most part, however, their relatively isolationist stance remained firm: identity was more important than extensive interaction.

China opted for a different choice. Trade was embraced, resulting in considerable profit for many Chinese. Long-distance trade was undertaken only by foreigners, but Chinese merchants settled and remained active in southeast Asia. Chinese leaders believed that new commercial connections did not jeopardize distinctive cultural traditions. They even welcomed a small number of Christian missionaries, partly to obtain access to European technological devices, so long as the missionaries adapted extensively to Chinese ways. The reversal of this tolerance for non-Chinese, in the 18th century, suggests new concern about identity, even though the number of conversions to Christianity remained fairly modest.

Like the Chinese, Mughal rulers were initially quite open to outside influences, but their tolerance later declined as well. The Ottoman Empire, cosmopolitan in many ways, and with extensive contacts with other societies, also limited cultural importations—this is one reason the use of printing was so long delayed in the region.

Even western Europe proved less interested in selective imitation than previously. Despite this, many Europeans learned more about other parts of the world than ever before. Asian products and animals were imported and often eagerly sought, as in the case of Chinese porcelain or Indian cottons. Tremendous interest developed in Middle Eastern coffee and coffeehouses, which became all the rage in the 17th and 18th centuries. But many Europeans did not feel that there was much to learn from other cultures. Most non-Europeans were seen as curiosities, as inferiors, or as heathens. Europeans' willingness to acknowledge the value of Islamic science and philosophy, so vivid during the previous period, now ceased; even when European scholars did borrow Muslim knowledge, they were now loath to admit it. In other words, here, too, a sense of separate identity reigned.

This early modern pattern of retaining identity to the greatest degree possible was inherently unstable. It was hard to juggle pride in cultural distinctiveness with the reality of increasing trade. But the predominant patterns were interesting, revealing impulses to have the best of both worlds—to profit while limiting the effects of contact—still visible today.

PART V

The World's First Industrial Period, 1750–1914

INTRODUCTION: THE INTERNATIONAL IMPACT OF INDUSTRIALIZATION

The century and a half after about 1750—often called the "long 19th century"—was dominated by the Industrial Revolution, one of the great changes in the human experience. This revolution did not occur overnight, but it ultimately reduced the importance of agriculture and agricultural labor relative to manufacturing and associated trade. Through new technology, it reshaped the processes of production, transportation, and communication. It reduced the link between families and work, spurring new definitions of family and new choices about roles for family members. This transformation, which continues today, was as significant as the earlier shift from hunting and gathering to agriculture.

Like the agricultural revolution after 9000 B.C.E., the Industrial Revolution massively changed where people lived and how they worked; it (gradually but fundamentally) altered family structures and gender relations, redefining the purposes of childhood. Also like the agricultural revolution, the Industrial Revolution increased available surpluses beyond basic material needs. The result supported not only a much larger global population than the agricultural economy could afford, but also higher consumer standards for many people and a growing number of specialists—from new government officials to an unprecedented number of professional entertainers. These consequences would ultimately have global impact, along with new economic divisions among regions; but they first showed in industrialization's initial home in Western society.

The long 19th century was defined not only by the Industrial Revolution, but by the fact that industrialization concentrated in western Europe and North America. Other regions were deeply affected—this was a global process from the start—but were forced to focus on food and raw materials production, and to suffer from the growing gap between agricultural and industrial economies, or to try and catch up to the industrial nations—or both.

Western Europe's industrial dominance during this period had two major consequences, both of which translated into new sources of power. The first was military. By the 1790s, Western armies were gaining new advantages over their rivals, even the great societies of Asia and Africa. More mobile artillery and the introduction of weapons such as the repeating rifle combined with an increasing capacity to mass-produce armaments thanks to new inventions such as interchangeable parts. During the 19th century proper, Western armies could and did overtake most societies not already under Western control. The armies were supported by steamships and railroads that enabled quicker movement of troops and supplies, in part because troops could now easily move not only across oceans but across rivers. All major societies in the world ultimately had to react to the new realities of military power.

The second change involved the world economy. The growing rate of production of factory goods in Europe displaced many traditional industries. Military force opened the way for European merchants where trade alone did not

suffice. By the second half of the 19th century, most of the world outside the West was busy producing foods, raw materials, and cheap craft products for Western markets, while importing Western manufactures. Increasing competition for goods, from vegetable oils to coffee to copper, drove prices up and wages down, further widening the gap between the prosperity of Western nations and the poverty of nonindustrial economies. In 1800, the average Mexican's income was only two-thirds that of the average citizen in the new United States; in 1900, the figure had dropped to one-third, thanks to simultaneously growing United States industrial prosperity and Mexican poverty.

The transformation of the world economy also began to have significant environmental impacts. Regions around Western industrial centers suffered water and air pollution, a result of factory smoke, urban waste, and chemical runoff. Only later in the 19th century did new measures, such as urban sewage systems, begin to address these problems. Conditions outside the West were changing as well. The pressure to produce more coffee, cotton, or rubber led to massive deforestation and, frequently, soil erosion, from Africa to Latin America.

Changes in global labor systems accompanied this first stage of the Industrial Revolution. Workers in many Western countries suffered great poverty, longer hours and greater danger on the job, and other problems, though conditions improved somewhat in the later decades of

Table V.1
ESTIMATED POPULATION OF THE WORLD AND THE CONTINENTS, 1650–1850 (IN MILLIONS)

Continent	1650	1750	1800	1850
Africa	100	95	90	95
Asia (excluding Russia)	327	475	597	741
Latin America	12	11	19	33
North America	1	1	6	26
Europe plus Asiatic Russia	103	144	192	274
Oceania	2	2	2	2
World Total	545	728	906	1171

Source: Adapted from Dennis Wrong, *Population and Society* (New York: Random House, 1969), p. 13.

the 19th century. Worldwide, the most striking change was the growing movement to outlaw slavery and serfdom—a historic shift for two of the most traditional labor arrangements. New Western humanitarian ideals, gradually accepted by other societies, were one cause of this shift. Another was global population growth, which increased the supply of labor available at low wages. As slavery declined, new forms of immigration filled the void. More than a million people from places such as China and India were sent as indentured workers to southeast Asia, the Caribbean, and Hawaii, to meet the continuing need for cheap labor in new ways.

Along with this, finally, came the gradual spread of new ideas, including nationalism, liberalism, and socialism. These ideas began to reshape political life, often in response to the new military and economic challenges generated by the Industrial Revolution. The new political ideas surged first in the Atlantic world, spreading among western Europe, North America, and Latin America, in part through the surge of revolutions and independence wars around 1800. Only later and more gradually did some of the ideas begin to make sense in Asia and Africa, sometimes as a means of resistance to Western economic and military pressure.

The massive shift to Western military and economic advantage during this period contributed to change in virtually every society during the 19th century, but societies responded to this shift in different ways. Nonindustrialized cultures' varying traditions and divergent forms of contact with the West, ranging from colonial status to efforts at independent reform, produced different 19th-century histories, despite the common framework. New forms of resistance to Western power arose in several places. This resistance often used religious symbolism, combined traditional values with reform interests, and expressed discomfort both with growing Western control and with local ineffectiveness in countering that control. Nationalist movements, an even more novel response, sought new bases for resistance to the West (in terms Westerners could understand, even if they tried to repress the movements) and attempted to balance tradition and change. Ironically, nationalism began in Europe itself, but the concept gradually spread to Asia and Latin America.

Chapters in this part first discuss the changes in the West, then turn to the rapid growth of and transformation caused by Western imperialism, then briefly cover the Western-dominated settler societies that developed in key regions. China and the Ottoman Empire constituted major civilizations that retained technical independence amid growing outside interference. Russia and Japan, also independent, reacted more successfully to the Western and industrial challenge. A final chapter deals with the late-19th-century tensions that exploded in the form of World War I—the event that ended this challenging chapter in world history.

GLOBAL CONNECTIONS

New technologies shrank the world during the long 19th century. With the steamship and the telegraph, both introduced during the 1830s, news and goods could travel around the globe in unprecedented quantity and at unprecedented speed. By the second half of the century, railroads were cutting across several continents, also with revolutionary impact. Joined with technology were other crucial shortcuts, provided notably by the Suez and then the Panama Canal. Never had goods moved so freely—in some ways, by 1900, more freely even than today. Small wonder that many historians now regard the later 19th century as the effective beginnings of globalization.

Buoyed by technology, Western imperialism also created new cultural connections. Though European powers were hesitant to impose too many changes on colonies they regarded mainly as economic property, they introduced some common patterns to most of their colonized cultures.

By the end of the 19th century, for example, European colonial governments sponsored new public health measures (as a matter of self-interest) that reduced common sources of disease in urban areas around the world. Countries such as Japan, eager to preserve independence through reforms, quickly imitated these Western systems, as did many Latin American governments.

Economic and political organizations reflected and furthered the process of connection. Major industrial firms in Europe and the United States began to set up production branches in other countries to increase profits and reduce shipping costs. Singer Sewing Machine Company, for example, formed one of the largest companies in Russia during the late 19th century. Western-based international companies were also eager to develop local raw materials and foods.

Two new kinds of political connections formed as well. First, Western governments, after 1850, began to sponsor international agreements to facilitate trade. The International Postal Union, for example, coordinated worldwide mail delivery for the first time in history. Such innovations were imposed by the West but had global application. Second, new kinds of nongovernmental organizations sought global impact and audience. The antislavery movement, though initially focused in the West, gradually founded branches elsewhere. By the 1880s, several international feminist organizations formed; they were primarily Western, but they gradually sought and found scattered membership in Asia and Latin America as well. The same applied to the new international socialist movement, which generated offshoots in many parts of the world.

Finally, there were even new kinds of global linkages in popular culture. Spread by European and American colonialists and merchants, certain kinds of sports began to gain worldwide interest by the later 19th century. Soccer football groups formed in places such as Latin America. Japan sported baseball teams by the 1890s.

Despite the breadth and depth of transformation that occurred during this period, it is important not to exaggerate its effects. Even amid new global industrial competition, many societies maintained traditional forms of production. Even though Western-style department stores began to spring up in places such as Tokyo and Shanghai, many people saw no reason to visit them, continuing to prefer locally made clothing and furniture styles. International political movements by no means dominated regional political patterns. Regional complexities, in other words, responded to the global trends of this new period.

CHAPTER 21

The First Industrial Revolution: Western Society, 1780–1914

The Industrial Revolution was the predominant development in western Europe during the 19th century. Along with industrialization came a host of new political movements associated in particular with the great French Revolution of 1789. New approaches in science and art constituted a third area of innovation. Developments in all three areas significantly altered western Europe. They had major implications for the rest of the world as well.

The Industrial Revolution transformed agricultural society much as the Neolithic revolution had once transformed hunting-and-gathering cultures. Associated with this economic and technological upheaval in western Europe and North America was the development of new political forms, ushered in by a variety of revolutions in many countries. Industrialization and political change also introduced major shifts in cultural life and basic social relationships, including class structure, family roles, and the locations of people's homes and work. The West did not lose all touch with its traditions in this sweeping process, but it was forced to reshape those traditions it retained.

This chapter deals with the transformation of the West itself, including the causes of change that evolved from previous developments in Western society, before proceeding to its global impact. With industrialization, the West utilized the social and intellectualized currents of the early modern period and the capital amassed from its role of world trade, in order to produce a society the likes of which had never been seen before in world history.

KEY QUESTIONS *How did the main changes in the West relate to each other? Did new political ideas such as liberalism and democracy fit easily with industrialization? Did new trends in art mesh or conflict with a machine age? How were daily lives, including family lives, affected by the key changes?*

PATTERNS OF INDUSTRIALIZATION

Typically, when we examine major historical periods within a civilization, political or cultural developments hold center stage. Thus, there are centuries during which new political organizations seem to dominate other activities, and other centuries in which new religions, scientific innovations, or shifts in popular beliefs are the primary focus. In 19th-century Europe, however, economic and technological change must be studied in advance of other features; economic change meant, above all else, industrialization.

In its essence, the Industrial Revolution consisted of a fundamental shift in technology and power sources. Instead of relying on human and animal power for virtually all production, the Industrial Revolution substituted fossil fuel power, first by means of coal to drive steam engines and later with electric and internal combustion engines. Along with the revolutionary power sources came new production equipment that could apply power to manufacturing (and later to other activities), with less dependence on

human effort. Spinning jennies wound fiber into thread, applying steam or, in the early days, waterpower through gear transmissions. The flying shuttle was adapted to steam engines for weaving. Hammering and rolling devices allowed the application of power machinery to metallurgy. Although, in early industrialization, textile manufacturing and metallurgy, along with coal mining, received the greatest attention, engines were also used in sugar refining, printing, and other processes. The industry of machine building arose to construct engines, looms, and presses—the new tools of production. Machine building was greatly aided by the American invention of interchangeable parts, initially introduced for the manufacture of rifles.

The technological breakthrough spread quickly to communication and transportation. The development of the telegraph, steam shipping, and the railway, all early in the 19th century, provided new speed in the transport of information and goods. These inventions were vital in facilitating Western domination in world affairs.

Innovations were applied to agriculture, particularly after 1850, with new harvesting and

Power loom weaving in a cotton textile mill, 1834.

planting equipment and gasoline-powered tractors. Scientific farming methods also produced artificial fertilizers and new strains of seeds and livestock. Technology also reached offices, through typewriters and cash registers, and homes, with sewing machines and refrigerators, although again, the major changes surfaced in the later 19th century on. By this point, virtually all kinds of work had been altered by new equipment and power sources.

Furthermore, technological change was a recurrent process once the Industrial Revolution was launched. New generations of equipment displaced earlier machines. By the late 19th century, when the United States assumed the lead in technological advances, many power looms were sufficiently automated for one weaver to operate 16 or more looms, in contrast to the one or two looms per worker in earlier decades. Metallurgy was transformed, beginning in the 1850s, by new blast furnaces that increased the capacity for refining iron ore and allowed the automatic reintroduction of minerals to convert iron into steel. Coal mining, although less open to modernization, saw the introduction of engines to move ore and then cutting devices to use in the pits. Clearly, the Industrial Revolution may be linked to no single change in methods, but to successive waves of innovation.

Along with revolutionary inventions came major changes in economic organization. Manufacturing was becoming concentrated in factories, rather than in small shops. With steam equipment, it was necessary for workers to cluster around the engines. Even apart from technological requirements, there were advantages to be gained from grouping larger numbers of workers: both discipline and specialization increased. Finance, too, became more sophisticated. New equipment and factories required growing investments. Banks began to play a greater role in funding industry. Corporations grew, particularly after 1850, to sell shares to large numbers of investors. In industrial economies, big firms assumed a dominant position. Even in sales, small shops increasingly faced the competition of department stores

and mail-order houses. Thus, the fundamental characteristics of economic organization were concentration, bureaucracy, and impersonality.

CAUSES OF INDUSTRIALIZATION

The Industrial Revolution first took shape in Great Britain, where key inventions, including the steam engine, had been introduced by 1780. British developments were quickly copied and other inventions added so that, by the 1820s, most of western Europe and the new United States were actively engaged in the early stages of the Industrial Revolution as well. Indeed, during the 19th century, the United States and Germany caught up with Britain, particularly in their emphasis on coal and iron production. The first Industrial Revolution was thus a Western-wide phenomenon, despite some interesting regional variations within the West.

The position the West had acquired in the world economy provided an active framework for the Industrial Revolution. European nations gained large amounts of capital from their colonial trading activities, including the slave trade. Businessmen also learned that there were markets for processed goods, which helped motivate them to devise new and cheaper ways to produce such goods. The great Asian manufacturing economies provided examples as well: early industrialization used machines to compete with Indian textiles or Chinese porcelain production. The privileged position of the West in world trade unquestionably explains why it was this society that first introduced industrialization and why it long maintained an industrial lead over other areas.

The internal causes of the Industrial Revolution were exceedingly complex, a fact that helps explain why many societies continue to find it difficult to complete the process the West first introduced. The factors that went into the West's Industrial Revolution range from a massive population increase, which forced many workers to accept factory jobs simply because they had no alternative, to new ideas and a business mentality that made some industrial entrepreneurs positively eager to introduce risky changes. Material resources and capital constituted other Western advantages in pioneering the industrial spirit.

Industrialization built on many of the trends in Western society prior to the 1780s. The new technologies were related to the rise of science. James Watt, the inventor of the first manufacturing steam engine, worked closely with scientists at the University of Glasgow. During the 19th century, the link between the economy and science grew closer, as university chemists worked on developing new dyes, fertilizers, and explosives. More widely, the outlook accompanying the rise of science promoted beliefs in change and control over nature that guided many manufacturing innovators even without specific exposure to formal science.

Industrialization required capital and a willingness to take risks. Western experience in colonial trade had encouraged a daring merchant spirit that was now applied to manufacturing. The colonial trade and earlier improvements in agriculture and domestic manufacturing had resulted in considerable capital, available for investment in the new equipment. New business forms emerged, through expanded joint-stock companies and banks, to mobilize capital for factories and railroads. Industrialization also required favorable natural resources, particularly coal and iron ore; parts of Europe and North America had these in abundance, along with rivers and canals that facilitated transport even before the rise of the railroads.

Along with science, an openness to risk and change, and the availability of capital, a massive increase in population growth spurred the Industrial Revolution in western Europe. Beginning early in the 18th century, the population began to soar, rising between 50 and 100 percent in all Western nations before 1800. The population

revolution was itself caused by relatively peaceful conditions, a temporary decline in epidemic disease, and above all, the introduction of new foodstuffs brought from the Americas. Europeans had initially hesitated to try new foods, but by 1700 they began to convert rapidly, particularly in their adoption of the potato into their diets. The use of new foods caused agricultural production to rise and the death rate to drop, which in turn allowed more offspring to live to adulthood and have children of their own. Hence, the population booms in a civilization that had not been particularly crowded previously. Population pressure rose rapidly, forcing many people off the land and creating a labor force for the new cities and factories. It also spurred merchants to take new risks in order to provide for their own growing families. The population revolution thus helps explain the timing of the West's Industrial Revolution as it combined with other factors.

Adding to population pressure was a new spirit of consumerism. Many people, in countries such as Britain, sought new forms of pleasure and identity in buying fashionable clothes and furnishings. Shopkeepers learned new methods of advertising and sales gimmicks to fuel this process. These new markets (along with colonial outlets) helped convince manufacturers to innovate in the interests of increasing production.

In several Western countries, full industrialization also depended on political change. In general, industrialization relied heavily on private capitalists, who built the new factories and offices. But governments played a role as well. In the United States, government provision of free land was vital to the development of the railroad network; in France and Germany, governments built rail systems outright. At the same time, governments had to abandon certain traditional practices in order for industrialization to occur. They could no longer, for example, defend the guild system, which tended to restrict technological innovation and the free movement of labor. Nor could they continue to defend slavery.

HISTORY DEBATE

CONSUMERISM AND INDUSTRIALIZATION

Until about 15 years ago, historians thought they completely understood the relationship between Western industrialization, which was a major new production system, and the advent of a society in which the consumption of goods played a transforming role in defining the economy and personal goals. Industrialization came first, and only later did output reach levels at which people gained both the time and the money needed for mass consumption.

Major discoveries in recent years, however, demonstrate that the first stage of a new kind of consumer society arose in places such as England during the 18th century. New shops opened, advertising and sales gimmicks gained ground, and ordinary people began to place new meaning on acquiring goods, particularly clothing and furniture. New levels of consumption helped cause industrialization, which then accelerated consumerism to yet another stage. What historians still debate, however, is *why* consumerism arose in advance of major new production levels. Enjoyment of products from the world economy—sugar, for example, or Asian textiles—played a role. So did prior changes in social structure, which created more fluid boundaries in which people sought to establish identities by wearing stylish clothes. So did a decline in religious fervor. But the precise causes remain to be established through fresh historical inquiry.

Political revolutions in France and its neighbors, and the Civil War in the United States, served a vital function in establishing governmental systems favorable to industrialization and promoting a sense among government officials that industrialization was a good thing. Although a host of factors, such as the bitter moral debate over slavery, entered into U.S. political conflicts, a key ingredient was the clash over how the economy should be organized, with the North urging mobile wage laborers tied to rapid technological change. In the 1861–1865 Civil War, Northern industrial strength provided a vital edge, and in turn, after the war, U.S. encouragement of rapid industrialization increased.

Industrialization was no simple development, even in its first, Western home. Many people resisted the changes in habits and the new, materialistic values it promoted. A complex set of causes, ranging from population growth to the dissemination of modern ideas, was needed to generate wide adoption of the new inventions and forms of organization.

EFFECTS OF INDUSTRIALIZATION

The economic effects of industrialization did not end with the rise of the factory system and the new equipment. Industrialization produced new wealth. With machines, productivity per worker rose rapidly. Even with the equipment available by 1800, a single worker using steam-driven spindles, for example, could produce as much thread as 100 manual spinners. Not all improvements in productivity were this vast, and the resulting new wealth was not evenly distributed. The West, already a wealthy society by world standards, became richer. Expanding wealth brought major changes in living standards and a desire for further improvements. By the later 19th century, the apparatus of a consumer society expanded further, as factories turned out growing quantities of goods. Advertising also developed, promoting a new mass press. Shopping gained public attention; even a new disorder, kleptomania, reflected the obsession with consumer goods.

Industrialization, which had depended on greater agricultural output through new crops, transformed farming in turn. Growing factories and cities required major improvements in the output of food. The average farmer had to produce more, so that an increasing percentage of society could live and work off the farms. New equipment, fertilizers, and scientific techniques promoted the spread of market agriculture. More and more European peasants tried to increase their landholdings and employ landless laborers, to take advantage of market opportunities. This kind of peasant was still tied to village traditions but more open than before to production growth and moneymaking. Some peasants specialized in dairy farming or vegetable production for the cities, buying more processed goods as a result. Finally, particularly after the rise of steam shipping, canning, and refrigeration in the later 19th century, western Europe looked to other parts of the world for some of its food. Grain imports from eastern Europe were surpassed by the highly productive commercial farms of the United States, Canada, Australia, and Argentina—where technological change far outstripped peasant levels—and meat was imported as well. Industrialization reduced the size of the agricultural population in the Western world while transforming economic life for those who remained on the farms.

Industrialization also created new needs for management skills and the handling of information. Early factories were small, often run by a single family. But with growth came larger and more complex hierarchies, with supervisors directing the workers, a sales staff, secretaries, and file clerks. Along with the spread of large department stores, the rise of management created an expanding white-collar workforce, which by 1870 had growth rates even more rapid than those of factory labor. Like factory workers, white-collar employees were highly specialized and closely supervised according to rules designed to encourage maximum productivity.

Another effect of industrialization was the development of cities, and particularly big cities located at transportation hubs, near coal fields, or as banking and political centers. During the Industrial Revolution, hundreds of thousands of people, mostly young, migrated from country to city, prodded by population pressure and the prospect of new, better-paying jobs. By 1850, for the first time in history, half of Britain's population lived in cities. By around 1900, the same was true of Germany, France, and the United States. The rapid growth of cities placed tremendous stress on existing urban structures and governments. Many early industrial cities suffered appalling conditions in housing and sanitation. Gradually, however, aided by industrial wealth, cities improved; by 1850, the worst was over in the West, as cities began to process sewage, pave streets, inspect the quality of food and housing, and provide parks and various other amenities. Adjusting to urbanization—or failing to adjust— was an important aspect of the whole industrialization process.

Closely related to urbanization were changes in health conditions. In agricultural societies, urbanization on the scale now introduced by the West would have been impossible, not only because of insufficient food supplies but also because cities had long bred disease. Indeed, during the first two-thirds of the 19th century, urban health was a serious problem in the West, as poverty and inadequate sanitation caused continuing high death rates. However, more efficient urban organization, particularly in the provision of better treatment of sewage and purer water supplies, plus related gains in medical knowledge through the development of

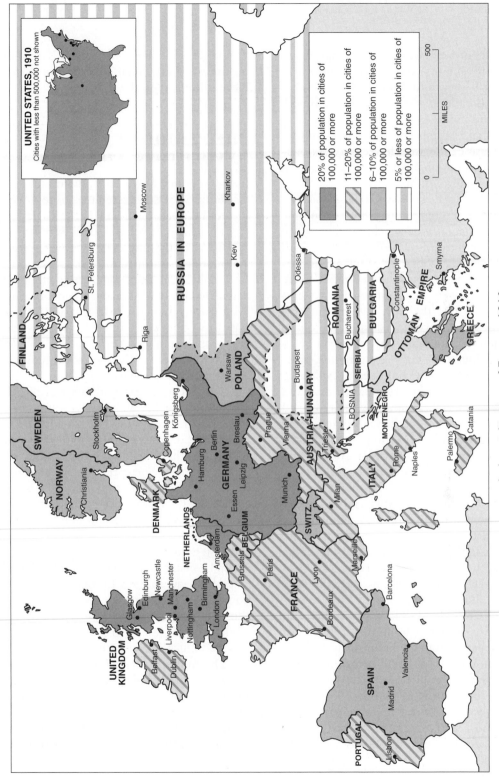

UNITED STATES, 1910
Cities with less than 500,000 not shown

20% of population in cities of 100,000 or more

11–20% of population in cities of 100,000 or more

6–10% of population in cities of 100,000 or more

5% or less of population in cities of 100,000 or more

500

0

MILES

Moscow

Kharkov

St. Petersburg

Kiev

RUSSIA IN EUROPE

FINLAND

Riga

Odessa

ROMANIA

Bucharest

Smyrna

SWEDEN

Stockholm

Königsberg

Warsaw

POLAND

Copenhagen

BULGARIA

Constantinople

OTTOMAN EMPIRE

GREECE

SERBIA

BOSNIA

NORWAY

Christiania

DENMARK

Hamburg

Berlin

Breslau

Prague

Vienna

AUSTRIA-HUNGARY

Budapest

MONTENEGRO

Catania

NETHERLANDS

Amsterdam

Essen

Leipzig

GERMANY

Munich

Trieste

ITALY

Rome

Naples

Palermo

BELGIUM

Brussels

SWITZ.

Milan

UNITED KINGDOM

Glasgow

Edinburgh

Newcastle

Belfast

Dublin

Liverpool

Manchester

Nottingham

Birmingham

London

Paris

FRANCE

Lyon

Marseille

Bordeaux

Barcelona

SPAIN

Madrid

Valencia

PORTUGAL

Lisbon

Industrialization of Europe, 1910

379

the germ theory of disease, caused significant health improvements after 1880. Child death rates, especially, began to drop rapidly. Instead of a third of all children dying before adulthood, by 1900 the figure was down to less than 20 percent and falling fast. Here was another important use of the wealth, technical knowledge, and organizational skills that resulted from the Industrial Revolution.

The Industrial Revolution, itself primarily a transformation in technology and economic organization, had wide-reaching effects on where people lived, how healthy and well off they were, and what jobs they had. The transformations engendered by industrialization were not sudden, nor were they uniform. Early factories were small, and the large factory run by a hierarchy of supervisors and managers was only a development of the later 19th century. Many groups continued to work along rather traditional lines, well into the Industrial Revolution. Artisans still produced luxury products and even some necessities such as housing; most women employed in the cities worked as domestic servants, with their jobs remaining largely traditional. But change, if sometimes gradual and uneven, was the primary characteristic of the West's industrial century. Even artisans faced pressures to become less creative and more efficiency-minded in their work, while rising factories eclipsed their overall importance. By 1900, most people in the West were not working at the same jobs their great-grandparents had performed in 1780; they were not living in the same place; they did not engage in the same recreational activities. In 1780, most people had worked in or near the home; by 1900, most work was separate from the home. In 1780, most people had used traditional herbal remedies when ill, viewing hospitals as places where the desperately poor went to die; by 1900, many people in the West were beginning to rely on hospitals and doctors regularly and to believe that many age-old health problems could and

should be eliminated. Here were some human measures of the change that the Industrial Revolution had produced.

THE PERIOD OF REVOLUTION, 1789–1848

Industrialization was a large, subterranean, often faceless process that altered the shape of Western society between 1780 and 1914. Particularly in its early phases, Western people were not always aware of exactly how their lives were changing. The concept of an industrial revolution itself arose only late in the 19th century, after the most basic changes had already taken place in the West. Along with industrialization, and more noticeable to most articulate observers, came a compelling number of political and intellectual innovations that produced a seemingly endless series of dramatic events.

The period began with a series of political revolutions, starting with the Revolutionary War in North America in the 1770s, which led to the formation of the United States. Americans, stirred by the liberal political values of the Enlightenment and pressed by new British restrictions on trade and political autonomy, engaged in the first modern struggle for national independence. They established a republican form of government, with a decentralized federal system and wide male suffrage. U.S. ties to Europe remained close, which enabled Americans to pick up quickly on European industrialization; European investment in the United States also supported economic change and expansion, while growing waves of European immigrants provided much of the necessary labor.

The American Revolution helped inspire a more sweeping revolution in France, starting in 1789. This great event resulted from an absolute monarchy grown inefficient, the power of Enlightenment ideas, and the discontent and confusion brought about by population growth and rising commerce in advance of outright industrialization. The French Revolution was the first of many struggles in various parts of the world that would stem from pressures to change that could not be contained within traditional political and social structures. Moreover, the French Revolution, although not fully successful, did alter the political and legal framework of French society and, through conquest and imitation, that of much of the rest of western Europe.

The French had grown restless under an absolute monarchy that was ineffective and unable to produce meaningful reforms. Many French people resented the powers of the church and the aristocracy. Population pressure added to the discontent, as did the growing popularity of Enlightenment ideas. Although France was not yet industrializing, groups of peasants and artisans were already hostile toward the increasingly commercial spirit of many merchants and farmers; they saw revolution not as a blow for new political forms so much as a way to regain older values. This complex mix came to a head in 1789 when the king, Louis XVI, strapped for funds, had to call a meeting of the Estates-General, the former medieval parliament that had not met for 175 years. Business and professional people, inspired by the Enlightenment, were unwilling to meet as a separate estate, giving greater power to the aristocracy and clergy as the first two estates. Peasants in many parts of France also rose against the remnants of manorial obligations. The great political revolution of modern Western history was underway.

The revolution went through several stages. For two years, relatively moderate leaders tried to set up a constitutional monarchy, which would protect the freedoms of the press, religion, and assembly. The idea was to scale down the power of the church, while abolishing serfdom and the guilds, thus abolishing the underpinnings of traditional social structure. The government divided up many of the estates of the aristocrats, making France a country of peasant owners. The Constitution of 1791 proclaimed the legal equality of all French people, as opposed to the traditional idea that different social groups had different rights of heredity. A parliament was established, with the vote confined to the relatively wealthy—a strong suggestion that middle-class rule, based on the power of money, was replacing aristocratic rule, based on legal privilege by birth. But, partly because of opposition inside France and attacks by foreign monarchies, the revolution turned steadily more radical. Many aristocrats and other opponents were killed in what was called, somewhat grandiosely, the Reign of Terror (1793–1794); radicals executed the king and proclaimed a republic. The power of the central government increased over traditional local bodies; every man was allowed a vote. The most important result of the revolution's radical phase was the organization of a new, mass conscript army—now that citizens were equal, they had equal obligations to serve—which helped the revolutionaries gain new territories in western Germany, the Low Countries, and elsewhere. This successful war spread many of the revolutionary principles to larger parts of western Europe.

The radical phase of the revolution was soon overturned, and in 1799 a military dictator, Napoleon Bonaparte, took charge of France. There followed 15 years of recurrent fighting as Napoleon sought to carve out a European empire. Within France, Napoleon confirmed revolutionary law and promoted new secondary schools to recruit talented bureaucrats. Napoleon's conquests outside France weakened the manor system and advanced the idea of equality under the law throughout much of western Europe. Wars during the revolution and under Napoleon also encouraged considerable popular nationalism. The French, armed with their new political rights, became enthusiastic about being citizens of France; Germans and Spaniards, angered by Napoleon's invasions, grew more nationalistic in

Respectable middle-class leisure in western Europe.

opposition. Nationalism supplemented the efforts of Europe's monarchies to put down the dangerous revolutionary upstart. Britain was a consistent enemy of France, with Austria and Prussia frequent opponents of Napoleon. The tsar of Russia, now intervening more in Western affairs than ever before, also played an important role in the final alliance that vanquished Napoleon. An attempt by Napoleon to invade Russia, in 1812, ended in disaster. As Russian forces retreated, the French armies followed and were subsequently caught in the frozen hold of a Russian winter; here was a sign of how much Russian military organization and size had changed since the days of the Mongols. The allies finally conquered France and exiled Napoleon in 1814–1815. A glittering diplomatic gathering, the Congress of Vienna, then tried to reassemble Europe's pieces.

For the next 30 years, Europe seemed dominated by conservative attempts to contain the forces that the revolution had unleashed. The monarchy was restored in France, and some, although not all, of the revolutionary legislation undone. The Catholic church, vigorously allied with the antirevolutionary cause, gained new rights in France and elsewhere—however, it never recovered the vast property lost during the revolutionary period. Conservatism was buttressed by a new intellectual current called *romanticism*, which opposed Enlightenment values. Romantic writers and artists wished above all to express emotion; they disdained the cold rationalism of the 18th century. They adored gothic styles and medieval adventures. Some romantic theorists went further, opposing Enlightenment political values in the name of religion or the mystical collective power of the state, which, they felt, should not be constrained by constitutions or individual rights.

Although conservatism gained new ground, the old order that had existed before the French Revolution and the Napoleonic Wars could not be recaptured. The Congress of Vienna, for example, did not restore the small states into which Italy and Germany had been divided; it thus encouraged Italian and German nationalists to hope that their respective countries could be unified outright. At the same time, liberals in France and elsewhere wanted to regain revolutionary achievements such as constitutions, parliaments, wider voting rights, and full religious freedom. And a new, small group of socialists began to encourage protest in the name of economic equality. Thus, western Europe was besieged by periodic efforts at agitation. Conservative leaders, headed by the tsar and the Habsburg monarchy, with its able minister Prince Metternich, tried in vain to keep the lid on popular unrest. Revolutions broke out in Spain, parts of Italy, and then Greece after 1820, with the Greeks winning independence from the Ottoman Empire. Again in 1830, further revolutions developed, leading to a new monarchy in France with a more liberal air, independence, and a liberal monarchy for Belgium, and upheaval elsewhere. A final series of revolutions, in 1848, swept over much of western Europe. It destroyed manorialism in Germany and Austria, encouraged Italian and German nationalists without, however, winning unity, and unseated the monarchy in France, this time for good.

A few Western countries were exempt from the tide of revolution. Britain, although strongly conservative in its opposition to the French Revolution, already had a parliamentary system. Popular protests in Britain sought political and social liberalization. In 1832, a reform bill gave most middle-class people the right to vote, and other reforms extended fuller religious tolerance, even to Catholics and Jews; regulated women and child workers in the factories; and granted new powers to city governments in improving material conditions. British politics became increasingly liberal, without revolution. Scandinavian governments also granted new powers to their parliaments and widened suffrage. In the United States, where revolution had already produced a constitutional republic and protection for individual liberty through the Bill of Rights, further pressures for political change were met, in the Jacksonian era of the 1830s, by reforms such as the secret ballot and extension of voting rights.

The revolutionary era in the West ended with the uprisings of 1848. There has been no major political revolution in this civilization since that time. The assurance of food supplies, prevention of famine, and stronger police forces contributed to the end of Western revolution, as did various political changes. On the surface, the revolutions of 1848 were political failures. Liberal leaders, eager for new rights and parliaments, grew afraid of the demands of the growing urban masses. Urban workers, pressed by the crowding and upheaval of early industrialization, sought economic reform, and a few fought for socialism as a means of creating economic equality. Socialists argued for group control over property and production, often urging governmental attacks on capitalist ownership and capitalist values. Revolutionaries were divided still further in many countries by their nationalist interests. German nationalists, for example, often wanted unity more than liberal political reforms. Amid these divisions, the forces of the traditional monarchs reasserted themselves, chasing revolutionaries from Hungary to Italy. In France, a nephew of the great Napoleon won popular election as president and soon established a new empire. The new or restored regimes proceeded to create police forces that helped stamp out political agitation.

The 1848 revolution in Berlin. After months of maneuvering, negotiation, and street clashes, the revolutionaries agreed on a liberal constitution that would have established a constitutional monarchy. When they offered the crown under these terms to King Friedrich Wilhelm IV, who had initially given in to the demands of the crowds, he politely declined, saying in private that he could not accept a crown "from the gutter." Friedrich Wilhelm believed he ruled by divine right—not by the consent of the governed. The great difference between the king's and the reformers' views of constitutional monarchy was indicative of the chasm that exited in mid-19th-century Europe between advocates of aristocratic and democratic government.

THE POSTREVOLUTIONARY ERA AND NATIONALISM, 1848–1871

Political repression was not the whole story after 1848. The revolutions had won new freedoms for the peasantry, in their complete abolition of the manor system. Most of western Europe now became a region of small peasant farmers; the aristocracy, although still powerful, was weakened. Furthermore, government leaders began to realize that concessions were necessary in the political arena, if a new round of revolution was

not to begin. So they granted constitutions and new powers to parliaments, plus a widened suffrage; these changes contented many liberals. Conservatism, in other words, became more adaptable. Two particularly flexible conservatives also worked to meet nationalist demands. In Italy, Count Cavour, the leader of a regional state in the north, engineered a series of wars beginning in 1859 that freed Italy from Austrian control and unified the entire peninsula. Otto von Bismarck, a Prussian politician, followed by orchestrating three regional wars, from 1864 to 1870, that unified the states of Germany. His final war, against France, also led to the downfall of Louis Napoleon's empire and the establishment of a new republic.

By 1870–1871, then, with the unification of Italy and Germany, political and diplomatic changes in western Europe had delighted most moderate nationalists. The new nations, and also Habsburg Austria-Hungary, had constitutions with some real protection for personal liberties, including religious freedom; they had parliaments with some real power over the budget. Germany even offered universal male suffrage, although the measure was qualified by a complex voting system. France, newly republican, also confirmed universal male suffrage. These developments, along with continued reforms in other states—as in Britain, where suffrage was extended in 1867 and 1884 so that a majority of men could vote—seemed to satisfy most Westerners sufficiently that basic issues of political structure no longer dominated the scene.

The United States also addressed a fundamental issue of political structure in the same period, through the Civil War. The preservation of the Union and the abolition of slavery did not end important political divisions in the United States or the continuing problems faced by the black minority. As in much of Europe, political change was qualified by conservative principles. Thus, while Germany granted parliamentary rights but kept basic sovereignty in the hands of the monarch, who appointed the state's chief ministers, the United States abolished slavery but then allowed new kinds of legal discriminations against black citizens after the Reconstruction period. However, such changes reduced internal friction, another of the adjustments that brought revolution to an end throughout the West and resolved some long-standing issues related to political and legal structures.

Western society had thus gone through several political phases by 1871: outright revolution and upheaval, dominated by the French Revolution and Napoleon (1789–1815); conservative–liberal contest (1815–1848); and consolidation, often under the auspices of flexible conservatives

(1849–1871). This last period had produced several sharp conflicts and the bloody American Civil War, which was the first war to signal the importance and destructive power of armies backed by industrial arsenals. The era of romanticism had ended in the West, and with it some of the more visionary political efforts; politicians now preferred hard facts and cold steel to enthusiasms either revolutionary or conservative. Bismarck, in fact, talked of having created the new, united Germany through "blood and iron."

"THE SOCIAL QUESTION," 1871–1914

Between 1871 and 1914, most Western governments were concerned with protecting the gains and compromises of earlier times. There was no major war within the Western world, although rivalries spilled over into struggles for colonial empires elsewhere. Germany's unification and the consolidation of the United States brought these powers increasingly to the fore, which automatically generated new tensions by altering the balance of forces in the West. One result was a new system of diplomatic alliances, as Germany sought to protect itself by linking with Austria and Italy, whereas France, eager to regain territories lost to Germany in 1871, gradually constructed its own alliance with Russia and then Britain. Diplomatic maneuvering among the leading Western powers won growing attention by the end of the century; ultimately, in 1914, it helped lead to unprecedented world war.

The final decades of the century saw two major developments in the internal politics of Western nations. Governments began to react more clearly to the pressures and problems of industrial society, taking on new functions. Many countries followed Germany's example and maintained mass conscript armies even in peacetime. Most countries extended a national system of compulsory education. National—or, in the United States, state—governments also took on new functions in inspecting factory conditions, setting housing standards, and the like; many began to provide health services to the poor. A number of governments, finally, led by Bismarck's Germany in the 1880s, passed social insurance laws, granting some state-sponsored protection against financial problems caused by illness, accident, or old age.

The expanded functions of governments were prompted in part by new political pressures, the second important domestic political development. Socialist parties arose everywhere after 1871. Many were inspired by the doctrines of Karl Marx, who had worked out his theories between 1847 and 1870. Socialist parties urged major reforms to protect working people; their goal was an alternative to capitalism that would provide economic equality. Some advocated revolution to reach this goal, but in fact most Western socialists worked within the political system, seeking to obtain power by a majority vote. Careful political organization and wide appeal made socialist parties the strongest single political force in Germany and an important third force, along with liberals and conservatives, in Britain, France, and (until after World War I) the United States.

The rise of socialism and the new functions of governments made what was called *the social question*—what to do about poverty and working-class demands—the leading domestic political issue in the last decades of the 19th century. Political alignments around this issue overshadowed the year-to-year shifts in parliamentary votes or presidential elections, as this level of politics became relatively routine. Thus, after a series of earlier periods in which the *form* of government had been the leading issue, Western politics settled increasingly into debates about the *functions* of government, about the role of government in the reshaping (or preventing the reshaping) of society, and, with growing urgency, about the role of government in international affairs, as the armies and arsenals of the Western nations were mobilized around a tense network of diplomatic rivalries. Some observers believed that divisions over the social question encouraged Western governments to think in terms of diplomatic initiatives that could unite their nations, thus distracting them from new signs of unrest.

Another key shift occurred in the final decades of the 19th century: the growth of military rivalries. As Western nations built or expanded overseas empires, they increased military spending, forming huge peacetime armies and navies. Soon after 1900, for example, Britain and Germany competed to see who could build the biggest battleships, providing new links between the state and the industrial economy in the process. The sense of national competition expanded, particularly with the rise of a powerful Germany. Government leaders spent much of their time on diplomatic and military issues, amid recurrent crises. The popular press also played up rivalries, creating a sense of tension and excitement that could push leaders to new adventures, particularly in the imperial field. Between the 1870s and the 1890s, two alliance systems took shape, one linking Germany, the Habsburg monarchy, and Italy, the other France, Britain, and Russia. The systems were defensive, but there was great potential for new conflicts. Both sides engaged in active planning for war. The West had long defined the state in part for its role in war and expansion, but with modern military technology, these functions took on new implications.

WESTERN POLITICAL INSTITUTIONS IN THE INDUSTRIAL REVOLUTION

The age of revolution in Western society recalled earlier political traditions in this civilization by calling for new balance against the power of the monarchy. However, this traditional impulse was reshaped by new political ideologies and the demands of an industrializing society. The result was a new kind of government, neither medieval nor absolutist in structure. Liberal leaders pressed for new protections for individual rights and for elected parliaments, and this led to new rights for newspapers, religious groups, even trade unions. Popular pressure and more radical leaders gradually persuaded some liberals to demand a democratic voting system.

Nationalism constituted another new force, fed by revolutionary beliefs in popular government and reactions to French invasions. Nationalists argued that the state should be linked to a single basic culture—a "national" culture, which should override minority differences within the society and should clearly delineate each nation in relation to others. Nation-states were partly invented—national cultures were not, in fact, so clear-cut—but the association of a state with a dominant language, literature, and history proved to be a powerful mix, first in Europe, then elsewhere in the world. Nationalists could either call for allegiance to existing territorial states, as in revolutionary France, or, as in Germany, they could claim ethnic cultural unity and urge its political expression. In Europe, nationalism fed the long-standing military and economic competition among states and ultimately encouraged a growth in the power of the state.

The result of liberal and popular pressure, through the decades of revolution and reform, was a new structure for most Western states. By the 1870s, the Western political framework involved parliaments, based on wide voting rights, which served as the source of most legislation and acted as a check on executive authority. Monarchies had either been abolished, as in France, or greatly reduced in power. The political activities of the Catholic and Protestant churches had been radically scaled down, and most governments no longer believed that they should perform significant religious functions. It is important to realize that Western governments varied in the extent to which they had embraced liberal goals; the new German state, for instance, was notably less liberal in structure and intent than the governments of France, Britain, and the United States. And there were important political movements in many countries that opposed liberal values in the name

of the older principles of monarchy and aristocracy. Nevertheless, despite variety and opposition, liberal values had significantly reshaped Western politics during the 19th century, among other things creating more similar political forms among the major Western states than had existed during the 17th and 18th centuries.

One key result of the development of liberal institutions was the rise of modern political parties, designed to organize members of parliament and to campaign for popular votes. In the United States, both major political parties espoused broadly liberal goals, although they differed significantly at important points of American history—for example, on the issue of slavery. In most European countries, liberal political parties competed with more conservative groups. By the 1870s, most conservative parties had added nationalist appeals to their political agenda, using this new force to advocate a strong state and military. Nationalism also gained force from the disruptions caused by industrialization. As people moved to the cities from their local villages, they were open to new loyalties, and a fascination with national achievements often served this purpose well. Finally, particularly after 1870, socialist parties began to grow, adding a new element to the political spectrum of most Western countries. Socialists were wary of nationalism and found liberalism too limited, although they largely accepted the importance of parliamentary institutions. Socialists pressed for major legislation on behalf of working people, and their revolutionary rhetoric often frightened liberals and conservatives. Nowhere, by 1914, had socialists won major positions in government, but their growing power helped generate new legislation to address important social questions.

Western politics, then, involved not only new political institutions, but also a multiparty system embracing a wide variety of political opinions. These views, expressed through a host of new "isms"—liberalism, socialism, nationalism, and formal conservatism—coexisted uneasily, and some politicians questioned the ability of the

WORLD PROFILES

MARY WOLLSTONECRAFT
(1759–1797)

Mary Wollstonecraft was one of the world's first explicit feminists. Her book *A Vindication of the Rights of Woman* (1792) applied the doctrines of the ongoing French Revolution to women's issues and effectively launched the modern women's movement, not only in her native Britain but throughout the Western world.

Wollstonecraft was the daughter of a tradesman who abused her mother and squandered his own inheritance. She early rebelled against some of the conventional practices applied to women, and her first writings addressed the lack of occupations open to them. She frequented radical circles in London and followed a deliberately unconventional lifestyle, bearing two children out of wedlock. (She died after the birth of her second child, Mary Shelley, the author of *Frankenstein*.) Wollstonecraft's sometimes shocking behavior caused subsequent feminists to shy away from citing her literary examples until a full century later. What combination of personal characteristics and more general social forces might have prompted such a radical life and outlook at this time?

This portrait, by John Opie, shows Wollstonecraft as a powerful woman with a trace of sadness. She may have been pregnant with her second child at the time.

parliamentary system to manage all the forces it had unleashed. But most groups accepted at least tentatively the possibility of working within the system, seeking to win enough votes to enact the government measures they sought. Continuing changes in voting rights opened the way to additional issues. A rising feminist movement in many countries by 1900 pressed for women's right to vote; this was mainly an issue for the future, but

several American states did grant women's suffrage, and Scandinavian governments did so shortly after 1900. Here was an important extension of the idea that basic political power should rest with the people themselves, expressed through equal voting rights.

Along with new constitutional structures and parties, the modern Western state assumed important new responsibilities and created the bureaucracy to carry them out. Some old functions were, of course, dropped or reduced, including the support of a single official religion and of aristocratic privilege. Governments after 1848 had also stopped defending the rights of groups such as guilds to establish work rules. But the new tasks of government were more extensive than those that were abandoned; one sign of this was that government staffs and budgets grew steadily, with rare exceptions, throughout the 19th century.

Western nations now clearly recognized their duty to encourage economic growth. Some used tariffs to protect particular industries. All supported the spread of railroad and canal networks. Governments also took on the function of mass education. All Western governments by the 1870s not only operated primary and secondary schools but also required attendance to at least age 12. Schools had as their role the teaching of useful economic skills to promote agricultural and manufacturing productivity. They also vigorously preached national loyalty, hoping the national literatures and histories would instill a new consensus among its citizens. Mass education was a new phenomenon, and levels of literacy, reaching 80 to 90 percent in Western society by 1900, had no precedent. The idea of the state, rather than the churches, serving as main educator was also novel. In addition, governments gained new contact with citizens through the practice of universal military conscription. The draft was used only in wartime by the United States and Britain, but even so, military forces grew larger than ever before. Because most male citizens spent a period in military service, as in France and Germany, they experienced firsthand the new power of the modern state—and, of course, had yet another occasion to learn national loyalties. Finally, as we have seen, governments began to take on responsibility for providing some protection for the health and well-being of all citizens. Laws regulating working conditions and consumer rights, efforts to build sewers and other public-health facilities, and social insurance measures were important signs of the new welfare functions of the Western state.

To meet the new demands, the Western state not only expanded its bureaucracies but also began to recruit according to talent. Secondary schools in many countries served particularly to train future bureaucrats. All Western governments introduced civil service examinations by the 1870s—imitating practices long ago developed in China. Although most upper bureaucrats still came from the aristocracy and wealthy business and professional groups, there was a new chance for ordinary people to rise on the basis of academic achievement and test results.

The Western state, as it had emerged by 1914, embodied some interesting tensions. Liberal structures implied controls on government power, through bills of rights and parliamentary limits. However, government functions and bureaucracies had grown, often with the blessing of liberals themselves. This tension was, in important ways, a restatement of older Western ambiguities about the state. It also reflected the fact that different political groups disagreed about the state's proper role. The tension over the state and its limits continued to color Western history into the 20th century.

WESTERN CULTURE IN THE INDUSTRIAL CENTURY

The 19th century produced a bewildering variety of intellectual movements. Major novelists abounded: Dickens, Austen, and many others in Britain; Hawthorne, Melville, and others in the United States; Balzac, Zola, and others in France. Poetry was slightly less important, as was drama, but here too literary production soared, and with it a host of new styles. In the arts, romantic painters focused on pastoral scenes, and then, in the last decades of the century, impressionists challenged old traditions of literal representation in their attempt to use the canvas to convey the essence, rather than the surface reality, of what the eye beholds. Interestingly, the 19th century did not produce a distinctive architectural style—revived gothic buildings predominated—but there was also classical and even Byzantine imitation. Science continued its advance, with major strides in biology, notably Darwin's theory of evolution; in electricity and magnetism as well as other aspects of physics; discovery of the germ theory in medicine; and important innovations in applied chemistry.

Industrializing society, as it generated growing wealth, almost naturally produced a growing array of cultural expressions. New money built new churches, new public buildings, new art galleries, and new laboratories. Industrial technology directly aided science, in promoting devices such as the X-ray machine or more powerful telescopes. New wealth also supported growing numbers of artists, even if many of them struggled lifelong with poverty. Inventions such as the camera and discoveries in optics also powerfully influenced artistic styles—impressionism rebelled against the camera's literalness, at the same time using new knowledge of how the eye perceives color. Rising literacy along with growing wealth supported new legions of writers; authors such as Dickens directly serialized their novels in middle-class newspapers, where payment by the word encouraged a rather long-winded writing style.

The role of religion in determining the intellectual agenda continued to decline. Christian faith remained important in the 19th century, even as the political role of organized churches waned. Many new churches were built, and Western society funded a vast missionary effort. In the United States, religion retained a particularly lively function, as revivals and immigrant churches powerfully shaped American culture. Religion faded more definitively as a popular force in Europe, where nationalism and socialism provided competing loyalties; here, however, Christianity continued to sustain many people. But as a formal intellectual force, religion was less vigorous even

than in the age of Enlightenment. Few leading writers cared greatly about the nature of God or the fine points of theology.

Two major examples reshaped the Western intellectual heritage: first, ongoing work within the rational, scientific tradition of the Enlightenment, and second, a vigorous artistic statement that new styles were essential to capture the meaning of life and provide an alternative to scientific modes of thought.

The Enlightenment heritage persisted, as we have seen, in political theory. Liberal writers modified Enlightenment beliefs. They no longer argued in terms of natural right, preferring instead to talk in terms of what was useful. However, they maintained the traditional beliefs that individuals were rational, education was worthwhile, and scientific and industrial progress was desirable. Most socialists also clung to Enlightenment beliefs. Karl Marx (1818–1883), the leading theorist of the entire century, used a historical rather than a strictly rationalist basis for his grand scheme. To Marx, history changed on the basis of who controlled the existing technology, or means of production. Class struggle resulted, with those in control fighting those below. In modern society, the middle class had wrested power from the aristocracy but had created a new class enemy, the property-less proletariat, or working class. This class grew until revolution became inevitable. But once the proletarian revolution had occurred, an Enlightenment-style utopia would result. The state would wither away as individuals rationally determined his or her own interests; goods would be distributed according to need; class struggle would vanish once the vestiges of the middle class had been eliminated. More prosaically, most socialist theorists agreed with liberals about the basic goodness and rationality of humankind and the importance of material progress, education, and science.

In addition to liberal and socialist theory, the rationalist tradition was also kept alive through scientific inquiry. Indeed, as scientists learned about new fertilizers and health measures, science became more firmly linked than ever before with the idea of progress on this earth. On the more theoretical level, science advanced on every front. The great contribution was Darwin's evolutionary theory. On the basis of careful observation, Darwin argued that all living creatures had evolved into their present form through the ability to adapt in a struggle for survival. Biological development could be scientifically understood as a process taking place over time, with some animal and plant species disappearing and others evolving from earlier forms. Darwin's ideas clashed with traditional Christian beliefs that God had created humankind directly, and the resulting popular debate, on the whole, weakened the intellectual hold of religion. The picture of nature that Darwin suggested was far more complex than the simple natural laws of Newton. Nature worked through random struggle. However, Darwin confirmed the idea that scientists could advance knowledge, and his theory was compatible with the idea that natural laws encouraged progress.

The social sciences also continued to advance, on the basis of observation, experiment, and rationalist theorizing. Great efforts went into compilations of statistical data concerning populations, economic developments, and health problems. Sheer empirical knowledge about the human condition had never been more extensive. At the level of theory, leading economists tried to explain business cycles and the causes of poverty; social psychologists studied the behavior of crowds. Toward the end of the century, the Viennese physician Sigmund Freud began to develop his theories of the workings of the human unconscious, arguing that much behavior is determined by impulses but psychological problems can be relieved by rational understanding. Like many other scientists, social scientists complicated the traditional Enlightenment view of nature and human nature by studying the animal impulses and unconscious urges of human beings. However, they continued to rely on standard scientific methods in their work, believing that human behavior can be rationally categorized, and most of them asserted that ultimately human reason would prevail, as manifested in appropriate economic, political, or personal behavior.

The artistic vision developed by the 19th century was rather different. To be sure, many novelists realistically portrayed human problems, believing that their efforts could contribute to reform. Artists, as we have seen, were aware of scientific discoveries. Beginning with romanticism, however, many artists looked to emotion, rather than reason, as the key to the mystery of life. They sought to portray longings and even madness, not calm reflection. They also deliberately endeavored to violate traditional Western artistic standards. They proclaimed their freedom from the traditional rules characterizing drama or poetry. This impulse was taken up, after romanticism declined around 1850, by new artists who attempted to defy literal representation. Leading poets shunned conventional rhymes and meters, writing abstract, highly personalized statements. Artists and sculptors sought suggestive images, while later 19th-century composers began to work with atonal scales that defied long-established conventions in music. Some artists talked of an "art for art's sake"—that is, art that had its own purposes, regardless of the larger society. Other artists and philosophers rejected rationalism outright, stressing the power of impulses or the human will. Artistic inspiration also came from new awareness of African and east Asian styles, a sign that global influences were affecting the West as well as other areas.

The new split in Western culture, between rationalists and nonrationalists, had institutional overtones. By the late 19th century, most scientists and social scientists worked in or around universities. Western universities, in a virtual eclipse since the end of the Middle Ages, now revived as great research centers that also trained society's elite. This model of the university developed first in

Bucolic romanticism: landscape by the British painter Constable, early 19th century.

Germany and spread quickly to France, the United States, and to a lesser extent Britain. Many artists, in contrast, worked outside any institution. Artistic communities, called *bohemian* by respectable middle-class observers who distrusted the artistic lifestyle, developed in most major cities, with the community in Paris the most glittering. Most artistic patrons preferred older styles, particularly in painting and music. But modern art continued to grow, its lack of clear standards and its defiance of ordinary taste and tradition clearly expressing an important aspect of Western culture in the modern age. It was revealing that in an age of great economic change, Western culture did not rely simply on existing artistic traditions as an anchor. The same individualism and secularism that helped spur business competition spilled over into culture, prompting many artists to seek

alternatives to ordinary values, scientific modes of inquiry, and the sheer ugliness of the industrial environment itself.

INDUSTRIAL SOCIETY

Industrialization left a decisive mark on the shape of society in Western nations. In combination with the legal changes ushered in by the decades of revolution, it produced a new social structure. Property and earnings, plus the level of education one had achieved, increasingly determined position in society. Former measures, such as birth, legal privilege, and purely landed estate, declined. In this new social structure, wealthy business executives and professional people gained growing prestige, at the expense of aristocrats and old merchant families. In the United States, where an aristocracy had never seriously existed and the Civil War decimated the landowning class in the South, the middle class reigned supreme. In most European countries, aristocrats continued to wield cultural and political influence, but they no longer dominated the social pyramid. Middle-class culture, evincing a broadly liberal faith in science and education and a passion for respectable, restrained behavior, increasingly set the social tone. The ranks of the middle class grew, with the expansion of business and the rise of professions such as engineering, law, and medicine, in which individuals could claim unique expertise on the basis of special knowledge, training, and licensing.

The second leading social class of modern Western society consisted of urban workers, particularly in the factories. This group, far larger than the middle class, had scant property and much lower earnings. It did not accept all middle-class values but was nonetheless influenced by their powerful expression in the popular media, notably books and newspapers, and the school system.

Not everyone fit into the basic middle-class/working-class division of industrial society, even aside from the important remnants of an aristocracy at the top. Artisans clung to older values, in some countries even hoping for a restoration of the guild system; they merged only gradually and incompletely with the new working class. The rural population, still massive, continued to reflect the distinctive features of a peasant tradition and agricultural life. Even here, however, the division increased between peasants or farmers who owned their land and employed others, on the one hand, and a growing number of landless laborers, on the other.

The rise of white-collar workers added another, newer complexity to the modern Western social structure. White-collar workers such as secretaries and telephone operators owned little property. Although they needed some education to perform their jobs, they could

HISTORY DEBATE

WOMEN IN INDUSTRIAL SOCIETY

Historians continue to disagree on what happened to women in Western industrial society. There are disputes of interpretation. Initially, for example, historians saw laws that limited women's hours of work as humanitarian gains. But feminist historians note that these laws made it less attractive to employ women and formed part of a new emphasis on the importance of the male breadwinner. Women were now supposed to maintain sexual respectability, but this power had a downside, for respectable women were not supposed to be sexually eager.

There are disputes of emphasis. Women were pushed out of the urban labor force, particularly after marriage. However, they were given greater moral esteem and power within the home. Women provided the "essential elements of moral government," and it was assumed that their purity overcame men's baser impulses. Educational gains for women did not result in equality, but they increasingly eliminated gender gaps in literacy.

Even feminism, rising in the second half of the 19th century, becomes controversial in this discussion. Did it result merely from new and old inequalities, or did it reflect women's new cultural status and other gains such as a reduction in family size? Is the 19th century to be seen as the triumph of a new form of patriarchy, or as a crucial, albeit complex stage of women's liberation?

not claim professional status. But white-collar workers did share styles of dress and values with middle-class people. They liked to think—usually incorrectly—that they or their children could rise into the managerial or professional ranks.

Family life was powerfully affected by industrialization. Family responsibilities changed, although gradually. The family ceased being the main center of production, as work moved outside the home. But the family gained or enhanced some other functions. It served as a consumer unit; most major purchases were affected within the family, and a new division of labor freed some family members—mainly housewives—for the important and time-consuming tasks of shopping, now that families did not make most of their own goods. Much leisure time was spent with the family. Holidays more and more became family occasions rather than community affairs. The idea of family vacations spread, first in the middle class and then to workers in the form of daylong excursions. The family also became the center of emotional gratification. Family members were supposed to love each other. The middle-class belief that the family should be a haven against the stress of the outside world was also reflected in some working-class sentiments. Courtship became increasingly romantic; at least in the working class, the importance of sexual pleasure deepened. Ironically, this emphasis on emotional satisfaction produced a noticeable growth in the divorce rate, with the United States taking the lead. As families declined as units of economic activity, it became more possible and perhaps more necessary to dissolve marriages that were not providing personal gratification.

Changes in family functions had vital implications for the roles of family members. The man was increasingly seen as the breadwinner, with his earnings from work his main responsibility. Married women were largely kept out of the formal labor force; in the middle class, even most girls did not work. According to middle-class family

ideals, women were to serve as the exponents of culture and the moral center within the family. This gave them a new significance, as women in fact came to dominate childrearing and the household more fully than before, but it also removed them from many public activities, because women lagged far behind men in political rights. Industrialization raised important questions about women's roles. Women were given new esteem, and their educational gains were more rapid than those of men although women started from a lower position on this scale. In the working class, moreover, women were vital to the labor force; girls worked in factories, as domestic servants, and later as clerks and public school teachers. However, in day-to-day activities, married women were increasingly separate from men. The rise of feminist movements, seeking expanded rights and opportunities for women, reflected the anomalies of this aspect of the Western family.

Attitudes toward children changed as well. Most middle-class children were expected to learn, not earn. Working-class children, on the other hand, were essential to the operation of early factories, maintaining the traditional assumptions that children should contribute to the family economy. But many people from all classes objected to the factory conditions to which children were exposed, particularly the frequency of accidents; in fact, as machines became more complex, children's usefulness declined. Moreover, the advent of compulsory education took most young children out of the labor force. Most adolescents still worked in 1914, although in the United States a high school education became more commonplace, even among working-class youth. Parents grew concerned with fostering their children's learning ability. Their emotional expectations of children also increased, their hope being that such attention and the resulting affection would compensate for the fact that offspring had become a greater economic burden. At the same time, parents' roles in children's lives decreased, and interaction among young people in schools heralded the development of separate generational cultures by the end of the 19th century. Being a child in the industrial West was different from being a child in a traditional agricultural society, but it was not necessarily easier.

The final impact of industrialization on the family involved population structure. In what is called the *demographic transition*, Western families quickly reacted to the population boom of the 18th century by reducing their birth rates. Birth rates began to fall gradually in the United States and France as early as 1790. The middle class led the way in this demographic transition. Middle-class culture emphasized the importance of sexual restraint, and most middle-class people married fairly late. Gradually, a birth-rate limit spread to the working class and peasantry, although under the new demographic regime, poorer families, on average, had larger families than the middle class—the reverse of traditional patterns. With children now an expense and parents expected to provide careful supervision and training to children, large families began to decline. By 1914, the average Western family included only three to four children. By this point, the medical advances that almost eliminated deaths in childhood were underway, making birth control even more imperative. Most families relied mainly on sexual restraint for this purpose, although new contraceptive devices became more common, particularly after the vulcanization of rubber in the 1830s; the incidence of abortion also increased. Thus, by 1914, the industrial, demographic regime was clearly in place in the West, with lower birth rates than ever before in human history, combined with low mortality rates for children as life expectancy steadily rose. This new demography produced important changes in family life and the roles of women, now that mothering required less effort than before; it also produced considerable tension, given the need for sexual restraint. The new demography had wider consequences, too, as the population of the West began to decline in relation to that of other parts of the world.

Despite all these changes, the family thrived in Western society, adopting new purposes and roles as old ones dwindled but also maintaining some traditional functions. Change itself was often concealed. As new household equipment made women's work easier, standards of household cleanliness increased, so the effort involved in housekeeping, in fact, remained the same. Mothers were praised despite the decline in the birth rate—the U.S. Congress, for example, enacted Mother's Day soon after 1900. Of all the traditional institutions from agricultural society—the village, the guild, even the church—the family survived the best. However, it did change, and Westerners worried out loud about the stability of this basic institution, as they continue to in the present day.

Along with social structure and family, popular culture altered its shape under the effects of industrialization. Growing literacy, exposure to political campaigns, and increasing wealth—at least, for most by 1914, slightly above subsistence—all had an impact. Ideas about the value of education, science, and technology spread more widely, and the gap between popular and elitist values narrowed by 1914.

However, industrialization imposed a general strain on society, as do ongoing changes in technology and business organization. The nature of work shifted, and probably its quality deteriorated. Before the Industrial Revolution, work for most people had been a social act, punctuated by gossip and naps, accomplished within a family context. With the rise of factories and offices, not only was work taken out of the home, but it also became increasingly regimented. Shop rules forbade workers from singing, chatting, or wandering about. The pace of work quickened, as a clock routinely timed workers' efforts. Strangers supervised more people than ever before, and workers performed specialized tasks, rather than creating whole products.

These changes were hard to integrate, and many argued that they have not been fully assimilated even now. In the early stages of the Industrial Revolution, particularly before 1850, the impact of new work forms was intensified by the rapid decline of popular leisure traditions. Festivals virtually vanished. As communities dissolved through migration to the cities, these highly local events were hard to maintain. Furthermore, the middle class disapproved of festivals as a threat to public order and sheer waste of time; the newly created police forces actively discouraged such public gatherings. Middle-class leisure consisted chiefly of useful activities such as family reading or piano playing that showcased cultural achievement and train the young. Many workers did not accept this utilitarian definition of leisure, but they had few alternatives. Tavern drinking became one of their major pastimes (one that middle-class temperance reformers fought in vain) because it provided a glimmer of former sociability.

Many workers protested the changes in their lives. The decades of revolution depended heavily on working-class protest in the name of older work values, with artisans taking the lead. Workers also sought to cushion the impact of industrialization on their lives, by taking time off from their jobs or changing employment with great frequency, to the fury of middle-class managers. Gradually, however, workers found some solace in the concept of instrumentalism; they recognized that they could not necessarily control the quality or conditions of their work, but they accepted their job's constraints for the sake of rising earnings. In other words, work became an instrument to other things. After 1850, working-class protest, although it increased as workers became better organized, largely changed from attempts to control the job itself, to demands for shorter hours and higher pay. The worker looked forward to new economic benefits, rather than backward to older values.

At the same time, new recreational outlets arose. Popular reading, vaudeville theaters, and professional and amateur sports proliferated in Western society after 1870, for various social groups. The new leisure was highly commercialized, signaling the growth of a consumer society. Sports also served to discipline people for the workplace, as they learned team cooperation and obedience to the rules imposed on every modern sport; sports also served to condition possible future soldiers. Some critics at the time and even today have blasted the new sports culture, its emphasis on pleasure seeking and physical release, and wondered if leisure was as satisfying and expressive as it should be, given the limits of industrial work. Whatever its quality, mass leisure was a uniquely modern creation and a vital part of the new culture spawned by industrialization. Some games, such as soccer football, first developed in industrial England, spread around the world much faster than industrialization itself.

GAIN AND STRAIN FROM INDUSTRIALIZATION

In 1900, heralding the advent of a new century, many Western newspapers looked back on the past century and found it satisfactory. Improved health conditions, new wealth, greater political freedom, more education—all suggested an improved quality of life, one that was getting better. Great change had unquestionably occurred, but by 1900 many people were becoming accustomed to it, bolstered by their belief in progress. Only a few groups in Western society, such as the new immigrants to the United States, were confronting urban, industrial life for the first time.

However, change had brought strain as well as apparent progress, and it continued to do so. An aristocratic German general, a Catholic bishop, and an old-fashioned New England intellectual all took issue with the idea of progress, believing that the values lost amid the change were more important than the material gains. From other vantage points, many workers, particularly those who found no meaning in their work, and many feminists also quarreled against progress, hoping that their satisfaction or ideals would some day come to fruition.

The strains within Western society spilled over into the West's world role. Industrialization brought new power to Western society, which it used to gain more complete control over more areas of the world than ever before. Imperialist expansion reflected not only business success but also the desire of aristocratic officers and Christian missionaries to find new arenas for their values, even as conditions at home became more challenging.

In turn, groups from China to Latin America, although proud of their own cultures, recognized that they had to copy some features of industrial society if they wanted to prevent total Western domination. A key question was which aspects of the Western industrial process had to be, and could be, imitated. Was it just the military technology and organization, or the wider economic revolution, or did Western-style politics, or art, or changes in women's roles also inextricably enter the process? Western history between 1789 and 1914 had brought profound transformations to one of the world's major civilizations; it also established a complex model for others to ponder.

PATHS TO THE PRESENT

The long 19th century expanded certain characteristics of Western society and introduced others—hardly surprising, as its key developments occurred only a century or two ago. Trends launched in the early modern period—such as the emphasis on science or consumerism—were extended. The French Revolution and liberalism revived and expanded the idea of parliamentary government.

New trends included the redefinition of the nature and purpose of art—the abstract styles associated with modern art continue to affect Western life. Another trend is the gradual, sometimes contested, separation of religious and political issues. Also, by the end of the long 19th century, feminism became a durable feature of Western life.

The Industrial Revolution created a host of features in its own right, including a new level of acceptance of recurrent technological change. Two points complicate this aspect of the Western picture: first, many characteristics of industrialized society first developed in the West but spread quickly to other societies. The idea of mass education is a case in point. The West was the first culture to decide that children should go to school rather than work and that the state should enforce this redefinition (though the process was completed only after 1914); but many other societies have made the same decision more recently. Is there, today, a distinctively Western childhood? Second, some characteristics changed life so profoundly that adjustments continue even in the present day, in the West and elsewhere. For instance, what should women's role be in an industrial society? The first Western answer was that women could obtain some education and rights, but still must stay home to take care of their families; a more recent Western answer has been that women should go to work in any profession and have families—or not—as they choose. The debate continues.

The Industrial Revolution prompted huge changes in the human condition. The West was the first to experience them and responded distinctly, but on the whole the process was a global one, in which the West participated along with most other regions.

SUGGESTED WEB SITES

For more information on the Industrial Revolution, see http://www.fordham.edu/halsall/mod/modsbook14.html and http://www.fatbadgers.co.uk/Britain/revolution.htm; for more information on society and culture

during industrialization, see http://www.bbc.co
.uk/history/society_culture/industrialisation/;
have a tour "Around the World in the 1890s," at
http://memory.loc.gov/ammem/wtc/wtchome
.html.

SUGGESTED READINGS

Recent work includes David S. Mason, *Revolutionary Europe, 1789–1989: Liberty, Equality, Solidarity* (2005); Peter Fritzsche, *Stranded in the Present: Modern Time and the Melancholy of History* (2004); Shirley Roessler and Reny Miklos, *Europe, 1715–1919: From Enlightenment to World War* (2003); Lynn Abrams, *The Making of Modern Woman: Europe 1789–1918* (2002); Rachel G. Fuchs and Victoria E. Thompson, *Women in Nineteenth-Century Europe* (2005); Brenda Stalcup, ed., *The Industrial Revolution* (2002); Robert Marks, *The Origins of the Modern World: A Global and Ecological Narrative* (2002); Joel Mokyr, *The British Industrial Revolution* (1999); Carolyn Tuttle, *Hard at Work in Factories and Mines: The Economics of Child Labor During the British Industrial Revolution* (1999); and E. J. Hobsbawm and Chris Wrigley, *Industry and Empire: The Birth of the Industrial Revolution* (1999).

Fine studies of the early industrial period include Phyllis Deane, *The First Industrial Revolution* (1980) (on Britain), and E. J. Hobsbawm, *The Age of Revolution: Europe 1789–1848* (1962) (on Europe generally). See also Peter N. Stearns, *The Industrial Revolution in World History* (1998). An excellent study highlights Europe by comparison: R. Bin Wong, *China Transformed: Historical Change and the Limits of European Experience* (1997). A more general survey of the social history of the period is Peter N. Stearns and Herrick Chapman, *European Society in Upheaval: Social History Since 1750*, 3rd ed. (1992); a more interpretive study is Barrington Moore, *Social Origins of Dictatorship and Democracy* (1966). For more specialized aspects of industrial change, see L. Tilly and J. Scott, *Women, Work and Family* (1978); F. D. Scott, *Emigration and Immigration* (1963); and E. P. Thompson, *The Making of the English Working Class* (1963). On leading developments in political history, a useful volume is R. R. Palmer, *The Age of Democratic Revolution: A Political History of Europe and America, 1760–1800* (1964); a good text survey is John Merriman, *Modern European Civilization*, Vol. 2 (1996). See also Harvey Graff, ed., *Literacy and Social Development in the West* (1982); Albert Lindemann, *History of European Socialism* (1983); David Kaiser, *Politics and War: European Conflict from Philip II to Hitler* (1990); Robin W. Winks and Joan Neuberger, *Europe and the Making of Modernity, 1815–1914* (2005); and Steven King and Geoffrey Timmins, *Making Sense of the Industrial Revolution* (2001).

World Economy and Western Imperialism: Africa and South Asia

European industrialization, supplemented by the growing industrial power of the United States, inevitably transformed the world economy. Merchants ventured forth from the industrialized nations, seeking markets and raw materials all over the world. Pressure to participate in world commerce increased everywhere. Previously isolated economies, such as Japan, now had to interact with the West. Economies already selling to the West now had to increase those levels of export; this was the case in Latin America.

The links in the world economy expanded steadily. New and speedier shipping played a vital role, making the crossing of the oceans a matter of a week or two rather than months. At the same time, railroads reached into continental interiors. More rapid communication, provided by the telegraph and later the telephone and the wireless, transmitted an unprecedented amount of information about business conditions around the globe. Levels of international trade rose as a result. By the 1830s, many industrial concerns were opening branch offices in major cities in various parts of the world.

Along with the great increase in volume came some alterations in the nature of the world economy. The Industrial Revolution gave the West new quantities of manufactured products to sell, including factory equipment, locomotives, and steamships. The West had already sold manufactured goods to other societies, but its capacity was now literally revolutionized, as was its intense need to find available markets for its soaring output. This was not just a matter of new Western gain: many traditional manufacturing systems were unseated, unable to match factory output and prices. Europe and North America also had capital to export, particularly after 1850. Earnings from early industrialization begged for profitable investment outlets; although domestic economies provided some of these, there was an avid search for opportunities, at higher interest rates, in less industrialized areas. The development of the U.S. West, including the rapid expansion of a railroad network, owed much to British and French investment, but significant capital also went to Latin America, Africa, and Asia—at a price. Western investment in Russia also increased rapidly.

New Western opportunities to export industrial products and capital were matched by growing needs for imports. There was one huge change: slaves were no longer necessary. The transatlantic slave trade was abolished between 1807 and 1834, mainly on British initiative; as of the latter date, slavery was ended in the British colonies. In succeeding decades, slavery was abolished in the Americas and elsewhere.

Cheap labor, however, continued to be essential. Nonindustrial societies intensified their commitment to food exports, as Europe's urbanization and growing wealth increased the market for both staples, such as wheat and beef, and specialty products, such as coffee and sugar. The need for raw materials became even more intense. Western transportation and recreational requirements opened a wide market for rubber, for example, which could be produced only in tropical areas. Growing production of steel made certain rare alloys vital, whereas other metals (such as copper) and chemicals were sought outside the West as well.

The new volume of economic exchange made the disparity between the West and most other civilizations far more significant than it had previously been. Spurred by Western merchants and capital, producers in other regions found themselves more deeply affected by the world economy than ever before. Huge numbers of Latin American peasants, for example, were now drawn into the production of coffee, or hemp for rope making, and away from their traditional village agriculture. The influx of Western capital into mining, transportation facilities, and market agriculture literally around the world also increased the direct involvement of millions of people in the international economy. There was another significant change: no part of the world could now isolate itself from Western commercial pressure.

The impact of the Western-dominated global economy was enhanced by the new surge of outright imperialism, based on growing European appetites and new military technology such as the repeating rifle. Western European nations and the United States claimed huge chunks of territory, from the islands of the Pacific to the interior of Africa. Land previously acquired, particularly in India and southeast Asia, was now more closely controlled, as Europeans had both the military and organizational means and the economic need to go beyond port cities and loose alliances with regional governments in the interior. The expansion of a Western empire and the subsequent changes in its nature bore most heavily on three non-Western regions: sub-Saharan Africa, India, and southeast Asia. But the threat of imperialist control, along with the expansion of the West's world economic role, affected all civilizations by 1900, accentuating the problem of what to do about the power and example of the West.

This chapter examines the new imperialism and the areas it most directly touched; the following chapters consider the varying reactions of other civilizations to what became, by 1900, a set of common themes in modern world history.

KEY QUESTIONS *What caused Europe's imperialist surge? This is the first question addressed in the following section. But more subtle questions are equally important. How did different parts of the world react to European pressure, and what caused the differences? What were the main differences among major colonial regions—comparing, for instance, Africa and India? What kinds of resistance and cooperation developed?*

THE REASONS FOR IMPERIALISM: MOTIVES AND MEANS

At the end of the 18th century, Western imperialism extended to North and South America, save for the newly independent United States; India, although the process of British control had yet to be completed; the islands of Indonesia; and scattered port holdings, particularly in parts of sub-Saharan Africa. The bulk of the Latin American empire was lost soon after 1800, through wars of independence, though this civilization nevertheless remained closely tied to the Western economy.

By 1900, Western empires included all the 1800 holdings outside Latin America; most of

---

HISTORY DEBATE

CAUSES OF THE ABOLITION OF SLAVERY

In 1833, arguing for the abolition of slavery in all British colonies, the British colonial secretary explained the need in terms of the "liberal and humane spirit of the age." For more than a century, historians echoed this explanation. It was new, humanitarian ideas that led to the abolition of slavery in Britain, France, and the northern United States after centuries of acceptance.

Then, in 1944, a West Indian historian, Eric Williams, took a radically different approach. He claimed that it was not humanitarianism but, rather, economic self-interest that explained the shifting viewpoint. British and other industrial capitalists were now in a position of power where the world economy was concerned. Slave economies were fading within this context. It was not idealism but simple materialism that now put slave owners on the defensive.

More recent work, by historians such as David B. Davis and Seymour Drescher, has complicated this picture even further. Drescher has shown that the slave economies were still very profitable apart from slavery, so it was not simple materialism that prompted the institution's abolition. Davis argues, however, that industrial capitalists now needed to defend wage labor being imposed (amid great hardship) on European workers themselves. To do this and distract workers from their own plight, industrial capitalists attacked slavery. Again, material self-interest rather than humanitarianism ruled the day, but such an analysis is complex. Drescher defends humanitarianism a bit more but contends that it was popularized among artisans and other people frightened by the industrial economy, who used abolitionism to bolster their own sense of morality. The current effort, then, is to combine a recognition that there were new humanitarian arguments involved in this historic change, with a belief that key changes in the capitalist economy were involved as well.

Can you think of other debates about the extent of idealism versus material self-interest in explaining historical change?

Two other points are worth mentioning. First, during the 18th century as a whole, as abolitionism spread in the nations of the Americas, rapid world population growth made it relatively easy to replace the slave trade with imported workers from Asia and Europe. Second, although slavery was increasingly abolished, it was often replaced with systems that were still coercive to some extent. For example, immigrant workers might be tied by indenture contracts. Company stores might place workers in debt, so they could not legally leave or change jobs. Practices of this sort continue into our own time.

How do these points affect the idealism versus materialism debate?

the mainland of southeast Asia, as the French conquered Indochina (present-day Vietnam, Laos, and Cambodia), while Britain seized Malaya and effectively controlled Thailand and Burma; the entire continent of Africa with minor exceptions, the most important of which was the proudly independent kingdom of Ethiopia; Australia and New Zealand; and the various Pacific islands, including Hawaii, Samoa, and Tahiti, which were divided mainly among Britain, France, Germany, and the United States. Western nations also had colonies along the coast of China, holdings on the eastern coast of the Arabian Peninsula, and a growing influence in Persia, Afghanistan, and parts of the Ottoman Empire. North African regions were colonies or about to become so. Britain proudly claimed that the sun never set on its empire, because of its worldwide span, and to many other Westerners the world seemed, for all intents and purposes, a Western holding. Never before had so much territory been acquired in so little time.

During the 19th century, moreover, the Western concept of empire changed. Earlier colonies had been regarded primarily as market outposts. Catholic powers, notably Spain and Portugal, had thought also in terms of Christian conversion, which extended European control in Latin America and the Philippines. The British colonization of the eastern coast of North America had also been an important exception to the common pattern. Outside the New World, limited control for trading purposes described the Western approach. After about 1800, this guiding viewpoint began to change rapidly. Trade alone was not enough when new market agriculture, transportation networks, and investment outlets had to be established. The redefinition of the world economy suggested more extensive penetration. Furthermore, Europeans and North Americans began to develop a greater sense of cultural superiority. Protestant groups now joined Catholics in seeking missionary contacts. More generally, Westerners began to claim a clearer mission to bring civilization to the peoples of the world—civilization,

of course, being as the West defined it. The English poet Rudyard Kipling described a widely held sentiment in arguing that the West had such superior moral and political values that it had a responsibility—the "white man's burden"—to reshape the rest of the world. Missionaries brought not only Christianity but also Western styles of dress and approaches to education and medical care. Business managers, convinced of the inferiority of "native" ways, tried to tell non-Westerners how to work and organize their businesses. Imperial governments sought to redefine marriage customs, caste systems, and tribal politics. In both old and new colonies, European imperialism now meant an effort to establish effective government and supervision over wide areas.

Why did Western imperialism change and advance into so many new parts of the world? The West's growing technological sophistication assumed a major role, although colonialists also played on ethnic and other divisions in the societies they conquered. European imperialism in Africa can be explained in large part by the ability of Western ships, steam-propelled, to navigate up the previously impenetrable African rivers. This allowed contacts with the interior that no people, including Africans themselves, had ever before achieved. Steam-driven iron boats were also basic to the European penetration of China. Western facility in weaponry continued to increase, even as Africans and Asians gained access to old-fashioned rifles. By the late 19th century, Western soldiers were armed with repeating rifles, which did not require separate reloading and thus represented a huge advantage. The introduction of the machine gun was another fundamental step. Winston Churchill, later the British prime minister, described an 1898 battle near the Upper Nile, pitting a small British force armed with 20 early machine guns against 40,000 Muslim troops:

The infantry fired steadily and stolidly, without hurry or excitement, for the enemy were far away and the officers careful. Besides, the

Fight between the German army and native troops in Tanzania: early 20th-century African art.

soldiers were interested in the work and took great pains. . . . And all the time out on the plain on the other side bullets were shearing through flesh, smashing and splintering bone . . . valiant men were struggling on through a hell of whistling metal, exploding shell, and spurting dust—suffering, despairing, dying.

When the battle ended, 11,000 Muslims and 48 British soldiers were dead, and the British had conquered the territory now known as the Sudan.

If technology, backed by medical advances that allowed Westerners to avoid contracting many tropical diseases, accounts for a key part of the Western advantage, particularly in Africa but to an extent elsewhere, it does not explain the motives for the new imperialism. Gains resulting from the Industrial Revolution, including not only technology but also improved organization, better health care, and expanded literacy, fed the growing belief that the West was superior to the rest of the world, with a right and duty to rule. This attitude now combined with Christian

beliefs in religious superiority, a current that had been evidenced in earlier Western expansion attempts from the Crusades on. Economic motives played a prominent role as well. Not only were Europeans eager for markets and raw materials, but they were also anxious about the stability of their own changing economy. Even confident U.S. business leaders sought secure markets and supplies through colonies or, in Central America, semicolonies. Many people believed that domestic sales and supplies were insufficient for an economy that depended on growth. They also saw imperialism as a way to excite and divert ordinary people who might otherwise join in social protest—and indeed imperial conquest did arouse popular passions in Europe and the United States, aided by the stirring headlines of the new mass press.

Certain groups in the West, left behind in the rush to industrialize, found solace in their empires. Aristocrats, increasingly displaced at home, could win prestige as imperial bureaucrats, living the good life while ruling the natives. Christian missionaries sometimes experienced greater satisfaction in preaching to the heathen than in facing the gradual decline of religion in their own lands. Individual adventurers, tired of the increasingly bureaucratic life of industrial corporations, found excitement in seeking fame and fortune in distant places. In various ways, then, imperialism expressed social tensions generated by industrialization, as well as the power that the Industrial Revolution provided.

The most direct factors in the imperialist scramble, however, were the claims and rivalries of various states in the West. Nationalist loyalty motivated many explorers and adventurers, such as the German Karl Peters, who staked Germany's claims to Tanganyika in eastern Africa, because of his desire to see his country assume its rightful place among the great powers—and who operated at first without official state backing. Patriotic assertions prompted European governments to intervene on behalf of individual missionaries or business entrepreneurs, who could not be tampered with lest national honor be impugned. Above all, chauvinist rivalries spurred new states to claim a share in imperial glory and old states to protect their existing holdings through expansion. Britain acquired many new colonies—such as Egypt, which guarded the quickest route to India after the building of the Suez Canal—to defend old ones against possible rivals. France sought additional territory in north Africa to protect its first north African colony, Algeria. Newly imperialist countries included Italy, which won important territory in north Africa; Belgium, which acquired the vast Congo region; and Germany, which displayed its greatness by taking possession of two major African colonies plus areas in China and the Pacific. To this list may be added the United States, which tended to oppose imperialism in principle, in part because of a long preoccupation with overland expansion to the west and in part because of its own national experience as a colony, but which in fact acquired extensive Pacific holdings, including the Philippines, won from Spain in the Spanish-American War in 1898, and several West Indian islands, most

notably Puerto Rico. The appearance of new imperialist nations heightened a growing French desire, after 1871, to gain colonies to compensate for defeat at Germany's hands back home in the Franco-Prussian War. The various pressures for conquest, which developed particularly after 1870, added to the belief that every available territory should be claimed as quickly as possible, for the sake of national security and national glory. Ironically, this same spirit of heedless rivalry later intensified conflict in Europe, when, after 1900, all available lands were taken and attention returned to competition nearer home.

IMPERIALISM IN INDIA AND SOUTHEAST ASIA

The new European imperialism focused particularly on conquering relatively populous territories that had important traditions of their own. It involved, in other words, ruling millions of other people and encountering considerable resistance in the name of established values. Most of the new colonies received European administrators and some business entrepreneurs, missionaries, doctors, and teachers, but few ordinary settlers. Important Italian immigration occurred in parts of north Africa, and some Europeans established themselves in the rich agricultural lands of east Africa as a new and privileged minority, but these were exceptional patterns.

European imperialism in Asia was completed—with the British conquest of India and extension of influence to Thailand and Burma and the French takeover of Indochina—without in any sense drawing these regions into the orbit of Western civilization. Revealingly, Christian missionary efforts in India and southeast Asia had little success, winning only small minorities of converts—a clear sign of the continued validity of traditional cultures. The new imperialism had a vital impact nevertheless. In India, Britain's rule had far more sweeping consequences than most previous periods of foreign control, including the recent Mughal Empire. Indeed, India and Dutch Indonesia became showcases for the kind of penetration that 19th-century imperialists sought. With such colonization, in turn, came important resistance, which itself established new patterns while confirming some older cultural values. One important result was that British rule lasted a considerably shorter time than had previous foreign occupations. This fact suggests some interesting features about the British commitment, which never evolved into a fully Indian regime, while also revealing important changes in the Indian

political tradition itself, which became less tolerant of foreign rule.

India

As Britain completed its conquest of India during the first half of the 19th century, it began also to take a more active hand in Indian affairs. Control by the British government substantially replaced that of the East India Company, and at the same time the respect British officials had for Indian culture declined. India became a place to change, to westernize. Thus, laws (not totally unlike those of the early Mughals) sought to limit child marriage and religious sacrifices; Hindu converts to Christianity were rewarded with government jobs.

British colonial officials at Delhi: a herald reads a proclamation that declares Queen Victoria empress of India.

British rule during most of the 19th century had a significant impact on Indian politics. The very fact of unification of the entire subcontinent was a major development. British rule permitted considerable autonomy for individual areas, with regional princes allowed to maintain governments under British advisors, but a uniform code of laws, derived from British precedent, was imposed over the entire country. Administration became steadily larger and more efficient. Direct taxation, based on land values, replaced earlier regional collection. Britain established tax levels it regarded as equitable; however, the fact that it gathered taxes directly, rather than using regional lords and village headmen, who in earlier times determined taxes based on how much their clients were able to pay, meant that taxes tended to rise—a source of considerable discontent among Indians who were unaccustomed to dealing with government without intermediary patrons. Britain also established a civil service, based on an examination system. Top officials were always British until 1864, and mainly so thereafter, but lower-level officials were drawn from high-caste Hindus, who were thus exposed to Western administrative ideas.

British rule had considerable cultural impact as well. Although relatively few Indians converted to Christianity, new missionary pressures prompted Hindu leaders to reexamine their own practices. They tended to downplay the worship of lesser gods, although this custom continued at popular levels, and to emphasize the monotheistic elements of Hinduism. This reaction was similar to that which had greeted earlier Muslim influence. It involved an attempt to adapt traditions to the standards of India's new leadership.

Still more important for Indian culture was a British-sponsored school system, seen as vital to reversing the decline of Indian education that had occurred under the later Mughals. British-sponsored secondary schools and universities were bent on teaching Western values. As one British liberal put it: "The great end should not have been to teach Hindu learning, but useful learning." This meant increased emphasis on science and technology, not totally foreign to Indian traditions in any event, and modern (mainly European) history. Many schools taught their subjects in English, which meant that English became a second language among many upper-caste Hindus and Muslim leaders.

Economic development was another British target. During the 1850s, the British began to construct railroad and telegraph systems. The new facilities aided the administration and military control of the vast country, but they also brought some prosperity. The governor general stated, in 1853:

> A system of railways . . . would surely and rapidly give rise to the same encouragement of enterprise . . . and some similar progress in social improvement that have marked the introduction of improved and extended communication in various kingdoms of the western world.

By 1900, India had more than 26,500 miles of rails, plus a number of new roads and canals. Britain also encouraged better agricultural methods, again along Western lines, and some industrial development. The subcontinent was no longer seen as a colony simply to exploit, but as a place where substantial economic activity could be pursued.

Socially, the British sought to change the caste system. Britain allowed different castes to mix in prisons and on trains, and lower-caste members could sue upper-caste people in British courts. The British also tried, although cautiously, to alter conditions for women. The biggest short-term impact of such attempts actually was an increase in women's economic difficulties, by reducing traditional manufacturing jobs. However, this ramification was not clearly understood, as respectable women were, according to the Western viewpoint, no longer supposed to work. Disdain for Hindu customs led to more explicit changes, as British observers claimed that, "Nothing can exceed the habitual

SOLVING PROBLEMS

RAILROADS

The spread of railroads from the early 19th century onward was meant to alleviate several problems. Most obviously, rails allowed heavy goods to be hauled relatively cheaply, over long distances. They were vital to bring coal to factories. As they spread in Asia and Latin America, they proved essential in bringing foods and raw materials from the interior to the sea, tying economies more fully to global trade. The more limited system built in Africa served the same function. But rails also had military uses, carrying troops and supplies more readily; this was a vital role in India, in helping the British put down local rebellions.

Not surprisingly, not everyone saw rails as problem-solvers. Some people did not want greater ties to the world economy. There was also fear of new dangers. A British firm in Shanghai built a short line to the outer harbor in 1876, but local opposition was so intense, particularly after a man was run over, that the Chinese provincial governor bought the line and had it torn up, shipping the rails to rust on a beach in

Taiwan. Resistance to a project to link coast to mountains in Ecuador also roused protest, put down by a firm liberal strongman. On the other hand, expected aversion to railroads in India—where the British feared general Indian traditionalism plus resistance to mixing castes on a train—never materialized, as Indians took to rail travel from the outset. And in general, whether there was some antagonism or not, railroad development proceeded everywhere, its extent determined by available capital and political backing. Not all the systems were as successful as the problem-solvers hoped—the lines in Ecuador did not pay off as fully as the government and the foreign investors had advertised—but they certainly advanced market economies, military mobility, and in key cases national integrations as well.

QUESTIONS: *Why were railroads seen as a threat by many people in the 19th century? What factors explain why rail systems in the United States or India were far more extensive than those in Africa?*

---

contempt which the Hindus entertain for their women." British officials attacked female infanticide and the practice of sati, and some Indian reformers soon joined the call for change. Colonial administrators also sought to modify marriage laws, by allowing widows to remarry. Here too was a theme that continued to inspire Indian reformers, including later nationalists.

The British presence had mixed results. Many measures did not reach the Indian masses, who remained largely illiterate and wedded to traditional family and religious practices. The caste system persisted for the most part. On the other hand, some Indians, particularly those educated in the upper schools, welcomed aspects of the Western occupation. Rammohun Roy blasted traditional

education and praised the British for promoting "a more liberal and enlightened system of instruction, embracing mathematics, natural philosophy, chemistry, anatomy, with other useful sciences."

Important resistance developed as well. Many Indians detested the more efficient tax collection, looking back fondly on the days when they could count on the informal patronage of local elites. Upper-caste Indians resented attacks on the caste system, and many lower-caste people also preferred traditional demarcations, disliking what they perceived as the demeaning treatment of the upper castes. Hindus and Muslims alike were suspicious of Christian missionary efforts and certain aspects of the new schools. Muslims also resented British preference for Hindus in government posts; they increasingly saw themselves as a belea-guered religious minority rather than, as in many past centuries, a ruling group. Rumors abounded, amid fears and resentments about British influence. For example, many Indians spread the word that colonial officials not only allowed widows to remarry, against Hindu custom, but forced them to. From various sources, then, tradition encouraged hostility to the new Western administration.

Indian soldiers, or sepoys, made up a large portion of the rank-and-file troops in the armies of British India. Commanded by European officers and armed, uniformed, and drilled according to European standards, troops such as those pictured here were recruited from the colonized peoples and became one of the mainstays of all European colonial regimes. The European colonizers preferred to recruit these soldiers from subject peoples whom they saw as particularly martial. In India, these included the Sikhs (pictured here) and Marattas, as well as Gurkhas recruited from neighboring but independent Nepal.

This antagonism led to one of the great 19th-century uprisings against Western imperialism. The Sepoy Rebellion of 1857 pitted Indian soldiers in the imperial army, numbering about 200,000, against 16,000 British troops stationed on the sub-continent. Many sepoys were of high caste and resented British officers. They also were disgusted by European customs such as eating beef; they insisted on traditional religious practices, for which the British refused to provide facilities. The incident that touched off the revolt was the greasing of bullets to fit in a newly introduced rifle. Animal fat was used for grease, and rumors spread among Hindu troops that the grease was from cows, among Muslims that it was from pork—in both cases, a highly offensive practice. Mutiny resulted, and for a time the rebels held the city of Delhi and much of north-central India, massacring many English families. British reinforcements broke the mutiny in 1858, aided by the fact that most Indian civilians had not joined the protest.

Britain responded to this challenge by introducing limited political representation for Indians, through local governments; they also established an advisory legislative council. Thus, some Indians gained new experience in parliamentary matters. Britain also ruled that no native of India should be barred from any job or office because of skin color or religion, and while Indians advanced only slowly into the upper reaches of bureaucracy, there were some gradual improvements. The number of Indians with civil service experience grew steadily. Britain also increased centralized supervision of the Indian regions, encouraged English-language education, and attempted new social reforms, including the abolition of slavery (never a very extensive institution in India since the classical age). In other words, pressures to westernize intensified, as Britain stepped up its efforts to alter the colony without undue repression.

During the later 19th century, moreover, the Indian economy began to develop in new directions. Many estate owners and peasants were encouraged to grow crops for a world market. During the American Civil War, for example, the production of cotton in India increased to compensate for the decreased availability of cotton in the American South. Some factories also were opened, in textiles and metallurgy, and directed by Indian entrepreneurs using equipment imported from Britain. In 1886, Jamshedi Tata, an Indian from a wealthy Bombay family, established a large steel plant in western Bengal, near India's richest coal and iron deposits. Although still dependent on imported machinery, the Indian steel industry began to export some of its products soon after 1900. Industrial development remained rather localized, and no full industrial revolution was underway, but change was taking place.

Economic transformation was a double-edged sword in India, however. British efforts to encourage higher agricultural production, including the sponsorship of large irrigation projects to reduce traditional problems with periodic droughts, stimulated rapid population growth in an already crowded country. Government attempts to introduce some Western medical procedures, through inoculations and sanitary reforms, worked to the same end. India's high birth rate, linked to the traditional desire to have enough sons to protect parents into their old age, rose further, and the death rate, although still high by Western standards, declined. Population growth seriously limited the effects of economic development, as did continued competition from British factories that displaced hundreds of thousands of traditional manufacturing workers; the prosperity of the average Indian did not increase.

Many Indian traditionalists continued to resent British practices. At the same time, a new opposition force emerged among educated Indians not only concerned about their own national identity but also influenced by key Western political and educational values that, in their view, argued against undemocratic foreign rule. Several Indian newspapers sprang up, resulting in lively political discourse. The first Indian National Congress, with Hindu and Muslim delegates drawn mainly from the ranks of civil servants, met in 1885. Its initial demands were modest, focusing on greater opportunities for Indians in the imperial bureaucracy. From this base, a nationalist sentiment spread among educated groups, particularly Hindus. This represented a new loyalty in Indian history, cutting across caste, regional, and to some extent religious lines. Nationalism encouraged Indians to think in terms of growing political freedom as well as a culture independent of Western influence. Successive National Congresses became increasingly vigorous in requesting reforms. They focused not only on civil service jobs, but also on British economic control, seeking the creation of an India that could advance to the ranks of industrial nations on its own. As one 1910 speaker stated: "India has come to be regarded as a plantation of England, giving raw products to be shipped by British moguls in British ships, to be worked into fabrics . . . to be re-exported to India by British merchants." Here was a resentment of the Western-dominated world economy that echoed through the 20th century in many civilizations.

Indian nationalism imitated European, and particularly British, political beliefs, while insisting on India's special qualities. Nationalist leaders opted for an inclusive definition of nationalism—including various religious, racial, and social groups—unlike the narrower ethnic nationalism that had developed in Germany. Key questions of precise definition, however, were overshadowed by the obvious need to reduce British control.

Before 1900, Indian nationalism did not pose a major threat to British rule. Periodic riots by peasant groups, against taxes or census taking (seen as a government plot to raise taxes), or in the name of traditional religion, were a greater problem, resulting in the assassination of several British officials.

India by 1900 was by no means westernized, but it had altered substantially because of both British initiatives and the new interests of Indian leaders themselves, particularly in education, nationalist politics, and industrial management. Indian cultural vitality had in many ways increased, spurred by the revival of Hinduism and active use of traditional artistic and literary styles.

At the same time, gaps had opened between Indian leaders, mostly upper caste in any event and now exposed to Western ideas and Indian nationalism, and the masses of Indians who revered traditional forms and viewed changes largely as impositions—new taxes, new and often poorly paid wage labor—by British or Indian masters.

Southeast Asia

Many developments in southeast Asia resembled trends in India—as had long been the case. The regional politics of this area continued, as different European powers controlled different countries. There was no substantial redrawing of the religious map, although a minority of southeast Asians, particularly in French Indochina, converted to Christianity. In Dutch Indonesia, the government built railroads and created a Dutch-language education system for the elite, along with a growing bureaucracy and new tax structure. New laws attempted to regulate the planters' use of native labor on the large estates devoted to export production. Essentially manorial controls, involving significant rights over peasant labor, were converted after 1870 to a wage labor system.

Particularly during the second half of the 19th century, increasing numbers of southeast Asian peasants were drawn into a market economy, employed as workers producing goods ranging from spices and tea to rubber, for sale on the world market. Many of these goods commanded relatively low prices; as a result, the system depended on low wages.

Imperial governments, as in India, began to introduce Western-style administrative measures. Bureaucrats busily collected census data. The independence of local leaders, including village headmen, was reduced. New police forces attempted to regulate crime and local unrest. As in India, more efficient administration and some agricultural improvements led to population increases, putting new pressure on available land.

Nevertheless, although traditionalists bitterly resented many European impositions, there was little systematic protest against imperialism before 1900. Nationalism was slow to surface, although soon after 1900, Indonesian civil servants sought greater equality with Dutch officials. Some local peasant uprisings occurred, expressing the need for land and resentment against tax collection, and in Indonesia a movement to renew Islamic fervor took shape. But the main wave of protest against European control, as in India, still awaited the future.

IMPERIALISM IN AFRICA

New Western penetration of sub-Saharan Africa became a dominant force only after the 1860s. During much of the 19th century, African history essentially followed an established path, with scattered innovations, although economic changes were significant. In the northern region, below the Sahara desert, Islam continued to spread through the popular missionary and holy war movement that had evolved in the later 18th century. A literature began to develop in Swahili, east Africa's written language linked to Islam. Later in the 19th century, the dissemination of Islam was furthered by Western imperialism, for Islam was seen as a vital, well-organized religion that had the merit of not being Western. Even before this, in the regions it touched, Islam attacked many African cultural traditions as superstitions, much as Western and Middle Eastern popular beliefs had been challenged by monotheism some centuries before. This process, in turn, helped launch a painful but exciting redefinition of African civilization to which Western imperialism ultimately contributed as well.

Africans did face a clear economic challenge. With the end of the Atlantic slave trade, the balance of trade shifted sharply. It became harder to acquire goods such as guns manufactured abroad. Many African leaders and merchants worked hard to develop alternative exports, such as vegetable oils made from peanuts or coconuts. In the process, they increased internal slavery as a means of providing cheap labor. Conditions for women often deteriorated, as their use as slaves expanded.

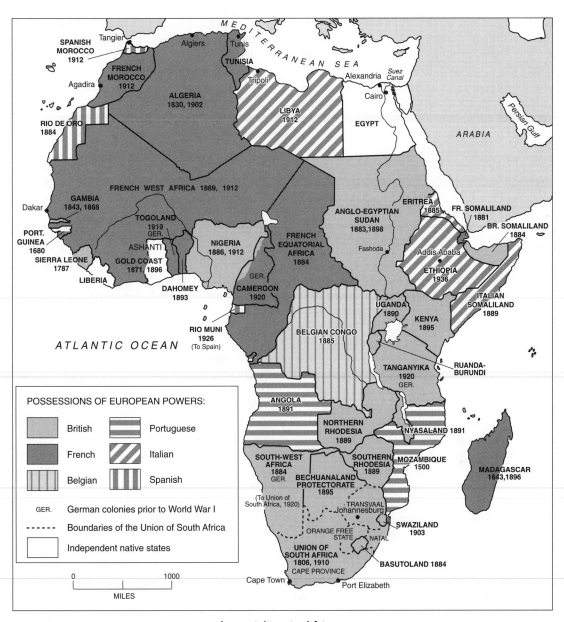

Imperialism in Africa

Some of this foreshadowed the economic impact of imperialism on labor conditions, even when outright slavery was abolished.

The same developments helped draw new European interest in Africa. Some European intervention was justified by the new desire to stamp out slavery. Probably more important was the incentive to push farther into Africa in search of profits, now that the slave trade no longer provided easy pickings.

In west Africa, before imperialism took firm hold, Britain and France gradually acquired new port territories. Britain, for example, took over the key city of Lagos, in what is now Nigeria; France, the city of Dakar, in Senegal. In European-controlled port cities, a small number of Africans converted to Christianity and had other contact with Western values. Some began to think in terms of developing African states along liberal political lines, although this remained as yet a dream. Finally, two small states were formed, Liberia and Sierra Leone, by freed slaves from the United States and British West Indian colonies, respectively. The freed slaves formed an elite governing group, which was heavily influenced by American and British governments, over the African majority in these states; here was another source of new Western influence in this region.

Greater change occurred in southern Africa. The migration of Boer settlers from the Cape province increased when Britain acquired control of this colony from Holland during the Napoleonic Wars. Boer farmers conducted many battles with African forces through the 1830s, gradually enlarging their own zone of settlement. At the same time, Bantu groups north of this zone faced crowded conditions because of their own population growth. The result was the formation of a number of tightly knit regional monarchies, organized along the traditional lines of a divine monarchy with highly ceremonial rule. Some of these kingdoms, such as the Zulus in Natal (now a state in South Africa), developed well-organized military forces and were able to hold their own against not only other Bantu states but also the Boers until the late 1880s.

In sum, most of sub-Saharan Africa continued patterns of regional government, mainly under a divine kingship, and traditional religion well into the later 19th century. Scattered European gains, more export-oriented farming, and the growth of Islam constituted new forces in some regions. On the other hand, there was no sweeping technological or political transformation.

Then came the new imperialism, bursting into this civilization with full force after 1870. To many

European leaders, as well as many Africans, its force seemed bewildering. The British foreign minister lamented in 1891, "I do not know the cause of this sudden revolution, but there it is." And there it was, indeed. By conquest and negotiation, by 1900, Britain had developed an extensive empire in west Africa, including Nigeria, and a north–south axis running from southern Africa toward Egypt and embracing the modern nations of the Sudan, Kenya, Uganda, Zambia, and Zimbabwe. The British also conquered the Boer states north of its Cape Colony through the bloody Boer War of 1899–1902, forming a united South African state with a large European minority. France concentrated on east–west expansion from its holdings in Senegal, winning control over most of the territory just south of the Sahara. Belgium had the Congo, Germany possessed Tanganyika and southwest Africa, and Portugal increased its control over Angola and Mozambique.

These new empires were not won without hard fighting. France and Britain both faced bitter resistance from Muslim forces below the Sahara, leading to battles such as the one Winston Churchill described. Full subjugation of this region occurred only in the late 1890s, because Muslim armies were well organized, if poorly armed, and consumed with a spirit of jihad, or holy war, against the intruders. In both their colonies, Germans met with vigorous African resistance, which they vanquished only by brutal massacres in which tens of thousands of Africans were killed. European intervention was compounded by frequent insensitivity toward local customs, as the imperialists tried to export or destroy religious symbols and some of the ceremonial apparatus of the divine kingship. In west Africa, for example, a British governor provoked a war when he tried to seize the traditional Golden Stool of the Ashanti king, to send back to Queen Victoria.

The consequences of new European rule in Africa were dramatic, although colonialism by no means overturned all African customs. As in India, Western institutions were only one among many forces at work. Furthermore, by 1914, the European regimes were barely in place,

WORLD PROFILES

JOHN MENSAH SARBAH
(1865–1910)

European imperialism created complex pressures for new African leaders. John Mensah Sarbah chose a path of utilizing Western standards in defense of African rights. A member of the Fante tribe on the Gold Coast, in the area now known as Ghana, Mensah Sarbah was a scholarly man who trained in English law and was the first African from his region to be admitted to the English bar. Mensah Sarbah used English constitutional arguments to claim that the British had no right to rule the Gold Coast and were consistently violating established African laws. He actively urged expanded responsibilities for educated Africans who could preserve Africa's traditional communal virtues. His multivolume *Fante National Constitution* (1906) followed from his elaborate research on customary law. He also founded several organizations designed to protect traditional African rights to land ownership, and his arguments did secure African land titles in British legislation of 1898. Mensah Sarbah thus worked in two worlds, an early example of a leader striving to unite Western methods and African goals. Was this a more effective approach than outright violent opposition to imperialism?

John Mensah Sarbah.

and much of the impact of the West became clear only later. Different imperialist countries followed somewhat different policies in their colonies. France, for example, was eager to educate an African elite in Western ways, whereas Britain concentrated more on basic education and medical care for a larger number of people while discouraging the formation of a new elite. However, some main lines of development were emerging by 1914, across the new political divisions of the continent.

The first consequence was the new political units themselves. Africa had always been divided, but now it was broken up into states artificially created by accidents of European competition and timing. None of the colonial states had any clear precedent. Many mixed different tribal, language, and religious groups that had long been rivals. A few regional kingdoms persisted under British supervision in southern Africa, and Ethiopia remained independent, defeating Italy in an 1896 war. Otherwise, however, the map of the civilization was entirely, and from an African standpoint arbitrarily, redrawn. European administrations tried to impose Western concepts of property law, sanitary regulation, and police on their new domains. Few Africans by 1914 were included in the new imperial bureaucracies.

The cultural impact of the Europeans was initially limited. Intense missionary activity created an important Christian minority in many parts of Africa, which added to the culture's religious diversity. But most Africans remained polytheist or, in the north, Muslim. Some combined Christianity with traditional beliefs, such as the witch doctors who converted but still prayed to other spirits for protection, relying on Christianity for favor in the afterlife. Knowledge of a European language spread among an educated minority, along with growing familiarity with Western science and some Western political ideas.

The economic impact of the Europeans was far greater than their cultural influence. The new rulers were eager to make the most profit from their colonies. Small numbers of white settlers claimed the most fertile land, a process already established in southern Africa and now applied to east Africa as well. Colonial administrations imposed new taxes, which forced many Africans to seek paying work on European-owned plantations and mines simply to obtain money in an economy that had previously relied heavily on barter. Colonial officials in some cases requisitioned labor directly, enforcing their demands by brutal physical punishments, including dismemberment. In general, Africans working the mines and the estates suffered harsh conditions—including frequent brutal physical punishments—and of course low pay. Europeans did improve port facilities and other aspects of the communication and transportation system, although there was much less railroad construction in the difficult African terrain than in India or southeast Asia. New medical facilities to combat traditional tropical diseases were also of some benefit, and the African population began to increase. Still, by

1900 and even beyond, the main economic results of European control were largely exploitative, as Africa supplied food and minerals—copper from the Congo, gold and diamonds from South Africa—to the Western market from the sweat of miserably paid laborers.

Most Africans, however, were not directly caught up in the institutions of imperialist rule. Village agriculture changed slowly, and other village institutions persisted; European ability to reach most Africans directly was quite limited in a vast and diverse continent where, even with European technology, communication remained difficult. At the same time, the relatively recent nature of European conquest hampered ongoing African reaction. Nationalist movements and other forms of resistance would come, but by 1914, the bloody defeat of initial opposition efforts was a setback to further response.

COMPARING COLONIES

Colonialism brought many similar experiences to otherwise different societies. Foreign rule raised some common issues, as did the subjection to an economic system dominated by industrial Europe. However, colonies often differed in their responses, depending on prior culture and institutions and variations in European policy.

India, with a major religion of its own and extensive experience of outside control in the past, adjusted its culture more selectively than did Africa; there were fewer Indian religious conversions, for instance. Indian civilization also had a longer time to come to terms with Western control, in comparison with the more sudden domination of Africa and the ensuing shock among local populations. Sub-Saharan Africa, by 1900, was beginning to experience the more systematic loss of traditional values, particularly in some areas where Christian missionaries had made advances. The rawest economic exploitation of India occurred around 1800. But in Africa, the European exploitation of resources and labor only increased from the 1890s on. Competition among European states also affected conditions in Africa, in contrast to India by this point. Although European beliefs in their racial superiority affected policies everywhere, the impact was sharper in Africa than India. Such differences impacted the colonial experience during the 19th century, and also native reactions later on, when independence became a viable possibility.

European imperialism had a worldwide impact, as a threat if not always fact. The balance of power among the civilizations of the world was dramatically shifted not only by European control of major civilizations—India, southeast Asia, and Africa—but also by the extension of essentially Western societies to North America, including the U.S. western frontier as well as Canada, and to Australia and New Zealand.

In India and southeast Asia, and ultimately in Africa, the fact of European control shaped vital questions of change and adaptation. New Western rule, efficiently administered, brought major innovations, including new political boundaries and new levels of commercialization. It was clear that the colonized societies were not going to become Western. Their traditional cultures were too deep rooted, their populations and territories too vast; European ambivalence about reforming the natives and seeing them as inherent racial inferiors, as children to be disciplined by wiser Western parents, also limited the process of westernization. However, European occupation did provide direct tutelage in Western ways, allowing leaders in southern Asia, and later in Africa, to decide what concepts they wished to borrow, which ones they wanted to reject. One idea that was assimilated, if only to give shape to what may have been an inherent desire for independence, was nationalism, as was already evident in India. Through nationalism, leaders attracted to some Western patterns, and others eager simply

to restore preimperialist traditions, could at least briefly join together in a fervent demand for independence. Imperialism clearly generated its own resistance, and this interplay dominated much of the history of the 20th century.

Nevertheless, imperialism also uprooted a host of traditional economic, social, and cultural patterns. An independent India or Africa would not go back to preimperialist ways of life. Imperialism also resulted in new political problems in uniting or dividing earlier units. It brought economic benefits, in the form of improved transportation and agricultural methods, along with the often harsh use of local labor and integration of colonies into a Western-dominated world market. Population growth posed its own new challenge to the economies of Africa and southern Asia. Limited medical advances, such as inoculations, swamp-draining, and other disease-control measures, had a tremendous impact just as Western population growth was ebbing. In 1914, the major question for Indian or Nigerian or Indonesian leaders was clear: how should we respond to Western rule? But imperialism raised wider political, economic, and cultural concerns also, which outlasted the struggle for independence in setting an agenda for world history well into the 20th century and beyond.

Many similar issues also affected those parts of the world not subject to full imperialist control, such as China and the Ottoman Empire, or newly freed from it—Latin America, for example. Would outright imperialist rule help or hinder a civilization in addressing problems of population growth, imbalance in the world economy, and new political tensions? Was India, to use the clearest example, better off for having experienced an intense if relatively brief period of Western rule than China, which faced Western depredations without the possible benefits of Western influence? Imperialism provided a shock to the civilizations that came under its full sway in the 19th century; its impact and the reactions it provoked conditioned the history of these areas even after independence was won.

PATHS
TO THE PRESENT

European imperialism has largely ended; decolonization is one of the great changes in world history that occurred after the long 19th century. Even the resentments imperialism caused have substantially cooled. Neither contemporary Africa nor contemporary India devotes much thought to getting back at their imperialists, though some sensitivities remain.

Imperialism encouraged a level of economic dependency that still affects the economies of most of Europe's former colonies. Africa in particular, colonized late by European powers eager to exploit cheap labor, mineral, and agricultural resources, has yet to recover from its colonial economic status.

The imperialism of the long 19th century differentiated among types of colonies, as we have seen. British control of India, though hardly benign, created not only a useful railroad infrastructure but also a degree of political unity that, in turn, built a framework for modern India, though that framework did not survive intact. In Africa, European colonies were carved without regard to prior political alignments. These colonies have also turned into new nations, but the illogic of their initial construction continues to complicate these new countries' political lives. The political and economic conditions of 19th-century colonies, in other words, are parallel to their political and economic conditions today, despite the many changes that have occurred in between.

SUGGESTED WEB SITES

For more information on European imperialism in the 19th century, refer to http://www2 .sunysuffolk.edu/westn/imperialism.html; on worldwide imperialism, see http://mars.wnec. edu/~grempel/courses/world/lectures/ imperialism.html; and for information on imperialism and colonialism, consult http:// andremeda.rutgers.edu/~jlynch/18th/.

SUGGESTED READINGS

Significant recent works on imperialism include Tony Ballantyne and Antoinette Burton, eds., *Bodies in Contact: Rethinking Colonial Encounters in World History* (2005); Karl Hack and Tobias Rettig, eds., *Colonial Armies in Southeast Asia* (2006); Ronaly Hyam, *Britain's Imperial Century 1815–1914: A Study of Empire and Expansion* (2002); Linda Cooley, *Captives: Britain, Empire and the World* (2004); Timothy Parsons, *The British Imperial Century, 1815–1914: A World History Perspective* (1999); Lester Alan, *Imperial Networks: Creating Identities in the 19th Century South Africa and Britain* (2001); and Caroline Elkins, *Imperial Reckoning: The Untold Story of Britain's Gulag in Kenya* (2005). See also Michael Adas, *Machines as the Measure of Men* (1989). On specific areas and imperialist powers, W. Baumgart, *Imperialism: The Idea and Reality of British and French Colonial Expansion* (1982), offers an excellent discussion. On Africa, worthwhile sources include Colin Turnbull, *The Lonely African* (1971); A. Moorehead, *The White Nile* (1971); Woodruff D. Smith, *The German Colonial Empire* (1978); Walter Rodney, *How Europe Underdeveloped Africa* (1982)—a vital study; and C. A. Bayly, *Indian Society and the Making of the British Empire* (1988). On peasant resistance, refer to J. Scott, *The Moral Economy of the Peasant: Rebellion and Subsistence in Southeast Asia* (1976). On women's conditions, see Clare Midgley, ed., *Gender and Imperialism* (1998). On other topics, see Robert D. Grant, *Representations of British Emigration, Colonization and Settlement: Imagining Empire, 1800–1860* (2005); Jennifer Pitts, *A Turn to Empire: The Rise of Imperial Liberalism in Britain and France* (2005); Alexei Miller and Alfred J. Rieber, eds., *Imperial Rule* (2004); John Marriott, *The Other Empire: Metropolis, India, and Progress in the Colonial Imagination* (2003); James L. Hevia, *English Lessons: The Pedagogy of Imperialism in Nineteenth-Century China* (2003); Bernd Hamm and Russell Smandych, eds., *Cultural Imperialism: Essays on the Political Economy of Cultural Domination* (2005); Arne Perras and Carl Peters, *German Imperialism, 1856–1918: A Political Biography* (2004); and Shigeru Akita, ed., *Gentlemanly Capitalism, Imperialism, and Global History* (2002).

CHAPTER

23 The Settler Societies: The West on Frontiers

In context of growing European economic and military power, the steady growth in European population through much of the 19th century had particular impact on several overseas regions, which, in turn, received the majority of their inhabitants and much of their political and cultural inspiration from Europe. The new United States, Canada, Australia, and New Zealand built on Western traditions, but they had to combine them with the values of more diverse peoples—native inhabitants, plus, in the case of the United States, African slaves and a small but important stream of Asian immigrants. These countries also faced frontier conditions long since eradicated from Europe, and in this respect they more closely resembled contemporary Russia and Latin America. These evolving centers became increasingly important in world history from about 1870 on, when their economic growth generated growing agricultural (and, in the case of the United States, industrial) exports.

The settler societies differed from Europe in several key respects. They did not have an established aristocracy or a peasant class. Innovative, profit-minded farmers increasingly dominated the agricultural market. Abundant land, plus opportunities to export to Europe, encouraged commercial farming. The societies were not initially as wealthy as their European counterparts, although their standards of living were high; they depended greatly on capital investments from Europe. These people were not as culturally creative as Europeans, looking to them for most basic styles, although a regional art and literature took shape during the 19th century (particularly in the United States). The settler societies escaped some of Europe's political tensions, establishing democracy relatively early, but they faced specific political problems of their own—as, for example, in the American Civil War between the antislavery North and the slaveholding South.

The settler societies also followed many of the same trends western Europe did during the 19th century, for example in the development of liberalism, nationalism, and (to a lesser degree in the United States) socialism. They underwent a demographic transition that cut their birth rates. Family patterns and women's roles were redefined in a similar fashion. Western-style science held a firm place, along with currents of thought derived from romanticism. On the basis of its economic power and political independence, the United States even participated in European-style imperialism by the 1890s, taking over islands in the Caribbean and assuming rule over the Philippines and other Pacific island territory.

Complexities in the settler society/western Europe relationship show clearly in the development of feminism and new women's rights. Feminist movements sprang up not only in many parts of western Europe, but also in the United States, from the mid-19th century onward. On the whole, settler societies were slightly quicker than western Europe in actually extending the vote to women, with New Zealand and some western American states leading the way, possibly reflecting frontier factors and a looser hand of tradition. On the other hand, Scandinavian countries moved swiftly also, and from a global standpoint the settler societies and the Protestant countries in western Europe can easily seem part of a common pattern.

Residents of the settler societies—aside from the native peoples whose numbers and power declined rapidly—had something of a love–hate relationship with western Europe. They recognized their affinity and dependence and in many ways felt part of Western civilization, but they were also proud of their differences and realized that their tasks of settlement and state-building differed from those of the mother countries. In addition, the United States maintained a tradition of isolation from Europe's diplomatic squabbles, while it tried (not always successfully) to discourage European intervention in the Western Hemisphere from the Monroe Doctrine (1823) on.

At the start of the long 19th century, the settler societies were only beginning to come into existence or, in the case of Britain's North American colonies, had only minor roles in world trade. The American Revolution provided an important example for other societies, but the real impact of the settler societies, in world history terms, developed after about 1850. By this point, Canadian, Australian, and New Zealand mining or agriculture contributed significant exports, mainly to western Europe, while some industrialization occurred as well. The United States combined industrial and agricultural exports. All the settler societies continued to attract significant immigration. And the United States began to take a hand in global diplomacy as well. The question was whether, in their growing global impact, the settler societies would merely reinforce European initiatives or whether they would add significant innovations of their own.

KEY QUESTIONS   *The overriding question is whether the settler societies were part of a single Western civilization or a major variant because of frontier conditions and different population mixes. Another comparative question involves the societies themselves: how similar were the main settler societies? Were Canada and New Zealand more "European" than Australia and the United States (as some observers believe), and if so, why? Finally, what were the main results of Western interaction with Polynesian peoples?*

THE UNITED STATES

After the American Revolution, the constitutional structure of the new United States was established in 1789. The republic launched a period of consolidation—interrupted by the War of 1812 with England—and westward expansion, as the new nation acquired the Louisiana Purchase from France in 1803. Democratic voting systems, with rights for free males, were widely completed by the 1820s. The nation's federal system led to a fairly weak central government, and many major developments were the result of state action or business initiatives. Thus, the Erie Canal, which helped link the Midwest with the East coast, was sponsored by New York State. However, the federal government was heavily involved in further westward expansion and warred with Mexico to acquire Texas in the 1840s. Within the federal government, there was also a growing tension between the Northern states and the slaveholding South, which culminated in the Civil War.

American culture began to take shape before the Civil War, personified by many New England writers and thinkers and a smaller group of painters and musicians. Also before the Civil War, new waves of European immigrants, particularly from Ireland and Germany, added to the size and mix of the American population.

The North's victory in the Civil War led to a new period of consolidation. Efforts to reform the South, beyond the abolition of slavery, were largely abandoned by 1877, as the United States settled into a succession of undistinguished presidencies and relatively modest basic divisions between the two major political parties. Settlement of the western territories continued, amid recurrent American Indian wars. The pace of industrialization increased, and labor agitation led to new unions, strikes, and occasional political assassinations. Waves of immigration from southern and eastern Europe brought much-needed labor to the nation's growing industries, and by 1914, the growing migration of African Americans from the South increased urban populations as well.

U.S. entry into the world economy, as more than a source of cotton or an investment opportunity, began in the 1870s. Massive agricultural exports combined with significant industrial ventures abroad. Several American companies,

HISTORY DEBATE

EXCEPTIONALISM

For more than a century, most approaches to U.S. history have emphasized the distinctiveness of American society—its "exceptions" to the norms of European history (or, presumably, any other history). American exceptionalism features arguments that the United States was unusually democratic, or unusually open to social mobility, or unusually free from political division. An exceptionalist argument can also be used in a less benign fashion: the nation as unusually racially divided or harsh to factory workers. Exceptionalism is, of course, a comparative statement, although many historians have not bothered to compare their observations. Should the United States be regarded as a separate civilization? If so, how can one account for similar dates and patterns of industrialization, demographic transition, and feminism? Should the United States be viewed as a somewhat unusual but definite part of Western civilization? If so, how can one account for the unusual per capita rates of American violence (well above European levels from the late 18th century to the present), the unusual hostility to the state as an active force in society? The comparative problems run deep, and they have not yet been resolved.

In terms of world history, the ongoing debate over American exceptionalism raises additional issues. If the United States differs from Europe, how much does it resemble other frontier societies, such as Australia or Latin America? As the United States gained a growing world role (particularly in the 20th century), did it behave differently from previous European great powers such as Britain, and if so, how? Finally, did the United States grow more or less different from west European nations as it became more industrial and a great power, and as Europe became more fully democratic?

such as the Singer Sewing Machine Company and International Harvester, established subsidiaries in Europe and Russia. American arms manufacturers sold weapons abroad after the Civil War's end, including among their clients a newly opened Japan. Although still importing technologies from Europe in industries such as the manufacture of chemicals, the United States contributed a number of inventions, including major developments in the uses of electricity. Even more significant were American innovations in the management of labor, where the democratic system sponsored new ways of regimenting large groups of workers. American initiatives in time and motion studies, designed by industrial engineers to speed the work process, and then the assembly line, spread widely to other industrial societies after 1900.

America's diplomatic expansion showed in not only imperialism but also its growing involvement in other international issues; President Theodore Roosevelt, for example, sponsored the conference ending the 1904–1905 war between Russia and Japan. American cultural influence was more modest outside its borders, although the introduction of the skyscraper in Chicago soon after 1900 suggested the new union and power of art and technology. Individual American artists and scientists went to Europe to learn and sometimes made their mark as creators or thinkers, but in most cultural arenas the United States remained largely a borrower until after World War I.

HAWAII

The 1890s saw the United States join the imperialist scramble, essentially adding to the list of Western powers involved. Territory was added in the Caribbean, including Puerto Rico, seized from Spain. The Philippines essentially became a colony. New interventions occurred in Cuba and Central America, including sponsorship of a new nation, Panama, taken from Colombia to facilitate American control of the new canal.

One new territory became a distinctive kind of settler society. Hawaii had been opened to the West by the voyages of British Captain James Cook, 1777–1779. Hawaiian rulers, headed by King Kamehameha, introduced Western-style reforms. American missionaries and planters began to move to the islands, causing major cultural and economic change. Western-brought diseases reduced the Hawaiian population of half a million to 80,000 by 1850. New workers were imported from Japan, China, and later the Philippines. Urged on by pineapple and sugar planters, the United States annexed Hawaii in 1898. The islands increasingly reflected American and (at a lower social level) Asian settlers. But there was little outside racism against native Hawaiians, and there was some respect for their culture even as a new, settler-dominated colony took shape.

THE NEWER SETTLER SOCIETIES

At the same time that the United States expanded, Canada, Australia, and New Zealand also filled with immigrants from Europe and established parliamentary legislatures and vigorous commercial economies that placed them effectively in the general orbit of Western civilization. Like the United States, these new nations looked primarily to Europe for cultural styles and intellectual leadership. They also followed common Western patterns in areas such as family life, the role of women, and the extension of mass education and culture. Unlike the United States, however, these nations remained part of the British Empire, although with growing autonomy.

Canada, won by Britain in its wars with France during the 18th century, had been preserved from the uprisings of the American Revolution. Religious differences between French Catholic settlers and British rulers and settlers troubled the area recurrently, and a number of revolts occurred early in the 19th century. Determined not to lose this colony in addition to the United States, the British began to grant increasing self-rule after 1839. Canada was permitted to establish its own parliament and laws, while remaining under the umbrella of the larger empire. Initially, this system applied primarily to the province of Ontario, but other provinces were gradually included, creating a federal system that describes Canada to this day. French hostilities were eased somewhat by the creation of Quebec, a separate province, where the majority of French settlers remained. Massive railroad building, beginning in the 1850s, brought settlement to western territories and a great expansion of mining and commercial agriculture in the vast plains. As in the United States to the south, new immigrants from southern and particularly eastern Europe poured in during the last decades of the century, attracted by Canada's growing commercial development and spurring even further gains.

Britain's Australian colonies originated in 1788 when a ship deposited convicts to establish a penal settlement at Sydney. Australia's only previous inhabitants had been the aborigines, a hunting-and-gathering people who were in no position to resist European settlement and exploration. Unfamiliar European diseases and guns took a predictable toll. By 1840, Australia had 140,000 European inhabitants, based mainly on a prosperous sheep-growing agriculture that provided needed wool for British industries. The exportation of convicts ceased in 1853, by which time most settlers were free immigrants. The discovery of gold in 1851 led to further pioneering, which resulted in a population of more than one million by 1861. As in Canada, major provinces were granted self-government with a multiparty parliamentary system. A unified federal nation was proclaimed on the first day of the 20th century. By this time, considerable industrialization, a growing socialist party, and significant welfare legislation had developed.

New Zealand, discovered by the Dutch in the 17th century and explored by the English in 1770, began to receive British attention after

This drawing depicts an Aboriginal Australian holding a rock and a long spear.

1814. Here the Polynesian hunting-and-gathering people, the Maoris, were well organized politically. Missionary efforts converted many of them to Christianity between 1814 and the 1840s. The British government, fearful of French interest in the area, moved to take official control in 1840, and considerable European immigration followed. New Zealand settlers relied heavily on agriculture (including sheep growing), selling initially to Australia's booming gold-rush population and then to Britain. As in Canada and Australia, a parliamentary system was created that allowed the new nation to rule itself as a dominion of the British Empire, without interference from the mother country.

New Zealand was something of a special case among settler societies because of the continuing importance of the native peoples, the Polynesian

WORLD PROFILES

HONGI HIKA

Hongi Hika is probably the most famous of all New Zealand's Maori warriors. Estimated to have been born around 1772, Hongi was from the Ngupuhi tribe and uncle of Hone Heke, chief of the Ngapuhi tribe in the north. Interestingly enough, *Hongi* not only means "smell" but is also a derivative of the word that represents the Maori greeting of pressing noses together. Nevertheless, Hongi Hika helped to single-handedly transform the nature of Maori warfare.

During Hongi's formative years, Thomas Kendell, a British missionary, formed a close and long-lasting friendship with him. Kendell believed that Hongi had converted to Christianity, and he invited Hongi to England. Kendell hoped to get Hongi's assistance in translating the Bible in the Maori language. Hongi, however, had his own agenda. He hoped a trip to Europe would enable him to obtain weapons for his intertribal wars. Thus, in 1820, Hongi embarked upon the long journey to Great Britain. Not surprisingly, Hongi's tattooed appearance caused quite a stir in England. Instead of the weapons he was hoping for, King George IV gave him many ceremonial gifts. However, thanks to innovative trading and a stop in Sydney, Australia, on the way to New Zealand, Hongi was able to obtain the muskets and ammunition he was seeking.

After he returned to New Zealand, Hongi was able to use the weapons he had secured, leading a series of successful raids against rival tribes. Suddenly, other tribes needed the modern weaponry that Hongi's tribe had. Consequently, his journey to England began

Hongi Hika.

a Maori trend of obtaining European weapons. Lacking the ceremonial gifts that Hongi had been able to exchange, other tribes began to trade preserved human heads for modern weapons. Hongi died in 1828 due to a bullet wound received in a battle.

Maoris. Initial British settlements on the coasts in the 1790s brought disruption, with increasing prostitution and alcoholism among the Maoris. Use of guns made traditional Maori warfare more dangerous. More important was the impact of disease, cutting an initial population of 130,000 by about 70 percent on the north island by the

1840s. But Maoris survived and began to use new Western tools for farming and cattle-raising (with animals purchased from Europeans). An influx of British farmers in the 1850s led to new disputes over land and a series of wars. The Maoris also developed frenzied new religious movements in the 1860s and 1870s that promised to drive the invaders out. But despite predictions of Maori collapse, the Maoris learned to use British laws to defend much of their land; they also adapted to Western education. The result was a settler society within the British Empire but with a distinctly multiracial flavor.

Like the United States, Canada, New Zealand, and Australia each had distinct national characteristics and national issues. These new countries were far more dependent on the European, particularly the British, economy than was the United States. Industrialization did not overshadow commercial agriculture and mining, even in Australia, so that exchanges with Europe remained unusually important. Nevertheless, these countries followed the basic patterns of Western civilization from this point on, from political forms to key leisure activities. Currents of liberalism, socialism, modern art, and scientific education, which described Western civilization to 1900 and beyond, thus largely characterized these important new countries.

It was these areas, finally, along with the United States and parts of Latin America, particularly Brazil and Argentina, that received new waves of European emigrants during the 19th century. Although Europe's population growth rate slowed after 1800, it still advanced rapidly on the basis of previous gains—that is, as more children reached adulthood and had children of their own. Europe's expansion was, in fact, greater than Asia's in percentage terms until the 20th century, and Europe's export of people helped explain how Western societies could take shape in such distant areas.

SPECIAL FEATURES OF SETTLER SOCIETIES

The extension of Western society through most of North America as well as Australia and New Zealand depended on the fortuitous absence of large previous populations, compounded by the continued ravages of Western-imported diseases on the indigenous people in these locations. Other parts of the world, more thickly inhabited, had quite different experiences under the impact of Western influence and some outright settlement. The spread of the settler societies also reflected the new power of Western industrialization. Huge areas could now be populated quickly, thanks to steamships and rails, while remaining in close contact with the Western home base in Europe. The expansion of the West revealed the power of Western values and institutions, as colonists deliberately introduced most of the patterns that had prevailed in Europe, from parliaments to standards for women and children.

PATHS TO THE PRESENT

The long 19th century was a formative period for the settler societies. Many Canadians argue that continuing differences between them and their United States neighbors to the south resulted from developments during this period: closer ties with Britain and with British reserve, for example, in contrast to the more demonstrative styles that characterize many Americans. Although Canadian westward expansion rivaled that of the United States, the free-wheeling cowboy image never emerged to the same extent north of the border. In a similar vein, New Zealand stayed closer to British models than Australia did, despite the important interaction with the Maoris; Australia's launching as a penal colony colored later utilization of British themes, despite its loyal participation in the Commonwealth. Key economic patterns were also set in this period that continued, broadly speaking, into the present, including the importance of agricultural and, for Australia and Canada, mineral exports within a high-wage economy.

All the settler societies expanded on the basis of inroads on native populations—New Zealand was the partial exception here. Canada, Australia, and recurrently the United States continue to discuss what, if anything, to do about past patterns of exploitation and abuse. The United States also still deals with its heritage of racial discrimination during and in the aftermath of slavery.

By 1900, the settler societies were only beginning to define their approaches to wider global interactions beyond those of economic exchange and acceptance of immigrants. Here was an opportunity that would await the 20th century.

SUGGESTED WEB SITES

To experience voices from the days of slavery, see http://memory.loc.gov/ammem/ collections/voices/; on revolutionary America and its era, refer to http://rs6.loc.gov/ammem/ gmdhtml/armhtml/armhome.html; for more information on the Thomas Jefferson Papers, see http://memory.loc.gov/ammem/collections/ jefferson_papers/; to interpret the Declaration of Independence by translation, see http:// chnm.gmu.edu/declaration/. A useful site for the history and culture of Hawaii can be found at http://www.everyculture.com/multi/Ha-La/ Hawaiians.html; and for resources on early migrants to New Zealand, see http://home-pages.ihug.co.nz/~tonyf/WHY/WHY.html.

SUGGESTED READINGS

On U.S. history, in addition to several excellent textbooks with good reading lists (e.g., Gary Nash and Julie R. Jeffrey, *The American People: Creating a Nation and a Society* [1990], and James Kirby Martin et al., *America and Its People*, 2nd ed. [2001]), see Eugene D. Genovese, *Roll, Jordan, Roll: The World the Slaves Made* (1974); Thomas Cochran, *Frontiers of Change: Early Industrialization in America* (1981); Steven Mintz and Susan Kellog, *Domestic Revolutions: A Social History of American Family Life* (1988); and Albert W. Niemi, *United States Economic History* (1987).

On Canada, Australia, and New Zealand, see J. M. Bumstead, *A History of Canada* (1992); Alastair Davidson, *The Formation of the Australian State* (1991);

Charles Wilson, *Australia, 1788–1988: The Creation of a Nation* (1988); and Miles Fairburn, *The Ideal Society and Its Enemies: Foundations of Modern New Zealand Society, 1850–1900* (1990). See also John Gascoigne and Patricia Curthoys, *The Enlightenment and the Origins of European Australia* (2005); and Annie Coombes, ed., *Rethinking Aettler Colonialism: History and Memory in Australia, Canada, New Zealand and South Africa* (2006);

For additional recent work, see Jonathan Glickstein, *American Exceptionalism, American Anxiety: Wages, Competition and Degraded Labor in the Antebellum United States* (2002); William Barney, *A Companion to 19th Century America* (2001); Alyson Greiner, *Anglo-Celtic Australia: Colonial Immigration and Cultural Regionalism* (2002); and Patricia Jalland, *Australian Ways of Life: A Social and Cultural History 1840–1914* (2002). Also refer to David Armitage and Michael J. Braddick, *The British Atlantic World, 1500–1800* (2002); Thomas Benjamin, Timothy Hall, and David Rutherford, eds., *The Atlantic World in the Age of Empires* (2001); Arnoldo De León, William Cronon, Howard R. Lamar, and Martin Ridge, *Racial Frontiers: Africans, Chinese, and Mexicans in Western America, 1848–1890* (2002); and David J. Weber, Jesus F. de la Teja, and Ross Frank, *Choice, Persuasion and Coercion: Social Control on Spain's North American Frontiers* (2005). See also Scott A. Silverstone, *Divided Union: The Politics of War in the Early American Republic* (2004); Robert E. May, *Manifest Destiny's Underworld: Filibustering in Antebellum America* (2002); Eric T. L. Love, *Race Over Empire: Racism and U.S. Imperialism, 1865–1900* (2004); Douglas Seefeldt et al., eds., *Across the Continent: Jefferson, Lewis and Clark, and the Making of America* (2005); Amy S. Greenberg, *Manifest Manhood and the Antebellum American Empire* (2005); Richard Waterhouse, *The Vision Splendid: A Social and Cultural History of Rural Australia* (2005); David Chennells, *The Politics of Nationalism in Canada: Cultural Conflict Since 1760* (2001); Philippa Mein Smith, *A Concise History of New Zealand* (2005); Charles Lockhart, *The Roots of American Exceptionalism: History, Institutions and Culture* (2003); Thomas Bender, *A Nation Among Nations: America's Place in World History* (2006); and Edward Davies, *United States in World History* (2006).

Latin American civilization had been a settler, frontier society of a sort in the early modern period. But the results of slavery and a plantation economy, plus the long period of Spanish or Portuguese political control, plus the dependent position of Latin America in the world economy made the Latin American experience distinctive. Settler society characteristics remained: frontier conditions, for example, prevailed in parts of Argentina; many Latin American nations received substantial immigration. But the larger native and mestizo populations in many areas, plus the greater degree of economic dependency, marked key differences from places such as Australia or the United States.

Latin American nations won independence, participating in the wave of Atlantic revolutions after 1810. The civilization as a whole further defined its identity as the century unfolded. In politics and culture, Latin American leaders combined a deep devotion to many Western styles and values with some distinctive features that resulted from the civilization's racial diversity, its own colonial past, and the social structure that stemmed from a semi-colonial economy. The result was a distinctive combination, in the 19th century and after.

One of the primary challenges to 19th-century Latin America was the formation of new nations where no clear precedent served to guide. These new nations were inevitably concerned with establishing territorial boundaries and with generating a leadership that could function despite the lack of prior political expression. Hereditary rule, for example, made little sense in this context because there were no indigenous ruling families. Previous American Indian regimes had long since been destroyed, and rule from Spain and Portugal was now ended as well. Along with new leadership, the nations had to set up legal structures and work to establish some kind of national loyalty. These were difficult tasks, yet for all their undoubted political problems, the new countries of Latin America achieved considerable success in addressing them during the 19th century.

█**KEY QUESTIONS**   *The most obvious question involves interpreting the combination of new political independence with Latin America's dependent position in the world economy. A second question involves culture: what were the key features of Latin American culture as it was further defined in the long 19th century, and did it provide a distinctive identity?*

THE WARS OF INDEPENDENCE

The 19th century began with the wars of independence from Spanish rule. Conflict broke out at several points in 1810, and the drive for independence was essentially completed by the mid-1820s. There followed another 30 years of consolidation, when the boundaries of the new nations were largely set, amid considerable strife, and the broad outlines of internal politics established. This was a period of economic hardship throughout most of Latin America, as the wars of independence disrupted earlier trade patterns and consumed substantial tax resources. It is important to realize that the countries of Latin America were formed in a harsh economic context, when material distress heightened the possibilities of discontent and disorder. After 1850, economic conditions tended to improve, as the civilization underwent extensive commercial development—although such development brought new hardship to important segments of the lower classes. Further imbalance divided a wealthy minority of landowners and merchants from the low-paid masses, even though slavery was abolished. Political instability did not end in this final 19th-century period, but it did follow some clearly established lines. The late 19th century also saw new pressures from the outside world, in the form of the imperialist actions of Western nations, particularly the United States, and a massive wave of immigration from southern Europe.

The wars of independence—unquestionably the most dramatic events in Latin America's 19th-century history—had several causes. Example was one. The revolution that had produced the United States showed that European colonial authority could be defeated. The French Revolution of 1789 also provided an example of the principles of political liberty and nationalist loyalty. Latin American leaders, particularly those drawn from the Creole class, racially European but native to Latin America and often of considerable education and wealth, were keenly aware of what was happening in the Western world, and the new examples became inspirations, along with the ideas of the Enlightenment more generally.

The French Revolution and its Napoleonic aftermath, indeed, provided an opportunity for Latin American leaders. Spain, with a somewhat inefficient government already, became distracted by the new danger on its northern borders, as the Spanish monarch sought to prevent revolutionary uprisings in his own land. Then Napoleon's armies invaded Spain, briefly establishing a regime that controlled most of the country. Neither this regime nor the beleaguered Spanish king Ferdinand had much time or resources to keep Latin American colonies in line. Ferdinand regained his throne in 1815, but by this point the drive for independence was well established. A later Spanish revolution, in 1820, led in fact by discontented troops about to be sent to put down colonial unrest, provided an additional diversion that allowed independence to be won.

Example and opportunity were fueled by serious grievances. In many regions, the colonial economy had depended on extensive slaveholding, and the slave population grew restless during the later 18th century. Material conditions and discipline were harsh. Many slaves expressed their

Latin American Independence

discontent by fleeing; by 1800, more than a quarter of all black slaves in Venezuela were fugitives, hiding out in self-governing communities in the jungles and mountains. Slave revolts also peppered 18th-century history in the Caribbean. In 1796,

Toussaint L'Ouverture, a black leader in the French West Indian colony of Haiti, proclaimed outright independence. L'Ouverture, inspired by French revolutionary doctrines and eager to capitalize on France's own distraction by the war and revolution at home, not only ended Haitian slavery but also established the first black republic in the New World. Because most West Indian islands remained under Spanish, French, British, or Dutch control throughout the 19th century and beyond—although slavery was abolished during the middle decades of the century—Haitian independence did not have widespread repercussions. But pressure from discontented slaves was a more serious factor in the Caribbean and Latin America around 1800 than it was in the United States.

American Indians and mestizos also had grievances. Many were bound to labor on haciendas run by Creoles, Spanish officials, or the church; others worked in the silver mines. Discipline was harsh, and there was little legal freedom. Most workers were forced to buy goods from estate stores and so suffered from a lack of economic options besides material misery. Revolts by American Indian and mestizo estate workers had broken out in the 1770s, centered at first in Peru and spreading to Colombia. The insurrections attacked both the estates system and the high taxes levied by Spanish administrators. These uprisings, although they led to initial success, were ultimately defeated by a combination of military force and trickery. However, they did greatly contribute to the desire for greater freedom from Spanish rule.

At the top of Latin American society, another set of grievances existed. Creoles, often aware of Enlightenment ideals, resented their lack of political opportunity. Although Creoles had been active in the colonial administration early in the 18th century, after 1750, Spain largely returned to a policy of appointing only Spanish-born officials. These officials often disdained Creoles, which only added to this group's resentment. Creole merchants and professionals, moreover, disliked Spanish taxes and economic restrictions, which prevented legal trade with the more prosperous nations of western Europe. As in the United States, revolt was fueled by regulations that seemed excessive and also arbitrary, because they were set without consultation, for

the benefit of the mother country. It was Creole leadership that largely sparked the drive for independence, tying it to the more general Atlantic revolutionary current but with clear moderation in key social issues. American Indian, slave, and mestizo dissatisfaction did not play a direct role, save in Haiti, in part because popular revolts had been recently vanquished. The Latin American wars of independence were not, then, truly mass uprisings, calling social as well as political institutions into question. And while the resulting regimes changed some economic conditions, abolishing slavery in a few cases, such as in Mexico, and weakening the estates system for a time, the social system of colonial Latin America, with its pronounced divisions between Creole owners and mestizo, American Indian, and black workers, remained largely intact.

The first blow in the war for independence occurred in Venezuela in 1810, when the Caracas city council debated whether it owed loyalty to the new Napoleonic regime in Spain. The council decided on disobedience and urged other city councils to do likewise. King Ferdinand's government in flight from Napoleon was greatly displeased by these actions, even though they were technically directed at his French enemy; he declared the new regimes in revolt and ordered the death of its leaders—an order he was powerless to enforce. The new administration in Venezuela promptly established its own army and proclaimed its independence, drawing up a constitution modeled on that of the United States and the French Declaration of the Rights of Man. Spanish forces were able to put down this regime in 1812, but their harsh retaliation against early leaders engendered further opposition. Simón Bolívar, a wealthy Creole trained in the Spanish army and deeply influenced by Enlightenment ideas, now took leadership of the northern independence movement, rather like George Washington in North America, with whom he was often compared. Several years of fighting ensued, in which Bolívar assembled an army composed of many former British, Irish, and German soldiers, along with Creole nationalists and some American Indian troops. By 1819, Bolívar was strong enough to defeat the Spanish army; he proclaimed a new republic, called Gran Colombia, which united Venezuela and Colombia. Spanish attempts to recapture this nation, hampered by its own 1820 revolution, ultimately failed. Bolívar's armies invaded Ecuador, adding this province to his country.

In 1810, independence movements sprang up in the south as well. In Buenos Aires, a provisional regime was formed with a strong liberal element. An army was organized, ultimately under the leadership of another able Creole general, José de San Martín. This army established a full-fledged government in Argentina and also aided the independence movement in Chile. Again, Spanish attempts to recapture these territories after 1815 were defeated, and the rebel armies also invaded Peru.

The final center of the independence movement took place in Mexico and Central America. Two priests, Miguel Hidalgo and José Morelos, led

WORLD PROFILES

SIMÓN BOLÍVAR
(1783–1830)

Simón Bolívar was perhaps the most well-known and revered leader for independence in Latin America, often compared to George Washington. Like Washington, Bolívar was born into the upper classes. A wealthy Creole officer with close intellectual ties to Europe, he developed a passion for national freedom and republicanism, and his fervor plus real military skill catapulted him to leadership of the Caracas-based independence movement in 1810. He was able to mobilize diverse support and won a series of victories against the Spanish in Venezuela, Colombia, and Ecuador between 1817 and 1822. Running the new country, Gran Colombia, was more difficult, however, and as it broke up into smaller nations, Bolívar became bitterly disillusioned. "America is ungovernable," he said, and "those who have served the revolution have plowed the sea." His principles remained firm, nevertheless, and he (again like Washington) refused popular efforts to crown him as king. Why is it often easier for individuals such as Bolívar to mobilize forces for national independence than to govern the new nation after victory?

Simón Bolívar (1783–1830), the great liberator.

a lower-class rebellion of Spanish-speaking American Indians and mestizos against the constraints of the hacienda system in 1810. Some Indians even talked of an Aztec government. The violence of the lower-class rebellion persuaded Mexico's Creoles to remain loyal to Spain until 1820. At this point, however, Spain's own weakness convinced the Creole elite that they should take matters in their own hands, so they would not end up powerless against further social upheaval. Hence, they supported an independent Mexico, hoping to create a monarchy that would attract a European prince. Finding no takers, a conservative Mexican emperor was crowned in 1822. Here was a clear case of decisive action as Creole landlords, in defending their own elite position, severely limited the social impact of freedom movements. Mexico's choice also foreshadowed political patterns in other Latin American areas, when strongman rule was seen as essential support for the elite against possible lower-class radicalism.

Independence for the Central American areas south of Mexico initially assumed more liberal lines. Centered in Guatemala, the movement proclaimed a United Provinces of Central America in 1823, with a constitution closely modeled on that of the United States.

No war was needed to bring independence to the final major nation of Latin America, Brazil. Threatened by Napoleon, the Portuguese ruler had fled to Brazil; when he was able to return to Portugal in 1815, his son, Pedro, remained as regent. Portugal then tried to reimpose colonial controls over Brazil, but Brazilian leaders, now accustomed to a government based in Rio de Janeiro, resisted. Pedro joined this movement, proclaiming Brazilian independence in 1822, with himself as emperor.

By 1825, then, virtually all of Latin America was free from colonial rule. Small European holdings persisted on the northeast coast of South America and in one part of Central America. And, of course, the bulk of the West Indies remained in European hands. Nonetheless, the spirit of freedom prevailed elsewhere.

THE PERIOD OF CONSOLIDATION

Following the intense activity of the liberation movement, a period of consolidation set in. Between 1825 and 1850, a number of the original nine new nations of Latin America split apart. Bolívar had cherished some hope of a political union among all the regimes, but this was clearly impossible because of disagreements among independence leaders, some of whom wanted to establish monarchies while others sought liberal republics. Similar kinds of disputes, plus personal rivalries, then divided even the original states. Gran Colombia fell apart by 1830, splitting into Colombia, Venezuela, and Ecuador. A brief union between Bolivia and Peru failed, in part because the stronger states of Argentina and Chile sought to avoid a powerful neighbor. The United Provinces of Central America had dissolved into five small states by 1840. Finally, a number of border clashes between some of the new nations marked this early period.

The period of consolidation also saw considerable instability in internal politics. Liberals dominated most governments, advocating free trade and a federal government system, but their policies were too idealistic. Debates soon surfaced between advocates of a central government and federalists. Mexico, for example, seesawed between the two systems, with one leader, the colorful general Santa Anna, taking contradictory positions at different points. Liberal rulers sought parliamentary institutions and religious freedom, whereas conservatives wanted to protect the church and upper classes; the latter controlled most regimes between 1830 and 1870. Many new governments were hampered by the lack of extensive political experience of the Creole group. Because Spanish administrators had so systematically excluded the Creoles, save at the level of city councils, few leaders could be found who knew how to operate a government. In this situation, military leaders, drawn from the independence armies, often played an unusually large role. They had a power base and organizational skills. They also characteristically enjoyed the support of landlords, who were eager for forceful military action against peasant unrest. But factional fighting plagued the military as well, leading to frequent coups and revolts. During the 19th century, for example, Bolivia experienced 60 revolts and coups, Venezuela 52. Lack of previous political activity, the important role in internal politics taken by the military, and the obvious lack of agreement on political principles ensured considerable instability for most Latin American nations. Even Brazil, under the steady rule of the Emperor Pedro and then his son until 1889, ultimately followed this pattern, as a republic was proclaimed that soon generated battles among liberals, conservatives, and army leaders.

By 1850, however, despite instability and dispute, many new governments managed to establish some key institutions. New legal codes were written, based largely on Spanish precedent. A number of countries opened school systems and assumed the task of developing port facilities and other public works. Few regimes set up particularly effective bureaucracies, and personal corruption played a frequent role in Latin American affairs. However, the military hierarchy helped compensate for weakly developed civil administrations, and the promotion of military and police functions was obviously vital to the preservation of public order, in turn a cherished goal of the Creole landlords and also church officials.

Although political instability by no means ended after 1850, it is possible to recognize some changes by this point, as initial consolidation was completed. A number of individual nations emerged from early disputes with a forceful government ready to pursue vigorous policies. By 1840, for example, Chile had settled several key issues of political structure, and during a series of administrations under capable presidents, it was able to expand the education system, offer wider voting rights for parliament, and open new lands in the south through the defeat of American Indian groups. A number of governments had also abolished slavery, although the institution survived in Brazil until 1888.

More impressive than internal political consolidation was the achievement of relative stability in foreign affairs. Many Latin American states remained rivals, sometimes contesting border areas. Britain prompted the creation of Uruguay in the 1820s as a buffer between Argentina and Brazil. However, the Latin American map remained quite fixed after 1850. The only major changes, all provoked by the United States, involved the massive loss of territory by Mexico (Texas, the U.S. Southwest, and California). Later, a semi-independent Cuba was established, after the Spanish-American War in 1898, and then an independent Panama, also under U.S. influence, was carved from Colombia to promote U.S. control of the canal constructed through the isthmus there. A few wars dotted Latin American history in the later 19th century. Paraguay took on Argentina and Brazil in the 1860s, provoking great devastation, and Chile warred with its Andes neighbors in the 1870s, taking Bolivian and Peruvian territories. But for the most part, Latin America was free from major strife between nations—far more free, certainly, than western Europe at the same time. The concentration of military leaders on their often repressive internal political role distracted Latin American countries from foreign exploits.

LATE-CENTURY TRENDS: DICTATORSHIP, IMMIGRATION, AND WESTERN INTERVENTION

No single political pattern describes Latin American developments during the late 19th century, but one significant trend was the tendency toward strongman rule. Venezuela, for example, went through three constitutions after 1870, but in fact was ruled mainly by a series of dictators, of whom the most successful was Antonio Guzmún Blanco. Mexico experienced a dizzying succession of changes before also settling into dictatorial rule. The final defeat of General Santa Anna had ushered in a period of liberal government under the American Indian leader Benito Juárez. Juárez sought to reduce the power of the church in Mexican affairs and to extend a secular system of education; he also wanted to decrease landlord influence, although he pressed less vigorously in this regard than he had initially promised his American Indian supporters he would. Even so, his efforts aroused the opposition of conservatives, who looked to France for help. During the 1860s, when France was eager to establish a new empire and the United States was divided by the Civil War, Mexico was ruled by an Austrian duke backed by French armies. However, these armies retreated and liberal insurgents captured and executed the hapless duke. Juárez returned, and with him another series of important liberal reforms. But on Juárez's death, a strongman regime was installed, under Porfirio Díaz, which lasted from 1876 to 1911. Díaz radically curtailed political rights, arranging for the assassination of major opponents. Even in Colombia, where a parliamentary regime had usually prevailed, a brief series of strongman governments assumed power after 1900.

The tendency to adopt strongman rule, amid the considerable shifting of regimes, was only one of the major trends in Latin American history during the second half of the 19th century. Liberals returned to power in most countries, after decades of conservative rule. They were eager for economic development and better, less constrained trade, but their policies were more authoritarian than before. Hence, a number of strongmen, such as Porfirio Díaz in Mexico, were actually liberal in orientation. Many regimes held regular elections but with very restricted voting rights, creating what some historians have called *oligarchic democracies*.

A third theme, steadily accelerating after 1870, was the surge of commercial development. Estate agriculture spread, as Latin American leaders sought to take advantage of new European markets for beef and coffee. Extensive mining resumed: a silver boom arose in Mexico, while the extraction of copper and other products took hold along the Andes. This economic expansion was encouraged by increased foreign investment in Latin America. It was also supported by the interest of a number of Latin American governments, including dictatorships such as that of Guzmán Blanco in Venezuela, in extending roads and rail networks to the interior.

In several regions, a massive new wave of immigration provided the backbone for the commercial upswing. Many governments promoted immigration, often inspired by a belief that American Indian and black labor could never be suitably trained in the ways of a modern society. The Argentine constitution even included a provision that "the Federal government will encourage European immigration," and by 1895, with three-fourths of all adults foreign born, it had a far higher percentage of immigrants than the United States. The end of slavery in Argentina and Brazil, by the 1880s, created a new need for labor. Freed slaves encountered far less complete discrimination in Latin America than in the United States. More intermarriage occurred, as blacks added to the racially mixed population along with mestizos. However, considerable prejudice continued against dark-skinned former slaves and American Indians. This created a favorable climate for the use of immigrant labor, which in fact decreased the number of job opportunities for former slaves in many regions. Latin American interest in immigration peaked just as population pressure in southern Europe crested. Hence, although some immigrants came from Britain and Germany, often bringing capital and organizational skills, the majority came from Italy, Spain, and Portugal. A small number of Asians, from China and Japan, also arrived. Immigrants

WORLD PROFILES

BENITO JUÁREZ
(1806–1872)

Benito Juárez was one of those rare but particularly significant individuals in world history who rose from humble origins to gain an important role in society and then helped shape events. Juárez was a Mexican Indian who acquired an education in law and became a state governor. He was an avid liberal, eager to reduce the privileges of church and army and to promote economic change. After a liberal revolt in the 1850s, Juárez became president of Mexico and undertook a sweeping reform program including the sale of church property. He also backed a land reform act that restricted traditional communal landholdings among Indians in favor of private property; his hope was to spur modern, independent farming, but in fact, the lands were often purchased by speculators, leading to increased landlessness. Conservatives in reaction removed Juárez from power and installed a French-backed emperor whom Juárez opposed in the name of Mexican independence. Juárez returned to office but became increasingly autocratic in reaction to the previous period of instability. Juárez's personality and goals had made him a national symbol by the time of his death in 1872. His legacy, however, was more mixed than he would have wished. A period of strong government and economic growth followed Juárez, but social reform for the groups from which Juárez had risen proved more elusive. Why do leaders such as Juárez sometimes fail to help their own people, despite a sincere desire to do so?

A portrait of reformer Benito Juárez by the artist Angel Bracho.

provided labor for the expanding economies and rapidly growing cities. They also represented new markets for the foods produced by estate agriculture. Many settlers adapted readily to Latin American life, often intermarrying with American Indians and mestizos. While immigrants promoted some European ideas, such as socialism, for the most part they accepted local beliefs, aided by the fact that many shared the Catholic religion with their new compatriots. Immigration thus brought important changes to Latin America, but it did not overturn established political or cultural patterns.

New problems with Western powers constituted the final major factor in late-19th-century Latin American history. Western nations had not left Latin America alone during the consolidation period; their businesses had a major impact on economic life. Britain, which ruled the seas, also blocked the slave trade. France and occasionally Britain interfered militarily, and both Britain and the United States also officially discouraged outside intervention, although the United States consumed approximately half the territory of Mexico between 1830 and 1860, through the annexation of Texas and other lands won by war.

From the 1870s on, however, foreign intervention increased. Heavy Western investment brought government action to enforce debt payments. British and French ships frequently threatened Latin American ports to compel fiscal reforms. U.S. ventures were still more significant. In addition to strong U.S. nationalist and imperialist sentiment, North American corporations acquired extensive estate and mining holdings and often called for military and diplomatic support against local reform movements. U.S. influence bore particularly heavily on governments in Mexico and Central America, although there were also important conflicts with Chile and other states. Through the war with Spain, the United States acquired the island of Puerto Rico directly and established a protectorate over Cuba. The building of the Panama Canal resulted in new pressure, leading to Panamanian independence

from Colombia, under U.S. auspices. And shortly after 1900, the United States began a policy of frequent military intervention in unstable countries in Central America and the West Indies, out of concern for its business interests in these regions. The problem of dealing with Western nations, especially the United States, began to rank high on the agendas of all Latin American states.

Events during the 19th century, and particularly after 1850, had established a number of distinctive regions within Latin American civilization. The great states of the south—Argentina, Uruguay, Chile, and Brazil—took the lead in the new prosperity of the late 19th century. They were most active in commercial development, and they also encouraged the highest levels of immigration. Several states, led by Argentina, prided themselves on their European airs. Buenos Aires became almost Parisian in its elegant boulevards, with stylish French and English shops serving the wealthy classes. Although Brazil had large black and American Indian populations, the southern states were overall more European racially than was Latin America generally. Places such as Argentina also saw considerably more industrial development in the late 19th century than was characteristic of Latin America as a whole.

A second group of countries covered the Andes region—Bolivia, Peru, and Ecuador. Here, the percentage of American Indian population was highest and the poverty greatest. Political instability and military rule were also somewhat more pervasive in this region than in Latin America generally.

Mexico, Central America, Colombia, and Venezuela all had sizable American Indian populations, although the majority was mestizo. This region also experienced some commercial and industrial expansion in the late 19th century. It was also the region most vulnerable to imperialist pressures, a major factor in the development of both foreign and economic policy.

Latin American regionalism, although significant, took shape amid a number of roughly common developments, from independence on, and amid some widely shared patterns of politics and cultural life.

POLITICAL INSTITUTIONS AND VALUES

The instability of Latin American politics became notorious in foreign eyes, particularly in the United States. Frequent violence and the collapse of one regime after another encouraged people in the United States to look down on the Latin American political style, because stability and a consensus on basic values seemed the hallmark of U.S. political life, at least after the devastating Civil War. Latin American politics were certainly distinctive, responding to factors rather different from those that described Western politics during the same period.

Politically active groups in Latin America tended to divide, from independence on, between liberals and conservatives. A small, mainly intellectual socialist movement arose in some places toward 1900, but it had yet to win political significance. Liberals, strongly influenced by their Western counterparts, stood for genuine parliamentary governments, constitutions, civil rights, and a reduction in the power of the Catholic church. They welcomed economic development and sometimes considered limited social or land reforms; they were eager to extend education. On the other hand, they had little commitment to social reform, often scorning or repressing peasant and American Indian values, and they supported elitist economic interests. After 1870, they increasingly supported the notion of strong governments that could back economic development but also regulate aspects of popular behavior that the liberals found distasteful.

HISTORY DEBATE

IS LATIN AMERICA WESTERN?

In 1997, a large number of Latin American historians, mostly but not exclusively from the United States, debated on the Internet whether Latin America should be judged a "non-Western" civilization. A few argued that Latin America should be viewed as part of the West because it shared a Western language and active participation in a common literary and artistic culture. Latin America is also the only society outside western Europe, North America, Australia, and New Zealand where political liberalism gained widespread support in the 19th century.

Other historians of Latin America, however, objected. Some argued that parts of Latin America—a city such as Buenos Aires or a group such as the middle class—were Western, but other key parts—the poor or a city such as Tucuman—were not. Costa Ricans may view themselves as Western, but the Quechua speakers in the Andean highlands do not. The majority of the debaters argued that the solution to the question was not to decide whether Latin America was Western or not, but to avoid the use of the term *Western*. For these historians, the term implied a certain superiority, and in their view such an interpretation did not reflect an accurate picture of any society. They further attacked the related tendency of many historians to lump together many civilizations in a "non-Western" category, as if a culture's not being Western was a coherent feature. Finally, they argued that Latin America should be seen as a syncretic civilization, combining many influences—but that other civilizations, including western Europe, were also syncretic. Interestingly, broad discussions of social and economic features did not loom large. The debate focused on culture and whether one was sympathetic or not to the viewpoint of Latin America as a Western civilization.

Conservatives, often attracted in the early days to the ideals of a monarchy, distrusted parliaments. They directly backed the power of the dominant landlord class and were less interested in commercial or industrial development than liberals. They also stood in firm defense of the rights of the Catholic church, which maintained a powerful role in education and possessed considerable wealth and land.

Disputes between conservatives and liberals helped account for political instability. When they were not clearly resolved, as in Colombia and Venezuela in the late 19th century, changes in regime were particularly frequent. Generally, however, liberal victory in the 1870s ushered in a period of greater political calm—it has been compared to the general triumph of democratic regimes in Latin America in the late 20th century. Liberals rarely gained a popular following, but they did ally with business interests and a growing urban middle class in promoting not only commercial expansion but also European-style urban renewal projects and efforts to improve public health and eliminate prostitution and other forms of crime.

Accompanying liberal and conservative conflicts was the frequency of strongman rule. *Caudillismo*, derived from the Spanish word for "leader," described this governmental form. Caudillos usually favored the conservative bastions of church and landlord but sometimes represented the liberal camp. Their tactics often cut through some of the conservative–liberal debate, if only by force. At times, some even worked for reform, scaling back church prerogatives and seeking economic development. By reducing liberal attacks on American Indian or mestizo traditions and offering public works, some conservative caudillos garnered ardent mass support. But all caudillos relied on force. They outlawed political opposition, regulated schools and newspapers, and used jails, police, and firing squads with abandon. Some, without question, were simply corrupt, lining their pockets and those of their cronies. Porfirio Díaz, the last Mexican caudillo, in addition to brutalizing his political opponents, encouraged landlords and U.S. investors to take over vast stretches of Mexican land, receiving extensive kickbacks in return. His government, indeed, sold off literally 20 percent of all the land in Mexico, much of it previously held by American Indians and mestizo villagers.

In the 19th century, Latin American politics had little contact with the masses; except for the times it exploited them. Few liberals were ardent democrats; they shared a distrust of American Indians and blacks. Liberal constitutions gradually increased the suffrage, but few liberals favored democracy; hence, mass political action was not an important feature of Latin America during this period. Liberals, indeed, were in some ways less sympathetic to mass interests than were conservatives, which helps explain their limited popularity. Liberals stood for individualized property rights; they promoted rationality and different, typically grueling, work habits; they attacked tradition, including, of course, popular religious customs. Liberal caudillos such as Porfirio Díaz brutally suppressed incipient trade union movements among urban workers. Other caudillos at times developed political symbols and public works projects that did have mass appeal. Even before 1850, for example, an early Argentine caudillo, Manuel de Rosas, won considerable popular support by requiring church prayers for his regime and by the widespread use of his image and his political symbol, a red rose, in public places. De Rosas and many other caudillos, particularly during the decades of consolidation, often helped build a national consciousness among elite groups and the masses, even when they were by Western standards unusually repressive. The tensions between the articulate political forces in Latin America and the somewhat separate masses were one of many traditions established in the 19th century that affect Latin American politics into our own time.

Most Latin American governments remained weak in the 19th century, even when caudillos officially claimed great power. The ability to regulate landlord or foreign business interests, or even, in some cases, roving bands of criminals, was limited (as was true to some extent in the United States). This was the context in which, after 1870, liberals often advocated greater state powers in the interests of economic development, government-sponsored education, or regulating Indians.

CULTURE AND THE ARTS

The Catholic church continued to provide one of the key cultural bonds throughout Latin American civilization. The institution operated schools and charitable facilities for the poor, in addition to maintaining its political role. Church ceremonies and buildings provided aesthetic as well as spiritual experiences for Latin Americans from almost all social classes and racial groups. Latin America thus remained largely separate from the assaults on religion as an intellectual and cultural force that arose in Western civilization during the same period, although liberals generated fierce attacks on the church as an institution. Debates such as that over Darwin's theory of evolution, in its implications for Christian belief, had little echo in Latin America. Indeed, Latin American culture, even at elitist levels, remained relatively disinterested in science. Although in most countries universities were established by 1850 that gradually developed some scientific and medical training, science remained less prestigious in this civilization than in the West, with its contribution to the general culture less significant.

Latin American culture was framed not only by religion but also by class structure. A considerable gap divided educated Latin Americans from the largely illiterate masses. A few governments, particularly in the southern region or under regimes such as that of Juárez in Mexico, made strides in promoting literacy. Argentina's literacy rate, 22 percent in 1876, jumped to 50 percent by 1895—the highest of any Latin American nation. These developments, along with a growing prosperity, help explain why cultural activity increased in Latin America during the later 19th century. Nonetheless, most formal intellectual activity still played to what was, by Western standards, a limited audience.

Culture was also shaped, again especially in the southern region, by the immense popularity of Western trends. Latin America developed no architectural style of its own during this period, in part because those who could afford major building projects thought in terms of replicating what they had seen in Paris or Madrid. Many artists and writers patiently reproduced European- style portraits and novels for an eager, wealthy audience. Even intellectuals who cultivated originality did not think in terms of an entirely independent Latin American culture, as they kept careful tabs on European, and particularly French, styles.

However, formal culture in Latin America, especially in literature, did achieve a distinctive tone. Poetry played an important role. Many poets were retained on university faculties, and in general, poetic expression became more vigorous in Latin America, in comparison with other literary output, than in the West. A number of women writers contributed to the impressive body of work in poetry. Using romantic styles, a number of poets and novelists also tried to convey the popular themes and concerns within their own civilization. They wrote of the frontier, American Indians, and slave life. Many were politically radical, using literature to spur social reform. They were joined by many historians and folklorists, who strove to describe the special features of the Latin American experience and its racial diversities. Finally, a number of writers, both conservative and radical, sought to convey something of the spirituality of life, and particularly Latin American life. In the 1890s, one Uruguayan novelist, Enrique Rodo, who achieved wide popularity in Spanish-speaking countries, highlighted what he perceived to be the special virtues of his civilization over the

The European look: section of Buenos Aires in the late 19th century.

materialism and mediocrity of Western culture, most notably in the United States.

Along with formal culture, a vigorous popular art continued to flourish. Many American Indian weavers and potters used traditional themes, designs, and vivid colors in their work. Festivals, even when organized around Christian celebrations, provided American Indians and former Africans with an opportunity to participate in lively folk dances. Popular dance music, using Spanish instruments such as the guitar but traditional American Indian or African melodies and rhythms, included the fast-paced tango and samba—styles that later influenced Western popular culture as well.

Overall, despite the limitations of poverty, illiteracy, and frequent political repression, a vibrant cultural life emerged at various levels of Latin American society. As in politics, Latin Americans worked toward a distinctive amalgam of Western styles and their own customs and values. Artistic expression became a vital facet of the maturing civilization.

ECONOMY AND SOCIETY

Economic and social patterns in Latin America most clearly separated this civilization from that of western Europe and the United States and indeed accounted for many of the distinctions visible in politics and culture. For the most part, dynamic sectors of the Latin American economies arose as suppliers to the West; manufacturing was weakly developed throughout most of the 19th century, except for the peasant production of cloth and other simple items for local use. Since colonial times, Latin America's great export facilities had been geared for the sale of goods in the Western-dominated world economy; this orientation endured after independence, which helps account for the long hold of slavery in a few states such as

An icon, probably Mary or a female saint, in a black robe is depicted on the wall of a monastery church in Mexico.

Brazil. As many regions became commercially active in the second half of the century, Latin American dependence on Western markets and a low-paid labor force actually increased.

The first half of the century produced bleak economic news for much of Latin America. The wars of independence disrupted previous economic activities. Because few of the new regimes attempted significant land reform, most commercial production remained in the hands of great estate owners; nonetheless, there was a good deal of confusion because of unrest and the disruption of trade with Spain. The abolition of slavery in places such as Mexico and Venezuela led to the erosion of a prime source of cheap labor that was not quickly replaced, with taxes rising to support growing armies. Furthermore, boundaries in several countries were drawn without regard to earlier economic patterns. Thus, Bolivia and Peru, centers of the great silver mines, were cut off from the rich agricultural plains of Argentina. More serious still was the decline in the production of precious metals, particularly in the Andes region, which reduced the availability of one of Latin America's chief exports. At the same time, independence opened Latin American markets to industrially produced cloth and tools from the West, especially Great Britain, which overwhelmed many local suppliers. Poverty among urban workers increased, and rural manufacturing was nearly eliminated.

By 1850, as we have seen, conditions often improved. There were exceptions, however—poverty increased in Mexico under Porfirio Díaz even as economic development advanced. Large estate owners, some of them foreign, tightened their grip on the American Indian and mestizo labor force. But many Latin American countries developed a key cash crop or mineral specialty that allowed them to capture a growing export market. In Cuba and part of Central America, the production of sugar was a primary focus. Brazil concentrated on coffee, and in 1889, the country produced 56 percent of the world's coffee; by 1904, the figure had risen to 76 percent. Argentina exported beef and wheat from vast ranches; Chile focused on copper and nitrates, Bolivia on tin. Mexico became a leading petroleum producer after 1900, spurred by U.S. investments and much foreign ownership. These concentrations on food and raw materials were highly vulnerable, however. Latin American production increased rapidly, but this risked flooding the market and thus lowering prices and total earnings. Brazil, for example, faced a devastating slump in coffee prices around 1900. The environment in many countries was also affected by deforestation and the promotion of crops such as coffee that were not native to the region.

At the same time, demand for products manufactured in the West tended to grow rapidly. Upper-class Latin Americans, often possessing new revenue from trade, mines, or estates, wanted European luxury items. They quite consciously backed the growth of export sectors as the basis for their style of life. Further, the railroads and ports that governments sought to promote required imports of equipment from the United States and Europe. Latin American nations accumulated rising foreign debts when their exports did not match their imports. Government indebtedness led to frequent Western intervention, which often averted bankruptcy but never addressed the problem of a basic economic imbalance.

Outright foreign economic control compounded the problem. Britain led in investments to Latin America during this period, but the United States and other Western nations were also heavily involved. Foreigners owned many of the most lucrative estates and industries. In Díaz's Mexico, they purchased a great deal of land; in Colombia and Chile, they owned most railroads, banks, and mines. Western investments brought frequent pressures on Latin American governments to protect Western property. They deprived Latin America's struggling business class of a full range of opportunities, for top management remained in foreign hands. And they removed much-needed profits from the region altogether.

Further, the economic development that did take place in the later 19th century, whether foreign-based or not, created intense pressures on the lower classes. While Latin American dependence on the world economy was not new, it had previously coexisted with village agriculture. Into the 1880s, many American Indians and mestizos operated village farms adequate for local subsistence needs. They were able to work according to traditional rhythms and organize frequent festivals, replete with dance, song, and drink. This pattern yielded quickly to the growing commercialization of the Latin American economy during the last decades of the 19th century. In virtually every region, more land than ever before was consumed by large estates. American Indians, accustomed to community ownership, were forced to sell out to individual owners. In Mexico, for example, a law of 1894 ruled that land could be declared vacant and open to purchase if legal title to it could not be produced, but few American Indians had such title, relying on traditional terms of use rather than modern notions of property. In Colombia and elsewhere, governments, often in liberal hands and eager to promote economic growth, opened new territories to bidding, which in fact displaced many traditional villages not regarded as having property rights. Other peasant owners were simply defrauded by shrewd speculators or encouraged to go into debt. Some of the new estates embraced thousands, even millions of acres; one Mexican estate was as large as West Virginia.

The peasants, once displaced, encountered still further indignities. They had little choice but to work on the large estates, where they were paid low wages or, even more commonly, paid in kind and kept permanently in debt. Virtual serfdom spread, as workers were not allowed to leave the land until they had paid their debts but were not able to earn enough money to have any hope of making their payments. Furthermore, hard-driving commercial estate owners tried to spur greater zeal on the part of workers. They clamped down on traditional festivals, regarded as a sheer waste of time. This was a pattern not entirely different from the pressures earlier placed on European or U.S. industrial workers, for a real commercial revolution was underway. But Latin American peasants suffered far less freedom and far more poverty than most Western workers, for the economy, because of its weak position in the world markets, depended on exploited labor. Investment in new equipment, which might have provided an alternative to cheap labor, lagged. And, although many estate and mine owners worked conscientiously to expand production, as opposed to the stereotype of idle drones living in luxury with no attention to management, the gap between the wealthy, mainly Creole or foreign, landowning classes and the impoverished masses grew ever wider.

Finally, many former peasants, forced off the land, sought refuge in the growing cities, where they faced competition for jobs from new immigrants from Europe. A large, often miserable property-less class spread in the cities, pitting sprawling slums on the outskirts against the impressive upper-class districts nearer the center of town. Because industrialization was slow, there were relatively few factory jobs to absorb the newcomers. Aided by foreign capital and European immigrants, countries such as Brazil did develop some industries in food processing, textile, and metallurgy. However, the numbers of workers these industries employed were small, as Western competition continued to cut into the available markets for manufactured goods. Hard-pressed governments had few resources to devote to welfare programs, so urban poverty and shantytowns grew unchecked.

The Latin American masses were not quiet under this new assault. The organization of urban trade unions was difficult, because of widespread misery and sheer confusion; government oppression also complicated any protest efforts. However, peasant uprisings to seize land and escape the commercially driven work routines became common from the 1880s on; indeed, they persist in many areas even today. Peasant rebellions were not regular occurrences, for peasants were usually repressed and could not be supported by legal organizations. But they also proved impossible to put down permanently. Mexico, Bolivia, and Colombia faced major revolts every 10 or 20 years. Rural banditry also

The drive for progress made Latin American nations eager to accept foreign investment. Railroads were needed to bring export goods to seaports so that they could be carried to foreign markets. They were built principally to serve the needs of foreign capital. Railroad workers, however, often proved to be the most radical segment of the Latin American workforce.

increased in many regions, recruiting displaced peasants and winning the quiet support of even larger numbers, who saw the bandits as expressing their discontent and hatred of landlords. Finally, rates of individual violence were high in many countries. Essentially frontier conditions existed in many places, as the formal presence of a central government was sporadic at best. Hence, many peasants took vengeance into their own hands. High levels of violence also reflected the deep grievances of landless peasants whose cheap labor sustained Latin America's production for trade.

The expansion of exports to the world economy placed new strains on the environment in many parts of Latin America. Mining or sugar growing had already reduced the forested areas in places such as Bolivia and Brazil. The spread of coffee growing in southeastern Brazil, introduced from Africa in the later 18th century, created additional pressure. During the 19th century more than 30,000 square kilometers of forest were cleared to allow coffee growing, and the extension of railroads and urban growth reduced forests still further. Soil erosion, particularly on mountain slopes where coffee is grown, was the principal environmental result. Many species of animals and plants also suffered as their habitat was destroyed. No attention was paid to these developments, however, until the 1930s, and few controls have proved successful even by the early 21st century.

Latin America during the late 19th century thus generated a paradox of rapid change and continued vulnerability in the world markets. Many sectors of the economy were out of Latin American hands. Emphasis on agriculture and mining continued, with only halting industrial development. Cities grew, but without a vigorous manufacturing base. Social structure remained oddly traditional, with great estate owners at the top of the heap, masses of peasants and property-less workers at the bottom, and a small middle class in between. Slavery had been abolished, but poverty and near-serfdom replaced it not only for many blacks but also for American Indians, mestizos, and many immigrants. Family structure remained rather traditional, with a strong emphasis

on the inferiority of women. Many lower-class women, in fact, entered the labor force, both on estates and in the cities, but officially and legally their place remained subordinate to men at virtually all social levels.

TENSION AND CREATIVITY

The tensions of Latin American society help explain the importance of strongman governments and the diverse roles of religion, through the late 19th century and beyond. One country, Mexico, was on the verge of revolution in 1900, driven by the unusually heavy hand of Porfirio Díaz and the extensive exploitation of American Indian and mestizo labor. However, most of Latin America long avoided outright revolution, although not recurrent protest, as army, church, and sometimes foreign intervention combined to keep the lid on unrest. Efforts by artists and intellectuals to voice the yearnings of the masses or to provide a spiritual identity distinct from Western values gained growing significance. Latin American civilization was formed under many unusual difficulties and under the strong tutelage of the more powerful West, yet it managed to generate not simply an array of problems but also a unique flavor that blended diverse traditions with the creation of new countries and rapid economic change.

PATHS TO THE PRESENT

Latin America today builds on many of the patterns established during the long 19th century. Economic dependency has lessened in some regions, but the struggle against it continues, even in areas that have become relatively independent. Some of the characteristic political patterns of the period, including frequent instability and caudillismo, have by now yielded to a more consistent commitment to democracy, but it remains to be seen whether stable democracies can be sustained in the region. Latin American high culture, with its interesting combination of Western styles and regional themes and flavors, persists as well. At the end of the 20th century, several Latin American authors worried about new global challenges to an identity that mixed Spanish-Portuguese with Indian and African elements, and their concern reflected the extent to which a creative identity had been forged earlier on.

The civilization's distinctive, though complicated, approach to race persists as well. In contrast to the United States, Latin American nations resisted tidy delineations between white and nonwhite; far more gradations were accepted. But another pattern was furthered in the 19th century: discrimination against darker-skinned people, and Indians generally, who encounter definite prejudice, sometimes falling lower on the economic scale than does the average African American in the United States.

One other tradition has persisted, though it invites diverse interpretations. As Latin American nations achieved independence, they did not define themselves in terms of territorial expansion or an aggressive world role (despite some bitter regional conflicts). Military establishments arose and persist—only Costa Rica took the unusual step, in the 1950s, of abolishing its army—but they operate mainly for domestic purposes. Even today, the civilization is noteworthy for a fairly low level of military adventurism.

SUGGESTED WEB SITES

On the Mexican Revolution, see http://www.ic.arizona.edu/ic/mcbride/ws200/mex-davi.htm; for more information on Mexican Independence, visit http://www.tamu.edu/ccbn/dewitt/mexicanrev.htm; on archeology at the Hispanic society, view http://www.hispanicsociety.org/hispanic/archaeology.htm. See also http://mexconnect.com/mex_/

history/jtuck/jtbenitojuarez.html for a comparison of leadership between Juarez and Lincoln.

SUGGESTED READINGS

Recent work includes Mark Thurner and Andrés Guerrero, eds., *After Spanish Rule: Postcolonial Predicaments of the Americas* (2003); Walter Mignolo, *The Idea of Latin America* (2004); Sylvia Chant, *Gender in Latin America* (2003); Guillermo M. Yeatts, *The Roots of Poverty in Latin America* (2005); David Bushnell, ed., *El Libertador: Writings of Simón Bolívar* (2003); Paul Hart, *Bitter Harvest: The Social Transformation of Morelos, Mexico, and the Origins of the Zapatista Revolution, 1840–1910* (2005); Eric Van Young, *The Other Rebellion* (2001); Ivan Jaksic, *Andres Bello: Scholarship and Nation-Building in 19th Century Latin America* (2001); David Lambert, *White Creole Culture, Politics and Identity During the Age of Abolition* (2005); David Eltis, *The Rise of African Slavery in the Americas* (2000); John Lynch, *Simon Bolivar: A Life* (2007); Carlos Forment, *Democracy in Latin America, 1760–1900* (2003); and Douglass Sullivan-Gonzalez, *Piety, Power and Politics: Religion and Nation Formation in Guatemala, 1821–1871* (1998).

A useful collection of sources is B. Keen, *Readings in Latin American Civilization* (1955). For discussions reflecting relevant scholarship, see T. Skidmore and P. Smith, *Modern Latin America* (1984); the book's only drawback is its concentration on single national or regional cases. See also David Bushnell and Neil Macauley, *The Emergence of Latin America in the Nineteenth Century* (1994), and Fernando Henrique Cardoso and Enzo Faletto, *Dependency and Development in Latin America* (1979), which disagree on the issue of dependency. On political patterns, see Tulio Halperin Donhi, *The Aftermath of Revolution in Latin America* (1973), and Claudio Veliz, *The Centralist Tradition in Latin America* (1980). On the Haitian Revolution, see Laurent Dubois and John D. Garrigus, *Slave Revolution in the Caribbean, 1789–1804: A Brief History with Documents* (2006). On key topics, see E. Bradford Burns, *Poverty or Progress: Latin America in the Nineteenth Century* (1973); Herbert Klein, *Bolivia* (1982); June Nash and Helen Safa, eds., *Sex and Class in Latin America* (1980); and Charles Berquist, *Labor in Latin America* (1986).

The Middle East and China in the Imperialist Century

China and the Ottoman Empire, like Latin America, were largely independent in the 19th century, though under great pressures from the West. The pressures were newer than in the Latin American case. This newness, combined with the proud traditions of both societies, complicated response. In some ways, the two societies resembled the West's outright colonies, but being technically independent did count for something.

The Islamic Middle East and China, although quite different as civilizations, displayed some similar reactions to the heightened pace of the world economy and the threat of Western imperialism during the 19th century. Neither the Middle East nor China came fully under Western control, in part because of the continuing strength of their governments and in part because Western rivalries canceled each other out, so that no one imperialist power could win predominance. Their patterns thus differed from those of southern Asia and sub-Saharan Africa. But both areas lost territory and increasingly felt the threat of further takeovers. Nonetheless, the Middle East and, particularly, China responded sluggishly to the transformations in the wider world during most of the 19th century, and both lost additional ground as a result. Change came, but haltingly. Traditionalist leadership and a long habit of looking down on foreigners, in the Chinese case, or Westerners, in the Muslim case, delayed vigorous reactions. Late in the 19th century, however, new forces arose in both societies that ardently sought fundamental reforms that would make their societies more competitive with the West and more like the West in certain ways. This outlook set the stage for a much more active period of development during the 20th century.

China and the Middle East, then, followed a 19th-century pattern somewhat in between the societies under outright imperialist control, such as India, and those that were stimulated during the century itself toward radically new kinds of responses. Ironically, it was China's east Asian cousin, Japan, that provided the most successful example of the latter type of approach. This means that China and Japan diverged increasingly despite shared traditions.

KEY QUESTIONS *What were the new forms of pressure from the West and the world economy, on both China and the Ottoman Empire? Beyond this are issues of causation and comparison. Why were both these societies somewhat slow to develop effective responses? But also why, and in what ways, were reform efforts in the Ottoman Empire more effective? Finally, there are additional comparisons, for example toward explaining why Chinese responses differed from Japanese. Compare both these cases also to colonial situations in India: some historians have argued that India, as a colony, was less seriously exploited than China was, precisely because no single Western power took real responsibility for China. Is this a plausible comparison, and how can degrees of damage or constructive impact best be assessed?*

THE ATTEMPT TO MODERNIZE EGYPT

The Middle East began the 19th century with a fascinating initiative, although one that ultimately failed. The Ottoman Empire had been rocked, in 1798, by Napoleon's successful invasion of Egypt. When Napoleon was forced out, by British pressure plus Napoleon's own ambition to gain power at home, an Ottoman military officer named Muhammad Ali took over Egypt as a virtually independent ruler, and indeed the Ottomans never did fully regain control of this vital province. At points, Muhammad Ali also conquered areas of the Arabian Peninsula adjacent to Egypt, although he was blocked by not only Ottoman resistance but also British fear of any strong power in this region so close to key routes to India.

As ruler of Egypt, Muhammad Ali represented one of the first non-Western leaders, and certainly the first in the Middle East, to adopt a self-conscious mission to modernize his society in Western terms. Unlike Peter the Great, Muhammad Ali never visited the West, but he greatly admired Western achievements and also realized that he must try to match some of them if he was to preserve the independence of Egypt. Under his sponsorship, Western, and particularly French, advisors flooded the country to aid in education, technology, and science as well as military affairs.

Muhammad Ali saw the need to alter traditional economic patterns. Although unable to spur outright industrialization, he introduced agricultural improvements and, in particular, developed an active export market for Egyptian cotton. The hold of landlords, traditionally uninterested in innovation, was weakened. Muhammad Ali also established a printing press and sponsored the translation of many Western books on science and technology into Arabic. In addition to using Western teachers, he sent a number of Arabs to study abroad. French became a second language to educated Egyptians. Despite these many developments, Muhammad Ali was unable to break through either the hold of tradition on much of Egyptian society or the limitations imposed by Western dominance of the world economy. Egypt became increasingly dependent, for export earnings, on the Western market for cotton; it thus had to compete with other producers of cotton, including the southern United States and India, and Egypt's cotton did not always command favorable prices. Its export earnings were frequently insufficient to pay for the machines and military equipment that Muhammad Ali sought, so his regime was increasingly forced to go into debt to Western banks. Here was a tragic irony, repeated many times in many countries, in the Middle East and elsewhere, throughout the 19th and 20th centuries. Governments seek to modernize, adopting new armaments, industrial machinery, and often an array of public buildings and urban amenities.

But these innovations, designed to spur independence, cost money at a time when the economy remains sluggish. Hence, nations must face the temptation to borrow, which gives foreign banks new powers to supervise policy in the interest of protecting their loans. Muhammad Ali, in sum, managed to change Egypt, but he saw Western control steadily increase; by 1849, when he died, he was bitterly disappointed in his limited achievements. His efforts stand more as an early example of an attempt to adapt in response to Western standards than as a successful revitalizing regime.

DECLINE OF THE OTTOMAN EMPIRE

The bulk of the Middle East remained largely immune to Muhammad Ali's influence. The Ottoman Empire reacted to growing Western pressure and the de facto loss of Egypt in much more limited terms. The sultans established somewhat more centralized controls over great estates, in the interests of ensuring higher tax revenues. The sultan Mahmud II (1808–1839) dismantled the corrupt janissary corps. This group had long since lost its military skills and morale and had turned to political intrigues while living well from state revenues. Mahmud II created a separate, modern artillery corps armed with a European cannon; on this basis, he was able to eliminate the janissaries and develop a new officer group eager to rival Western military organization and technology.

These reforms, focusing on military structure primarily, were not sufficient to revive the decaying Ottoman Empire or to limit the growing Western strength in the region. Important provinces of the empire were lost during the first half of the 19th century. Not only Egypt (although it technically remained a province until 1914) but also the north African states of Algeria, Tunisia, and Libya (Tripoli) became independent; these last regions had never been fully integrated into the empire in any event.

Piracy from the north African shores provoked a military response from Europe and also the United States, which attacked the shores of Tripoli. In 1830, France began its outright conquest of Algeria, the first of many European takeovers in this area. On the Arab Peninsula, new, religiously inspired rebellions against the Ottoman Empire broke out, although with the help of Muhammad Ali, they were defeated. Finally, the European provinces of the empire became increasingly restless, inspired by the example of liberalism and nationalism in the French Revolution. In 1820, a major war for independence erupted in Greece, which after a decade, and with wide if informal support from western Europe, won its independence. Nationalist agitation also stirred in Romania and Serbia, putting new pressure on the Ottoman regime.

Western European economic influence in the Middle East intensified during the first part of the 19th century. Outside the boundaries of the Ottoman Empire, on the east coast of the Arabian Peninsula, Britain established a number of protectorates to limit piracy. London established steamship routes between India and eastern Arabia; by the 1830s, Britain and France operated steamship routes across the Mediterranean to Egypt and the Ottoman Empire itself. Thus, Middle-Eastern shipping and foreign trade lay increasingly in Western hands. British companies even operated some river shipping within the Ottoman Empire. Western economic power severely limited the revenue capacity of the empire, which was barred from taxing foreign enterprise. World economic position, in other words, greatly constrained the Ottoman political response.

Finally, pressure on the Ottoman Empire continued from yet another traditional source—the surging Russian Empire. Several regional wars occurred between Russia and the Ottomans during the first half of the 19th century, resulting in a loss of territory. Russia could have gained still more save for the intervention of France and Britain, who now had their own stake in this region and feared Russian dominance. The Crimean War of 1854–1856 resulted from

British-French opposition to further Russian expansion in the Mediterranean, and indeed the Russians were defeated. Another Russo-Turkish war occurred in 1877–1878, and again only Western intervention prevented Russian dismemberment of the empire, which lost new territory even so.

By this point, the Ottoman Empire risked becoming the puppet of forces beyond its control. The empire was not fully carved up only because the Europeans and Russians could not agree on the spoils; each power feared that the others would gain too much. The Middle East was too close to Europe to allow the kind of free-for-all that ultimately occurred in Africa; the danger of all-out war was too great. So the empire survived until 1918. Various sultans continued to experiment with reforms. Occasionally, they granted constitutions, in an effort to follow Western practices, but in fact the rule of the sultan and the bureaucracy remained unchecked. Slavery was abolished in 1908—quite late, of course, by some standards. Substantial military reforms concentrated much of the impetus for change within the ranks of the armed forces. Many Ottoman officers were trained in Europe, and European—particularly German—advisors were brought in to improve technology and modernize military administration. However, the Ottoman army remained weak and relatively backward, in part because military reforms were unable to transcend the loose political organization and largely agricultural economy. Tax revenues and morale were both inadequate to provide new vigor to the Ottoman state as a whole.

Nevertheless, there was some real change. Particularly important was the Tanzimat reform movement between 1839 and the 1870s. The reforms aimed at a partial westernization of the Ottoman state and society, through greater centralization and partial secularization of law and education. All subjects, regardless of religion, gained equality under the law. Penal codes and commercial law were revised according to French models. But Islamic law was also embraced in new codes. A constitution was issued in 1876, providing for a parliament, but the experiment did not last long. Outside the government proper, the rise of modern journalism and other developments added to the reform current.

But the overall results were limited. Efforts at land reform actually strengthened the hold of large landowners over peasants. Periodic revolts, for example in the Balkans, were usually put down, but this helped create an atmosphere of repression as well as provoking European hostility. After 1876, the regime became more autocratic and religious, and the reform current dwindled.

Hence, the empire continued to lose territory on its fringes and suffer growing Western economic penetration. Nationalist uprisings in the Balkan area, supported by Russia and some of the Western powers, produced a network of small, independent states by the end of the 1870s: Serbia, Romania, and a few still smaller states joined Greece. As a result of further Balkan agitation, which led to an independent Bulgaria, the Ottoman Empire had, by 1914, lost almost all hold in Europe, save for a patch of territory including Constantinople.

Direct imperialist conquest in north Africa also continued, although this region, of course, had already been lost to the Ottomans. In 1869, a French company completed construction of a canal through the Isthmus of Suez, the narrow strip of land that had connected north Africa and the Middle East. By using the new Suez Canal, European ships could save immense time in reaching the Indian Ocean, by sailing from the Mediterranean to the Red Sea rather than around Africa. Egypt's importance increased because of its new strategic position. Britain, anxious as always to safeguard its interests in India, began to interfere more and more in Egyptian affairs, mainly to preempt French influence. Heavy Egyptian debts to British banks provided an obvious opening. Britain was able to buy controlling shares in the Suez Canal and then, in the 1880s, established a protectorate over the Egyptian government; the Egyptian ruler

The building of the Suez canal.

became a virtual figurehead. In response, France took over outright control of Tunisia. Soon after 1900, Italy gained Libya; France captured Morocco. All of Muslim north Africa lay in European hands.

To the east of the Ottoman Empire, British and Russian representatives divided influence over the kingdom of Persia, while direct British hold over the small states of the eastern Arab coast continued. Within the empire itself, European interests gained increasing economic power. German businesses, backed by the government, constructed a major railroad linking Berlin to Baghdad. French and English merchants bought quantities of luxury items. In Turkey proper, a number of rug factories were established, utilizing machines imported from the West and displacing many traditional hand-workers, to fill the growing markets of western Europe and the United States, where Turkish carpets and other furnishings became the rage in middle-class homes in the later 19th century. Although some Turks and Arabs gained experience and wealth as factory owners or agents for Western companies, the new industry rested heavily on low-paid labor, and its basic directions were determined by Western merchants, not those in the Middle East. The Ottoman Empire, bounded by Western colonies, new and aggressive Balkan nations, and the ambitious Russian state, was no longer master in its own house.

THE RISE OF NATIONALISM

Although the Ottoman government proved unable to respond successfully to these new developments, several important events occurred that shaped Middle-Eastern history in the 20th century. A strong current of Arab nationalism began to emerge, directed against both European imperialists and the hold of the Ottoman state. In Turkey, a modernizing movement arose among younger army officers. Finally, some efforts were made to rouse new Islamic fervor.

In contrast to India, a large Middle-Eastern nationalism did not take clear shape, although there were efforts to encourage patriotic loyalty to the Ottomans. Nationalism increasingly meant particularism, associated with a smaller region, such as Egypt, or an ethnic-linguistic group, such as the Turks.

Arab nationalism developed most vigorously in Egypt, where Muhammad Ali had first opened the way to growing European influence and example. There nationalism, in fact, emphasized Egypt more than Arabs in general, and a full nationalist statement did not emerge until the early 20th century. Many educated Egyptians followed Muhammad Ali's goal in wanting to create a modern state and economy, along something like Western lines, but they also desired a proudly independent Egypt, inspired by the same nationalism they saw in western Europe. Nationalism was a new force in the Middle East (as in India), in its quest for loyalty to secular states and specific peoples instead of Arabs or Muslims in general. Nationalism's newness for a time limited its appeal, particularly to peasant masses, but it did focus attention on the important twin goals of independence and political change. As the Egyptian government grew weaker and more indebted toward the middle of the 19th century, nationalist opposition increased. It was inflamed still further by a British takeover. Britain regularized Egyptian finances and helped sponsor some railroad construction and a massive dam on the Nile at Aswan, which increased the amount of water available for irrigation in agriculture. London also abolished slavery in Egypt and expanded the school system. However, these reforms did not daunt the new nationalism. Egyptian nationalists resented economic controls that, in their view, prevented full industrialization. They also resented the lack of political rights and the arrogance of many British colonial administrators. As mostly educated city dwellers, the nationalists were able to easily see firsthand the privileged position and luxury of foreigners in their own country.

Arab nationalism also sprang up elsewhere in north Africa, in response to new imperialist regimes. In Tunisia, for example, the French built port facilities, rails, and a telegraph and telephone system; they also introduced new schools and hospitals. However, they did not encourage much industry and were careful to retain control of most export trade. A handful of French settlers took over some of the most fertile land in the country. These developments, as well as the gap between French and Tunisian culture, were more than enough to stimulate nationalist concerns. As in Egypt, north African nationalism before 1900 mainly took the form of political rallies and newspaper diatribes—themselves new political experiences for the Arabs involved. Little nationalist rioting occurred. But there was no question that a new political force was rising in this ancient region.

Some Arab nationalism also spilled over to the Ottoman Empire. A number of governors of Arab provinces, including the one that contained Mecca, flirted with nationalism; their loyalty to the sultan was questionable by 1900. In 1913, Arab nationalists were able to meet in Persia to discuss independence for Iraq.

Other kinds of nationalism also entered the field. A movement among European Jews, called *Zionism,* arose in the later 19th century in response to European patriotic claims and new kinds of intolerance against the Jews. The Zionists argued that Jews should reestablish their homeland in Palestine, and by 1914, a number of Jewish settlers were entering the area. This current had no great political consequences as yet, but it proved vital in the region's future.

Further north, in the Ottoman heartland, more serious reform currents from the early 19th century set the basis for Turkish nationalism. Even though the Ottomans lost the ability to rule

WORLD PROFILES

LALLA ZAINAB

Between 1897 and her death in 1904, Lalla Zainab directed a major Islamic religious center in southern Algeria. Her role was shaped by the continuing power of Islamic belief in north Africa and the Middle East, by hostilities roused by French conquest of Algeria (from 1829 on), and by her own convictions and personality. Zainab's father, who claimed descent from the prophet Muhammad, had established the religious center. He provided an extensive religious education for his daughter, who was raised in a large harem. Zainab decided not to marry, and her celibacy, as well as her simple style of life, enhanced her reputation for spirituality. Clearly impressed with her abilities, Zainab's father gave her an inheritance equal to that of his sons. When her father died, Zainab successfully resisted the efforts of a male cousin to take over the community, as well as interference by the French colonial administration. To carve out considerable autonomy, Zainab was able to use a French lawyer and the French governor's new interest in establishing better relations with Islamic religious groups. Zainab used her power, including superb understanding of how the French administration operated, to provide assistance to many Muslim refugees, women, and the poor throughout the region. Her life demonstrates the role unusual individuals could gain even under imperialism, and the place an exceptional woman, with a clear record of piety, could obtain under Islam.

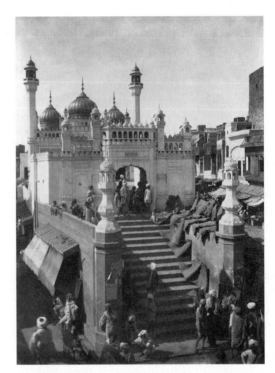

An Algerian mosque around 1900.

their empire vigorously, they did introduce changes affecting Turkey proper. The strengthening of the military, following the courageous dissolution of the janissaries, brought many Turkish officers into contact with Western training. University education was reorganized along Western lines, and the government launched new postal and railway services in Turkey. These changes were important, but they whetted appetites for more. Muslim leaders clashed with the westernizing elite, and Sultan Abdul Hamid reestablished authoritarian rule after 1878. This was the context, around 1900, in which a number of younger army officers began to push for reform of the sultan's government and modernization of the empire. This movement of *Young*

Turks, as they were called, sought political rights similar to those promised in a constitution of 1876 that the sultan had quickly withdrawn; they wanted an end to political corruption and a more vigorous foreign policy. They demanded new limits on European economic activities in their land. As one Young Turk put it, "We follow the path traced by Europe . . . even in our refusal to accept foreign intervention." Young Turks participated in a number of violent attempts to overthrow the sultan's government, although without initial success.

The Young Turk movement was long unclear as to whether it wanted to revive the Ottoman Empire or form a modern nation-state in Turkey. It talked mainly of the empire, but the movement relied so heavily on Turkish pride and the imposition of Turkish force that it was, in fact, more narrowly nationalistic. Nonetheless, the movement proved to be the basis for the modern Turkish nation that emerged after the larger Ottoman Empire collapsed.

In 1914, the Middle East was caught between the pressures of imperialism and the structures of the Ottoman state on the one hand, and the forces of a modernizing nationalism on the other. These latter forces, including the Young Turks, constituted an important new ingredient in the region, a sign of Europe's great influence but a symbol also of a vigorous desire for independence. Nationalism was not a native Middle-Eastern development. The idea of breaking up the region into separate states, which even most Arab nationalists suggested in their concentration on Iraq, or Egypt, or Tunisia, had some precedent in earlier periods of regionalism in the Middle East, but it ran against the Islamic as well as the Ottoman tradition. The nationalists were not worried about precedent, however. They wanted not only independence but also a new society, no matter how vague their definitions. They often embraced a reformist version of Islam, but they were positively hostile to the traditional social structure and educational system of their region. They wanted new political regimes, not only independence but

also parliaments and voting rights. For them, as many admitted, the West was both the example and the enemy.

Most people in the Middle East were still peasants and only vaguely affected by the new currents. They remained faithful to Islam, educated in the laws and ceremonies of the Qur'an. Some were drawn into new economic endeavors, such as the rug factories or cotton estates, but most continued to work by traditional methods and to rely heavily on village institutions. No serious change occurred in the lives of Middle-Eastern women, still largely isolated in extended family households according to Islamic law. Even in the upper classes, few women came into contact with Western ideas, as even imperialist regimes did not try to alter this basic feature of Islamic life. A few Muslim leaders talked of trying to adapt the religion to modern life, and to use Islam as a unifying force for the whole civilization against Western pressure and nationalism alike. Islam was not an unchanging force, although it embraced strong traditionalist elements. Several religiously inspired revolts broke out against Europeans in north Africa, and Islamic belief in the superiority of their religion continued unabated, easily sufficient to doom Christian missionary movements in the region. In this context, Islam conveyed anger and anxiety, a role that was to continue into the 21st century.

CHINA FACES IMPERIALISM

China by the end of the 18th century had been able, proudly if not entirely realistically, to maintain its empire's isolation, which remained far more complete than in the days of Mongol rule, when Western travelers such as Marco Polo had roamed widely through the vast country. The Chinese economy remained largely self-sufficient at this point, despite modest exports in return for gold. The Qing dynasty, although past its prime, was still functioning fairly smoothly in the hands of the fabled bureaucracy.

A mere 40 years later, China was forced to open its borders to new Western trading and cultural activities as a result of one of those imperialist wars barely noticed in Europe, involving handfuls of Western troops, which dramatically revealed the new balance of power between a declining imperial China and the industrial West.

From the 1820s on, Western traders became increasingly insistent on gaining access to the vast Chinese markets and the products of Chinese artisans. Growing wealth at home spurred new demand for Chinese vases, porcelain, and other artifacts. At the same time, the Qing dynasty lost vigor rapidly, in a process familiar in Chinese history but now fatefully juxtaposed against the new Western strength. Local rebellions began to increase early in the 19th century, partly because Western interventions intensified. A major uprising, the Taiping Rebellion, arose in the 1850s. Led by a man who claimed to be the younger brother of Jesus Christ, the rebels sought traditional peasant goals: lower taxes and more land. The rebels also sought newer reforms, such as the end of foot binding. Hundreds of thousands were involved in the conflict, which was put down with great difficulty. More generally, peasants were pressed by a rapidly rising population; simultaneously, the efficiency of the central government declined. The bureaucracy could no longer collect taxes effectively, and the quality of the imperial army deteriorated. This made unrest harder to put down and more difficult to prevent. The government struggled for years with the Taiping rebels, finally requiring Western military support to conquer them. Increasingly, the government was forced to rely on locally trained militias, but these forces, newly armed, often turned against the emperor as well, stepping up rebellion and banditry. The costs were staggering. Overall, the rebellion resulted in the loss of more than 20 million lives, disrupting China even after the fighting ended.

The first clash between a waning empire and the greedy West occurred in the Opium War of 1839–1842. British merchants in India had been exporting opium for sale in China. Ironically, they still had trouble finding goods that appealed to the

British East India boats destroy Chinese junks during the Opium Wars period, 1841, in this 19th-century line engraving.

Chinese market. Because of the adequacy of traditional Chinese manufacturing, factory-made textiles, for example, had little appeal. So opium was seen as an important item of exchange that allowed the West to pay for Chinese goods without offering valuable gold. However, the Chinese empire objected to the opium trade. Opium use was not traditional in China, and there was widespread knowledge of its harmful effects. Furthermore, the government continued to treat British representatives as annoying inferiors. A government effort to seize all opium in the harbor of Canton (Guangzhou) led to a fight with British sailors and an attempt to prohibit all British trade in the area. War followed, as the British blockaded the entire coast; the Chinese were powerless to resist because they had no effective navy, and because, thanks to the Industrial Revolution, the British now had steamboats that could penetrate the Chinese interior by going upstream on key rivers. The Chinese finally yielded, opening several ports including Canton and Shanghai to British merchants, and giving Britain the island of Hong Kong.

The defeat in the Opium War was a huge blow to Chinese leaders, who long remembered not only the loss but also the fact that Britain was willing to fight for the right to export a substance that resulted in the addiction of many Chinese people. But bitter memories did nothing to stop further Western penetration. On the heels of British gains came France and the United States, demanding new trading rights. By 1850, foreign colonies existed in a number of ports. A second war, in 1857, led to the opening of still more ports and additional rights that allowed Westerners to trade and conduct missionary activity even in the interior. An Anglo-French army pushed to Beijing, driving the emperor from the city, in order to enforce these concessions.

These early imperialist advances did not alter the basic direction of Chinese policy. The Chinese leadership still believed that traditional ways were best, seeing Western gains as temporary setbacks like other brief invasions that had occurred earlier in Chinese history. No new measures were taken to either imitate or counter Western developments. For their part, Western nations, led by Britain and France, were learning that China was a weak empire, not all that different from the Ottomans in basic strength, and hence an easy victim for any modern state with a good navy. Ironically, by the middle of the 19th century, the Chinese government was not particularly interested in copying Western military technology—in contrast even to the Ottoman regime. Chinese officers regarded technology as uninteresting, treating engineers with contempt as social inferiors. The reverence for tradition and for cultural as opposed to military or business concerns in the Confucian value system, plus the real weakness of the imperial administration at this point, combined to make innovation seem both undesirable and impossible.

Nonetheless, beneath the level of imperial administration, China was changing. Population growth continued, creating a great demand on the part of many peasants for land. A relatively small number of peasants even sought relief in emigration—an unusual development in Chinese history—as they were recruited by railroad or estate bosses in the United States and some parts of Latin America. This movement, however, had no real impact on continued unrest at home. At the same time, Western influence affected some Chinese as well. Missionary efforts converted

An English church in Shanghai, late 19th century: transporting Europe to China as literally as possible. Compare this style to the Jesuit approach in China, illustrated in chapter 20.

small groups of Chinese to Christianity and promoted some wider interest in Western ways. More importantly, Western business activity in the open, or treaty, ports helped sponsor wider economic development on a regional basis. The ports grew rapidly in population and wealth; they stimulated market agriculture and some manufacturing, even a few mechanized factories, in the surrounding countryside; and they gave some individual Chinese business executives experience with Western commercial methods, often resulting in profitmaking zeal. A few entrepreneurs and Christian converts began to gain experience abroad, some attending foreign universities, although this was for the time being the merest trickle against the backdrop of centuries of isolation.

Western imperialists remained uninterested in trying to take over China directly—it would have been a difficult task and was an unnecessary one, given their new access to Chinese trade. They even aided the Qing dynasty in putting down the Taiping uprising during the 1850s; Western regimes preferred a weak imperial administration to outright disorder. Given growing

HISTORY DEBATE

CHINA'S 19TH-CENTURY SLUGGISHNESS

A key task in exploring culture is to understand its role in causing historical or current developments. But cultural causation, although real, is difficult to measure. China in the 19th century provides an important case in point. Historians debate the balance among three factors: the nature of Chinese culture, and particularly Confucianism, long a strength but now perhaps a weakness in response to unprecedented change; the deterioration of Chinese government and society—in other words, internal problems that were not however primarily cultural; and the nature and destructive force of outside intervention, including of course the pressure to expand the use of opium.

There is no question that China was resistant to imitating Western models, despite its proud tradition of strength. The Confucian tradition—a core component of Chinese culture—is often blamed, not only by historians but also by subsequent Chinese leaders. Confucianism did engender two weaknesses in China's responses to modern Western pressure. It encouraged traditionalism, as opposed to praising innovation, and it tended to downplay science in favor of more literary cultural emphases. Chinese bureaucrats, in resisting Western models, reflected these Confucian principles.

Nevertheless, other Confucian societies, notably Japan, found it possible to modify but use the Confucian legacy as part of a commitment to change. Reduce the traditionalism and aversion to science, but keep the emphasis on group loyalty, obedience, and education, and a society could emerge with a strong basis for successful change. This basis was perhaps different from that of the West, but no less effective.

Too much emphasis on culture, in China's case, may therefore be misplaced. Of course, there are other cultural components to consider, such as the long-standing aversion to foreigners (Japan shared this perspective to a degree, although earlier it had successfully and very deliberately imitated China). But in addition to culture, maybe as important, was the abusive manner of Western intervention, with its stress on opium trade, which hardly encouraged imitation. And there was a period of ineffective government as the Qing dynasty declined, plus massive population pressure. Cultural causation, and particularly Confucianism, needs to be understood in a more complex context in contemplating China's 19th-century dilemmas.

unrest over land, taxation, and corruption among many officials, the Qing dynasty became increasingly dependent on European—particularly British—assistance during the second half of the 19th century. Western advisors were employed to improve the army and also increase efficiency in tax collection—a real paradox for an empire with the greatest bureaucratic tradition in the world. The use of Western advisors signaled a new awareness of the need to change. Some Chinese officials grew more interested in Western weaponry—as one writer put it, "Learn the technology of the Barbarians in order to control them." However, there still was no commitment to significant reform. Indeed, after the Taiping Rebellion was finally crushed in 1864, the government directed most of its efforts to restoring the prestige of the emperor and traditional Confucian principles. The government even tore up a rail line built by private interests in the 1870s, in the hopes of maintaining traditional ways. Such actions showed a firm desire to avoid westernization—indeed, some clashes with Christian missionaries occurred—but no grasp of what measures might be necessary to keep the Westerners out. Furthermore, the revival of traditional culture did not effectively deal with internal problems, as bureaucratic corruption increased and regional officials became harder to control. Some economic change occurred, in part because of Western influence in the port cities, but most Chinese manufacturing continued with traditional, hand-labor methods. The Chinese imported machine-made thread from Europe and the United States but continued to weave cloth manually. A handful of Chinese bankers and merchants built prosperous enterprises in the port cities, but most economic patterns stagnated. Products exported to the West, such as tea and craft goods, were generated by small-scale operations, not the big estates characteristic of India or southeast Asia. China was moving only slowly toward the new principles of world commerce.

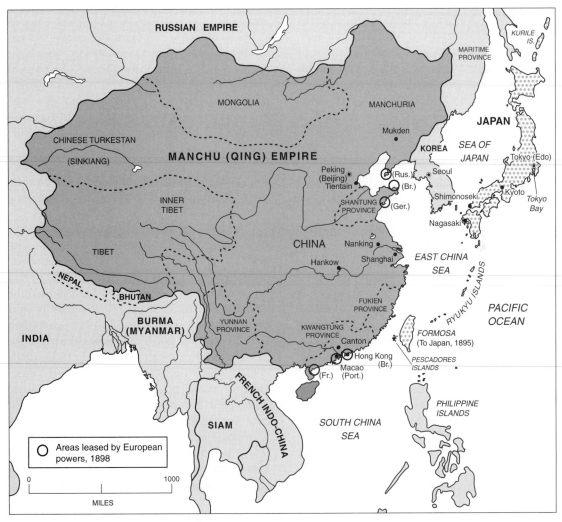

China and Japan in the 19th Century

China, in fact, was faced with a situation that had no precedent. With the lone exception of Buddhism, foreign influence had never been seen as a source of inspiration—only as a nuisance to be outlasted through superior Chinese traditions. Most other cultures, including Japan, India, and even the Ottoman Empire, had more experience with selective borrowing. Chinese politics had long stressed not only tradition but also the prevention of conflict; it was not well suited for promoting change. Bureaucrats saw no particular reason for new, Western-style efficiency, because they defined bureaucratic talent more in terms of cultural interests and the promotion of harmony. The expansionist, profit-seeking values of Western-dominated trade were also at serious odds with Chinese tradition, despite the vigor of many Chinese merchants even in the past. An old Confucian adage held: "Acknowledgment of limits leads to happiness." This was hardly the capitalist spirit. Added to these cultural impediments were the growing weakness of the reigning dynasty and the stark pressure of rapid population growth, which diverted resources and political attention from other issues. Thus during most of the 19th century, China changed less rapidly than not only the West or Japan but also colonial India or Turkey.

This lack of change, in the context of 19th-century world history, meant an invitation to Western imperialism. France's conquest of Indochina from the 1850s on was a blow to Chinese prestige, as Vietnam had long been a protectorate of the emperor. Russia, again on the advance, took over some territory in northern China in 1860.

The huge blow, however, came in 1894–1895, in a war with Japan. The Sino-Japanese War was triggered by a rebellion in Korea. Both Japan and China intervened to suppress this revolt. China had long treated Korea as a vassal state, whereas Japan, now rapidly industrializing, sought new spheres of influence. Both China and Japan also wished to prevent Russian action in Korea. But the two nations attacked each other as well, and Japan, with a modern navy, easily won—to the astonishment of literally the whole world outside of Japan. China was forced to yield not only Korea but also the island of Taiwan to the Japanese, plus the Liaotung Peninsula. This region was regained only by the intervention of Western powers, who wanted no Japanese influence in China proper. China was shown to be a hollow power, unable to fend off its much smaller Japanese rival. This fact, plus concern about Japanese gains and the intense rivalry among the European states, which had by now consumed most of Africa and was searching for new pastures, produced a scramble for Chinese holdings.

The result, by 1900, was a series of new treaties giving France, Germany, Britain, and Russia long-term leases on a number of key ports and surrounding territories. This was not outright imperialist annexation, but it amounted to much the same thing as the European governments established their own local administrations. Russia also seized some additional northern territory outright. Western nations proceeded to expand their business influence from their new centers, building rail networks and setting up river shipping toward the Chinese interior.

At last, China started to decisively react. A new young emperor, Kuang-hsu, ordered military reforms, railroad building, and the extension of education. But Tzu-hsi, the widow of the previous emperor, seized power in 1898 and canceled these reforms, executing several of the leaders of the westernization movement. Tzu-hsi believed that China could still go its own way despite the presence of foreigners. She gave secret support to a society called the Righteous Harmony Fists, or Boxers, who began killing Europeans and Christian Chinese in 1899. The Boxer Rebellion was suppressed fairly easily by a combined European–American military force, and China was required to grant additional legal privileges to foreigners, making them virtually immune from Chinese jurisdiction throughout the country. Tzu-hsi herself established a Western-style military structure and updated the education of imperial bureaucrats.

Colonial-era Customs House in Shanghai, China.

nationalism but also liberalism, democracy, and socialism. There was no full agreement on what the new China should look like. Some reformers wanted only a limited imitation of the West, in purely practical matters; others desired a full parliamentary regime, new roles for women, an attack on Confucian tradition. However, there was agreement that change was essential and, increasingly, a sense that the existing regime had to go. Students returning from experiences abroad were joined by other students influenced by missionary schools or simply impressed by the growing translations of Western science and literature. Forced finally by defeat to open the gates to change, China's old regime could not contain the resulting flood.

THE NEED FOR FURTHER CHANGE

Even more clearly than the Ottoman Empire, China was poised on the brink of revolution by 1900. Population pressure caused more internal unrest in China than the Middle East, whereas the intellectual minority, newly aroused by Western ideas, was more excited in China than the Middle East, where Islam continued to exercise cultural control. Both areas, of course, suffered from weak imperial administrations and infuriating levels of interference from the Western powers and Russia. The resulting mixture was too unstable to last, and it did not survive. Revolution was to break out in China in 1911, ending the Qing dynasty the following year and installing a republic in its stead—ending the world's oldest imperial government. The Ottoman Empire crumbled in the aftermath of World War I, and the political cohesion of the Middle East was shattered as well. Both these developments highlighted the tensions that had developed as a result of internal change and external pressure, particularly during the last decades of the 19th century.

But by this point, shortly after 1900, it was clear that the waning Qing dynasty could not master the three forces bedeviling China: internal problems of decline and population growth; imperialist pressure; and a new force among Chinese who were aware of Western ways and eager to "modernize" their country along partially Western lines. From 1896 on, a flood of Chinese students began to attend schools in Japan, Europe, and the United States, to gain access to the knowledge that their country so painfully lacked. They wanted to learn new technology, new science, and to an extent new organizational methods. In the process, they also learned about new political ideas, including

PATHS TO THE PRESENT

This period's most obvious legacy for China and the Middle East was the humiliation of persistent setbacks in the face of Western pressure. Chinese leaders in the 20th century were strongly motivated to reverse the world perception of China's weakness, though they disagreed on how to do so. Leaders in the Middle East—especially the new Turkish nationalists—had the same goal. These two civilizations possessed proud traditions but were faced with a century of increasing ineptitude: here was a call to arms. Not surprisingly, both of the regimes that had staggered through the later 19th century were gone soon after 1900.

The long 19th century also generated some of the forces that could be used to renew these regions. Turkish, Arab, and Jewish nationalists continue to play a major role in shaping the contemporary Middle East, with agendas—and divisions—that reflect their 19th-century origins. The Chinese students who eagerly set out to learn lessons from the West and Japan around 1900 have many heirs in modern China, as this giant nation, after a century of turmoil, establishes a new power position in world affairs.

SUGGESTED WEB SITES

On the Boxer Rebellion, see http://www.wsu.edu/~dee/CHING/BOXER.HTM; for more on Ottoman rule, see http://www.jewishvirtual-library.org/jsource/History/Ottoman.html; for a virtual tour of current Chinese art, see http://china.arts.ubc.ca/. Additional insights on Islam and Central Asia can be found at http://www.ucalgary.ca/applied_history/tutor/islam/fractured/centralAsia.html.

SUGGESTED READINGS

Recent works on China include David G. Atwill, *The Chinese Sultanate: Islam, Ethnicity, and the Panthay Rebellion in Southwest China, 1856–1873* (2005); Erik Mueggler, *The Age of Wild Ghosts: Memory, Violence, and Place in Southwest China* (2001); Peter Harrington, *Peking 1900: the Boxer Rebellion* (2005).

Recent works on the Ottoman Empire include Iris Agmon, *Family & Court: Legal Culture and Modernity in Late Ottoman Palestine* (2006); Huri Islamoglu-Inan, ed., *The Ottoman Empire and the World Economy* (2004); Jakub J. Grygiel, *Great Powers and Geopolitical Change* (2006); Donald Quataert, *Ottoman Manufacturing in the Age of the Industrial Revolution* (2002); Maya Jasanoff, *Edge of Empire: Lives, Culture, and Conquest in the East, 1750–1850* (2005); Elisabeth Ozdalga, *Late Ottoman Society: The Intellectual Legacy* (2005); Levy Avigdor, ed., *Jews, Turks, Ottomans: A Shared History, Fifteenth Through the Twentieth Century* (2002).

On the Middle East, see also W. R. Polk and R. L. Chambers, eds., *Beginnings of Modernization in the Middle East: The Nineteenth Century* (1968); Juan Cole, *Napoleon's Egypt: Invading the Middle East* (2007); Alan Palmer, *The Decline and Fall of the Ottoman Empire* (1992); and M. G. S. Hodgson, *The Venture of Islam* (1971). On China, an excellent short survey is M. Gasster, *China's Struggle to Modernize* (1983); for related studies, see Gilbert Rozman, *The Modernization of China* (1981), and Jonathan Spence, *The Search for Modern China* (1999). A useful source collection is Ssu-yu Teng and J. K. Fairbank, *China's Response to the West: A Documentary Survey, 1839–1923* (1954).

For additional relevant work, see S. A. Smith, *Revolution and the People in Russia and China: A Comparative History* (2008); Pamela Kyle Crossely, *The Manchus* (2002); Timothy Brook and Bob Tadashi Wakabayashi, eds., *Opium Regimes: China, Britain, and Japan, 1839–1952* (2000); Jonathan D. Spence, *God's Chinese Son* (1996); Fatma Gocek, ed., *Social Constructions of Nationalism in the Middle East* (2002); Joseph Tse-Hei Lee, *The Bible and the Gun: Christianity and South China, 1860–1900* (2003); and R. K. Schoppa, *Revolution and Its Past; Identities and Change in Modern Chinese History* (2002). See also Michael Axworthy, *The Sword of Persia: Nader Shah, from Tribal Warrior to Conquering Tyrant* (2006); Ann Chamberlain, *A History of Women's Seclusion in the Middle East: The Veil in the Looking Glass* (2006); James Onley, *The Arabian Frontier of the British Raj: Merchants, Rulers, and the British in the 19th Century Gulf* (2007).

Russia and Japan: Industrialization Outside the West

Among societies outside the West or the settler societies, Japan and Russia alone launched industrial revolutions by the late 19th century in response to the Western challenge. They escaped full Western economic dominance. Russia remained backward by Western standards, and its leaders grew painfully conscious of this fact. Even after 1900, its economy depended heavily on Western trade, technology, and capital; only revolution, in 1917, seriously altered this situation. However, Russia had displayed dynamism in previous centuries despite an economic lag, and this pattern persisted during the 19th century. Russia continued to expand, although it met Western and, at the end of the century, Japanese resistance at key points. The nation gained territory in central Asia and the Far East, and it achieved important influence over new, small states in southeastern Europe. Finally, the Russians began to sketch their reaction to the Western example of industrialization. Without becoming Western, Russia tried to alter its social pattern to conform to the requirements of an industrial society, and by 1890, it had launched the early phases of a real industrial revolution.

The response of Japan was even more striking. Continuing its policy of isolation until the 1850s, when Western pressure forced new contacts, the Japanese then rapidly transformed their basic political and social institutions, generating initial industrialization and a military reform that soon made Japan Asia's leading power. These events more clearly than ever before divided Japan from its Chinese neighbor, although in fact they still shared many cultural and artistic customs. For a time, indeed, the Japanese seemed bent on imitating everything Western, as the tradition of isolation made it difficult to sort out which Western habits were essential to economic and military strength and which were optional. But no more than Russia did Japan become Western: a key aspect of both Japanese and Russian development was an ability to industrialize without sacrificing all the distinctive features of their societies.

Japanese and Russian efforts form the first examples of what can be called "latecomer" industrial revolutions, in that they began after the West had established a pronounced lead in the process. Latecomer industrialization involved certain factors that had not been necessary in the West. Capital was hard to come by for essential investment; neither Japan nor Russia had the West's advantage of prior colonial and merchant wealth. Unfamiliar technology must be mastered. There may be an inevitable tendency for the government to assume a greater role in latecomer industrializations than was true in the West, to amass scarce resources through taxation and to guide manufacturers in the adoption of foreign techniques. At least this was clearly the case in both Russia and Japan, where, in any event, previous political structures made a strong government seem logical. Latecomer industrialization may also impose greater strain on the population involved, because change is even more abrupt than it was in the West, where innovation caused enough tension even without these additional factors.

Although sharing both the ability to respond strongly to Western example and some common features of the latecomer pattern, Russian and Japanese initiatives differed in crucial respects. Russian efforts to change, and failures to change rapidly enough, produced a revolutionary climate by 1905, when the first Russian revolution broke out. Japan avoided revolution in a literal sense, although in some ways revolutionary transformation was imposed from the top down after an intense internal struggle in the 1860s. At the same time, Japan shifted its traditional policies more radically than Russia, in not only industrializing so rapidly but also adopting an aggressive diplomatic stance quite foreign to its own precedents.

Neither Russia nor Japan was fully industrialized by 1914; both continued to lag behind the West for some decades. Nevertheless, the 19th-century breakthroughs were crucial in both countries. They ultimately had an influence even beyond national borders, in showing people in other parts of the world that Western economic tutelage was not the only way to produce change, and that a strong response could keep Western imperialism at bay.

KEY QUESTIONS   *Causes head the list here: why were Russia and Japan able to respond relatively successfully to the Western/world economy challenge? What factors did they share? Then of course, there were dissimilarities: how did the two reform processes differ, and why by 1914 was Russia, but not Japan, headed for revolution?*

RUSSIAN CONSERVATISM: AN ALTERNATIVE TO THE WEST

The first half of the 19th century saw relatively little change in Russian culture and society. Russian leaders were indeed proud of their seeming immunity to the revolts and tensions that plagued western Europe during the same period. After the defeat of Napoleon's armies, the Russian state viewed itself as one of the guardians of conservative order in Europe. Its acquisition of new territory in Poland at the Congress of Vienna, in 1815, furthered its long-standing interest in expansion. The Russian tsar Alexander I flirted with liberal ideas, and a few reforms were introduced, notably to improve the training of Russian bureaucrats. But neither the authoritarian state nor the tight system of Russian serfdom was seriously altered.

In December 1825, a minor revolt broke out, led by Western-minded army officers who wanted to see their country change. The Decembrist revolt was easily vanquished, but it inspired the new tsar, Nicholas I, to embrace more outright conservatism. The repression of political opponents increased, as the secret police expanded. The press and schools were tightly supervised. What political criticism survived did so mainly in exile, in places such as Paris and London, and with little impact on Russia itself. In 1830–1831, Nicholas I brutally put down a nationalist uprising in Poland led by Catholics and liberal aristocrats who chafed under foreign rule. He also intervened in the revolutions of 1848, sending troops to Hungary in 1849 to help the Habsburg monarchy restore their government. Russia itself remained untouched by the revolt and agitation that spread virtually throughout western Europe.

Although the situation in Russia seemed calm, the country was, in fact, falling farther behind the technological and economic levels of the West. Russia responded to Western industrialization initially with a further tightening of labor obligations of the serfs, so that the great grain-growing estates would have more to export. Individual factories did sometimes use Western equipment, but there was no significant change in overall manufacturing or transportation methods. Russia remained a profoundly agricultural society based on essentially unfree labor. Russian aristocrats, conscious of the West's greater dynamism, attempted to conceal the differences by their enthusiastic embrace of European cultural styles, remaining up-to-date on the latest fashions in dress, dance, or painting, but this important cultural current did not close the economic and social gap between the two societies.

This gap was dramatically highlighted by an apparently minor though bloody war in the Crimea in the mid-1850s. Russian leaders had continued to peck away at Ottoman holdings in central Asia, maintaining what was by now a traditional foreign-policy interest. However, British and French power in the Middle East constituted a new force of opposition. When Nicholas provoked war with the Ottomans in 1853, the Western countries came to the sultan's aid. Essentially because of industrialization, which provided superior equipment and relatively rapid transport, the Western forces, far from home, prevailed over the Russian army in its own backyard. Both sides, however, suffered huge loss of life. The war's result was a particularly severe blow for a Russian regime that prided itself on military dynamism.

The Crimean War contributed to the greatest event of 19th-century Russian history, the emancipation of the serfs. Some aristocratic landlords were no longer sure that serfdom provided the most profitable system of labor. Many Russian leaders were also concerned with the periodic peasant uprisings against their lack of land and freedom, which continued to punctuate Russian history even after the collapse of the great Pugachev Rebellion. Some upper-class Russians were swayed by ideals of liberty and humanitarianism, finding serfdom wrong in principle. Above all, Russian leaders, including the new tsar Alexander II, wanted to rid Russia of a social system that seemed to be holding it back in relation to the West. If Russia were to develop a more dynamic economy, it needed workers who were free to move to cities and factories. It needed to encourage better methods even in agriculture, which the easy reliance on servile labor prevented. It needed, in sum, a partial revolution from above.

THE BEGINNINGS OF RUSSIAN INDUSTRIALIZATION

The decision to emancipate the serfs came at roughly the same time as, in the United States and, shortly before, in Brazil, the decision to free slaves. Some of the motives, including humanitarianism and a desire to convert more fully to a free labor market, were also similar. No more than slavery did rigorous serfdom suit the economic needs of a society that could hold its own in modern world trade.

In some ways, the emancipation of the serfs in 1861 was more generous than the liberation of slaves in the Americas. Although aristocrats retained part of the land, including the most fertile holdings, the serfs got most of it—in contrast to slaves who received their freedom but nothing else. But Russian emancipation was careful to preserve essential aristocratic power and above all the tight grip of the tsarist state. The serfs obtained no new political rights at a national level. They were still tied to their villages until they could pay for the land they were given—the money from such a redemption going to the aristocrats. Many peasants, as a result, could still not travel freely or even sell their land, although some became more mobile. High redemption payments, in addition to state taxes, kept most Russian peasants miserably poor. Emancipation did bring change; it helped create a larger urban labor force. However, it did not spur a revolution in agricultural productivity, as most peasants continued to use traditional methods on their small plots. And it did not bring contentment; indeed, peasant uprisings became more rather than less common, as hopes for a brighter future now seemed dashed by the limits of change.

Alexander did, to be sure, introduce further reforms during the 1860s and 1870s. He created local political councils, the *zemstvos,* that had a voice in regulating roads, schools, and other conditions. The zemstvos gave some Russians, particularly middle-class people such as doctors and lawyers, new political experience, but they had no influence on national policy, where the tsar resolutely maintained his own power and that of the extensive bureaucracy. Alexander liberalized legal codes and created new courts. Reformers modernized the army, by encouraging promotion by merit and other organizational changes. Recruitment was extended, and many peasants learned new skills, including literacy, through their military service.

These adjustments, like emancipation itself, were important. They imitated some Western principles; the new law codes, for example, provided milder punishment for crimes and enforced equality before the law. However, they were not designed to create a Western society: they

did not attack the fundamental power of the aristocracy and modify political authoritarianism. The reforms were sufficient to spur the beginnings of Russian industrialization. They were not sufficient to provide a stable social base for economic upheaval. Political as well as peasant unrest increased and provoked a return to more repressive measures.

From the 1870s on, Russia began to construct an extensive railway network. It served as a vital link in the giant country—the establishment of the Trans-Siberian Railroad, connecting European Russia with the Pacific, was the crowning achievement of this drive, largely completed in the 1880s. Railroad facilities were also necessary to integrate Russia's wealth in coal and iron and to bring these resources, in turn, to markets—Russia's river system, running south to north, was not particularly useful in this regard. Moreover, rails aided Russia's drive to export grain, essential for earning capital to purchase Western machinery. The rail system, finally, helped spur a modern coal and metallurgical industry, for although some key equipment had to be purchased from the West, the government stimulated native industry as much as possible. By the 1880s, when Russia's railroad network had almost quintupled compared to 1860, modern factories had sprung up in Moscow, St. Petersburg, and several Polish cities, and an urban working class was growing at the same pace.

Russian industrialization was not unopposed, however. Quite apart from impoverished factory workers, who soon proved susceptible to revolutionary doctrines, some Russian leaders worried about the unsettling impact of this Western force. But industrialization appealed to the widespread desire to catch up with the West. It allowed further Russian territorial expansion in central Asia and northern China, for rails enabled Russia's massive armies to be moved more quickly and established technological superiority over many Asian states. Furthermore, Russian industrialization flowed in part from the authoritarian position of the state. Railroad development was a state-run operation. Many factories were also state-run, and the government oversaw some of the industrialization effort.

Under Count Witte, minister of finance from 1892 to 1903 and an ardent economic modernizer, the government enacted high tariffs to protect new Russian industry, improved its banking system, and encouraged Western investors to build great factories with advanced technology. As Witte put it, "The inflow of foreign capital is . . . the only way by which our industry will be able to supply our country quickly with abundant and cheap products." By 1900, approximately half of Russian industry was foreign-owned and much of it foreign-operated, with British, German, and French industrialists taking the lead. Witte and others were confident that government controls could keep the foreigners in line, rather than converting Russia into a new imperialist playground, and for the most part, they seemed correct. By 1900, Russia had surged to fourth rank in the world in steel production and was second to the United States in petroleum production and refining. Russian textile manufacture was also impressive. Long-standing Russian economic backwardness was beginning to yield.

This was still, however, an industrial revolution in its early stages. Russia's world position was a function more of its great size and population, along with rich natural resources, than of really thorough mechanization. Agriculture remained backward, as peasants had neither the means nor the motive to change their ways. Literacy was gaining and peasant habits did begin to change—for example, thanks to urban contacts, the rules of courtship relaxed, with more sexual overtones permitted—but agricultural methods lagged. This, in turn, retarded the growth of cities and made periodic famine a recurrent threat. Many Russian factories were vast—the largest, on average, in the world—and urban artisans also gained ground in fields such as printing. But the urban labor force, although expanding rapidly, was still a minority, and many workers had yet to convert to new work values.

Nor did a powerful business class arise in Russia. Government controls and foreign investment produced industrialization without a surging middle class. Some Russian entrepreneurs showed impressive dynamism, and the number of businessmen and professionals increased, but Russian industrialization did not engender the kind of assertive, self-confident middle class that had arisen in the West. Industrialization was, in sum, still tentative, and it was definitely proceeding along distinctive lines in Russia.

THE FOUNDATIONS OF REVOLUTION IN RUSSIA

The nation's early industrialization increased the already fearsome tensions within the society. Peasant discontent, although not a constant force, continued to rise. Famines regularly provoked uprisings. Peasants, who deeply resented aristocratic estates and the redemption payments and taxes that burdened them, were also pressed by rapidly growing population levels, which augmented land hunger. Along with the peasantry, many educated Russians, including some aristocrats, clamored for revolutionary change. Their goals and motives varied, but in general they wanted political freedoms while maintaining a Russian culture different from that of the West, which they saw as hopelessly plutocratic and materialist. Upper-class radicals claimed that a spirit of community lay deep in the Russian soul, which could serve as the basis for an egalitarian society free from the injustice of the capitalist West. Many Russian radicals were anarchists who sought the abolition of all formal government. Although anarchism was not unknown in the West, it took on particular force in Russia in opposition to unyielding tsarist autocracy. Many anarchists turned to extremely violent methods, forming the first large terrorist movement in the modern world. Terrorism, in the form of assassinations and bombings, seemed an essential

approach, given the lack of other political outlets. It appeared that anarchist terrorist tactics
often focused more on destruction than on
coherent political goals for the future. As the
anarchist leader Bakunin put it:

> We have only one plan—general destruction.
> We want a national revolution of the peas-
> ants. We refuse to take any part in the work-
> ing out of schemes to better the conditions of
> life; we regard as fruitless solely theoretical
> work. We consider destruction to be such an
> enormous and difficult task that we must
> devote all our powers to it, and we do not
> wish to deceive ourselves with the dream that
> we will have enough strength and knowledge
> for creation.

Not surprisingly, the recurrent waves of terrorism merely reinforced the tsarist regime's resolve
to avoid further political change, in what became
a vicious circle in late-19th-century Russian
politics.

By the late 1870s, Alexander II pulled back
from his reform interest, fearing that change was
escalating out of control. Censorship of newspapers and political meetings tightened; many
dissidents were arrested and sent to Siberia.
Alexander himself was assassinated by a terrorist
bomb in 1881, and his successors, while escalating the effort to industrialize, continued to
oppose further political reform. New measures
of repression were also directed against minority
nationalities, as a conservative nationalism, hostile to internal minorities and Western influence
alike, swelled in praise of Russian values. The
Poles and other groups were carefully supervised,
and persecution of the large Jewish minority
increased, resulting in many executions and
seizures of property; as a consequence, many
Russian Jews emigrated. In general, moreover,
the late-19th-century tsars sponsored a vigorous
drive to impose Russian culture and language on
the minority peoples. They thus tried to
Christianize many Jewish children by force,
while forbidding Poles and other minorities

This late 19th-century roadside scene depicts the
poverty of a Russian peasant village. What forces
produced such poor conditions, even after serfdom
had been abolished?

from using their own language for public purposes. In response, many minority nationalist
movements spread on an underground basis,
joining the anarchists in their energetic, if illegal,
resistance to the tsarist regime.

One final political current arose by the
1890s. A number of radical leaders, drawn from
the same educated circles as the anarchists, were
attracted to the Marxist doctrines that were being
disseminated in the West. Largely underground
or in exile, Marxist groups formed, committed
to a tightly organized proletarian revolution.
Although the Marxist movement remained small,
its ideas took hold among some urban industrial
workers, who chafed under the harsh conditions
of the early factories and the illegality of ordinary
trade union activity.

Searching passersby in Riga during the Revolution of 1905.

By 1900, the contradictory currents in Russian society may have made revolution inevitable. Although the forces demanding change were not united, and although extensive police work and military repression kept most uprisings in hand, the combination of pressures may have been too powerful to resist. Peasants had little concern for the more formal political ideas; indeed, anarchist efforts to reach out to the people in previous decades had been largely ignored. Marxists and anarchists, in fact, often disliked each other, for indeed both their methods and goals were different. The small middle class, interested in some political voice but not eager for full-scale social upheaval, was yet another piece on the complex Russian chessboard. Revolution did come in 1905, after Russia had suffered another disastrous and surprising military defeat, this time at the hands of Japan, who opposed further Russian expansion in northern China and Korea. Defeat unleashed massive general strikes by urban workers and a tumultuous series of peasant insurrections. In response, the tsarist regime relaxed the constraints of the post-emancipation rural system, allowing peasants greater freedom to buy and sell land and operate independently of redemption payments and village controls. However, a halting pledge to appease middle-class sentiment by creating a national parliament, the Duma, was soon dashed by renewed political repression; the Duma became a hollow institution, satisfying no one. And no gains were offered to the Marxists at all. The prospect of further revolution loomed large and then became reality when Russia plunged into yet another conflict—World War I—hoping that battle would bring new territory and distraction from internal stress. The gamble failed and, in 1917, one of the great revolutions in world history took place.

THE CULTURE OF EASTERN EUROPE

Many smaller east European countries followed patterns similar to those of Russia during the later 19th century. New nations such as Romania, Bulgaria, and Serbia, free from Ottoman control, liberated the serfs, but amid restrictions that retained the bulk of the land for the aristocracy. Parliaments were established on superficially Western lines, but they had little power and were based on very limited voting rights. Most of the smaller east European nations industrialized less extensively than Russia and remained even more dependent, as agricultural producers, on Western markets.

Despite economic problems and political tensions, however, eastern Europe, including Russia, enjoyed an impressive cultural surge, a final ingredient in the complex developments that accompanied reactions to Western industrialization. Many Western artistic styles were appropriated. Russian and other east European novelists and essayists wrote in the romantic vein, glorifying national ways; the Russian novel enjoyed unprecedented popularity in the hands of writers such as Tolstoy, Turgenev, and Dostoyevsky. Composers such as Tchaikovsky brought romanticism to music. Modern art currents in the West also found an echo, as abstract painting and atonal music took shape in the hands of Russian practitioners soon after 1900. East European intellectuals also participated in the scientific developments of the later 19th century. The important experiments on conditioned reflexes conducted by a Russian physiologist, Ivan Pavlov, advanced the understanding of unconscious responses in human beings.

In many ways, then, eastern Europe seemed to be drawing closer to the West in cultural activity, continuing a pattern visible since the time of Peter the Great. With growing industrialization and some political impulses borrowed from the West, including Marxism, it seemed possible that, despite its political peculiarities, Russia might produce a version of Western civilization, just as it had moved into the Western diplomatic orbit in many respects.

However, east European culture remained ambivalent about the West. Although some intellectuals were ardent admirers of Western culture, others used only partially Western styles to comment on the distinctiveness of the Russian or Slavic spirit. Many novelists joined political conservatives in finding a unique soul in their people, which they believed should be exalted and protected against Western influence. Romanticism, in its east European manifestation, encouraged a vigorous set of cultural and political nationalisms, designed to capture the glories of Russian, or Ukrainian, or Serbian peoples. A Pan-Slavic movement also arose—particularly in Russia, which claimed leadership of Slavic Europe—that argued for Slavic unity against the more materialistic and individualistic West.

Furthermore, the masses in eastern Europe, mainly peasant, remained firmly attached to older traditions, including the Orthodox religion, different from those of the West and the partially westernized upper classes. Popular culture changed through the impact of growing literacy, rising urbanization, and military service, but it did not merge with the popular culture of the West. Indeed, popular resentment against growing Western influence, including the power of foreign capitalists, was yet another revolutionary rallying cry during and after World War I.

By 1900, then, Russia and much of the rest of eastern Europe represented a distinctive amalgam of tradition and change. Principles of authoritarian rule remained virtually unaltered, but they now joined with diverse political opposition concentrated for the most part on sweeping revolution rather than purely liberal reforms. The tradition of territorial expansionism, although checked by resistance from the West and Japan, still ran strong. Pan-Slavic sentiments indeed encouraged new Russian influence in southeastern Europe. Massive social change had resulted from emancipation and

---

HISTORY DEBATE

THE PRECONDITIONS FOR REVOLUTION

Historians debate at what point a great Russian revolution became inevitable. We know that such a revolution occurred in 1917, partly triggered by additional hardships and frustrations during World War I. But some scholars argue that it had become unavoidable well before then, at least at the point when the responses to the 1905 revolution led to little real change.

Arguments about inevitability are inherently difficult, because they cannot be definitively proved; they can only be judged strongly probable. The case for inevitable revolution rests on several factors. The regime of Nicholas II became increasingly incompetent. It defended its own autocracy and the rights of the aristocracy and the Orthodox Church with little flexibility, which merely built discontent from the small but growing middle class, the new working class and the huge peasantry. There were no legal outlets for protest. Strong ideological alternatives existed in Russian populism and in the small but well-organized and fervent Marxist movements. Weak regime; buildup of revolutionary ideas; large and diverse social base ready to countenance violence because no other expression was available—this can be taken as the stuff of revolutionary inevitability.

On the other hand, we know that major revolutions are hard to predict. Without the further challenge of World War I, and the specific circumstances that led to the clash of 1917, the revolutionary spark might have been avoided. Another decade to grow out of the worst stresses of early industrialization, more chance for the reforms that had been offered the peasantry to bring greater capacity to take advantage of market agriculture—the picture might have changed. The debate helps sharpen questions about Russia, but it can hardly be resolved.

The debate also raises intriguing comparative questions. Japan would avoid major revolution, despite cultural and social strain. The regime was more effective than its Russian counterpart, and Meiji reforms had modified aristocratic control, giving other social sectors some voice. Japanese culture may have been more cohesive, and its foreign policy certainly brought greater successes than the Russian government managed in the same period. Can analysis of the causes of one revolutionary situation be used to explain why revolution did not occur in another case?

---

early industrialization, but east European society continued to be more agricultural and in many ways more traditionalist than its Western counterpart. Finally, a larger ambivalence toward Western values persisted. East European intellectuals contributed creatively to general European artistic and scientific work, but a desire to define distinctive features, to resist full westernization, remained all-important in many quarters, both elitist and popular. Eastern Europe was, in sum, developing its own pattern of change as it entered the industrial age. This pattern soon embraced a distinctive kind of revolution as well.

THE OPENING OF TRADE IN JAPAN

Even more than Russia, Japan faced new pressure from the West during the 1850s, although it took the form of a demand for more open trade rather than outright war. After a tense debate during the 1850s and 1860s, Japan's response was more direct than Russia's and, on the whole, more immediately successful. Despite the long history of isolation, Japanese society was better adapted than Russia's to the challenge of industrial change. Market forms were more extensive, reaching into peasant agriculture; levels of literacy were higher. Japan, nevertheless, had to rework many of its institutions during the final decades of the 19th century, and the process produced significant strain. The result, by 1900, was different from both purely Western patterns and the more obvious tensions of Russian society.

On the surface, Japan experienced little change during the first half of the 19th century. The Tokugawa shogunate remained intact, although there were signs that it was becoming less effective. The shogunate ran the country through a combination of central bureaucracy and alliances with the regional daimyos. It also encouraged some business interests and provided a central banking system. Japanese culture still relied heavily on Confucianism, and participation in Confucian schools grew rapidly. Traditional artistic and dramatic styles remained lively. The interest in Western science that had developed among a small number of scholars continued, through 18th-century contacts with the Dutch trading outpost in the port of Nagasaki, but no technological breakthroughs occurred. The Japanese boasted a productive agriculture and considerable rural manufacturing, but there were signs of economic stagnation, particularly in a growing number of peasant riots

against poor conditions. Nevertheless, there is no reason to believe that Japan was on the verge of significant change before change was thrust upon it.

In 1853, the American commodore Matthew Perry arrived with a fleet in Edo Bay, near Tokyo, insisting through threats of bombardment that Americans be allowed to trade. In 1854, he returned and won the right to station an American consul in Japan; two ports were opened to commerce. Britain, Russia, and Holland quickly won similar rights. As in China, this meant that Westerners living in Japan were governed by their own representatives, not by Japanese law. Other privileges soon followed, along with a few military skirmishes. Leading Western nations simply insisted on their need and right to trade, as part of the expanding world economy, while also seeking fishing rights in Japanese waters. For several decades, they limited Japan's ability to decide on its own tariffs. Russian pressure was a problem as well, as the nation's eastward expansion had already produced a few small clashes over control of islands in the North Pacific.

Some Japanese had already grown impatient with strict isolation. More important was the now obvious fact that Japan could not compete with Western navies and so had to defer to their interests. But many Japanese leaders, including conservatives who feared Western influence, wanted to strengthen their government in order to control their nation's future. Their interest caused them to bypass the shogun and appeal directly to the emperor for support. Long secluded as a religious figure, the emperor now began to gain power.

In the 1860s, a political crisis came into the spotlight, involving a clash between many samurai and the shogunate. The crisis was marked by attacks on foreigners, including one murder of a British official, matched by the Western naval bombardments of feudal forts. Virtual civil war broke out in 1866 as the samurai eagerly armed themselves with surplus weapons from the

Commodore Perry's "Black Ship" as seen by the Japanese, 1854.

American Civil War, causing Japan's aristocrats to finally come to terms with the sheer power of Western armaments. When the samurai defeated a shogunate force, a number of Japanese finally were shocked out of their traditional reliance on their own superiority, with one author arguing that the nation was, compared to the West with its technology, science, and humane laws, only half-civilized.

This multifaceted crisis came to an end in 1868, with the proclamation of rule by a new emperor named Mutsuhito, whose regime was soon called *Meiji,* or "enlightened rule." Backed by some samurai leaders, the new emperor managed to put down the troops of the shogunate and gradually built up support, establishing his capital in Edo, now named Tokyo. The crisis period had been shocking enough to allow further changes in Japan's basic political structure—changes that went much deeper at the political level than those introduced by Russia from 1861 on. With the chief ministers actually taking the major initiative, the imperial government sponsored three decades of rapid change, designed to make Japan competitive with the West and thus save national independence in what was, for Japan, a radically new and perilous environment.

The key to the Japanese response was heightened governmental centralization. Meiji leaders abolished feudalism, as the regional lords surrendered their land rights to the government. Ministries in the central government now directed national policy in a surprisingly quick political adjustment. The ministers in the Meiji period were committed to further reform, as a government-sponsored reshaping of Japanese society was underway. Such reshaping, however, did not call into question the Japanese belief in their independence and basic superiority of their culture. An early Japanese visitor to the White House wrote a self-satisfied poem that captured part of the national mood:

> We suffered the barbarians to look upon the glory of our Eastern Empire of Japan.

JAPANESE INDUSTRIALIZATION IN RESPONSE TO THE WEST

The Japanese combination of rapid adaptation and firm belief in the validity of their own values and institutions may explain the distinctive Japanese response in matching Western pressure without outright revolution and full-scale westernization. Japanese leaders carefully blended economic political change with existing institutions and values.

Reform interests, in the Meiji period, focused on several targets. A new army was established, modeled on the German system. It was based on the universal conscription of young males. The training of officers improved, as new men replaced older feudal generals. Military armament was brought up to Western standards, and a navy was formed, initially with the aid of Western advisors. The government also quickly introduced Western public-health measures, which promoted population growth.

Mass education spread rapidly from 1872 on, for women as well as for men. Elite students at the university level often emphasized science, many of them studying technical subjects abroad. The rapid assimilation of a scientific outlook was a major new component of Japanese culture. Other cultural changes ranged farther afield. Fearful of embarrassment in Western eyes—a factor of growing importance in world history—the Japanese government even tried to outlaw homosexuality around 1900 and to increase differences in dress between boys and girls.

Reform also meant further political change. A new constitution took effect in 1890, again based on the German model. A two-house parliament, elected by men of property, served under the supreme emperor. The parliament did not develop extensive powers, as the emperor named his own ministers and controlled basic policy. But several political parties competed for votes. The Japanese political style

SOLVING PROBLEMS

MAINTAINING IDENTITY

Japan faced an obvious challenge when, in 1868, it decided to open to the outside world and imitate many institutions and values from the West. Of course, the fact that the nation had a prior, postclassical experience of imitation (with China) that had not cost its identity may be one of the reasons the venture seemed feasible in the first place (in contrast to societies that had less precedent in this area). Still, there was a key danger that imitation of the West would be too sweeping, erasing cherished values and leading to an inconclusive identity of any sort.

Indeed, in the 1870s, boundary lines were unclear. Western standards seemed to dominate the field of education, and many foreign experts were brought in to guide reform. Many consumers began to prefer Western products like toothpaste. At this point, and periodically thereafter, many conservatives worried that Japanese ways were at risk of extinction.

By the 1880s, the government reached in to try to solve the problem, without resorting to pulling out of the global economic and diplomatic system (which is an approach other societies would try, periodically, even into the early 21st century). Western standards for science and technology were promoted, but

access to Western political and values was constrained. The educational system began to urge attention to group cohesion as well as national loyalty. Worship of the emperor was touted as a key tradition, even though, from the standpoint of historical fact, it was a recent precedent. (Invented traditions were a key part of world history in the later 19th century, as the United States for example introduced an invented tradition of Thanksgiving celebration in the 1860s as a gesture of national solidarity.)

This solution worked, as the Japanese maintained interest in relevant foreign patterns—even beginning to pick up enthusiasm for American baseball in the 1890s—without losing a sense of shared identity and an array of distinctive social values. Later developments would require modifications in the specific solution—emperor worship had to be dropped after World War II—without jeopardizing the basic achievement of identity amid globalization.

■QUESTIONS: *Why have identity issues become so common in modern world history? Was Japan unusually successful—compared to other societies—in addressing the problem?*

now combined centralized imperial rule with limited representative institutions; the combination gave great power to a new oligarchy of wealthy businessmen and aristocrats, who influenced the emperor and also pulled strings within parliament. This rule by an elite echoed earlier Japanese reliance on cooperation rather than competition in politics, as well as a tradition of considerable deference to the authority of the upper classes. Here was a clear case of blending Japanese values with Western-style institutions.

Above all, reform meant industrialization, with the government taking a far more active role than its Russian counterpart. New banks were created by the government to fund growing trade and to provide capital for industry. State-built railroads spread across the country, and rapid steamers connected the islands. Although Japan still relied heavily on home or small-shop production, particularly of goods such as silk cloth that were widely exported, factory industry expanded steadily. Finally, the market emphasis on agriculture increased, as

The first Japanese parliament meets, 1890.

new methods were introduced to raise output to feed the growing cities.

Japanese state initiative not only built transportation and banking systems but also led to the government operation of mines, shipyards, and metallurgical plants. Scarce capital and the unfamiliarity of new technology seemed to compel state direction, which also served to supervise the many foreign advisors the Japanese required. Japan established a ministry of industry in 1870, and it quickly became one of the key government agencies, setting overall economic policy as well as operating specific sectors. However, private initiative played a role as well. In textiles, private businessmen, many of them from older merchant families, ran the leading companies. In other industries, government concerns, tax-financed, were later sold to private interests, to the profit of the latter. Close collaboration between government agencies and private firms, especially big business concerns, early formed a hallmark of the new Japanese economy.

Although Japanese big business developed rapidly, early industrialization also depended on the massive exploitation of workers, particularly women workers. Tens of thousands of women were sold for labor service by fathers or husbands in the overpopulated Japanese countryside. They worked particularly in the silk industry, developed by the state on a labor-intensive basis to capture vital export earnings as Japan surpassed China in producing this luxury commodity.

CULTURAL AND ECONOMIC EFFECTS OF JAPANESE INDUSTRIALIZATION

As had earlier occurred in the West, industrialization altered the existing social structure. Only a handful of aristocrats and people from the samurai warrior class entered the ranks of successful businessmen. A new elite was formed that embraced leading entrepreneurs for the first time, and while old merchant families contributed to this group, talented people from diverse backgrounds, including former peasants, now rose to the top. Among the masses, the rise of a huge, propertyless class of urban workers was a new development. Both peasants and workers endured low wages and high taxes, as Japanese leaders used cheap labor to compete with Western enterprise and to amass the capital needed for further investment. And while the new elite did not cultivate the luxurious lifestyle of Western business magnates, being content with lower profit rates, it did insist on retaining power. Unions and lower-class political parties, although they began to emerge by 1900, made only slow headway, and a militant socialist movement was outlawed without difficulty.

Many Japanese copied Western fashions as part of the effort to become modern. Western-style haircuts replaced the samurai practice of a shaved head with a top knot—another example of the fascinating westernizing of hair throughout modern world history. Western standards of hygiene spread, and the Japanese became enthusiastic tooth brushers and consumers of patent medicines. Japan also adopted the Western calendar and the metric system. Few Japanese converted to Christianity, however, and despite fads imitating Western popular culture, the Japanese managed to preserve an emphasis on their own values. What the Japanese wanted and got from the West involved practical techniques; they planned to infuse these with a distinctively Japanese spirit.

Thus, in education, an initial surge of interest in Western schooling in the 1870s, which included the use of hundreds of European and American teachers, yielded in the 1880s to a reassertion of Japanese group loyalty and attacks on excessive individualism. New exposure to science changed culture, but the growing stress on nationalism provided a new focus for traditional beliefs in Japanese cohesion and distinctiveness.

Japanese family life retained many traditional emphases, as opposed to Western customs. To be sure, unprecedented population growth forced increasing numbers of people off the land, which disrupted families and caused the unusual reliance on women's work in industry. However, the Japanese were eager to maintain the traditional inferiority of women in the home. A new law promoted monogamy, but in practice, mistresses were still widely accepted in the upper classes. The position of Western women seemed repellent. Official Japanese visitors to the United States were appalled by what they saw as the aggressive, domineering ways of women: "The way women are treated here is like the way parents are respected in our country." Standards of Japanese courtesy also contrasted with the more open and boisterous behavior of Westerners—particularly Americans. "Obscenity is inherent in the customs of this country," noted another samurai visitor to the

Women of Fashion Sewing, Japanese woodblock print, 1887.

United States. Other basic features of Japanese life, including diet, were maintained in the face of Western influence. Japanese religious values were also distinctive. Buddhism lost some ground, although it remained important, and Confucianism was undermined through the new emphasis on science in the schools. But Shintoism, which appealed to the rising nationalist concern with Japan's own unique mission and the religious functions of the emperor, won new interest.

JAPAN AS AN INTERNATIONAL PLAYER

By 1900, Japan's industrial success had not brought the country to Western levels, and the Japanese remained intensely fearful for their independence. Economic change, and the tensions as well as the power it generated, however, produced a shift in Japanese foreign policy. With only one previous exception, the Japanese had never before been interested in territorial expansion, but by the 1890s, they joined the ranks of imperialist powers. Partly this shift was an imitation of Western models, and at the same time it was an effort to prevent Western encroachment. Imperialism also relieved some strains within Japanese society, giving displaced samurai a chance to exercise their military talents elsewhere and providing symbols of nationalist achievement for the populace as a whole. The Japanese economy also required access to markets and raw materials. Because Japan was poor in many basic materials, including coal and oil for energy, the pressure for expansion was particularly great.

Certainly, Japan's quick victory over China, in the quarrel for influence over Korea in 1894–1895, proved to be just a first step. Japan convincingly demonstrated its new superiority over all other Asian powers. Humiliated by Western insistence that it abandon the Liaotung peninsula, the Japanese planned a war with Russia as a means of striking out against the nearest European state. A 1902 alliance with Britain was an important sign of Japan's arrival as an equal player in the Western-dominated world diplomatic system. The Japanese were also eager to undermine Russia's growing strength in east Asia, after the completion of the Trans-Siberian Railroad. Disputes over Russian influence in Manchuria and Japanese influence in Korea led to the Russo-Japanese War in 1904, which Japan won handily on the basis of its superior navy. In 1910, Japan annexed Korea outright; it was now not only a modern industrial power but also a new imperialist force as well.

As Japan consolidated its control of Korea, from this point, it used the opportunity to generate cheap imports, not only of foods and raw materials but inexpensive factory products, while exporting Japanese industrial goods in ways that helped balance the nation's vulnerable position in the larger world economy. This experience, in turn, would help explain later efforts to carve out an even larger colonial sphere in east and southeast Asia.

THE STRAIN OF MODERNIZATION

Japan's success by 1900 was amazing. Its victories over China and then Russia surprised virtually every observer outside of Japan. There is no question that Japan's rapid transformation, like its more recent success in becoming one of the most advanced industrial societies in the world, constitutes a unique achievement. Furthermore, Japan—unlike Russia or major parts of the West—prepared the groundwork for industrialization without the serious threat of popular revolution.

However, this achievement, even combined as it was with significant currents from earlier Japanese culture and political styles, had its costs. Many Japanese conservatives resented the passion that some Japanese displayed for Western fashions. Their concern helped ensure that Japanese women, initially the subject of some reform interest, were mainly confined to family roles. Nevertheless, disputes between generations, with the old clinging to traditional standards, the young more interested in Western culture, were commonplace and very troubling in a society that stressed the importance of parental authority. Social tensions added to the strain, as expectations rose more rapidly than standards of living. Crowded conditions in the growing cities produced misery at least as great as in earlier Western slums. Rising divorce rates—Japan had the highest in the world by 1900—showed another kind of strain.

Some tension translated into politics, even with the narrow voting system. Political parties in Japan's parliament, the *Diet,* sometimes clashed with the emperor's ministers over rights to determine policy. The government frequently had to dissolve the Diet and call for new elections, seeking a more workable parliamentary majority.

Another kind of friction emerged in intellectual life. Many Japanese scholars emulated Western philosophies and literary styles. But other intellectuals retained an interest in more traditional forms and expressed a deep pessimism about the Japanese loss of identity in a changing world. Some wanted the government to become more fully Western; many were concerned about jobs, as universities tended to turn out more graduates than the economy could handle. The underlying theme was confusion about a Japan that was no longer traditional, but not Western either. What was it? Thus, some writers spoke of Japan heading for a "nervous collapse from which we will not be able to recover."

As an antidote to social and cultural insecurity, Japanese leaders urged national loyalty and devotion to the emperor, and with considerable success. The official message promoted Japanese virtues of obedience and harmony that the West lacked. School texts thus stressed:

> Our country takes as its base the family system; the nation is but a single family, the imperial family is our main house. We the people worship the unbroken imperial line with the same feeling of respect and love that a child feels towards his parents. . . . The union of loyalty and filial piety is truly the special character of our national polity.

Nationalism was a partially new force in Japan, and of course it was common in the West and other parts of the world in 1900 as well. However, Japanese nationalism built on traditions of superiority and cohesion, deference to rulers, and the new tensions generated by rapid change. It became if not a deeper force in Japan than elsewhere, at least one that played a unique role in justifying sacrifice and struggle in a national mission to preserve independence and dignity in a hostile world. Nationalism, along with the firm police repression of dissent, certainly helps explain why Japan avoided the revolutionary pressure that plagued Russia, China, and other countries after 1900, and also the kind of unrest that had characterized early Western industrialization around 1848.

Japan's traditions thus enabled it to foster rapid change from above, without the need for a literal revolution to either purge the existing system or respond to the undeniable tensions that modernization produced. The result, by 1900, was a dynamic country newly powerful on the world scene, shaping a distinctive kind of industrial society. No other country matched its achievements for more than half a century.

PATHS TO THE PRESENT

Two legacies from the long 19th century, and particularly its final decades, stand out in modern Russia and Japan. The first involves the results of successful latecomer industrializations. Both countries maintained strong positions in world affairs into the 21st century, building on reforms of the late 19th century. Japan's achievement—the nation was the world's second largest industrial economy by 2006—is particularly impressive.

Indeed, Japan continues to embellish the approach it had worked out by 1900: balancing great commitment to global activities and considerable openness to learning from outside example with the capacity to maintain a distinctive identity. This equation has shifted, of course, with Japan's growing global influence, but many elements of the formula persist. Russia, however, differs from Japan: its reform responses by 1900 were less thorough than Japan's, creating a framework for more radical changes that loosened the nation's connections with its 19th-century past.

SUGGESTED WEB SITES

On 19th-century Russian literature, see http://www.wsu.edu/~brians/hum_303/russian.html and http://web.archive.org/web/20000815095939/www.ucr.edu/history/seaman; on industrial structure in the era of Japan's industrial revolution, see http://ideas.repec.org/p/tky/jseres/2005cj128.html; on the empire that was Russia, see http://www.loc.gov/exhibits/empire/.

SUGGESTED READINGS

Recent works on Japan include John H. Sagers, *Origins of Japanese Wealth and Power: Reconciling Confucianism and Capitalism, 1830–1885* (2006); Masayuki Tanimoto, *The Role of Tradition in Japan's Industrialization: Another Path to Industrialization* (2006); Andrew Gordon, *A Modern History of Japan: From Tokugawa Times to the Present* (2003); Donald Keene, *Emperor of Japan: Meiji and His World, 1852–1912* (2002); Midiso Hane, *Peasants, Rebels, Women and Outcastes: The Underside of Modern Japan,* 2nd ed.

(2003); Thomas C. Smith, *Native Sources of Japanese Industrialization, 1750–1920* (1988); Marius B. Jansen, *The Making of Modern Japan* (2000); and Morris Low, ed., *Building a Modern Japan: Science, Technology, and Medicine in the Meiji Era and Beyond* (2005).

Recent work on Russia includes Anthony J. Heywood and Jonathan D. Smele, *The Russian Revolution of 1905: Centenary Perspectives* (2005); W. Bruce Lincoln, *The Conquest of a Continent: Siberia and the Russians* (2007); Michael Khodarkovsky, *Russia's Steppe Frontier: The Making of a Colonial Empire, 1500–1800* (2002) and John P. LeDonne, *The Grand Strategy of the Russian Empire, 1650–1831* (2004).

A. Gerschenkron, *Economic Backwardness in Historical Perspective: A Book of Essays* (1962) helps define the conditions of latecomer industrialization. Russian reforms and economic change are discussed in W. Blackwell, *The Industrialization of Russia,* 2nd ed. (1982) and Jerome Blum, *Lord and Peasant in Russia from the Ninth to the Nineteenth Century* (1961). On social and cultural developments, see Victoria Bonnel, ed., *The Russian Worker: Life and Labor Under the Tsarist Regime* (1983); Barbara Engel, *Mothers and Daughters: Women of the Intelligentsia in Nineteenth-Century Russia* (1983); and Jeffrey Brooks, *When Russia Learned to Read: Literacy and Popular Culture* (1987).

Japan in the 19th century is viewed from the perspective of modernization in R. Dore, ed., *Aspects of Social Change in Modern Japan* (1967). For a comparative view, see Peter N. Stearns, *Starting School: The Rise of Modern Education in France, the United States, and Japan* (1997). See also J. C. Abegglen, *The Japanese Factory: Aspects of Its Social Organization,* rev. ed. (1985); Hugh Patrick, ed., *Japanese Industrialization and Its Social Consequences* (1973); Andrew Gordon, *The Evolution of Labor Relations in Japan* (1985); R. H. Myers and M. R. Beattie, eds., *The Japanese Colonial Empire, 1895–1945* (1984); and E. O. Reischauer, *Japan, the Story of a Nation* (1981). For comparison, see Rudra Sil, *Managing Modernity: Work, Community and Authority in Late-Industrializing Japan and Russia* (2002).

27 World War I and the End of an Era

One of the most devastating wars of all time broke out in Europe in 1914. World War I had international significance and international causes. It marked the beginning of the end of western Europe's world supremacy and ended a major period in the world's history. The factors that led to the massive conflict also help explain why the conflict was so decisive.

Dramatic events are involved in the end of many eras in world history, of course. The collapse of the great classical empires might be compared to World War I, although their collapse occurred over a far longer period of time. World War I had its own character, however. Although many Europeans launched the war almost eagerly, thinking it would lead to glory and power, the mood soon changed. By the end of the war, many people knew that an age had ended. The causes of the war highlighted the century of imperialism, but they also led to the erosion of Europe's dominance.

KEY QUESTIONS   *What major changes were accumulating by 1914? What were the causes of World War I? Did the war result from purely diplomatic issues and miscalculations among the European powers, or did it suggest wider breaks in the patterns of world history that had developed during the previous century?*

SIGNS OF CHANGE

Events soon after 1900 signaled an end to what some historians have called the "long 19th century."

Item: Women in several Scandinavian countries and Australia obtained the right to vote, and feminist agitation heated up in other parts of Western society.

Item: Australia became fully independent in 1900, a symbol of the changing role of the European settler societies in world history.

Item: A Chinese revolution in 1911 toppled the imperial system for the first time since the collapse of the Han dynasty. China was in the throes of massive change.

Item: A Mexican revolution began in 1910 that called into question some of the political and social arrangements that had been common in 19th-century Latin America.

Item: Japan's victory over Russia and the Russian revolution of 1905 signaled dramatic new power alignments and the potential for turmoil in one of the world's major empires. The long period of Russian expansion had not ended, but it was becoming more complicated.

Developments around 1900 suggested two kinds of change. First, some patterns that had long characterized the agricultural period in human history were beginning to come to an end. Second, some patterns more specifically characteristic of the long 19th century were also encountering new challenges.

In the first category, the breakthrough of women in getting the vote—though at this point a limited, not global phenomenon—suggested that new ideas were challenging basic notions of patriarchy, far more than earlier changes, like the advent of the world religions, had done. Just as formal slavery was now on the way out, so fundamental gender issues were brewing as well. The fall of the Chinese empire had implications that were almost as great. Here was one of the perennial systems of the history of civilizations from the classical period onward. Chinese rejection of this aspect of their past suggested that basic political institutions that had long been assumed as normal, like monarchies and empires, were beginning to lose their viability. As with feminism, these developments were just being suggested by 1914, but we know in retrospect that they foreshadowed sweeping, global changes in both categories—both gender and political systems.

Other changes applied more specifically to patterns of the long 19th century. The rise of Japan, as an industrial and imperial power, clearly showed that the easy period of Western industrial monopoly and Russian territorial growth was coming to an end. The Mexican revolution might also suggest that some characteristic Latin American politic responses, that had surfaced during the 19th century, also had to be rethought, though patterns here proved complicated over the next several decades.

It was World War I, however, that really drew the long 19th century to a close. It was a major event in its own right, showing for the first time, despite earlier hints in the American Civil War, the full power of industrial technology and organization applied to war. It weakened the economic role of Europe in the world, contributed to the growth of both American and Japanese power, toppled a number of monarchies and empires, and contributed to nationalist resistance to Western imperialism in many regions. In all these respects, it truly formed the end of one era—the era of Western industrial monopoly and imperialism—and suggested some of the features of the world history period that would come next.

CAUSES OF WORLD WAR I

The outbreak of World War I in 1914 launched a conflict that had massive effects in Europe and the Middle East, with important spillover in east Asia and the Pacific, south Asia, Africa, and North America. The war pitted Britain, France, and Russia against Germany and the Habsburg monarchy—the world's most heavily armed nations came to blows through rival alliance systems. Other areas joined as colonies of the European powers or independently in hope of territorial gains or other advantages. By the time the war ended in 1918, the 19th-century world order had been severely disrupted, although many Western leaders, eager to return to what they called *normalcy,* refused to recognize this fact.

HISTORY DEBATE

RESPONSIBILITY FOR WORLD WAR I

For many decades after World War II historians and others passionately discussed the causes of World War I in terms of national responsibility. The big issue was whether the Germans were solely, or almost entirely, responsible. This was the assumption in the Versailles Treaty that punished Germans so badly. The argument was that Germany was war-hungry, could and should have restrained the Habsburgs, was so anxious about the two-front war that they launched action early, and so on. Not everyone agreed. There were discussions of early Russian mobilization: Russia, less efficient and huge, took longer to mobilize its armies than did Germany, so Russia started even earlier, which helped scare the Germans. How much were the Habsburgs at fault for being so edgy about southern Slav nationalism that they wanted to punish Serbia once and for all? How about the British, who might have held back and tried harder to prevent all-out war?

Today, these discussions seem outmoded, though the issues are still interesting. More attention today goes to larger factors, such as industrial competition, or the spill-over impact of imperialist rivalry. The focus, in other words, is on deeper causes, many of them affecting both sides in the emerging war, rather than trying to place blame. Did World War I suggest fundamental flaws in European society? Or is the idea of national faults or even the deficiencies of individual leaders even relevant?

The obvious fear displayed by an assortment of European leaders in this 1912 *Punch* cartoon is eerily prescient of the bafflement and concern that later seized European and world leaders in the midst of the Balkan wars of the 1990s.

The causes of World War I hardly sum up all the major trends that had emerged by the end of the 19th century, but they capture a fair number. The specific trigger for the war lay within the small nations of southeastern Europe, recently independent from Ottoman control. Ottoman decline had created a vacuum of power in this region that continues to this day. The new Balkan states, all highly nationalistic, frequently quarreled among themselves, conducting two regional wars before 1914. Russia and the Habsburg monarchy vied for influence in the area, hoping to distract their own peoples from internal tensions. Russia sponsored Slavic nationalism, whereas the Habsburgs, with large and restless Slavic minorities, tried to suppress the same force. In 1914, a Serbian nationalist assassinated a member of the Habsburg royal family. Austria threatened war. Russia backed Serbia. Then, the larger European alliance system

came into play. Germany feared abandoning Austria lest it face Russia and France alone. France and, more reluctantly, Britain decided they had to support Russia. Rigid diplomacy and fervent nationalism among all the European great powers parlayed a regional crisis into full-scale war. Europe's alliance system, combined with growing military rivalry and massive armaments, thus trapped the major powers into decisions that led inevitably to war.

Larger issues were at play, as the causes of war revealed massive fault lines in Western society. Huge weapons industries had evolved in all the powerful European nations, partly because of imperialist rivalries, partly to ensure sales to influential industrialists. Arms races—particularly navy-building competitions, especially between Britain and Germany—heightened public anxiety and made it more difficult for nations to compromise when disputes broke out. Russia,

During the Great War, the 33rd division in a front line trench near Forges, France, fires through a fence.

Germany, and France all had rigid strategic plans that encouraged prompt military action—in the hope, which proved completely illusory, of delivering quick knockout blows to the enemy. Germany, for example, hoped to knock France out quickly, to concentrate on Russia. But this plan involved moving through Belgium, which galvanized British fear and outrage.

Imperialism had created a growing sense in Europe that aggressive expansionism was normal state policy. But by 1914, the opportunities for further colonies were essentially exhausted, and the fervor that had gone into empire building now turned back on Europe itself. Politicians had increasingly pointed to nationalist triumphs as a means of wooing voters, and the habit persisted. Russia and Austria–Hungary, keenly aware

that they had fallen behind in imperialist races, hoped for triumphs that would divert public opinion.

European political and military leaders also worried about broader social tensions within their societies. Labor unrest was mounting, joined in some cases by feminist agitations and the push for independence by other repressed groups such as, in Britain's case, the Irish. Many officials worried that internal difficulties would erode national power—believing that it would be wisest to engage in war now, while strength was still high. Others argued that a successful war would unify the population, reducing the strength of socialist dissent. Ordinary people, bored or oppressed by industrial life, saw war as an exciting option—unaware of how devastating industrial warfare would actually be. Boys in various social classes had been raised on a diet of toy soldiers and aggressive sports—war seemed a glorious prospect in societies in which the importance of masculinity was asserted but not always easily expressed. The enthusiasm for war, in sum, drew on a number of tensions and anxieties created by industrial society.

Europe's decision to embark on a war also reflected its position in the world, strengths and weaknesses alike. Europeans were feeling at least vaguely threatened by the rise of societies outside their borders. Japan's industrial and military surge, plus stirrings in China, made some European nationalists talk of a new "yellow peril" that might displace Western supremacy. U.S. economic rivalry was keenly felt. British observers, greeting the new century in 1900, wondered if their days of easy empire were numbered, given new rivals and the sheer numbers of its colonial peoples. Oddly but revealingly, given Britain's strength, they looked forward to the new century with real dread. These anxieties might, of course, have prompted a new European unity, in order to protect their general interests, but national divisions ran too deep for this. Instead, countries concerned about their future turned to the familiar, nationalist military response. In essence, Europeans worried about their world position, but at the same time they assumed a position of assured dominance, believing it was safe to engage in internal conflict. This confidence led, among other things, to the extension of European warfare to the colonies and to the use of colonial troops on the European front. The result was a genuine world war and one that would redefine world alignments.

But war in an industrial age, and in the changing world context, had itself changed. Although many Europeans entered this conflict optimistically, assuming a quick and glorious end, World War I resulted in unprecedented dislocation and death, and a host of unforeseen consequences. A new period in world history was baptized in blood, as the most powerful civilization tore itself apart.

WORLD WAR I: EUROPE

As the war broke out in the late summer of 1914, Germany hoped for a quick strike into France, knocking this nation out of the conflict, so it could concentrate on what it anticipated would be a longer battle with Russia. France and Belgium, aided by the British army, resisted the Germany invasion, and a long trench war opened, mainly in northern France, that would last for over three years. Soldiers on both sides dug themselves in, to try to protect themselves against artillery and machine gun fire. Periodically, a general would order an offensive against the opposing trenches that would routinely yield hundreds of thousands of casualties in a few days. The devastating power of industrial weaponry had never been so starkly demonstrated. Later developments—the beginnings of air warfare, the use of tanks and submarines, and the introduction of poison gas—simply amplified the deadly effects of military technology.

Organization of production for this kind of war affected civilians as well as soldiers. All the European combatant governments increasingly took over economic control, rationing goods and assigning labor to maximize war output. Other government measures sought to control spies and to mount strident, nationalistic propaganda to whip up morale. This demonstration of government power, unprecedented in world history, would have its own repercussions in 20th-century world history.

Other fronts opened up. Austria quickly invaded Serbia. A larger battleground opened up in Eastern Europe. Military lines between German/Austrian and Russian forces were more fluid than those in Western Europe, but there was still massive loss of life on both sides. German cannon and machine guns took a huge toll on Russian peasant forces, leading to growing political discontent in Russia that would ultimately trigger outright revolution in 1917.

Italy was persuaded to enter the war on the side of Western allies, in 1915, hoping to grab territory from the Habsburg monarchy and to increase its overseas empire. The Italian-Austrian front was another bloody one, opening new political fissures in Italy.

The European war did come to an end, in 1918. The Russian Revolution had closed the eastern front, as Russian revolutionaries ultimately withdrew from combat. On the western front, German exhaustion plus the entry of the United States in 1917 (with hundreds of thousands of troops arriving by early 1918) finally tipped the balance, after a final German offensive failed. At the same time the Austrian effort against Italy collapsed and the Austro-Hungarian Empire split. German generals reluctantly agreed to an armistice in November, after the German emperor had abdicated in favor of a new republic (another sign of the move away from traditional political forms).

Loss of life in Europe was staggering. Britain lost almost a million soldiers, France 1.3 million, Russia 1.7 million, Germany 1.8 million, with many more millions wounded—a total of over 10 million dead and 20 million wounded. Economic losses were huge as well, at hundreds of billions of dollars and massive devastation particularly in northern France and Serbia.

From a world history standpoint, the European aspects of World War I constituted in a way a massive, murderous civil war within Western civilization, as nations literally tore each other apart. Loss of life, loss of leadership, loss of production all ensured that it would be impossible for Europe to regain its full role in the world at large even when the conflict ended. This was not fully realized at first, but it proved inescapable. As European production had focused on military goods, Japanese and American economies began to take advantage of export opportunities, to Europe and elsewhere. They gained ground in Europe in ways that could not be reversed. The British economy, particularly, never recovered the world position it had enjoyed in the later 19th century.

The war's disruption of Europe's role was compounded by tensions that persisted into the following decade. Germany and, ironically, Italy were aggrieved powers, eager for new nationalist gains. France was on the defensive. With the end of the Austro-Hungarian Empire and the distraction of Russia, east central Europe split into a host of small nations, not clearly economically or politically viable. Further European tensions were virtually guaranteed.

WORLD WAR I: THE WORLD

World War I was a global event not only because of Europe's new wounds, but because of direct involvements from other parts of the world. These followed, above all, from the ramifications of European imperialism, but also reflected the appetites of Japan and the United States and a fatal decision by the Ottoman Empire to align itself with the German side.

A small amount of fighting took place in Africa, mainly around the German colonies. And of course Germany's ultimate loss in the war raised the question of what to do with these colonies. The war effort also disrupted African exports. More important, Britain and particularly France recruited thousands of African troops to fight in Europe. They learned new military skills, they learned the vulnerabilities of European soldiers, and they learned more about the importance of nationalism.

Massive British use of Indian troops (mainly for use in the Middle East, against the Ottomans) had even greater effects in further stimulating nationalism. To sustain Indian involvement, Britain offered many promises about greater self-government, which for the most part it did not honor after the war's end. This gave a huge boost to a new generation of Indian nationalist leaders, including Mohandas Gandhi.

Britain and France angled for Japanese participation in the war, mainly to put pressure on Germany's Pacific colonies. The Japanese gladly took over German-held islands and also its lease in the Shandong peninsula of China, setting up new Asian conflicts after the war's end.

SOLVING PROBLEMS

MOBILIZING FOR TOTAL WAR

The casualty figures in World War I and the agonies of trench warfare draw primary attention, but behind the scenes the war also led to an unprecedented mobilization effort that demonstrated and extended the power of governments in industrial societies. This effort, in turn, has generated the idea that contemporary warfare can become unprecedentedly total, in terms of its involvement of economic resources, labor, and even culture. The problem to be solved was how to organize the production necessary to sustain the vehicles and weapons needed for, and often destroyed in, the war effort, and how to persuade ordinary citizens, through propaganda, that this kind of effort was justified.

In Germany, for example, generals were given the power to decide which workers should be sent to the front and which were needed for agriculture and industry. Joint boards were set up, representing labor as well as management, to enlist support—a sign that prewar social divisions had to yield in favor of war production. Because Britain blockaded imports, Germany faced significant problems of food supply, and authorized officials to tell farmers what to grow and what animals had to be slaughtered, while also regulating food prices to prevent urban riots. University professors were mobilized to provide justifications for German conquests in east-central Europe, including a "civilizing mission" in Slavic lands. Nationalist propaganda also included concealing defeats, so that many Germans were truly surprised, in 1918, to learn that they had lost the war.

British policies, if anything, went further, particularly in terms of regulating industry. Propaganda featured lurid (and fictitious) pictures of German soldiers killing Belgian babies and other atrocities designed to rouse deep anger. In most nations, political strife was frowned upon, with many opposition figures arrested, in favor of united support for the war effort. And growing concern about spies and news items that could undermine the war effort led to new police controls and censorship.

■**QUESTIONS:** *What is a good definition of total war, and how many total wars have been fought in the world since 1914? What were the implications of wartime mobilization for developments after the war had ended?*

The war had huge effects in the Middle East and Egypt. Led by Britain, which used many troops from Canada, Australia, and New Zealand, the Western powers opened a front in Turkey, with mixed results. Seeking to press the Ottoman government, once it entered the war on the German side, Western countries also encouraged Arab nationalists while simultaneously making promises to Jewish leaders about a homeland in Palestine. The war effectively completed the process of destroying the Ottoman Empire—another historical marker, reversing a pattern launched centuries before—and at the same time effectively prevented alternative political unity in the Middle East. New, sometimes conflicting nationalist aspirations and divisive interventions by Britain and France after the war guaranteed a new, but also a troubled future for this region in the next phase of world history.

Overall, the global effects of World War I involved heightened nationalism, new diplomatic tensions, and new challenges to European power—this last compounding the effects of the war in Europe itself. Here too, the war marked the end of the previous era—the long 19th century—and the opening of a new one.

And the watershed was a violent one. New weapons promoted a new willingness to kill unprecedented numbers of people, often from great distances. New or intensified hatreds, particularly between conflicting nationalistic entities, might promote violence as well. Here was a legacy to contemporary world history that is still being sorted out.

PATHS
TO THE PRESENT

World War I and the great revolutions that surrounded it—China's in 1911, Russia's in 1917—set huge changes in motion. The Great War's most obvious legacy is the disruption it caused, particularly the military, economic, and demographic blows to the West and the West's position in the world. Whether or not the war was the result of flaws in Western culture, it created major problems for the world's future.

The war also, of course, provided new opportunities. Women in Europe and the United States gained new working roles, and while this newfound freedom was quickly taken away after 1918, a precedent was set. Nationalists in India, Africa, and the Middle East gained new confidence, while amplifying their goals for independence. Business leaders in Japan and the United States saw new chances for global profit, the results of which echo through today's world economies.

The war's most obvious legacy to the present, however, was the change in the nature of war itself. Governments learned new forms of control and manipulation, which showed up in several ways in subsequent decades. Leaders in many nations learned the importance of new military technology. Perhaps most important, the war blurred the boundaries between military and civilian populations and activities—a change that affects many struggles in the contemporary world.

SUGGESTED WEB SITES

For recordings from World War I and the 1920 election, see http://rs6.loc.gov/ammem/nfhtml/nfhome.html; for more information on World War I, refer to http://www.worldwar1.com/ and http://www.lib.byu.edu/~rdh/wwi/. See also http://www.gwpda.org/photos/greatwar.htm.

SUGGESTED READINGS

Recent works on the war includes Richard F. Hamilton and Roger H. Herwig, *Decisions for War, 1914–1917* (2004); David Fromkin, *Europe's Last Summer: Who Started the Great War in 1914?* (2004); Michael E. Brown, ed., *Offense, Defense, and War* (2004); Richard S. Fogarty, *Race and War in France: Colonial Subjects in the French Army, 1914–1918* (2008); Hew Strachan, *The Outbreak of the First World War* (2004); Janet S. K. Watson, *Fighting Different Wars: Experience, Memory and the First World War in Britain* (2004); Gail Braybon, ed., *Evidence, History and The Great War: Historians and the Impact of 1914–1918* (2004); Richard F. Hamilton and Holger H. Herwig, eds., *The Origins of World War I* (2003); Annika Mombauer, *The Origins of the First World War: Controversies and Consensus* (2002); William N. Tilchin and Charles E. Neu, eds., *Artists of Power: Theodore Roosevelt, Woodrow Wilson, and Their Enduring Impact on U.S. Foreign Policy* (2006).

On the causes of World War I, see James Joll's *Origins of World War I* (1980), and K. Robbins's *The First World War* (1984). For a wider view, see Eric Hobsbawm's *The Age of Extremes: A History of the World, 1914–1991* (1996).

On other topics, see Sean Cashman, *America Ascendant: From Theodore Roosevelt to FDR* (1998); Niall Ferguston, *The Rise and Demise of the British World Order and the Lessons of Global Power* (2003); Aviel Roshwald, *European Culture in the Great War* (1999); and Robert Zieger, *America's Great War: World War I and the American Experience* (2000).

The World's First Industrial Period, 1750–1914

CONTACTS AND IDENTITIES

The long 19th century created unprecedented challenges for established identities because international exchange and Western intrusion were so far-flung. Groups in virtually every society sought to reject outside models, but they were increasingly hard-pressed to maintain a sense of local identity.

Some of the tensions were familiar from earlier passages in world history. As Christianity spread in Africa, for example, it roused opposition from those who benefited from, and found meaning in, the older, indigenous, polytheistic religions and the village power structure they sustained. But Christianity gained ground anyway (along with Islam in many regions), because it was associated with success and because many Africans, including young people or women who had less stake in the existing order, found various merits in it.

Other clashes were novel. The Chinese officials who destroyed the first regional railway may not have been interpreting Chinese technological traditions correctly, but they certainly thought they were defending established values. Japan's virtual civil war in the 1860s involved many samurai who sought to ban foreign influence, however unrealistic their hopes, given the country's new power imbalance with the West. Egyptians, around 1900, debated whether women should be veiled. Some reformers argued that requiring Egyptian women to wear veils branded Egypt as hopelessly backward and that change was essential, but others, including many women, rallied around the veil as a vital symbol of cultural identity—and this debate continues today in Muslim society. Protest movements such as the

Taiping rebellion in China combined new religious and reform interests with an effort to maintain some sense of Chinese identity as separate from the world at large.

Precisely because these tensions intensified, the availability of an apparently new agent of reconciliation—nationalism—was widely welcomed. Nationalism, though of European origin, spread widely around the world precisely because it promised to protect at least some aspects of established identity in terms that were also unassailably modern, given the West's acceptance of national loyalties. Small wonder that Arab, Indian, Turkish, Japanese, and Chinese nationalism—and by 1900, African as well—joined the nationalist parade that already included various eastern European and American countries.

Nationalism allowed Japan, for example, to accept huge changes that unquestionably undercut established feudal and Confucian identities, by proclaiming that key virtues of group loyalty and deference were being maintained. Nationalism allowed Arab and Turkish leaders to urge modernization of their societies, and even potential modifications of Islam, in the interests of enabling greater competitiveness with the West because nationalism also allowed—even urged—identification and preservation of older identities.

As a new loyalty bent on protecting identity, nationalism often "invented" some of the traditions it sought to maintain. Thus, by the 1880s, the Japanese imperial government was emphasizing loyalty to the emperor and the revival of Shinto as if they were age-old parts of the national heritage—which was not the case. American president Abraham Lincoln established Thanksgiving as a national holiday in an attempt to cement the country's fractured loyalties, strongly implying that this was an observance steeped in tradition—which, again, was not the case. Russian nationalists praised idealized peasant communities as models of Russian group loyalty far preferable to damaging Western individualism at a time when many Russian peasants suffered from growing poverty and participated in recurrent protests. Earlier, Latin American nationalists urged loyalty to governmental entities such as Venezuela or Argentina that were themselves new political units. In all of these cases, nationalism won growing acceptance and accommodated a need for identity in a changing world—in the process, however, it also introduced considerable further change.

Not surprisingly, in this context, some groups found nationalism itself a threat to identity. Ethnic minorities in Russia, for example, who were directly and sometimes violently attacked by conservative nationalists, began to generate small-group nationalism of their own. Zionism arose in western Europe in part out of fears that Jewish identity might be lost in the wave of larger German or French nationalist currents.

Thus, in a period of dramatic new connections around the world, defense of identity evoked both traditionalism and innovation.

PART VI

The Contemporary World, 1918 to Present

INTRODUCTION: A NEW PERIOD IN WORLD HISTORY

Almost everyone agrees that a new period opened in world history during the 20th century, but determining its main themes is a challenge. We remain close to events, chronologically and emotionally, which makes it hard to sort out durable priorities. The very fact that a major new period began complicates definitions, for we are probably still in the early stages of establishing the dominant new trends. It is easier to figure out which themes have abated. Finally, the 20th and 21st centuries themselves seem internally divided: the decades of world war and economic depression, 1914–1945; then the decades of cold war and decolonization, to the late 1980s; then the decades since 1991. What themes transcend these familiar subperiods?

It helps to begin the way historians usually start in setting up a new period: what events signal the transition? As we have seen, World War I launched or accelerated a process of relative Western decline that depression and World War II intensified. The West retained its important position on the world stage, but exhausted so many resources between 1914 and 1945 that its grip on the rest of the world slipped. Correspondingly, pressures for independence in the rest of the world increased from the 1920s on.

The new period of world history was marked, then, by a decline in the West's relative power—a decline that reversed several centuries of fairly steady gain. Decolonization was the most obvious countervailing process, as the West lost its direct political control over most of its overseas territories. But new military rivalries, new military capacities on the part of newly independent states, and expanded tactics such as guerrilla warfare also reduced the West's military dominance. The West retained great military power, particularly as the United States' role expanded, but it could not deploy its military assets as easily or as decisively as it had in the past, particularly after 1945. This was a huge change, particularly compared to those of the long 19th century.

Western economic power held up better than its military might, though Japan and the Pacific Rim increasingly became factors in the global picture. A world economy still existed, with relationships of great prosperity and economic dependence, and the West still shared the summit, though it no longer monopolized it. But a growing number of countries managed to carve out some independent space above outright dependence, without necessarily managing to rise to the top levels of fully industrialized, "developed" countries. Many societies expanded their industries, reducing the need to import items from the West. Here, too, was a process that began in the 1920s, with new policies in places such as Turkey and Iran, and that had expanded significantly by the early 21st century. Defining the world economy, in other words, became more complicated. The 19th-century divisions between industrial and dependent economies no longer applied so clearly.

The new world history does not yet have a terminus; societies around the world are still engaged in the new trends that took root after 1914—including, of course, adjusting to the changes in the West's position of power.

NEW THEMES

One of the major challenges in the process of determining the main themes of the current period in world history is that there are so many changes to record. Three profound trends stand out, however, along with realignment of global power relationships and the impact of wider participation in factory industry on the world economy and on regional economies alike.

First, global population exploded, more than tripling during the 20th century alone, to more than six billion people. This is a result, above all, of improved public-health measures and (despite continuing problems) increases in the food supply. By 1970 there were more people living than had ever reached adulthood in the entire previous history of the human species.

Population growth at this level triggered other major changes, such as widely expanding industry and unprecedented pressure on the environment. Crowding and poverty in some regions led to new patterns of emigration, with people from Africa, southeast and south Asia, and Latin America seeking jobs and homes in industrial centers. Population increase also caused unprecedented urbanization: by the 21st century, worldwide, more than half of all people lived in cities, a pattern previously achieved only by industrial societies. Latin America and the Middle East became heavily urban, with poor people seeking in cities resources that they could no longer find in the countryside. Giant cities containing many millions of people grew in India, China, and Latin America. The pressure of the world population explosion also helps explain the frequent unrest of urban and rural groups in the 20th and 21st centuries, whether the outlet is revolution, nationalism, or terrorism.

The second overriding trend involved the series of new technologies that revolutionized the speed of international transportation and, particularly, communication. Radio and international telephone connections were in place early in the 20th century, soon followed by air travel, and in more recent decades, satellite transmissions, international cell phones, and the Internet—all of which created opportunities for contact and cultural exchange had no precedent in world history. By 2000, more than a quarter of the world's population might watch a single event, such as World Cup soccer. The same communications revolution opened new capabilities for organizations, including the new multinational business corporations, and for military operations.

The third set of changes highlighted decisive, global shifts in social and political arrangements, essentially replacing characteristics of agricultural societies with new, though sometimes varied, patterns. In 1914, the dominant social class in most of the world's societies was the landed aristocracy. By 2009, it was an upper middle class of educated managers and big-business owners, a huge change. In 1914, most political regimes were empires or monarchies. By 2009, monarchy, except for figure-head rulers, was quite rare, and multinational empires had largely disappeared. Concerning gender, while men and women were still unequal by the 21st century, patriarchal conventions had been seriously modified, almost everywhere, by voting rights for women, new educational access, and other legal and social changes. By the end of the 20th century, rapidly declining birth rates added another dimension to the changing lives of women. The core challenges to the traditions of agricultural societies did not produce uniform responses. Monarchies might be largely gone, but there was massive divergence between democratic and authoritarian replacements. Women had new rights almost everywhere, but their economic conditions and even their gender goals varied widely. Finally, the method of innovation varied from one place to the next. Huge revolutions spurred changes in some cases, not only in social structure and politics but also (at least in principle) on women's conditions. In other places, new kinds of contacts and the process of decolonization set the context for innovation, though with less sweeping drama. It is also important to note that cultural changes were less decisive than those in politics and society.

Still, the third set of changes, in combination with the first two, was fundamental. The contemporary period differs markedly from the long 19th century in key themes. Power balances shifted, including a relative decline for the West; population explosion and the revolutions in global communications were supplemented by the new social and political trends. All this was punctuated and shaped, of course, by the criss-crossing of wars and revolutions that marked the birth of world history's newest era.

All major civilizations interacted with the century's leading themes, but as always, differences in circumstance and tradition created varied responses. Chapters in this part reprise the areas of major civilization, but in relation to the new challenges and opportunities, from Western civilization to eastern Europe, east Asia, south and southeast Asia, the Middle East, Latin America, and Africa. The part's final chapter looks at the trends that emerged at the dawn of the 21st century, some of which provide further definition for the themes of the period as a whole.

GLOBAL CONNECTIONS

With the new communications and transportation facilities as a base, the new period in world history was substantially defined by the unprecedented array of international links that developed. Literally every society had to react to an array of new contacts. Many societies hesitated in the initial decades of the new period. In various ways, Russia, Germany, Japan, the United States, and China sought to pull away from full entanglement with global politics or economics. By the 1970s, however, the new and unprecedented round of globalization was in full swing, with only a few, small holdouts.

New contacts included familiar items; for instance, missionaries fanned out to new areas. American evangelical missionaries flooded into eastern Europe and Latin America at the end of the 20th century. More conventional Christian and Muslim missionaries were widely active, often supported by the new facilities for global communication. During much of the 20th century, Marxist movements also supported essentially missionary activity, to convert new groups to this powerful political faith.

Student exchanges were not new in world history, but they became far more numerous and common from the 1920s on, save in wartime. Many universities in the United States, Europe, Australia, and Russia came to depend on substantial international attendance. New patterns of long-distance migration brought people from Asia and Africa to industrial centers. Transportation facilities allowed many to return home, often just for visits, bringing new habits with them. International tourism developed widely after World War II, bringing people from industrial centers, including Japan, to tropical paradises in Hawaii, Thailand, and the Caribbean—wherever sun and beaches could be found. Again, local workers in the tourist industry could pick up some new ideas—or new reasons to distrust foreign ways.

Commercial organizations deliberately fostered new types of global contacts. Far-flung international corporations used workers and sold products literally around the world. Corporations also developed to sell cultural products. By 1919, Hollywood was already emerging as the global capital for movies, and major film studios had branch offices in Latin America, South Africa, Lebanon, Australia, and elsewhere. By the 1970s, cultural exports—films, music, and TV shows—formed the second largest category in the United States (after aircraft), and by 2004, lifestyle exports constituted the largest category for Japan.

New political organizations also brought global influences. After 1945, the United Nations and its agencies disseminated new international standards for human rights or health care, often urging changes in family practices. The World Health Organization pressed individual countries to improve reporting and quarantine practices. International nongovernmental organizations flourished, particularly after 1970. They pressed governments and corporations to improve human rights policies, including the treatment of women and children, labor conditions, and environmental standards.

And of course there were events themselves, that increasingly became global. The 20th century's two world wars and the cold war touched every major society in some way—again, there was no precedent for this range of impact in world history. Even natural disasters took on global overtones. The horrific tsunami that occurred at the end of 2004 directly affected virtually all the land masses in and around the Indian Ocean, provoking intervention and humanitarian aid from every part of the world.

These previously unimagined shifts in connection among the world's populations created a spectacular framework for exchange, and it is essential to emphasize the situation's novelty. Two cautions, however. First, not everyone was equally exposed to the changes. By 2009, less than a third of the world's population, for example, had regular access to the Internet, though the percentage was rising rapidly. Rural areas were far less affected by global contacts than were urban centers. Access to global contacts indeed created new differentials within societies—American Midwesterners were more cautious about global contacts than their conationals on the two coasts; huge distinctions opened between rural and urban residents in India and Africa.

The second caution is familiar in world history, even amid the great changes of the contemporary period: societies and groups might still react quite differently to the same contacts. They might embrace them, they might selectively adapt to them, they might seek to ignore them, they might actively resist them—the permutations were considerable. Much of the world history of the past century involves the interaction between unprecedented, unavoidable contacts and the ways different regions sought to handle them.

28 The West in the Contemporary Period

Although one of the themes of 20th-century world history is the relative decline of the West, particularly for Europe, Western civilization remained a standard-bearer in many ways. By the early 21st century, it still was the wealthiest society in the world along with Japan. The artistic and popular cultural forms it generated had more influence on other civilizations than those of any other single society. One sign of the West's continued importance has been its role as a target for people in many parts of the world who dislike not only Western power but also the threat it poses to traditional values.

KEY QUESTIONS *The West encountered unusual troubles during the world war decades. What significant changes resulted? Do they still affect the West? What is the best definition of the principal features of Western civilization by the early 21st century, in light of 20th-century developments? Finally, are the United States and western Europe part of the same civilization, or have they parted ways?*

PATTERNS OF WESTERN HISTORY: 1914–1945

Picking up the pieces after World War I was extremely difficult, however, with the more than 10 million people who had been killed and the vast amounts of property destroyed. The European economy had suffered a shattering blow through the loss of investments abroad and huge debts accumulated internally to fund the wasteful war effort. A peace conference was held at Versailles; its work divided between desires for revenge

491

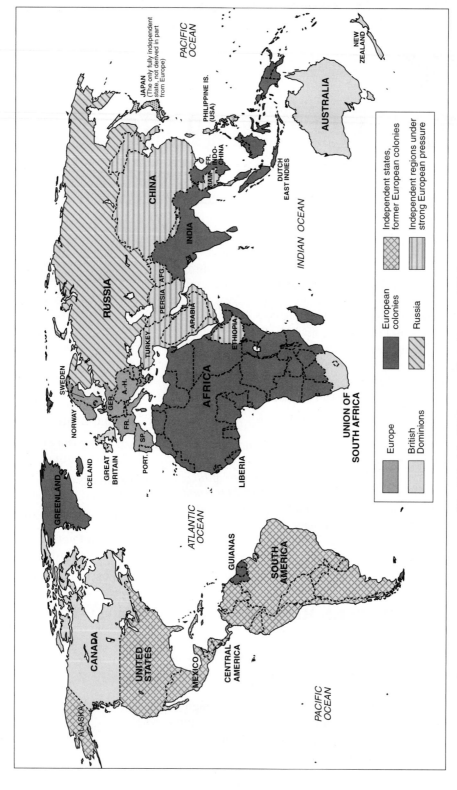

The World of Western Dominance, 1914

against Germany and the idealism represented by President Woodrow Wilson of the United States. Idealism led to the establishment of the League of Nations, designed to promote international harmony in the future, and the creation of a series of new states in central and eastern Europe, from the territory of Russia, the Habsburg monarchy, and Germany. Poland resurfaced, along with other new Slavic states and an independent Hungary. The new states were weak, however, and this created a source of tensions in European diplomacy for the foreseeable future. The League of Nations, although not insignificant in world affairs during the next 15 years, proved largely ineffective as well. At the same time, motives of revenge resulted in huge reparation payments and a loss of territory for Germany, generating further resentments. Even the victorious allies were unsatisfied: France still feared its German neighbor, the United States pulled back from European entanglements into an unrealistic isolationism—not even joining the League of Nations—and Italy bemoaned its lack of success in acquiring vast new territory.

World War I and the Versailles Peace Conference set the stage for the next two difficult decades of Western history. Diplomatic tensions eased somewhat during the 1920s, as Germany made some efforts to adjust to its reduced position, but fears and resentments still ran high. European and U.S. internal politics were largely ineffectual as a series of mediocre leaders gained power. Germany, now a republic, suffered at the hands of a number of groups who opposed democracy. Communist movements, linked to the Soviet regime that now ruled Russia, emerged to the left of socialist parties in many countries, serving as small but frightening revolutionary forces. The liberal middle sector of Western politics weakened, as many erstwhile liberals became more conservative in their desire to prevent major social reform. The absence of a strong center made effective government difficult, even in Britain,

where the parliamentary tradition was particularly strong.

New political tensions might have been manageable had postwar economic trends not proved so disastrous. Many nations suffered from massive inflation during much of the 1920s, the result of wartime debts and postwar dislocations. Prosperity returned toward the middle of the decade and the United States, in particular, enjoyed an industrial boom. But in 1929, a major economic depression occurred, as banks failed first in the United States and then throughout the Western world. The Great Depression resulted from a number of factors. Purchasing power was too low among many peasants and workers to sustain increased industrial production. Many peasants and American farmers faced a rapid decline in agricultural prices, due to overproduction; mechanized agriculture outstripped the demand for food in the Western world, and this limited farmers' ability to buy. Nonindustrial countries in eastern Europe and many other parts of the world also saw prices for their raw materials tumble as their production increased faster than Western demand; this crisis also weakened markets for Western goods. High tariffs, imposed by many nations to protect their own economies, added to the difficulties of trade. In essence, Western productive capacity outran available markets. As a result, speculative investments finally proved hollow, causing the stock market crash and bank failures of 1929.

The ensuing economic depression was the worst in modern memory. Millions of workers lost their jobs. Wages plummeted, and insecurity spread even among those who were employed. Levels of production collapsed, as up to a third of the economic capacity of countries such as Germany and the United States was idled by 1932. Although the worst of the Depression was over by the mid-1930s, its traces remained strong throughout the rest of the decade.

Only a few Western governments responded constructively to this economic crisis. Scandinavian states increased government spending, providing

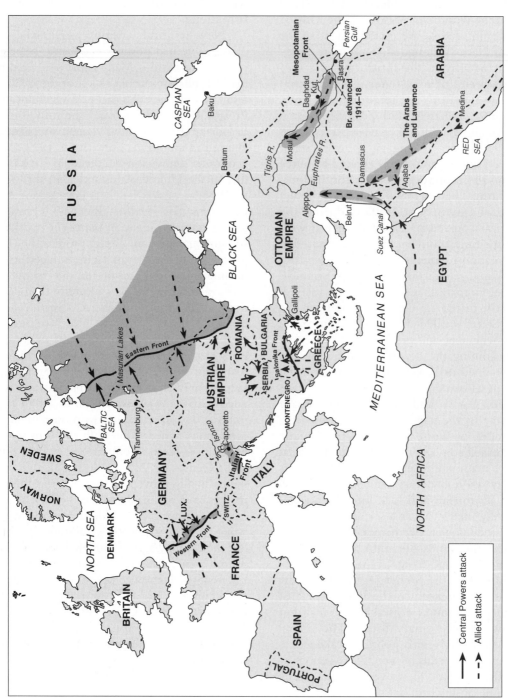

World War I

Central Powers attack

Allied attack

new levels of social insurance against illness and unemployment and foreshadowing the modern welfare state. In the United States, Franklin Roosevelt's New Deal, from 1933 on, enacted a number of social insurance measures and used government spending to stimulate the economy. The New Deal did not cure the American Depression, but it alleviated the worst effects and provided new hope that forestalled major political pressure against the established order. Britain and France, however, reacted weakly to the economic catastrophe. Both countries continued to be plagued by inept leadership. They were also torn between socialist and conservative forces, and their allies on the political extremes; effective action seemed impossible.

Nazism

The Depression led directly to a fascist regime in Germany in 1933. Fascism was a product of World War I; the movement's advocates, many of them former veterans, attacked the weakness of parliamentary democracy and the corruption and class conflict of Western capitalism. They proposed a strong state ruled by a powerful leader, who would revive the nation's forces through vigorous foreign and military policy. Fascists vaguely promised social reforms to alleviate class antagonism, and their attacks on trade unions and socialist parties pleased landlords and business groups alike. The first fascist regime arose in Italy in 1923, and fascist parties complicated the political process in a number of other nations during the 1920s. However, it was the advent of the National Socialist, or Nazi, regime in Germany, under Adolf Hitler, that made this new political movement a major force in world history.

Hitler appealed to a country bitter about its defeat in war and unusually hard hit by economic disorder. He promised many groups a return to more traditional ways; thus, many artisans voted for Hitler in the belief that preindustrial economic institutions, such as the guilds, would be revived. The middle class, including the leaders of big business, were attracted to Hitler's commitment to a firm stance against socialism and communism. Although Hitler never won a majority popular vote in a free election, his party did attain the largest single vote total by 1932. By this time, the effects of the Depression were compounded by the weak, divided response of Germany's parliamentary leadership in a country that had never fully accepted the validity of liberal political forms.

Once in power, Hitler quickly set about constructing a totalitarian state—that is, a new kind of government that exercised massive, direct control over virtually all the activities of its subjects. Hitler eliminated all opposition parties; he purged the bureaucracy and military, installing loyal Nazis in many posts. His secret police, the Gestapo, arrested hundreds of thousands of political opponents. Trade unions were replaced by government-sponsored bodies that tried to appease workers with low pay by offering full employment and various welfare benefits. Economic planning on the part of government helped restore production levels, with a particular emphasis on the manufacture of armaments.

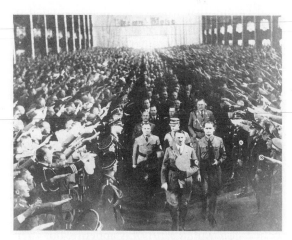

Nazi Party Congress in Nuremberg, Germany. The Führer is saluted by his "storm troopers," in a demonstration of the effective Nazi use of mass orchestrations.

Hitler solidified the power of his regime with constant, well-crafted propaganda, strident nationalism, and an incessant attack on Germany's Jewish minority. Hitler's hatred of Jews ran deep; he blamed them for various personal misfortunes and also for movements such as socialism and excessive capitalism that in his view had weakened the German spirit. Obviously, anti-Semitism served as a catchall for a host of diverse dissatisfactions. Anti-Semitism also benefited Hitler's cause by providing a scapegoat that could rouse national passions and distract the population from other problems. Measures against Jews became more and more severe, as Jews were forced to wear a letter on their clothing identifying them as Jews, their property was attacked and seized, and increasing numbers were sent to concentration camps. After 1940, Hitler's policy took an extreme turn, focusing on the total elimination of European Jewry. In this Holocaust, six million Jews were killed in the concentration camps of Germany and conquered territories; other groups, such as gypsies and homosexuals, were targeted as well.

Hitler's policies were based on preparation for war. He wanted not only to recoup Germany's World War I losses but also to create a land empire that would extend across much of Europe, particularly toward the east into the territory of allegedly inferior Slavic peoples. Progressively Hitler violated the provisions of the Treaty of Versailles that had limited German rearmament. In 1936, he intervened in a civil war in Spain, on the side of fascist forces. Within two years, he had annexed Austria and seized part, then all, of Czechoslovakia. To all these steps, the other European powers responded only weakly. France and Britain were too divided to pursue a resolute foreign policy. They negotiated with Hitler at Munich in 1938, offering him part of Czechoslovakia in the hopes that this concession would satisfy his appetite, but their feeble attempt at appeasement merely inspired Hitler to further demands. The United States remained isolationist; the Soviet Union was worried but too isolated from potential Western allies, who feared its communism, to pose an effective counterbalance.

World War II

With nothing standing in his way, Hitler moved forward, forming an alliance with the Soviet Union in 1939 that allowed both powers to attack Poland. This act finally convinced Britain and France that they could no longer sit idly by, and war was declared in September 1939. Hitler was far better prepared for conflict than were his opponents, and during the first three years of the war, his forces, in alliance with Italy, swept over much of western Europe. By 1942, Germany held France, Norway, the Low Countries, and the small Balkan states. However, an invasion of Russia in 1941, following the collapse of the brief alliance between Russia and Germany, resulted in Germany's armies being bogged down much as Napoleon's had been 130 years before. Furthermore, the United States, goaded by the Japanese attack on Pearl Harbor, entered the war in December 1941 on Britain's side. Three years of bitter fighting in Europe, the Pacific, and elsewhere followed. The Russian armies gradually recovered, with some assistance in the form of armaments from the United States, and pressed inexorably toward Germany's eastern borders. American and British forces, aided by resistance movements against Nazi occupation, drove Germany first from north Africa, then gradually from Italy. In 1944, a massive invasion force moved across the English Channel into France, and within a year the allies entered Germany from the west. Hitler committed suicide, and the European war drew to a close.

Like its predecessor, World War II resulted in a massive loss of life. Russia and Germany were hardest hit, along with the Jewish population of central and eastern Europe. Economic devastation was even greater than before. Hitler had drained the occupied countries of labor and productive

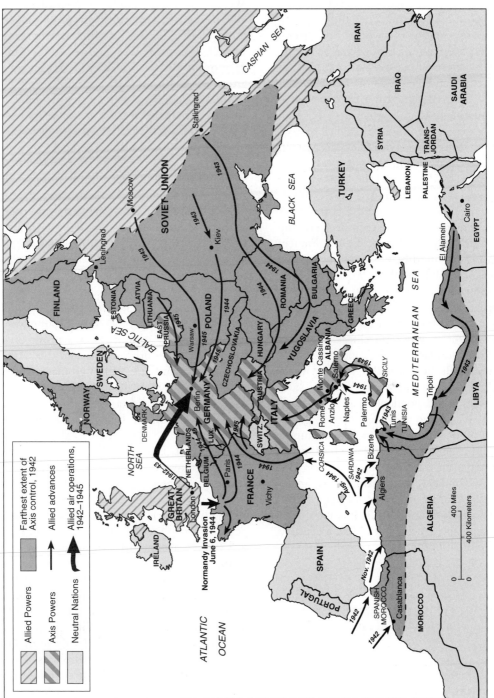

World War II: European and North African Theaters

goods, as part of his frenzied war effort. Massive bombing had destroyed many cities and factories, as well as transportation networks. For several years after the war, western Europe was the scene of grinding poverty, massive movements of dislocated people, and seeming hopelessness.

The war also redesigned the European map more fundamentally than World War I. Russian dominance extended through virtually all of eastern Europe. Only two countries in eastern Europe preserved any real independence: Greece, which was aided by Britain and the United States in maintaining a noncommunist government, and Yugoslavia, which established a communist regime independent of Soviet control. Germany was divided. Initially, the Soviet Union, France, Britain, and the United States each occupied a zone of Germany. But the three Western powers gradually allowed their zones to be united in an independent Federal Republic, whereas the Soviet zone converted into a communist state heavily dependent on Russian military support.

The new boundaries of Europe initiated a prolonged struggle between the Soviet Union and the United States, each with a network of European allies and dependencies. A "cold war" started in 1947, pitting the two postwar giants against each other. Russia, with its virtual empire extending into central Europe, saw the United States construct an alliance system among the leading Western states and retain a substantial military presence of its own to guard against possible Soviet attack. Here, within Europe's own boundaries, was the cruel result of half a century of disarray and violent internal struggle.

PATTERNS OF WESTERN HISTORY: 1950 TO THE PRESENT

To many observers, by 1950, the future of the Western world, or at least its traditional European base, seemed unbelievably bleak. If World War I had caused two decades of virtually unqualified confusion, could the consequences of a second conflict be anything but worse? In fact, the West seemed to recover both economic and political vigor in the decades after 1950; although the results were far from problem-free, they were certainly more constructive than the record of the years between both world wars.

Postwar Europe did not regain its previous diplomatic position. The dominance of the superpowers, the Soviet Union and the United States, continued. The United States formed the North Atlantic Treaty Organization (NATO) with most other Western governments in 1949, to oppose the Soviet threat; creation of the alliance ensured American influence over western Europe in dealing with the Soviet Union. At the same time, weakened by world war and pressed by surging nationalist movements throughout the world, western Europe lost most of its colonies, sometimes as a result of bitter struggle. India, southeast Asia, and then Africa all gained independence. Although many Europeans resented this sign of decline, attempts to reassert some shadow of earlier authority largely failed. In 1956, for example, Britain and France tried to seize control of the Suez Canal from a newly independent Egypt, only to be forced into retreat as a result of Egyptian resistance and U.S. and Soviet pressure. Even aside from the great power of the United States as a representative of generally Western values, the West did not suffer perpetual diplomatic decline. Decolonization was largely accepted by the people of western Europe, who did not attempt to hold out at the expense of political stability and economic growth at home. West European cultural and economic influence in many former colonies remained considerable. With time, leading European powers also gained a more independent voice vis-à-vis the United States. Although not military equals, individual states such as France were able to oppose American policies at key points.

Make no mistake: after World War II, the world's diplomatic framework decisively changed, and in many ways this transformation worked to the West's disadvantage. The balance of power within the West shifted to the United States. When the age of imperialism ended, the West's direct voice in Asia and Africa was dramatically lessened. The cold war between the United States and the Soviet Union meant that even the West's leading power could not set the tone for world affairs, instead facing a roughly equal rival. By 1949, when the Soviet Union developed the atomic bomb, it became clear that centuries of Western military superiority over all other civilizations had ended, and that eastern Europe now shared this claim of strength. The fearsome power of modern weapons and the intense East–West rivalry left many Westerners concerned that a new war could destroy their own civilization and that of most other parts of the world. At times, diplomatic processes seemed to have escaped human control.

Nonetheless, the Western world itself remained free from war after 1945. Early cold war tensions, particularly over the new divisions of Germany, brought war scares. In 1948–1949, the Soviet Union blocked off the city of West Berlin, a western enclave within East Germany, and only a massive American airlift relieved the pressure on supplies. Colonial wars also involved the West. France lost a bitter war to retain its possessions in and around Vietnam and then faced a long, ultimately unsuccessful struggle to keep Algeria. Finally, in 1949, the United States, with wider world interests now than western Europe, became involved in a war in Korea and then, in the 1960s, in a long and disheartening struggle in Vietnam, both against communist forces. These regional wars were important, of course, but the fact remains that even major threats of war within the West now receded, as at least for a time the West became one of the world's more internally peaceful civilizations.

A key ingredient of the West's new diplomatic environment involved explicit initiatives by western Europe to set its own diplomatic house in order after 1945, with some American encouragement. Eager to prevent further nationalist wars and also anxious to promote economic development, leading west European nations joined hands in economic cooperation. Initial moves to coordinate industrial policies led in 1958 to the formation of the European Economic Community, which promoted full-scale exchange across national boundaries. Although the Common Market, as it is called, ultimately broadened to include Britain, Ireland, Denmark, Greece, Spain, and Portugal, in addition to its initial members, West Germany, France, Italy, and the Low Countries, it did not become a single government. However, the organization did develop common policies and a common bureaucracy to oversee economic relations and, to an extent, coordinate other policies. Nationalist tensions receded to a lower point than ever before in modern European history. In 1993, the organization—now known as the European Union or EU—created full tariff unity and planned further integration, possibly involving a single currency and exchangeable rights of citizenship. The new currency unit, the euro, was launched in 1999, even as additional countries moved closer to membership in the EU. In 2004, a number of east-central European countries joined the EU.

More striking still were new economic and political trends. Particularly during the 1950s and 1960s, the doldrums of the interwar decades were reversed. Political tensions declined, while economic growth soared. Western society avoided major economic depressions, although there were years of slackening prosperity; most Western nations enjoyed a 2–8 percent growth rate per year. The West easily retained its lead over most other civilizations in terms of per capita prosperity, and indeed the gap between its wealth and that of many agricultural societies widened. Only Japan caught up in this regard. Within the West, mass affluence, now exhibited by widespread ownership of cars, refrigerators, and the now ubiquitous television set, reached unprecedented levels. The United States, whose population had achieved affluence earlier, found its prosperity rivaled by dynamic European countries such as West Germany and France.

Western economic development was spurred by the widespread transformation of leadership after World War II. In western Europe, men and women who had fought in resistance movements against Nazism vowed to avoid the errors of the past and to create a new society. The influence of the older aristocracy was further reduced. Training for west Europe's elite now broadened to recruit more talented people from worker and peasant families, as support for higher education and the availability of scholarships increased. University education itself was revamped to focus on more technical subjects. A new generation of managers, with a redefined mission and educational background, brought new dynamism to the West in various fields.

During the crucial years immediately after 1945, Western society also forged new political institutions. Carefully wrought democratic constitutions were developed in West Germany and Italy, providing more stable parliamentary institutions than ever before. France revived its parliamentary system after the years of Nazi occupation; in 1958, government instability in the face of the paralyzing colonial war in Algeria prompted the nationalist leader Charles de Gaulle to engineer a new constitution, providing for a strong but democratically elected presidency overseeing parliament. Spain, Portugal, and Greece installed new democratic systems in the 1970s. Democracy and relative political stability were encouraged by the virtual destruction of the radical right in politics, discredited by Nazi excesses and defeat in war. Most Western countries had a strong conservative party fully committed to the democratic system. On the left, although significant communist movements remained in a few countries, reformist socialist parties, also committed to the democratic process

and extensive personal liberties, won wide support outside North America. The communist minority itself declined by the 1980s. The new political spectrum thus provided a multiparty system, with leadership characteristically alternating between major parties, depending on the performance of the economy, but the spectrum was bounded by the commitment of most groups to the basic political process. Even communist parties in western Europe relied mainly on election efforts, abandoning attempts at revolutionary agitation.

The political system was altered, finally, by the construction of more extensive welfare institutions. In France and Italy, coalition governments combining conservatives, socialists, and communists enacted new welfare programs between 1945 and 1948. These programs provided state-sponsored medical insurance, payments to large families, and greater regulation of working conditions. France and other countries also created more formal state economic planning, to guide in postwar recovery and then further industrial development. Between 1945 and 1951, Great Britain extended its welfare state under the leadership of the Labor Party. The British welfare state featured an unusually elaborate program of socialized medicine, with the government paying most medical bills from tax revenues; it also entailed government housing programs and other social measures. Most other Western nations extended their welfare and economic planning activities; Canada, for example, enacted a state-funded medical insurance program. Even the United States, which had a more restricted array of welfare programs than most other Western countries, initiated the Great Society measures of the 1960s, providing medical insurance for the indigent and elderly, expanding the Social Security system, and passing a number of laws to protect the rights of minorities and women.

The pattern of economic growth and political stability that took shape in the postwar West

Rubble on the streets of Notting Hill after a race riot in London in 1958.

feminism and environmental protection, entered the arena during the 1970s partly as an aftermath of the student protests; in some western European countries, a terrorist movement, focused on the kidnapping of political and business leaders, and sometimes their assassination, caused anxiety as well. Economic growth also slowed during the 1970s, partly because of rising energy costs; in the late 1970s and early 1980s, the Western world faced its greatest economic recession since the postwar recovery. New leadership sprang up within the British Conservative Party and the U.S. Republican Party, seeking to reduce the costs and size of the welfare state to spur new economic growth. Additional political currents arose in other Western countries, including new rightist parties and "Green" environmentalist movements.

Key problems intensified in the 1990s and early 2000s. Global economic competition hit the West hard. In Europe, the result was substantial unemployment, up to 12 percent or more, as goods requiring less skilled labor now came from elsewhere. The United States faced similar pressures but created a larger number of low-paying jobs; here, the new trend involved growing inequalities in income, greater than in any other industrial society. All Western nations, amid economic pressure, had to reconsider welfare state expenditures, and most cut back; again, the United States, with a smaller welfare system than most others, reduced protections for the poor most systematically. Various political changes accompanied these developments. More zealous conservatism surfaced particularly in the United States. Liberal and socialist movements in western Europe as well as in North America developed a more moderate stance, less wedded to welfare traditions. A few new currents of protest developed: a racist, neofascist movement in France called the National Front, a surge of paramilitary groups in the United States on the far right.

Terrorist activity was another problem. This activity involved usually random attacks, with

was disrupted in the late 1960s by a series of student protests, compounded in the United States by civil rights demonstrations and rioting among urban blacks. Campus unrest at major American universities focused on the war in Vietnam, which many students regarded as futile and immoral. Young people in Europe and the United States also targeted the materialism of their societies, seeking the embrace of more idealistic goals and greater justice. Student uprisings in France in 1968 created a near revolution. By the early 1970s, new rights for students and other reforms, combined with police repression, ended the most intense student protests. But some ongoing political concerns, including guns or explosives, to dramatize a cause. Some terrorist activity within Europe lingered from the protests of the 1960s, with radical gangs in Italy, for example, periodically attacking businessmen. Some activity resulted from nationalist agitation, as in violence by people advocating independence for the Basque ethnic group in Spain. Irish nationalist battles with British control over Northern Ireland also resulted in terrorism. A right-wing zealot in the United States bombed a federal building in Oklahoma City. By the 1990s, tensions with some elements in Islam generated terrorism. Countries such as France, with a growing Islamic minority, saw small groups generate some incidents, designed to protest Western activities in the Middle East or to attack Jews. Czechen rebels in Russia used bombs in Moscow. On September 11, 2001, individuals associated with the militant Al Qaeda movement flew jetliners into the World Trade Center in New York and the Pentagon in Washington, DC. Subsequent terrorist attacks hit Indonesia (with Australians a particular target), Spain, and Britain. This produced growing international police and military activity against terrorism.

Despite these important issues, Western society after 1950 has been relatively free from traumatic events, compared to the frenzy of the 1920s and 1930s. Decolonization created tension; U.S. involvement in world diplomacy produced a number of new concerns; the student movement of the late 1960s was an indication that all was not well in the affluent society. Cushioned by the rapid rise in wealth, however, the Western world remained considerably freer from major upheavals than most other civilizations in the postwar decades. Indeed, boredom itself became an issue, as observers worried that the welfare state created too much security, and political apathy was so pervasive that many people no longer bothered to vote. Had Western society achieved a new harmony, or were the postwar decades a period of deceptive tranquility before a new storm?

WESTERN POLITICAL INSTITUTIONS IN THE 20TH CENTURY

Two somewhat contradictory themes ran through the political development of Western society after 1900. On the one hand, the power of the state increased; on the other hand, a commitment to democratic and liberal values remained strong and, after 1945, gained ground.

The rising power of the state showed in both world wars. Governments in democratic nations such as Britain and the United States increased their regulation of economic activities, introducing rationing and the allocation of labor. Governments mounted massive propaganda campaigns to win the passionate loyalty of citizens to the military effort; enemies were pictured as the epitome of evil; newspapers were censored and the new media of radio and motion pictures were used to further intensify patriotism. The powers of wartime government helped inspire the totalitarian dictatorships of Nazi Germany (and also communist Russia). Nazism demonstrated that under stress, a major Western society could abandon liberal values in favor of a government dedicated to the destruction of all competing sources of power and the manipulation of individual citizens through mass education and propaganda. Authoritarian governments in some other states, such as fascist Italy and, after 1936, a semifascist Spain, also used new police and propaganda powers to repress opposition.

More generally, the rise of the welfare state throughout most of the West after 1945 represented a major extension of government power. Government expansion under the New Deal greatly increased the importance of the American state, which was then extended by the growth of military spending from World War II until the end of the cold war. Throughout the West, governments assumed the responsibility for providing some coverage of health-care costs, adequate

HISTORY DEBATE

CONVERGENCE

The Western world split apart during the 1930s, between fascist and democratic systems. After 1945, however, European nations became more similar than ever (although not identical)—a phenomenon called *convergence*. Industrial growth reached countries such as Italy. The results of World War II eliminated some German peculiarities, such as a rabidly conservative aristocracy. The spread of democracy was obviously a convergent development. So were key social trends, such as an aging population and new roles for women. Nationalism declined. Growing west European unity both reflected and furthered the convergence phenomenon.

Convergence also reduced some key differences between Europe and the United States. On the west European side, the elimination of the traditional peasantry and the final demise of the aristocracy, along with rapid economic growth, made social and economic structures more similar on both sides of the North Atlantic. A prosperous Europe also opened the door to the consumer culture of the United States, providing a growing (if occasionally critical) market for American TV shows, fast foods, even a Euro Disney. Because of new immigration, Europe also developed some racial tensions similar to those in the United States, although usually less severe. On the American side, the New Deal and World War II had created a stronger government, more like its European counterparts, though the United States did not develop as extensive a welfare state. Although American popular culture predominated, European contributions such as the miniskirt and the Beatles moved easily across the Atlantic in the other direction.

Differences remained. The United States participated with Europe in more open sexuality, but the nation was more prudish; topless beaches, the norm in Europe, were not popular in the United States. American moralism also showed in an unusually intense antismoking crusade. The largest new distinction involved obvious differences in military policy. The United States, the world's greatest power, rapidly increased its peacetime army and armaments expenditures—spending rose 300 percent in the 1950s alone. American foreign policy, as a result, was more influenced by military pressures than was true in Europe, which often boasted of pioneering a civilian welfare society. Correspondingly, Europe depended on American military protection while its own global military capacity steadily diminished.

Indeed, from the 1990s on, Europe and the United States seemed to be diverging once again. European resentment against aggressive United States military policies crested with massive protests against the invasion of Iraq in 2003 (even though some European countries participated). The United States proved much more comfortable with free market capitalism than western Europe did, where there was greater reluctance to dismantle the welfare state (and, some critics argued, lower prospects for economic growth as a result). The United States also remained a far more religious society with a significant Protestant fundamentalist movement largely absent in Europe but gaining ground on American shores from the 1970s onward. Europeans also accepted new values such as opposition to the death penalty—outlawed as a condition of membership in the EU—whereas the United States was more conservative. The undeniable convergence of the postwar decades may have begun to unravel.

working conditions, and protection against dire poverty. The United States, more fully committed to older liberal values that relied on individual initiative, stood slightly apart in this movement. But even here, by the 1970s, 21 percent of total

tax income was applied to social welfare payments. Expanding welfare functions and growing involvement in economic planning obviously broadened the role of the state in individual lives. Taxes increased, and so did the regulation of how employers could hire and fire, what crops farmers could plant, where poor people could live. Government bureaucracies expanded steadily.

The rise of the state has been balanced, however, outside the period of fascist regimes, by the West's continued devotion to a multiparty democracy and substantial freedoms of speech, press, religion, and assembly. The West has developed a mixed system, in which important governmental authority is combined with private enterprise. In the economy, for example, state planning has left the operation of most businesses in private hands. West European countries did nationalize some economic sectors, such as railroads and mines. The nationalization movement took place primarily during the period of recovery after World War II, but a French socialist regime extended nationalization again in the early 1980s. Even here, however, most businesses have operated through private decision-making within frameworks partly established by government.

The extension of liberal, democratic systems after 1945 showed the continuing strength of parliamentary institutions in Western political culture. West Germany established a far more solid democracy than it had managed in the 1920s. Political debate has centered on significant disagreements between conservatives and socialists about the extent of the welfare state or diplomatic policy, but it has not called the system into question. Although conservatives dominated German politics through most of the 1950s and 1960s, and again in the 1980s and early 1990s, socialist leadership took power peacefully at a number of points. The 1989 collapse of the Soviet empire brought about German unification in 1991, partly because of extensive East German demands for democracy. By the mid-1980s, the Western world was more fully characterized by a single political system—liberal democracy—than at any time since the decline of feudalism. From Australia and New Zealand through North America to western Europe, a

tension between multiparty rivalry and personal freedom on the one hand, and powerful state planning, taxation, and welfare systems on the other, has constituted the core of modern politics. Alternative political ideologies such as fascism and even Marxism have declined.

The rise of a strong state democracy was accompanied by the decline of classic diplomatic and military issues in Europe. Old antagonisms between France and Germany or Britain and the continent declined. So did commitments to imperialism. Although west European governments participated in the cold war, military issues and expenditures receded. U.S. military concerns, however, increased, as did American diplomatic influence in European affairs—even after the cold war had ended, the United States continued to take a lead in new issues such as the strife in the former Yugoslavia. Tensions between the United States and western Europe occurred at times, particularly during surges of French nationalism or when American policy became high-handed, but they were rarely acute—never reaching the pitch of the former nationalist rivalries within the West. In 2009, a new American president, Barack Obama, worked to restore greater collegiality in Western relations.

CONTEMPORARY WESTERN CULTURE

Western culture continued to display great vitality during the 20th century, although at times it seemed to lack coherence. Artists and composers stressed stylistic innovation, against older traditions and even the efforts of the previous generation. Scientific work flourished, as the West remained the center of most fundamental inquiry in the theoretical sciences. However, complex discoveries, such as the principle of relativity in physics, qualified older ideas that nature can be explained in a few sweeping scientific laws. And the sheer specialization of scientific research removed much of it from ready public understanding. Because no unifying assumptions represent the essence of formal intellectual activity in the contemporary West, neutral terms such as *modern* or *postmodern* are used even in the artistic field. Disciplines that once provided an intellectual overview, such as philosophy, declined in the 20th century or were transformed into specialized research fields; many philosophers, for example, turned to the scientific study of language, rather than writing basic statements about the nature of life and the universe. Although work in theology continued between both Catholic and Protestant thinkers, it no longer commanded center stage in intellectual life. No emphasis was placed on an integrated approach; no agreement was reached on what constitutes an essential understanding of human endeavor.

The dynamism of scientific research formed the clearest central thread in Western culture after 1900. Growing science faculties commanded the greatest prestige in expanding universities; individual scientists made striking discoveries, while a veritable army of researchers cranked out more specific findings than scientists had ever before produced. In addition, the wider public continued to maintain a faith that science held the keys to understanding nature and society and to improving technology and human life. Finally, although scientific discoveries have varied widely, a belief in a central scientific method persists: form a rational hypothesis, test through experiment or observation, and emerge with a generalization that will show regularities in physical behaviors and thus provide human reason with a means of systematizing and even predicting such behaviors. No other approach to understanding in Western culture has had such power or widespread adherence.

The first scientific breakthrough of the 20th century took shape with the discovery of the behavior of atomic particles. Experiments with X-rays and uranium produced the knowledge of electrons and the nucleus of the atom. At about the same time, by 1905, the work of Albert Einstein in Berlin transformed the former idea, central to Newtonian physics, of physical matter as a solid essence that behaved in absolutely uniform ways. According to Einstein's theory of relativity, space and time are not absolutes but are always relative to the observer measuring them. Einstein used time as a fourth dimension to explain behaviors of light and planetary motion that had been misstated in Newtonian physics. Radiation and other electronic activity are not regular but occur in discontinuous waves. Increasingly complex mathematics, involving the abstract language of differential equations, was essential in understanding the actual behavior of both planetary bodies and particles within the atom. By the 1930s, physicists began to experiment with bombarding basic matter with neutrons, particles that carry no electric charge; this work was to culminate during World War II in the development of the atomic bomb. Research in physics continued after World War II with a combination of increasingly sophisticated observation, made possible by improved telescopes and then lasers and space satellites, and the complex mathematical theories facilitated by the theory of relativity. Astronomers made substantial progress in identifying additional galaxies and other phenomena in space; the debate about the nature of matter also continued.

Breakthroughs in biology have primarily involved genetics. The identification, in the 1860s, of inheritance characteristics received wide attention only after 1900. By the 1920s, researchers experimenting with the increasingly familiar fruit fly determined exact rules for genetic transmission. In the 1940s, the discovery of the structure of the basic genetic unit by British and American scientists, the famous double helix pattern of deoxyribonucleic acid (DNA), advanced the understanding of how genetic information is transmitted and can be altered.

Biologists were also responsible for major improvements in health care. New drugs, beginning with penicillin in 1928, revolutionized the treatment of common diseases, whereas immunization virtually eliminated scourges such as diphtheria. Findings on hormones and their connection to certain behaviors, leading in the 1920s to the science of endocrinology, also had widespread medical applicability. Genetics itself, by the 1970s, gave rise to a host of industries that utilized scientific principles to produce new medicines, seeds, and pesticides.

Nevertheless, the new science has also had some troubling features, even apart from its use in weapons of destruction and its sheer complexity. The physical world is no longer considered neatly regulated, as it had been by Newtonian physics. Genetics made it clear that evolution proceeded by a series of random accidents, not through any consistent pattern. The use of the rational, scientific method thus has not produced the kind of simple worldview that it had resulted in a century or so before, and the ensuing uncertainties have influenced some artists in their attempts to convey an irrational, relativist universe. However, for most people in the West, the belief in progress, defined in terms of both better technology and a rational understanding of nature, largely persists.

The rational method, broadly conceived, also advanced in the social sciences from 1900 on. The German sociologist Max Weber worked to characterize general features of institutions such as bureaucracies, for analysis and comparison. Many sociologists promulgated theories of human society, or aspects of it such as the behavior of elites, on the assumption that rationally conceived models captured the essential reality of human affairs. In economics, quantitative models of economic cycles or business behavior have increasingly gained ground. Work by the British economist John Keynes, stressing the importance of government spending to compensate for loss of purchasing power during an economic depression, played a great role in the policies of the American New Deal and efforts by European planners to control the economic cycles after World War II.

Like the sciences, the social sciences became increasingly diverse and specialized. As in the sciences, many social scientists sought practical applications for their work. Psychologists became involved, for example, in not only defining and treating mental illness but also trying to promote greater work efficiency. Governments called on economic forecasting. Social science thus added to the impression of an explosion of rationally generated and useful knowledge, even when research pointed to deterministic or irrational aspects of human affairs. Most leading social scientists continued to emphasize the quest for consistency in human and social behavior. After World War II, the increasing use of mathematical models and laboratory experiments in the social sciences enhanced this emphasis.

Most 20th-century artists, concerned with capturing the world through impressions rather than through reason or the confinements of literal reality, worked against the grain of science and social science. Painting became increasingly nonrepresentational. The cubist movement, headed by Pablo Picasso, rendered familiar objects as geometrical shapes; after cubism, modern art moved even further away from the tenets of normal perception, stressing purely geometrical design or other expressionistic techniques. The focus was on mood, the individual reaction of viewers to the individual reality of the artist. Musical composition involved the use of dissonance and experimentation with new scales; after World War II, a growing interest in electronic instrumentation added to this diversity. Because writers are, in fact, constrained by words, their stylistic innovation was generally less extensive. However in poetry, the use of unfamiliar forms, ungrammatical constructions, and sweeping imagery continued the movement of the later 19th century. Playwrights experimented with new types of staging and unconventional dramatic norms, often seeking to involve the audience in direct participation. In literature, the novel remained dominant, but it turned toward

This 1945 painting, *Figuras* (Figures), by Pablo Picasso, a leading figure in 20th-century modern art who was born in Spain but worked primarily in France, is closer to Surrealism than to the cubist style that characterized his work during the early years of the 20th century, although elements of Cubism are on display in this painting. *Source:* Artists Rights Society, Inc.

and public taste, generally continued. Some politicians, including Adolf Hitler, campaigned against what they saw as the decadence and immorality of modern art, urging a return to more traditional styles. Certainly art did not hold its own against the growing prestige of science.

However, artistic vision was not simply a preoccupation of artists. Designs and sculptures based on abstract art began to grace public places from the 1920s on; furnishings and films also reflected modernist themes. Most revealing of a blend between art, modern technology, and public taste was the development of a characteristic 20th-century architectural style, the "modern" or "international" style. The use of new materials, such as reinforced concrete and massive sheets of glass, allowed the abandonment of much that was traditional in architecture. The need for new kinds of buildings, particularly for office use, and the growing cost of urban space also encouraged the introduction of new forms such as the skyscraper, pioneered in the United States. In general, the modern style of architecture sought to develop individually distinct buildings—sharing the goal of modern art to defy conventional taste and cultivate the unique—while conveying a sense of space and freedom from natural constraints. Soaring structures, free-floating columns, and new combinations of angles and curves were features that described leading Western buildings from 1900 on. Following World War II, when reconstruction in Europe and the growth of the U.S. West and Southwest provided massive opportunities for building, the face of urban space in Western society was greatly transformed.

There were a few unifying themes between the artistic and scientific approaches. A constant quest for the new was one feature: as artists sought new styles, scientists sought new discoveries. Furthermore, Western culture in the 20th century, in both art and science, became increasingly secular. Individual artists, writers, and scientists might proclaim religious faith, but

the exploration of moods and personalities, rather than the portrayal of objective events or clear story lines. A vast gulf grew between the scientific approach and the artistic framework as to how reality can be captured and, to an extent, what constitutes reality.

Many people ignored the leading modern artists and writers, in favor of more commercial artistic productions and popular stories. The gap that had evolved earlier, between avant-garde art church institutions had long since lost control over basic style or content. In western Europe, despite an important reform movement within the Catholic church that abandoned traditional ceremonies in favor of more direct contact between priest and worshippers, religion played a minor role in both formal and popular culture. Regular church attendance tended to be of interest only to a minority—5 percent of the British population, for example, by the 1970s. In the United States, religion maintained a greater hold, and both church attendance and popular belief remained at much higher levels than elsewhere in Western society. The United States also witnessed, both in the 1920s and again after World War II, a greater variety of popular revival movements and attempts to use religion to maintain or restore traditional values. Here was a clear indication that, for some individuals, neither the artistic nor the scientific approach to understanding was fully satisfactory—and this became yet another ingredient in the cultural diversity and tension of Western society.

Western culture was not a monopoly of European civilization in the 20th century. Modern art forms, particularly in architecture, spread widely. The achievements of Western science, at least those related to technology and medicine, often had to be taken into account by societies seeking their own industrial development. Western arts and sciences were, by the same token, greatly enriched by many practitioners from other cultures—by Japanese artists, for example, or Indian medical researchers and computer scientists. Elements of Western culture thus became international, and in tracing their roots, we must link most accomplishments to a number of other civilizations. Yet no other culture, not even the Japanese, created quite the same balance between an overwhelming interest in science and an all-important concern for stylistic innovation and individual expression in the arts.

ECONOMY AND SOCIETY

During the 20th century, rapid transformation characterized the economy and social organization of Western civilization. By the latter part of the century, some of the changes seemed almost as fundamental as those that had ushered in the Industrial Revolution two centuries before. The recurrent shifts in technology, economic organization, and social structure in Western industrial society had significant effects on the rest of the world as well, making it hard for industrializing nations to "catch up" to Western levels.

To begin with, economic change involved new products. During the first decades of the century, synthetic textile fibers, such as rayon and nylon, introduced variety into the clothing industry. Radios and, by the 1950s, early television brought instant entertainment and news into homes across the land (see Table 28.1). The automobile, although invented before 1900, increasingly became a consumer staple, first in the United States and then, after World War II, in western Europe.

Economic change involved, in addition, new forms of organization. The growing role of the state in formal planning was one aspect of this. In the private sector, corporate business became increasingly common, furnishing giant companies with extensive funds for widespread investment. Older family enterprises declined

Table 28.1
TELEVISION OWNERSHIP IN 1957 AND 1965

Country	1957	1965
France	683,000	6,489,000
Germany	798,586	11,379,000
Italy	367,000	6,044,542
The Netherlands	239,000	2,113,000
Sweden	75,817	2,110,584

Sources: The Europa Year Book 1959 (London, 1959) and The Europa Year Book 1967, vol. 1 (London, 1967).

further. By the 1920s and again after World War II, many corporations established an international base of operations. U.S. firms took the lead here, for the extensive American market provided both capital and experience in dealing with large markets. However, a number of European-based firms became multinational as well. They had marketing and supply offices, and production subsidiaries, on several continents. In domestic markets and to an extent internationally, the concentration of ownership among a small number of corporations was the rule. A multitude of aspiring automobile producers before World War I thus settled into a handful of big producers in most Western countries between the wars, and further concentration, including international operations, occurred after World War II. As one result, the Ford Motor Company manufactured cars in Britain and Germany, whereas German and French automakers stepped up operations in the United States, Mexico, and Brazil.

Agriculture experienced an organizational revolution of its own, particularly after World War II. In western Europe, peasant farming gave way to cooperatives for purchases and sales; most small landholders acquired new market skills as well as modern equipment, making them more like rural business executives than peasants. In the United States, Canada, and Australia, great concentrations of land operation, called *agribusiness*, arose after 1950, as purely family farms became increasingly marginal. Organizational change plus improved machinery, seeds, and fertilizers steadily raised agricultural productivity in the Western world, although some worried about a decline in the actual quality of foods and also growing environmental damage from the chemical spraying and other measures designed to maximize production.

Refinements in organization also affected the structure of work. Early in the 20th century, U.S. firms took the lead in developing ways to increase the pace of manufacturing by defining jobs and supervising workers more closely. By 1910, early forms of the assembly-line system were in effect, pioneered at Henry Ford's automobile plant. Such operations had workers performing repetitious tasks with a minimum of motion and thought, becoming as much like the machines they worked with as was humanly possible. After World War II, assembly-line procedures were modified by the use of more automated equipment, with machines themselves—including, by the early 1980s, robots—performing some of the most routine functions.

As it had since industrialization began, economic change meant new technologies. The growing use of the internal combustion engine in manufacturing and transport, and growing use of petroleum instead of coal for fuel, marked important steps early in the century. Coal mining, long a staple of Western industrialization, declined, and some regions, particularly western Europe, became dependent on fuel imports since their own oil holdings were small. Faster and more mechanized equipment steadily increased manufacturing productivity. Early in the century, the production of machines was revolutionized by the use of automatic riveters, drills, and other equipment that provided the technological basis for an assembly-line operation in what had been a craft industry. The production of chemicals and ubiquitous plastics required automated procedures for transporting, mixing, and molding ingredients. After World War II, a technological revolution took shape in communications and information storage as well, with the introduction of computers; in the 1970s, the development of the microchip made computers smaller and more flexible and increased the speed and volume of information flow, while displacing conventional storage operations such as manual filing.

The economic advance of Western society was not, of course, without its setbacks.

During the decade of the Depression, many wondered if the economy could ever recover its former vitality. The two world wars resulted in immense loss and dislocation. The economic slowdowns of the late 1970s and early 1980s, with rising rates of unemployment and fierce foreign competition, particularly from east Asia, raised anxieties anew. In the 1990s, global competition produced high unemployment in western Europe, while inequality in income increased in the United States. Furthermore, not all Western nations fared equally well in the economic development process; previous leaders such as Great Britain fell behind until the 1990s. Australia and Canada produced large quantities of foods and minerals for export, which made them unusually dependent on the prosperity of more fully industrial centers such as Japan or the United States, although they maintained considerable industries of their own. By 2000, and again with the global economic crisis of 2008, many people in the West worried about job loss to rising industrial, but low-wage giants such as China and also about the outsourcing of services or jobs to English speakers in India or French speakers in Morocco.

Nevertheless, for the past six decades as a whole, the theme of continued economic vitality and change remains valid. Western society was quick to recover from wartime destruction, for example, bouncing back rapidly from the bombings of World War II, a sign that basic industrial capacity and know-how accounted for considerable resilience once they were firmly established.

Yet another area in which economic change had an impact was the class structure of Western society. A basic division between the middle class and working class continued. But the middle class was defined increasingly by its managerial skills and education, rather than property ownership; the working class became less distinctive as its affluence increased. In the United States, indeed, the majority of workers identified themselves as middle class, on the basis of earnings. Furthermore, increased mobility, particularly in the decades after World War II, blurred class lines somewhat. Making the most

of new educational opportunities, a number of people from working-class backgrounds entered corporate upper management and the top levels of government service, although they still formed a minority. Interestingly, social mobility in western Europe soon matched that of the newer nations of the Western world, such as the United States, despite a more explicit class structure.

The greatest change in social structure, however, was the rise of workers in the service sector of the economy. The percentage of farmers, already small, dropped further. But by the 1920s, the number of factory workers began to stabilize as well, as production increased mainly through continuing mechanization. By the 1950s, it was clear that service work—that is, jobs involving steady interaction with people and the processing of paperwork rather than producing goods— was the wave of the future. Restaurant workers, health-care workers from hospital janitors to doctors, teachers, recreation workers—all rapidly expanded in number, as did the secretaries and salespeople needed in a bureaucratized, consumer-oriented economy. By the 1970s, more than half of all workers in Western society were employed in the service sector.

Finally, again particularly after 1945, a new wave of unskilled workers entered the labor force, many of them immigrants. Western Europe drew hundreds of thousands of workers from the Middle East, north Africa, the West Indies, and Asia; immigration to the United States reached higher levels than ever before, drawing mainly from east Asia and Latin America. Not all the newcomers were unskilled, but many filled the ranks of agricultural laborers, maintenance workers, fast-food personnel, and other slots where pay was low and rates of unemployment often high. Many urban blacks in the United States also fit into this growing category, which often seemed tragically isolated from the prosperity and security of most sectors of Western society.

Racial antagonisms flared periodically, for example, in attacks on Turkish workers in

WORLD PROFILES

SIMONE DE BEAUVOIR

Simone de Beauvoir was a vigorous French intellectual, particularly known for her feminism. Born in Paris in 1908, she received a Catholic upbringing but went on to a career of philosophical radicalism. She wrote widely, not only in philosophy but also in literature. She advocated greater protection for workers, better treatment of the elderly, abortion rights, but above all equality for women. Her book *The Second Sex*, published in 1949, provided the intellectual foundations for later 20th-century feminism. The American feminist leader Betty Friedan, for example, helped popularize de Beauvoir's ideas and apply them to contemporary American women.

De Beauvoir graduated from university in 1929 and spent about 15 years teaching in secondary school. During these early years, she formulated not only her basic philosophy, associated with the movement called *existentialism*, but also her passionate social voice. She also formed a close friendship with Jean-Paul Sartre, another leading philosopher. De Beauvoir's final active decades saw her become increasingly involved in political activism, including feminism. Sartre's death in 1981 hastened her own physical and mental decline, and she died in 1986. She is buried next to Sartre.

Simone de Beauvoir.

Germany. A number of political groups worked to limit immigration. The United States worked hard, though with limited effect, to control illegal immigration from Latin America. The new mixture of peoples, in both western Europe and the United States, produced important changes—opportunities as well as tensions.

Like social structure, family life changed considerably during the 20th century without being totally transformed. Birth rates remained relatively low. Western society experienced an increase in birth rates from the late 1940s until the early 1960s—the famous baby boom. The boom was caused by growing prosperity, after many families had delayed births during the Depression, and in some cases in response to government aid to families. But even the baby boom, while it severely pressed schools, day-care facilities, and so on, produced relatively modest birth rates. After 1963, the baby boom ended, with birth rates again dropping rapidly. Further decreases in death rates for most age groups, due to improved medicine and a new interest in exercise and fitness, have maintained the basic population pattern of the later 19th century: low birth rates and low death rates adding up to a stable or slightly rising population and a growing number of elderly people. The increase in the elderly population, while a significant burden on social security systems, has had only limited impact on families, as older people in the Western world now live apart from younger relatives—a major change in residential patterns that began in the 1920s.

Western family life continued to emphasize the importance of close emotional ties, between spouses and between parents and children, along with a new emphasis on sexual satisfaction before and during marriage. The role of the family in recreational activities increased. The annual family vacation became a standard experience as time at work was shortened. After 1945, the advent of television made the home an attractive place to spend leisure hours.

Although family functions and family demography displayed striking continuities with the past, but with some interesting new twists, the roles of family members were revolutionized by new patterns of women's work. During World War I, with many men away in battle, women entered the labor force in vast numbers. This movement was largely cut off in the 1920s. But in World War II, women returned to the factories and offices, and after the war they tended to remain there. Increasing numbers of women in western Europe and North America, now as well educated as men, with relatively few children to care for, and in a society where earnings bring self-fulfillment and power, sought an identity and income through work. At the same time, the rise of service occupations deemed suitable for women facilitated the movement of women into the labor force, while increased expectations—a desire for better housing, travel, or education—encouraged women to work. In all Western countries, women's participation in the labor force rose steadily, reaching roughly 45 percent of the total by the late 1970s. Women of all social classes were now working, and they were doing so after marriage and even during active

motherhood. Their earnings lagged behind those of men, and in response to this, an active feminist movement seeking fuller equality sprang up by the 1960s. Nonetheless, the change in work patterns easily reversed the earlier trends of Western industrial society, in which women had been encouraged to concentrate on family life.

Women's work fostered greater equality in family decision-making. However, although the authoritarian position of husbands declined, new roles for women brought great confusion as well, for all parties concerned. Men rarely shared equally in household work, even when women found their time at home with the family decreased. Child care was another key issue. Increasing numbers of children, particularly in western Europe, were raised, in part, in day-care centers, one of the new functions of the welfare state. But worry persisted about the quality of children's upbringing, as older values of maternal nurturing changed less rapidly than mothers' activities did. Many thus professed that mothers, at least those of young children, should not work.

Tensions of this sort easily fed concern about the family itself, a theme already raised during the Industrial Revolution. Many people complained about changes in family roles, claiming that children were receiving too little adult supervision and spending too much time in front of television sets. Certainly, the Western family became unstable. Divorce rates rose during most decades of the 20th century, with the United States leading the way. By the 1970s, one marriage in two in the United States, and one in three in Great Britain, ended in divorce. The fact that changing laws made divorce easier to obtain was merely a symptom of a growing tension between individual fulfillment and continued interest in family ties. The family has survived in the West and in many ways adapted to new functions. One of the reasons for rising divorce rates has indeed been the high expectations Western people have about the family, as they seek love, sexual pleasure, and freedom from dispute. However, there is no question that the concept of the family often failed in practice, and the resulting strains on and conflicts

In Houston, in November 1977, the U.S. government sponsored a National Women's Conference. In order to symbolize the direct link between earlier American feminists and the women at the Conference, a torch was lit in Seneca Falls, New York—seat of the famous women's right convention of 1848—and carried 2600 miles by relay runners to Houston. In this photograph, feminist leaders accompany the torch and its three bearers on the last mile of the journey. Here, from left to right, are Susan B. Anthony II; Representative Bella Abzug; Sylvia Ortiz, Peggy Kokernot, and Michele Cearcy (the torch bearers); and Betty Friedan.

for family members occasioned great anxiety in the 20th-century West.

Along with social structure and family, pleasure seeking became an important theme of Western society in the 20th century, most obviously during the 1920s and again in the affluent era following World War II. With growing prosperity and shorter working hours—by the 1940s, most people worked an eight-hour day—interests in leisure exploded. Mass media, including popular novels as well as movies, radio, and television, brought escapist entertainment to millions. Professional sports commanded growing attention, particularly soccer in western

Europe and football and baseball in the United States. Sex also garnered more open public interest than was the case during the 19th century. Birth control remained an essential consideration, but it was provided increasingly by artificial devices, not abstinence. A society concerned with pleasure and the consumption of goods found sex an important consideration. More revealing fashions, particularly those for women; the more open use of sexual themes in films and on television; and manuals devoted to teaching methods of greater sexual pleasure all marked this new chapter in Western history. Whether people actually experienced greater sexual pleasure than before is open to question, but there was no doubt of great public interest in the subject. Sex or sexual allure became a vital part of having fun and of selling products. To some observers, indeed, sports and sex seem to have taken the place that religion once held in popular Western culture.

The changes in Western society during the 20th century—including technological advances as well as setbacks such as the Depression—caused considerable social tension. Burgeoning unionization and rising rates of strikes into the early 1950s expressed class conflict, as workers reacted to automation and the power of their middle-class bosses. However, with growing affluence and the rise of the service sector, where unionizing came harder, strikes and unions receded somewhat. Other protest movements, including the student risings in the 1960s and feminism, reflected social change, including discontent within the family. Overall, though, collective protest did not surge in the West. But there were also more individualized signs of distress. Rates of violent crime increased in Western society after World War II, initially because of the dislocation of war itself but then as a result of new conflicts among youth and also racial minorities. For the most part, the United States had the highest per capita crime rates, but western Europe faced an upward trend as well. The growing use of drugs was also interpreted as a reaction to boredom and the lack of meaning in Western life.

Western society, like Western politics and art, seemed enmeshed in a fundamental contradiction of the 20th century. On the one hand, the society encouraged individualism. Children were raised to think of themselves as individuals, to rise above their parents' achievements if possible, to embrace new educational and employment opportunities. Leisure interests appealed to individual pleasure seeking. But individualism was severely curtailed by the growing bureaucratization of society. Most jobs involved routine activities, controlled by an elaborate supervisory structure; individual initiative counted for little, in not only factories but also the offices of giant corporations. Leisure, appealing to individual self-expression in one sense, generally meant mass, commercially manipulated outlets for all but a handful of venturesome souls. By the 1950s, television watching had become far and away the leading interest of Western peoples, and most television fare was deliberately standardized. Individualism also came into conflict with the continued devotion to family bonds, as we have seen. Ironically, individualism and its manifestations often made collective protest against bureaucratization and routine extremely difficult.

To critics, inside Western society and without, late-20th-century Western society seemed confused, in constant conflict. Poverty and job boredom coexisted with affluence and continued appeals about the essential value of work. Youthful protest—as expressed in defiant styles of dress and jarring forms of music—family instability, and crime might be signs of a fatally flawed society. Rising rates of suicide and an increasing incidence of mental illness were other troubling symptoms. At the least, Western society continued to display the strains of change. People displaced by change or troubled by the rejection of former values, as well as people caught up in new styles but disappointed by their results, showed the tensions of adjusting to a society still in rapid flux.

A POSTINDUSTRIAL AGE?

Many people in Western society came to believe that they were facing greater changes than ever before, whether for better or for worse. By the late 1960s, a new concept of a *postindustrial* society took shape in both western Europe and North America. It held that Western society was the leader in a transformation as fundamental as the Industrial Revolution had been. The rise of a service economy, according to this worldview, promised as many shifts and changes as those precipitated by the rise of an industrial economy. Control of knowledge, rather than control of goods, was the key to the postindustrial social structure. Technology allowed the expansion of factory production with a shrinking labor force, and attention shifted to the generation and control of information. The advent of new technology, particularly the computer, supported the postindustrial concept, by applying to knowledge transmission the same potential technological revolution that the steam engine had brought to manufacturing.

Changes in the role of women paralleled the postindustrial concept, and some observers began to talk of a postindustrial family in which two equal spouses would pool their earnings for a high-consumption lifestyle. Postindustrial cities increasingly became entertainment centers, as most work could now be decentralized in the suburbs, linked by the omnipresent computer. Postindustrial politics were less clearly defined, although some noted that the old party structure might loosen as new, service-sector voters sought issues more appropriate to their interests. The rise of environmental and feminist concerns that cut across former political alignments might thus prove an opening wedge to an unpredictable political future for the West.

The postindustrial society was not an established fact, of course, even by the late 1990s. Important continuities with earlier social forms, including political values and cultural directions, suggest that new technologies might modify rather than revolutionize Western industrial society. It is clear, however, that Western society has taken on important new characteristics, ranging from age brackets to occupational structure, that differentiate it from the initial industrial patterns generated during the 19th century. And this fact, even if more modest than the visions of some of the postindustrial forecasters, raises an important question for the West and the world: how would a rapidly changing, advanced industrial society

fit into a world that has yet to fully industrialize? How could the concerns of an affluent, urban, fad-conscious Westerner coexist with the values of the world's peasant majority?

PATHS TO THE PRESENT

Many characteristics of Western culture were shared by non-Western societies by the early 21st century, as industrialization and consumerism spread and democratic forms of government were more widely adopted. The West introduced important additional changes during the contemporary era, under the spur of events such as the world wars. It adjusted to shifts in world position, including the loss of colonies and, consequently, of economic and political control over those colonies. The force of nationalism diminished in western Europe amid a new capacity for political unity. The questions that existed during this period about the relationship between western Europe and the United States were redefined as the United States gained superpower status. Some social issues affecting the West were common to industrial economies more generally, such as rapid birth rate reduction and, by the 21st century, rapid aging. The extent of change in gender relations also marked the West during this period, as did the challenge of immigration, as many Western countries struggled to deal with an increasing volume and diversity of immigrants.

SUGGESTED WEB SITES

For lectures on 20th-century Europe, refer to http://www.historyguide.org/europe/europe .html; to visit the United States Holocaust Memorial Museum, go to http://www.ushmm .org/; to explore more U.S. history, see http:// chnm.gmu.edu/exploring/; on the Great War and the 20th century, see http://www.pbs.org/greatwar/thenandnow/ and http://www.mtholyoke.edu/acad/intrel/ww2.htm.

SUGGESTED READINGS

Recent work includes Michael Adas, *Dominance by Design: Technological Imperatives and America's Civilizing Mission* (2006); Jonathan Rosenberg, *How Far the Promised Land? World Affairs and the American Civil Rights Movement from the First World War to Vietnam* (2006); Elizabeth Borgwardt, *The New Deal for the World: America's Vision for Human Rights* (2005); David Harvey, *The New Imperialism* (2005); Robin W. Winks and John E. Talbott, *Europe 1945 to the Present* (2005); Volker R. Berghahn, *Europe in the Era of Two World Wars: From Militarism and Genocide to Civil Society, 1900–1950* (2006); Eric Dorn Brose, *A History of Europe in the Twentieth Century* (2005); Sally Marks, *The Ebbing of European Ascendancy: An International History of the World, 1914–1945* (2002); and Arthur Marwick, Clive Emsley, and Wendy Simpson, eds., *Total War and Historical Change: Europe, 1914–1955* (2001). See also Gabrielle Hecht and Paul Edwards, *The Technolopolitics of the Cold War: Toward a Transregional Perspective* (2007); Lizabeth Cohen, *Consumer's Republic* (2003); Walter Laqueur, *Europe Since Hitler* (1982); D. A. Low, *Eclipse of Empire* (1991); Helen Wallace et al., *Policy-Making in the European Community* (1983); Alfred Grosser, *The Western Alliance* (1982); and R. Paxton, *Europe in the 20th Century*, 2nd ed. (1985). On the Holocaust, see R. Hilberg, *Perpetrators, Victims, Bystanders: The Jewish Catastrophe* (1992). The following excellent national interpretations provide important coverage of events since 1945 in key areas of Europe: A. F. Havighurst, *Twentieth-Century Britain* (1982), and John Ardagh, *France in the 1980s* (1982). Volker Berghahn, *Modern Germany: Society, Economy and Politics in the 20th Century* (1983) is also useful. On post–World War II social and economic trends, see C. Kindleberger, *Europe's Postwar Growth* (1967); V. Bogdanor and R. Skidelsky, eds., *The Age of Affluence* (1970); R. Dahrendorf, ed., *Europe's Economy in Crisis* (1982); and Peter Stearns and Herrick Chapman, *European Society in Upheaval*, 3rd ed. (1991). On the welfare state, see Stephen Cohen, *Modern Capitalist Planning: The French Model* (1977), and E. S. Einhorn and J. Logue, *Welfare States in Hard Times* (1982).

On the relevant Commonwealth nations, see Charles Doran, *Forgotten Partnership: U.S.–Canada Relations Today* (1983); S. M. Lipset, *American Exceptionalism: A Double Edged Sword* (1995), which compares Canada and the United States; Edward McWhinney, *Canada and the Constitution, 1979–1982* (1982); and Stephen Graubard, ed., *Australia: Terra Incognita?* (1985). On the United States during the cold war decades, see Walter LaFeber, *America, Russia and the Cold War, 1945–1980*, 4th ed. (1980); Thomas Patterson, *On Every Front: The Making of the Cold War* (1979); David Oshinsky, *A Conspiracy So Immense: The World of Joe McCarthy* (1983); Richard Polenberg, *One Nation Divisible: Class, Race and Ethnicity in the United States Since 1938* (1980); Harvard Sitkoff, *The Struggle for Black Equality, 1954–1980* (1981); and William Chafe, *The American Woman: Her Changing Social, Economic and Political Roles* (1972).

CHAPTER

29 Eastern European Civilization

The Russian Revolution and its aftermath dominated eastern European history in the 20th century. Russia experienced many of the events that also rocked the West during these decades, but it also developed a distinctive kind of industrial society under a communist system. This society reflected earlier Russian traditions and the massive innovations produced by the revolution of 1917, following on the huge devastation of World War I. Until the 1940s, the smaller nations of eastern Europe stood apart from this system, but as the Soviet Union extended its military influence, they too were brought under a communist economic and political framework. The result was not only considerable unity, but also significant tensions in east European civilization as a whole. Then, in the late 1980s, the whole communist system split apart, within Russia as well as its empire.

The fundamental transformation in Russian society during the 20th century resulted from industrialization and the creation of a new social structure, freed from traditional aristocratic control and supported by mass education. The communist regime installed in 1917 was an instrument of change. Revolution itself resulted from the conflicts of a society in which population pressure, new political aspirations, and the early stages of Russian industrialization challenged older social and political forms without reforming them. As in France in the later 18th century and China and other countries in the 20th century, massive revolution was essential in responding to the initial forces of change and in opening the way for further shifts. However, the Russian Revolution did not alter every facet of society—no revolution does. The new Soviet political system, although vastly different from tsarist times, preserved the authoritarian tradition in Russian life, including many specific institutions such as the secret police. An expansionist foreign policy continued as well, but it was one shaped by the results of two world wars. Russia's expansionism, combined with its new industrial strength, cata-pulted the country into superpower position, along with the United States, after 1945. Russia also preserved its long-standing ambivalence regarding Western culture, at once seeking to imitate features of the West but then trying to avoid its influence in the name of distinctive east European values. Thus, although science and a secular outlook gained ground in Russia, bring-ing it closer to modern Western culture in many respects, deliberate efforts to avoid Western artis-tic and popular cultural styles created divisions between the two civilizations. The events of 1989–1991 reopened the relationship to the West, redefining yet again the question of Russia's identity.

■**KEY QUESTIONS**   *What were the main changes the 1917 revolution brought to Russia and, later, eastern Europe more widely? What caused the collapse of east European communism in the 1980s? What were the principal changes and continuities in Russia's relationship with the West from 1917 into the 21st century?*

THE RUSSIAN REVOLUTION

The impetus behind Russia's 1917 revolution was its suffering during World War I. Russian forces encountered many defeats, particularly at the hands of the better-equipped German armies, and civilian conditions deteriorated dreadfully as the country sought to sustain the war effort. Food shortages and high prices spurred massive discontent. However, the underlying problems ran deeper. The govern-ment had refused to provide meaningful politi-cal rights, as the parliament (Duma) remained a shallow exercise. The Tsar Nicholas II was both impervious to the legitimate grievances of the masses and stubborn; he surrounded himself with corrupt advisors who weakened the regime's reputation. Urban workers formed the

clearest revolutionary class, as they were sub-jected to harsh conditions in the early industrial factories that only intensified the resentments they had harbored from their peasant back-ground. But middle-class liberals and the peas-antry had grievances of their own, and a variety of revolutionary movements and factions, mostly operating illegally, were eager to channel any and all discontent. In essence, Russia consti-tuted a traditional rural society being hurried into the industrial age at a dizzying pace, with an unresponsive political system—the formula for 20th-century revolution.

In March 1917, strikes and food riots broke out in Russia's capital, and they quickly assumed revolutionary proportions, calling for not just material aid but a new political regime. A coun-cil of workers, called a *soviet*, took over the city government and arrested the tsar's ministers. The tsar abdicated, thus ending the long period of imperial control. For eight months, a liberal pro-visional government struggled to rule the coun-try. But liberalism was not deeply rooted in Russia, if only because of the small middle class, and the regime also made the mistake of trying to continue the war effort. Nor were liberals ready to grant massive land reforms, for they respected existing private property and thus dis-appointed the peasantry. So a second revolution took place in November (October, by the Russian calendar) that soon brought the radical wing of the Communist party—the Bolsheviks—and their dynamic leader—Vladimir Ilyich Ulyanov, known as Lenin—to power.

The Bolsheviks formed one of the smaller revolutionary forces in Russia, but they had the advantage of tight organization and a coherent plan of action. They also had, in Lenin, one of the great revolutionary organizers of all time. Although in exile during most of the early years of the 20th century, Lenin had hammered out a distinctive version of Marxist theory, arguing that a country such as Russia, even though not fully industrialized, could have a working-class revolution on the basis of a

A massive demonstration of women marching during the Russian Revolution, demanding the right to vote.

well-organized vanguard of the proletariat. This vanguard would operate in the proletariat's name, initially as a dictatorial force. Revolution was further possible, according to Lenin, because international capitalism had extended so widely in the world. Here was a powerful statement in the age of imperialism, facilitating Marxist movements not just against native capitalism but against Western domination as well. Lenin built a cadre of trained, professional revolutionaries under his leadership. He dominated other Marxists, many of whom believed that Russia must first pass through a middle-class phase; he outmaneuvered other radical groups as well. His organization became known as the Bolsheviks, or *majority*, even though they were, in fact, outnumbered. His most formidable opponent was the Social Revolutionary party, which had anarchist roots and won wide appeal among the peasantry by arguing for the primary importance of land reform. During the early months of the revolution, Lenin also worked for peasant support, pressing for state control of all the land, and he gained growing influence among urban workers by backing their spontaneous revolutionary councils, the soviets. Above all, Lenin surpassed his rivals by calling for radical revolution immediately, rather than taking the cautious approach that most others advocated. As popular discontent persisted, with urban strikes and rural riots, Lenin's firm position won growing prestige. By October, Lenin had a majority in the leading urban soviets. On November 7, Bolshevik leaders seized power throughout the capital city, and a national Congress of Soviets established a Council of People's Commissars, headed by Lenin, to govern the state.

WOMEN AND THE RUSSIAN REVOLUTION

Following the revolution, Russia's new communist leadership proudly claimed major advances for women. The Marxist assumption was that the destruction of capitalism would cure social ills for women, eliminating sexual exploitation and prostitution, for example. Women were carefully included on key government committees, though rarely in a leadership role. Russian industrialization had already emphasized women's work, and this continued. Leaders proudly noted women's economic roles in contrast to Western patterns of housewifery.

But Western critics often attacked this vision, often as part of cold war debates. They argued that while women worked, they received low pay and status. Most doctors were women, for example, but their wages were quite low. Furthermore, women often had to combine full-time jobs with full responsibility for housework, for in this respect the attitudes of Russian men changed little. The long lines associated with shopping added to women's burdens here.

Recent work by historians paints a more subtle picture. During the early phase of the construction of communist society, in the 1920s, women's groups had considerable freedom. All sorts of innovations were discussed, including alternatives to the traditional family. It was also in this context that the birth rate began to drop and educational opportunities for women began to expand. These changes continued, but under Stalin's government, family policy turned far more conservative, emphasizing the dominance of husband and father. Some problems, such as prostitution, were swept under the rug in an effort to emphasize communist achievement. Women's conditions had changed, but not as far as official rhetoric suggested.

Questions continued after the fall of communism in 1991. Rising consumerism meant, for some women, new opportunities to be fashionable, but other women could find the need to dress stylishly a constraint. New levels of unemployment were another challenge. Sexual exploitation and more open levels of prostitution were one consequence throughout the former Soviet realm.

Bitter struggles remained after the Bolshevik seizure of power, however. Popular elections produced a majority for the Social Revolutionary group, but Lenin forced this party to dissolve, concluding that "the people voted for a party which no longer existed." The assembly was shut down, and the Bolshevik-dominated Congress of Soviets took its place; Russia was to have no Western-style, multiparty system. A greater problem was posed by massive resistance in various parts of the country. The Bolsheviks had only a vague notion of what to do after power was obtained. They ended the war effort, signing a humiliating peace treaty with Germany that cost considerable territory.

And they redistributed land to the peasantry. Gradually, they also nationalized basic industry under the Council of People's Commissars. But tsarist generals fought the new regime in many regions, backed at points by troops from Japan, France, Britain, and the United States, all appalled at the radical regime that ruled Russia. Civil war raged for three years, until the communists managed to construct a powerful Red Army of their own and win widespread popular support against foreign intervention. Internal opposition, including competing revolutionary leaders, was gradually crushed, with numerous executions. Lenin also found it necessary to curry popular favor by issuing a New Economic Policy in 1921, which promised greater freedom for small businesses and peasant agriculture than the Bolsheviks had intended. Under this temporary policy, food production began to recover after years of widespread famine, and the regime had time to formulate the more permanent policies of the communist system.

By 1923, the Bolshevik revolution was an accomplished fact. A new constitution established a federal system of socialist republics, which gave minority nationalities some sense of freedom while preserving the dominance of ethnic Russians. The new nation was known as the Union of Soviet Socialist Republics, but firm Communist party control over the state governments, and centralization of all basic decisions in the new capital of Moscow (moved from St. Petersburg, now named Leningrad, to provide a more Russian, less Western tone to the revolutionary state), formed the basis of an authoritarian rule more effective than the tsarist regime had ever been. The revolutionaries also began to concentrate more exclusively on Russian affairs, after a brief period in which great hopes had been pinned on promoting a communist revolution in other European states. The Bolsheviks maintained a Communist International Office (Comintern) to support and guide communist parties elsewhere, but their main focus was on building their own state.

The Russian Revolution was one of the most important transformations in human history. Building on widespread if diverse popular discontent and a firm belief in centralized leadership, the Bolsheviks beat back foreign intervention and avoided even a partial restoration of the "old regime," as had occurred in France after Napoleon. Although the Bolsheviks utilized features of the tsarist system, including its authoritarian principles, they managed to create a new political, economic, and cultural structure without serious internal challenge after the initial years of chaos.

PATTERNS OF SOVIET HISTORY AFTER 1923

Lenin died in 1924, and after a few years of jockeying, Joseph Stalin succeeded him as undisputed leader of the Soviet state. Stalin, with his base in the Communist party, which now clearly dominated the new government, was a man of working-class background, with limited education and scant interest in theoretical Marxism, but he had a relentless obsession with power. Under his rule, Russia was to develop its own version of a socialist society—"socialism in one country," as Stalin put it, as opposed to the vision of worldwide revolution that had inspired many earlier leaders. By the time Stalin had fully eliminated potential rivals in 1927, Russia had advanced only slightly toward a socialist system, although its revolutionary momentum had not ended. Much of the land was in the hands of wealthy peasants, or kulaks, who seemed attuned to a profit-based market agriculture; even in industry, state-run enterprises and planning had only limited effect. Stalin devoted himself to a double task: to make the Soviet Union a fully industrial society, and to do so under the full control of the state, rather than private initiative. In essence, Stalin wanted modernization, but with a revolutionary, noncapitalist twist.

A massive program for collective agriculture began in 1928. Collectivization meant large, state-run farms, rather than individual holdings as in the West. Communist party agitators pressured peasants to join the collectives. The vast majority of kulaks refused, but through threats and mass executions and deportations to Siberia, they were forced to submit. Agricultural production fell drastically as a result, and although it gradually recovered during the later 1930s, the Soviet Union was saddled with the persistent problem of lack of peasant motivation. Although collective farms allowed peasants small plots of their own and job security, they created an atmosphere of factory-like discipline and rigid planning from above that left many peasants reluctant participants.

The collective farm system did, however, facilitate control of the peasantry so that rural profits could be reduced, in favor of providing capital for industrialization, and excess workers could be forced into the ranks of urban labor. If Stalin's handling of agriculture had serious flaws, his approach to industry was in many ways miraculously successful. A system of five-year plans under the state planning commission began to construct massive state-run factories in metallurgy, mining, and electric power, to make Russia an industrial country without foreign capital or more than very limited foreign advice. The focus was on heavy industry, which built on Russia's great natural resources and also served to prepare for possible war with Hitler's Germany. This unbalanced allocation, which slighted consumer goods, was to remain characteristic of the Soviet version of an industrial society. Further, Stalin's ambitious hope to replace market forces with government choices led to many allocation bottlenecks plus a wasteful use of resources and labor, as production and supply quotas for individual factories were set in Moscow. However, there was no question that rapid industrial growth had occurred. During the first two five-year plans, to 1937—the period when the West was mired in the Depression—Russian output of machinery and metal products grew 14-fold. Russia had become the world's third industrial power, behind only Germany and the United States. Russia's long history of backwardness seemed to have ended.

Along with forced industrialization, Stalin continued to maintain the police powers of the state. Opponents and even imagined opponents were executed. During the great purge of high party leaders in 1937–1938, hundreds of people were intimidated into confessing imaginary crimes against the state, and most of them were executed. Party congresses and meetings of the executive committee, or Politburo, became mere rubber stamps, and a zealous internal police,

renamed the MVD in 1934, perpetuated an atmosphere of terror in Russian society.

Ironically, Stalin's purges had weakened the nation's ability to respond to the rising threat of Hitler, the self-proclaimed leader of anticommunism. Along with an understandable suspicion of the motives of the Western powers, this internal weakness encouraged Stalin to sign his pact with Hitler in 1939. The alliance bought some time for greater war preparation and also enabled Russian troops to attack eastern Poland and Finland in an effort to regain territories lost in World War I. Here was the first sign of a revival of Russia's long interest in conquest, which was borne out by the results of World War II.

The war itself was devastating for the Soviet Union. German invasions, although ultimately unsuccessful, brought massive death and hardship. Russia's new industrial base, hastily relocated to the Ural Mountains and beyond, proved vital in providing the material needed for war, along with some U.S. and British aid, but the effort was extremely costly. Great cities such as Leningrad and Stalingrad were besieged by the Germans for months, with a huge loss of life. The war heightened Russia's age-old fear of invasion and foreign interference, already enhanced by World War I and Western intervention during the revolution. However, as the Red Army pressed westward after 1943, finally penetrating to the Elbe River in Germany, there was new opportunity for aggrandizement as well. Russia was able to regain its former western boundaries, at the expense of nations such as Poland; some small states, established by the Treaty of Versailles, were swallowed up entirely. Larger east European states were allowed to remain intact, but their regimes were quickly brought under the control of communist parties backed by the Soviet occupation forces.

Most of the small nations of eastern Europe had encountered serious problems between the world wars. They were mostly new, the product of particular nationalisms honored by the Versailles treaty and carved from the western

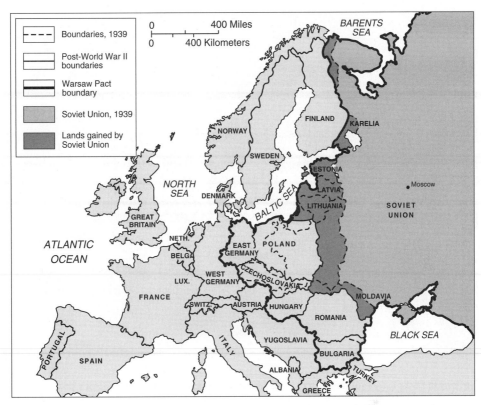

Soviet and East European Boundaries by 1948

parts of the Russian empire plus the now defunct Habsburg realm. Only in Czechoslovakia did a democratic, parliamentary regime achieve durable success. Most states, after a brief democratic experience, had turned to authoritarian rule under a monarch or army general. Land reform had been ignored in favor of continued aristocratic dominance. Bickering over boundaries had added to severe economic distress; industrialization lagged, and agricultural productivity actually declined. Then came the Nazi attack that easily overwhelmed the smaller, more backward armies of states such as Poland. This was followed, between 1944 and 1948, by effective Russian control. Through a combination of sheer military might and collaboration with local communist movements, opposition parties were crushed and an essentially Soviet political system installed in Poland, Hungary, Romania, Bulgaria, Czechoslovakia, and East Germany, in an unprecedented westward extension of Russian power. Only Yugoslavia and Albania, with separate communist regimes, plus Western-oriented Greece escaped the new Soviet empire. Elsewhere, Russian-style agricultural collectivization and state-run industrialization began to take shape along with a single-party communist government. Ultimately, the Soviet Union forged the Warsaw Pact alliance of military cooperation, to confront NATO in the West.

Although the extension of Soviet control to the rest of eastern Europe was the most dramatic diplomatic result of World War II, there were other significant developments as well. Russian

Uprising in Budapest, 1956. At this stage of a temporary victory, the citizens control a tank.

participation in the late phases of the war against Japan presented the Soviets with an opportunity to seize some islands in the northern Pacific. Russia established a protectorate over the communist regime of North Korea, to match the American protectorate in South Korea. Russian aid to the victorious Communist party in China resulted in new influence in that country for a time. In the 1970s, Russia gained a new ally in communist Vietnam, which among other things provided naval bases for the Russian fleet. Russia's growing military and economic strength gave the postwar Soviet Union new leverage in the Middle East, Africa, and even parts of Latin America. Communist ideology, attacking Western domination and capitalist exploitation, won wide followings in many parts of the world. The Soviet Union's superpower status was confirmed by its development of the atomic and hydrogen bombs and deployment of missiles and

naval forces to match the rapid expansion of U.S. arsenals. Russia had become a world power.

Internally, the Stalinist system remained intact during the first postwar years. The regime was supported by the growing cold war with the United States, which convinced many Russians that firm authority was essential to counter the new foreign threat. But Stalin died in 1953, and from that time on no single leader gained comparable power. Choice of single leaders by ruling committees balanced various interest groups in the Soviet hierarchy—the army, the secret police, the bureaucracy of the Communist party. The Soviet government had rigidified, with entrenched bureaucratic interests ready to defend their prerogatives, and no ruler could produce sweeping change. But in 1956, a new Russian leader, Nikita Khrushchev, attacked Stalin's dictatorial policies, blasting the late dictator's crimes against opponents. The de-Stalinization current roused great interest in the satellite states of eastern Europe, chafing under Russian control. More liberal communist leaders arose in Hungary and Poland, seeking to create states that, while communist, would permit greater diversity and certainly more freedom from Soviet domination. In Poland, the Russians accepted a new leader more popular with the Polish people; among other results, Poland was allowed to halt agricultural collectivization. However, a new regime in Hungary was brutally crushed by the Russian army—de-Stalinization clearly had limits. Within the Soviet Union itself, de-Stalinization produced a reduction in the number of political trials and the most overt forms of police repression. But the apparatus of the state, including the one-party system and centralized economic planning and control, remained intact.

After the furor of de-Stalinization, patterns in Russia remained unusually stable until the 1980s. Economic growth continued, but with no dramatic breakthroughs and with recurrent worries over sluggish productivity and especially over periodically inadequate harvests, resulting in expensive grain purchases from Western nations including the United States. A number of leadership changes occurred, as party chieftains aged and died, but such transitions occurred smoothly. Russian military development continued, including substantial troop deployment throughout eastern Europe; the Soviets' world position was dramatized by leadership in many space probes and space flights and by growing success in international athletic competitions, including the Olympic Games. The Soviet hold over eastern Europe loosened slightly after the trauma of 1956, for heavy-handed repression cost considerable prestige. East European governments were given a freer hand in economic policy and allowed to experiment with greater cultural freedom in a limited sense. As a result, Hungary emerged as a state with considerable intellectual diversity and extensive consumer-goods industries. However, severe limits remained, as Soviet leaders insisted on basic political and military control of the border states. An attempt to create a more liberal regime in Czechoslovakia, in 1968,

brought Russian army repression, while renewed agitation in Poland during the late 1970s, although controlled by the Polish army, was carefully monitored by Soviet leaders. Finally, in the one direct military thrust outside the postwar orbit, Russian troops entered Afghanistan in the late 1970s, to protect a regime friendly to Soviet interests against Muslim opposition. Russian foreign policy, in other words, while not literally imperialist, remained opportunistic and particularly bent on buffering Soviet borders against a potential threat, although Russia's only actual war after 1945 was in Afghanistan.

SOVIET POLITICAL INSTITUTIONS

The political system that the Soviet leaders built after the revolution, and then extended to the smaller states of eastern Europe, maintained the authoritarian traditions of the tsar in many ways. Stalin's brutal treatment of opponents and his paranoid suspicion of potential rivals were accurately compared to the actions of tsarist predecessors such as Ivan the Terrible. Even forced industrialization, although it represented a dramatic shift in Russia's economic structure, bore the marks of Peter the Great's state-sponsored westernization. Finally, the parliamentary system that evolved under Stalin, creating impressive-sounding institutions that were elected under Communist party supervision, with no opposition tolerated, bore more than a small resemblance to the essentially powerless Duma that the last tsar had created to try to pacify liberal opposition. By Western standards, the Soviet Union had no more parliamentary power than the tsars had allowed, despite carefully worded constitutions and a universal suffrage system that, in fact, compelled most Russians to vote but offered no choice save the officially sponsored candidates and policies.

Nonetheless, the Soviet system was far more efficient and sweeping than tsarist authoritarianism had been. It utilized modern technologies, including rapid communications, and the experience of Western governments in mobilizing their societies during World War I. The Soviet system, like Hitler's Germany, was sometimes called a totalitarian government in that it sought to reach citizens directly, to shape their thoughts and actions and command their loyalties. Thus, it developed far more extensive functions than the tsarist regime had attempted. Under Stalin, control of virtually all agriculture and industry, under state planning ministries, meant that the economy and the state were fully intertwined. Peasant garden plots, a few small shops, and an often extensive black-market system were the only economic forces that escaped state direction. The state was also responsible for cultural policies, and although this had been foreshadowed by the church–state links under the tsars, it had no full precedent. The communist regime tried to shape a secular population that would believe in the political doctrines of Marxism and embrace a scientific outlook on the world, monitoring artistic and literary styles as well as purely political writing. The educational system was greatly extended, yielding rapid gains in literacy and considerable access to higher education for talented students; this system, too, was designed to promote the state's vision of a loyal and productive citizenry.

Soviet leaders also constructed an elaborate state-sponsored welfare system. Able-bodied citizens, men and women alike, were required to work; the Soviets permitted no unemployment, although extensive underemployment often existed. But the state operated medical facilities, day-care centers, and youth organizations and provided payments to the disabled and elderly. Many of these programs were administered by Communist party organizations, including the loyal trade unions that were not permitted to strike but did mobilize many group recreational activities. Athletic clubs and beach resorts in southern Russia were among the state-run operations that cemented the welfare system. Far more literally than the welfare system developed in the West, the Soviet version embraced its citizens from cradle to grave.

Networks of political police and police informers attempted to ensure loyalty to the state, continuing and extending the tsarist tradition.

In Memoriam to Y. Gagarin, a painting of Yuri Gagarin, a leading early cosmonaut, by A. Shmarinov, member of the U.S.S.R. Academy of Arts, 1971.

Communist party members monitored all major operations, from youth groups to collective farms. Foreigners visiting Russia and Russian groups traveling abroad were carefully supervised. Groups and individuals suspected of dissidence were intimidated, often arrested. In the Stalinist era, in addition to the widely publicized purge trials and executions, millions of suspected opponents were sent to forced labor camps in Siberia. Under de-Stalinization, intimidation was moderated somewhat. Some opponents of the regime were allowed to go into exile; others were sent to psychiatric clinics. Outright political executions became rare, but an atmosphere of considerable fear remained.

Along with policing came extensive positive efforts at persuasion and propaganda. The press and other media were strictly state-controlled, offering carefully filtered versions of the news. Massive banners, pictures of leaders, and patriotic parades stimulated devotion and a sense of identification with the regime. The Soviets introduced a new set of holidays, commemorating the revolution and other anniversaries, including the international workers' day, May 1. Under Stalin, efforts to instill Marxist loyalty to the cause of the proletariat were blended with more traditional nationalism against foreign enemies, a powerful brew that unquestionably created a high level of commitment among many Russian people.

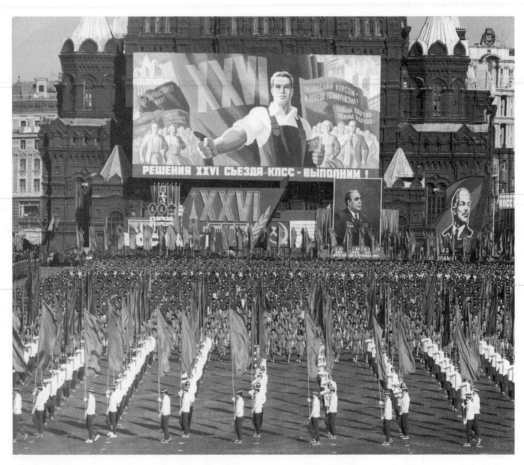

Parade of athletes and workers: Red Square, Moscow, May 1, 1981. May Day was a major civic celebration in the U.S.S.R. and for workers' movements in many other countries.

The construction of the Soviet state was in many ways a remarkable achievement. The tsarist precedent helped, but tsarist officials and church leaders were cast aside during the revolution, while a host of new functions were undertaken. The Soviets tapped vast reservoirs of popular talent and enthusiasm to construct their new bureaucracy. At the same time, this very creation became increasingly unwieldy. After important new access to political power for able workers and peasants in the 1920s, recruitment to the party and the bureaucracy increasingly came within the ranks of bureaucratic families, which favored their own. The Communist party itself was effectively run by a top committee, the Political Bureau, or Politburo, consisting of 20 people who were the real rulers of the country. Decisions were made at the top tier, often in secret, and then transmitted to lower levels for execution; little reverse initiative, with proposals coming from lower bureaucratic agencies, was encouraged. Just as the new bureaucracy replaced the tsarist aristocracy in ruling the country, so it raised some of the same problems as a power elite often more concerned with self-perpetuation than innovation.

SOVIET CULTURE

As in politics, Russian culture in the 20th century exhibited a fascinating blend of new elements, products of the revolution and industrialization, and more traditional themes. Soviet leaders from the beginning viewed key features of traditional Russian culture as forces to be attacked and undermined. Religion headed the list. Although the new regime did not attempt to abolish the Orthodox church outright, it greatly limited the church's outreach. Thus, the church could not give religious instruction to anyone under 18, and state schools vigorously preached that religion is mere superstition. The Soviet regime also limited freedom of religion for the Jewish minority, often characterizing Jews as enemies of the state in what was, in fact, a manipulation of traditional Russian anti-Semitism. The larger Muslim minority was given greater latitude, on the condition of firm loyalty to the regime.

The Soviet state also opposed the strong Western orientation of the 19th-century tsarist elite, although it should be pointed out that this preference had never widely touched the masses. Modern Western styles of art and literature were attacked as decadent. Earlier styles, appropriated as Russian, were maintained. Thus, Russian orchestras performed a wide variety of classical music, and the Russian ballet, although rigid and conservative by 20th-century Western norms, commanded wide attention. Soviet culture emphasized a style of "socialist realism" in the arts, intent on glorifying heroic workers, soldiers, and peasants. A vigorous strand of modern art in prerevolutionary Russia was repressed under Stalin, in favor of grandiose, neoclassical paintings, and sculpture. Russian architecture emphasized functional, classical lines, with a pronounced taste for the monumental, although various sorts of historical buildings were carefully preserved.

Russian literature remained diverse and vibrant, despite official controls sponsored by the communist-dominated Writers' Union. Leading Russian authors wrote movingly of the travails of the civil war and World War II, maintaining the earlier tradition of sympathy with the Russian people, great patriotism, and a concern for the eternal Russian soul.

The most creative Soviet artists, particularly writers, often tread a fine line between conveying some of the sufferings of the Russian people in the 20th century and courting official disapproval. Their freedom also varied depending on the mood of Russia's leaders; thus, censorship eased after Stalin and then tightened again, although not to previous levels. Nonetheless, even authors critical of aspects of the Soviet regime maintained distinctive Russian values. Aleksandr Solzhenitsyn, for

In a Designing Office, an example of socialist realism. Notice bust of Stalin at left of painting.

example, was exiled to the West after the publication of his history of Siberian prison camps, *The Gulag Archipelago*, but found the West too materialistic and individualistic for his taste. Although barred from his homeland until 1993, he continued to seek some alternative to both communist policy and westernization, clinging to his belief in the durable solidarity and faith of Russia's common people.

Along with an interest in the arts, Soviet culture placed great emphasis on science and social science. Social scientific work, heavily colored by Marxist theory, nevertheless produced important analyses of current trends and history. Scientific research was even more heavily funded, and Soviet scientists generated a number of fundamental discoveries in physics, chemistry, and mathematics. At times, scientists also experienced the heavy hand of official disapproval. Biologists and psychiatrists, particularly, were urged to reject Western theories that called human rationality and social progress into question. Thus, Freudianism was banned, and biologists who overemphasized the uncontrollability of genetic evolution were jailed. But

Russian scientists overall enjoyed considerable freedom as well as great prestige. As in the West, their work was linked with advances in technology and weaponry.

Shaped by substantial state control, 20th-century Soviet culture was neither traditional nor Western. Considerable ambivalence about the West remained, as Russian leaders shared Western enthusiasm for science while trying to redefine artistic styles and popular beliefs.

ECONOMY AND SOCIETY

The Soviet Union became a fully industrial society between the 1920s and 1950s. The rapid growth of manufacturing and rise in city populations to more than 50 percent of the nation's total were measures of this development. Most of the rest of eastern Europe was also fully industrialized by the 1950s. East European modernization, however, had a number of distinctive features. State control of virtually all economic sectors was one key element: no

SOLVING PROBLEMS

UPDATING THE TREATMENT OF CHILDREN

By the 20th century, Western society had established a fairly clear model for crucial changes in the nature of childhood. In contrast to agricultural norms, in industrial societies children should go to school rather than work; birthrates should be limited, but infant death should become quite rare. There were still some finishing touches on this model—the United States had more child laborers between 1910 and 1920 than ever before (or since), and only after this did work reforms take full hold. But the pattern, and the huge transformations involved, was near completion, bolstered by new arguments about how much attention children deserved.

The problem was, for societies not fully part of Western culture and poorer besides, how to react to these standards. Communist leaders, initially in Russia and then elsewhere, did not hesitate. Soviet officials made it clear that traditional family attitudes toward children needed drastic updating, with the state providing expert guidance. With their leadership and investment, primary school attendance had doubled by 1929, and secondary school enrollment rose eightfold; experts began to devote considerable research to improvements in teaching methods. Great attention was paid to children's health, with local clinics established for prenatal care. State policy on birth control oscillated during the 1920s, but in fact parents began to cut average family size quite vigorously. The result, by the 1930s, was the Russian installation of the modern patterns of childhood as a key product of the great revolution.

Of course there were distinctive twists. Communists eagerly formed youth groups to indoctrinate children (and wean them from religion), and they also established some work service during the summer (an understandable move given Marxist emphasis on the laboring class and the needs of a still-poor society). But these special features were arguably less important than the insistence of the more basic changes in the functions and treatment of children.

QUESTIONS: *Why did Soviet leaders, bent on establishing a different society from that of the capitalist West, implicitly imitate Western standards of childhood? How did modern changes in childhood affect the experience of growing up and the treatment of children in families?*

other industrialized society gave so little leeway to private initiative. The unusual imbalance between heavy industrial goods and consumer items was another distinctive aspect. Because of the low priorities it placed on consumer goods, the Soviet Union lagged behind in not only Western staples such as automobiles but also housing construction and simple items such as bathtub stoppers. Consumer-goods industries were poorly funded and did not achieve the advanced technological level that characterized the heavy manufacturing sector. The Soviet need to amass capital for development, in a traditionally poor society, contributed to this inattention to consumer goods; so did the need to create a massive armaments industry to rival that of the United States, in a society still poorer overall. Living standards improved greatly, and extensive welfare services provided security for some groups that was lacking in the West, but complaints about poor consumer products and long waiting lines to purchase desired goods remained a feature of Soviet life.

East European industrialization also paid little regard to the environment. Chemical pollution and the exhaustion of waterways endangered large stretches of the region; some estimates held that as much as 40 percent of Russian agricultural land became endangered, whereas more than 20 percent of Soviet citizens lived in areas of "ecological disaster." Damage in parts of eastern Germany and other centers was also extensive. The effort to force-feed industrial and military growth was costly, and some environmental problems may prove irreversible.

The communist system throughout eastern Europe also failed to resolve problems with agriculture. Capital that might have gone into farming equipment was often diverted to armaments and heavy industry. The arduous climate of northern Europe and Asia was a factor as well, dooming a number of attempts to spread grain production to Siberia, for example. But it seemed clear that the east European peasantry continued to find the constraints and lack of individual incentive in collective agriculture a deterrent to maximum effort. Thus, eastern Europe had to retain a larger percentage of its labor force in agriculture than was true of the industrial West and still encountered problems with food supply and quality.

Despite the importance of distinctive political and economic characteristics, eastern European society echoed a number of the themes of contemporary Western social history—simply because of the shared fact of industrial life. Work rhythms, for example, became roughly similar. Industrialization in Russia brought massive efforts to speed the pace of work and introduce regularized supervision. Incentive systems designed to encourage able workers resembled those used in Western factories. In the 1930s, the Soviets adopted a practice of rewarding the heroes of labor—workers who exceeded production quotas—with extra benefits and prestige. Along with similar work habits came similar leisure activities. For decades, sports provided excitement for the peoples of eastern Europe, as did mass media such as film and television. Family vacations to the beaches of the Black Sea were cherished.

Russian social structure also grew closer to that of the West, despite the continued importance of the rural population and the impact of Marxist theory. The aristocracy ended. Particularly interesting was an increasing division of urban society along class lines, between workers and a better-educated, managerial middle class. Wealth divisions were not as great as in the West, to be sure, but the perquisites of managers and professional people—particularly if they were Communist party members—set them off from the masses and their lower standard of living.

Finally, the Russian family had to cope with some of the same pressures of industrialization that the Western family experienced. Massive movement of people to the cities and crowded housing helped to undermine the nuclear family unit, as ties to a wider network of relatives loosened. The birth rate dropped. Official Soviet policy on birth rates varied for a time, but the basic directives became similar to those in the West. Falling infant death rates, with improved diets and medical care, plus growing periods of schooling and some increase in consumer expectations, made large families less desirable than before. Wartime dislocations contributed to a decline in the birth rate at various points as well. By the 1970s, the Russian growth rate was about the same as that of the West. Also as in the West, some minority groups—particularly Muslims in southern Russia—maintained higher birth rates than the Russian majority.

Patterns of childrearing showed some similarities to those in the West, as parents, especially in the managerial middle class, devoted more attention to their children's education and ensuring good jobs for them in the future. At the same time, children were more strictly disciplined than in the West, both at home and in school, with an emphasis on authority that might have political implications as well. Russian families were never afforded the domestic idealization of women that had prevailed in the West during industrialization. Most married women worked, an essential feature of an economy struggling to industrialize and offering relatively low wages to individual workers. As in the peasant past, women performed many heavy physical tasks. They also dominated some professions, such as medicine, although they were far lower in status than their male-dominated counterparts in the West. Russian propagandists took some pride in the constructive role of women and their official equality, but there were signs that many women suffered the psychological burdens of demanding jobs with little help from their husbands at home.

By the 1970s, many Russians seemed satisfied with their political and social system. Police repression remained, but Stalinist excesses had been reduced. Pride in Russian space and athletic achievements were coupled with a realization of the improvements in living standards and opportunity that had grown with the Soviet system. Many Russians also noted weaknesses in the West that enhanced their faith in their own institutions. Family instability, greed, and crime seemed lesser problems in the Soviet context, and only partly because the regime concealed accurate statistics. Except for the unpopular war in Afghanistan, Russian foreign policy had remained fairly prudent; American diplomacy could be construed as more unpredictable and warlike. In 1962, for example, the Soviets pulled back their missiles from Cuba, rather than risk outright conflict with the United States. Furthermore, of course, the Soviet system had partially isolated much of eastern Europe, allowing only limited trade outside the communist system and only carefully regulated cultural contacts. The imagery of an "iron curtain" enclosing this civilization was not entirely an exaggeration.

THE EXPLOSION OF THE 1980s

Despite its many achievements, Soviet society began to come unglued by the early 1980s, opening a dramatic new chapter in east European and central Asian history. The initial cause of this extraordinary upheaval lay in deteriorating economic conditions, intensified by the costs of a military rivalry with the United States. The Soviet economic system, after a strong growth rate in the 1950s and 1960s, stopped functioning well by the late 1970s. Industrial production began to stagnate and even drop, as a result of rigid central planning, health problems, and poor worker morale. Growing inadequacy of housing and common goods resulted, further worsening motivation. As economic growth stopped, yet cold war military competition continued, the percentage of resources allocated to military production escalated toward a third of all national income. This reduced the funds available for other investments or for consumer needs. Disease rates, infant mortality, and alcoholism all increased. Younger leaders began to recognize, at first only privately, that the system was near collapse.

Nevertheless, the Soviet system was not incapable of change, despite its complex bureaucracy. In 1985, after a succession of leaders whose age or health precluded major initiatives, a new, younger official rose to the fore. Mikhail Gorbachev quickly renewed many of the earlier attacks on Stalinist rigidity and replaced some of the old-line party bureaucrats. He conveyed a new and more Western style, dressing in fashionable clothes (his wife, Raisa, publicly did the same), holding relatively open press conferences, and even allowing the Soviet media to engage in active debate and reporting on problems as well as successes. Gorbachev also urged a reduction in nuclear armament, and in 1987, he negotiated a new agreement with the United States that limited medium-range missiles in Europe. He ended the war in Afghanistan and brought home Soviet troops.

Gorbachev proclaimed a policy of *glasnost*, or "openness," which implied new freedom to comment and criticize. He pressed particularly for a reduction in bureaucratic inefficiency and unproductive labor in the Soviet economy, emphasizing more decentralized decision-making and the use of some market incentives to stimulate greater output. In many ways, Gorbachev's policies constituted a return to a characteristic Russian ambivalence about the West as he reduced Soviet isolation while continuing to criticize particular aspects of Western political and social structure. Gorbachev clearly hoped to use some Western management techniques and was open to certain Western cultural styles, without, however, intending to abandon the basic controls of the communist state. Western analysts wondered if the Soviet economy could improve worker motivations without embracing a Western-style consumerism or whether computers could be more widely introduced without allowing the free exchange of information.

Gorbachev also sought to open the Soviet Union to fuller participation in the world economy, recognizing that isolation in a separate empire had restricted access to new technology and limited the motivation to change. Although the new leadership did not rush to make foreign trade or investment too easy—considerable suspicion did persist—the economic initiatives resulted in symbolic changes, such as the opening of a McDonald's restaurant in Moscow, and a whole array of new contacts with foreigners. Participation in cultural as well as economic globalization increased.

The keynote of the reform program was *perestroika*, or economic restructuring, which Gorbachev translated into more leeway for private ownership and decentralized control in industry and agriculture. Farmers, for example, were given the chance to lease land for 50 years, with rights of inheritance, whereas industrial concerns were authorized to buy from either private or state operations. Foreign investment was newly encouraged. Gorbachev urged more self-help among Russians, including a reduction in the consumption of alcohol, arguing that he wanted to "rid public opinion of . . . faith in a 'good Tsar,'; the all powerful center, the notion that someone can bring about order and organize perestroika from on high." Politically, he encouraged a new constitution in 1988, giving considerable power to a new parliament, the Congress of People's Deputies, and abolishing the communist monopoly of elections. Important opposition groups developed both inside and outside the party, wedging Gorbachev between opposing factions—liberals pressing for faster reforms versus conservative hard-liners. Gorbachev himself was elected to a new and powerful position as president of the Soviet Union in 1990.

DISMANTLING THE SOVIET EMPIRE

Gorbachev's new approach, including his desire for better relations with Western powers, prompted more definitive results outside the Soviet Union than within, as the smaller states of eastern Europe uniformly demanded greater independence and internal reforms. Bulgaria moved for economic liberalization in 1987 but was held back by the Soviets; pressure resumed in 1989 as the party leader was ousted and free elections were arranged. Hungary changed leadership in 1988 and installed a noncommunist president. A new constitution and free elections were planned, as the Communist party renamed itself "Socialist," and Hungary moved rapidly toward a free-market economy. Poland installed a noncommunist government in 1988 and again acted quickly to dismantle the state-run economy; prices rose rapidly as government subsidies were withdrawn. The Solidarity movement, born a decade before through the merger of noncommunist labor leaders and Catholic intellectuals, became a dominant political force. East Germany displaced its communist government in 1989, expelling key leaders and moving rapidly toward unification with West Germany, which occurred in 1990—a dramatic sign of the collapse of postwar Soviet foreign policy. Czechoslovakia installed a new government in 1989, headed by a playwright, and again sought to introduce free elections and a more market-driven economy.

Although mass demonstrations played a key role in several of these political upheavals, only in

Romania was there outright violence as an exceptionally authoritarian communist leader was swept out by force. As in Bulgaria, the Communist party retained considerable power, although under new leadership, and reforms moved less rapidly than in countries such as Hungary and Czechoslovakia. The same held true for Albania, where the unreconstructed Stalinist regime was dislodged and a more flexible communist leadership installed.

New divergences in the nature and extent of reform in eastern Europe were exacerbated by clashes among nationalities—as in the Soviet Union itself, where both Baltic nationalists and Asian Muslims raised new demands. Change and uncertainty brought older traditions to the fore. Romanians and ethnic Hungarians clashed, while Bulgarians attacked a Turkish minority remaining from the Ottoman period. In 1991, Yugoslavia, where an existing communist regime—although not Soviet-dominated—also came under attack, a bloody civil war developed from nationalistic disputes as Slovenia, Croatia, and Bosnia-Herzegovina proclaimed independence and then Bosnia divided among warring Serb, Croat, and Muslim factions. Czechoslovakia was peacefully broken up into a Czech republic and Slovakia.

Amid many conflicts and uncertainties, the Soviet empire was dismantled. Gorbachev reversed postwar imperialism completely, stating: "Any nation has the right to decide its fate by itself." In several cases, notably Hungary, Soviet troops were rapidly withdrawn, and generally it seemed unlikely that a change of heart, toward an attempt to reestablish a repressive empire, was possible.

RENEWED TURMOIL AFTER 1991

The uncertainties of the situation within the Soviet Union were confirmed in the summer of 1991, when an attempted coup was mounted by military and police elements. Massive popular demonstrations, however, asserted the strong democratic beliefs that had developed in the Soviet Union since 1986. The contrast with earlier Soviet history and with China's suppression of democracy two years earlier was striking. But Gorbachev's authority ironically weakened. The three Baltic states gained full independence, although economic links with the Soviet Union remained. Other minority republics proclaimed independence as well, but Gorbachev struggled to win agreement on a continued economic union and some form of political coordination. By the end of 1991, leaders of the major republics, including Russia's Boris Yeltsin, proclaimed the end of the Soviet Union and a commonwealth of the leading republics in its stead, including the economically crucial Ukraine.

Amid the disputes, Gorbachev fell from power, doomed by his attempts to salvage a presidency that depended on the survival of a greater Soviet Union. His leadership role was assumed by Boris Yeltsin, president of Russia and an early critic of communism, who now emerged as the leading, although quickly beleaguered, political figure in Russia.

Most of the now independent republics tentatively agreed to the resulting Commonwealth of Independent States. But tensions immediately surfaced about economic coordination amid the rapid dismantling of state controls; about control of the military, where Russia—still by far the largest state—sought predominance, including nuclear control, amid challenges from the Ukraine and Kazakhstan (the two other republics that could claim nuclear weaponry); and about relationships between the European-dominated republics, including Russia, and the cluster of central Asian states. Unity within the former Soviet Union had largely ended, although Russia retained economic influence in central Asia and close ties with some new Slavic states such as Belarus.

The fate of economic reform was also uncertain, as Russian leaders hesitated to convert

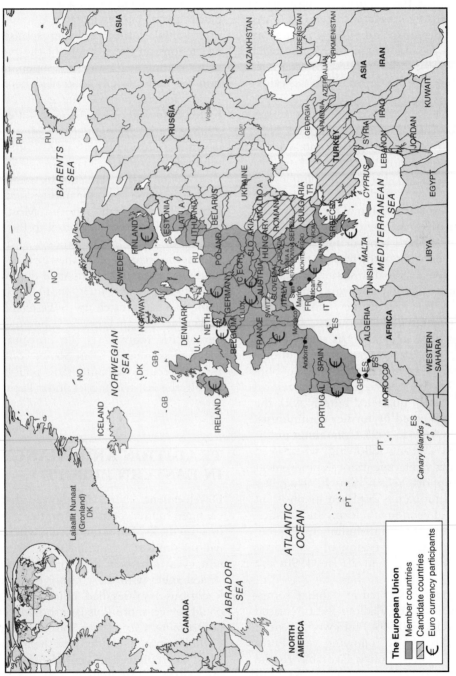

Present-Day Europe

The European Union
- Member countries
- Candidate countries
- € Euro currency participants

to a full market system lest transitional disruption further antagonize the population. Here again, more radical plans emerged at the end of 1991, calling for the removal of most government price controls. Economic conditions improved by the late 1990s; food supplies, for example, were plentiful. A growing middle class, called *New Russians*, eagerly engaged in consumer delights. However, inefficient state-run factories persisted. Government revenues dropped. New gaps between rich business groups and workers and retirees resulted in important tensions.

Political directions also became complicated. Russian leaders outlawed the Communist party, in retaliation for its leadership of the failed coup, but an alternative party system emerged only slowly. Soviet citizens took delight in tearing down the old emblems of the revolution, including massive socialist–realist statues of Lenin. Even old tsarist flags and uniforms were trotted out for display. But effective new emblems had yet to be generated. Nonetheless, in some republics, including in central Asia, party leadership retained considerable vigor, and political strife in several now independent republics allowed the Russian army to regain some role. In Russia itself, Yeltsin quarreled bitterly with the parliament dominated by former communists, dissolving it by force in 1993. Communist politicians retained a strong following, whereas an equally vigorous, militaristic nationalist movement won some support. Yeltsin himself, struggling with personal problems, displayed inconsistent attitudes toward economic reforms and politics. Finally, regional conflict in Muslim areas within Russia, particularly the region of Chechnya, resulted in bitter fighting in the late 1990s and early 2000s.

Russian politics seemed to stabilize somewhat, particularly when Vladimir Putin replaced Yeltsin as president in 1999. Putin won a general election handily in the following year. Putin maintained a foreign policy favorable to the West. He talked of democratic commitment but introduced new controls over the media and took other steps to tighten central authority. Elections in 2002 showed a decline of democratic liberal parties in favor of supporters of presidential authority. Putin sponsored new restrictions on the freedom of the press; newspaper commentary was fairly open, but television was rather strictly controlled. Economically, Russia's fortunes improved in the early 21st century, particularly with an increase in oil exports. In 2008, a Putin colleague, Medvedev, easily won election as president and named Putin his prime minister.

By the early 21st century most of east-central Europe was separating further from Russia and Russian patterns. Most of these countries either were admitted to the European Union or were in the process of admission, and some had joined the NATO alliance. Commitments to Western-style democracy and capitalism spread widely, though standards of living had yet to catch up to Western levels. The 2005 elections in Ukraine ushered in a more democratic regime. Of the European nations that had sprung up from Soviet collapse, only Belarus retained an autocratic political system akin to the Russian model under Putin.

TRADITION AND CHANGE IN EASTERN EUROPE

Developments after 1990 showed that less had changed under communism than some had imagined, in Russia and elsewhere. Strong nationalism had persisted despite the Soviet system, even in parts of Russia proper, and it blossomed anew with the collapse of communism. Religious loyalties had quietly persisted and could revive: more Russians showed an interest in Orthodox Christianity, Polish commitment to Catholicism strengthened, and the importance of Islam was renewed in central Asia and among minorities within Russia. The 2008 Russian presidential election saw most voters seeking a president who was a believer, but not too fervent—a far cry from the communist decades. Gender equality had not been completely achieved—despite communist rhetoric, women juggled work roles with disproportionate domestic responsibilities—and progress toward it suffered further from the fall of communism. Many women lost their jobs, emphasis on the importance of (male-defined) female beauty and sexuality increased, and a significant sex trade affected many women in several east-central European countries.

Once the Soviet mantle of protection was withdrawn, several key issues dominated any analysis of the new eastern Europe and central Asia. The first involved basic stability. Conversion to a market economy and a democratic political system was bound to be difficult. Many experts thought Poland, Hungary, and the Czech Republic stood an excellent chance of succeeding in their attempts at conversion because of their relatively advanced industrial structures and unusual degree of adoption of Western cultural and political values. Prospects for southeastern Europe and Russia itself were less clear, however, and efforts to move toward market structures and abandon the economic patterns upheld by former communist leadership were less rapid in these areas. Ethnic and religious battles generated more instability in the former Yugoslavia, central Asia, and other parts of the Balkans.

Finally, Russia's relationship to not just the West but also the wider world focused new attention on global questions. The Soviet empire, although somewhat closed to outside contact, had organized politics and economics in a huge part of Europe and Asia, building on the tsars' territorial expansion. Much of this was now undone. The empire had also played a vigorous role in world affairs, providing political guidance and economic and military aid to every continent. Russia's economic weakness ended this role, at least temporarily. But what world role would Russia and its neighbors now play? In the immediate aftermath of communist

collapse, particularly after 1991, Russian leaders carefully supported most Western diplomatic initiatives. This included many aspects of the United States–led campaign against terrorism, with particular attention to rebellious forces in Islamic countries. Under Putin, Russia defined more separate interests and sought to reestablish greater influence over former territories such as Ukraine and Georgia. Russia's new role continued to unfold as the 21st century advanced.

RUSSIA AND THE WEST IN COMPARATIVE ANALYSIS

Russia has had a close relationship with Western society since the time of Peter the Great. Its political, military, and cultural patterns have often overlapped. At the same time, it has usually maintained distinctive features as well, as when it maintained tsarist autocracy in the 19th century or struggled longer with the issue of serfdom. Correspondingly, its 1917 revolution, though influenced by the West and certainly influential in turn on Western society, was clearly a Russian process.

In the last several decades, new sets of questions emerged about how to analyze the Russian–Western relationship. Russia became an increasingly industrial, urban society. It participated in an emphasis on science broadly shared with the West. After 1989 it accelerated involvement in consumer interests very similar to those of the West, and links in popular culture and art accelerated. It is important to see these parallel trends, even amid cold war divisions and certainly since the cold war ended. By the early 21st century Russian universities accepted standards developed by their West European counterparts, an extraordinary statement of shared interests.

Yet differences remain. Russia's modification of open democracy, through a dominant single party under Vladimir Putin and through growing state control of television, differed from Western norms. It was true that Russia remained more democratic than ever before in its history, so the difference might be one of degree. But many Russians remained more pre-occupied with carefully maintaining political order than was true in the West. Russian reliance on oil production for its growing prosperity, its interactions with a growing but regionally based Muslim minority added other distinctive features. Not only the analytical challenge but the goals of many Russians themselves involved a complex relationship to Western patterns.

PATHS TO THE PRESENT

The turmoil of the past 15 years in eastern Europe should not distract us from the huge and important changes that the Russian Revolution and then Soviet expansion introduced in the region. Most of eastern Europe is now urban and industrial; the long dominance of the peasantry had ended. Correspondingly, the landlord class had been destroyed. A policy of mass education was instituted and persisted; in fact, communist regimes were crucial in converting the focus of childhood from work to schooling. None of these shifts was reversed by the fall of communism, which meant that the region's characteristics remained profoundly altered from what they had been a century and a half before. Even the area's largely secular culture persisted, despite some religious revival, including a substantial commitment to the funding and exploration of science. Strong traces of the precommunist past remained as well, even in the Soviet state itself, but the current characteristics of the region reflect the massive redefinition caused by the events of the first half of the 20th century.

SUGGESTED WEB SITES

View the Marxist Internet Archive at http://www.marxists.org/; to learn more about the former Soviet Union, visit http://memory.loc.gov/frd/cs/sutoc.html; visit the Cold War Museum at http://www.coldwar.org/; for more information on the "Gulag: Soviet Forced Labor Camps and the Struggle for Freedom," see http://www.gulaghistory.org/exhibits/nps/. Details on the Russian Revolution may be found at http://www.barnsdle.demon.co.uk/russ/rusrev.html.

SUGGESTED READINGS

Recent work includes Rex A. Wade, *The Russian Revolution, 1917* (2005); Alexei Yurchak, *Everything Was Forever, Until It Was No More: The Last Soviet Generation* (2006); Steven G. Marks, *How Russia Shaped the Modern World: From Art to Anti-Semitism, Ballet to Bolshevism* (2003); Evgeny Dobrenko, *Aesthetics of Alienation: Reassessment of Early Soviet Cultural Theories* (2005); Mosheé Lewin, *Lenin's Last Struggle* (2005); Sarah Davies and James Harris, eds., *Stalin: A New History* (2005); Thomas C. Wolfe, *Governing Soviet Journalism: The Press and the Socialist Person After Stalin* (2005); Marc Garcelon, *Revolutionary Passage: From Soviet to Post-Soviet Russia, 1985–2000* (2005); Olav Njølstad, *The Last Decade of the Cold War: From Conflict Escalation to Conflict Transformation* (2004); David Ost, *The Defeat of Solidarity: Anger and Politics in Post-Communist Europe* (2005); Daniel Gros and Alfred Steinherr, *Economic Transition in Central and Eastern Europe: Planting the Seeds* (2004); Ronald Powaski, *The Cold War* (1998); Jeffrey Brooks, *Thank You, Comrade Stalin! Soviet Public Culture from the Revolution to the Cold War* (2000); Stephen F. Cohen, *Bukharin and the Bolshevik Revolution* (1980); Sheila Fitzpatrick, ed., *Stalinism: New Directions* (2000); Lewis Siegelbaum and Andrei Sokolov, eds., *Stalinism as a Way of Life: A Narrative in Documents* (2000); Orlando Figes, *Whisperers* (2006); Vasily Grossman, *Life and Fate* (2006); and Joseph Rothschild, *Return to Diversity: A Political History of East Central Europe Since World War II*

(2000). See also Sabrina Ramat, ed., *Eastern Europe: Politics, Culture and Society Since 1939* (1998); Rex Wade, *The Bolshevik Revolution and the Russian Civil War* (2001); Terry Martin, *The Affirmative Action Empire: Nations and Nationalism in the Soviet Union* (2001); Lee Edward, *The Collapse of Communism* (2000); Stephen Kotkin, *Armageddon Averted: The Soviet Collapse, 1970–2000* (2001); Sheila Fitzpatrick, *Everyday Stalinism: Ordinary Life in Extraordinary Times: Soviet Russia in the 1930s* (2000); Terry Martin, ed., *A State of Nations: Empire and Nation-Making in the Age of Lenin and Stalin* (2001); Anders Aslund, *How Capitalism Was Built: The Transformation of Central and Eastern Europe, Russia and Central Asia* (2007); and Wendy Goldman, *Women at the Gates: Gender and Industry in Stalin's Russia* (2002).

Later Soviet history is examined in David Childs, *Two Red Flags: European Social Democracy and Soviet Communism Since 1945* (2000); Harald Wydra, *Communism and the Emergence of Democracy* (2007); Martin McCauley, *The Soviet Union, 1917–1991* (1993); Richard Barnet, *The Giants: Russia and America* (1977); A. Rubinstein, *Soviet Foreign Policy Since World War II* (1981); Alec Nove, *The Soviet Economic System* (1980); Stephen Cohen et al., eds., *The Soviet Union Since Stalin* (1980); Jeffrey J. Rossman, *Worker Resistance Under Stalin: Class and Revolution on the Shop Floor* (2005); and Ben Eklof, *Gorbachev and the Reform Period* (1988). On the Russian Revolution, see B. Wolfe, *Three Who Made a Revolution* (1955); D. Footman, *Civil War in Russia* (1962); and T. Skocpol, *States and Social Revolutions* (1979), a major interpretive effort.

Other areas of eastern Europe are explored in Joseph Held, *The Columbia History of Eastern Europe in the 20th Century* (1992); F. Fetjo, *History of the People's Democracies: Eastern Europe Since Stalin* (1971); J. Tampke, *The People's Republics of Eastern Europe* (1983); Timothy Ash, *The Polish Revolution: Solidarity* (1984); H. G. Skilling, *Czechoslovakia: Interrupted Revolution* (1976), on the 1968 uprising; and B. Kovrig, *Communism in Hungary from Kun to Kadar* (1979).

On the early signs of explosion in eastern Europe, see K. Dawisha, *Eastern Europe, Gorbachev and Reform: The Great Challenge* (1988). Bohdan Nahaylo and Victor Swoboda, *Soviet Disunion: A History of the Nationalities Problem in the USSR* (1990), provides important background information. An excellent recent study is Ron Brady, *Kapitalism: Russia's Struggles to Free Its Economy* (1999). On women's experiences, see Barbara Engel and Christine Worobec, eds., *Russia's Women: Accommodation, Resistance, Transformation* (1990).

CHAPTER

30 East Asia in the 20th and Early 21st Centuries

In the 19th century, east Asia had been divided by the differing responses of Japan and China to Western pressures. These divisions continued into the 20th century. Japan maintained an aggressive foreign policy that helped launch World War II and then developed one of the most successful economies in the world. China, in contrast, continued to struggle in order to industrialize. The giant nation was wracked by two revolutions, the second initiating a communist regime that resembled Soviet Russia in important ways.

Nevertheless, east Asia has maintained something of its own character. Japan, although an advanced industrial nation and a democracy, continued to differ from the West in many ways. China, although ultimately a communist society, showed marked variations from the Soviet model. It borrowed selectively from the Soviet example, somewhat as Japan had earlier picked and chosen from the West. There were some signs, also, that the unique characteristics of east Asia propelled much of the region, and not just Japan, into the ranks of fully industrialized nations by the early 21st century. Certainly, the rapid economic growth of South Korea, Hong Kong, and Taiwan, and the probability that China itself will make the turn to full industrialization, has raised new discussion of east Asian "advantages" in the process of late-comer modernization. Finally, even amid great diversity, east Asian nations continue to interact. Japan's invasion of China in the 1930s colored the development of both nations. New economic exchanges by the 1970s again focused some attention on the links within this historic region.

East Asia in the 20th century thus split between the Chinese communist pattern, shared to an extent by Vietnam, and Japan's rapid industrialization, joined after the 1950s by other parts of the Pacific Rim, including parts of southeast Asia. Both sections of east Asia continued to utilize former traditions of strong government and Confucian values, blending them with new ingredients—in China's case, outright revolution—to gain increasing impact in the world at large.

KEY QUESTIONS *Both China and the combined area of Japan and the Pacific Rim were unusual centers of 20th-century activity and change. Can you think of reasons for this, compared to other areas? What were the major changes that communism brought to China? What did Japan westernize, and not westernize, during the century? (This question has two parts, one for the war period and one for after 1945.) In what ways have China and the Pacific Rim been drawing closer together since 1978? What are the key remaining differences?*

A CLASH OF CULTURES: REVOLUTION AND WAR

During the first two decades of the 20th century, Japan continued its policies of rapid industrialization and imperialist expansion. The exploitation of Korea developed rapidly from 1910 on. Japan's participation in World War I involved little major fighting, but it provided Japan with a chance to acquire former German colonies in the Pacific islands. At the same time, Japan was not granted high status at the Versailles Peace Conference, which Japanese leaders found humiliating. Internal pressure mounted for a more aggressive foreign policy that would compel the Western powers to recognize Japan's greatness. Internal stresses were also accumulating within Japanese society. A growing radical-socialist movement attempted to address working-class grievances, although it was successfully outlawed. Intellectuals continued the discussion of Japan's identity.

But as important tensions swirled in Japan, China faced more dramatic events in the century's first decades. Growing Western penetration of the empire, combined with the government's sluggish response and the wave of students eager to see major reform, produced a revolutionary climate. A new republican movement sought to replace the age-old empire. Headed by Dr. Sun Zhongshan, the educated son of a poor family who had spent time in both British-controlled Hong Kong and Hawaii, the republicans believed that China should imitate Western principles of nationalism and democracy while introducing socialist policies to protect the people's welfare. Sun Zhongshan was no blind admirer of Western values; his emphasis on socialism was designed to guard against the excesses of capitalism and individualism. Nonetheless, he and his student followers advocated a radical departure from Chinese political traditions.

In 1908, the death of the dowager empress brought government promises of a written constitution and an examination of other aspects of Western government. But these vague assurances were not enough to prevent widespread student rioting, which led to outright revolution in 1911. Sun Zhongshan hurried back from a trip abroad to head the provisional government, as the empire was ended in 1912.

The revolution demonstrated the weakness of the imperial regime, victim of the long decline characteristic of earlier Chinese dynasties but heightened by its inability to counter growing Western imperialism. However, although the old regime was easily displaced, the issue of what to do next was far less quickly resolved, for China was not ready to spring into a modern, Western lifestyle. Sun Zhongshan's movement had attracted student support because of its optimistic belief that China could regain its full independence and become politically like the West with no difficulty. However, the Chinese had never had direct experience with voting or representative bodies. The decline of the imperial institutions made it difficult simply to govern the country, much less reform it. The revolutionaries appointed a military general, Yuan Shi-h'ai,

HISTORY DEBATE

JAPAN AND WESTERNIZATION

Japan had copied the West extensively in the late 19th century. Imitation proceeded even farther under American occupation after World War II. Japan's industrial success, its democratic political system, its increasingly ardent embrace of consumerism all suggested a society that was increasingly Western, despite its history and geography. Conservative critics who attacked modern Japan because of loss of tradition implied the same judgment.

Yet many observers insisted that Japan remained different from the West in crucial ways. They used the country, in fact, as an illustration of how a society could become successfully modern without westernizing entirely. Personal and family values formed one distinctive area. Respect for the elderly, though challenged by the costs of an aging society by the early 21st century, seemed different from the West. So, in subtle ways, did the status of women. Advertisers rated Japan one of the industrial societies in which commercials slanted toward strong masculinity had the greatest success. Business forms and the close links between business and the state were another area in which Japan was not just like the West. Many interpreters, in Japan and outside, pointed to the ongoing impact of modified Confucian values in instilling respect for group loyalty and respect for hierarchy. By the 1990s, when Japan's economy slowed, some Americans argued that the Japanese government was too cozy with business, tolerating inefficiency and subsidizing bad decisions. But it was not clear whether this judgment was correct, or that Japan would choose to change its distinctive habits even if it was.

as president of the new republic, to conciliate the army and prevent foreign, particularly Japanese, intervention. The choice also reflected the fact that Sun Zhongshan and his colleagues had no government experience, and they proved to be indifferent administrators. But the new president was no reformer; although he briefly tolerated an elected parliament, he worked to consolidate his own power as a possible future emperor. He was not capable of improving government efficiency, as tax revenues dwindled and Western influence expanded. In fact, China by 1916 was collapsing into a series of regional governments, headed by competing warlords, each with his own local army. Sun Zhongshan and his associates tried to counter the growing chaos by forming a political party of their own, the Guomindang, but they gained influence only in part of China, mainly around the city of Canton (present-day Guangzhou). Thus, the 1911 revolution had

destroyed key traditional institutions, but it had not created adequate substitutes for them. For this reason, revolution simmered in China throughout the next few decades, producing one deficient new regime after another until after World War II.

There was, briefly, a more hopeful interlude. During the later 1920s, the Guomindang armies were able to subdue a number of the warlords. The regime also induced the major Western powers to renounce their claims on Chinese territories; the Western-controlled treaty ports thus returned to Chinese hands, with the exception of Portuguese Macao and British Hong Kong. Revolutionary leaders became more skeptical of Western political models and capitalist economics, and the values behind them, and the idea of a Chinese version of modern society gained ground. The new leader of the Guomindang, Jiang Jieshi (Chiang Kai-shek), formulated a constitution that established authoritarian rule but was designed to lead the country to democracy. New laws also attacked traditional constraints on women in Chinese society, including the practice of footbinding; growing numbers of students attended modernized universities, some run by Christian missionaries, where Western-style science and social science were taught. Nonetheless, this period of renewal was short-lived. Jiang Jieshi did not effectively rule the whole country, and the warlords soon resurfaced. Jiang's own government became increasingly opportunistic, making deals with warlords and business leaders rather than focusing on political reform, and the hope for a complete democracy increasingly dwindled. Furthermore, the Guomindang faced another internal opponent in a strong communist movement, inspired by Marxism and the Russian Revolution. Driven out of the Guomindang itself, the communists staged the heroic Long March to the distant Shensi province in the northwest, where they held out under the leadership of Mao Zedong.

It was in this confusion that Japan's path fatefully crossed China's once again, as Japan's industrial strength continued to grow. As in the Soviet Union, the 1920s and 1930s constituted an important second stage in the Japanese process of industrialization. Heavy industry expanded rapidly; the Japanese developed their own machinery production, and the use of electrical systems spread widely. With a growing and skilled labor force, mostly male, the Japanese also reconsidered earlier industrial policies. Many workers were given security of employment in return for hard work and loyalty to the firm, whereas the government itself increasingly combined worship of the emperor with nationalism in order to prevent social unrest. Political stability, however, proved elusive.

After a period of moderate politics during the 1920s, in which Japan seemed to accept a multiparty political system, even allowing nonaristocrats to serve as prime ministers for the first time, Japan abandoned liberalism after 1930. The nation suffered severely from the early stages of the economic depression, as international trade plummeted. Dependent on exports for food and fuel, Japan saw unemployment rise steadily when the depression in the West reduced its available markets. The silk industry, long an export staple, suffered when Western synthetics, such as nylon, cut into sales—a sign of Japan's continuing industrial vulnerability. Furthermore, population growth contributed to the pressure, as 65 million inhabitants were crowded into territory about half the size of the state of Texas. A million people a year were added through the combination of high birth rates and falling death rates.

New Militarism

Economic chaos, although short-lived, allowed Japan's military leaders, allied with conservative business and agricultural interests, to regain the upper hand in politics. This group rebelled against the cautious liberalism of the reigning politicians, using assassination and the threat of mass unrest as weapons. Japan's powerful oligarchy turned to an essentially fascist approach that was foreign, in its violence and methods of intimidation, to Japan's political tradition. This transformation reflected not only the crisis of the economic depression but also the strains that rapid industrialization had placed on Japanese society—strains that did not produce outright revolution but did lead the ruling oligarchy to its militaristic lines of defense. Parliamentary rule became increasingly shallow, as military leaders manipulated the politicians or, like General Hideki Tojo, held office directly. With this authoritarianism came renewed interest in foreign expansion; the Japanese sought a sphere of influence in eastern Asia to deal with the nation's overproduction and overpopulation. The more aggressive foreign policy aided, and was aided by, Japan's quick rebound to renewed industrial growth.

In 1931, the Japanese launched an unde-
clared war on China, seizing the province of
Manchuria and turning it into a satellite state.
This was the first act of aggression in the interwar period that led toward World War II;
Chinese leaders were unable to gain Western
support, beyond moral condemnations of
Japan, and this failure helped teach other rulers,
such as Hitler, that aggression reaped worthwhile dividends. Jiang Jieshi hoped to satisfy the
Japanese by agreeing to the loss of Manchuria,
but in fact the Japanese soon resumed their
advance, extending control over additional
provinces in 1935, and in 1937 mounting a new
war against China, which effectively continued
until Japan's World War II defeat in 1945. Thus,
China, already internally divided, faced 15 years
of invasion and occupation. Vast stretches of the
country were seized, many resources diverted
to Japanese war industries, and millions of people killed or uprooted. Jiang Jieshi's regime was
driven from the great cities, but he was able to
maintain control of many rural provinces. Both
the warlords and the communists now joined in
opposition to the Japanese, the communists
gaining prestige and important military experience through their role in the resistance.

Stalemated in China, Japan used the outbreak of war in Europe as an occasion to turn its
attention to other parts of Asia. It seized

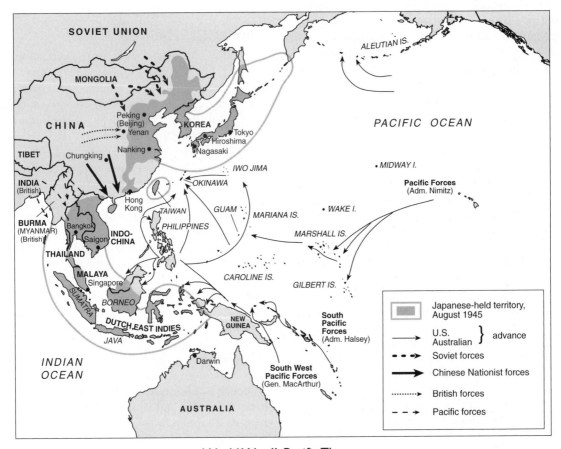

World War II: Pacific Theater

Indochina from France's troops and then allied with Germany and Italy in a pledge of mutual military assistance. This alliance, along with continued expansion in southeast Asia as the Japanese attacked Malaya and Burma, put the Japanese on a collision course with the United States, which as a Pacific power itself was unwilling to allow Japan to become a predominant force in the Far East. U.S. holdings in Hawaii and the Philippines, the fruit of earlier imperialism, convinced Japanese leaders that a clash was inevitable. Negotiations with the United States broke down with the American insistence that Japan renounce all lands acquired since 1931. It was within this climate that the Japanese attacked Pearl Harbor on December 7, 1941, and then in the following months seized American possessions in the western Pacific, including the Philippine Islands. Only toward the end of 1942 did the United States begin to turn the tide, making the most of its superior level of industrialization. Scattered islands were reconquered, followed in 1944 by the Philippines, while massive air raids began an onslaught on Japan itself. Meanwhile American, British, and Chinese forces continued to bog down a considerable Japanese army on the Asian mainland. Finally, in 1945, the United States dropped atomic bombs on the cities of Nagasaki and Hiroshima, forcing the full surrender of Japan and a period of American occupation.

Hiroshima, 1945, after the first atomic bomb was dropped.

RETURN TO STABILITY IN JAPAN

The end of World War II separated the paths of Japan and China once again. Japan's imperialist surge ended, seemingly for good. It had been an anomaly in Japanese history in any event, and American-imposed changes in government personnel and limitations on military activity further reduced the potential for military adventurism. Victims of the only actual use of atomic weapons, many Japanese advocated an antimilitarist stance, whereas official Japanese policy accepted American protection against possible Soviet aggression rather than mounting a significant defense capacity directly.

Internal politics were restructured as well, as American occupation forces helped produce a more liberal constitution, which enhanced the power of parliament, reduced the emperor from a religious figure to a national figurehead, and provided important safeguards for freedom of speech and press. Universal suffrage, first granted during the moderate period of the 1920s, was restored, and a number of political parties contested the major elections. In fact, a single party, the Liberal Democrats, held the reins of government throughout most of the postwar decades, but extensive political criticism and continued potential opposition affected its policies. Japan produced a new era of political stability, in which major concentration turned to economic development, and the Japanese soon entered the ranks of the world's most technologically sophisticated nations.

UPHEAVAL AND ONGOING REVOLUTION IN CHINA

With Japan's defeat, China emerged as the leading power in the Far East. Jiang Jieshi was welcomed as a postwar leader, particularly by his U.S. allies; the Chinese were treated as a great power, along with Britain, France, the United States, and the Soviet Union, in forming the new United Nations. This was the first time an Asian nation had been accorded such status in Western-dominated diplomacy. However, the honeymoon was short-lived. Jiang Jieshi was unable to assert a firm hold on China, for communist opposition began to mount.

The communist struggle with the Guomindang dated back to the aftermath of China's first modern revolution. Inspired by the revolutionary atmosphere and also the example of Russia's Bolshevik success, a communist movement formed among students in Beijing between 1919 and 1921; the movement quickly came under the leadership of Mao Zedong, a librarian who was from a wealthy peasant family. Communists and Guomindang collaborated for a time, both interested in establishing a revolutionary regime and opposing the warlords. But the goals of the two groups were quite different, and Jiang Jieshi expelled the communists in 1927, summarily executing anyone who wore the emblematic communist red scarf. Recurrent battles continued, for although the communists were weakened, they were not eliminated. Then a renewed military effort in 1934 culminated in the historic Long March, in which Mao led his followers to a remote northwestern province, where they built a strong reform movement among the peasantry and an independent power base. World War II gave the communists a chance to display their solid organization and guerrilla fighting techniques, and they also gained important new territory in their resistance effort against Japan.

By the war's end, the communists claimed to control more than 70 million Chinese, with an army of almost a million. The Guomindang, in contrast, had been exhausted in its war effort, as the Japanese had taken over the coastal cities where the movement had its power base. Economic problems and internal divisions and corruption further weakened the Guomindang, which could not prevent communist guerrilla attacks and sabotage that undermined support for the existing regime. The communists offered not only successful military strategies but also a much clearer program of land reform to China's peasant majority than the Guomindang, which increasingly seemed little more than a Western-dominated militarist group, its heritage from Sun Zhongshan mere rhetoric. Soviet aid to the communists also helped, whereas American support for the Guomindang actually enhanced the government's organizational confusion. While Stalin had no love for the Chinese communists and Mao had long since diverged from the Russian model in peasant issues, a temporary union between the two was a critical factor in communist success.

Mao Zedong poster helps intimidate election workers as they count the vote during elections to the National People's Congress.

Civil war between the communists and Jiang Jieshi's armies broke out in 1945, and the Guomindang lost ground steadily. Indeed, the speed of communist success surprised everyone, including the communists themselves. By 1949, the communists were in full control of mainland China. By 1950, Jiang Jieshi had been driven to the island of Taiwan, which the communists could not capture because they had no navy. There, Jiang and his army imposed an authoritarian regime, while still plotting an eventual return to the mainland. But, in fact, the mainland now squarely belonged to Mao and the communists.

Communist victory, in turn, meant a second revolution in modern Chinese history—or a culmination of almost half a century of revolutionary agitation. The new rulers executed at least 800,000 political opponents and arrested many more. Their goal was to destroy all traces of China's forming ruling class—educated bureaucrats, landlords, and capitalists alike. In their place, the communists constructed a strong centralized state dedicated to economic modernization and social change. Five-year plans were issued, based on the Soviet model, to encourage heavy industry. Agriculture was collectivized, with peasant communes replacing traditional villages. With property seized from landlords, the revolution in the countryside reached major proportions. The government strictly controlled education and information, mounting a major attack on the various religions of China.

In its early years, Mao's regime maintained its close alliance with Soviet Russia. This alliance, plus a desire to assert China's traditional power in Asia, prompted the communist regime to resist U.S. advances in the Korean War. Divided between a communist north and a noncommunist south after World War II, Korea had become a battleground in 1950 when the communists invaded South Korea. The United States came to the aid of its southern protectorate and then crossed into North Korea. This move resulted in massive Chinese intervention, which ultimately

Peasants threshing rice on an agricultural commune near Beijing.

the two giants of the communist world had become virtual enemies.

The rift with Russia prompted Chairman Mao to experiment with a different path to communism during the 1960s. Instead of five-year plans for heavy industry, Mao began to emphasize small-scale workshops in which intensive labor would substitute for advanced technology. Peasant communes stressed the need for a new Chinese personality, with common dining halls and large-scale propaganda attacking the evils of traditional family ties and Confucian hierarchical values. Finally, schools were transformed into pure agencies of Maoist propaganda, and technical and scientific study was abandoned. Many teachers and other intellectuals were ordered to the countryside to perform agricultural work. During the 1960s, China seemed engulfed by this new revolutionary fervor, as Mao sought to solidify his power, to defy the Soviet model, and, above all, to attack many of the traditions of Chinese society, in order to produce a modern nation that was also free from the trappings of Western modernization or the bureaucratic conservatism of the Soviet Union. During this period of the Cultural Revolution, bands of youths were organized to attack any vestige of traditional hierarchy in schools, family, and even the army. As one manifesto proclaimed, "We are bent on striking down not only the reactionaries in our school, but the reactionaries all over the world. Revolutionaries take it as their task to transform the world."

The Cultural Revolution in China began to yield, however, by the late 1960s. Disruption of the schools and the attempt at backyard industry had worsened the Chinese economy. Pressure from the Soviet Union, including outright border fighting in 1969, prompted Mao to seek a partial reconciliation with the United States, which occurred in 1971. More moderate communist leaders also regained influence, and on Mao's death, in 1976, they assumed control. Under the leadership of Deng Xiaoping, the communist regime, although maintaining tight

forced American retreat and a restoration of the previous Korean regimes and boundaries. China thus served notice that no outside power could claim east Asian dominance, in contrast to the humiliating decades of Western and Japanese imperialism. However, this same new strength soon caused a rift between Chinese and Russian communists. Mao began to attack post-Stalinist Soviet policy as a violation of true Marxism. Russian aid and advisors to the new Chinese regime were withdrawn, and tensions along the Soviet-Chinese border increased. Although ideological differences colored the new disagreement, it became clear that territorial disputes were an important consideration as well: the Chinese had not forgotten the earlier Russian seizure of some northern lands, whereas Russian rulers were keenly aware of the potential pressure of China's massive population on their sparsely peopled Asian republics. By the 1960s, political authority, began to devote itself to intensive but rather conventional modernization efforts, stressing technical education and industrial development. In fact, an important student movement for democracy in 1989 was vanquished in favor of continued authoritarianism. By the early 21st century, Chinese leaders worked hard to combine continued authoritarian political controls, with periodic arrests of dissidents and forceful moves against a new, Buddhist-derived religious movement, with rapid industrial growth and great openness to foreign contacts. The surge of industry—with growth rates of 10 percent a year—inevitably gave China a new or renewed importance in the world economy and triggered unprecedented Chinese efforts to secure needed resources, particularly oil, in central Asia, Africa, and elsewhere.

EAST ASIA TOWARD THE END OF THE CENTURY

The major events of east Asian history in the 20th century may seem bewildering in their complexity. Japan moved from imperialism and authoritarianism to democracy and a concentration on economic advance. China endured two revolutionary periods punctuated by Japanese invasion and then, under the communists, three distinct phases: Russian-style consolidation, radical experimentation during the Cultural Revolution, and more pragmatic modernization since the late 1970s. Clearly, east Asian nations struggled for appropriate political forms during much of the 20th century. Stability in Japan since World War II and considerable stability in China since the end of the Cultural Revolution suggest that such a goal has finally been achieved.

East Asia was also adjusting to new power alignments. Along with the period of conflict between Japan and China, the region was engaged in limiting Western influence and preventing major new Soviet gains. China's expulsion of special Western treaty rights, Japan's attack on Western-held territories, and China's Korean intervention all worked to this end, albeit in different ways. Although Soviet and American influence in east Asia remained considerable, there was little question by the 1970s that the region had regained substantial freedom of action. Internal conflicts subsided as well, so that since the end of the Korean War, a period of effective peace took hold within the region. Tensions continued, to be sure: the regimes of North and South Korea faced each other across a precarious border, the Chinese People's Republic officially claimed sovereignty over a now separate regime on Taiwan, and China encountered tensions with Vietnam to the south. Japan's power and its behavior in World War II caused ongoing tensions with South Korea and China. But compared to many other parts of the contemporary world, the region became fairly trouble-free—as it had so often been in earlier periods of history. Relative stability and a reduction in the turmoil that had marked the earlier decades of the century have given the major regimes of east Asia a chance to define their own characters.

JAPAN, INCORPORATED

Japan in the 20th century, for all its transformations in political regime and foreign policy, displayed two consistent traits: an ability to combine adaptation to selected Western imports and technologies with a distinctive cultural identity, and a dynamism that brought the nation to world prominence first as a military force and then as one of the economic giants of the final decades of the 20th century. The two traits were interrelated. Japan's skill in borrowing without a loss of identity, and its ability to utilize traditional characteristics such as strong group cohesion, had much to do with military and economic success. Such was Japan's impact

WORLD PROFILES

SUN ZHONGSHAN
(1867–1925)

Dr. Sun Zhongshan was an important figure in 20th-century Chinese history; he helped solidify the revolution that toppled the traditional imperial government. Sun failed, however, to create a fully successful alternative, becoming one of those world leaders whose reach exceeds their grasp. Sun was born into a poor family near Canton (present-day Guangzhou), but he acquired an education at that point in history when students experienced new influences from the West and became resistant to Chinese traditions. Because of his opposition to the conservative imperial regime, Sun was forced to spend much time abroad, particularly in the United States, and he was thoroughly familiar with Western political thought. His writings proclaimed goals of nationalism, democracy, and ultimately socialism for a China that would be new, but not necessarily a victim of some of the social ills that plagued the West. These writings made him the hero of Chinese students educated overseas.

When a revolution broke out in China in 1911, Sun rushed back to China from the United States and became its provisional president. At his insistence, no compromise was struck with the imperial regime, and China's boy-emperor resigned in 1912. Sun could not control the presidency, however, which passed to a military general. Sun formed the Guomindang (Nationalist party) to join forces with the military as part of an effort to organize a parliamentary state. However, these efforts to unite communists and conservatives in one movement failed with his death in 1925. China remained deeply divided for another two

China's great modern revolutionary, Sun Zhongshan.

decades. Was Sun Zhongshan the best kind of leader to create a new state in China? What were the main barriers he faced in fulfilling his self-proclaimed tasks?

that by the 1970s, along with continued Japanese interest in Western ways, came an almost obsessive Western eagerness to learn Japanese secrets, including traditional social traits that seemed so strikingly useful in an advanced industrial age. Western business and labor leaders began to

make pilgrimages to Japan with some of the same zeal that Japanese students had displayed in their visits to Western nations during the previous century.

Japanese politics certainly blended modern democratic forms with traditional elitist ties. As in the Meiji era and to an extent during the authoritarian period of the 1930s, postwar politics were dominated by civil servants and business leaders. Although democratic suffrage prevailed and a number of political parties showed strength, the fact was that postwar Japan experienced no shifts in party leadership. Opposition groups were less important than factional jockeying within the Liberal Democratic party. Few major policy shifts occurred after World War II. Only in 1993, amid growing evidence of business payoffs, did the Liberal Democrats split and lose their parliamentary majority, opening the possibility of more innovative politics. Up to this point, unusual stability in party dominance made Japan less similar to the Western political system than the constitutional structure suggested. The other distinctive feature of the contemporary Japanese state was an unusual alliance with business interests toward the promotion of economic development and the expansion of exports. Government economic planning remained extensive, and business leaders willingly acquiesced to government production guidelines and other regulations; there was no sense of a division of interests between public and private spheres, as still prevailed to an extent in the West. Small wonder that the coordination of economic policies produced the half-admiring, half-derisory Western label of "Japan, Incorporated."

Close business and political interaction resulted, in part, from the needs of a wartime economy and then postwar reconstruction. It was supported by Japan's precarious position in terms of resources, as the nation needed to import petroleum and most other vital raw materials, and so depended on active exports, which, in turn, the government helped promote. However, the interaction also followed from a long cultural tradition in which group cohesion was seen as the logical basis of society's functioning, a cohesion that easily blurred what Westerners saw as the lines between private enterprise and the role of the state. Government initiative also played a key role in ending Japan's rapid population

increase. Once imperialist expansion ended, Japanese leaders realized that population must stabilize, and they used government, in the late 1940s and 1950s, to organize an active campaign promoting birth control and legalized abortion, which indeed reversed a century-long trend of demographic expansion. Unlike the West, where government policy had little to do with population trends and sometimes ran counter to such trends, Japan's more integrated political-social system allowed concrete action in a vital area of human behavior, which, in turn, encouraged more orderly economic growth and an improvement in living standards.

Important segments of Japanese culture were also oriented toward the goal of economic development. The extensive school system established during the Meiji period was further expanded. Japanese children were encouraged to achieve academic success, with demanding examinations for entry into the university becoming the primary goal of ambitious young men and women. Higher education, in turn, placed a major emphasis on technical and scientific subjects, although general research and teaching in the social sciences gained ground as well. Growing university enrollments, based on examination performance, thus recruited students on the basis of educational merit, creating one of the most open social systems in the world.

Japanese culture also preserved important traditional elements, however, providing aesthetic and spiritual satisfaction amid rapid economic change. Japanese films and novels recalled earlier history, including the age of the samurai warriors; they also stressed group loyalties, as opposed to individuality or strong assertions of personal will. An interest in rituals, including tea ceremonies and traditional costumes for recreation, remained an important theme as well. Japanese artists participated actively in the "international style" developed in the West, but they typically infused it with earlier Japanese motifs such as stylized nature painting. Japanese architects, also working in the modern style, incorporated traditional themes as well. Finally, both Buddhism and Shintoism, despite a largely secular culture, sustained religious forces in Japanese life. Overall, Japan during the 20th century produced a blend of new cultural interests, many of which originated in the West, and older approaches, which allowed Japan, in turn, to make distinctive contributions to international artistic and scientific movements.

Particularly after World War II, however, it was through rapid economic growth that Japan made its clearest mark. Industrial development had continued at a steady pace through the 1920s, and again in the late 1930s, as Japan built upon its efforts during the Meiji era and produced a fully industrialized society. Then from the 1950s on, the Japanese moved into the orbit of advanced industrial nations, easily surpassing the level of technological development current in eastern Europe and challenging Western nations for world leadership. Beginning in the middle of the century, economic growth rates

were among the highest in the world. By the 1970s, Japan became the world's chief producer and exporter of automobiles and many kinds of electronic equipment.

Japan's economic success rested on several factors. Wages remained lower than those common in the West, although living standards improved rapidly, particularly by the 1960s. The collaboration of business and government was supplemented by the large corporate combines, called *zaibatsu*, which emerged by the 1920s as a means of reducing competition within Japan itself. Business concentration took place in the West as well, but the mutual arrangements among large Japanese concerns, backed by government planning, went further still. The Japanese also cultivated an unusual degree of worker loyalty and diligence. Although some labor unrest occurred both in the 1920s and after World War II, strike rates were low by Western standards and Japanese workers were noted for their careful workmanship and productivity. In the large

Employees inspect automobiles along an assembly line of a Nissan plant in Tokyo.

companies, workers were assured of job security; they could not be fired. They were often consulted on possible technical improvements. At the same time, businesses sponsored group exercises and other collective activities that increased worker morale. Japanese managers also showed less interest than their Western counterparts in high profits, while emphasizing group decision-making and loyalty over individual ambition within a corporate hierarchy.

The Japanese approach to labor relations had some serious political and social costs, however. Many workers were forced to join company unions, as Japan's ruling oligarchy continued to find ways to undermine protest. Pressure to maintain high productivity was intense, and some workers who would not toe the line were forced to retire. Workers were divided between those with job security and a large number, about 60 percent of the manufacturing labor force, including most working women, who faced more unstable market pressures. The *zaibatsu* system, effective in economic coordination, also helped suppress political competition, although less completely and arbitrarily than in the 1930s. But at least into the early 1990s, the Japanese way, in the eyes of a significant number of Westerners and many Japanese themselves, was a powerful economic instrument, creating unprecedented productivity and economic growth and a rising margin of exports over imports that steadily increased Japan's role in the world economy. Economic growth slowed in the 1990s, partly because of new global competition, but the nation remained a world powerhouse.

An additional element in Japan's economic success was the application of distinctive social relations to an advanced industrial technology. By Western standards, the Japanese seemed extremely nonindividualistic, loyal to group endeavors and not very concerned with personal reward or private expressions of discontent. Continued elaborate expressions of politeness, plus a heavy emphasis in the schools on the importance of patriotism, helped explain this unique national psychology. So did Japanese methods of childrearing. Children were encouraged to conform to group standards, among other things by the use of shame as a punishment for nonconformity—an approach in childrearing that the West had largely abandoned by the early 19th century. Japanese social solidarity showed even in the nation's legal practices. Lawyers were uncommon in 20th-century Japan, for it was assumed that people could resolve certain issues on the basis of mutual agreement and that individuals had no reason to use the courts to protest the activities of neighbors or business leaders, or the government.

Not surprisingly, Japanese family customs and important aspects of personal behavior continued in ways that were significantly different from those of the contemporary West. Male authority remained preeminent in 20th-century Japan. Relatively few women worked after marriage, and women's wages lagged well behind male levels—about 40 percent compared to the 70 percent that was common in the West. Women's role in the family, particularly in rearing young children, was heavily stressed. Japanese family structure stabilized after the high incidence of divorce around 1900, but it emphasized more than ever the domestic functions of women. Although a few Japanese feminists emerged, there was no movement comparable to that in Western society demanding new rights for women. However, Western influence showed, for example, in growing tolerance toward expressions of romantic love. In intimate life as in culture, Japan blended diverse ingredients. In the area of personal behavior, Japanese psychiatrists reported a distinctive pattern of mental illness. Problems of loneliness and alienation were far less significant than in the West, as the Japanese remained highly dependent, emotionally, on group activities. Conversely, in situations where individuals encountered competition alone, as in university entrance tests, stress levels were much higher than in analogous Western experiences. The Japanese also had their particular ways to relieve tension. Bouts of drunkenness were more readily tolerated than in the West, as a time when normal codes of conduct could be suspended. Businessmen had recourse to traditional geisha houses as a normal and approved activity.

Japanese popular culture was not static. Western influences permeated this area too. During the 1920s, Western styles of dress, sports, and music gained acceptance in the cities. Fashionable residents of Tokyo were even called *modan boi* (modern boy) and *modan garu* (modern girl). The U.S. presence after World War II resulted in a growing fascination with the sport of baseball, and a number of professional teams were established. In the early 1980s, a new passion for television game shows, adapted from their American progenitors, took hold, although the Japanese typically altered the characteristic format of such shows to engender more elaborate humiliation (or shame) for losers. Romantic soap operas hit Japan with *Tokyo Love Story*, in 1989, quickly the most watched TV show in the nation's history. In popular as well as formal culture, Western domination caused some concern among conservatives, who worried that important traditions—such as the use of chopsticks—might be lost for good. But to Western eyes, the Japanese ability to assimilate imported culture within a distinctive context seemed far more striking.

In terms of the global economy and culture, Japan was no mere imitator but an active contributor. Japanese firms were among the most powerful multinational organizations, gathering resources, locating production sites, and selling products literally around the world. Japan played a lead role in global consumer culture. Japanese animated films had wide audiences in regions such as the Middle East. Japanese toys gained large markets in the West and other parts of the world. The Japanese doll series "Hello Kitty" won a large following by combining Japanese styles with growing Western beliefs in children's cuteness. The Pokémon toys (derived from traditional Japanese games and figures) also sold

massively. Japanese rock music groups toured widely. By 2003, Japan had become a model for "cool," at least to many parts of the world, and exports of popular culture constituted a leading economic sector for the nation.

As noted, Japan was not without its problems amid economic success. Many nations both in the West and in Asia resented Japanese competition, often seen as unfair because the Japanese were slow to open their own markets to outside goods. Japanese dependence on imported oil and other products made the nation vulnerable to events in distant areas, such as the oil-producing Middle East. Pollution became an increasing problem with industrial growth and the rapid expansion of cities; traffic police, for example, often had to wear protective masks simply to breathe. New regulations after the 1970s did reduce pollution problems and helped generate growing environmental industries. Competition from other parts of Asia increased. Some Japanese experts, worried that the nation's economic vigor would prove fragile, wrote articles with titles such as "The Short, Happy Life of Japan as a Superpower," and growing unemployment plus sluggish production rates caused new concern by 1995. Economic stagnation continued into the first years of the 21st century, with higher-than-average unemployment and slow overall growth. This situation prompted other kinds of change, including an increase in the percentage of wives seeking jobs.

THE PACIFIC RIM

A number of other east Asian nations developed an extensive industrial economy from the 1950s on, although none could rival the advanced methods and accomplishments of Japan. South Korea, Taiwan, the British colony in Hong Kong, and, farther to the south, the city-state of Singapore (whose population is largely Chinese) produced rapid economic growth. By the 1980s, Malaysia, Thailand, and Indonesia joined in. Most of these nations were long ruled by authoritarian regimes; political opposition was suppressed. Governments and business leaders collaborated to develop new factory industries, with an emphasis on both consumer goods and metallurgy. Growing exports earned revenues needed for the import of raw materials and advanced Western or Japanese technology.

As in Japan, the Pacific Rim states—the coastal countries of east and southeast Asia—stressed national and group loyalties and limited what they saw as excessive individualism, including undue consumerism, which they considered to be wasteful and a threat to economic growth. Korean leaders emphasized traditional Confucian morality as part of this effort. The intent, as in Japan, was to change traditional values and social structures sufficiently to modernize the economy but to preserve enough of these same values to avoid westernization. The success of these nations suggested that east Asia, led by but not confined to Japan, was becoming the world's second industrial civilization, along with the West, as the region easily outstripped eastern Europe. The prospect was made all the more probable by the region's ability to maintain the world's highest rates of economic growth during the 1970s and early 1980s. Greater openness to democracy was an important additional development in much of the Pacific Rim by the 1990s. A near revolution generated a more democratic regime in Indonesia by 1999, whereas greater political diversity in Taiwan contrasted that country with communist China. The Pacific Rim weathered a major financial crisis in 1998, but growth trends soon resumed. By the early 21st century, an updated Korean popular culture, including music and dance styles, generated wide interest throughout east and southeast Asia, another sign of the dynamism and connectedness of the region.

CHINA UNDER COMMUNISM

China, the mother country of east Asian civilization, did not participate fully in the initial east Asian economic boom until the end of the 20th century. The political system remained resolutely authoritarian. Once again, east Asia was a divided region, in politics and economic patterns, as the fits and starts of the communist regime in China abundantly demonstrated.

Communism took hold in China for a number of reasons. Historical accident played a role: the Japanese invasion distracted the Guomindang and thus prevented a concerted attack on the communist forces and allowed the latter to consolidate their provincial power base. The inspired leadership of Mao Zedong was another important ingredient; as in Lenin's Russia, the communist revolution depended heavily on individual talent. Mao converted to communism during his student years, in 1918, seeing it as a means of challenging Western economic dominance while also facilitating fundamental changes within China. The all-encompassing belief system that Marxism provided played a role here as in the West and Soviet Russia. But Mao adapted Marxism to Chinese circumstances early on, particularly in his emphasis on the power of the Chinese peasantry. He argued in 1927 that "the force of the peasantry is like that of the raging winds and driving rain. . . . The peasantry will tear apart all nets which bind it and hasten along the road to liberation." By promising land reform and conciliating peasants during the revolutionary struggle, Mao's forces gained crucial support in their war against the better-armed Guomindang.

Although communism was a new force in Chinese history, with the goal of genuine revolution and not simply the seizure of power, it coincided with traditional features of Chinese society—as had been the case in the Soviet Union. The Chinese legacy of a strong state, with an elaborate bureaucracy, lent itself readily to a communist system, in which state power was further extended and in which government bureaucrats, although recruited from new sources and held to a new political faith, regulated large sectors of the economy and even family life. Mao's success, after the earlier failure of more liberal politics during the 1920s, was in this sense no accident. From the late 1940s on, communist officials prevented political opposition, monopolized the main sources of information and propaganda, and abandoned all pretense of establishing a Western-style parliamentary regime. The Communist party ruled the new People's Republic of China, and Mao dominated the party. Although the communist state was more efficient in its use of police and active promotion of political loyalty than the empire had been, there were some strong similarities between the two. Indeed, Communist leaders themselves soon found that they had recreated a complex bureaucracy that posed some of the same barriers to change that the old Confucian bureaucracy had. By the 1970s, appeals to bureaucrats to recognize the importance of new technologies and management methods became standard, as the Chinese continued to seek a reconciliation between a strong state authority and revitalized economic growth.

Mao's state and that of his more pragmatic successors were bent on transformation outside the political arena. China had been changing even before the communist revolution. During the 1920s, the port cities continued to expand, and factory industry took root. Modernized patterns of work and education gave a new voice to young people, weakening the Confucian tradition of ancestor worship. The importance of student groups expressed this shift. The position of women also began to change, as women in the cities acquired formal education and practices such as footbinding declined. More and more marriages were based on mutual affection rather than economic arrangements alone. Educational reforms brought even greater shifts in outlook, as science began to play a more significant role; many educated Chinese, at home and abroad,

contributed actively to scientific and technological research.

Mao sought to extend and formalize the pattern of cultural and social change. He attacked Confucian values head-on. Promotion of harmony, ceremony, and ancestor worship were impediments to the liberation of China's masses, in his view. He encouraged the new importance of youth, the validity of attacks on established hierarchies and even on the authority of parents within the family. Officially, at least, revolutionary China mounted a far more sweeping attack on the traditions of its civilization than did the other societies of east Asia, including Japan. Plays, operas, and art embraced the revolutionary regime, abandoning older themes in favor of praise for the heroic peasant and worker and attacks on China's enemies, among them the United States. The commune system in the countryside, which placed children under the charge of nurseries long before formal schooling began, and limited young people's contact with parents, was designed to eliminate traditional values at their root. Here, Mao's regime went further than Russian revolutionaries had ever attempted.

Chinese habits, however, were not easily undone. The Communist regime dislodged the former landlord class, putting the land directly in the hands of the peasantry, who were then organized into state-directed communes. smoothly than had been the case in Soviet Russia during collectivization. Foreign business interests and native capitalism were unseated in favor of state-directed enterprise. However, more subtle traditions, including family values and a tendency to venerate the elderly, seemed to persist. The Communist party itself was soon dominated by older men, as Mao's group aged. After the furor of the Cultural Revolution, it was not clear that youth would become the new heroes in China. Women gained greater equality and participated actively in the labor force, as had long been the case, but particularly in the countryside, older traditions such as arranged marriages persisted. Other customs, such as extreme politeness and the careful control of emotions, proved durable as well.

Furthermore, Communist leaders were eager to utilize some traditional practices as an alternative to a simple imitation of the West. In health care, for example, teams of "barefoot doctors"—hygiene officials rather than formally trained medical specialists in the Western sense—were dispatched to numerous rural villages, where they were responsible for raising health standards without fully imposing the concepts of modern medicine. Traditional remedies, including acupuncture, were maintained along with Western-style hospitals.

The Communist regime had a mixed impact on the Chinese economy, particularly in the area of industrialization. State control furthered the accumulation of resources for mechanization but resulted in some of the same problems of inflexible planning that plagued the Soviet Union, though industry did expand under Mao's regime. The sheer chaos of decades of Japanese invasion and then civil war, and the renewed turmoil of the Cultural Revolution, retarded economic advance. Furthermore, Chinese population growth continued at high levels. Mao wavered in his approach to this issue, at times believing that China's great resource, militarily as well as economically, lay in increasing numbers. However, as before, population growth consumed immense resources and produced widespread poverty. By 1979, China's population stood at 23 percent of the world's total, but the nation accounted for only 3 percent of the world's industrial product. Clearly, a full industrial revolution had yet to occur, although most observers agreed that the country was farther along the path than most other agricultural nations.

Chinese leaders after Mao's death, especially under Deng Xiaoping, worked more single-mindedly toward the goal of industrialization. High-level technical and scientific training returned to the universities, after the disruption of the Cultural Revolution. In 1978, the government began to favor more competition and also wider outside contacts, to spur economic expansion. Many groups and individuals were sent abroad to study. The regime adopted an unprecedented rigorous policy toward the population problem, aiming at zero growth almost immediately. Marriage before the age of 25 was forbidden, and couples having more than one child were punished. Here, not only the policing apparatus of the communist state but also earlier traditions of state control over society combined to produce a startling reversal in social customs. Again, official policy and reality, particularly rural reality, may differ. There were reports that the new rigor produced a wave of female infanticides, as couples were more interested in producing male heirs. However, the regime claimed, with apparent justification, that the birth rate had radically slowed. Finally, the regime collaborated with Western and Japanese enterprises, seeking more advanced technology. Individual managers and also rural producers were given greater authority and some profit incentives to obtain higher output, as the communists sought a new balance between state control and individual initiative. Industrial development was given clear priority over military concerns, as China returned, more clearly than under Mao, to a position of largely defensive foreign policy. China's new leaders projected an essentially completed process of industrialization by the year 2020. Improvements in living standards, most notably in the cities, were an early and popular result of the new policies, and economic growth rates stood at 10 percent a year by the 1990s. A rising pollution problem resulted as well, as Chinese cities filled with industrial gases referred to as the "yellow dragon."

China (and, in its wake, Vietnam and North Korea) firmly resisted the democratizing trends of the 1980s that so altered eastern Europe. Even as more democratic systems were installed in South Korea, Taiwan, and the Philippines, and in the face of their own massive student rebellion

Merchandising for the Beijing 2008 Olympics carried the theme, "One World, One Dream."

of 1989, Chinese leaders maintained an authoritarian regime. Russia's troubles in combining political and economic reform further convinced them that tolerating dissent was a significant mistake. The regime eagerly moved forward toward a more market-based economy, with profit incentives and private initiative along with state planning. Chinese exports soared in order to pay for new equipment and expertise from abroad. However, China insisted—as it had so often done in the past—on its own political formula. Assimilation of the former British colony of Hong Kong, from 1997 on, exposed China to not only another dose of ardent capitalism but also another set of issues concerning freedom of expression.

Rapid change continued into the early 21st century. Chinese industrial growth maintained 10 percent annual rates, and the nation became a leading exporter of goods to places such as the United States. Cities such as Shanghai

mushroomed. Some state-run enterprises stagnated, and there was growing unemployment. Foreign companies often exploited low-wage labor, as did export-minded Chinese firms—the downside of globalization for China as for other areas. Peasant and worker protests emerged periodically. Political tensions surfaced as well. Hong Kong was promised its own political system, but the national government imposed a somewhat authoritarian leader. Another challenge was the Falun Gong, the new, widely popular religious movement in a strongly secular society. The government viewed the movement as subversive and arrested many proponents. The challenge of running an authoritarian state in a global environment was not simple. Rising levels of environmental pollution posed another problem, as China moved into second place, behind the United States, as a generator of carbon emissions and as many of its massive cities became engulfed in a permanent haze.

EAST ASIA AND
THE WORLD

As the communist revolution spread across China, while Japan adapted to a more democratic political structure after World War II, the differences among east Asian societies seemed overwhelming. Even by the 1990s, the variations in levels of economic development and political forms constituted major distinctions not only between Japan and China, but also among the smaller nations. Japan, along with the leading Western industrial states, was a key participant in annual "free world" economic conferences, because of shared political concerns as well as world market interests. Countries such as South Korea and Taiwan were industrializing rapidly; they also faced periodic protest against their authoritarian political structures, which liberalized somewhat toward the end of the 1980s. On the other hand, China and Vietnam, still partially isolated, attempted economic reforms while maintaining their communist systems.

Over time, some enduring common features among east Asian societies have reemerged. An emphasis on strong social cohesion is one such element. China's communist regime seeks tight social solidarity, whereas Japanese values stress group ties from the family through the nation. From a common Confucian past, admittedly one much altered by recent events, east Asian nations also preserve an interest in ceremony and emotional restraint. They share a desire to develop or maintain industrial dynamism without necessarily becoming a carbon copy of either Western or Russian society.

Both China and Japan, although open to more international influences than ever before in their history, have continued to stand somewhat apart from other civilizations. Visitors to Japan report a polite but somewhat detached welcome, as the Japanese continue to honor the distinctiveness and superiority of their own culture, to which foreigners are rarely, if ever, fully admitted. China, although embarking on renewed contacts with the West after the vigorous attack on all foreign influences during the Cultural Revolution, continues to monitor outside influences, particularly in politics making it clear that selective imitation should not make the Chinese people fully tolerant of foreign ways. East Asia, more influential in the wider world by the early 21st century than at any previous point in history, has maintained its ability to see the world through its own lens.

PATHS
TO THE PRESENT

East Asia, and particularly China, had long emphasized "change within tradition," and strong traces of tradition persisted in the region at the dawn of the 21st century. Chinese commitment to state leadership and political order was hardly a communist invention. The attacks on the Falun Gong religious movement strikingly recalled the later Tang dynasty's hostility to Buddhism—independent religions have a history of making China's political leaders nervous. Other cultural legacies in the region include Japanese investment in group loyalties and Korean reliance on elaborate codes of politeness.

On the whole, however, developments in the 20th century at least temporarily unseated the "change within tradition" motif. Japan's experience with war and defeat, and China's massive revolution and its key phases, shattered traditions. The region's industrialization, including China's rapid growth by the 21st century, represented a huge shift. So did the widespread interest in consumerism, despite some hesitation. The degree of interaction with and openness to the outside world in Japan after 1945, in South Korea after the 1950s, and in China after 1978 was unprecedented. The region retained its various identities and distinctions, but it did so amid an exceptionally rapid process of transformation.

SUGGESTED WEB SITES

To discover more about China's Middle Kingdom, see http://library.thinkquest.org/26469/history/; on World War II in the Pacific, see http://www.historyplace.com/unitedstates/pacificwar/timeline.htm; on Japanese remembrance of World War II, see http://spice.standard.edu/docs/154.. For a directory of resources on East Asia, see http://newton.uor.edu/Departments&Programs/AsianStudiesDept/index.html.

SUGGESTED READINGS

Recent works include Xu Guoqi, *China and the Great War: China's Pursuit of a New National Identity and Internationalization* (2005); Mariko Asano Tamanoi, ed., *Crossed Histories: Manchuria in the Age of Empire* (2005); Susan Greenhalgh and Edwin A. Winckler, *Governing China's Population: From Leninist to Neoliberal Biopolitics* (2005); Xiaoyuan Liu, *Frontier Passages: Ethnopolitics and the Rise of Chinese Communism, 1921–1945* (2004); Barbara Molony and Kathleen Uno, eds., *Gendering Modern Japanese History* (2005); Daniel V. Botsman, *Punishment and Power in the Making of Modern Japan* (2005); Andrew Gordon, *The Modern History of Japan* (2003); Linda K. Menton et al., *The Rise of Modern Japan* (2003); Ian Inkster, *Japanese Industrialization: Historical and Cultural Perspectives* (2001); and Toshiaki Tachibanaki, *Confronting Income Inequality in Japan: A Comparative Analysis of Causes, Consequences, and Reform* (2005).

For an overview on China, see George Zhibin Gu and William Ratliff, *China and the New World Order: How Entrepreneurship, Globalization and Borderless Business Are Reshaping China and the World* (2006); Joseph Fewsmith, *China Since Tiananmen* (2007); Joseph W. Esherick, Paul G. Pickowicz, and Andres G. Walder, eds., *The Chinese Cultural Revolution as History* (2006); and I. Hsu, *The Rise of Modern China*, 2nd ed. (1975). For an excellent interpretive study, using a modernization model, see G. Rozman, ed., *The Modernization of China* (1981); see also Edward Friedman et al., *Chinese Village, Socialist State* (1991) and *Revolution, Resistance, and Reform in Village China* (2005); and Wolfgang Franke, *A Century of Chinese Revolution* (1970). On the Chinese revolutions, J. Spence, *The Gate of Heavenly Peace: The Chinese and Their Revolution, 1895–1980* (1982), is invaluable; on the communist revolution specifically, Edgar Snow, *Red Star Over China* (1968) is quite readable. On women's roles, see Margery Wolf, *Revolution Postponed: Women in Contemporary China* (1988). Consult also, as a source, A. Freemantle, ed., *Mao-Tse Tung: An Anthology of His Writings* (1962). On developments after Mao, I. Hsu, *China Without Mao: The Search for a New Order* (1983), is worthwhile.

On Japan, an excellent cultural interpretation is E. O. Reischauer, *The Japanese* (1988). See also Linda K. Menton et al., *The Rise of Modern Japan* (2003); M. Howe, *Modern Japan: A Historical Survey* (1986); and Daniel V. Botsman, *Punishment and Power in the Making of Modern Japan* (2005), as well as H. Patrick and H. Rosovsky, *Asia's New Giant: How the Japanese Economy Works* (1976). An important specific topic is covered in R. Story, *The Double Patriots: A Story of Japanese Nationalism* (1973). Japanese economic success and its significance are addressed in Ezra Vogel, *Japan as Number One: Lessons for Americans* (1980). On the Pacific Rim, see Philip West et al., eds., *Pacific Rim and the Western World: Strategic, Economic and Cultural Perspectives* (1987). See also G. Rozman, ed., *East Asian Region: Confucian Heritage and Its Modern Adaptation* (1991), and Bruce Cuming, *Korea's Place in the Sun: A Modern History* (1997).

See also Merle Goldman, *Historical Perspectives on Contemporary East Asia* (2000); Alexander Pantsov, *The Bolsheviks and the Chinese Revolution, 1919–1927* (2000); Ian Cook, *China's Third Revolution: Tensions in the Transition Towards a Post-Communist China* (2001); Edward Beauchamp, ed., *Women and Women's Issues in Post–World War II Japan* (1998); Vera Simons, *The Asian Pacific: Political and Economic Development in a Global Context* (1995); and S. Ichimore, *The Political Economy of Japanese and Asian Development* (1998).

31 India and Southeast Asia

During the first half of the 20th century, nationalist pressures built steadily on the Indian subcontinent and in southeast Asia. Dislocations produced by World War II prompted the end of European controls. In a few cases—most notably Vietnam—the struggle to achieve independence continued well after World War II, but in most instances, including India, decolonization occurred quickly and without much further conflict with the former imperialist powers. Thus, the history of India and southeast Asia since the late 1940s is characterized by the formation of newly independent nations and the establishment of their distinct political styles. India became the world's largest democracy, building on older political traditions as well as the legacy of British rule and nationalist struggle. Other nations on the Indian subcontinent and in southeast Asia were more authoritarian in political structure, though democracy gained ground by the 1990s, whereas Vietnam became communist. Problems of economic development also loomed large. Again, there was great diversity; a few new nations, such as Bangladesh, proved to be among the world's poorest. But in India itself, significant economic change took place, while parts of southeast Asia were pulled into the dynamic orbit of the Pacific Rim. India also experienced rapid population growth, becoming the world's most populous country early in the 21st century.

■KEY QUESTIONS *The Indian subcontinent and southeast Asia were part of the larger process of decolonization. But results varied. Why, compared to most other new nations, was India able to maintain a democracy? What was the balance between tradition and change in India and southeast Asia generally?*

THE RISE OF NATIONALISM

India provided a key example of the growing struggle for independence after 1914, just as it helped lead the movement of new nations after World War II. Rising nationalism in much of southeast Asia proved somewhat similar to patterns in India. Throughout southern Asia, indeed, the issue of national freedom moved to the top of the agenda during the years between the world wars. Problems in Europe weakened the hold of the imperialist nations, although they remained militarily dominant until the 1940s. Many Europeans became increasingly open to the idea that their colonies should work toward ultimate freedom. New currents in India and southeast Asia provided an even greater impetus to nationalism. The example of the Russian Revolution and the Leninist concept that a massive social revolution was possible as part of the struggle against an empire also attracted some Indian and southeast Asian leaders. Outside Vietnam, where nationalism and Marxism were closely linked, Marxism had less impact in southern Asia than in China, but it was a significant element none theless.

Religious commitments played a great role in shaping nationalist currents in the region. India's nationalist leaders tried to unite Muslims and Hindus, but in the end they failed, as heavily Islamic regions split from the country. Buddhism played a significant role in Burmese nationalism. The bad treatment of religious minorities created issues in Thailand (where a restive Muslim minority developed) and in Indonesia, where a Christian region, East Timor, chafed under national rule and ultimately gained its independence. At the same time, the continuing importance of religion helps explain why Marxist loyalties won only limited hold in most of the region.

Also important was a new wave of peasant unrest in various parts of south and southeast Asia. Peasant agitation resulted from growing population pressure combined with the more efficient tax collection and commercial agriculture that were part of imperialist rule. Peasants had their own idea of social justice, which included the more tolerant leadership of village headmen and greater access to land; they were rarely directly concerned with national independence, but their goals were compatible with liberation movements in that they resented the economic and administrative measures induced by outside rule.

Nonetheless, it was nationalism itself, gaining new vigor and popularity, that characterized the political history of southern Asia during the first half of the 20th century. Copied from Europe initially, nationalism took on, if anything, greater importance in India and southeast Asia. Here, it meant freedom from foreign domination and a chance to come to terms with the modern world while preserving important features of traditional civilization. In India, nationalism promised a kind of unity that the country had almost never known and a self-expression that had not been possible for many centuries. The Indian patriot Chittaranjan Das, writing early in the century, advanced the nationalist cause as follows:

> What is the ideal, which we must set before us? The first and foremost is the ideal of nationalism. Now what is nationalism? It is, I conceive, a process through which a nation expresses itself and finds itself, not in isolation from other nations, not in opposition to other nations, but as part of a great scheme by which, in seeking its own expression and therefore its own identity, it materially assists the self-expression and self-realization of other nations as well: Diversity is as real as unity. . . . I contend that each nationality constitutes a particular stream of the great unity, but no nation can fulfill itself unless and until it becomes itself and at the same time realizes its identity with Humanity.

The idealistic fervor of southern Asian nationalism, and especially the form of nationalism that took root in India, was a real force on its own, quite apart from specific issues and grievances.

Indian nationalism was given direct impetus by the events of World War I. Three million Indian soldiers fought in British armies during the war. At the same time, taxes and food shortages at home created discontent, bringing new strength to the Indian National Congress and an alliance between the Hindu leadership of the Congress party and the nation's Muslim League. This united front called for self-government within the British Empire. Britain did indeed establish new provincial legislative councils as a result, providing voting rights for 6 million of the nation's 250 million people; the councils had jurisdiction over such areas as education and public health. But this 1919 measure was obviously halfhearted, indicating London's continued suspicion of India's ability to rule itself. The central government remained firmly in British hands, with advisory councils elected by only a million Indian voters. The British followed a classic pattern of offering enough reform to encourage new expectations—along with the excitement caused by World War I and the principles of national self-determination discussed at Versailles—but not enough to satisfy all. At the same time, the British tightened police measures against those they viewed as troublemakers. The new repression resulted in a wave of rioting across the subcontinent. Police anxiety even prompted clashes at Hindu religious festivals; in one such confrontation, 379 celebrants, all unarmed, were killed by British-led troops. Police brutality here, and in major labor strikes, heightened Indian nationalism and helped unite upper-caste leaders with large numbers of workers and peasants. British policies also increasingly played Hindus and Muslims against each other. A new organization, the Muslim League, gained increasing support, particularly when Hindu nationalists seemed to fail to represent Islamic interests adequately.

Popular agitation continued in the 1920s. An influenza epidemic and crop failures that killed 5 million people led to a wave of rural uprisings against landlords and moneylenders. Some urban protest developed as well, with strikes among textile and railroad workers; Marxist doctrines made some headway. This diverse discontent was grist for the nationalists' mill, as it served to pressure the British. Middle-class nationalists even discussed a boycott of British goods, to protest India's economic dependence.

GANDHI'S NONVIOLENT STRATEGIES

In this context of growing agitation, the emergence in 1920 of Mohandas Gandhi as the leader and master tactician of the nationalist forces was a key development. Gandhi became an almost universally respected symbol of India's political awakening, the most important political figure in Indian history since the Mauryan and Gupta dynasties of the classical period. Gandhi had been born into a merchant family that also wielded great political influence in a small princely state north of Bombay, under British rule but shielded from the most direct Western pressure. His family had been devout Hindus, keenly persuaded of the importance of group loyalties. Gandhi himself studied law in Britain and practiced it for a time in South Africa, where he became keenly aware of the desperate plight of many Indians whom the British had imported as indentured laborers and who, like Gandhi himself, were often victims of brutal discrimination in public. Gandhi's reaction was not just one of indignation, but a deep search for a strategy by which the weak could overcome imperialist strength. His conclusion, drawn from his version of Hindu tradition plus other religious reading,

WORLD PROFILES

MOHANDAS GANDHI (1889–1948)

Mohandas Gandhi was unquestionably the leading figure in India's independence movement and one of the most important individuals in 20th-century world history. Gandhi spent part of his early life in South Africa, where growing movements by white leaders to segregate Asians as "colored" prompted his development of nonviolence opposition tactics. Trained in part in England, Gandhi later turned to modifications of Hindu tradition in his nonviolent mass protests against British rule. In particular, he attacked traditions of caste and the subjugation of women. He also projected an Indian alternative to modern society as it had developed in the West. He urged a craft-based, rather than factory- and common-based, economy. Gandhi's protest tactics worked, although his goals were less completely realized. Tragically, he was killed by a narrow Hindu nationalist group hostile to tolerance for Muslims. How much did Gandhi shape and reflect a distinctive Indian experience, and would India's independence have occurred differently without his guidance?

Mohandas Gandhi.

was collective nonviolence in resistance to injustice. He organized a campaign of peaceful marches to protest discrimination in South Africa, including nonviolent resistance to police attacks and arrest, which was successful in removing some of the most overt forms of discrimination against Indians in that colony.

Then, in 1915, Gandhi returned to India, and after a few years of reflection and experimentation with different tactics, he seized the opportunity provided by growing popular and nationalist unrest to mount a campaign of nonviolent resistance. Gandhi's great gift was to unite educated nationalist leaders with the rural masses, who saw in Gandhi an incarnation of deep spiritual values and whose own Hinduism was in accord with his emphasis on nonviolence. Gandhi told the Indian masses, who had long left the fighting to the warrior castes, that they too could be courageous:

> Wherein is courage required—in blowing others to pieces from behind a cannon, or with a smiling face to approach a cannon and be blown to pieces? Who is the true warrior—he who keeps death always as a bosom-friend, or he who controls the death of others? Believe me that a man devoid of courage and manhood can never be a passive resister.

Under Gandhi's leadership, the Congress movement became a mass political force for the first time, giving Indians a far greater taste of political participation than Britain's timid legislative experiments had allowed. Gandhi served also as a significant figure in a revived and revised Hinduism, in which ethical principles were stressed over both ceremonialism and the caste system.

Gandhi was also a master of tactics. His simple, holy style of life, which included a renunciation of sex, brought him the title *Mahatma,* or "saintly one." He could attack castes, and so please the masses and Muslims, while also wooing Brahmin religious leaders by praising tradition. He could converse with both striking workers

and moderate reformers. He appealed to new public interests for women, urging women to abandon domestic isolation for the sake of national freedom. However, he did not renounce Hindu family ideals. Above all, his stress on nonviolence confounded British authorities, who found it difficult to respond with all-out repression. Gandhi was frequently arrested, but his sentences aroused so much mass furor—heightened by well-publicized refusals to eat during imprisonment—that he was always ultimately released. Although Gandhi was not able to prevent periodic violence against British officials, he did direct most attention to peaceful mass disruption, refusals to pay taxes, and other tactics that were hard to counter. "We must voluntarily put up with the losses and inconveniences that arise from having to withdraw our support from a government that is ruling against our will." In this spirit, Gandhi and his followers boycotted elections, blocked trains by lying down on the tracks, and surrounded government buildings with thousands of quiet demonstrators so that officials had to walk over bodies in order to get to work.

By the 1930s, the British realized that they had to offer further reforms. However, a series of conferences with Indian leaders convinced the British that there was no way to please Hindus and Muslims, radicals and princes. Indeed, many Muslim leaders were increasingly antagonized, despite Gandhi's efforts at reconciliation, by the development of an Indian nationalism based largely on Hindu symbols and customs. They began talking of the need for their own nation, a *Pakistan,* or "land of the pure," instead of a unified India. Britain also played its own role in encouraging Hindu-Muslim divisions, in spite of considerable Muslim support of Congress party goals. In this context, the British issued a new constitution, in 1935, that provided for a federal system of 11 provinces, each with an elected assembly and ministers responsible for it, with a British-appointed governor to oversee the administration. At the center, a two-house parliament had some real power, although British officials remained in charge of defense and foreign affairs. The vote was extended to 35 million people.

Although disappointed at the lack of full self-governance, the Congress party ran in the new elections and won majorities in most states. Gandhi himself advocated service in the new governments as long as the British did not unduly interfere, whereas more radical leaders, including Jawaharlal Nehru, preached continued resistance. But all leaders agreed on the need for ultimate independence, and when Britain became unresponsive on this point after 1940, they refused to cooperate in the government's World War II effort. Gandhi, Nehru, and other leaders were arrested as a Japanese attack seemed imminent, and Britain ruled India through military control until the war's end. With Congress Party leaders in jail, the British turned to the Muslim League for support, promising acknowledgement of Pakistan when independence came.

NATIONALISM IN SOUTHEAST ASIA

A similar national awakening developed in southeast Asia during the 1920s and 1930s, although without such a compelling figure as Gandhi. In French-ruled Indochina, an advisory council was permitted, but as in India, such halfway reforms proved insufficient. Rioting broke out in major cities in 1930–1931. Although it was suppressed by force, nationalist agitation continued. Serious peasant outbreaks occurred as well, caused more by economic hunger than by nationalism, as the market for agricultural exports collapsed during the economic depression. A significant Marxist movement also took shape under the leadership of Ho Chi Minh, who became an enthusiastic convert to Marxism while working as a waiter in Paris, finding it a faith that could sustain him in his

country's long battle for national freedom. But amid the new unrest, the French were determined to preserve their power. A similar pattern prevailed in Indonesia. Dutch rulers granted local leaders half the seats in a national assembly, but when nationalist and socialist unrest spread against the limited reforms, the government responded by jailing the leaders—which only stimulated further agitation. In 1937, the nationalists petitioned the Dutch crown for dominion status within ten years.

Nationalism and peasant unrest against lack of land and high taxes created new ferment in Burma and Siam, where British influence predominated. In Siam, nationalist sentiment prompted a successful attack on Western control of tariff policy and special legal rights for foreigners. The nationalists celebrated their achievement by renaming their nation *Thailand,* or "land of the free." Finally, nationalists attacked U.S. control over the Philippines, where a popularly elected legislature already had real powers. Although Americans talked of ultimate independence for this land, they also discriminated against native Filipinos, whom they tended to treat with the same racism that they expressed toward blacks at home. Thus, Filipino nationalism persisted, though dominated by a land owner elite, and it also was enhanced by the economic problems brought about by the Great Depression, as U.S. resistance to Filipino exports grew amid that crisis. In 1934, the U.S. Congress increased Philippine rights to self-government and promised outright independence in 1944.

Southeast Asian nationalism generally was stimulated by the results of World War II. Japanese control of the Philippines, Indochina, and other areas was often harsher than Western imperialism, but it demonstrated that the West was vulnerable and to this extent spurred hopes for ultimate freedom. When Tokyo surrendered in 1945 to the Allies, many Westerners prepared to return to the southeast Asian plantations and social clubs as if nothing had happened, but in fact, a new era had begun in the whole region. Imperialism, difficult in the 1930s, had now become impossible.

DECOLONIZATION AFTER THE WAR

It was not surprising that the current of decolonization, which soon swept the world, bore its first postwar fruit in southern Asia. With nationalist resistance already well established in places such as India, most European powers, now exhausted, were unwilling to experience the trouble and risks of hanging on any further—even assuming that they could have done so successfully. The new Labor party in Britain was positively eager to leave India after 1945, for the costs of operating a government there had become too great to bear. A crucial issue remained—the split between Hindu and Muslim—which, to the sorrow of leaders such as Gandhi, occasioned bitter rioting as independence neared. The deepest conflict was resolved in 1947 by the creation of two states, a Muslim Pakistan and a predominantly Hindu India. Religion-based nationalism triumphed over the larger territorial nationalism in the Congress tradition, although this tradition persisted in India along with frequent religious and ethnic challenges.

Britain extended its decolonization policy by granting freedom to Ceylon (present-day Sri Lanka) and Burma (present-day Myanmar) in 1948. Malaysia also won independence after the British successfully suppressed a communist guerrilla movement. The United States made good on its earlier pledge by freeing the Philippines in 1946, while retaining substantial military bases on lease. The Dutch retreat from Indonesia was somewhat less graceful, as there was an attempt to reconquer the territory after the end of World War II. However, this effort failed, and an independent Indonesia was recognized in 1949.

Only in Indochina was national independence seriously delayed after World War II. The French, particularly eager to reassert their military strength after their disastrous loss to Hitler's armies in 1940, were unwilling to recognize the strength or validity of the nationalist movement. They were aided by the United States, which was hostile to communism, especially after the success of the Chinese revolution, and eager not to "lose" another Asian region to their cold war enemy. Ho Chi Minh, however, proved to be a stubborn opponent, successfully organizing a guerrilla warfare that depended on widespread peasant support and was impossible to suppress by conventional tactics. A series of defeats suffered by French troops led to a peace settlement in 1954, which brought division between a communist North Vietnam and a noncommunist, though politically authoritarian, South Vietnam. The French also withdrew from Laos and Cambodia. North Vietnam soon began to press its southern neighbor, with aid from the Soviet Union and China. As South Vietnam faced guerrilla attacks, it relied increasingly on the United States for aid. American participation in the conflict escalated in 1964, after North Vietnamese ships allegedly attacked American vessels, and over the next 10 years, more than 2 million U.S. soldiers were sent to fight in Vietnam. Despite massive American bombing raids, however, communist guerrilla forces gained ground, and the fighting also spread to Laos and Cambodia. Opposition to the war effort within the United States helped prompt peace talks, begun in 1969, which finally resulted in an end to the war in 1973. With U.S. forces withdrawn, and amid accusations from both sides about treaty violations, North Vietnam increased its troop levels in South Vietnam, and by 1975 it had gained full control of this region. For a time, communist Vietnam also imposed military control over Laos and Cambodia, partly to destroy a brutal and aggressive Khmer Rouge regime in the latter country. Laos and Cambodia regained independence after 1989.

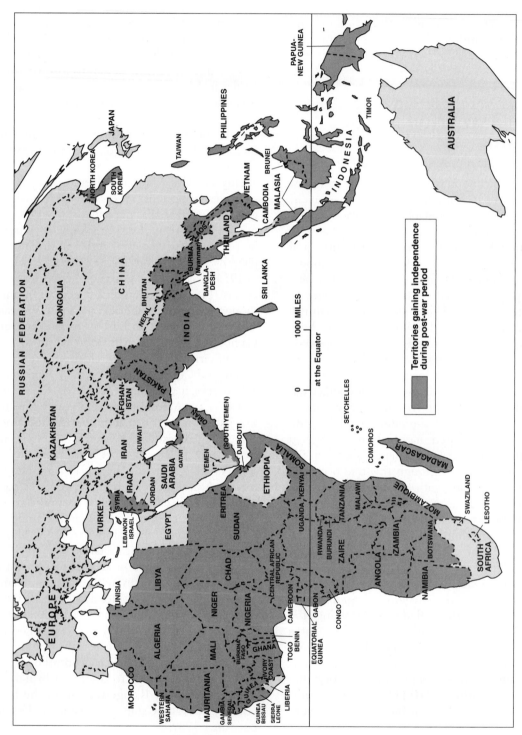

Decolonization in Africa and Asia After World War II

Territories gaining independence during post-war period

1000 MILES at the Equator

0

568

The rise of a communist regional state in southeast Asia was an extremely important development. The bitter warfare that had led to this state played a significant role first in French and then U.S. politics. More importantly, the same warfare resulted in massive devastation and loss of life within the region itself, creating long-lasting scars and severe problems of economic reconstruction. Military experience and a communist regime distinguished this part of southeast Asia from the majority of the new nations, where independence had come earlier and with far less trauma.

SOUTHEAST ASIA AFTER INDEPENDENCE

The rise of nationalism during the first half of the 20th century had provided most of southern Asia with such a compelling cause that the problems independence would generate were often obscured. The focus was on freedom from outside control. Leaders were less clear about what would be constructed when and if the Westerners left. Most nationalists assumed a democratic, parliamentary structure—to this extent, they copied Western values. However, there was profound division among religious groups, as in India, and between educated leaders and the peasant masses. This could make democracy difficult. Nationalists were also typically vague about economic and social issues. Gandhi, for example, had little interest in economic development in the sense of industrialization. He was not opposed to factory production but insisted on preventing its dehumanizing effects on workers; at times, he seemed to prefer enhancing peasant agriculture and home-based manufacturing. But other Indian leaders called for an aggressive drive toward economic modernization. Peasants, although often drawn to the nationalist cause, were far more interested in land and protection from world market fluctuations

than in purely political reforms or economic modernization. Urban workers, poorly paid and badly housed amid the conditions of early factories, also pressed for greater social justice. Dealing with these various pressures, while also establishing the institutions of government, was an arduous task after the excitement of attaining national freedom.

The new or revived nations of southeast Asia illustrated the range of possibilities and problems that followed from decolonization. Southeast Asian civilization had always been diverse. Traditional variations continued to be important, as differing religious and ethnic backgrounds determined distinctive policies. However, new distinctions now arose as well, as in the split between communist Vietnam and the noncommunist—sometimes anticommunist—policies of the other states of the region. With encouragement from the United States, a number of southeast Asian governments formed a loose alliance to coordinate resistance to Chinese and Vietnamese communist influence and to discuss common economic interests. Nonetheless, this grouping was not a significant unifying force amid the region's fascinating cultural and political diversity.

Most southeast Asian nations attempted to establish democratic parliamentary institutions after attaining independence, but most found these institutions impossible to maintain. Lack of political experience among the peasant masses, divisions within the population that prompted frequent rioting, and, often, the ambitions of individual nationalist leaders tended to turn governments toward more authoritarian policies. In the Philippines, for example, a parliamentary system modeled on that of the United States lasted until 1963, when President Ferdinand Marcos seized full power, which he retained, amid considerable corruption and political violence, for more than two decades. The Philippine government faced attacks from communist guerrillas, which were mostly controlled. It largely avoided any effort at land reform; a wealthy elite dominated the country, sharing power with the military. The gap between rich and poor was significant, and there was little progress toward economic development. The government nevertheless received substantial U.S. aid and support, from postwar reconstruction on, in part because of American concern for maintaining its military bases on the islands. Only in 1986 was the Marcos regime toppled, after trying to rig a new election, and replaced by a reformist regime that initiated more genuine democracy.

In Malaysia and the monarchy of Thailand, parliamentary institutions functioned somewhat more effectively than in the Philippines, and the repression of political opposition was less complete. By the 1970s, Thailand faced considerable pressure from the powerful Vietnamese armies on its northern border. Malaysia had earlier suppressed a communist guerrilla movement run mainly by the ethnic Chinese minority on the peninsula. Tension between native Malays and the Chinese minority continued to cause friction, however. It also made impossible a brief union with the city-state of Singapore, dominated by the Chinese; Singapore split off under a strong-willed leader bent on rapid economic growth and tight control of the city's population.

Burma, a largely Buddhist nation like Thailand, opted for considerable isolation soon after independence, hoping to avoid the influence of both the West and communist nations. A series of generals ran the country, the culture of which remained highly traditional—one of the only nations in the world that isolated so fully from broader international currents. Only a few indications of greater openness occurred by the early 2000s, as the country adopted the new name Myanmar. A courageous leader, Suu Kyi, galvanized democratic sentiment in the country, but she was kept under house arrest from 1999 on. The military regime tightened controls in 2008, strictly limiting foreign contacts.

Indonesia gained independence under the leadership of Achmed Sukarno, who soon established authoritarian rule, in part, as a means of unifying a diverse population. A strong communist movement influenced Sukarno, but an outright communist uprising in 1965 was defeated and the army seized power, killing at least half a million communists and radicals. The military also attacked the ethnic Chinese minority, who were resented for their hold over merchant activity in the cities. Sukarno was forced out of power, and the army generals ruled with no pretense of democracy. Firmly Muslim, the new government supported Islamic law and customs, although without the rigor of some other nations in the Islamic orbit. The authoritarian regime did, however, attack several minority nationalities as it retained its hold against the currents of democracy into the late 1990s. After 1998, however, popular uprisings forced the general out. Indonesia constructed a new, democratic regime that managed transitions according to election results, despite significant issues of economic development, internal ethnic clashes, and several bombings by international Islamic terrorists.

In Vietnam—first the North, after 1954, and then the larger nation after 1975—a different kind political and social system developed. Private businesses were seized, and land was taken from the large landowners and turned over to government-controlled communes. Vietnamese society was colored by the heavy toll of prolonged war, including the military outlays needed for the conquest of Cambodia against considerable resistance. The Vietnamese regime relied heavily on Soviet support, as relations with China soured. China had never welcomed a strong Vietnam and objected strenuously to the attack on Cambodia. Border tensions, including one brief war, further encouraged the strong militaristic tone of the Vietnamese version of communism. Economic development remained meager into the later 1980s, because of wartime dislocations and continuing military costs. By the 1990s, however, Vietnam followed China's policy of greater openness to the outside world and a more market-oriented economy, still

By the mid-1990s, the failed efforts of the United States to isolate Vietnam gave way to increasing economic and diplomatic contacts. One example of American corporate penetration is depicted in this street scene from Hanoi in 1993. The opening of Vietnam to foreign investment, assistance, and tourism accelerated through the 1990s. In this atmosphere it has been possible to begin to heal the deep wounds and animosities generated by decades of warfare waged by the Vietnamese people against advanced industrial nations such as Japan, France, and the United States.

combined with a strong communist state. Ties with the outside world increased, with many study trips sent abroad. A growing number of foreign firms located factories in Vietnam to take advantage of cheap labor.

Except for Vietnam, and the Philippines until 1986, most of southeast Asia tried to combine an interest in social reform, including aid to the peasantry, with considerable private enterprise. A number of nations experienced noteworthy economic growth. More productive crops were developed in the 1960s as part of the Green Revolution, which brought the aid of Western science to bear on the food problems of agricultural countries, thus allowing most southeast Asian nations to feed themselves. Particularly important were new strains of rice, which grew faster and had higher yields than those grown formerly. The Green Revolution favored wealthy farmers who could afford expensive seeds and fertilizers, but it nevertheless helped many nations regain self-sufficiency in food production. Even so, economic advance was modified by considerable population growth. Most southeast Asian nations continued to depend heavily on raw materials and cash crop exports to the industrialized nations of the West or Japan, and this dependence brought the usual problems of low and uncertain incomes on the world market. Except in dynamic Singapore, full industrialization had yet to come.

INDIA AND PAKISTAN

India presented an unusual mixture of strengths and weaknesses as it attained independence in 1947. It lacked a consistently successful political tradition, having far more often been divided and ruled through outside conquest than by self-government. It embraced a wide array of religions and languages. Despite important pockets of modern industry, it had a largely agricultural economy pressed by a rapidly growing population. On the other hand, India had an unusually well-established nationalist movement, which had a recognized and experienced leadership. Because of roughly two centuries of British rule, it had also been exposed to Western political ideas and institutions, including an effective civil service system.

The birth pains of the new nation were a severe disappointment to Gandhi and other nationalist leaders. Growing Muslim insistence on a separate nation met vigorous Hindu opposition,

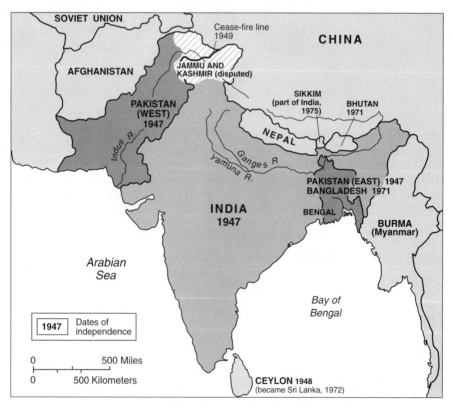

The Partition of South Asia: The Formation of India, Pakistan, Bangladesh, and Sri Lanka

as Congress-style nationalism ultimately failed to override religious divisions, but massive violence during 1946 convinced both sides that unity was indeed out of the question. The new nation of Pakistan comprised two regions: the heartland was West Pakistan, to the northwest of India, in the portion of the subcontinent nearest the Middle East, where Islam had the strongest roots; the second area was East Pakistan, to India's northeast. Even partition was insufficient to prevent further religious antagonisms. In the weeks after independence, Hindus and Muslims battled each other, causing at least 200,000 deaths (and possibly many more) and forcing 3 million people to flee their homes to seek sanctuary with coreligionists in one of the two new nations. Gandhi and the Congress party were powerless to stop the bitter hatred. Gandhi, who started a fast to protest Hindu persecution of Muslims and to restore the "best friendship" between the two peoples, was shot by a Hindu fanatic. Tensions with a Muslim minority continued to affect India. Furthermore, relations between the nations of India and Pakistan were hostile, each eyeing the other warily and devoting hard-won tax revenues to military expenditures designed to keep the other at bay.

Pakistan followed a political pattern rather similar to that of the southeast Asian nations. It adopted an authoritarian form of government in 1958, under military leadership. Even under these conditions, the nation proved unable to maintain unity between its two main provinces, as East Pakistan constantly complained of neglect. In 1971, a revolt in the east produced the new nation of Bangladesh, the eighth most populous country in the world and one of the poorest. Pakistan itself, although less crowded, faced serious problems of economic development. Land reform was slighted in favor of supporting the regional elite. In the 1970s, in an appeal to religious tradition, Pakistan's military government adopted increasingly rigorous Islamic laws. The nation also faced tensions with the Soviet Union as a result of the invasion of Afghanistan,

and this too became a burden despite U.S. aid. More democratic elections occurred in the 1990s, but political stability was fragile and the army kept a watchful eye. A military regime returned in 1999, just after Pakistan tested its first nuclear bomb and as tension with India mounted. Pakistan cooperated with the United States in attacks on terrorists in neighboring Afghanistan from late 2001 on. Islamic political agitation within Pakistan continued, however. Tensions with India, particularly over control of the disputed region of Kashmir (whose population was largely Muslim), continued to simmer as well.

India, which controlled the majority of the territory and population on the subcontinent despite the 1947 partition, developed a distinctive political and cultural pattern that combined tradition and change. Most striking was its ability to maintain democracy; indeed, India has been one of the few newly independent nations to preserve this political form with any consistency since World War II. Equally important was India's resolve to combine serious social reform with economic development and esteem for many aspects of Hindu culture.

Politically, India retained a federal system, which reflected the nation's regional diversity and the pattern set under British rule. Individual states had considerable power, although there were disputes with the central government at various points. The nation was ruled by the nationalist Congress party with only two exceptions—in the late 1970s, when a coalition of conservative groups assumed office briefly, and again through the 1990s and early 2000s in what was a significant political change. However, multiparty competition was free and fierce, and freedoms of the press and association were not normally limited. Control of many state governments, indeed, passed to parties other than the Congress group, including the Communist party. Congress party leaders, although mainly drawn from the political elite, learned to campaign effectively among the masses, combining the prestige of high status with genuine popular appeal.

There were some questions about Indian democracy, to be sure. The Congress party dominance prevented a great deal of experience with partisan shifts at the central government level. As in the Japanese Liberal Democratic party, more political maneuvering took place among factions within the dominant group than among different parties. India also experienced few leadership changes at the top. The first prime minister, the nationalist Jawaharlal Nehru, held power for 17 years. He was succeeded by his daughter, Indira Gandhi (no relation to Mohandas Gandhi). Although Indira Gandhi was initially selected by Congress party stalwarts for her presumed susceptibility to manipulation, she proved to be a tough-minded leader who was very conscious of her power. Indeed, it was under her rule that liberal rights were suspended, from 1975 to 1977, as she tried to clamp down on a number of opposition groups and arrested many political critics. These policies led, however, to the Congress party's defeat in 1977, which suggested that the curtailment of democracy within India was costly. New elections in 1980 restored Indira Gandhi to power, but there was no attempt to revive authoritarian rule. Regional disunity, however, remained a serious problem. Gandhi faced growing opposition from the minority Sikh religion, which demanded greater autonomy for the Sikh-dominated state of Punjab. This led in the early 1980s to renewed religious rioting, this time between Hindus and Sikhs, and Indira Gandhi's assassination by Sikh militants. Her successor was her son Rajiv, which raised concern about a new dynasty ruling India; again, the formal institutions of a liberal democracy continued to function, doubtless solidified by some popular faith in the ruling family. Rajiv's assassination by southern Tamil separatists ended his family's reign. The Congress party also yielded its control, but a new political coalition assumed power smoothly. India had produced four decades of strong political performance, suggesting that its democratic forms responded to traditions and needs alike and had become part of the nation's political heritage.

India also took the lead in establishing a distinctive diplomatic policy. The new nation remained friendly with its former British rulers and participated actively in Commonwealth meetings to discuss mutual concerns with Britain, Canada, Australia, New Zealand, and the growing number of other former British colonies. At the same time, Nehru and his successors were firmly resolved to avoid entrapment in alliances that were irrelevant to India's needs. The government thus assumed the initiative in organizing interested non-Western nations in a nonaligned, or "third force," bloc that sought to deal with both the West and the Soviet Union while shunning military pacts with either side. The first meeting of this neutral group took place in 1955, and although the cohesion of the group oscillated, India persevered in establishing good relations with both the United States and Soviet Union, often lecturing the great powers on the evils of their competition. India itself faced diplomatic problems, particularly with Pakistan and, periodically in the 1960s, with China as well. However, the nation avoided extensive involvement in issues outside its regional concerns, except perhaps for a sometimes moralizing rhetoric.

Congress party leaders from Nehru on were eager to remake their nation without losing its identity; independence and political power were not enough. Their vision differed somewhat from that of Mohandas Gandhi's in that they were more concerned with economic modernization and less disdainful of factories and sophisticated commerce. Nevertheless, Gandhi, too, had sought some changes in India's old order. Key targets in early legislation were the caste system and traditional gender relations, as India sought to institute equality under the law. The nation's constitution granted equality to women, including the right to vote, and allowed

HISTORY DEBATE

WOMEN'S CONDITIONS IN INDIA

For many Indian women, conditions changed during the 20th century. Early in the century, a number of Western feminists encouraged new schools; Christian missionaries also worked for schooling. Gandhi actively combated traditions of domestic isolation, or purdah. This was one of the changes he had to promote in order to form an effective mass political movement, and women played a prominent part in many of his demonstrations. There was no hesitation about granting the vote to women when independence came.

But patterns were complex, and scholars debate about how to sort out the complexity. Two issues predominate. First, there were huge variations by region and social class. Rural women, still usually uneducated, saw only gradual change. Their family lives were heavily defined by patriarchal traditions. Birth rates gradually dropped, but they remained high enough to condition women's lives.

The second complication, affecting urban women aware of Western models, involved some degree of backlash against change. Many women found Western models irrelevant or harmful. A woman's magazine argued that Indian traditions were much better for women than the styles of the modern West. With arranged marriages, women did not have to think constantly about finding a man or sacrificing everything to beautification. Many urban women worked for their own combination of tradition and change. They enjoyed many global consumer forms, often spoke English, but also tried to live up to the expectations of being a good Hindu wife and mother. Would this kind of approach prove temporary, as more pressure for westernization set in, or was it a potentially durable mixture?

women to seek divorce and marry outside their caste. The caste system itself was outlawed. The government tried to encourage former untouchables to participate more fully in Indian society, by establishing quotas for "ex-untouchables" in universities and government jobs. But India's attack on these ancient social traditions was of necessity less forceful than China's war on ancestor worship and other family practices, for outright coercion or the formation of radical new institutions such as communes would have been incompatible with democratic forms. India had no revolution. Therefore, in fact, strong remnants of the caste system remained in India, although not enforced by law. Most government leaders were drawn from the traditionally higher castes, as were most of the growing numbers of university-trained professionals and managers. At the family level, the authority of men continued to be strong, particularly among the rural majority.

Practices such as arranged marriages, often with the partners pledged during their teens and not even necessarily meeting before their wedding, continued to be widespread at all social levels.

In economic policy, India's leadership professed a nondoctrinaire socialism. This meant, in practice, considerable economic planning toward the allocation of scarce resources; it also meant government operation of key services such as airlines and railroads. But substantial private enterprise remained as well. Government welfare services focused mainly on basic hygiene, as the nation's poverty prevented a more elaborate social security system. The government also encouraged widespread peasant landownership, dismantling some former estates and helping to clear new land toward this end. This policy, along with progressive taxation, reduced the economic power of the old princely aristocracy.

A key concern, even in the heady early days of independence, was economic development. Congress party leaders had long wanted fuller economic equality for India, as a weapon against Western dominance. Furthermore, steady population growth virtually compelled attention to the issue of economic growth. Government planning and private enterprise, plus some foreign economic aid, promoted substantial growth during the 1950s; the national income expanded by 42 percent. However, the nation's population grew from 360 to 439 million during the same decade, which eliminated half the economic gain. During the 1960s, per capita income stagnated, and India was forced to import food to prevent starvation. This prompted greater concern for improved agricultural production. The government helped sponsor Green Revolution research on better seeds; it also promoted the widespread use of fertilizers and pesticides. These measures yielded impressive results; despite continued population growth, the nation remained self-sufficient in agriculture from 1970 on.

The government also attacked the population problem directly. Under Nehru, official measures were half-hearted, but with a growth rate of 2.4 percent per year, it became increasingly clear that no serious improvement in living standards for the impoverished masses could occur without birth control. Indira Gandhi's government stepped up propaganda efforts, with slogans such as "A Happy Family Is a Small Family," and medical personnel provided free birth-control devices and procedures, including vasectomies for men. But the campaign met massive popular resistance. Men and women alike feared to tamper with God's ways. Men worried that an operation such as a vasectomy would destroy their "male power," making them as docile as castrated animals. They also continued to value a large family as a sign of good fortune, seeking particularly a sufficient number of sons to ensure their own care in old age. Popular resistance to birth control helped prompt Indira Gandhi's suspension of liberties in 1975 as the government launched an effort to force poor men with large families to undergo vasectomies. This campaign stopped, however, in 1977, as the government returned instead to a policy of intense propaganda and widespread medical services. India's birth rate did begin to slow in the later 1970s, as people became more aware of family planning as an alternative to grinding poverty, but birth rates remained high.

Despite population pressure, which diverted extensive resources to increasing agricultural production and was unquestionably responsible for massive poverty in the countryside and crowded cities alike, India managed to resume its pattern of economic growth in the 1970s. Modern industrial technologies were applied to metallurgy and chemical production, creating pockets of advanced factory industry in a still agricultural nation. India produced cars and tried to limit imports. As a result of its technological interchange with the West and Soviet Russia, India for a time during the early 1980s surpassed China technologically. Modern factories as well as rising agricultural productivity accounted for a 4 percent annual growth rate in the years after 1975. India remained vulnerable in the world economy, and its export performance has lagged despite important industrial sales in the Indian Ocean region. The nation's growth record fell well behind that of the Pacific Rim, particularly after the mid-1980s. Elections of new leadership in 1991 that broke the hold of the Congress party greatly reduced state economic regulation in favor of freer market activities. This created the context for the rapid growth of India's software industry and a considerable acceleration of economic expansion, including the rapid growth of an urban, consumerist middle class. Indian economic growth remained strong in the decade after 2000, and many predicted that the country would become one of the world's economic leaders within a few decades.

Indian cultural life showed a predictable balance between new themes and old. India's leaders encouraged a rapid expansion of education, which gradually cut into widespread illiteracy. By the 1970s, literacy rates had doubled from the 1947 figure to 30 percent. At the elitist level, scientific training spread widely, and Indian researchers participated actively, in both India and foreign laboratories, toward advances in physics, biology, medicine, and computer science. The Indian government even mounted its own space program. Cultural change was also encouraged, although particularly among the elite, by the continued reliance on the English language, which helped maintain India's openness to developments in Western culture. Congress party leaders had hoped to promote Hindi as a new national language, but regional resistance was so great that English remained the only language with countrywide currency in government, the universities, and the press. A number of leading writers also relied primarily on English. Because Indian universities produced more trained professionals than the society required, a large number of doctors and lawyers emigrated to Britain or North America, giving India further ties with the West, although at some economic cost.

At the popular level, however, traditional cultural forms wielded strong influence, albeit sometimes in new guises. An active film industry produced innumerable stories of adventure and romance, couched in the terms of traditional popular literature. Few foreign movies penetrated beyond elitist levels, while at the same time Indian films almost never reached beyond the country's borders. By the 1990s, however, a new fusion of Hollywood and Indian styles occurred in the film industry in Mumbai (formerly Bombay), whose center was dubbed "Bollywood" and whose work presented some international box office appeal. Along with films, literature in the various traditional languages remained active, as did traditional artistic styles. Indian painters and sculptors did not participate widely in modern or "international" artistic developments, preferring to continue working mainly in older modes. Artistic imagery, both old and new, remained a vital part of Indian popular life, as did religion. Devotion to Hindu ritual and belief was widespread among the majority, and reverence for holy men continued to be a high priority.

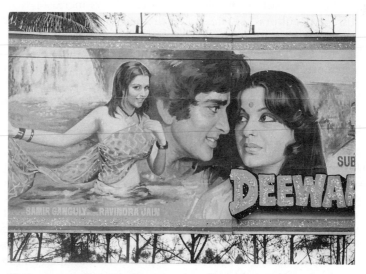

Movie poster in Bombay, advertising actor Shashi Kapoor in the film *Deewangee*.

Part of India's distinctiveness rested in the ongoing divisions between the elite and popular culture. The elite, drawn mainly from higher castes, were responsive to new educational opportunities as well as to the new outlets for political and managerial leadership. In this group, both men and women played a meaningful role, for here India's attack on gender divisions had a significant result. Women graduated from universities in growing numbers and held important government and professional positions. The elite did not become Western. Traditional patterns such as arranged marriages continued among this group, as did distinctive religious and cultural interests. However, there was significant change in elitist values, including significant contact with Western (particularly English-language) cultural and scientific developments. Popular culture was quite a different matter, which helps explain the widespread resistance to government-sponsored measures such as birth control in the name of religion and family. India's masses did change, as a minority entered jobs in modern factories and a larger number altered some of their agricultural methods. But change here definitely took place amid vigorous devotion to a number of earlier values. Distinctive religious and cultural interests showed even in basic outlook, as Indians preserved a greater place for imagination in their childrearing practices, putting less stock than Westerners (or east Asians) on careful lessons in the distinction between pretend and "reality."

India's divisions were regional and religious as well as social. Lacking a highly centralized culture, India had long experienced religious diversity. Despite Mohandas Gandhi's hopes to use nationalism to transcend these differences and a long tradition of considerable tolerance, relations among Hindus, Muslims, and Sikhs grew tenser by the 1990s and early 2000s. Cultural change, including the partial secularism of the elite, helped explain new concerns among religious leaders; so did the older tensions with Muslims. The result was recurrent clashes that threatened the stability of the government. A Hindu fundamentalist movement arose, calling on the government to promote Hinduism at the expense of other religions—a fascinating, perhaps ominous development. Large numbers of new temples arose, often small but often placed in ways that disrupted traffic—an interesting sign of renewed popular piety. Fundamentalist political power increased in the 1990s and early 2000s, and Hindu nationalists assumed control of the government, increasing military spending and nuclear development and occasionally talking tough in confrontations with Pakistan. While the Hindu government largely avoided extreme intolerance, it was under pressure from its supporters to attack the Muslim minority within India and to limit foreign influence. The Congress party regained power in 2005, however, and adopted a more conciliatory approach to Pakistan.

Change and continuity remained complex. The boom in high-technology sectors helped expand a middle class, estimated at as many as 80 million people. Along with the new vigor of Hinduism, a secular popular culture emerged. This was the context in which Bollywood moviemakers increasingly combined traditional themes with Hollywood techniques. Film stars enjoyed great prestige. Some practitioners also combined traditional musical forms with rap and other Western styles, drawing attention outside India as well as within. Another contested sign of cultural change was the proliferation of beauty contests.

INDIA AND CHINA

Because India established an independent democracy just as China underwent its communist revolution, comparisons between the two Asian giants became commonplace. Which path would produce greater political success? Which path would prove most compatible with economic development? American observers initially pinned their faith on India, convinced that democracy and real modernization ultimately went hand in hand. But just as India's democracy proved incapable of stemming population growth—and as India insisted on neutrality rather than an alliance with the West, to the annoyance of many Americans—opinion veered, and China often seemed the better bet. Indian traditions, including religious beliefs and a certain idealism coupled with the country's phenomenal population growth, now seemed less favorable than forceful Chinese methods to the necessary reforms. As China became friendlier with the United States in a number of well-publicized moves, enthusiasm for China's development prospects increased.

By the early 21st century, neither China nor India had managed to achieve a full industrial revolution in the style of Japan, and their economies, through growing rapidly, remained smaller. At the same time, both have experienced significant economic change. Both have health rates and per capita income rates significantly above those in the poorest agricultural nations, with China, however, now in the lead. Both have seemingly vigorous governments, albeit with quite different institutions, styles, and problems. A comparison is complicated, to be sure, given our ignorance of some Chinese developments, as official control of information remains extensive. Nonetheless, it seems certain that, building on government tradition and communist zeal, China has become more effective than India in reducing its rates of population growth. Most experts assume that India will indeed surpass China as the world's most populous country in the early 21st century. On the other hand, India has advanced more consistently in technological development and higher education, and it has also had more regular contacts with the outside world. Each nation, then, uses both distinctive traditions and distinctive current political forms to produce its own balanced mix of strengths and weaknesses. Ongoing differences between India and China recall different traditions established in the classical period, particularly in terms of political values and institutions but also in terms of attitudes toward the outside world. Later developments are also compelling examples of other important distinguishing factors: India's complex experience as a colony compared to the Western treatment of China, the fact that China had a revolution and India did not, perhaps even the different creative styles of Gandhi and Mao as seminal 20th-century leaders. If China has ultimately gained the edge in economic growth, it may have suffered more in terms of cultural instability and dislocation.

PATHS TO THE PRESENT

The rise of nationalism and the subsequent achievement of national independence are the central features of south and southeast Asian history in the contemporary era. This theme encouraged the maintenance or revival of many traditional elements, including widespread religious commitment and considerable attention to customary art forms.

Nationalism, however, also promoted change. In India, nationalist leaders actively pushed for historic reconsideration of the caste system and traditional patriarchy, as well as the establishment of a modern democratic political structure. Independence of India involved far more than the removal of British control, with major innovations built into the structure of the new nation. The dedication to economic development and the new level of success from the 1990s on, also had wider implications for change.

The impact of nationalism in other parts of southeast Asia was varied. Communists in Vietnam worked directly for major reforms. Burmese leaders, in contrast, discouraged change while themselves introducing new methods of political repression. In countries such as Indonesia and Malaysia, a considerable degree of industrial development and then, in the 1990s, the greater acceptance of democratic politics opened the door to potential additional changes, even as religious affiliations and regional religious divisions remained strong.

SUGGESTED WEB SITES

On colonialism and nationalism in Southeast Asia, see http://www.seasite.niu.edu/crossroads/ wilson/colonialism.htm; on the wars for Vietnam, see http://vietnam.vassar.edu/; on the story of India's independence struggle, see http://www.kamat.com/kalranga/freedom/. For information on other countries in South Asia, see https://www.cia.gov/library/publications/ the-world-factbook/index.html.

SUGGESTED READINGS

Recent work includes Ramachandra Guha, *India After Gandhi: The History of the World's Largest Democracy* (2007); Robert W. Stern, *Changing India: Bourgeois Revolution on the Subcontinent* (2003); A. G. Noorani, *The Muslims of India: A Documentary Record* (2003); Ranabir Samaddar, *A Biography of the Indian Nation, 1947–1997* (2001); C. J. Fuller and Véronique Benei, *The Everyday State and Society in Modern India* (2001); Kiran Dhingra, ed., *The Andaman and Nicobar Islands in the Twentieth Century* (2005); P. N. Dhar, *Indira Gandhi, The "Emergency," and Indian Democracy* (2000); Peter John Brobst, *The Future of the Great Game: Sir Olaf Caroe, India's Independence, and the Defense of Asia* (2005); Meghnad Desai, *Development and Nationhood: Essays in the Political Economy of South Asia* (2005); Donald E. Weatherbee with Ralf Emmers, Mari Pangestu, and Leonard C. Sebastian, *International Relations in Southeast Asia: The Struggle for Autonomy* (2005); Gianni Sofri, *Gandhi and India* (1999); Susan Bayly,

Caste, Society and Politics in India from the 18th Century to the Modern Age (1999); Nicholas Dirks, *Castes of Mind: Colonialism and the Making of Modern India* (2001); S. Rushdie and Elizabeth West, *Mirrorwork: 50 Years of Indian Writing, 1947–1997* (1997); and Vikrameditya Pradash, *Chandigarh's Le Corbusier: The Struggle for Modernity in Postcolonial India* (2002).

A provocative general study of Asian politics, with particular reference to southern Asia, is L. W. Pye's *Asian Power and Politics: The Cultural Dimensions of Authority* (1985), which argues for the difficulty of using Western concepts to understand the Asian state. See also William H. Overholt, *Asia, America, and the Transformation of Geopolitics* (2007) and Ornit Shani, *Communalism, Caste and Hindu Nationalism* (2007).

On southeast Asia, D. G. E. Hall, *A History of South-East Asia* (1981) is a good survey; see also Alan Wood, *Asian Democracy in World History* (2004) and R. N. Kearney, *Politics and Modernization in South and Southeast Asia* (1974). See also M. C. Ricklefs, *A History of Modern Indonesia* (2002).

Recommended readings on Vietnam include G. Kolko's profound *The Anatomy of a War (1985); Qiang Zhai, China and the Vietnam Wars, 1950–1975* (2000); David W. P. Elliott, *The Vietnamese War: Revolution and Social Change in the Mekong Delta, 1930–1975* (1985); George C. Herring, *America's Longest War: The United States and Vietnam, 1950–1975*, 4th ed. (2002); Duong Van Mai Elliott, *The Sacred Willows: Four generations in the Life of a Vietnamese Family* (1999).

Excellent source reading on 20th-century India is provided by various English-language novelists, who write directly of Indian life, although using Western languages as well as literary conventions. A well-known example of such a writer is Rabindranath Tagore. More strictly contemporary authors are Kamale Markandaya, Shanta Ramarao (on women), T. Shivasankara Pillai (on the south), and R. K. Narayan (on peasants). Also relevant is the work of novelist and essayist V. S. Naipaul, who is of Indian extraction but, because he was raised in the West Indies, writes as an outsider.

Several major themes weave together in the most recent historical patterns of the oldest area of civilization in the world. Political unity in the Middle East, already tenuous during the 19th century, ended completely after World War I. A few subsequent efforts to revive larger segments, usually under the banners of Arab nationalism or Muslim brotherhood, failed. As new nations were carved out of the former territory of the Ottoman Empire, semi-imperialist controls by various European states coexisted with the independence of several regional states between the wars. After World War II, the entire region gained independence. Divisions among Middle Eastern nations were compounded by a diversity of political forms. Monarchies arose in a few cases—virtually the only recent instances in which monarchy remained a serious political force in the 20th century. Strongman regimes were even more characteristic. Some Middle Eastern states worked vigorously to modify age-old traditions, including the force of Islam, in the name of more secular goals. Others sought to preserve older values above all else.

Partly because of political divisions, the Middle East became the world's leading trouble spot after World War II. The oil wealth discovered in the Middle East during the 20th century gave the region new importance in the world economy, but it also attracted greed; this intensified the potential for outside interference in Middle Eastern affairs. Further, the creation of a new Jewish state after World War II produced a seemingly irresolvable tension that provoked internal warfare within the region and a series of interventions from the leading powers in the cold war.

Finally, the Middle East generated an unusually complex pattern of reform efforts and counter reactions. A new regime in Turkey, installed in the wake of the collapse of the Ottoman Empire, provided the first of many secularization attempts that succeeded in producing some industrialization and agricultural development, as well as new systems of education and relationships both in society at large and within the family. Nonetheless, change came painfully in the Middle East, and a number of Islamic leaders, in the name of traditional ideals, helped mobilize reactions against the new trends. A current of Islamic fundamentalism arose, particularly from the 1970s on; by the 1990s, acts of terrorism against apparent enemies of Islam increased as well. Thus, the Middle East produced a more bitter and overt clash between reformist and conservative forces than any other civilization in the contemporary world. Friction was often heightened by disputes over political form and rivalries among the new nations, adding greatly to the intricacy, and often the tragedy, of recent Middle Eastern history.

■**KEY QUESTIONS**   *The Middle East is in the daily news. Because we know the region is troubled, and because we know that some Middle Easterners dislike the United States, it is sometimes tempting to generalize about the region only in terms of religious fervor and political violence. What were the main patterns in the region during the 20th century, in addition to the persistence of Islam? What features has the region shared with other civilizations in the 20th century, for example, in terms of the impact of anticolonialism or of globalization?*

REPLACING THE OTTOMAN EMPIRE

The Ottoman Empire's alliance with Germany during World War I opened the most recent chapter of Middle Eastern history. Britain and France worked to undermine Ottoman rule as part of their own war effort; they encouraged Arab nationalism, against Turkish control, and the British also vaguely promised Jewish leaders a new homeland in Palestine. Wartime pledges plus the ringing ideals of President Wilson at the Versailles Peace Conference prompted many Arab

leaders to hope for outright freedom. Instead, they encountered victorious Western allies bent on extending imperialism to their region; not only Britain and France but also Italy and Greece were eager for new territory as the spoils of war. Thus, Middle Eastern nationalism was at once stimulated and frustrated, a dangerous combination.

One point was clear, however: the Ottoman Empire could no longer be supported. Arab leaders, united in their hatred of the Turks, agreed on this point with European imperialists, who hoped to carve up the region for their own purposes. Arab uprisings were led by the chief magistrate of Mecca, Hussein Ibn Ali. Then at the war's end, French and British forces moved into the Middle East; the French taking over Syria and Lebanon; the British occupying Palestine, Jordan, and Iraq. The 1920s Treaty of Sèvres proclaimed the end of the Ottoman Empire. Efforts to conquer Turkey itself failed, however. A young Turk military leader, Mustafa Kemal, organized a Turkish resistance movement, defeating both Greek and Western invasion forces. Kemal's success resulted in new negotiations with the European powers and produced a 1923 treaty that created Turkey as a new, separate nation. This treaty not only ensured Turkish independence but also guaranteed the nation's continued strategic importance in European and Russian diplomacy because of its important geographic location.

Buoyed by his military and diplomatic success, Kemal unseated the sultan and proclaimed a secular republic in the new Turkey. Like Muhammad Ali in Egypt a century before, Kemal intended to lead the modernization of an Islamic nation, to achieve parity with the European states on their own terms. He carefully fostered a new Turkish nationalism separate from religious faith. He moved the country's capital from Istanbul to Ankara, in the Turkish heartland. Profoundly influenced by Western political ideas, Kemal introduced parliamentary institutions and a new voting system. But his version of democracy was tightly controlled, with a single party—the People's party—preventing any legal opposition.

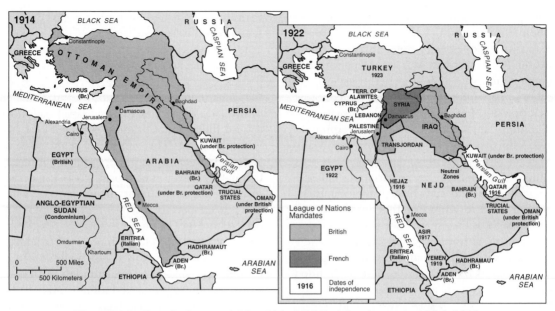

The Middle East Before and After World War I Settlements, 1914–1922

Like other notable westernizing leaders—including Peter the Great—Kemal believed that authoritarianism was an essential precondition of change, for the people had to be forced to accept reforms. Kemal, who took the name *Atatürk*, or "father of the Turks," vigorously attacked the hold of Islam. He abolished the religious caliphate and made the state secular. Civil marriage was required, and a secular school system was established. The regime outlawed many Muslim customs and symbols, including polygamy and traditional clothing— Western dress was mandatory. Sunday rather than Friday was proclaimed the national day of rest, and Muslim law was superseded by the laws of the state, which were modeled after Western codes. Arabic script was replaced with a Latin alphabet for the Turkish language, judged easier to learn and thus more appropriate for modern education. Against Islamic tradition also, Atatürk granted women the right to vote and to receive an education. A concerted effort to extend primary schools reduced illiteracy from 85 percent in 1914 to 42 percent in 1932.

Atatürk's reforms, like those in Peter the Great's Russia or Meiji Japan, included stirring attacks on traditional clothing. It is important to recognize, and to explain, the passions involved. Here is how Atatürk framed his views on the fez, a traditional cap for upper-class Ottoman men: "It was necessary to abolish the fez, which sat on our heads as a sign of ignorance, of fanaticism, of hatred to progress and civilization, and to adopt in its place the hat, the customary head-dress of the whole civilized world, thus showing that . . . no difference existed between the Turkish nation and the whole family of civilized mankind."

Atatürk's regime also promoted industrialization. A number of factories were established under state guidance. Cities grew. Turkey vigorously pursued the training of engineers and other technical personnel, to make foreign experts unnecessary. At the same time, unions were forbidden to strike, in order to prevent any barriers to economic growth. By 1939, a year after Atatürk's death, the economy had advanced enough so that foreign railroad companies could be bought out—a major blow against lingering economic imperialism.

Atatürk's hopes were not entirely fulfilled, however. His power base was secure; nationalism unquestionably gained ground; traditional culture yielded to new interests in science and economic development. However, the rural majority was not entirely supportive of the new regime, as Muslim objections to secularism persisted. Many crusading schoolteachers reported persistent traditionalism—in their view, superstitious belief— among their students and village leaders. Atatürk's successors had to allow for this deeply rooted religious faith, as they slowed the pace of reform. Furthermore, although Turkey became a new nation and successfully maintained its independence, bolstered by the largest, best-disciplined army in the region, it did not fully industrialize. Economic growth was slow, poverty widespread. Despite the genuine revolution in Turkish politics and culture, this was no Japanese-style leap forward in terms of economic change.

Turkey was the most dramatic case of new Middle Eastern politics after World War I, but it was not the only one. Persia, dominated before the war by British and Russian influence, proclaimed new independence as well, shaking off British efforts to maintain control. Persian nationalists selected an army officer, Riza Khan, soon known as the shah, or king, as their new leader. The new ruler worked for economic change as well as independence, building rail lines and schools and creating a banking system. The government encouraged enough factory industry to provide for national needs in clothing and metals, reducing dependence on Western imports. The regime benefited from important oil revenues, developed by a British company under Persian license. In 1935, to signal the beginning of an era, the kingdom's name was changed to Iran. But the shah was deposed during World War II, in favor of his son, in part because of efforts to gain advantages from both sides in the war. Islamic opposition to modern trends, along with hostility to the luxurious lifestyle and dictatorial methods of the shah himself, created far more tension than persisted in Turkey.

One policy that Iran explicitly introduced from the 1920s on deserves particular note, because countries in other regions soon moved in the same direction: import substitution. At the end of the 19th century, Russia and Japan had moved toward full industrialization, hoping to catch up with the West. This approach required active exports, particularly in Japan, and it was motivated by military as well as economic goals. Import substitution suggested a more modest approach: build enough factory industry to reduce dependence on Western goods in areas such as textiles and basic machinery (later, automobiles were added to this list). Success in this realm made Iran more economically independent, although not enough so to become a world economic power. Turkey followed this policy to a degree, as did India after 1947; Latin American nations did the same from the 1930s on. Successful import substitution had its own impact on the world economy and did not preclude countries from taking a more active export stance later.

ASSERTIONS OF ARAB NATIONALISM

Although important new regimes arose in the northern Middle East, marked by commitment to reform and authoritarian rule, the bulk of the Middle East lay under European control during the 1920s and 1930s. North Africa, of course, was held as colonies by France, Britain, and Italy. The major areas of the Middle East proper, now taken over by France and Britain, were governed as League of Nations mandates, rather than as outright possessions, which implied some commitment to ultimate independence. Nevertheless, Arab indignation at this new foreign rule was a further impetus to nationalism. Riots and demonstrations forced Britain to recognize the technical independence of Egypt in 1922, and Iraq and Jordan soon followed, although in all these cases, Britain continued to regulate economic and military affairs. France made fewer early concessions to nationalism in its territories. It split Lebanon off from Syria, encouraging division between Christians and Muslims in Lebanon as well. And while Lebanon achieved independence under French protection, and Syria won promise of the same in 1936, European influence remained strong. Indeed, in oil-rich territories such as Iraq, European and U.S. companies quickly acquired ownership rights, which actually increased the Western stake in the region even as formal imperialism was declining.

Another key issue for Arab nationalists during the 1920s and 1930s was the growing Jewish presence in Palestine. Although Jews constituted a mere 11 percent of the total population of the region in 1914, Jewish emigration from Europe, encouraged by Zionist organizations and also by Hitler's anti-Semitic onslaught, increased the number of Jewish residents rapidly, to half a million by 1940. The Jewish population was still outnumbered by Palestinian Muslims and Christians, but Arab nationalists were alert to this threat to what they regarded as their land. They pressed Britain, as the mandate power in Palestine, to restrict immigration, but British policy in fact vacillated, failing to satisfy either Muslims or Jews. In the meantime, Jewish organization of agriculture and industry in Palestine, around communal farms known as kibbutzim, gained ground steadily, greatly increasing traditional productivity and developing new export crops such as citrus fruits.

Arab nationalism thus had a number of targets. Although nationalism became more intense, it was also a divisive force in the Middle East. Not only were nationalists distracted by the boundaries drawn among mandate territories, such as Lebanon and Syria, but they also disagreed about the future of the Middle East. Some, as in the new kingdom of Saudi Arabia, advocated traditional Muslim ways, whereas others talked of Western-style parliamentary democracy; still others, such as the Iraqi Kamil Chadrichi, preached

an Arab form of socialism. Few groups in the Middle East were outright Marxists, for Marxist hostility to nationalism and religion, demonstrated by attacks on Islamic groups in the Soviet Union, was too severe even for most secular reformers. However, no single non-Marxist formula for a Middle Eastern future emerged.

Then World War II exploded, which further weakened western Europe's tenuous hold on the region. Turkey remained carefully independent during the conflict, bent on developing its own state without distraction. But much of the rest of the area was drawn into the hostilities, as German forces invaded north Africa and then faced defeat at the hands of the British–American alliance in 1942. More important was the sheer weakness of Britain and France after the war, which gave new hope to Arab leaders. France yielded to riots in 1945, abandoning all government powers in Syria and Lebanon. Britain followed suit, although this was delayed by its attempts to find a solution to Arab–Jewish conflicts in Palestine. Riots and terrorist attacks by the two groups and even against the British marked the period of 1945–1948. When the British finally pulled out of the area, the Jews simply declared a new state of Israel (May 1948), beating off an attack by the surrounding Arab countries and conquering more territory. Almost a million Muslim refugees were expelled from Palestine, creating a legacy of great hostility between the Arabs and Israel and its political allies, including the United States.

Defeat at Jewish hands triggered a revolution in Egypt, where the army colonel Gamal Abdel Nasser drove out the corrupt, pro-Western king in 1952. The goal was a secular, reformist state under one-party leadership. Nasser, who for a time spearheaded Arab nationalism generally, seized the Suez Canal in 1956, provoking a British-French-Israeli attack that managed to invade Egypt but was forced back by U.S. and Russian pressure, as the two superpowers were bent on courting Arab favor. A fully independent Egypt, which proved its technical competence by running the Suez Canal efficiently, was a major

The Middle East Today

new player in the Middle East from this point on. Nasser quickly demonstrated his reformist inclination internally by dividing the great estates along the Nile and awarding land to the peasants, thus ending the long-standing manorial system.

Arab independence was completely achieved between 1956 and 1962; the final north African colonies won their freedom as the states of Libya, Tunisia, Morocco, and Algeria. The key battle here focused on Algeria, a French holding since the mid-19th century and symbolic, to many French leaders, of France's battered claims to greatness in the world of power politics. Nationalist agitation led to outright civil war for almost a decade, as the minority of European settlers supported the French army against a pattern of guerrilla attacks and terrorism that proved impossible to suppress. Finally, the French, rightly worried about the effects of the long, brutal struggle on their own internal political stability and national morality, pulled back, agreeing in 1962 to Algerian independence.

With independence achieved, through an assortment of individual states, the most coherent thread in Middle Eastern affairs remained the dispute between the Arab states and Israel. Israel's immediate neighbors were most directly involved, but other Arab leaders found Israel a convenient target to generate popular enthusiasms at home, and a genuine affront to Arab and Islamic authority in the region. For its part, Israel created a strong military force, with far more modern armaments than the Arab states could boast and an aggressive outlook designed to avoid any further scapegoating of the Jewish people. Wars broke out between Israel and its neighbors in 1967 and 1973. The first war led to substantial new Israeli-controlled territory, including the entire city of Jerusalem, regarded as a religious center by Muslims and Christians as well as Jews. Even apart from outright war, guerrilla attacks and terrorism were widely employed by Palestinian groups hostile to Israel, whereas Israel frequently retaliated with bombing missions against refugee camps suspected of

The Palestinian issue, 1979: Israeli soldier patrolling Arab village during a Palestinian general strike against Israeli-ordered expulsion of a mayor sympathetic to Palestinian independence.

harboring terrorists. In 1982, Israel invaded Lebanon in order to unseat Palestinian terrorists, producing literal anarchy in this nation, as no group seemed capable of ensuring order. There were few bright spots in the seemingly irresolvable conflict over Israel. In 1977, the Egyptian president, Anwar Sadat, made a stunning gesture by visiting Israel in the hopes of negotiating a peace. Although this initiative reduced tension, it led to no overall settlement, because Israel refused to surrender most of the territories it had gained in 1967 and many Arab nationalists refused to recognize Israel's right to exist.

In 1993, Israeli agreements with the Palestinians in some autonomous regions, followed by a 1994 peace treaty with Jordan, renewed optimism for settling a number of wider disputes. Tensions again increased after 1996 with the victory of a more right-wing party in Israel. The peace effort resumed in 1999 but seemed to collapse amid new violence beginning in 2000. Palestinian terrorist bombings increased, as did Israeli state violence. Israel later began to build a wall to limit Palestinian entry. In 2005, Israeli settlements were removed from the Palestinian Gaza region, but West Bank settlements were extended; in 2006, the Palestinians, in a democratic election, returned a majority for Hamas, which many regarded as a terrorist group and which refused to recognize Israel's existence. Also in 2006, bitter war broke out between Israel and the Shiite Hezbollah movement in Lebanon. Prospects for Arab–Israeli relations remained complex at best.

In addition to the issue of Israel, questions of alignment with the world's superpowers were the focus of many nations in the Middle East. Israel was a firm Western ally, receiving significant financial and military aid from the United States. Turkey, anxious about its Soviet neighbor to the north, was also in the Western camp as a member of NATO. Most other Middle Eastern nations, however, oscillated in their alignments. Egypt's Nasser helped organize "neutral" nations in the world, along with India during the 1950s, as an alternative to an alliance with either side during the cold war. Most Middle Eastern leaders would probably have preferred an essentially neutral course, so they could concentrate on foreign and domestic objectives of their own. However, Western influence continued to loom large. Western nations were often the target of attacks as allies of Israel, remembered imperialists, or capitalist exploiters. They were also valuable sources of arms, purchasers along with Japan of most of the oil produced in the region, and usefully hostile to Marxism. Most of the more conservative Arab states thus tended to develop relatively close

ties with the West, whereas more secular regimes either alternated between the cold war superpowers—as did Egypt, which used Russian aid after the Suez war and later renounced it in favor of American support—or leaned toward heavy reliance on Russia—as did Syria during the 1970s. Or they tried to win support from both sides. In any event, competition between the cold war camps continued to weigh heavily on the Middle East, which could not resist substantial outside influence because of internal divisions and military and economic weakness. At the same time, superpower rivalry gave many states a chance to play off the two sides and thus gain room for independent maneuvers. Differences among U.S., Russian, and European policy remained long after the cold war ended.

Two other factors played a considerable role in Middle Eastern events after the end of outright imperialism: local rivalries and efforts at economic coordination. A number of newly independent states clashed over territory or policy. Egypt and Libya developed a rivalry; Morocco and Algeria disputed territory; in 1978, a fundamental policy dispute opened up between a secular state in Iraq and the fervent religious revolutionaries who had seized power in Iran, resulting in a particularly brutal and protracted war over territory between Iraq and Iran in the early 1980s. Hundreds of thousands of people, from both sides, died in this war, which ended inconclusively. Iraq's own expansionism led to the invasion of Kuwait in 1990. This was followed by the 1991 Persian Gulf War, in which an alliance among Saudi Arabia, Egypt, Syria, and the major Western powers beat back the Iraqis while trying unsuccessfully to replace their strongman leader, Saddam Hussein.

Against this backdrop of frequent fighting, a few institutions of greater scope provided partial balance. The Arab League existed to help reconcile quarrels in the name of the larger ideal of renewed Arab unity. Periodic efforts to unite different nations surfaced; Syria thus briefly merged with Egypt. Although these attempts seldom had much substance, they served as a reminder that a higher political dream for the region persisted and might someday have greater impact. Finally, and more pragmatically, oil-producing Arab states, headed by Iran, Iraq, and Saudi Arabia, took the lead in forming Organization of Petroleum Exporting Countries (OPEC) in 1961, although there were important non–Middle Eastern participants as well. The formation of OPEC resulted from successful Arab and Iranian efforts to reduce the independence of Western oil companies operating in their region, as either nationalization or at least significant government supervision took hold. OPEC nations also attempted to coordinate production levels and pricing policies, and during the 1970s, they had considerable success in raising the price of oil and therefore the earnings of member nations. Here, at least briefly, was an important change in the customary dependency of raw material suppliers in the world market. By the end of the 1970s, however, competition from other regions and even among OPEC members, plus Western conservation efforts, reduced OPEC's effectiveness in maintaining revenues. Nevertheless, OPEC, along with individual efforts by wealthy Arab states such as Saudi Arabia to provide economic support to petroleum-poor states such as Jordan and Egypt, again demonstrated that narrow nationalist rivalries did not alone capture the complexities of Middle Eastern politics. By 2000, coordination again improved, producing higher oil prices and revenues. Surging demand boosted the prosperity of many oil-producing states again after 2007.

THE NEW ROLE OF THE STATE

With growing nationalism and then independence, the states of the Middle East developed a number of similar functions. Most assumed new responsibility for providing systems of education; an economic infrastructure including roads, ports, and airlines; and some limited welfare programs.

Most regulated foreign companies to some extent, and the region gained leverage against the West. Universities were created, teaching secular subjects along with or instead of the basic principles of Islamic faith. Even conservative regimes such as the Saudi Arabian monarchy spurred technical training. The new functions of government demonstrated the novelty of many of the forces impinging on this region during the 20th century. What was happening in the Middle East, as elsewhere in the world, was a common pattern of political modernization, defined simply as the extension of government functions to new areas, such as mass education and economic planning, and the attempt to focus new loyalty on the state. At the same time, Middle Eastern nationalists had to tread very carefully in the area of religious devotion, insisting that nationalism did not contradict true belief and emphasizing a common interest in the glorious Islamic past, while urging some reforms in Islam itself. Definitions of nationalism also varied and clashed. Was a nation a region with boundaries established by Europeans after World War I? Should it embrace all Arabs? Should it be secular or Islamic?

Changes in government functions and the rise of nationalism did not mean Western-style political forms in the typical Middle Eastern states. Liberal democracy did not take hold in this region; here was another common denominator in the Middle Eastern political style. Along with China, the Middle East indeed proved most resistant to the spread of democracy in the 1980s and 1990s. The one consistent exception was Israel, where a parliament achieved great power and a multiparty system flourished. Even here, Israel's focus on military development and repression of its Palestinian minority at times clouded the nation's liberal vision, as did the power of extremist religious groups in winning government support for Orthodox Jewish practices.

Most Middle Eastern states either did not establish parliaments or, as in the more secular states, limited their effectiveness by preventing multiparty competition. Even Turkey, which periodically experimented with opposition parties and a fairly free press after World War II, sometimes retreated into military regimes. A multiparty system did gain ground, producing the first woman prime minister in the 1990s. Then victory by a pro-Muslim party caused the military to intervene in 1997 and install secular politicians, although on the basis of a party coalition in parliament. Restoration of democrasy led to the victory of a moderate Islamic party early in the 21st century. Elsewhere, monarchy or strongman rule normally prevailed. Islamic political tradition constrained liberal political values, while the tensions within Middle Eastern society convinced many leaders that their power could not be preserved within a framework of political competition. Most countries, then, imposed restrictions on the press, used political police extensively, and relied heavily on military support in an essentially authoritarian approach.

Nevertheless, there was no single vision of how the state should operate. A key division erupted between the monarchies—Morocco, Jordan, Saudi Arabia, Iran before 1978, and some smaller states on the Persian Gulf—and the secular republics, where individual strongmen typically wielded power, often backed by a single political party. Most of the monarchs, while working for economic development, not only discouraged political opposition but also tended to support the existing social hierarchy and conservative Islamic social values. Saudi Arabia was the most extreme example, in part because the country emphasized the Wahabi version of Islam, which was quite puritanical. The country sought to use oil revenues to develop a wider industrial base as well as new cities and extensive education. But it also enforced traditional Arab dress and social segregation of women, as well as significant penalties for sexual misconduct or other violations of Islamic law. The government forbade women to drive cars, even though many had learned to drive during visits to the West. It promoted active Islamic education combined with intolerance for other beliefs.

Most republics, on the other hand, although just as hostile to political opposition as the monarchies, sought to encourage not only industrial development and agricultural reform but also a more secular outlook. They worked for new educational and job opportunities for women, while discouraging traditional dress. Like Atatürk's regime, they tried to limit Islamic habits—such as fasting during the day for the month of Ramadan—that would affect economic productivity. A number of the republics worked toward a policy of what was called *Arab socialism*, designed to produce a society different from the West and the communist nations alike. Arab socialism meant regulations for business—particularly foreign-owned business—but not state control of the entire economy. It involved attempts to limit inequality, through heavier taxation on the rich and land reforms to benefit the peasantry. Arab socialism did not, however, represent a full-scale attack on religion or devotion to elaborate political doctrine; it was an impulse more than a well-defined movement.

Many regimes developed extensive police powers, including arrests of political opponents and frequent torture or even assassination. In no sense did they express popular support, though some people benefited from stability and from favors from the government. Opinion polls in the early 2000s made it clear that most people in the Middle East preferred democracy. One poll indicated that 92 to 99 percent of all Middle Easterners favored democracy (in contrast to 89 percent in the United States). This was a huge change from the 1930s and 1940s, when many had preferred some kind of fascism. But it was hard for these opinions to win through, because of the police powers of the state. One reaction was an increase in Islamic fervor as a means of expressing political frustration as well as sincere belief. Amid internal political divisions and a host of essentially new nations, it was clear that the Middle East had not yet settled on a durable political form.

SOLVING PROBLEMS

REVIVING RELIGION IN CONTEMPORARY HISTORY

Huge forces encouraged a more secular culture, throughout most of the world, in the 20th century and into the 21st. Science continued to gain ground, often encouraging a nonreligious approach to physical nature and even to human experiences such as serious illness or death. Powerful belief systems, such as Marxism, and even many versions of nationalism encouraged a focus on this world. The spread of consumerism, though not necessarily contradicting a religious interest, could be a challenge. Global urbanization pulled people away from established community rituals, in which religion had often been involved.

For people for whom religion remained important, including key leaders, there was a new problem: how to maintain or revive religious interests in what by many measurements was an increasingly secular society.

Several approaches could help resolve the problem, often in combination.

- Join forces with some contemporary trends to help counter others. Thus religion might often be joined with nationalism, or sometimes (as in the United States) with consumerism, but against other currents such as Marxism.

- Use contemporary technology. Many religious leaders became skilled in television preaching or, as in Islam, appeals through the Internet.

- Target groups left behind in global change. Though it is important not to oversimplify, many religious revivals, in Islam and in missionary Christianity, focused on urban lower classes who were not participating in the gains of the global economy.

- Attack key modern trends (such as permissive sexuality) and even other religions. Many religious movements veered away from tolerance, as when Hindu fundamentalists urged new levels of hostility to Indian Muslims.

- Seek assistance from the state. Russian Orthodox leaders, after the fall of communism, turned to the state for support against outside missionaries— not a new trend in this religion, but an important development. Christian, Islamic, and Hindu revivals often looked for state assistance against extremes of secularism.

The religious revival of the late 20th century, in many regions of the world, depended on many factors, but the capacity of religious leaders to use several specific strategies to deal with the problem of secularism played a key role.

■QUESTIONS: *Why have secular cultures faced new challenges, in many parts of the world, in the past 40 years? How can religions combine appeals to older traditions with significant innovations in techniques and arguments?*

THE RISE OF FUNDAMENTALISM

Political and economic change produced an important backlash in Middle Eastern political and cultural life, which became increasingly dominant from the 1970s on. Furthermore, failures of reform—in the continuation of massive

poverty—created pressure to use religion for protest. The spiritual power and pervasive legal framework of Islam explain why many people, ordinary peasants as well as religious leaders, were tempted to use their Islamic faith as a rallying point against change or for different kinds of reform, and especially against any signs of Western cultural influence. Thus, the Ayatollah

Khomeini, ultimately the leader of Iran's 1978 revolution, reacted to educational change:

> Our universities must become Islamic. . . . They have served to impede the progress of the sons and daughters of this land; they have become propaganda arenas. Our young people may have succeeded in acquiring some knowledge, but they have not received an education, an Islamic education. . . . The universities do not impart an education that corresponds to the needs of the people and the country; instead they squander the energies of whole generations of our beloved youth, or oblige them to serve the foreigners.

The rise of Islamic fundamentalism was part of a broader global current, in which various groups sought to reemphasize the importance of religion, usually amid new levels of intolerance for other beliefs. For example, Christian and Hindu fundamentalisms were important developments in the United States and India, respectively. Islamic fundamentalism nevertheless gained particular importance as a means of protesting political and economic conditions within many Middle Eastern states and expressing resentment at what were perceived as outside attacks and belittling of Islam.

The Islamic fundamentalism that took shape after 1970 sought, in essence, a return to the original Islamic political ideals of a state committed to religious values and the enforcement of these values as its first priority. This was not pure traditionalism; fundamentalists used novel methods, including the Internet, and often displayed an intolerance that was not characteristic of Islam. Most leaders were urban and educated, but there was a protest against change. Many Islamic scholars and other religious leaders, including the ulema scholars, raised important objections to trends occurring in the Middle East (and also in neighboring Islamic societies such as Sudan, Afghanistan, and Pakistan). They viewed their society's concentration on economic advance as evidence of improper priorities:

An Iranian revolutionary trains women in military skills.

adherence to religious duties should come first. Westernized clothing—particularly for women and especially in recreational areas and on beaches—and other imports, including films, were attacked as scandalous and immoral. The tendencies of more secular states to promote education without a firm basis in religion and to cooperate with Christian Westerners were condemned, while Islamic purists also insisted on a more concentrated attack on the problem of Israel. In short, Islamic fundamentalists called for a restoration of many traditional values, including a reorientation of political actions.

Deeply committed Muslim groups emerged in most Middle Eastern states by the 1970s. Even in conservative Saudi Arabia, they exerted pressure on the regime to follow Muslim laws more faithfully. Thus, as the result of some court trials intended to set an example, adulterers were stoned or beheaded. A group of fundamentalists was responsible for the assassination of President Anwar Sadat in 1981, although Egyptian policy was not greatly affected by the conservative current. Fundamentalist pressure in Pakistan prompted the military regime to introduce a new code of law more in line with Muslim tradition, providing, among other things, harsher punishments for crimes such as sexual immorality. In the 1990s, fundamentalist pressure increased in Turkey, although the military tried to curtail it and although more moderate Islamic political parties predominated. Algerian military rulers faced an even tougher battle with a larger fundamentalist faction, and considerable violence ensued between both groups. In general, Islamic fundamentalism added an important ingredient to the Middle Eastern mix, even when states largely resisted the pressure.

The greatest victory of the Islamic militants occurred in Iran. It was revealing that the most dramatic revolution in the 20th-century Middle East was religious in spirit, unlike all other contemporary revolutions in the world. The Iranian Revolution has been called, in fact, the first real "third-world revolution," in that it sought not a special national path to modernization using ideas such as Marxism first created in the West, but a commitment to the ideals of Islamic law. The revolutionaries were zealous Shiites, a majority in Iran although a minority in Islam overall. Shiites had long been bent on creating a purer religious state, against what they saw as the errors of the Sunni, the majority group of Muslims. This aspect of the Iranian struggle renewed a conflict that had existed for centuries within Islam.

The specific framework for the Iranian Revolution involved a rapid reform program that had taken place in Iran, building on the efforts of the 1920s and 1930s, combined with brutal political repression. The shah's government, which with U.S. help had defeated a 1953 protest, had launched a crash program of modernization rather like that of Atatürk earlier in

Turkey, but with the added development of substantial oil revenues and greater contact with the West. The regime supported education, including the training of many Iranians abroad, plus industrial and military development. These changes caused much discontent. The rural majority was neglected. Inflation ran high, for even with significant oil earnings, the country's many new projects were expensive. The shah's brutal repression of political opposition, through a powerful secret police, antagonized additional, liberal segments of Iranian opinion, as did extensive corruption. Other grievances rested with the Muslim faithful. Islamic leaders were appalled at the new surge of Western influence, visible in the 100,000 foreigners who helped run

The Iranian Revolution, 1979: anti-American demonstration, with posters of the Ayatollah Khomeini.

the economy. They protested the resort areas developed for foreigners' use, where the use of liquor and skimpy bathing attire openly clashed with Muslim law.

Revolt broke out in 1978, forcing the exile of the shah early the following year. The new leader was the aged holy man, the Ayatollah Khomeini, who had long campaigned against the "godless and materialistic" regime of the shah. The revolutionary government quickly suppressed other discontented groups, including liberals and communists. It banned Western music, bathing suits, and liquor and set out to create a holy Shiite state. Traditional dress, including a veil or *chadur*, was required of women. During the long war Iraq launched against Iran, leaders hoped to export its political principles to other Islamic states; the ayatollah talked of a new *jihad*, or holy war, that would unite the whole Middle East in a literal version of the Islamic state. A high level of religious and revolutionary excitement continued in Iran through the mid-1980s. Fundamentalists, mainly Shiites, were also active in the troubled nation of Lebanon, after the 1982 Israeli invasion, and they stirred elsewhere; in Syria, for example, a fundamentalist insurgency was vanquished, but only after considerable brutality. By the late 1990s, however, more moderate policies gained ground in Iran. Democratic elections produced a reformist government. Controls by Islamic clerics, however, prevented the government from changing policies too dramatically, and a 2006 election returned a more radical regime to power. The situation remained volatile, even as Iran's regional foreign policy became more assertive.

Fundamentalist reaction to change in the Middle East generally formed an important current in the late 20th century. There was no way to determine its durability; certainly key states such as Iraq and Syria, as well as most north African regimes, managed to maintain their secular policies that were, in any event, not in full opposition to Islam. But fundamentalists put massive pressure on governments, as in Algeria, and fundamentalist groups were responsible for frequent acts of terrorism. Even the Soviet Union worried about a potential fundamentalism current among its own Islamic minority; this was one reason for the invasion of Afghanistan, to guard against a fundamentalist regime in this neighboring state. Debates over Islamic policy resumed in the new central Asian republics that followed the Soviet collapse. Finally, the incompleteness of industrialization and divisions of outlook, even in well-established secular states such as Turkey, suggested that Islam and some aspects of a conventional reform program were not easily compatible. Again, Islam's spiritual hold, its emphasis on obedience to Allah, and its tradition of regulating social life in some detail gave it an unusual role among world religions in the 20th century.

The continued strength of the Muslim faith and the fundamentalist upsurge increased the complexity of Middle Eastern politics in the later 20th century. At the same time, it is vital to realize that Islamic fundamentalism has by no means been uniformly triumphant. Its surge reflects the fact that significant political and social change has already touched Middle Eastern civilization—for example, steady urbanization has brought more than 65 percent of the population of major countries such as Egypt into cities, away from rural roots and economies. Even during the early 2000s, Islamic fundamentalism was not the only force for cultural change in the region. For instance, global consumerism exerted its own pressure, with massive shopping malls spreading in the oil-rich states. Even in Iran, a Japanese animated cartoon character became an important emblem of independence for many women. In leading Turkish cities, Christmas shopping took hold, even though the holiday was religiously irrelevant to Muslims. Many Muslims also began exchanging gifts and cards during Ramadan, a remarkable development for a holiday traditionally devoted to self-denial. Westernization does not fully influence the contemporary Middle East, politically or culturally, but nor does unaltered religious traditionalism.

HISTORY DEBATE

TERRORISM

Americans developed a new awareness of terrorism on September 11, 2001, and many thought the world would never be the same. Understanding brutal attacks that could kill 3000 people, totally at random, is no easy exercise. Some people simply refer to terrorists as evil and assume that the dark side of human nature is all one needs to know.

There are, however, historical perspectives on terrorism that may be illuminating. The first recognizes that terrorism, in anything like a modern sense, began in the later 1880s. It reflected the frustration of groups confronting powerful established forces—for example, Russian protesters attacking the tsar's regime—and it reflected the new technology of guns and explosives. It was a terrorist act, the assassination of the Austrian archduke by a Serbian nationalist, that precipitated World War I. As today, terrorists were powerfully motivated, organized in secret, and willing to die for a cause. Then, as now, many terrorists believed they were responding to terrorism by governments—the attacks or torture sponsored by political police, for example.

However, two aspects of terrorism changed around 2000. First, terrorist activities became increasingly associated with religious extremism, and not only from Islam. (It was a Buddhist-derived extremist sect that unleashed poison gas in a Japanese subway, for example.) Second, terrorist acts were increasingly directed not at government officials so much as civilian targets. Changes in terrorist weapons, including miniaturized bombs, contributed to this second change. Terrorists obviously believe that they have no alternative in expressing the need to destabilize governments and the economic and cultural influences they find repellent.

Two final points about terrorism are frustratingly inconclusive. In the first place, modern terrorism has rarely produced the results terrorists desire. Usually, terrorist acts galvanize resistance and counterattack. But in the second place, no one has yet figured out how to end terrorism, either by force or by providing other channels for effective expression of deep grievance.

MIDDLE EASTERN CULTURE AND SOCIETY

One fully industrial country emerged in the Middle East after World War II: the state of Israel. The new nation, although severely pressed to defend its existence, benefited from extensive foreign aid, a deeply felt nationalism on the part of many of its citizens, and its experience in developing an industrial economy. Most initial Israeli leaders were immigrants. Hundreds of thousands of European Jews migrated to the new nation after the Nazi Holocaust of World War II. Substantial immigration from the cities of the Middle East developed as well, as hostilities

between Arabs and Jews disrupted earlier patterns of tolerance and the new Israeli state served as a beacon for the Jewish faithful. With immigration came population growth and the infusion of a multitude of skills in business and manufacturing. Israeli commitment to industrial output and market agriculture, including extensive projects of desert reclamation, produced a dynamic economy that easily placed Israel among the most technologically advanced nations of the world. Although the new country faced economic problems, particularly because of heavy military expenditure, it had easily jumped the basic hurdles of 20th-century economic development. The country turned increasingly to consumerism by the 1990s, which caused concern among religious groups and secular nationalists alike.

In contrast, manufacturing, market agriculture, and levels of technology lagged in most other parts of the Middle East. Indeed, the gap in technological sophistication between Israel and its rivals was one of the bases of Israeli survival, as Israeli production of up-to-date armaments became a major industry. Variety among the Islamic states in economic conditions increased. The region embraces about 60 percent of the world's known petroleum reserves, but they are not evenly distributed. Nations with substantial oil production and small populations—among them some of the traditionally poorest desert states—suddenly surged to immense per capita wealth. The Persian Gulf state of Kuwait thus ranked in 1980 as the richest in the world in terms of average income. Saudi Arabia also rose to great wealth. Lavish new urban construction and extensive medical and educational services followed from oil revenues in these nations, particularly during the heyday of OPEC price manipulation. Regional manufacturing did gain ground, generating additional import substitution and a new minority of factory workers. However, although the oil-rich states struggled to invest their earnings in industries that could sustain a better-balanced economy and provide wealth even when oil production declined, they encountered serious difficulties. Many, indeed, invested substantial funds abroad, especially in the West, because there simply were insufficient productive opportunities at home. Lack of other resources, continued limitations in technical training and interest, a pronounced gap between rich and poor that restricts consumer demand—these were some general factors that inhibited the translation of oil wealth into industrialization. Heavy military expenditures also played a role, for these investments involved purchases from abroad rather than a stimulus to domestic production. When military expenditure turned into war, as in the Iran–Iraq

conflict, the impact on economic conditions could be devastating.

Nations without oil wealth faced even more severe economic problems. Here, too, military expenditures and, in some cases, political instability limited economic development. Many countries were also burdened by significant population growth. Lack of available land haunted many rural people, whereas opportunities in the cities did not keep pace with need, even as urbanization accelerated. Muslim beliefs slowed conversion to new birth-control methods. A number of governments attempted massive projects to expand production. Egypt's President Nasser, for example, with substantial Soviet aid, orchestrated the construction of a huge dam at Aswan, on the Nile, designed to increase agricultural land through irrigation while providing low-cost electrical power for industry. The dam was also meant to symbolize Arab greatness and recall the glory days of ancient Egypt; thus, Nasser described the dam as "more magnificent and seventeen times greater than the Pyramids." Unfortunately, the Aswan project, although successful, did not keep pace with Egypt's population growth. Both the urban masses and the peasant population of this key nation remained desperately poor.

New oil revenues, land reform, and some real growth in urban manufacturing did bring economic change to the Middle East, particularly after World War II. City populations outstripped rural populations in most countries as Middle Eastern urbanization levels exceeded those of India and China. However, outside of Israel, a breakthrough to a fully industrial economy has yet to occur, and standards of living in the larger countries tend to stagnate. One result was considerable emigration in search of jobs, as many Turks and north Africans sought work in western Europe, whereas other Arab peasants took unskilled jobs, often at low pay, in the oil-rich states. Masses of Egyptians and Palestinians (and also Indians and Pakistanis) worked in Saudi Arabia and the United Arab Emirates.

Middle Eastern culture, like the economy, also straddled the fence between tradition and change. Outside of Israel, few Middle Eastern artists participated in international styles. Most Muslim art continued to use traditional styles and themes, although "modern" architecture did find a place in the urban development of countries such as Saudi Arabia and prerevolutionary Iran. Although some Western films were shown in the more secular nations, Islamic filmmaking remained largely separate from patterns developed in the West, partly of course for religious reasons. The Muslim world retained an active allegiance to traditional musical styles, relying, even for most popular music, on instruments and singing techniques different from those in the West. Although important work has been done in art and literature—an Egyptian novelist won the Nobel Prize for literature in 1994, for instance—and also in Islamic theology and law, there was little sense of a revival of a creativity that might recall the brightest periods of Middle Eastern culture.

Most Middle Eastern governments encouraged a growing interest in science. Nasser established a Supreme Science Council in Egypt, arguing that "we have to keep up with the new world and new discoveries. We suffered so much in the past because we were left behind by the ages of steam and electricity. What suffering awaits those who fail to keep up with the new dawn will certainly be much greater than whatever we have experienced in the past. . . . In this world of breathtaking discoveries, to be left behind is to forfeit one's right to existence."

By 2008, the Iranian regime was sponsoring high-level scientific and technical training, and many other states sponsored new, sometimes Western universities to promote skills in technology and management. Although improved scientific training added an important dimension to Middle Eastern culture, it did not propel the region into the top ranks of scientific creativity; the Middle East remained heavily dependent on the West for basic scientific research. The dissemination of a scientific outlook to a larger population through the expanding school systems, along with growing literacy, established a basis for further change in the future, although at times this viewpoint clashed with Islamic fundamentalism.

Society in the Middle East reflected the growth of cities and the policies of reform-minded governments. It also reflected population pressure and, in places, the impact of war. But there were important continuities with the past as well. Many Middle Eastern villages have changed only slowly. Some new agricultural equipment was introduced, and contacts with urban markets expanded. However, the pace of life and work remained recognizable in traditional terms. Although landlord dominance was reduced throughout most of the region, the gap between peasant masses and local notables was an important fact of life.

A key tension in Middle Eastern society involved the position of women. In a major break with the past, increasing numbers of women gained access to formal education. By 2006, more than half of all university students were women in countries such as Iran and the United Arab Emirates. In the more secular states, such as Turkey, Egypt, Algeria, and Syria, many women also cast aside traditional clothing, abandoning the veil and adopting Western dress. Many governments tried to encourage new work patterns among women, seeing them as a vital resource for fledgling industrial economies. Thus, some women entered the ranks of factory and office workers. But the economic and social segregation of women remained severe. Work outside the home, and especially a commitment to professional jobs as doctors or lawyers, was widely disapproved of, and few women could hope to support themselves without family resources. The gap between male and female school attendance remained greater than in any other civilization. Male dominance within the household was still pronounced, and the relatively high birth rate both caused and reflected

In late 2006, Burj Dubai was under extensive construction, as the emirate enjoyed a massive building boom.

the domestic emphasis of women's lives. Conservative states such as Saudi Arabia enforced even more pronounced separation between men and women, including severe penalties for sexual infidelity. The Iranian Revolution showed that even reformist regimes such as the shah's could yield to more traditional practices concerning women.

Again, the result was not uniform. Countries such as Turkey had large numbers of "westernized" women, wearing cosmetics and European-style clothes, active in urban jobs, including politics, and pursuing a secular education. They shared the streets with women in traditional dress, those enmeshed in a more traditional Islamic culture and family life. In a few cases, they also faced attack from the

fundamentalist movement. Yet in many countries, including Iran, women university students began to outnumber the men by the early 21st century

NEW TENSIONS IN THE EARLY 2000s

The early 2000s saw an escalation of violence in parts of the Middle East and neighboring countries. Renewed violence between Palestinians and Israelis fueled wider tensions. This conflict, along with larger grievances about authoritarian regimes and economic frustrations, helped engender wider efforts by Islamic terrorists. Attacks occurred in other countries and also in east Africa and western Europe.

The presence of United States forces in countries such as Saudi Arabia, a result of the 1991 Persian Gulf War, fanned resentment as well. Terrorist preparations were particularly widespread in Afghanistan. Terrorist attacks on Russian forces had flourished during the 1980s, often encouraged by the United States. The organizations remained intact after the Russians left, and they were supported by an extreme Islamic government, the Taliban. Then, on September 11, 2001, agents of the Al Qaeda organization managed to seize commercial airliners to crash into the World Trade Center and the Pentagon, in the United States, causing about 3000 deaths. This massive assault prompted an American invasion of Afghanistan, where the Taliban regime was removed. Concern about armaments and potential terrorist support from the authoritarian regime of Saddam Hussein, in Iraq, motivated a U.S.-led invasion in 2003, which occupied the country relatively easily, but then encountered stubborn and violent resistance. The aggressive U.S. policies raised the question of whether a new American empire was being formed in the region. More modest questions, about whether the Americans would be able to bring order to

Moroccan shoppers wear traditional clothing, while looking at Western-style shoes.

their new, if temporary, territories in Afghanistan and Iraq, much less build prosperous, democratic societies, were hard to answer. Nor was the terrorist threat eliminated.

As the United States tried to build a new regime in Iraq, which was badly divided among factions including Sunni and Shiite Muslims, it tried to encourage greater democracy in the whole region. Several countries introduced new elections, at least for local councils, and greater, if still limited, tolerance for opposition movements arose in places such as Egypt. Islamic parties seemed to be the biggest beneficiaries of this opening. Shiite groups gained new voice in Iraq, though the country was still under American occupation; the more militant regime emerged in Iran and vowed, among other things, to develop a nuclear program despite Western protests; and Islamic groups gained strength in Palestine and Egypt. Secular policies did not vanish, but they were clearly under renewed

attack, and the issue of democracy in the Middle East added another complication to the web of the region's politics.

A TROUBLED REGION

Many more question marks dot the appraisal of trends and prospects in the Middle East than is the case for other major Asian civilizations. The region has produced no unity in political forms. The existence of divisions and diversity is no novelty in Middle Eastern tradition, of course, as periods of chaos often punctuated efforts at unification in the past. However, there is certainly no clear end in sight to some of the fundamental conflicts that describe political and military life in the region. Disputes between secular reformers and Islamic fundamentalists continue to constrain many national governments and divide behaviors among women. The precise blend of tradition and change that will continue to define a Middle Eastern civilization has yet to be found, even as some of the region's tensions directly affect other parts of the world.

Adding to the complications facing Middle East politics was the collapse of the Soviet Union and the emergence of the new Muslim nations in nearby central Asia. These nations had their own problems: what kind of political system to establish, how to treat minorities such as Armenian Christians in their region, and how to plan economic development in an area long used by Russia as a raw-materials center. They also had a new opportunity to reach out to their Muslim brethren. Iranian fundamentalists hoped to guide central Asia toward their version of Islam. Diplomats from more secular Turkey tried to persuade the region of the virtues of top-down reform. Links between the Middle East and restive Muslim minorities in Europe created another set of issues. Questions about the eventual role of Islam, though centered in the Middle East, clearly had a global reach.

PATHS TO THE PRESENT

The discovery of oil and the creation of the state of Israel brought profound change to Middle Eastern civilization in the contemporary period. Despite the importance of these events, however, the area's most central event in many ways was the collapse of the Ottoman Empire after World War I. This change, along with new Western intervention, deprived the region of any unifying political force. Atatürk's decision to end the caliphate also reduced the capacity to provide any centralized direction for Islam. These developments opened the way for reform regimes, as in Turkey itself. Here, despite tensions, widespread Islamic faith seemed compatible with major change and considerable tolerance

for secular groups. But these developments also promoted the formation of states with little by way of established tradition or legitimacy, which encouraged authoritarian regimes and fostered renewed religious loyalties as a means of providing the region's peoples with a means of maintaining their identities.

Other changes resulted from processes familiar in many societies during the contemporary era. Massive urbanization, the growth of new industry, and the spread of education were unsettling changes in numerous ways, but positively altered many lives, nonetheless. Birth rates declined, though more slowly than in some other regions of the world and amid ongoing debate about the new roles many women had gained.

The shifting balance between tradition and change created tensions and divisions particular to the Middle East, though the basic issues were common to many other societies.

SUGGESTED WEB SITES

For more information on the Hagop Kevorkian Center, New York University, see http://www.nyu.edu/gsas/program/neareast/index.html; for a historical overview of the Iraq crisis and war, see http://www.mideastweb.org/; on present-day and historical Middle East, see http://www.arab.net/; on the Arab–Israeli conflict, see http://www.ict.org.il/arab_isr/frame.htm; on U.S. conduct in the Middle East since World War II and the folly of intervention, see http://www.cato.org/pubs/pas/pa-159.html.

SUGGESTED READINGS

Recent work includes Fred Halliday, *100 Myths About the Middle East* (2005); Mehran Kamrava, *The Modern Middle East: A Political History Since the First World War* (2005); James L. Gelvin, *The Modern Middle East: A History* (2005); Reinhard Schulze, *A Modern History of the Islamic World* (2002); Beverley Milton-Edwards and Peter Hinchcliffe, *Conflicts in the Middle East Since*

1945 (2001); D. K. Fieldhouse, *Western Imperialism in the Middle East 1914–1958* (2006); Keith David Watenpaugh, *Being Modern in the Middle East: Revolution, Nationalism, Colonialism, and the Arab Middle Class* (2006); Steven Heydemann, *War, Institutions, and Social Change in the Middle East* (2000); Shlomo Ben-Ami, *Scars of War, Wounds of Peace: The Israeli-Arab Tragedy* (2006); Ian J. Bickerton and Carla L. Klausner, *A Concise History of the Arab-Israeli Conflict* (2005); James L. Gelvin, *The Israel-Palestine Conflict: One Hundred Years of War* (2005); Paul Mendes-Flohr, ed., *A Land of Two Peoples: Martin Buber on Jews and Arabs* (2005); Rebecca L. Stein and Ted Swedenburg, eds., *Palestine, Israel, and the Politics of Popular Culture* (2005); Tom Segev, *1967: Israel, The War, and the Year That Transformed the Middle East* (2007); Gerges Fawaz, *America and Political Islam: Clash of Cultures or Clash of Interests?* (1999); Beverley Milton-Edwards, *Contemporary Politics in the Middle East* (2000); and Elizabeth Thompson, *Colonial Citizens: Republican Rights, Paternal Privilege and Gender in French Syria and Lebanon* (2000). Several valuable sources are available on the Middle East in this period; see David Ben-Gurion, *Israel: Years of Challenge* (1963), and

I. Khomeini, *Practical Laws of Islam* (1983) and *Islam and Revolution: Writings and Declarations of Iman Khomeini*, trans. Hamid Alger (1981). Mahmud Makal, *Village in Anatolia* (1951), is an exceptionally interesting account of the tension between a modernizing Turkish schoolteacher and the environment and response in his village. Also see M. Hakan Yavuz, *The Emergence of a New Turkey: Democracy and the AK Parti* (2006).

Useful overall surveys include Birgit Schaebler and Leif Stenberg, eds., *Globalization and the Muslim World: Culture, Religion and Modernity* (2004), and G. Lenczowski, *The Middle East and World Affairs*, 4th ed. (1980); see also Hain Faris, *Arab Nationalism* (1986), and Juan Cole, ed., *Comparing Muslim Societies* (1992). See also E. Boserup, *Women's Role in Economic Development* (1974), which covers a vital aspect of Middle Eastern development (and also the patterns in other non-Western areas), although within a controversial theoretical framework, and Nikki Keddie and Bill Baron, eds., *Women in Middle Eastern History* (1991). For information on the individual Muslim states, see Ira M. Lapidus, *A History of Islamic Societies* (2002).

33 Latin America in the 20th Century

Many Americans regard Latin America as a highly traditional area. In fact, the 20th century resulted in a number of rapid economic and political changes, although Latin America retained a great deal of its distinctive cultural identity. This society did not have to contend with the problems of new nationhood that preoccupied so many other parts of the world. Superpower intervention remained a concern, particularly because of the economic and military outreach of the United States in the Caribbean and Central America. Responding to North American influence was not a novel issue, however, although it took on some new twists, especially after World War II. Latin America also remained free from major warfare except for the 1932–1935 Chaco War between Bolivia and Paraguay. Nationalist rivalries existed and led to some conflict, but the region was far more peaceful, in terms of formal diplomacy, than most of its counterparts elsewhere in the world. There were no regional arms races, and military arsenals, although they expanded after World War II, were modest for the most part. (One nation, Costa Rica, abolished its army entirely.) Major internal violence was generally directed against peasant protesters and American Indian minorities, as landowners and caudillos, or military dictators, sought to maintain their power.

Nonetheless, after 1900 there were new themes and strains in Latin American society. The revolution in Mexico, early in the 20th century, reflected some of the same tensions that plagued China and Russia during the same period, although the revolution yielded a distinctive result. Latin American politics were redefined by the growing role of central states, beginning in the 1930s. Popular unrest in Latin America rivaled that of other peasant societies, although it did not always lead to significant political reform until the early 1980s, when a new democratic trend gained ground. The 20th century, in sum, saw important new political contests and governmental forms.

A second area of change focused on economic growth. Issues of economic development inevitably assumed a new urgency, as growing numbers of Latin American governments, both democracies and caudillo-led authoritarian regimes, sought a more active economic role. Moreover, rising levels of population brought Latin America new social problems, as the region became one of the most rapidly growing areas of the world. A number of societies further developed significant industrial sectors, modifying the economic weakness that had long characterized Latin America's place in the international economy in the past. Economic inequality, between a growing middle class and impoverished urban and rural groups, was considerable by world standards. New problems, but also new approaches, thus described economic patterns during this period.

Finally, the Latin nations continued to develop their distinctive cultural amalgam, blending styles generated in the West with a variety of local patterns. Indeed, the 20th century proved to be a rich period in Latin American culture, with major innovations in painting, architecture, and literature. Even as economic and political tensions garnered attention, the cultural and religious creativity of the region suggests a civilization still actively expanding its range.

KEY QUESTIONS *How can significant economic change in Latin America be described, given the fact that the society remained quite poor by Western or Japanese standards? What were the most important new political currents? Amid growing consumerism and outside influence, was there a definable Latin American culture?*

LATIN AMERICA IN 20TH-CENTURY WORLD HISTORY

Latin America may sometimes seem a society apart. It did not participate significantly in the world wars, although the cold war had significant impact in the region. Nevertheless, international themes were vital. Industrial development coexisted alongside the older tradition of economic dependency. Most countries continued to depend, at least in part, on cheap exports produced by low-paid workers. Even the drug trade fits into the patterns of Latin American dependency in certain key respects.

Older racial issues had left their own particular legacy. Slavery was gone and explicit racism was less pervasive than in the United States. African-inspired cultural and religious movements gained wide audiences. But the color of one's skin nonetheless counted. In societies such as Brazil, with large black minorities, economic inequalities increased on racial lines.

Population movement was another important theme. Latin America and the Caribbean sent growing numbers of emigrants to the United States and western Europe.

Cultural influences, finally, reflected new global invlovements. Latin America continued to import cultural forms, including different versions of Christianity. However, popular music, dances, and costumes from the area also became part of international culture, providing much variety. Latin American interaction with the wider world was thus vitally important.

THE MEXICAN REVOLUTION, 1910–1920s

Revolution in Mexico, from 1910 to 1917, was the great event of the early 20th century in Latin America, although it directly affected only one major nation. The Mexican conflict articulated some of the same peasant grievances that simultaneously surfaced in Russia, as the peasantry was caught in the pressures of an expanding market agriculture while still lacking full access to the land. Discontented intellectuals also played a role, attacking a political regime seen as corrupt and inefficient—although in the Mexican case, the regime lacked the deep

CANADA

UNITED STATES
OF AMERICA

*ATLANTIC
OCEAN*

MEXICO

Gulf of Mexico

Mexico
City

Havana

Nassau

BAHAMAS

HAITI (1804)

DOMINICAN REP. (1844)

Santo Domingo

CUBA (1898)

**JAMAICA
(1962)**

Port-au-
Prince

San PUERTO RICO (U.S.)
Juan

BARBADOS (1967)

CARIBBEAN SEA

Port of Spain **TRINIDAD & TOBAGO (1962)**

GUYANA (1966)

Caracas

Georgetown

Paramaribo

**VENEZUELA
(1811)**

Cayenne **FRENCH GUIANA**

*PACIFIC
OCEAN*

CENTRAL AMERICA
See Inset Below

Bogotá

**COLOMBIA
(1821)**

**SURINAM
(1975)**

Equator

GALÁPAGOS IS.
(Ecuador)

Quito

ECUADOR (1822)

Amazon R.

**PERU
(1821)**

**BRAZIL
(1822)**

| 0 | 1000 | 2000 |

MILES

Lima

**BOLIVIA
(1825)**

Brasilia

La Paz

Sucre

CENTRAL AMERICA

**PARAGUAY
(1811)**

Rio de Janeiro

**CHILE
(1818)**

Asunción

**GUATEMALA
(1821)**

Belmopan

**JAMAICA
(1962)**

BELIZE (1981)

Kingston

Guatemala

HONDURAS (1821)

Tegucigalpa

CARIBBEAN SEA

Santiago

Buenos Aires

URUGUAY (1828)

Montevideo

Salvador

**EL SALVADOR
(1821)**

**NICARAGUA
(1821)**

**ARGENTINA
(1816)**

La Plata R.

Managua

*Panama
Canal*

San Jose

Panama

**COSTA RICA
(1821)**

*PACIFIC
OCEAN*

**PANAMA
(1903)**

FALKLAND IS.
(Br.)

CAPE HORN

Dates indicate year of independence

Latin America Today

historical roots of the Russian or Chinese empires. Resentment against foreign economic influence, visible in China and Russia, played an even more obvious part in Mexico. Although the Mexican Revolution produced no single leader of the stature of Lenin or Sun Yat-sen, it had its share of dramatic figures and, at least in a strictly political sense, proved more successful than its Chinese counterpart during the same period of time.

The specific roots of the Mexican Revolution dated back to 1900, when a small group of intellectuals began to agitate against the authoritarian and corrupt regime of General Porfirio Díaz. The agitators sought democracy, a more liberal economic policy, and new restrictions on the church; the movement soon broadened to include social issues of concern to urban workers and the peasantry. Landless rural laborers, receiving low wages for work on land that had once been theirs but under Díaz had been seized by a small landlord class, were particularly restless. Their resentment focused on foreign owners; economic nationalism, or a desire to return control of economic life to Mexican hands as opposed to outsiders, especially U.S. investors, formed an important part of the revolutionary movement. Peasant leaders included Emiliano Zapata, whose motto was "Land and Liberty" and who saw revolution as the uprising of rural and urban workers against capitalist owners of all sorts. Bandit leaders were also active in some rural regions. Pancho Villa established something of a Robin Hood reputation, robbing the rich and befriending the poor. Revolution, in sum, drew on diverse groups with varied goals—as successful revolutions must always do.

Fighting broke out late in 1910. At first a moderate leader, Francisco Madero, came to the fore, arranging for a new presidential election after Díaz escaped the country. Madero thought too strictly in terms of political reform to satisfy the working class and peasant leaders, however, and the revolution soon escaped his control.

Zapata, in particular, organized new revolts, which in turn terrified business interests, including many Americans'; with U.S. backing, a military leader replaced Madero, executing him and many other rebel leaders. Revolutionary forces continued to operate, however, and in the south Zapata established a regional government of his own. In 1916, a change in U.S. policy lent support to a more moderate leader, Venustiano Carranza, who seized power in that same year. Carranza began to solidify key revolutionary gains. A new constitution, in 1917, proclaimed Mexican ownership of all mineral rights, thus reducing the role of foreign investment; landownership was reserved for Mexicans, and many large estates were broken up, to the benefit of mestizo and Indian peasants. The power of the Catholic church, which had supported Díaz and then the repressive regime that attacked Madero, was also restricted.

Carranza's reform goals were limited in practice, however. He showed little interest in a liberal political government, preferring to hold power directly; he did not, in fact, carry land reform too far. In 1920, revolutionaries pressed for new leadership; under the presidency of Álvaro Obregón, the long period of disorder drew to a close, and the results of revolution took clearer shape. Obregón continued the land redistribution in the south that Zapata had initiated; Pancho Villa and his bandit forces were bought off by the gift of a cattle ranch. Obregón moved slowly with further changes, however, lest conservative opposition overturn the new regime. Fearing U.S. hostility, he even allowed existing foreign owners to retain their holdings. Instead of a full attack on the social system, comparable to that in the new Soviet Union, Obregón preferred to concentrate on selective reforms that would encourage economic development. He advanced a widespread system of primary education that taught Spanish, and Mexican nationalism, to many American Indians for the first time. The government worked actively on public-health measures and also expanded cultivable lands through irrigation. However, the regime did not try to seize control of the urban economy from business groups, nor did it unseat the entire landlord class. And although the Catholic church found its political influence reduced, there was no effort to uproot it. Revolution in Mexico, in social terms, meant change but not upheaval.

Politically, the revolution during the 1920s ended the nation's long history of instability, creating a system that differed from both liberal democracy and caudillismo. A single political party, the PNR (National Revolutionary Party), dominated political life, co-opting opposition leaders and vigorously repressing dissent. Presidents, who were selected from within the party and thus faced election with an assurance of victory, wielded huge power; some grew rich on public funds, much as old-style caudillos had done. Nonetheless, the new system prevented any one person from ruling the country permanently, for the presidency had to change hands every six years, and so the worst excesses of caudillismo were avoided. Furthermore, the PNR withstood the process of regular elections and thus remained responsive to many wider concerns. At times, its rhetoric and slogans, which boasted of worker and peasant rights, outstripped its achievements. But there was no question that the power of the traditional ruling classes was now limited by the PNR's desire to retain popular loyalty, or that foreign influence in Mexican affairs had been dramatically reduced. The regime's successful balance between forces old and new was reflected in its durability, amid only occasional, usually minor, political attacks. Into the mid-1990s, as the former PNR, now renamed the PRI (Institutional Revolutionary Party), began to allow freer elections, Mexico experienced considerably more political stability and considerably more independence in policy than many other Latin American nations— particularly those close to the orbit of the United States.

Unlike many revolutions, Mexico's had limited spillover to other areas. Though it helped inspire later peasant protest in other countries, the revolution did not produce a single doctrine, like Marxism, capable of rousing wider support elsewhere. U.S. opposition to political radicalism also helped limit the revolution's impact in Central America. Furthermore, although the revolution generated important reforms and encouraged a vigorous cultural movement, it did not propel Mexican economic development to new heights, nor did it lead to a full industrial revolution, again in contrast to the Soviet regime in Russia. Overall, the Mexican Revolution did not usher in a new period in Latin American history as a whole.

Effects of the Depression, 1930s–1950s

The worldwide economic depression of the 1930s had widespread, catastrophic effects on Latin America, which in turn triggered a new round of political turmoil. The value of Latin American exports decreased by a full two-thirds; the economy had depended on selling agricultural goods and minerals to the industrial nations of the West, which now simply could not afford to buy them. As unsold goods piled up in warehouses, poverty increased. No sweeping revolutionary movement resulted, although popular rioting broke out in many areas. But the results of the Great Depression encouraged the nation to press for fuller economic independence and to use government power to gain greater economic control. Various kinds of political regimes evinced this new, nationalistic concern.

The despair caused by the Depression did encourage Marxist movements in several countries, including Chile and Brazil, but these were generally kept in check by firm military rule. A revolutionary movement in Peru produced a doctrine combining socialism, fierce anti-Americanism, and a stress on American Indian cultural values; although it promoted agitation, it did not seize power.

The tide of economic nationalism proved more successful. Unequal land distribution, illiteracy, and poor production methods spurred a number of governments to take remedial action. Many of the regimes proved willing to run some industries directly, and most saw the need to regulate foreign investment and required foreign firms to employ Latin American managers. Most importantly, state-sponsored programs of import substitution increased the size of the industrial sector.

A series of populist leaders came to the fore in many countries, building multi-class alliances, including urban workers (whose importance was obviously growing). In Mexico, a spirit of reform was rekindled by the election of Lazaro Cardenas as president in 1934. Cardenas seized foreign oil companies, establishing a state corporation, Pemex, to manage the industry. A series of land reforms broke up additional estates. Education spread and with it an effort to integrate Indian culture more fully into national life. A state bank was organized to encourage industry; as a result, Mexican production increased more rapidly than that of any other Latin American country from 1940 to 1960, although immense poverty persisted.

In Brazil, weak political leadership and deteriorating economic conditions led to a military revolt, headed by Getulio Vargas, which produced a reasonably mild caudillo-style dictatorship that lasted from 1930 to 1945. Vargas abolished elections and parliament, while regulating the press and operating a secret police that kept the opposition divided. Deeply committed to economic modernization, Vargas hoped to free Brazil from its dependence on coffee exports. Under his administration, the state constructed important steel mills, and the nation began to produce most of the industrial goods it required. The Amazon basin was opened to agricultural development. Cities expanded, their centers graced by modern office buildings and apartment houses. Brazil remained a largely agricultural nation, but one capable of considerable economic growth.

The government of Chile responded to the effects of the Depression without dismantling its liberal, parliamentary system. A state-run development corporation was established during the 1930s to provide funds and planning for industrial projects.

Other parts of Latin America reacted less forcefully to the economic and political stress of the 1930s. Poverty and static social and economic conditions were particularly apparent in the Andes nations of Peru, Bolivia, and Ecuador, with their large American Indian populations. Here, as in a number of other countries, army-backed caudillos often ruled without great vision beyond the maintenance of power, amid recurrent rural unrest and frequent changes of regime.

A military and landholding elite governed Argentina during the 1930s. Only in 1943 did real change take place under the populist authoritarian Juan Perón (elected president in 1946). Even more than Brazil's Vargas, Perón appealed to the masses with a policy of benefit programs. His government crushed free trade unions and opposition parties, while directing the main branches of the economy. Foreign-owned companies were bought out, and the power of former landholders was diminished by state controls over the price of their goods. Perón promoted the general thrust of economic nationalism, but with a populist twist—an effort at frenzied mass appeal that was suggestive of European fascism. The expense of Perón's massive welfare programs limited Argentina's real economic growth, even as popular loyalty to Perón remained high. A military coup in 1955 displaced the Argentine strongman, with an attempt to restore parliamentary democracy. But worried by the continued strength of Perón, and eager to ensure stability, the military took political control in 1966 and again in 1976, each time with vigorous police repression of opposition political forces.

Mass demonstration for Perón in Buenos Aires, with a heroic statue.

REVOLUTION AND RESPONSE, 1950s–1990s

Despite important variations in political forms and economic development, by the late 1950s, there was considerable optimism about Latin America's prospects. Leading countries, including Mexico, post-Vargas Brazil, and post-Perón Argentina, were firmly bent on economic development, some social reform, and some degree of political freedom, though not usually through a full-fledged, multiparty system. Despite Marxist currents, radical political efforts had little appeal. U.S. opposition to anything that smacked of communism combined with the strength of conservative forces. A reform-minded regime in the Central American nation of Guatemala was unseated with U.S. aid in 1954, as the giant to the north briefly resumed the tradition of intervention from a half-century before. Nevertheless, the United States did not consistently oppose the nationalist policies that had emerged since the 1930s. A major social revolution in Bolivia in 1952–1953 produced significant agrarian reform.

Although U.S. business interests exercised great power in many countries, Washington also welcomed the economic growth of nations such as Brazil and Mexico despite the fact that considerable planning and investment on their part were involved. "Good neighbor" policies initiated during the 1930s, during Franklin Roosevelt's administration, took some of the rougher edges off U.S.-Latin American relations, although a profound disparity in power remained and much of the good-neighbor rhetoric was purely cosmetic.

Hopes for a new level of stability were challenged by the revolution in Cuba. Long a U.S. protectorate, Cuba had suffered from weak political institutions. A strongman leader, Fulgencio Batista, had ruled since 1933, despite the great corruption of his regime. A pronounced gulf divided a rich minority from the impoverished masses, as in many Latin American nations. Although the Cuban economy was relatively prosperous, it was dangerously dependent on sugar exports to the United States, and the trade was controlled by U.S. firms. Peasant grievances against external capitalist control recalled the causes of the Mexican revolution. During the 1950s, a guerrilla rebellion arose against the Batista regime, headed by a magnetic leader, Fidel Castro. Castro's long-term political goals were unclear, but his attack on corruption and foreign influence, and his plea for land reform constituted an important new revolutionary current, blending peasant grievances with explicit political concerns. Military victory came in 1959–1960. The new regime frightened away or expelled wealthy Cubans, while deteriorating relations with the United States followed from, and also encouraged, the increasingly communist orientation of the Castro government. The Cuban Communist party, initially hesitant to do so, soon came to embrace Castro fully. A U.S. effort in 1961 to topple Castro failed miserably, leaving the new regime free to build a society along modified Soviet lines. State ownership combined with worker committees in factories,

while the great sugar estates were confiscated and turned into collective farms. The new regime promoted greater racial equality. The result was, in many ways, a more complete revolution than had occurred in Mexico—and it also led, thanks not only to Castro's policies and rhetoric but also to the U.S. response, to the development of cold war tensions within Latin American politics. Revolution in Cuba came to mean a close alliance with the Soviet Union, and a leadership cult evolved around the strong and persuasive personality of Castro.

The Cuban revolution did not have the unsettling effects on the rest of Latin America that its supporters had hoped for or its opponents had feared. Many Latin American governments maintained good relations with the new regime, rather pleased at Cuba's success in defying the North American giant but not eager to install a communist system in their own nations. U.S. policy shifted, in reaction to its failure to dislodge Castro, toward more significant economic aid to other Latin American countries, although momentum in this effort dwindled by the 1970s. A radical regime arose in Peru in 1968, but the reform results were meager, and military coups soon killed off most of the civilian revolutionaries. Much later, in 1979, a radical uprising in Nicaragua, with assistance from Cuba, unseated a U.S.-backed dictator. The new regime promoted land reform, seizing great estates (many of them owned by U.S. concerns), and enacted education and public-health measures. It also encouraged guerrilla movements in other Central American nations, notably El Salvador. During the early 1980s, the United States provided military aid and encouraged its own guerrilla activity in defense of more conservative regimes in the region. By the 1990s, peace had been largely restored as the regime sponsored, and lost, a democratic election.

The establishment of a communist system in Cuba encouraged a new round of authoritarianism in some other countries, as military and civilian leaders sought the fullest possible protection against any new subversion. Populist regimes also seemed to have failed by the 1960s in places such as Argentina, whereas economic development increased internal disputes, often pitting workers against the middle class and elite. The resulting series of military regimes, although they did not affect every country in the 1960s, became increasingly common. Fear of communism encouraged the military regimes of Argentina, beginning in 1966. In 1970 in Chile, a Marxist-led coalition of communists, socialists, and radicals won a free election. No carbon copy of Castro's, the new regime proceeded to enact a number of key reforms, including nationalization of U.S.-owned copper mines and division of the great landed estates. This, in turn, provoked a reaction from the middle and upper classes, and the conservative resurgence won U.S. support. A military coup toppled the reformist government, amid considerable bloodshed, and a strongly authoritarian dictatorship was installed that lasted into the late 1980s.

The spread of democratic systems began to overtake the surge of conservative military dictatorships in the 1980s, starting with the new Argentine regime of 1982. At first, the trend seemed merely a renewal of the oscillations long characteristic of Latin American politics. Free elections occurred in Brazil in 1984. A newly elected leader in Uruguay noted that "there are winds that blow in favor, winds that blow against. It is evident in this era the winds are favorable to democracy." Chile's authoritarian ruler yielded to democracy. Mexico gradually abandoned one-party dominance as contested elections became more common and opposition groups controlled some state governments; elections in 1997 were freer than at any point since the revolution, and early in the 21st century an opposition political leader won the presidency. Paraguay, one of the classic authoritarian states, adopted democracy in 1993. At least for the moment, Latin American leaders decided that democracy spared societies the painful costs of repression and encouraged economic development.

The surge resembled the rise of liberalism in the late 19th century, but it was not only democratic but less authoritarian. Amid changes in regimes and oscillations in the form of governments, Latin American political values unquestionably changed during the 20th century, even before the democratic surge. More groups gained political consciousness. In Mexico and many of the Andes nations, American Indians obtained new rights and political involvement. Women were given the right to vote for the first time in many countries—in Mexico, this occurred in 1954. By the 1990s, a significant minority of women served as elected officials in that country. The extension of education to the poorest classes was another important development in countries such as Brazil.

Still more significant was the growing commitment of Latin American governments to programs of economic development, although there had been some precedents for this trend in the 19th century. By the 1950s, few caudillos remained who sought only personal power and riches for themselves and their followers. Cuba's Batista was one such leader; so was the Nicaraguan head of state deposed by a revolution in 1979. Most authoritarian leaders, such as Perón or Vargas, now adopted a new stance, extending the functions of government in important new directions; the same held true for the Mexican regime and expanding democratic systems at the end of the 20th century.

The new-style authoritarian leaders might be just as brutal toward political opponents as their more traditional predecessors had been, but they were increasingly likely to sponsor economic planning, to encourage new technologies, and to regulate foreign investment in order to achieve greater economic nationalism. In most cases, their interest in development led to some concern for social reform, as authoritarian as well as liberal leaders moved to dismantle at least some of the vast landed estates and provide some welfare protection for urban workers. Except for Cuba, no government sponsored revolutionary

Urbanization: Belo Horizante, Brazil, 1967. Then only 70 years old, the city had more than a million inhabitants.

social reform during the 20th century. However, with rare exceptions, governments did assume new functions, including the extension of education and public-health measures and the development of certain economic sectors. Here was a significant, evolutionary transformation of the Latin American political style under various constitutional arrangements. Authoritarian rulers might now appeal directly to popular support and engage in vigorous reforms unsettling to conservative interests.

The democratic current in the 1980s and 1990s emphasized greater free enterprise. Governments sold off many state-run businesses, as the international emphasis on freer trade and capitalism strongly affected Latin America. Mexico, for example, reduced the government's role in the economy as part of its participation in the North American Free Trade Agreement (NAFTA) with the United States and Canada. Government activities remained extensive, and in some areas, such as environmental regulation, they increased somewhat. Latin America did not return to the weak government structures that had predated the 1930s.

Partly because of more vigorous efforts on the part of government, leading Latin American nations also managed to become increasingly independent from outside influence during the 20th century. The Mexican Revolution did not eliminate foreign economic activity, but it unquestionably reduced U.S. ability to determine key political or diplomatic policies. The nationalization of some crucial foreign enterprises, inaugurated by Mexico's control of its oil industry, was embraced by diverse governments in several Latin American countries. In the Caribbean islands, many former colonies gained political freedom after the 1950s, leading to a number of new island nations formed from previously British and Dutch holdings. In 2000, the United States finally surrendered control of the Panama Canal to the nation of Panama—another sign of the waning of the imperialism that had surged around 1900.

At the same time, Latin American independence was far from complete—again, a sign of continuity amid change. Cuba exchanged U.S. domination for Soviet influence in its economy and diplomacy. France, the Netherlands, and the United States still maintained some outright colonies, although they upgraded their status, as in the case of the Commonwealth of Puerto Rico. Britain maintained control of the Falkland Islands claimed by Argentina and rather easily vanquished a military uprising there in 1982. The ability of the United States to intervene in Central America, reasserted in the 1980s, remained an important factor, although it was not clear that such intervention could be as straightforward, or as successful, as in the past. Most importantly, the continued economic power of the United States and western Europe, in the still-dependent economies of Latin America, seriously qualified the general tendency toward greater national freedom and self-assertion.

Several factors raised new questions about Latin American democracy by the early 21st century. In Venezuela, a more authoritarian leader, Hugo Chavez, emerged who delighted in criticizing the United States. Argentina faced near economic collapse in 2002, raising questions about whether a free-market economy and globalization were benefiting Latin America. Similar issues arose elsewhere. After several short-term governments, however, Argentina elected a new president through democratic elections. Brazil embraced a popular social reformer as president. Similarly, in 2006, embryonic democracy extended to Chile, which elected its first woman president, a socialist, and to Bolivia, which elected its first Native American president, also a socialist. The retirement of Fidel Castro as Cuban leader, in 2008, brought new concessions to consumerism and private enterprise, but no relaxation of political controls. Generally, however, aside from Cuba and Venezuela, democratic regimes seemed reasonably solid in the region, though some of them turned toward greater economic intervention and social reform, in contrast to the more conservative politics of the United States in the same period.

LATIN AMERICAN CULTURE

In culture, even more clearly than in politics, the close interaction with the West left a definite mark, as Latin Americans participated vigorously in Western-initiated artistic developments of the 20th century. However, this was no simple extension of Western culture either, for a new artistic and literary vigor resulted in a growing emphasis on distinctive styles and themes.

Most wealthy Latin Americans shared Western tastes in fashion, furnishings, and art. Throughout the 20th century, a considerable market existed for Western imports of this sort, and some Latin American artists produced for

SOLVING PROBLEMS

ADAPTING CONSUMER VALUES

The pressure of foreign (mainly west European and U.S.) consumer forms and other societies' responses to them was one of the great cultural issues of the 20th century and promises to remain one in 21st-century world history. Western consumerism stands for the importance of acquisition, secular values, and new products as a measure of personal and national success and modernity. Some groups deeply resist this kind of pressure—Islamic fundamentalists, for example, who promote a religious alternative to consumer culture. Other groups gleefully join in, such as the many Japanese who made McDonald's and the Disney theme park near Tokyo instant successes.

The pressures of the consumerist model create a number of problems. Some individuals and groups simply don't like consumerism: for them, the problem is how to resist or avoid the phenomenon. A second problem: people in many regions can't really afford significant consumerism, though they may wish they could. Adjusting expectations and resources, amid global inequality, is a substantial issue. Many groups and regions, finally, are attracted to consumerism and can afford at least some elements, but they do not want to lose identity entirely, or become slaves to foreign models. Here, in what is in some ways the most subtle problem, the question is how to manage a modification process.

To solve this problem, a common response involves adding a distinctive regional twist while embracing a consumer trend. This is, in fact, a common pattern in cultural contact, involving the blending, or syncretism, of an outside model with local elements. But it is particularly important to grasp this in terms of contemporary consumerism, because otherwise it becomes easy to mistakenly assume that the whole world, except for pockets of resistance, is

largely becoming American. Even contemporary Western Europe, for example, modifies American patterns by insisting on larger amounts of leisure time—notably, through longer annual vacations—instead of accumulating quite so many goods.

The history of comic books in Mexico provides a specific example of an adaptation pattern. Comic books were imported from the United States to Mexico as early as the 1930s, and they caught on quickly thanks to the prestige of U.S. products and the low levels of average literacy. However, comics were soon modified to meet Mexican standards of beauty and political values. Thus, one series noted: "He was no vulgar bandit, he shared with the poor who live under the lash of vile capitalism"—this was hardly a common theme in the United States at that time. Macho exploits were touted, but there was also great emphasis on kinship and community ties. In contrast to American warriors, Mexican heroes were not loners. Indeed, they were often pitted against American villains, such as the "Invincible Jack Superman of Indianapolis," and in these imagined conflicts, the gringos lost almost every time. By the late 20th century, comic books were read far more regularly in Mexico than in the United States, precisely because Mexico had changed the medium to make it part of a national culture. In another example: many Indian beauty pageant organizers, while copying the basic global format, have blended requirements about demonstrating knowledge of local culture and dance styles. Important regional ingredients thus combine with the influence of American styles.

■QUESTIONS: *What aspects of American consumerism differ from larger global patterns? Why is some engagement with consumerism so attractive in the contemporary world?*

Mural by Diego Rivera (1886–1957) on elements of Mexico's rich historical heritage.
Source: Instituto Nacional de Bellas Artes INBA - Mexico

this market as well. A number of Latin American composers made a mark in symphonic music after 1920, and major cities boasted orchestras performing a wide repertoire of Western-style music. Still more impressive was the region's contribution to modern architecture. Economic and political development encouraged new building in most Latin American cities, as hotels and office complexes sprang up in the sleek styles familiar in the West. Particularly breathtaking was the erection of an entire city, Brasília, constructed in the 1960s as Brazil's new capital. Although criticized for its costliness, Brasília became a powerful symbol of modern architectural and urban-planning concepts.

Latin American initiatives in science lagged somewhat, as in the past. Major universities trained their students in science and technology, but the expense of elevating research to a more prominent position, and traditions in a civilization that still placed greater emphasis on the artistic and spiritual aspects of culture,

limited the overall importance of science in intellectual life, compared to other contemporary civilizations.

In art and literature, Latin America contributed vigorous 20th-century styles, although with an ongoing link to Western influences. The Mexican Revolution spurred innovative developments in painting. Two great muralists, Clemente Orozco and Diego Rivera, created numerous and powerful epics depicting the struggle of the Mexican lower classes from colonial days to the 20th century. Their forceful human figures and stark colors emphasized the suffering and courage of agricultural and factory workers, women as well as men. Their decision to paint wall murals, rather than conventional canvases, was a result of their social commitment to the public good, for their art decorated many public buildings and was not confined to museums or private collections. Both painters achieved international reputations. A number of other artists, from several

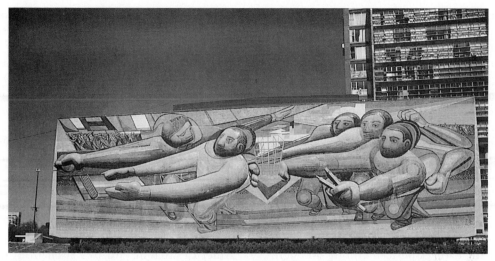

Mural to Students, by David Siqueiros, University of Mexico, Mexico City.   *Source:* Artists Rights Society, Inc.

countries, moved toward less representational styles after World War II, but an interest in the forms and coloration derived from Latin America's Indian and black heritage remained.

Contributions to Latin American literature, although at times constrained by political repression, involved both poetry and the novel. Major writers emerged in Chile, Mexico, Brazil, and Argentina. The Mexican Revolution inspired realistic novels that dramatized the plight of American Indians and other labor groups. Masterpieces of the Mexican revolutionary period include Mariano Azuela's *Los de abajo* (1916) and Martin Luis Guzmán's *El Aquila y la serpiente* (1928). The award of three Nobel prizes for literature to Latin American writers symbolized the rise of Latin American fiction after World War II. Major writers embraced many themes—history and anthropology, foreign domination including U.S. imperialism, and a strong current of fantasy that built on earlier poetic traditions. Both fantasy and stark realism, sometimes combined in the same novel, were intended to convey the special features of the Latin American experience; they represented a

balance of subject matter different from 20th-century European fiction. In addition to the use of American Indian themes and a strong social awareness, Latin American literature often addressed problems of identity—the attempt to define this part of the world's culture amid strong European and North American influences. At the same time, Latin American and Western writers worked in similar styles as well as languages, and they shared the same body of literature and criticism.

A final feature of Latin American culture, both formal and popular, was its dynamic Christianity. Although the political power and wealth of the Catholic church declined in some countries, such as Mexico, religion remained a much more pervasive force in Latin America than in Europe and North America. In terms of sheer numbers and pious devotion, Latin America indeed became the most significant Christian civilization by the mid-20th century, with 233 million people listed as Catholics—not all, to be sure, fervent believers—by 1985. Nonetheless, Latin American Catholicism was not simply a traditional force. From the 1960s on, a new generation of priests and theologians was responsible for increasing social commentary, urging Catholic involvement in the cause of social and political reform. Some Catholic leaders aided peasant guerrilla movements, whereas sympathetic bishops pressured governments for improved welfare programs, land reform, and popular political rights. Statements about the church's social responsibility became known as "liberation theology." The new currents within Latin American Catholicism resulted in clashes with some authoritarian governments and also criticism from the papacy, which by the 1980s was not enthusiastic about political activism. Catholic debate formed another important channel for Latin American culture and additional evidence of a new level of intellectual vigor. Catholicism was itself challenged, however, by popular religions that mixed Christian and African elements—particularly in Brazil—and by a surprising current of conversion to fundamentalist Protestantism, creating a vibrant new religious minority spurred by missionary activity. The advance of Protestantism, particularly among poorer groups seeking cultural outlets, was truly striking: by the late 1990s, 30 percent of the Guatemalan population was Protestant, and similar changes had occurred in Brazil. These developments complicated the society's cultural map but confirmed the unusual importance of religion in 20th-century Latin America.

ECONOMY AND SOCIETY

Latin America experienced rapid social and economic change, particularly after 1950, although important traditions continued from the past. In most countries, the social division between rich and poor remained great. The wealthy minority controlled landed estates in many countries—in some cases, only 4 percent of the population owned 80 percent of the land—and also operated the leading commercial and manufacturing concerns. In many cities, luxurious mansions and

lifestyles juxtaposed with mass squalor. The widespread employment of female domestic servants remained a standard prerogative of upper-class households. Social reform efforts, even in revolutionary Mexico, rarely did more than scratch the surface of such a basic division, although some changes occurred. Regional disparities remained considerable as well. The Andes nations were particularly impoverished. Argentina maintained its position as a significant exporter of grains and meats, but the Argentine economy was often hampered by political problems and a level of government spending that encouraged paralyzing inflation.

Another troubling continuity involved Latin America's inability to free itself from reliance on vulnerable export items. Despite concerted policy attention and some diversification, the civilization continued to depend on imported Western technology, and exports consisted disproportionately of agricultural goods such as coffee, sugar, raw materials, and oil, all vulnerable to low and fluctuating prices. Furthermore, most Latin American nations, because of their poor earnings position in the world economy, remained heavily indebted to Western banks. Ambitious development programs often merely increased the debt, which by the 1980s severely burdened both the rich and poor economies within the civilization. Even Cuba, which defied tradition in many ways, proved unable to escape economic dependency, as it relied for its export earnings on sales of sugar to eastern Europe and million-dollar-a-day Russian aid. The Soviet collapse brought new problems to the island that highlighted its failure to industrialize.

Nonetheless, many areas of Latin America gained new economic strength. Agricultural production improved in many countries, as new techniques, including the innovations of the 1960s, the Green Revolution, were adopted. Tourism expanded, resulting in foreign earnings and influences. Chile dramatically expanded its exports in commercial agriculture, growing in prosperity by the 1990s. Manufacturing output

HISTORY DEBATE

LATIN AMERICA AND THE THIRD WORLD

During the cold war, the idea of a "third world," siding with neither the West nor the communist bloc, emerged. India was a leading example. Because most of these neutral nations were also poor, the term *third world* came to imply poverty and lack of industrial development, and this is its key meaning today.

Latin American countries are often described as third world countries. Certainly they are far less wealthy and industrial than societies such as Japan and western Europe; standards of living and technologies lag. Many foreign companies set up branch operations in countries such as Mexico to take advantage of cheap labor and weak environmental regulations.

But the third world idea can be misleading. Most Latin American countries have fairly high rates of literacy (more than 70 percent), and life expectancy has increased. They have large middle classes, with high consumer standards including routine ownership of items such as televisions and refrigerators. Significant industrial sectors have emerged in Mexico and Brazil, while commercial export agriculture has promoted greater prosperity in Chile. Many analysts argue that *third world,* as a term, does not capture the variation among the countries and regions to which it is applied, and that it also does not capture significant change. Ironically, some of the same foreign companies that located in Mexico have since moved to China and southeast Asia, because Mexican wages have risen somewhat—while still remaining far below Western standards. What kind of terminology makes most sense for Latin American countries? Should the terminology used for countries in Africa or southern Asia be used for Latin American countries?

increased, too, and the wealthier Latin American nations began to produce most of the industrial goods they required for normal consumption. Textile and metallurgical industries spread widely, and a few countries, headed by Brazil, began to export basic manufactured goods to other parts of the world, including the United States. Brazil also developed the world's fourth largest computer industry, specializing in less sophisticated computers than those from Japan or the United States, but ones deemed reliable in other less developed, less technologically advanced nations.

To be sure, advancing mechanization still fell short of a full industrial revolution. It did not bring Latin America to the levels of economic development being achieved in the Pacific Rim. The high birth rate, averaging between 2 and 3 percent annually after World War II, limited gains

in the standard of living. Catholic hostility toward birth-control measures and the strong traditionalism of many Latin American families contributed to this growth in population, which in many countries literally consumed the gains in food and manufacturing production. One result of population pressure was the extraordinary rate of emigration, both legal and illegal, to the United States. Another result was a low-wage economy that induced many U.S. and some European and Japanese firms to establish factories in Latin America for inexpensive exports to industrialized areas of the world.

Many Latin American countries, however, did make a turn to greater population control. Mexico, for example, underwent a demographic transition in the 1960s, resulting in markedly smaller families even though population expansion continued on the basis of earlier growth.

Furthermore, the manufacturing gains—the evolution toward a more industrial society—engendered measurable improvements in living standards for many people. Brazil's economic growth, at 6 percent per year during some decades, expanded both the middle class and urban working class. Many began to participate in new consumerism. By 1990, 22 percent of all Brazilians owned cars, 56 percent had televisions, and 63 percent had refrigerators. These gains, which were echoed in Mexico and elsewhere, surpassed levels in eastern Europe or the Pacific Rim (apart from Japan). Not yet industrialized, Latin American economies were nevertheless carving out a distinctive position among the major societies of the world.

Both population pressure and industrial gains furthered the rapid urbanization of Latin America from the 1930s on. Here too, the society held an unusual place, becoming more urban than most of Asia and Africa although less so than the industrialized societies. City growth was itself distinctive, combining new manufacturing with huge enclaves of dire poverty. The rural populations simply could not be accommodated in the countryside, particularly when the land was held in large estates. Cities provided some factory jobs to a privileged segment of the masses; to even more people, they offered some hope of occasional work plus charity or welfare.

In 1925, only 25 percent of Latin America's population was urbanized; by 1975, 60 percent lived in cities—in contrast to a mere 30 percent in China or India. Massive shantytowns arose in Mexico, Brazil, and elsewhere, as a largely unemployed population constructed houses out of cans and boxes. The world's largest city took shape in the Mexican capital, which had 3 million people in 1950 but an overwhelming 9 million by 1970, and 24 million by 2009. Excruciating problems of pollution as well as dire poverty resulted from this extraordinary urban development.

Population pressure and urban problems inevitably added to earlier social grievances,

Urban slums in Caracas, Venezuela. Migrants to the city stake out their unauthorized living spaces.

notably the unequal distribution of land and the gap between rich and poor, to produce recurrent popular protest. Rural rioting occurred in many countries in the 20th century, even aside from the major revolutions. Peasant attacks on landlords paralyzed much of Colombia in 1947. Indian peasants formed guerrilla bands that controlled stretches of Bolivia and Peru in the 1970s and 1980s. A rural rebellion erupted in southern Mexico in 1994. Urban strikes and riots dotted the 20th-century landscape as well. Violence spilled over into other areas. Mass sports events often featured fights between partisan crowds. In Mexico and Venezuela, murder rates were among the highest in the world.

Nevertheless, there were strengths in Latin American society as well as fearsome tensions. Family structure remained tight, characteristically under male domination. Yet women made some gains, through new voting rights, education, and legal protections. The number of women in parliaments increased. It was often women, acting even against the wishes of priests and husbands, who made the decisions that limited population growth. Popular festivals and religious celebrations featured traditional dances and music and provided joyful release to many groups. The ability of Latin Americans to preserve family institutions and cultural forms in the face of rapid population movement to the cities set some limits on the worst confusions of social transformation, although the same traditionalism enforced limitations on the conditions of women under the sway of *machismo* traditions and a strong emphasis on sexuality. Amid problems common to many parts of the world—such as underemployment—Latin American popular culture retained a distinctive flavor.

TOWARD A GREATER WORLD ROLE?

Latin America has long occupied a somewhat ambiguous place in world history. The civilization first developed as one dependent on the West, a status still not fully shaken off. Although Latin Americans participate fully, if not always influentially, in the world economy, they have generated neither dramatic cultural forms nor catastrophic military upheavals with international impact. Nationalism and literary preoccupation with issues of Latin American identity follow from a sense of being ignored or misunderstood in the wider world. The United States, which continues to play a powerful role in Latin American affairs, stands particularly accused of ignorance and neglect.

However, the trends in Latin American history in the later 20th century suggest an increase in the civilization's visibility. Latin America constitutes a growing share of the world's population. Its economic advance, although often troubled, places it in the middle rank of developing nations. Its importance in the world religious sphere is on the increase. Some observers believed that the civilization's potential for social upheaval remains unusually great, although the 20th-century experience suggested a balance between unrest and conservative continuities. Brazil and a few other leaders may soon make the turn to a self-sustaining industrialization. But the likelihood of growing international impact in the future seems high, as the newest world history period brought new self-consciousness and millions of new people to a civilization increasingly proud of its achievement, if still resentful of its economic dependency.

PATHS TO THE PRESENT

Although striking events marked Latin America's landscape over the past century, greater change resulted from more everyday processes. The conversion to a largely urban society was a huge development, as was the expansion of the manufacturing sector. Modifications in family structure, including a reduction in the birth rate, also had major implications for Latin American society. The recent, substantial, commitment to democracy is built on earlier liberal currents in the region's politics but was a major shift, nonetheless. Latin American voices began to exert influence on a variety of human rights and environmental issues, particularly within Latin America itself but also to an extent on a larger world stage; the number of the area's nongovernmental organizations, bent on marshalling public opinion, increased rapidly from the 1970s on.

The Latin America of 1906 was largely peasant, largely authoritarian, and highly patriarchal. This was not the Latin America of 2009, thanks to the various economic and social processes in which the society had participated over many decades, even while preserving important links to earlier cultural forms, including an active popular religion.

SUGGESTED WEB SITES

For more information on Mexico, see http://www.mexonline.com/revolution.htm; on women in the Mexican Revolution, refer to http://www.ic.arizona.edu/ic/mcbride/ws200/mex-jand.htm; on Cuban history, see http://www.fiu.edu./~fcf/history.html; and for resources on Latin America past and present, see http://lib.nmsu.edu/subject/bord/laguia/.

SUGGESTED READINGS

Recent work includes Peter H. Smith, *Democracy in Latin America: Political Change in Comparative Perspective* (2005); Howard J. Wiarda, *Dilemmas of Democracy in Latin America: Crises and Opportunity* (2005); Jean Franco, *The Decline and Fall of the Lettered City: Latin America in the Cold War* (2002); Di Tella S. Torcuato, *History of Political Parties in Twentieth-Century Latin America* (2004); Ben Schneider, *Business Politics and the State in Twentieth-Century Latin America* (2004); Martin Hopenhayn, *No Apocalypse, No Integration: Modernism and Postmodernism in Latin America* (2001); Courtney Jung, *The Moral Force of Indigenous Politics: Critical Liberalism and the Zapatistas* (2008); Francisco Vidal Luna and Herbert S. Klein, *Brazil since 1980* (2006); Silviano Santiago, *The Space In-Between: Essays on Latin American Culture* (2001); Peter Winn, *Americas: The Changing Face of Latin America and the Caribbean* (1999); David Craven, *Art and Revolution in Latin America* (2002); John Peeler, *Building Democracy in Latin America* (1998); Carlos Alonso, *The Burden of Modernity: The Rhetoric of Cultural Discourse in Spanish America* (1998); John C. Chasteen, *Born in Fire and Blood: A Concise History of Latin America* (2001), a survey of developments since 1945; Alezandro de la Fuente, *Race, Inequality, and Politics in Twentieth-Century Cuba* (2001); Gilbert Joseph et al., eds., *Close Encounters of Empire* (1998), on United States' impacts on Latin America; and Greg Grandin, *Blood of Guatemala* (2000), on social tensions and reform.

CHAPTER

34 Sub-Saharan Africa: From Colonies to New Nations

Africa south of the Sahara had been fully consumed by European imperialism only 20 years before the 20th century began. For several decades after 1900, when other areas of the world were rousing to new nationalisms, African history continued to be characterized by the operations of the colonial governments and western Europe's increasing economic impact. However, nationalism took root here as well, and after World War II it gained momentum. The result, occurring only slightly later than in most of Asia, was the independence of a number of new nations. From the 1960s on, their efforts to establish the institutions and loyalties of nationhood represented the primary focus in the region. Problems of economic development, and in some areas recurrent famines and disease, complicated national politics. And the continued existence of a powerful, white-dominated South African nation long cast its shadow over the continent.

Even before independence was achieved, and certainly after its first results were taken into account, issues of cultural identity and social and economic transformation played a vital role in the patterns of Africa. Imperialist policies brought fuller contact with the world economy and encouraged some internal economic development along with great dislocation. One result was a marked resemblance to earlier characteristics of Latin America, the other society most fully touched by Western economic dominance and cultural and political influence. African civilization, to be sure, was not obliterated to the extent that American Indian cultures had been. Nonetheless, Africa displayed patterns of economic dependency comparable to colonial and 19th-century Latin America, including a reliance on vulnerable cash crops and mineral exports; of tensions of new nationhood, including frequent reliance on authoritarian political forms; and even of considerable cultural innovation, the result of both Muslim and Christian missionary efforts that made this civilization, again like that of Latin America earlier on, the scene of great religious fervor and creativity.

Africans, on the other hand, were less closely linked to Western cultural styles than were Latin Americans, and they faced more acute problems of defining their identity amid new or outside influences. And Africa emerged from its brief colonial experience less developed—in terms of city size, literacy levels, amount of manufacturing, and commercial agriculture—than any of the other major contemporary civilizations. Generating further change, particularly toward industrialization or a better-rounded economy, and adjusting to 20th-century trends such as population increase and urbanization have posed acute challenges for contemporary Africans. Efforts to combine cultural and family traditions with modernization reflect a desire to maintain a distinctive African character and to cushion the impact of new political and economic styles.

■**KEY QUESTIONS**   *What were the characteristic problems of African new nations? Why and how were some countries more successful than others in resolving the problems?*

EMERGING NATIONALISM

World War I triggered some new currents in colonial Africa. Scattered fighting took place in the German colonies in the south, which were then taken over by the British, with one possession, South West Africa, or what is now called Namibia, administered as part of South Africa. The French used large numbers of loyal African troops in their European campaigns. Discussion of national rights after World War I encouraged a rethinking of the future of the African colonies. European diplomats spoke of their holdings as "a sacred trust of civilization" to help educate peoples "not yet able to stand by themselves under the strenuous conditions of the modern world." This outlook produced new efforts to better the standard of living of the colonial

peoples by building local schools, hospitals, libraries, and so on. Belgium, known for its harsh exploitation in the Congo, shifted its policies significantly. Colonial-run police forces tried to prevent tribal warfare, and attention was paid to improving agricultural techniques.

Western imperialism hardly changed entirely, however. Assumptions of African inferiority continued. Schools reached only a minority of Africans, and they often taught details of European history and culture that made little sense in the African context. Belgian officials in the Congo, for example, insisted that educated Africans learn Flemish as well as French, although the language had little wider applicability, simply because the society back home and its languages were regarded as the pinnacle of culture. Many schools were run by missionaries, including large numbers from the United States, who attacked local religious traditions in the name of Christianity; a Christian minority, both Catholic and Protestant, did develop in most colonies as a result. Most colonial governments allowed Africans to enter only the lower levels of the bureaucracy and military. French policy encouraged an African elite to enroll in schools in France and assimilate into French culture, but there was little real concern for the African masses. Britain paid attention to a larger number but reserved the upper ranks of administration for British officials. Few African soldiers could rise above the rank of sergeant. Thus, 20th-century imperialism, although it involved new expenditures for the colonies—Britain may have spent more in Africa during the 1920s and 1930s than it earned there—remained very much an imposition from the outside.

Imperialism also resulted in continued pressure for economic change, toward generating more low-cost exports of foods and raw materials. In largely British-ruled eastern Africa, where population levels were low and prior political forms relatively loose, a wealthy minority of white colonists established estates on the rich agricultural lands of the plateaus, using African

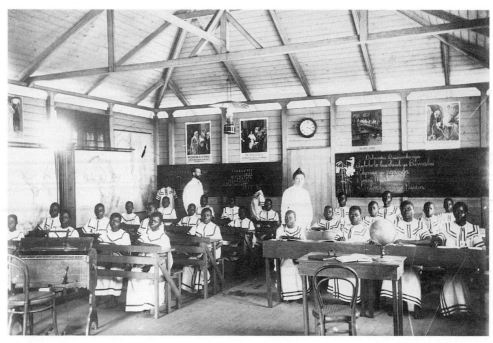

African mission school run by Europeans. Probably from the Belgian Congo, 1920s.

labor; other Africans preserved a hunting-and-gathering existence or worked as farmers on the less fertile lands. In Portuguese Mozambique, many Africans were required to grow cotton, because Portugal thought this would feed its own industrialization. But cotton was not best suited to the soil, resulting in environmental damage, and the workers, mostly women, did not have time to grow much food for themselves. The result was increasing poverty and malnutrition. In western Africa, with more of its own commercial experience, African business entrepreneurs along with Europeans introduced cash crops, such as peanuts and cocoa, for sale on the world market. Railroads and shipping lines also opened further access to raw materials. Belgium drew rubber, copper, and vital minerals from the Congo; British Rhodesia exported copper; South Africa mined gold and diamonds. Mining operations were owned and operated by Europeans, or by white South Africans, using poorly paid gangs of African labor. Thus, the ties

of Africa to the world economy became more extensive, but largely on terms that reaped profits for Europeans.

The impact of this burgeoning economic activity on Africans was mixed. Some businessmen drew substantial profits while becoming accustomed to the ways of international commerce. In the boom years of the 1920s, rich business leaders in British West Africa acquired an extravagant lifestyle: "Motor cars were purchased right and left, champagne flowed freely, and expensive cigars scented the air." This elite also participated in local elections, for governing bodies that had a limited voice over issues such as roads and public health. Larger numbers of Africans were drawn into the emerging cities and the mining centers as laborers. Many traditions and family ties were disrupted by the move to the cities, particularly because women were often left behind. As custom conflicted with the attractions of a partially westernized urban life, tension developed that influenced African culture from this point on. Finally, large numbers of Africans remained generally isolated from the economic transformation, in scattered agricultural or hunting settlements rarely reached by Europeans.

In South Africa, a special pattern of European–African relations continued to develop. Here, white settlers, some of English origin but primarily Afrikaners of Dutch extraction, were more numerous than in any other African region. Clashes between the English and the Boers, the name given to the Dutch settlers, intensified the friction. The Afrikaners increasingly supported the Nationalist political party, which talked of leaving the British Empire and vowed to keep black Africans, the majority, in a subordinate place. The party slogan was "South Africa: A White Man's Land." During the 1920s, the Nationalists sponsored the Color Bar bill to prevent blacks from holding skilled jobs. In 1936, blacks were excluded from voting in elections. White South Africans were gradually creating two separate societies, preventing any contact between whites and blacks save that between employer and unskilled laborer.

Nowhere, of course, did Africans have extensive political rights. What was unusual in South Africa is that representative institutions did exist but were reserved mainly for whites. In other colonies, voting rights, if any, were limited to an urban minority of Africans, and the bodies they elected had few powers and were dominated by whites.

African bitterness toward white rule broke out periodically. To promote black rights, a group ultimately named the African National Congress formed in South Africa as early as 1912. In 1921 in the Congo, a carpenter named Simon Kimbangu formed a religious movement with impressive rituals and revolutionary political doctrines, drawn in part from the Bible. His movement aroused considerable mass support until Kimbangu was arrested and executed. In Kenya, a government clerk, Harry Thuku, organized the East Africa Native Association to protest

a reduction in wages; his arrest in 1922, on charges of sedition, led to a wave of riots.

Outright African nationalism developed only gradually. The experiences of the African elite, some trained at European universities, brought growing awareness of nationalist ideas. The Pan-African Congress met in Paris in 1919 to press for national independence, and similar meetings occurred periodically through 1945. Pan-African nationalism, bent on not only freedom from European control but also a glorification of the strengths and traditions of Africa and the hope for a new, unprecedented African unity, received powerful stimulus from the writings and political leadership of U.S. and West Indian black leaders in the 1920s and 1930s. Figures such as the American Marcus Garvey, who sought new links with Africa as part of the black struggle for freedom in the United States, helped African nationalists, particularly in the British colonies, articulate their own strivings. However, the limits to Western-style education in Africa meant that nationalist ideas spread slowly. To many Africans, the concept of nationhood was an abstraction, compared to the known loyalties of the tribe and extended family. Even more than in the Middle East after 1918, most African colonies were arbitrary units, embracing many tribes and language groups with no precedent in Africa's earlier political history. Loyalty to these nations thus came hard. Nationalist leaders themselves debated inconclusively about whether to pursue a larger African unity, tribal units, or nation-states based essentially on colonial boundaries. This was a period of genesis for African nationalism, not, before 1945, a full flowering. Many individual leaders who emerged after World War II developed their nationalist convictions during this period, however. For example, Jomo Kenyatta, educated at the London School of Economics and later in Moscow, began to write of the strengths of African traditions as opposed to Western materialism and corruption. Kenyatta later led the nationalist movement in Kenya and become its first president. Leopold Senghor, a Catholic native of Senegal who lived in Paris, learned of the cultural traditions of Africa and also admired the achievements of blacks from the United States and West Indies. He began to write of the beauties of *négritude*, or blackness, seen as a source of racial pride and confidence in black creativity, particularly within the arts.

The worldwide economic depression hit Africa hard. The region's growing dependence on the sale to the West of low-price items such as cocoa beans, and on Western companies that directly organized raw-materials production, was vividly highlighted. Loss of jobs and wages increased unrest and spurred the nationalist movement as strikes and riots attacked the power and greed of European and U.S. companies.

World War II heightened nationalism still further. A number of black leaders in French colonies supported the resistance movement against Nazi control of France. They felt real loyalty to France, but they expected growing political rights in return. The rise of anticolonial movements in other parts of the world and the retreat of once-proud empires in Asia served as an obvious inspiration in Africa. For their part, European administrations recognized the need to work harder for social and economic improvements in Africa. France thus poured more money into its African colonies between 1947 and 1957 than it had done in the whole previous half-century. British leaders began to talk of ultimate self-government, suggesting that the role of the mother country was now to train its colonies in nationhood. Nonetheless, many Europeans seemed in no hurry to admit that Africans were ready to take over their own government. Their belief in African inferiority and a desire to hold fast to this one vestige of imperialism, while the rest of the empire was crumbling, posed obvious barriers. In many colonies, particularly in British East Africa, the demands of the influential white-settler minority also slowed change: how could this group be protected if colonialism came to an end?

European hesitation was met by a new generation of nationalist leaders, most of them trained in European or North American universities; many had experience in trade unions or local governments. They thought in terms of independent nations built on the basis of existing colonies; ideas of African unity or a return to tribal organization now faded. The new leaders mounted mass rallies of urban Africans. Often arrested, they used imprisonment to dramatize their cause. Many also battled traditional African leaders, including the tribal chiefs, to whom the concept of nationalism remained foreign. Direct raids on European settlers, as in Kenya, added to the pressure from yet another source, as villagers and hunters protested the white control of the best lands.

THE TRANSFORMATION TO INDEPENDENCE

Between 1957 and the mid-1970s, the colonial era drew to a close. The country named Ghana arose first, based on Britain's western Gold Coast colony; Kwame Nkrumah was its nationalist leader. A schoolteacher, he had studied for a decade in the United States, where he was deeply influenced by both European socialism and American black nationalists who called for a rebellion against white domination. Returning to the Gold Coast in 1945, Nkrumah built a mass political movement among urban elements and commercial cocoa farmers with the slogan "Self-Government Now." Many of his followers saw independence as a key to a brighter future across the board, in which economic as well as political problems would be swept away by the searchlight of freedom. Nkrumah organized a series of riots and strikes, which landed him in jail; he dominated local elections from 1951 on. Britain conceded the inevitable, and Ghana, drawing its name although not its boundaries from the historic kingdom, won its freedom in 1957.

A Nigerian village with housing made of corrugated iron and women engaged in traditional tasks.

Other British colonies in West Africa gained independence soon after. France sought to prevent a complete rift within its colonies, after its bitter experiences in Indochina and then Algeria, by granting commonwealth status to its 13 sub-Saharan holdings in 1958. African leaders deeply loyal to France supported this move, although Sékou Touré, a radical leader in the colony of Guinea, insisted on full independence immediately. The other nations gained national status in the early 1960s, but most retained close ties to France. Belgium lost the Congo in a series of riots in 1959—one of the only cases outside southern Africa where the granting of

independence did not come peacefully. Britain's east African colonies also gained national freedom, despite the agitation of white settlers. Only in Southern Rhodesia did a major delay in independence arise, as the white minority broke away from Britain in 1965 and held out for over a decade against a guerrilla war conducted by black nationalists and against substantial diplomatic pressure from Britain and the United States. Here too, independence triumphed, through the creation of a black-run government with assurances of white minority representation; in 1980, the new nation shook off its colonial name and took on another historic

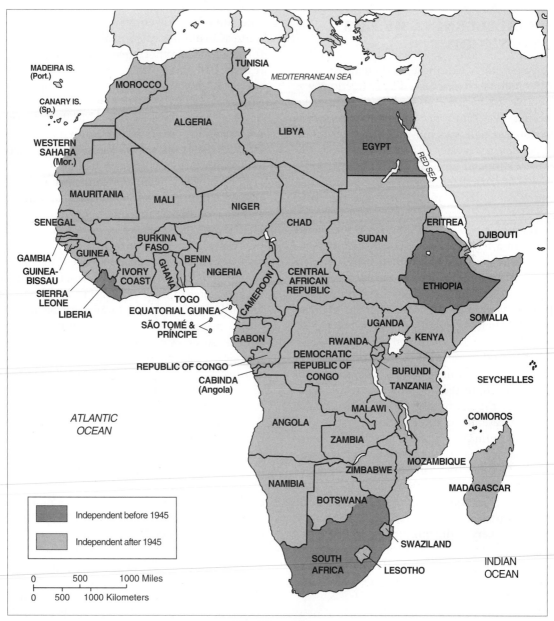

The New Africa

name—Zimbabwe. Finally, also in the 1970s, a change in the political regime of Portugal, along with significant guerrilla warfare and some backing from the Soviet Union and Cuba, led to independence for Angola and Mozambique. In the space of two decades, approximately 40 new nations had been born in sub-Saharan Africa.

THE CHALLENGES OF NEW NATIONHOOD

The ease with which most—although not all—former colonies had achieved their freedom was deceptive. Many Africans and Westerners alike expected great gains once imperialism ceased to be a distraction. In fact, most African states found independence a greater challenge than the battle against European control had been. Although conditions varied widely in a civilization still quite diverse, most of the new nations were poor. Independence did not transform the economy or promote new power on the world market. In a few cases, as in the former Belgian Congo, initial disorder disrupted trade patterns and caused the flight of Western managers and technicians, a situation that was only later repaired. Many new nations, such as Nigeria, adopted policies of "indigenization," or partial nationalization, which required that business and landed estates pass from European hands to majority African control within a decade or so. This approach, in seeking fuller national command over the economy, was understandable; indeed, it resembled the economic nationalist policies of Latin American countries in the earlier decades of the 20th century. But indigenization efforts had to be balanced against continued needs for Western technologies and capital. Nor could indigenization free most economies from the previous status of dependency. For many African workers, indigenization merely substituted African for European capitalists in a cash-crop or mining operation, as land was not widely redistributed and reliance on poorly paid labor remained extensive.

Leadership was also a problem in the new nations, along with agonizing economic issues. Some stirring nationalists proved inept or corrupt once in power—Ghana's Nkrumah was a case in point. Filling bureaucracies with competent staff was not easy when so few Africans had prior political experience. Here was one reason for frequent reliance on authoritarian rule, after brief attempts at parliamentary systems, as firm lines of control might compensate for political inexperience. The fact that army leaders had more organizational training—of the modern, bureaucratic type as opposed to the personalized, tribal sort—than most and national rather than local loyalties help account for frequent periods of military control. However, this reliance on the army for effective leadership was no panacea. Generals who the year before had been sergeants now ran many armies; although some quickly learned the lessons of complex management, others were inefficient.

Many of the new nations faced periods of civil war soon after independence. This experience resembled that of Latin America and the United States in the 19th century, but precedent was of little comfort. Divisions by tribe and language group made central administration difficult, in some ways more difficult than when Europeans had ruled. Leadership could now be ascribed to one group, which tended to antagonize other groups. The former British colony of Nigeria, in west Africa, dramatically illustrated a common problem. A large, populous nation, potentially one of Africa's wealthiest because of rich oil holdings as well as commercial farms, Nigeria was divided among three major language groups. Each group had distinctive political and cultural traditions—some emphasized military values, others business success. Nigerians in the north were Muslim; southerners were Christian or polytheist. Independent Nigeria was thus initially organized as a federation of three regional governments, but internal warfare resulted nevertheless. A group of army officers, committed to national unity, took control in 1965 and abolished these regions, but because most of the new leaders were from a single tribe, the Ibos, the result was a fierce attack by the Muslim north. The attempt by the Ibo region to form an independent state in 1967 led to three years of bloody warfare in which hundreds of thousands died of starvation. However, national unity survived; the central military leadership held on and then made peace with the defeated Ibos through economic aid and local autonomy.

Internal warfare also surfaced in Congo, whose name was changed to Zaire in 1971, although in this case regional conflicts were heightened by Western and Soviet interference. With backing from European business leaders and military forces, a pro-Western dictatorship was ultimately established. Warfare between majority and minority tribal groups also plagued Zimbabwe after independence, although outright civil war was avoided.

There were also other complications. Boundary disputes led to regional warfare in a few instances. Ethiopia and Somalia engaged in a bitter territorial quarrel in the late 1970s. The Pan-African Congress met periodically to resolve disputes, often with considerable success, and the civilization was far freer from warfare than the neighboring Middle East. Cold war tensions also affected the new nations for a time. Soviet backing for Angolan independence included the provision of Cuban troops. The Ethiopian–Somali dispute was fueled by aid from both the Soviet Union and the United States, as first Somalia and then Ethiopia became Soviet allies. Most African nations tried with some success to stay clear of a firm alignment with either cold war side, but superpower rivalries could be an undeniable distraction.

South Africa proved to be one of the most intractable problems of the late 20th century. White minority rule continued in this powerful country, long defying the movement toward black independence. South Africa boasted the only industrialized economy on the continent, built on unusual mineral wealth and rich agriculture; it also maintained the continent's strongest military force. Afrikaner power in South Africa, which had increased gradually during the first half of the 20th century after the Boer War, culminated in outright victory in the 1948 national elections. The National party ruled the country until 1994, seceding from the British

Commonwealth in 1961. The Afrikaners progressively constructed a system called *apartheid*, or separation, to keep the black majority in economic and political subjugation. In most public places, blacks were not permitted to use white facilities; intermarriage was forbidden; blacks, even when working for white-owned firms, were required to live in segregated urban compounds; and many rural blacks were forced onto artificially created homelands, usually on the worst lands, where superficial self-government barely masked white control. Protests from a liberal white minority were silenced by police action and censorship, although moderate opposition was allowed to continue. Agitation from black groups, and also from Indian and mixed-race minorities, surfaced periodically, only to be crushed amid widespread brutality.

However, pressures from blacks for political rights and against an economic discrimination that confined them to unskilled jobs could not undo the existing system of apartheid. Unrest developed particularly among black workers in the urban compounds. Many parts of the world supported these actions, which also prompted some superficial concessions in apartheid policy during the 1970s, although in 1984–1986, a new series of bloody riots led to the reinstatement of martial law. Only at the end of the 1980s did a breakthrough begin, as a new white leader, F. W. de Klerk, negotiated with Nelson Mandela of the African National Congress. Apartheid was legally dismantled and negotiations continued toward election-based universal suffrage with some protections for the white minority. Conditions remained uncertain, and violence between whites and blacks and among black groups continued to run high, but the long era of white domination ended. Mandela was elected president in the first elections based on universal suffrage, in 1994.

For most of sub-Saharan Africa, which remained rather separate from South Africa while denouncing apartheid, three themes dominated the decades after independence.

A colorful mural on display at the BAT Center in Durban, South Africa, reflecting the vibrancy of the postapartheid era.

First, national unity was successfully maintained in most cases, though there were agonizing exceptions. Administrations were extended over the new nations, school systems expanded, national loyalty preached through the government-dominated press and the ubiquitous transistor radio. In key cases, as we have seen, secessionist movements were defeated, and except in a few cases, a full commitment to either side in the cold war was avoided.

Second, initial attempts to maintain democratic political structures were quickly abandoned. Despite Western expectations, in part because of the limited political experience that had been possible during the colonial period, virtually all the new nations dismantled parliamentary institutions, multiparty political systems, and guarantees of political freedom. In Ghana, Kwame Nkrumah soon jailed his political opponents and outlawed all parties save his own. His goal was a one-party state capable of arousing the kind of loyalty that would hold together the nation and maintain his personal power. Nkrumah finally failed, victim in part of poor economic management that bankrupted the new nation. Military leadership replaced him. Most other African countries converted to either military rule or one-party systems that brooked no legal opposition. One-party governments arose in Kenya and Tanzania and in most of the former French colonies. Military rule predominated in Congo, Ethiopia, Liberia, and elsewhere. During the 1950s and 1960s, Africa experienced at least 70 attempted military takeovers (20 of which succeeded), and the pattern continued in later decades. Nigeria's military government turned power over to an elected civilian government in 1979, but another military coup soon followed.

Third, determined efforts were pursued in many nations to promote economic change. Most of the new African leaders saw economic development as a vital expression of independence, an essential component to the national unity they worked hard and successfully to preserve. Such a goal proved far more compelling than Western-style liberalism, although its achievement remained elusive amid a particularly daunting set of economic and demographic barriers.

AFRICAN POLITICS

The almost uniform conversion of independent African states to authoritarian political structures in the later 20th century is not surprising. Latin America and many Asian nations have shown a similar pattern in response to new nationhood. African political traditions, which so often emphasized the divine power of kings and had been shaped more recently by repressive colonial administrations, offered scant basis for a more liberal political approach in the Western or Indian sense.

African leaders, many personally ambitious and almost all eager to defend the unity of their new countries as the top political priority, found it hard to countenance opposition that seemed a personal affront and often expressed regional or tribal loyalties that threatened the nation. Success in maintaining unity—and the new African nations fared better in this regard than the initial Latin American nations had done in the first half of the 19th century—seemed to require strong police effort. Authoritarian rule also came naturally to many military leaders, who represented one of the more solid national institutions in most new nations. Many ordinary Africans, particularly in the fast-growing cities, placed great faith in the more charismatic leaders. Rural Africans might be less involved politically, but their loyalties, more traditional, corresponded to smaller segments of society such as family, village, and tribe, not to a national force of opposition. Although a number of Africans defended liberal values, the extent of support for

parliamentary politics that helped forge an oscillation between liberal and authoritarian forms in the Latin American tradition did not surface, at least during the first decades of independence. The authoritarian style went largely unchallenged until the 1990s, except for attacks by rival aspirants to authoritarian power.

Although authoritarian government in Africa characteristically meant attacks on opposition leaders, monopoly of the press and radio, and an emphasis on an internally strong army, other policies of authoritarian leaders varied widely. At one extreme was the brutal corruption of a number of leaders in Uganda, where at least two dictators used their armies to attack rival tribes and kill hundreds of thousands of civilians. This kind of brutality resulted in no stability, as rival claimants to power chased each other out of office with some frequency. Another authoritarian style involved emulation of the Soviet Russian example. Ethiopian Marxists, who took power after a revolt toppled the nation's ancient monarchy, talked in terms of a totalitarian state that would represent workers and peasants. But the Soviet model was unusual in Africa. Few Africans found that doctrinaire Marxism described their political or economic conditions. Even in Ethiopia, the active power of the government, in an impoverished agricultural economy and amid great regional strife, hardly permitted the political controls of the Soviet state. A few kingdoms bordering South Africa, in yet another pattern, maintained some of the trappings of divine kingship, with rulers enjoying lavish ceremonies. The ruler of the giant state of Zaire (which after he was ousted resumed the name Congo) similarly stressed ritual demonstrations of power and receipt of tribute, along with a strong army, but the actual administration of government under his rule was very loose.

A number of nations with one-party systems achieved impressive political stability. Kenya faced tensions between two main tribal groups, but the ruling party created considerable unity and produced able leaders who transferred power without engendering strife. Kenya's capital city of Nairobi gained stature as the headquarters for several UN agencies and a meeting place for African organizations.

Several African nations pursued non-Marxist socialist policies, hoping to combine economic advance with social reform. In Tanzania, Julius Nyerere tried to build on African community traditions to create a distinctive form of rural socialism. The government supported village cooperation. Nyerere argued that "socialist societies in different parts of the world will differ in many respects . . . reflecting both the manner of their development, and their historical traditions." An African definition of socialism appealed to nationalist sentiment and reflected an unquestionable distaste, on the part of many Africans, for the greed and competitiveness of Western capitalism. Nyerere's practical policies in Tanzania, however, were hampered by poor economic management, and the country did not develop rapidly. Zimbabwe, although late in winning its independence, was a more hopeful example. Robert Mugabe, the prime minister, although a Marxist in theory, devoted himself to a program of practical reforms, which would redistribute some land and offer a degree of protection to manufacturing workers but would not antagonize the white minority or repel foreign investors. The regime degenerated into greater authoritarianism, however, in the early 21st century.

Several west African governments made little reference to socialist ideas. Leaders in Nigeria supported private enterprise while also using government funds and planning to encourage further economic development. Great hope existed in the 1970s that government oil revenues could be channeled into industrial investment, although the decline of oil prices in the early 1980s threatened economic advance and resulted in widespread unemployment.

Two trends surfaced, or resurfaced, by the 1990s, extending for at least two decades. Early in the 1990s, a resurgence of democracy began to emerge. Africa (including the now democratic regime in South Africa) was strongly influenced by international trends and pressures toward more open political regimes. By 1997, 17 countries had installed freer elections with multiparty competition. Nigeria joined this list in 1999. In 2006, after years of bloody civil strife, Liberia not only elected a new president, but its first woman president, Ellen Johnson Sirleaf.

While the spread of democracy suggested African links to political trends in the wider world, the subcontinent continued to generate situations in which effective government gave way to long-standing bloodshed—this was the renewed trend. Military coups continued. Strife among different ethnic groups remained another source of friction, as did intervention by neighboring states. In the mid-1990s a fearsome clash between Hutus and Tutsi, traditionally rival groups in Rwanda, led to a genocide that left hundreds of thousands dead, with many others raped or deliberately maimed. Civil war engulfed major parts of the Sudan, northern Uganda, Congo, and several sites in west Africa. Outside intervention and policing by forces from the African Union kept an uneasy peace in some instances, but tensions often spilled beyond anyone's control. Boy soldiers—children of 11 or 12, heavily armed, who had known little but warfare in their lives—were a noteworthy feature of the strife. An African definition of a stable political order that was not simply authoritarian proved to be no easy task, amid the stresses of new nationhood and widespread poverty. Former colonial powers, such as France, and also the United Nations periodically tried to intervene. But the outside world hesitated over Africa, not sure what to do and not sure that African problems were as important as issues in other areas. The end of the cold war, reducing competition for loyalties in Africa, also reduced interest to some extent.

On the other hand, many states succeeded, sometimes despite prior tensions. Liberia and Sierra Leone, for example, at least for a time, rebounded from civil war with the election of effective rulers. Several countries also worked on the difficult art of remembering and sometimes punishing past misdeeds while also promoting reconciliation—South Africa tried this course after apartheid, as did Rwanda after its bloodbath. The African political path, despite some common problems remained divided.

AFRICAN CULTURE

Men and women who, as artists or writers, attempted to articulate African culture in the 20th century faced an important contradiction. On the one hand, a widespread awareness existed of traditions that should be maintained, as a bridge between the civilization's past and its future and as alternatives to Western (or Marxist) styles. In this sense, contemporary African culture served many of the same purposes as cultural traditions in the Middle East or India. On the other hand, a defense of African culture has often involved the use of alien languages and forms of expression. For example, the novel, as a work of literature, did not evolve from the African heritage. Moreover, except for those who wrote in Arabic or Swahili, most novelists turned to Western languages—English, French, or Portuguese. They thus were detached from the African masses, many of whom remained illiterate, even as they tried to express and further guide public values. Here was a source of friction inherent to some extent in any formal intellectual life, in a culture that had long been largely oral. In Africa, the newness of many cultural outlets, particularly the educational system and the written word, posed a fundamental challenge to the preservation of vital traditions.

Indeed, one sign of the tension of intellectual life showed in the characteristic education of the small minority that passed beyond the primary level in the independent African nations. African secondary schools preached nationalism and taught African history; to this extent, they departed from the conventions of the former colonial schools. However, the schools taught in Western languages, of necessity. They maintained a strong interest in European history and social science, as well as some Western science. Large numbers of British, American, and French schoolteachers served the system, which was still linked to examination procedures in European countries. Zambia's standardized secondary tests, for instance, were prepared and graded in England. Despite the drawbacks, genuine progress resulted as the educated African leadership expanded. Nonetheless, the challenge to older cultural habits was far greater than in any other 20th-century civilization.

An important group of African writers emerged after 1920. Crafting essays and poetry, but particularly the novel, these writers came to terms with a number of contemporary African issues. White South African writers, many critical of the policy of apartheid but deeply loyal to their homeland, wrote of the tensions and brewing trouble within their society. Black writers typically stressed the virtues of African traditions, pointing out that their people had a rich heritage long before Europeans arrived on the scene. The Senegalese poet and political leader Leopold Senghor thus criticized Western scientific traditions that separate humankind from nature; he advocated, instead, an African tradition of intuition about nature through experience in it. The Angolan Agustinho Neto praised the power of African culture, again attacking many Western standards and describing a unique black point of view. Jomo Kenyatta, glorifying tribal culture in Kenya, elevated the position of women in African society. A West Indian poet, popular in Africa, praised the new black consciousness of superiority over Western values:

> Hurrah for those who never invented anything hurrah for those who never explored anything hurrah for those who never conquered anything hurrah for joy hurrah for love hurrah for the pain of incarnate tears.

HISTORY DEBATE

THE QUESTION OF IDENTITY

During the 20th century, intellectuals in a number of societies worried about what they called *identity*. They saw their societies changing rapidly, in part because of heavy influences from the outside world—particularly western Europe and the United States. They did not necessarily object to all the changes, but only to the crucial loss of what was distinctive or traditional about their societies. With this, they further argued, came a loss of cultural value. The notion of identity is abstract, and certainly many people prefer newer identities as Western-style consumers or economic modernizers. But for some, including certain leading intellectuals, the concern was very real.

Africa was one of the centers of discussion around the issue of identity. African nationalist leaders did not worry too much about identity when there was a common enemy—European colonialism—to attack. But once independence was achieved, nationalists faced several difficulties in the area of identity. First, their nations lacked traditions, for the boundaries had been defined by colonialists. Second, key tribal customs had to be opposed, for they might undermine fragile loyalty to the new nations, which were usually made up of several groups. In contrast to the Middle East or India, there was no great religion to uphold with pride, as part of a valid tradition, for the religions that were spreading most rapidly, Islam and particularly Christianity, came from the outside. Third, certain cultural imports from the West—for example, science and medicine—continued to seem attractive. Where was identity in all of this? Some leaders emphasized a common African character, one that cut across national boundaries; ideas about blackness, or *négritude*, had a similar ring. Nationalists also stressed what they saw as key African virtues, such as communal and family loyalty as opposed to excessive individualism and exploitation, reverence for nature, distinct artistic styles, and a spirituality that transcended specific religions. Were these virtues enough to provide an identity to a people experiencing rapid change?

Chinua Achebe, the Nigerian novelist, wrote directly (in English) about the issue of identity. His book *Things Fall Apart* told of how traditional religion was undermined by Christian missionaries. He bemoaned the loss, although he could not bring himself to advocate a complete return to traditional religious practices, some of which now seemed either superstitious or cruel. Another novel, *No Longer at Ease*, discussed how Western urban culture, with its emphasis on consumerism and sexuality, attacked traditional family values. Again, however, Achebe did not expressly advocate a return to the past. His work raises a question that still preoccupies many: where does African identity lie?

More soberly, Nigeria's leading novelist, Chinua Achebe, stated "the fundamental theme" of the rising group of African writers:

the African people did not hear of culture for the first time from Europeans; . . . their societies were not mindless but frequently had a philosophy of great depth and volume and beauty, . . . they had poetry and above all, they had dignity. It is this dignity that many African peoples all but lost in the colonial period, and it is this that they must now regain. The worst thing that can happen to any people is the loss of their dignity and self-respect. The writer's duty is to help them regain it by showing what happened to them, what they lost.

However, the new African novelists were not simply apostles of tradition and black pride. They also wrote of the anxieties that accompany modernization. Achebe's brilliant novels dealt with the corrosive effect of Western ideas, including Christianity, on powerful village characters. In his works, he examined the stress of city life on popular traditions and expressed the disillusionment of many African intellectuals with corrupt and power-hungry rulers, worrying that the masses "had become even more cynical than their leaders and were apathetic in the bargain." African culture, with writers such as Achebe, combined traditional values with new forms of expression to present powerful dramas of a changing society.

African artists and craftspeople preserved a thriving legacy, working in older stylistic conventions largely apart from the "modern art" styles of the West, which, ironically, had been partly inspired by African forms. Design and decoration in village houses retained their distinctive quality. Sculptors continued to create powerful figures for both religious and aesthetic purposes. African artistic productivity continued at very high levels in the early 20th century and

beyond, using traditional masks and sculpture, though often incorporating objects, such as glass beads, imported from the West. French colonials, sending some of this art back home around 1900, helped inspire modern art forms such as cubism in Europe. Later in the 20th century, African dance and music remained lively art forms, both at the popular level and in formal government-sponsored troupes that toured internationally. African culture was not isolated, however, and many craftsmen and musicians interacted with the proponents of other styles. Some crafts, catering to tourism, pandered to Western ideas of what African art should be like.

The interactions that dominated 20th-century African culture showed clearly in the area of religion. Africa remained a religious society, although in the cities, secular values competed for center stage. Islam, which gained many new converts in the north and center, maintained a trajectory as the most rapidly growing popular religion, claiming about 40 percent of all Africans

Modern African art showing traditional themes: a pair of male and female antelope headdresses, from the mid-20th century.

south of the Sahara. Africa's Christian minority, almost as large, grew rapidly as well. Black Protestant leaders played a leading role in moderate resistance to apartheid in South Africa. African Catholicism assumed a growing role in the Roman church, as the first African cardinal was named and the pope visited the continent for the first time in the 1970s. Catholicism in Africa expanded more rapidly than in any other area, as the number of African Catholics more than doubled from 29 million in 1965 to 66 million in 1985. Christian and Muslim gains meant that Africa experienced the kind of growth of monotheism and new spirituality that had characterized civilizations such as western Europe after the classical age. The result, as in these earlier cases, was both exciting and unsettling. New converts often retained former beliefs in part, for syncretism was common. African Christianity characteristically combined conventional Christian doctrine with traditional values—including, in some areas, a continued belief in polygamy and a definite scorn for Catholic celibacy—and traditional rituals. At the same time, outright polytheistic beliefs retained some vitality, in both the city and the countryside. Traditional remedies were often used to treat disease, following the quite logically presented principles of spirit-caused illness and its cure. Popular religious leaders, some of them women, helped arouse fervor in several regional 20th-century revolts, in which faith in divine guidance combined with worldly grievances against colonial rule or economic exploitation. A number of movements, focusing less on protest than on healing by prayer and the promise of the millennium, blended traditional animist creeds with ideas adapted from the Bible. Overall, although religious diversity—and sometimes bitter conflict—continued, a general esteem for the applicability of religion to life, society, and nature continued to dominate African culture.

The surge of literary creativity and the complex religious transformations were not the only cultural innovations in 20th-century Africa.

Nationalist leaders obviously urged cultural change, away from purely traditional concepts; while attacking imperialism, they usually argued for the adaptation of some concepts from the West, including new kinds of science and medicine. However, they also tried to highlight important African qualities, such as community and family solidity. In the cities, other Western cultural influences, including consumerism, constituted yet another force, adding to changes in belief and creating complicated combinations of old and new.

ECONOMY AND SOCIETY

Changes in African culture, and particularly the spread of education and Western-language literature, raised some basic questions about the relationship between culture and social change. Even as praise for traditional styles and values resounded, there were signs of the unusually rapid disruption of many customary social forms. Writers such as Achebe wondered whether the breakup of long-held beliefs had not weakened Africans' ability to find an anchor amid so much change. Other intellectuals, however, stressed the continuing validity of basic religious orientations and family ties, contrasting African strength in this regard with what they saw as the demoralization of Western society.

Most of sub-Saharan Africa did not face, throughout the 20th century, the kinds of pressure for land redistribution that deeply affected Latin America and parts of Asia. White minorities opened large estates in east and south Africa; many of these remained, after independence, in white or African hands, although some African governments were able to introduce limited land reform. In more populous west Africa, peasant small-holding remained the norm, except for the cash-crop estates that relied on low-wage labor.

Nevertheless, the persistence of village-based agriculture raised issues of its own. During the colonial decades, Western governments pressured African peasants to convert to cash crops such as peanuts or cotton. Some farmers made profits on such crops, but others had to minimize the production of basic foods for subsistence in favor of meeting commercial quotas. Although a few village headmen made money on market sales and then bought bigger homes, bicycles, and even art reproductions, the bulk of the population suffered.

Commercial pressures often continued after independence was gained in Africa, although some areas reverted to more localized agriculture. Major gains in agricultural production came slowly, as peasants lacked both the capital and the education to undertake new methods. Many governments were more concerned with creating public works and factories than with modernizing agriculture. Despite the clearance of new lands for farming, agricultural production lagged in many parts of Africa. Dependence on root crops in the drier lands meant that the gains of the Green Revolution were irrelevant. Agricultural stagnation plus population growth made key regions vulnerable to disasters of climate. In the early 1970s and again in the early 1980s and 1990s, drought conditions on the Sahara's southern rim and down the east coast caused widespread famine. Intense cultivation in some areas was exhausting the soil and expanding the desert, creating more than temporary problems in places such as Ethiopia. More generally, agricultural lag promoted inadequate nutrition and helped explain widespread poverty, even when severe weather problems did not add to the burdens. Finally, reliance on cash crops such as cocoa, cotton, or peanuts for export continued to distract from well-balanced agricultural production, leaving many nations divided between export farmers and a subsistence-minded peasantry wedded to largely traditional methods.

Development of the cash-crop system continued to tie many African countries closely to the Western-dominated world economy. This dependence did not disappear with decolonization. Despite their nationalism, many African countries remained firmly linked to the markets, shipping, and commercial know-how of their erstwhile European rulers. Despite a brief flurry of radical rebellion against Belgian business in Congo, for example, Belgian capital and expertise remained fundamental to the nation's economy, as the mineral wealth of the mines continued to be directed toward Western markets almost exclusively. No African country aside from South Africa created a large industrial base of its own. Government encouragement promoted factories for local food processing and clothing and tool production in countries such as Kenya. By the late 1990s, a few countries, including Botswana and Uganda, reported rapid manufacturing growth, leading some observers to wonder if Africa might finally begin to participate in the kind of industrial evolution that had taken root in Latin America and parts of the Middle East some decades before. Everywhere, however, reliance on the technologies and manufactured imports of the West remained significant. Many African nations ran up huge debts because of the gap between export earnings and import needs.

Despite the limits of economic change, a new class of wealthy, urban Africans took shape both under colonialism and with independence. Merchants, the cash-crop landlords, and top government officials stood apart from the African masses in their luxurious lifestyle, as Africa joined other agricultural societies in a radical division between the wealthy and the masses. In Swahili-speaking east Africa, common people called the new elite *wa Benzi*, meaning "those who ride in a Mercedes-Benz." In stark contrast, per capita annual income for the general population often stagnated; in mineral-rich Congo, for example, average income stood at $137 in 1976 and $160 in 1985.

Furthermore, substantial population growth hit sub-Saharan Africa during the 20th century. Medical and public-health measures promoted by colonial regimes and extended by independent

African governments accounted for some of the gain. So did disruption of village community controls as a result of new market earnings from commercial agriculture or labor in the mines and cities. Population increase occurred despite the absence of a real agricultural revolution and the severe limits of climate and soil fertility in many regions. Indeed, population growth helped worsen agriculture in some cases. As land was over-farmed, its fertility declined—hence, there were recurrent famines in key regions that, ironically, did not halt population growth.

From the 1970s on, the spread of AIDS in east Africa added to economic woes, as many children and young adults became afflicted— more than 25 percent in some regions—thus curtailing the available active labor force. The AIDS crisis hit eastern and southern Africa particularly hard. Local governments were often slow to respond, amid some belief that this was a crisis manufactured in the West as a means of regulating African sexuality. The big problem, however, was poverty, as no African nation could afford the drug costs for the best available treatments. By 2003, a few countries, such as Uganda, were making progress in preventive campaigns, emphasizing condom use.

Rapid population growth continued despite the AIDS crisis, as Africa remained one of the regions in which new forms of birth control spread most slowly. This growth, new transportation facilities, and more modern forms of government, along with some growth in commerce, spurred the rapid expansion of African cities, particularly after World War II. Only 8 percent of the population throughout the entire African continent was concentrated in cities in 1925 and only 13 percent in 1950, but by 1973, the percentage had soared to 23 and this trend gained momentum. Most urbanization did not depend on the expansion of factories; it was based on trade, political concentration, and above all, the absence of alternatives in the countryside, as population

growth and cash-crop estates increased the number of property-less poor. As in Latin America, urban populations crowded into hastily built slums, hoping for survival by means of occasional unskilled jobs, begging, or prostitution, or peddling in the omnipresent open markets of the African city.

African urbanization, unlike that in Latin America, involved considerable family disruption. Because far more men than women moved to the cities, a significant number of families, particularly in the countryside, were headed by women. Indeed, Africa resembled the West, by the 1970s, in the dissociation of a growing minority of men from their families and the problems, economic and psychological, that occurred when women had to raise children on their own. The African tradition of an extended family modified these pressures to some extent, as relatives provided moral support and more tangible assistance to female-headed households. While their husbands toiled in urban centers or mining villages, some women found their new independence challenging and exciting, as the traditions of male domination faded. Nevertheless, issues of family disruption in Africa—a civilization proud of its close and supportive family ties— seemed inescapable as part of social change in the later 20th century. Changes in social structures and personal values stood in stark contrast to more traditional expectations, in one of the several urgent dramas of 20th-century Africa.

A weekly newspaper in Zambia featured a "Dear Josephine" column that mirrored the process of change, as urban Africans developed new and more individualized patterns in a society long characterized by strong family traditions and tightly knit communities. Africans wrote to ask if they could marry despite the fact that older brothers in their families remained unwed; tradition held that the eldest should marry first, but what should the middle son do when he found the right girl? Or how was a city dweller to pay a bridal dowry in cattle, which his intended's family, back in the village, insisted on? Or how might the tribal traditions of mutual support be continued? For example,

> I am well-known, with a big family to feed. My house is by the bus-stop and every day I receive visitors from the home village. It is my duty to give my tribes folk food and money for their journey needs. But my family suffers from hunger and I go without the decent clothes my position calls for. Though I have a good job I am kept poor by home-people. I do not dislike them, but what can I do to be saved from them?

Women's activities also began to shift. The impact of larger changes—social, economic, and political—on African women provoked important debate. On the one hand, women gained new roles as men's ties to their families loosened. On the other hand, women were typically concentrated in more traditional economic sectors, including agricultural areas, in order to protect their economic status. As governments became more effective, first under colonial rule and then with independence, the informal local power of women often declined. Some observers argued that women were net losers in this process, despite certain new freedoms. In addition, in some areas, such as the Muslim northeast, traditional limitations on women persisted, including practices of circumcision that were designed to limit a woman's sexual pleasure and consequently promote fidelity. Nonetheless, growing educational opportunities and even some of the social disruptions promoted new ideas among women, including a growing belief that women should stick together; here, traditional ideas of family unity combined with a desire for education and birth control to create a novel outlook. Upper-class urban women also managed to pressure some governments to improve legal rights for all women. But battles over outside influences often complicated this process. Many women won rights to property by appealing to UN declarations on women's rights. By 2000, some courts overturned these rulings in the name of African tradition.

By the late 1990s, another change entered the mix. A growing number of multinational companies, from Korea and Japan as well as the West, began to set up factories in impoverished areas such as Lesotho. The aim was to take advantage of cheap labor, including many women. Conditions were rigorous, with long hours and strict regulations against leaving the factory because of fears of theft. As in other parts of the world, it was not clear whether these developments would bring benefits in the long run, by cutting into high rates of unemployment, or whether they would merely confirm and perpetuate economic dependence.

DEFINING THE NEW AFRICA

Disruptive transformation was no African monopoly in the 20th century. Most civilizations faced challenges to established institutions and values. Africans in various ways remained able to rely on traditions; their lifestyles were not totally disturbed or undone by surrounding change. Nonetheless, the upheaval brought about by colonial impositions, population growth, and new urban and commercial institutions was considerable, particularly when it was not matched by significant improvements in the standard of living. At the same time, change brought new hopes to many Africans. Intellectuals proud of their culture and politicians enthusiastic about national independence were joined by more humble people, such as the young woman in Kenya who noted the opportunities available for the self-sufficient and the resourceful. Describing her mother's large family and hard physical labor on a subsistence farm, she discussed how her own views had been shaped by the experience of school:

> My life is very different from my mother's. . . . Women have to get an education. Then if you get a large family and don't know how to feed it, you can find work and get some cash. That's what I will teach my children: "Get an education first."

Africa remained the poorest of the world's civilizations through the end of the 20th century, as its vulnerability to famine starkly attested. Modernization, including political independence, had not reaped all the benefits that many had hoped for and may have jeopardized some sources of cultural strength. However, change continued to generate aspirations for the future, in a culture still defining its relationship to the contemporary world.

PATHS TO THE PRESENT

Two primary forces reshaped Africa during the contemporary period, linking trends launched before the 1920s to modern Africa. The first was the rapid colonization of the economy, pushed by European powers and Western business interests to take precedence above everything else. By the 21st century, multinational companies from east Asia, including Chinese government oil interests, were also exploiting Africa's natural resources. Considerable urbanization and family destabilization resulted from these economic shifts. The second force was nationalism, which ultimately led to political independence. It did not, however, reverse the artificial national boundaries earlier imposed by European colonizers. Political independence brought further change and fluctuation, but it did not manage

to sever Africa's economic dependency on the West and parts of Asia.

Another pattern of change also acted on the continent's cultures during this period. Though less blatant than the forces discussed above, its impact was equally dramatic: during the 20th century, millions of Africans changed or modified their cultural systems. These changes occurred largely in the arenas of religion and lifestyle: Christianity and Islam made striking gains on the continent, and more Africans than ever before embraced urban, consumerist values and nationalist identity. Most Africans managed to combine traditional styles and beliefs with new commitments—even with one of the world religions—but innovations were considerable. Few other civilizations participated in such fundamental cultural shifts during the past century.

SUGGESTED WEB SITES

View the African timeline at http://web.cocc.edu/cagatucci/classes/hum211/timelines/htimelinetoc.htm; on South African history, see http://www.sahistory.org.za/; for information on Africa's culture and African studies, visit http://www.h-net.org/~africa/ and http://sociolingo.wordpress.com/; visit the National Museum of African Art at http://www.nmafa.si.edu/index2.html.

SUGGESTED READINGS

Recent work includes Robert H. Bates, *When Things Fell Apart: State Failure in Late-Century Africa* (2008); Ronald Hyan, *Britain's Declining Empire: The Road to Decolonisation, 1918–1968* (2007); James E. Genova, *Colonial Ambivalence, Cultural Authenticity, and the Limitations of Mimicry in French-Ruled West Africa, 1914–1956* (2004); Jon Abbink, Mirjam de Bruijn, and Klaas Van Walraven, eds., *Rethinking Resistance: Revolt and Violence in African History* (2003); Martin Meredith, *The State of Africa: A History of Fifty Years of Independence* (2005); Frederick Cooper, *Africa Since*

1940: The Past of the Present (2002); Toyin Falola, *Nationalism and African Intellectuals* (2001); Goran Hyden, *African Politics in Comparative Perspective* (2006); Charles O. Chikeka, *European Hegemony and African Resistance, 1880–1990* (2004); Taisier M. Ali and Robert O. Matthews, eds., *Durable Peace: Challenges for Peace Building in Africa* (2004); A. B. Assensoh and Yvette M. Alex-Assensoh, *African Military History and Politics: Coups and Ideological Incursions, 1900–Present* (2001); Cheryl Mawaria, ed., *African Visions: Literary Images, Political Change and Social Struggle in Contemporary Africa* (2000); Adebayo Adedeji, ed., *Comprehending and Mastering African Conflict* (1999); and Einar Bratthen, ed., *Ethnicity Kills? The Politics of War, Peace and Ethnicity in Sub-Saharan Africa* (2000).

Various source materials have contributed to research in African history. W. E. B. Du Bois, *The World and Africa* (1974), presents an American black nationalist perspective. Works by nationalist leaders include J. Kenyatta, *Facing Mount Kenya* (1953), and from South Africa, A. Luthuli, *Let My People Go* (1962). F. Fanon, *Wretched of the Earth* (1965), is a stinging indictment of Western colonialism. Novels by C. Achebe, particularly *Things Fall Apart* (1978), deal with changes in African society and culture. See also B. Fetter, *Colonial Rule in Africa: Readings from Primary Sources* (1979); Ali Mazrui and Michael Tidy, *Nationalism and New States in Africa* (1984); Martin Meredith, *The First Dance of Freedom: Black Africa in the Post-War Era* (1984); and S. A. Akintoye, *Emergent African States* (1976). Competent works on South Africa under apartheid include R. W. Johnson, *How Long Will South Africa Survive?* (1977), and Gail Gerhart, *Black Power in South Africa* (1978). On women in African society, see N. H. Afkin and E. Bay, eds., *Women in Africa* (1977).

CHAPTER 35

The Early 21st Century: World History and the Future

The 20th century witnessed huge changes in world history. The relative decline of western Europe helped usher in the cold war and decolonization. Alterations in political, social, and cultural forms affected all societies, though in different ways. By the 1990s, decolonization was largely completed, the cold war was over, and a new framework was taking shape. This framework furthered the definition of the contemporary period in world history that had begun in the 1920s and 1930s.

The new framework was built from three primary components, which did not neatly combine. First, the end of the cold war left the United States as the world's only superpower, the only power capable of independent global military action. It also furthered new regional conflicts and alliances and reinvigorated old conflicts. The world is still working out the implications of the cold war's demise.

Second, globalization accelerated after having slowed during the middle decades of the 20th century. The pace and impact of global economic and cultural contacts, fed by new technologies, had no precedent in the human experience. As a result, some people thought a revolutionary new phase of human society was imminent.

Third, the revival of religion and regional religious identities, beginning in the 1970s, affected Christianity and Christian missionary outreach, Islam, Hinduism, and some new forms or adaptations of Buddhism, such as the Falun Gong movement in China. Religious revival did not necessarily contradict globalization, but it pushed cultures in different directions. Many groups focused on religious identities more than global consumer standards, for example.

The combination of these three new forces influenced some of the other changes taking place in the contemporary world. Again, the results were not always tidy. Shifting global standards, for example, generally pushed further changes in women's roles, toward lower birth rates, more personal freedom, and more participation in consumerism. The global economy, however, could disrupt women's work, providing them only with difficult factory jobs or reducing their role in the workplace altogether. Religious revival, on the whole, prompted a traditional approach toward women, including hostility to the impact of Western consumerism on women's dress and perceived sexuality. Globalization and religious revival also had different implications for ongoing discussions of political forms, including definitions of individual rights.

The result, a sense that change was overwhelming, generated confusion and uncertainty during the early 21st century. This, in turn, caused some cultures to move away from the leading progressive issues of the 20th century. The sense if being overwhelmed also shaped some of the fundamental questions about the world's future. Despite this, important continuities from the past were sustained. The previous positions of different societies in the world economy and commitments to cultural traditions and identities continued to mark the world in the 21st century. Many groups sought new ways to defend or revive what they saw as key elements of their pasts. This is another set of components to fold into an understanding of the world's present and future.

KEY QUESTIONS *How can the diplomatic and military framework of the post–cold war world best be defined? How can globalization be defined, and why has political globalization not kept pace with culture and economics? How do new religious interests relate to the rise of science, consumerism, and other secular attachments? What are the best ways to use history to help sort out predictions about the world's future?*

AFTER THE COLD WAR

The economic collapse of the Soviet Union and the division of the Soviet empire, between 1985 and 1991, obviously limited the power of the new Russia (see chapter 29). President Vladimir Putin largely embraced a partial pro-Western diplomatic policy, but his firm political control plus improvements in the Russian economy permitted some gestures of independence. Russia joined France and Germany in opposing the U.S. war against Iraq in 2003. Many Russians questioned the benefit of a close relationship with the United States, and the popularity of the United States and any "American model" had declined in Russia by 2004. However, Russia no longer provided a strong military opposition to U.S. power. By 2001, Russian military spending, at $4 billion a year, was one-thirtieth that of the United States.

Other countries worried visibly about unchallenged American strength. China, particularly, alternated between seeking favorable economic arrangements with the U.S. government (China enjoyed a great balance of trade advantage with the United States) and seeking to increase military strength. China's claims to control Taiwan, combined with U.S. involvement in defense of the island, were a particularly fruitful source of tension. China's military buildup, however, did not threaten the United States directly. Efforts to forge alliances against U.S. power, by greater cooperation with Russia or with other countries such as Iran, roused U.S. concern, but no full-fledged partnerships emerged.

By 2001, even western European countries expressed some misgivings about U.S. strength, particularly when the United States seemed to ignore international collaboration in areas such as the environment. In 2001, in an interesting gesture of anti-Americanism, the United Nations (UN) excluded the United States from membership on its Human Rights Commission, the first time this had happened since the commission was formed.

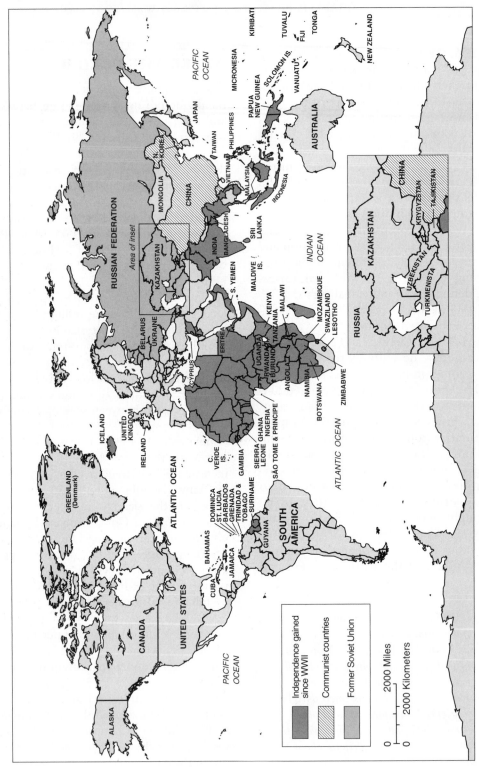

Global Relations in the 21st Century

Still, no systematic counterpoise to U.S. power emerged after the cold war's end. U.S. power was indeed enhanced, through most of the 1990s, by unusually rapid economic growth and by U.S. leadership in burgeoning new fields of information technology and bioengineering. Even Japan did not keep pace with U.S. innovations in technology and business organization, as the Pacific Rim encountered new economic difficulties at the very end of the 20th century.

Free from the cold war, the United States continued a high level of military spending, with levels above the next 13 countries combined. Indeed, of the $700 billion spent annually on the military worldwide, the United States generated 60 percent. Not even western Europe kept pace with American military technology, especially in the air. Early in the 21st century, the United States expressed new resistance to international agreements, on the environment, the use of mines, and international prosecution of war crimes. The nation successfully appealed for extensive international cooperation after the terrorist attacks of September 11, 2001. It tried to organize international pressure against governments that were not aligned with U.S. policies and that had active weapons programs; its leaders sometimes called nations such as Iran and North Korea "rogue states" or part of an "axis of evil." But in 2002–2003, the invasion of Iraq, and pronouncements about an American right to strike preemptively against nations capable of developing weapons of mass destruction, sounded a new note. Some observers saw the emergence of a new American imperialism. Others worried that American power was being stretched dangerously thin. As with Russia, the implications of the end of the cold war on American participation in world politics were not easy to evaluate.

There were other results in the cold war's end, including a new boost to democracy as a political form (a trend already underway before the Soviet collapse); a realignment of east-central Europe toward the West, marked by the admission of several countries into North Atlantic Treaty Organization (NATO) and the European Union (EU); a new band of independent states in central Asia; a new set of ethnic tensions in parts of the former communist world; an encouragement to general forces of globalization; and, ironically, a new expression of old as well as new regional conflicts. The failure of communism also contributed to revival of religious interest in several east European centers, again a part of a larger world movement that had begun before 1985.

THE SPREAD OF DEMOCRACY

The end of the cold war was clearly associated with another large trend in the world at the end of the 20th century: the spread of multiparty democracy with (reasonably) freely contested elections. This trend helped end the cold war, and its end, in turn, accelerated the trend. We have seen that, through much of the century, several different government forms competed for success amid a general climate of change: communism, fascism and other authoritarianisms, and democracy itself. But from the late 1970s on, the tide seemed to turn toward democracy in many regions that had long been inhospitable.

Economic and political success in western Europe, including the drawing power of the Common Market, helped propel Spain, Portugal, and Greece to democratic systems in the mid-1970s, after long periods of authoritarian control. Then the democratic wave hit Latin America, backed by U.S. and western European support. Beginning with new regimes in Argentina and Brazil, authoritarian controls were replaced by free elections. The process continued through the 1990s, when literally all Latin American countries except Cuba were in the democratic camp. Revolutionaries in Central America accepted the system in the late 1980s; Paraguay was the final authoritarian regime to

Supporters of Ukrainian President Viktor Yushchenko waved orange flags of support as they listened to his speech in Independence Square in Kiev, Ukraine, in late 2005.

yield a decade later. In 2000, Mexico elected its first president from a party other than the PRI, the party that had monopolized control since the revolution.

Democratic systems gained ground in South Korea and Taiwan in the 1980s. In the Philippines, an authoritarian ruler was cast aside, amid considerable popular pressure, in favor of an elected government. By this point, of course, the democratic current captured the Soviet bloc, with democratic systems winning out in most of east-central Europe, Russia, and to a degree in some former Soviet republics in central Asia.

While much of Africa remained authoritarian, democratic change spread to this region by the 1990s, headed by the triumph of democracy over apartheid in South Africa. Nigeria, the continent's most populous country, turned to democracy in 1999 after new assertions of military control. In

Indonesia at this time, a near revolution toppled its authoritarian system and replaced it with competitive elections. Early in the 21st century, democratic systems triumphed in the former Soviet states of Ukraine and Georgia.

Never before had democracy spread so widely, among so many otherwise different societies. Only China and parts of the Middle East and central Asia seemed to stand apart. In China, the major democratic demonstration in Beijing, in 1989, echoed the global democratic current but was brutally put down. Elsewhere, the political stability, cultural prestige, and economic success of Western democracy, supplemented by the strength of democratic systems in Japan and India, seemed to win the day. The fall of European communism both reflected and encouraged the trend. One of democracy's main competitors was now discredited. The end of the cold war worked to the same effect: there was no superpower support for authoritarian systems in return for military alliance. The United States, in particular, became more consistent in its encouragement to democratic reforms, under Jimmy Carter and again in the 1990s.

Huge questions remained about democracy's future. The link to economic expectations—the sense that democracy was a precondition for freer markets and economic growth that supported many Latin American conversions and also Gorbachev's reforms in Russia—was an obvious vulnerability: what if the economy did not improve? New uncertainties emerged by 2000, particularly with the greater authoritarianism of the Russian regime, including new controls over the media and intimidation of potential opponents. Still, the global trend was undeniable at least for a time, and it conjoined with the hopes born of the reduction of cold war tensions.

The spread of democracy had one ironic result, however, which became quite apparent by the early 21st century: open elections produced diverse results. Some voters in the Middle East, newly free to express themselves, opted for Islamic parties that were quite different from what Western proponents of democracy had in

---

HISTORY DEBATE

20TH AND 21ST CENTURIES—CHANGE OR CONTINUITY

An eminent historian writes of a "short" 20th century, 1914–1990, dominated by the world wars and the cold war and struggles for supremacy in Europe, followed by something new in the past two decades. Another historian writes quite simply that the 21st century will be "very different" from the 20th century.

But if the 20th century opened a significant new period in world history, one might not expect the next century necessarily to break totally new ground.

Sorting out the present in historical terms is both challenging and fascinating, a key use of historical analysis. Obviously, the 21st century will differ from the 20th in specifics—there will be no 21st-century Stalin or Hitler. Even more important: we cannot know how new, in more fundamental terms, the 21st century will be because we cannot know what has not happened yet. It is all worth thinking about, to orient our sense of relationship between past and future, but conclusions are speculative at best.

If the 20th century featured a decline of the relative importance of the West and a rebalancing of power in the world at large, the 21st century may continue this theme. Specific developments such as decolonization will not recur, because the process has largely been completed, but the theme of rebalancing in relation to the West will persist.

If the 20th century featured a rise of globalization, first through new technologies, then through new policies in places in China and Russia, then the 21st century may well maintain this trend. Of course the details will be different, and the process may go farther, but it will not be unrecognizable.

On the other hand, the huge population surge of the 20th century is already slowing. It will continue to impact at least the first half of the 21st century, but it will not define it in the same way; and soon the key issue may be population stability and ageing.

If environmentalists succeed—and this is an if—the hugely wasteful 20th century will be replaced by dramatic new energy policies and changes in consumerism—genuinely new trends.

Will the 21st century further resolve questions about appropriate political forms (given the virtual disappearance of monarchy) or women's roles (given the decline of traditional patriarchy)? Will a global middle class continue to gain ground? Here, the particular features will of course be new, but the framework may continue from the recent past.

A new century does not necessarily mean a basic new period in global characteristics. Defining what the basic themes of the 20th century turn out to have been is a vital aspect of thinking about the future, because we can then ask which themes persist and which themes were time-bound.

This is a debate that must continue.

---

mind when championing electoral democracy for the region. Latin Americans returned to power socialists bitterly opposed to United States capitalism. Much to the unpleasant surprise of Western policy makers, it turned out that the implementation of democracy in previously undemocratic societies did not always produce a more uniform world.

A WORLD OF REGIONS: ALLIANCES AND DISPUTES

The end of the cold war framework highlighted certain regional rivalries. Many of them were not new, but they became more acute as the controlling influence of U.S.–Soviet rivalry disappeared. At the same time, efforts to form regional cooperative arrangements also gained ground. Europe took the lead here, in building further on its Common Market structure, but there were developments also in Asia and the Americas.

The collapse of the Soviet empire raised obvious questions for the principal alliance systems in western Europe. NATO had been formed specifically to block Soviet expansionism. What was its purpose now that the Soviet threat had receded? NATO officials continued to see the alliance as a desirable stabilizing force in Europe and perhaps beyond. We will see that NATO did play a direct role in one of the greatest pockets of instability, in the Balkans. Coordination of military planning continued. And several former Eastern bloc countries requested admission to NATO, to herald their new orientation toward the West and to insure against Russian intervention. NATO did grant admission to several east-central European countries at the end of the 1990s and again in 2002.

The economic alliance of western Europe—the EU—was another matter, because its purposes of economic integration and stimulus to growth were unaffected by the cold war's end. Most eastern European countries, along with Turkey, sought entry into the EU. Their economies were in the throes of conversion from communist systems to market arrangements, and their standards of living were noticeably below those of western Europe. In some cases, questions persisted also about commitments to democracy and human rights. Full integration with the EU clearly would be a drawn-out process. But by 2003, candidacies of several countries where market reforms had been most successful, such as Poland and Hungary, resulted in agreement to enter (as of 2004). In the meantime, the EU continued to strengthen internal integration. Amid dispute, many existing members agreed on a common currency, the euro, which went into effect in a number of EU countries in early 2002. The experiment in European unity continued.

Other areas sought benefits from economic alliances, though without moving to the level of integration Europe had achieved. During the 1990s, the North American Free Trade Agreement (NAFTA) joined the United States, Mexico, and Canada. Opponents worried about loss of jobs to cheaper Mexican labor and about environmental damage as firms moved to more loosely regulated regions. But a considerable trade increase resulted, seeming to benefit all participants but particularly Mexico.

East and southeast Asia and the Pacific Rim formed the final center for new discussions about new levels of international economic arrangements. Several discussions explored opportunities for tariff reduction and policy coordination. Clearly, economic issues had replaced cold war rivalries as the motor for regional diplomatic experiments.

But the continued potential for regional diplomatic and military conflict was striking as well. Most of the conflicts were not new. But the end of the cold war at the very least highlighted regional clashes and the maturing military power of many regional players, including nuclear capacity in several cases. By 2009, even Russia was reasserting regional military power with efforts to use military or economic pressure against neighbors such as Georgia and Ukraine. The United States and the UN sought to keep the peace in most instances, but their efforts were not always successful.

The Middle East remained a trouble spot. Even before the end of the cold war, Iraq and Iran had conducted a long, casualty-filled war, with the ambitions of Iraq's dictatorial leader, Saddam Hussein, pitted against the Islamic revolutionary regime in Iran. After this bloody conflict, in 1990 Iraq invaded the small, oil-rich state of Kuwait. This galvanized the international coalition of Western and moderate Arab states, which defeated Iraq in the 1991 Persian Gulf War but left Saddam Hussein in power. The United States maintained a large military presence in the Persian Gulf region, which drew

Arrival of the euro.

criticism from many Arabs and Muslims. In 2003, when a predominantly U.S. and British coalition invaded Iraq and toppled Saddam Hussein, a further component was added to the region's power politics. The rise of Iran, with new technological prowess combined with sponsorship of Shiite movements elsewhere, was another key factor.

Israeli relations with the huge Palestinian minority served as another Middle Eastern flashpoint that, on the whole, deteriorated after the cold war ended, despite some promising peace moves in the mid-1990s. Though an autonomous Palestinian government was set up over two territories within Israel, hostilities escalated in the early years of the 21st century.

Tensions between India and Pakistan also escalated, with various border clashes particularly around the disputed territory of Kashmir. By 2000, both countries had conducted tests of nuclear weapons. War seemed to threaten in 2002, but both sides pulled back. This was the most open case of nuclear dissemination, as the limited nuclear group of the cold war began to expand. Increased Hindu nationalism within India was matched by fiercer Muslim rhetoric in Pakistan.

No clear global pattern of activity resulted from the end of the cold war. The tensions between impulses toward integration, based primarily on economic goals, and the indulgence of rivalries, sometimes spiced by military expansion, were obvious.

ETHNIC CONFLICT

The upsurge of ethnic conflict in several areas constituted a more strikingly novel feature of the post–cold war scene. Ethnic rivalries were not new, but several components helped explain the new and troubling outbreak. Globalization provided one element. New levels of global interaction increased the potential for group identities to generate hostilities. Some groups clearly increased their investment in ethnic identity as a means of countering outside influences and global pressures. At the same time, the collapse of several key multinational states, notably the Soviet Union and Yugoslavia, opened the door to a reassertion of ethnic identity as a means of replacing discredited ideologies, such as communism, and as part of the conflict for control within new political units.

Within Europe, a number of ethnic groups developed new opportunities for expression, as the hold of the classic nation-state declined. The British government, for example, gave limited autonomy to Scottish and Welsh governments. France and Spain became more tolerant toward linguistic minorities such as the Catalans and Bretons. During the 1990s, a number of European countries saw the rise of new political movements bent on reducing immigration in favor of protecting jobs and cultural identity for the majority national group. A National Front group in France won up to 10 percent of all votes during the mid-1990s, though it then fell back a bit. Austria generated a controversial right-wing national government rhetorically hostile to immigrants. In 2001, a new government leader in Italy emphasized an antiforeign plank. Violence against immigrant groups, such as Turks in Germany, flared recurrently as well.

More systematic violence broke out in several of the territories of the former Soviet empire. Czechoslovakia split peacefully into two ethnic segments, the Czech Republic and Slovakia, but this was not the common pattern. New or newly freed states witnessed frequent ethnic conflicts. Hungarian minorities in Romania and Turkish minorities in Bulgaria faced new pressures during the 1990s. A bloody revolt broke out in a Muslim region of Russia, Chechnya, where a regional leader proclaimed independence in 1990. On two occasions during the ensuing decade, heavy fighting broke out between rebels, seeking an independent Muslim nation, and the Russian military. Acts of terrorism, including bombs placed in several Moscow apartment buildings and theaters,

helped push Russian public opinion to greater acceptance of military action. Neither side had achieved full victory by 2004, though Russian resistance to this kind of regional and ethnic claim seemed firm.

Ethnic tension also surfaced in southeastern Europe and central Asia. Recurrent fighting occurred among ethnic groups in the newly independent nation of Georgia. More serious warfare erupted periodically between Armenian Christians and their Muslim neighbors in Azerbaijan.

Yugoslavia was the most important case where elimination of a multiethnic state, successfully united under communism, brought bloodshed and turmoil. Ethnic patterns were unusually complex in this region. Slavs differed linguistically from Albanians, many of whom were Muslim. Slavs were divided into groups such as Serbs and Croats, with different alphabets, religions, and historical experiences. There were also Muslim Slavs in the territory of Bosnia. Groups had been pitted against each other from the Turkish conquest to, more recently, the German occupation in World War II. After the death of the strong communist leader in Yugoslavia, Marshall Tito, ethnic divisions

The Implosion of Yugoslavia

became more open, with rising tensions between Albanians in the region of Kosovo and the dominant Serbian group. Individual Serbian nationalist leaders, such as Slobodan Milosevic, began to gain increasing attention.

Then the Soviet Union collapsed, which emboldened several regions to seek independence. Slovenia and Croatia pulled away in 1991, and fierce fighting erupted between Croats and Serbs before the latter reluctantly agreed to a dismemberment of a country they believed they should dominate. The government of Bosnia and Herzegovina declared independence in 1992, but this led to bitter fighting among internal groups—Catholic Croats, Orthodox Serbs, and Muslims—aided by outside intervention particularly from Serbia. Massive killing resulted, with many atrocities against civilians under the heading of "ethnic cleansing"—which often meant killing or removing non-Serb populations to facilitate Serb control. Tremendous diplomatic pressure from western Europe and the United States, supplemented by Russia, led to tenuous cease-fires, but finally, in 1995, an international military force had to step in to impose an uneasy peace. At the end of the 1990s, warfare broke out between Serbs and Muslims in the province of Kosovo, with atrocities on both sides. Purely diplomatic efforts to stop the killing failed, and NATO forces, headed by the United States, began a bombing campaign against Serbia, which finally forced an end to hostilities and the installation of another international occupying force. By 2000, demonstrations within Serbia expelled Milosevic from the presidency. A few years later Montenegro became independent, adding to the welter of small states.

Ethnic attacks were not confined to the lands once ruled by communism. In 1990, bloody conflicts broke out in central Africa, pitting tribal groups, the Hutus and the Tutsis, against each other, particularly in the nation of Rwanda. Here, too, old rivalries blended with disputes over current power; the Tutsis had long ruled, but resentful Hutus outnumbered them. Intervention from neighboring states such as Uganda contributed to the confusion. Tremendous slaughter resulted, with hundreds of thousands killed and many more—more than two million—driven from their homes. While outside powers, the Organization of African States, and the UN urged peace, there was no decisive outside intervention. Bloodshed finally ran its course, but ethnic disputes continued in central Africa, contributing to civil war in countries such as Congo. Major warfare in 2003 brought tens of thousands of deaths. Ethnic and religious disputes were also involved in a number of other African trouble spots, including Muslim attacks on Christians in Sudan, and warfare among military gangs in Sierra Leone and Liberia.

Clearly, ethnic tensions were leading not just to warfare, but to renewed acts of genocide that targeted civilians, including women and children, and the creation of massive refugee populations. Reactions from the world at large varied. In some instances, violence seemed sufficiently menacing to major powers that intervention

Displaced and sick Sudanese women and children await medical treatment at an Egyptian centre at Abu Shouk refugee camp, home of tens of thousands of refugees from Sudan's western province of Darfur in the early 21st century.

occurred, though never without great hesitation. No policies emerged that offered great promise in abating ethnic conflict.

GLOBALIZATION

The collapse of the Soviet Union and the Warsaw Pact alliance, which effectively ended the long cold war stalemate, abruptly opened up possibilities for transglobal connections that had been limited after 1914 by successive wars and international crises. In many instances, the new linkages between states and regions that were created or greatly expanded after 1989 represented revivals of processes that had begun to flourish in the decades before World War I. But major, late-20th-century innovations in communications, banking, and computing—all of which came together in quite remarkable ways on the Internet—made possible transmissions of information, economic exchanges, and cultural collaborations at a speed and intensity beyond anything imaginable in earlier epochs. Particularly noteworthy was the rapidity with which the republics that emerged from the former Soviet Union, including Russia, and the former communist states of eastern Europe were incorporated into expanding global networks. Mainland China, which remained communist politically, also moved to adopt market capitalism and increase its trade with the United States, Japan, and the industrial nations of the EU.

Many experts saw what they called *globalization* as the dominant theme of present and future world history. Globalization meant the increasing interconnectedness of all parts of the world, particularly not only in communication and commerce, but in culture and politics as well. It meant accelerating speed for global connections of various sorts. It meant openness to exchanges around the world.

The new focus on globalization in the 1990s legitimately reflected several new developments beyond the networks established from the later 19th century on. First, the end of the cold war and the absence of systematic patterns of international conflict meant new opportunities for, and new attention to, global connections. China, as well as the former Soviet Union, became much more fully open to international trade and many, if not all, other facets of globalization. More broadly, the growing commitment around the world to more free market arrangements, and less state intervention, opened up opportunities for foreign investment and the extension of manufacturing operations to additional areas. Latin America, India, and other places participated in this movement, along with the communist and former communist world. By the 1990s, only a handful of spots—Myanmar, North Korea, the former Yugoslavia—were largely outside the network of globalization.

Second, the late 20th century saw a new round of technical developments, associated particularly with the computer, that greatly accelerated the speed and amount of global communication. The new technology particularly facilitated international commerce, but there were global cultural and political implications as well.

Finally, though more tentatively, more people around the world became accustomed to global connections. At least in some areas, intensive nationalism declined in favor of a more cosmopolitan interest in wider influences and contacts. The spread of English as a world language, though incomplete and often resented, was part of this connection. English served airline travel, many sports, and the early Internet as a common language. This encouraged and reflected other facets of global change.

THE NEW TECHNOLOGY

A globalization guru tells the following story. In 1988, a U.S. government official was traveling to Chicago and was assigned a limousine with a cellular phone. He was so delighted to have this novelty that he called his wife just to brag. Nine years later, in 1997, the same official was visiting the Ivory Coast in west Africa, and he went to a remote village, reachable only by dugout canoe, to inaugurate a new health facility. As he prepared to leave, climbing in the canoe, a government official handed him a cellular phone and said he had a call from Washington. Cellular phones became increasingly common, one of the key new communication devices that, by the 1990s, made almost constant contact with other parts of the world feasible and for some people unavoidable. Western Europe and east Asia led in the cellular phone revolution, but leading groups in all parts of the world participated.

During the 1980s, steady improvements in miniaturization made computers increasingly efficient. By the 1990s, the amount of information that could be stored on microchips increased by more than 60 percent annually. Linkages among computers improved as well, starting with halting efforts in the 1960s, mainly for defense purposes. E-mail was introduced in 1972. In 1990, a British software engineer working in Switzerland, Tim Berners, developed the World Wide Web, and the true age of the Internet was born. Almost instantaneous contact by computer became possible around the world, and with it the capacity to send vast amounts of text, imagery, and even music (both legally and illegally). While the Internet was not available to everyone—by 2001 only 25 percent of the world's population had any access to it—it did provide global contacts for some regions otherwise fairly remote. In eastern Russia, for example, international mail service was agonizingly slow, telephone access often interrupted—but a student could sit at an Internet café in Vladivostok and communicate easily with counterparts in the United States or Brazil.

Satellite linkages for television formed a final communications revolution, making simultaneous broadcasts possible around the world. A full quarter of the world's population now could, and sometimes did, watch the same sporting event, usually World Cup soccer or the Olympics, a phenomenon never before possible

or even approachable in world history. Global technology gained new meaning.

BUSINESS ORGANIZATION AND INVESTMENT

Thanks in part to new technology, in part to more open political boundaries, international investment accelerated rapidly at the end of the 20th century. Stock exchanges featured holdings in Chinese utilities or Brazilian steel companies as well as the great corporations of the West and Japan. U.S. investments abroad multiplied rapidly, almost doubling in the first half of the 1970s. By the 1980s, foreign operations were generating between 25 and 40 percent of all corporate profits in the United States. Japan's foreign investment rose 15-fold during the 1970s. During the 1980s, Japanese car manufacturers set up factories in the United States, Europe, and other areas. German cars, French tires, German chemicals and pharmaceuticals, and Dutch petroleum all had substantial U.S. operations. At the end of the 1990s, the German Volkswagen firm introduced an imaginative new car design with production facilities entirely based in Mexico, but marketing in the United States and around the world.

Globalization in business involved rapid increases in exports and imports, the extension of business organization across political boundaries—creating the so-called *multinational corporations*—and division of labor on a worldwide basis. Cars in the United States were manufactured by assembling parts made in Japan, Korea, Mexico, and elsewhere. Japanese cars often had more American-made parts in them than Detroit products had. Such was the new structure of global manufacturing. Firms set up operations not simply to produce closer to markets in order to save transportation costs; they also looked for centers of cheap labor and relaxed environmental regulations. Computer boards were made by women in the West Indies and Africa. India developed a huge software industry, subcontracting for firms in the United

States and western Europe. The linkages were dazzling.

International firms continued a long-standing interest in finding cheap raw materials. Companies in the West and Japan thus competed for access to oil and minerals in the newly independent nations of central Asia, after the collapse of the Soviet Union. International investments also followed interest rates. During the 1990s, relatively high U.S. interest rates drew extensive investment from Europe, Japan, and the oil-rich regions in the Middle East.

Multinational companies often had more power, and far more resources, than the governments of most of the countries within which they operated. They could thus determine most aspects of labor and environmental policy. They could and did pull up stakes in one region if more attractive opportunities opened elsewhere, regardless of the impact in terms of unemployment and empty facilities. Yet the spread of multinationals also promoted industrial skills in many previously agricultural regions, and they depended on improvements in communications and transportation that could bring wider changes.

American factories located in northern Mexico, designed to produce goods largely for sale back in the United States, showed the complexity of the new international economy. The factories unquestionably sought low-paying labor and lax regulations. Factories often leaked chemical waste. Wages were barely 10 percent of U.S. levels. But the foreign factories often paid better, nevertheless, than their Mexican counterparts. Many workers, including large numbers of women, found the labor policies more enlightened and the foremen better behaved in the foreign firms as well. Evaluation was tricky. A key question, not yet answerable, was what would happen next. Would wages improve, and would the industrial skills of the new factory workers allow a widening range of opportunities? Or would the dependence on poverty-level wages persist?

MIGRATION

Broad international patterns of migration had developed by the 1950s and 1960s, with the use of "guest workers" from Turkey and north Africa in Europe, for example. Here, patterns in the 1990s built clearly on previous trends. But the fact was that easier travel back and forth plus the continued gap between slowly growing

Muslim school children in France.

populations in the industrial countries and rapidly growing populations in Latin America, Africa, and parts of Asia maintained high levels of exchange. A few areas, such as Italy, Greece, and Japan, had almost ceased internal population growth by the 1990s, which meant that new labor needs, particularly at the lower skill levels, had to be supplied by immigration. Japan hoped to avoid too much influx by relying on high-technology solutions, but even here, worker groups were brought in from the Philippines and southeast Asia. Migration into Europe and the United States was far more extensive, producing truly multinational populations in key urban and commercial centers. By 2000, at least 25 percent of all Americans, mostly people of color, came from households where English was not the first language. Ten percent of the French population in 2003 was Muslim. Here was an important source of tension, with local populations often fearing foreigners and worried about job competition. Here also was a new opportunity, not just for new laborers but for new cultural inspiration as well.

CULTURAL GLOBALIZATION

Thanks in part to global technologies and business organization, plus reduced political barriers, the pace of cultural exchange and contact around the world accelerated at the end of the 1990s. Much of this involved mass consumer goods, spread from the United States, western Europe, and Japan. But art shows, symphony exchanges, scientific conferences, and Internet contact increased as well. Music conductors and artists held posts literally around the world, sometimes juggling commitments among cities such as Tokyo, Berlin, and Chicago within a single season. Science laboratories filled with researchers from around the world, collaborating (usually in English) with little regard for national origin.

The spread of fast-food restaurants from the United States, headed by McDonald's, formed one of the most striking international cultural influences from the 1970s on. The company began in Illinois in 1955 and started its international career in 1967 with outlets in Canada and Puerto Rico. From then on, the company entered an average of two new nations per year and accelerated the pace in the 1990s. By 1998, it was operating in 109 countries overall. The company won quick success in Japan, where it gained its largest foreign audience; "makadonaldo" first opened in Tokyo's world famous Ginza, already known for cosmopolitan department stores, in 1971. McDonald's entry into the Soviet Union in 1990 was a major sign of the ending of cold war rivalries and the growing Russian passion for international consumer goods. The restaurants won massive patronage despite (by Russian standards) very high prices. Even in gourmet-conscious France, McDonald's and other fast-food outlets were winning 26 percent of all restaurant dining by the 1990s. Not everyone who patronized McDonald's liked the food. Many patrons in Hong Kong, for example, said they visited the chain's restaurants mainly to see and be seen and to feel part of the global world.

Cultural globalization obviously involved increasing exposure to American movies and television shows. Series such as *Baywatch* won massive foreign audiences. Movie and amusement park icons such as Mickey Mouse, and products and dolls derived from them, had international currency. Western beauty standards, based on the models and film stars, won wide exposure, expressed among other things in widely sought international beauty pageants. MTV spread Western images and sounds to youth audiences almost everywhere.

Holidays took on an international air. American-style Christmas trappings, including gift giving, lights, and Santa Claus, spread not only to countries of Christian background, such as France, but also to places such as Muslim Istanbul. Northern Mexico picked up American Halloween trick-or-treating, as it displaced the more traditional Catholic observance of All Saints' Day.

Consumer internationalization was not just American. The steady gains of Japanese popular culture have been noted. The Pokémon toy series, derived from Japanese cultural traditions, won a frenzied audience in the 1990s among American children, who for several years could not get enough. A Japanese soap opera heroine became the most admired woman in Muslim Iran. South Korea, historically hostile to Japan, proved open to popular Japanese rock groups and cartoon animation, and Korean culture exports expanded in turn. European popular styles, including fashion and music groups, gained large followings around the world as well.

Dress was internationalized to an unprecedented extent. American-style blue jeans showed up almost everywhere. A major export item for Chinese manufacturing involved Western clothing pirated from famous brand names. A "Chinese market" in the cities of eastern Russia contained entirely Western-style items, mainly clothing and shoes.

Cultural internationalization obviously involved styles from industrial countries, wherever the products were actually made, spreading to other areas, as well as within the industrial world itself. Degrees of penetration varied—in part by wealth and urbanization, in part according to degrees of cultural tolerance. Foreign models were often adapted to local customs. Thus foods in McDonald's in India (where the chain was not very popular in any event) included vegetarian items not found elsewhere, while McDonald's in Morocco offered special banquets after sunset during Ramadan. Cultural internationalization was a real development, but it was complex and incomplete.

INSTITUTIONS OF GLOBALIZATION

On the whole, political institutions globalized less rapidly than technology or business, or even consumer culture. Many people worried about the gap between political supervision and control, and the larger globalization process. UN activity accelerated a bit in the 1990s. With the end of the cold war, more diplomatic hotspots invited intervention by multinational military forces. UN forces tried to calm or prevent disputes in a number of parts of Africa, the Balkans, and the Middle East. Growing refugee populations called for UN humanitarian intervention, often aided by other international groups. UN conferences broadened their scope, dealing, for example, with gender and population control issues. While the results of the conferences were not always clear, a number of countries did incorporate international standards into domestic law. Women in many African countries, for example, were able to appeal to UN proclamations on gender equality as a basis for seeking new property rights in the courts. By 2001, the UN became increasingly active as well in encouraging assistance to stem the AIDS epidemic.

As more nations participated actively in international trade, the importance of organizations in this arena grew. The International Monetary Fund (IMF) and the World Bank had been founded after World War II to promote trade. Guided by the major industrial powers, these organizations offered loans and advice to developing areas and also to regions that encountered temporary economic setbacks. Loans to Mexico and to southeast Asia, during the 1990s, were intended to promote recovery from recessions that threatened to affect other areas. Loans were usually accompanied by requirements for economic reform, usually through reduced government spending and the promotion of more open competition. These guidelines were not always welcomed by the regions involved. The IMF and the World Bank were widely viewed as primary promoters of the capitalist global economy.

Annual meetings of the heads of the seven leading industrial powers—four from Europe, two from North America, plus Japan—usually with Russia as an eighth member, also promoted global trade and policies toward developing regions. The regional economic arrangements that had blossomed from the 1950s on gained growing importance as globalization accelerated. The EU headed the list, but the NAFTA and other regional consortiums in Latin America and east Asia also pushed for lower tariffs and greater economic coordination. A massive global economic crisis, stemming initially from unsound bank loans in the United States, opened in 2008. The crisis revealed how closely major economies were tied together, as virtually every region suffered from financial instability and declining sales. The crisis also suggested a global response. Most countries were careful to emphasize collaboration in dealing with the crisis. The United States, late in 2008, triggered an international conference to deal with the problems, carefully including not only the familiar European industrial powers plus Canada and Japan, but China, India, Brazil, Turkey, and others as well—a 20-nation power list that suggested how the global balance had widened.

PROTEST AND ECONOMIC UNCERTAINTIES

Accelerating globalization attracted a vigorous new protest movement by the end of the 1990s. Meetings of the World Bank and the industrial leaders were increasingly marked by huge demonstrations and some violence. The current began with massive protests in Seattle in 1999, and they continued at key gatherings thereafter. Protesters came from various parts of the world, and they featured a number of issues. Many people believed that rapid global economic development was threatening the environment. Others blasted the use of cheap labor by international corporations, which was seen as damaging labor conditions even in industrial nations. Rampant consumerism was another target.

Many critics claimed that globalization was working to the benefit of rich nations and the wealthy generally, rather than the bulk of the world's population. They pointed to figures that suggested growing inequalities of wealth, with the top quarter of the world's population growing richer during the 1990s while the rest of the people increasingly suffered. This division operated between regions, widening the gap between affluent nations and the more populous developing areas. It also operated within regions, including the United States and parts of western Europe,

Protest against the World Trade Organization in Seattle.

where income gaps were on the rise. Bitter disagreements increasingly divided the supporters and opponents of globalization.

Quite apart from formal protest, different regions interpreted globalization variously, depending on economic results. From the mid-1990s on, new economic problems affected areas such as southeast Asia, Russia, and Turkey, where unfavorable balances of trade drove down the values of national currency, while production declined and unemployment increased. International economic organizations such as the World Bank tried to help, but on condition of reforms that might, for example, force the closing of less effective enterprises, which would temporarily drive up unemployment. By 2001–2002, major economic crises hit Argentina and to a lesser extent Brazil. These led to widespread beliefs that globalization was hurting, not helping, local prosperity. Whether global ties could survive these continuing regional problems was unclear.

NATIONALISM AND RELIGIOUS CURRENTS

Several trends ran counter to globalization as the 21st century began. Nationalism was one. While many nations were partially bypassed by globalization—within many countries much less powerful than the multinational corporations—nationalist resistance to globalization surfaced in many ways. Many countries opposed the erosion of traditions by global cultural patterns. The French government periodically resisted the incorporation of English words into the French language. Many European countries tried to regulate the number of immigrants from Africa, Asia, and the West Indies, in the interest of preserving dominance for families and workers of European background. The United States rejected a wide variety of international treaties, including a provision for regulation against war

crimes, because they might interfere with national sovereignty. China and other states periodically bristled against international criticism of internal policies concerning political prisoners and other human rights issues. The Chinese government attempted to block Internet sites that, in the government's perception, criticized it or promoted democratic movements. Middle Eastern leaders, deeply concerned about undue foreign influence, proved notably uninterested in translating foreign books into Arabic: by the early 21st century, the annual number of translations of Western books in the Middle East was no larger than the number of books translated in the small nation of Greece. Clearly, this was an impediment to Middle Easterners' participation in global intellectual life.

The global religious revival also developed during the final decades of the 20th century, and while religious movements used global ties, they also added complexities. Religious movements tended to resist a uniform global culture and to insist on the distinctiveness of their own respective cultures. These movements also bred suspicion of the consumerism and sexuality highlighted in many manifestations of globalization, including films and tourism.

As communism collapsed in eastern Europe, many people returned to previous religious beliefs, including Orthodox Christianity. Protestant fundamentalists, often from the United States, were also busy in the region. Protestant fundamentalism also spread rapidly in parts of Latin America such as Guatemala and Brazil. In India, Hindu fundamentalism surged during the 1990s, enabling Hindu nationalist politicians to capture the nation's presidency. Fundamentalism also gained ground in Islam, particularly in the Middle East and nearby parts of Africa and south-central Asia. Whether Christian, Hindu, or Islamic, fundamentalists urged a return to the primacy of religion and religious laws. They often opposed greater freedoms for women, and they criticized Western-style consumerism. Frequently, fundamentalists urged government support for religious values.

Religious fundamentalism ran counter to globalization in several ways, even though many religious leaders became adept at using new global technologies such as the Internet. It tended to appeal particularly to impoverished urban groups who seemed to be left behind in the global economy. Fundamentalism also tended to increase intolerance, even in religious traditions that had historically been reasonably open. Hindu fundamentalists thus frequently clashed with Muslims in India. While some advocates of globalization assumed that religious traditionalism would decline, the balance was in fact unclear as the 21st century opened.

GLOBAL TERRORISM

A new wave of international terrorism built on some of the nationalist, subnationalist, and religious currents in various parts of the world early in the 21st century. The new terrorism used some of the apparatus of globalization, particularly to reach across regional boundaries; it also attacked key institutions and principles of globalization in some instances.

Terrorists used secret military operations to counter the power of regular military forces, often targeting civilians. Terrorism was not new: bombing and assassination attempts had dotted the later 19th century, for example in Russia they were directed against political regimes the terrorists viewed as oppressive. It was a terrorist assassination of an Austrian prince that had launched World War I. By the later 20th century, terrorism usually involved a minority nationalist movement, such as the Basque terrorists in northern Spain or an Indian separatist group in Sri Lanka, or a religious cause. Technological advances, including the miniaturization of bombs, expanded the destructive power of terrorist acts and their

capacity to sow fear. As governments improved security protections for political leaders, terrorists increasingly turned to more random civilian targets, in hopes of destabilizing a society and undermining a hated political regime.

The terrorist attack on the United States on September 11, 2001, which killed about 3000 people, was an unusually brazen act by a group of Islamic terrorists. It obviously protested American power and policies in the Middle East, but it also chose a symbol of economic globalization, the World Trade Center in New York.

Terrorism normally provoked extensive retaliation by the police and military in societies under attack. This retaliation sometimes caused far more casualties, even among civilians, than the terrorist acts themselves. Terrorists seldom seemed to achieve many of their stated goals, but eliminating the threat of terrorism proved very difficult. As terrorism went global, particularly with the attacks on the United States, it threatened to complicate some of the institutions of globalization—for example, by provoking new limitations on international travel. Here was a key theme for at least the early 21st century.

GLOBAL WARMING AND A PLANET IN PERIL

Perhaps the most sobering problems with globalization were those associated with the environment. Increased access for travelers and reporters to once restricted areas of the Soviet Union and eastern Europe made it clear that the drive for industrial development in the communist nations had been even more environmentally devastating than the capitalist variant of that process, even in its colonial manifestations.

The impact of these revelations was intensified by the prospect of communist China's new "market-Leninist" path to industrialization, which stressed grafting free market capitalism onto dictatorial, highly bureaucratized political systems such as those long associated with communism. In China, a population of more than a billion people is building on a resource base already severely depleted and degraded; widespread water shortages are another crucial problem. Long-term prognoses of the dire outcomes of unrestrained global "development" may prove to be understatements. Equally alarming have been reports on the ecological fallout of rapid development in southeast Asia, where multinationals based in Japan and in the newly industrialized countries of east Asia are extracting resources with abandon, and the rain forest is disappearing even more rapidly than in Brazil. Similar trends have been documented in sub-Saharan Africa, where economic collapse and environmental dangers are now routinely predicted.

On a more literally global scale, most scientists now agree that the greenhouse effect caused by the buildup in the atmosphere of excessive amounts of carbon dioxide and other heat-trapping gases has led to a substantial warming of the Earth in recent decades. Some of the chief sources of the pollutants responsible for the atmospheric buildup are industrial wastes—including those resulting from energy production through the burning of fossil fuels such as coal—and exhaust from millions of cars, trucks, and other machines run by internal combustion engines that burn petroleum. But other major sources of the greenhouse effect are both surprising and at present essential to the survival of large portions of humanity. Methane, another greenhouse gas, is introduced into the atmosphere in massive quantities as a by-product of the stew of fertilized soil and water in irrigated rice paddies, which feed a majority of the peoples of Asia, the world's most populous continent.

If scientific predictions are correct, global warming has already and will increasingly cause major shifts in temperatures and rainfall

Fish killed by industrial waste.

throughout much of the globe. Fertile and well-watered areas now highly productive in foods for humans and animals may well be overwhelmed by droughts and famine. If widely accepted computer simulations are correct, coastal areas at sea level—which from Bangladesh and the Netherlands to New Jersey are among the most densely populated in the world—are likely to be inundated. They are threatened not just by rising water levels in the world's oceans but by hurricanes and tropical storms that may in the coming decades generate winds up to 200 miles an hour. As climates are drastically altered, vegetation and wildlife in many areas will be radically altered. Temperate forests, for example, may die off in many regions and be replaced by scrub, tropical vegetation, or desert flora. Some animal species may migrate or adapt and survive, but many, unable to adjust to such rapid climatic changes, will become extinct.

The destruction of the rain forests is especially troublesome; unlike the temperate woodlands, they cannot regenerate themselves. In terms of evolution, the rain forests have been the source of most of the species of plant and animal life that now inhabit the earth. In this and other ways, human interventions now affect global climate and weather in the short term and will determine the fate of the planetary environment in the centuries, perhaps millennia, to come.

International discussions of environmental regulation increased from 1997 on. A major conference in Kyoto, Japan, set limits on greenhouse gas emissions in order to curtail global warming. It was not clear, however, whether these limits would have any effect. Many individual nations, including the United States and Russia, opposed the limits proposed because of potential damage to national economies. Here was another area where global politics did not seem to be keeping pace with other aspects of globalization. A new American administration in 2009, under President Barack Obama, prepared to take the United States into greater engagement in environmental issues.

By 2008, rising prices of basic commodities added another dimension to this global discussion. Soaring fuel prices reflected growing demand from places such as China and India and continued high oil use in the industrial nations. Energy costs helped in turn to prompt rising food prices. Along with environmental change, these developments constituted clearly global issues, but solutions were less apparent.

DISEASE

Changes in global contacts have usually involved disease, and late-20th-century globalization was no exception. More rapid international travel helped spread the AIDS epidemic from the 1980s on. Southern and eastern Africa were hit most severely, but AIDS also spread to the United States and western Europe. The epidemic took on even larger proportions in places such as Brazil. By the early 21st century, rates of increase in parts of Asia and in Russia began to accelerate. These were regions that had initially felt relatively safe but where global contact ultimately brought new levels of contagion. In 2003, another new disease, Severe Acute Respiratory Syndrome (SARS), spread rapidly from Asia.

The result, to be sure, was less severe than some of the earlier epidemics associated with global contacts, though some experts warn of even greater disease problems in the future, including a possible spread of avian flu to humans. Environmental issues, newer on the global scale, may have replaced disease as the clearest downside of international connections.

PROJECTING FROM TRENDS

Human beings have always wanted to know what the future will hold. Various societies looked to the configurations of the stars for predictions, and astrology still has partisans in the contemporary world. Some societies generated beliefs in cycles, so that the future would repeat past patterns; many Chinese scholars, for instance, developed a cyclical approach. Still other societies assumed that the future would differ from the past; from the Enlightenment on, Western culture developed a belief in progressive change.

History suggests the futility of many efforts at forecasting. It has been estimated that well over half of the "expert" forecasts generated in the United States since World War II have been wrong. This includes predictions that by 2000 most Americans would be riding to and from work in some kind of airship or that families would be replaced by promiscuous communes. Yet if history debunks forecasts, it also provides the basis for thinking about the future.

The most obvious connection between history and the future involves the assessment of trends that are likely to continue at least for several decades. Thus we "know" that global population growth will slow down, because it is already slowing down. Many forecasts see stabilization, based on rapidly falling birth rates literally around the world, by 2050. We also "know" that populations will become older. This is already happening in western Europe, the United States, and Japan and will occur elsewhere as the birth rate drops. What we do not "know" of course is how societies will react to the demands of older people or how much the environment will have deteriorated by the time global population stabilizes. Even trend-based forecasts can be thrown off by unexpected events, such as wars. Thus, in the 1930s, experts "knew" that the American birth rate would fall, because it was already falling; but then war and prosperity created a totally unexpected baby boom, and the experts were wrong for at least two decades.

Trend-based forecasting is even chancier when the trends themselves are already fragile. The late 20th century saw a genuine global spread of democracy, though admittedly not to every region. It was possible to venture predictions about the triumph of this form of government. But by 2004, it was hard to be confident that democracies were entirely secure in parts of Latin America or even in Russia. The hold of earlier, less democratic political traditions or the sheer pressure of economic stagnation might unseat the trend.

Forecasting is at least as complex when two different trends are in play. The 20th century saw a fairly steady rise in consumerism, which spread to all parts of the world. The appeal of mass media, commercialized sports, and global fashions reaches across traditional boundaries. But the last 30 years have also seen a pronounced increased in religious interest, in many if not all parts of the world. Some people participate in both trends, but overall, the priorities are different. Is one of the two trends likely to predominate? Or should we think of the future in terms of division and tension among cultural interests?

PATHS TO THE PRESENT

The two decades since the mid-1980s have generated a host of new, or partly new, questions for the world's present and future: will current democratic trends hold firm, and perhaps spread to new regions, such as the Middle East? Is a standard model for gender relations available to replace those prescribed by patriarchy, yet accommodate different cultural norms? Will societies such as India, China, and Brazil become fully industrialized—and become, perhaps along with the United States, the economic giants of the mid-21st century? How long will the United States remain the world's sole superpower—an unusual and, many argue, inherently unstable status?

Of the many threads that unspool from our recent past and are weaving themselves into our future, the most obvious is the tension between ongoing globalization and its countercurrents: this issue may be the one that most radically alters the fabric of world history. Globalization has created a world in which contacts have never been so important and varied. Some pundits argue that international influences and crosscutting identities such as *youth* or *scientists* will replace the definable separate civilizations that so long organized human history. But countercurrents to these changes run deep: aside from numerous explicit protests against globalization, myriad ethnic and regional conflicts and the rise of religious affiliations and fundamentalism directly and indirectly counteract the forces of globalization. Will one or another force triumph? Or, more likely: what is the blend of the global and the particular that will provide a stable framework for world history's next stage?

SUGGESTED WEB SITES

For more information on the Council on Foreign Relations, see http://www.cfr.org/; on global policy forum, see http://www.globalpolicy.org/; view the September 11 digital archive at http://911digitalarchive.org/. For matters regarding genocide and related issues, see http://www.un.org/preventgenocide/rwanda/preventgenocide.shtml.

SUGGESTED READINGS

Recent work includes Ignacio Ramonet, *Wars of the 21st Century: New Threats, New Fears* (2004); Elbe Stefan, *Strategic Implications of HIV/AIDS* (2003); Makere Stewart-Harawira, *The New Imperial Order: Indigenous Responses to Globalization* (2005); Eric Hobsbawm, with Antonio Polito, *On the Edge of the New Century* (2000); David Runciman, *The Politics of Good Intentions: History, Fear, and Hypocrisy in the New World Order* (2006); Robert Pinkney, *The Frontiers of Democracy: Challenges in the West, the East and the Third World* (2005); John Agnew, *Hegemony: The New Shape of Global Power* (2005); Edgar Grand and Louis W. Pauly, eds., *Complex Sovereignty: Reconstituting Political Authority in the Twenty-First Century* (2005); Barbara Harff and Ted Robert Gurr, *Ethnic Conflict in World Politics* (2004); Paul Richards, ed., *No Peace, No War: An Anthropology of Contemporary Armed Conflicts* (2005); Karen J. Greenberg, ed., *Al Qaeda Now: Understanding Today's Terrorists* (2005); William V. Spanos, *America's Shadow: An Anatomy of Empire* (2000); and Dieter Senghaas, *The Clash Within Civilizations: Coming to Terms with Cultural Conflicts* (2002).

On U.S. power, see Eric Hobsbawn, *On Empire: America, War and Global Supremacy* (2008); Niall Ferguson, *Colossus: The Price of America's Empire* (2004); Chalmers Johnson, *The Sorrows of Empire: Militarism, Secrecy and the End of the Republic* (2004); and a very interesting book by the specialist in Soviet affairs, Jerry F. Hough, *Changing Party Coalitions: The Mystery of the Red State–Blue State Alignment* (2006); and David S. Mason, *The End of the American Century* (2008).

Globalization is covered, and debated, in Thomas Friedman, *The Lexus and the Olive Tree* (2000); John Gray, *False Dawn* (1999); Alison Brysk and Gerson Shafir, eds., *People Out of Place: Globalization, Human Rights and the Citizenship Gap* (2004); and Thomas Frank, *One Market Under God* (2000). On cultural ramifications, see Peter N. Stearns, *Consumerism in World History* (2002); Alf Hronborg and Carole L. Crumley, eds., *The World System and the Earth System: Global Socioenvironmental Change and Sustainability Since the Neolithic* (2007); Walter LaFeber, *Michael Jordan and the New Global Capitalism* (2000); Stephen Rees, *American Films Abroad* (1997); and James Watson, ed., *Gold Arches East: McDonald's in East Asia* (1998). See also Bruce Mazlish and Ralph Buultjens, eds., *Conceptualizing Global History* (1993); Theodore von Laue, *The World Revolution of Westernization* (1997); Harold Perkin, *The Third Revolution: Professional Elites in the Modern World* (1996); and Francis Fukayama, *The End of History* (1991).

On globalization and women, see Jean H. Qaataert, *The Gendering of Human Rights in the International Systems of Law in the 20th Century* (2006), and Kathryn Ward, ed., *Women Workers and Global Restructuring* (1990). On religion, see Dilip Hiro, *Holy Wars: The Rise of Islamic Fundamentalism* (1989); Richard Antoun, *Understanding Fundamentalism* (2001), which emphasizes Christianity; and Gurdas Ahuja, *BJP and Indian Policies* (1994).

On environmental change, helpful texts include Ramachandra Guha, *Environmentalism: A Global History* (2000), and Judith Shapiro, *China's War Against Nature* (2001). On forecasting, see Daniel Bell, *The Coming of Post-Industrial Society* (1974); D. John Shaw, *Global Food and Agricultural Institutions* (2008); and Robert Heilbroner, *An Inquiry into the Human Prospect* (1974).

Studies of key diplomatic developments include David Halberstam, *War in a Time of Peace* (2001), on U.S. interventionism; Walter Laqueur, *War Without End: Terrorism in the 21st Century* (2003); Walter Russell Mead, *Power, Terror, Peace and War: America's*

Grand Strategy in a World at Risk (2005); Misha Glenny, *The Balkans: Nationalism, War and the Great Powers* (2000); Tim Judah, *Kosovo, War and Revenge* (2001); Ben Kiernan, *Blood and Soil: A World History of Genocide and Extermination from Sparta to Darfur* (2007); and Levon Chorbajian and George Shirinian, *Studies in Comparative Genocide* (1999). See also Henry E. Hale, *The Foundations of Ethnic Politics: Separatism of States and Nations in Eurasia and the World* (2008); Charles S. Maier, *Among Empires: American Ascendancy and Its Predecessors* (2007); and Alberto Alesina, *The Future of Europe: Reform or Decline* (2006).

The Contemporary World

CONTACTS AND IDENTITIES

A key question for the future involves the fate of individual civilizations. World history has been shaped by the characteristics of key civilizations for more than 5000 years, granting that not everyone has been part of a major civilization and that *civilization* can be difficult to define. Some observers argue, however, that by the 21st century the separate characteristics of civilizations are yielding to homogenizing forces. Many scientists, athletes, and businesspeople, for instance, feel more commitment to their professional interests than to their region of origin—which means that global professional identities can override civilization loyalties. The downtowns of most cities around the world look much alike. The same products, stores, and restaurants are found in most urban areas. Globalization may be outpacing regional labels.

Yet we have also seen that globalization can falter, as it did during the middle decades of the 20th century. Even when it accelerates, as in the 1990s, it is balanced by efforts to reassert separate identities. Even as China participates in the global economy, for example, it remains distinct, reflecting some of the political and cultural characteristics it initiated 3000 years ago. The Japanese move easily in the global economy and culture but simultaneously adhere to a group identity measurably different from the individualism emphasized in the United States. Major religions such as Hinduism and Islam continue to mark their regions; in some ways, their influence is increasing.

World history has long been defined by tension between regional features and larger connections. The specifics change, for example, with shifts in technology and organizational capacity. But it probably is premature to assume that some kind of global homogeneity is going to alter the equation completely.

A crucial question raised by this tension involves identities. Many people enjoy aspects of globalization—such as a sense of participating in the hottest trends—but they also, often, cherish a sense of their particular identity. This need to retain a sense of localized identity is expressed by the current revival of religion, especially fundamentalist religion, and nationalism, as well as by smaller, subnational, ethnic loyalties, some of which cause further conflict and tensions in the form of regional disputes and terrorism. Change, including globalization, has widely challenged identity in the past half-century. What balance will be struck between identity and larger connections is far from clear.

Credits

Chapter 11

188: Erich Lessing/Art Resource, NY; 191: The Granger Collection, NY; 192: Robert Frerck/Odyssey; 193: Archivo Iconografico, S. A./Corbis; 198: Dorling Kindersley Media Library/Barnabas Kindersley © Dorling Kindersley

Chapter 12

210: Dorling Kindersley Media Library/Nigel Hudson © Dorling Kindersley; 211: Jochen Helle/Bildarchiv Monheim Fotofinder/IPN; 213: Giraudon/Art Resource, NY

Chapter 13

223: National Palace Museum, Taipei; 226: Metropolitan Museum of Art, New York. Gift of John M. Crawford Jr., in honor of Douglas Dillon, 1981. 1981.276; 229: Freer Gallery of Art, Smithsonian Institution, Washington, D.C., 1935.10; 231: Werner Forman Archive/Peking Palace Museum/Art Resource, NY; 233: "Night Attack on the Sanjo Palace, from the Illustrated Scrolls of the Events of the Heiji Era (Heiji monogatari emaki)", 13th century, Japanese, Kamakura period, Handscroll, ink and color on paper, 41.3 × 699.7 cm (16-1/4 × 275-1/2 in). Photograph (c) 2010 Museum of Fine Arts, Boston. Fenollosa–Weld Collection (11.4000); 238: Kawanabe Kyosai Memorial Museum, Japan

Chapter 14

244: Dorling Kindersley Media Library/Demetrio Carrasco © CONACULTA-INAH-MEX; 247: Dorling Kindersley Media Library/© Judith Miller/Dorling Kindersley/Arte Primitivo

Chapter 15

255: The Granger Collection, NY

Chapter 16

272: The Granger Collection, NY; 278: Courtesy Lyndon Baines Johnson Library and Museum; 283: The Granger Collection, NY; 284: AP/Wide World Photos; 286: Museo de America, Madrid, Spain/Erich Lessing/Art Resource, NY; 289: Dorling Kindersley Media Library/Tony Morris © Dorling Kindersley

Chapter 17

296: Metropolitan Museum of Art, Bequest of Benjamin Altman, 1913 (14.40.627); 297: Alinari/Art Resource, NY; 299: Getty Images/ De Agostini Editore Picture Library; 304: Dorling Kindersley Media Library/Peter Hanneberg © Dorling Kindersley; 308: Dorling Kindersley Media Library/Laurence Pordes © Dorling Kindersley, Courtesy of The British Library; 309: Alinari/Art Resource, NY

Chapter 18

324: Dorling Kindersley Media Library/Peter Visscher © Dorling Kindersley; 328 (left): Beniaminson/Art Resource, NY; 328 (right): Sovfoto; 329: Dorling Kindersley Media Library/Demetrio Carrasco © Dorling Kindersley

Chapter 19

340: Dorling Kindersley Media Library/Tony Souter © Dorling Kindersley; 346: Tretyakov Gallery, Moscow, Russia/Scala/Art Resource, NY

Chapter 20

353: Dorling Kindersley Media Library/© The British Museum; 355: Giraudon/Art Resource, NY; 356: The Nelson-Atkins Museum of Art, Kansas City, MO; 360: The Granger Collection, NY; 361: The Granger Collection, NY; 362: The Granger Collection, NY

Chapter 21

374: Public domain; 382: Mary Evans Picture Library; 384: The Granger Collection; 388: By Courtesy of the National Portrait Gallery, London; 392: The National Gallery, London

Chapter 22

403: M. and E. Bernheim/Woodfin Camp & Associates; 405: The Granger Collection, NY; 408: (c) The British Library Board. WD 2413.

Chapter 23

421: Dorling Kindersley Media Library/© Dorling Kindersley; 422: Alexander Trumbull Library/National Library of New Zealand

Chapter 24

429: Archives Charmet/Bridgeman Art Library;
433: Dorling Kindersley Media Library/Linda
Whitwam © Dorling Kindersley; 438: Horacio L.
Coppola; 439: Pearson Education Corporate
Digital Archive; 441: No credit information
available

Chapter 25

448: Dorling Kindersley Media Library/Piter
Visscher © Dorling Kindersley; 450: William
Henry Jackson/Corbis; 452: The Granger
Collection, NY; 453: Courtesy Peabody
Essex Museum, Salem, MA; 457: Dorling
Kindersley Media Library/Chen Chao
© Dorling Kindersley

Chapter 26

464: Keystone-Mast Collection, UCR/California
Museum of Photography, University of California,
Riverside; 465: Sovfoto; 468: Courtesy of the
Mariner's Museum, Newport News, VA; 471:
The Art Archive; 472: Adachi Ginko (Japanese,
1874–1897), "Illustration of Ladies Sewing (Kijo
saiho no zu)", 1887, Japanese Meiji Era, woodblock
print (nishiki-e), ink, color and silver on paper,
Vertical oban, one sheet of triptych, 36.5 × 25.2 cm
(14-3/8 × 9-15/16 in.). Photograph (c) 2010
Museum of Fine Arts, Boston. William Sturgis
Bigelow Collection (11.18171.73)

Chapter 27

479: National Archives and Records
Administration

Chapter 28

495: AP/Wide World Photos; 501: Getty Images,
Inc.–Hulton Archive Photos; 507: Dorling
Kindersley Media Library/Alex Robinson
© Dorling Kindersley, Courtesy of Museu de Arte
Contemporanea; 511: Hulton Archive/Getty
Images; 513: Time & Life Pictures/Getty Images

Chapter 29

519: Getty Images, Inc.–Hulton Archive Photos;
524: Bettmann/Corbis; 526: The Art Archive;
527: Sovfoto; 529: Sovfoto

Chapter 30

545: AP/Wide World Photos; 547: Liu Heung
Sh'ing/Contact Press Images; 548: AP/Wide
World Photos; 550: Sovfoto; 552: Pearson
Education/PH College CHET 2; 558: Rough
Guides Dorling Kindersley

Chapter 31

564: Margaret Bourke-White/Time Life
Pictures/Getty Images; 571: Bettmann/Corbis;
577: Jahangir Gazdar/Woodfin Camp & Associates

Chapter 32

587: William Karel/Corbis Sygma; 592: Patrick
Chauvel/Corbis Sygma; 593: Francis Duhamel/
Corbis Sygma; 598: Rough Guides Dorling
Kindersley; 599: Jacques Pavlovsky/Corbis Sygma

Chapter 33

608: Baldwin H. Ward & Kathryn C. Ward/Corbis;
611: AP/Wide World Photos; 614: Dorling
Kindersley Media Library/Diego Rivera
(1886–1957) Mexican. "Teatro de los Insurgentes
on Avenida Insurgentes Sur, Mexico City." Mural.
(Detail) Photo: Peter Wilson. © Banco de Mexico
Diego Rivera and Frida Kahlo Museums Trust.
Av. Cinco de Mayo No. 2, Col. Centro, Del.
Cuauhtemoc 06059, Mexico, D.F. Reproduction
authorized by the Instituto Nacional de Bellas Artesy
Literatura; 615: Photo by Stuart Cohen. (c) 2009
Artists Rights Society (ARS), New York/SOMAPP,
Mexico City; 618: Peter Menzel/Stock Boston

Chapter 34

623: The Art Archive; 626: Dorling Kindersley
Media Library/Adam Hook © Dorling Kindersley;
630: Dorling Kindersley Media Library/Roger de la
Harpe © Dorling Kindersley; 635: Dorling
Kindersley Media Library/© Judith Miller/Dorling
Kindersley/Elms Lesters

Chapter 35

646: Efrem Lukatsky/AP/Wide World Photos; 652:
Beatrice Mategwa/Corbis/Reuters America LLC;
656: Jacques Pavlovsky/Corbis Sygma; 659: Dan
Kraus/AP/Wide World Photos; 662: Sergio
Moraes/Time Life Pictures/Reuters/Getty Images

Index